IN A PEACEFUL CAPE COD PINE WOOD THE HORROR BEGAN . . .

THE VICTIMS

Each one of the young women was lovely. Each one was unsuspecting. And each one fell too easily under the spell of one charming man.

THE KILLER

He was polite and attractive. He was a poet and a bit of a liar. And he was a serial killer who performed a grisly ritual for death.

THE COPS

They had seen and heard of too many runaway girls to take the missing persons reports seriously. They were off-hand about a boyfriend's pleas and a parent's inquiries. They never even considered murder until they found the first grave . . .

IN HIS GARDEN

ALSO BY LEO DAMORE

The Cape Cod Years of John Fitzgerald Kennedy
The "Crime" of Dorothy Sheridan
Cache
Senatorial Privilege: The Chappaquiddick Cover-up

IN HIS GARDEN

THE ANATOMY OF A MURDERER

LEO DAMORE

A DELL BOOK

Published by
Dell Publishing
a division of
Bantam Doubleday Dell Publishing Group, Inc.
666 Fifth Avenue
New York, New York 10103

Printed in the United States of America
Published simultaneously in Canada

July 1990

10 9 8 7 6 5 4 3

RAD

For Alice and Russell Dexter
and
Sarah Kenney Walker

And He walks with me,
And He talks with me,
And He tells me I am His own;
And the joy we share as we tarry there,
None other has ever known.

"In the Garden"
Traditional Hymn

CONTENTS

PART ONE: Pat and Mary Anne   1

PART TWO: Susan and Sydney   129

PART THREE: Christine   251

PART FOUR: Barbara and the Diggers   343

PART FIVE: Tony   491

EPILOGUE: Walpole   617

PART ONE

Pat and Mary Anne

———

1

A downpour greeted Robert Turbidy's arrival in San Diego on Saturday, January 25, 1969. On Thursday night he had phoned Providence, Rhode Island, and promised Patricia Walsh that he would buy her a "nice present"; then their long distance conversation was interrupted by the Los Angeles operator, asking him to relinquish the line for an emergency call. Hastily saying goodbye, Turbidy had told Pat, "I'll see you next week for sure." Now he was having second thoughts about the gift he had in mind.

He entered the tattoo parlor and asked the price of having the name "Pat" inscribed on his arm.

"Two bucks," the grizzled shop owner replied.

Turbidy left, undecided. He spent fifteen minutes in his green and white 1965 VW camper making up his mind. The tattoo was an antic idea sure to delight Pat; in his view "a very giving thing."

Returning to the shop, he ordered the job done. Wiry and muscular, he retained at twenty-six the lineaments of an appealing boyishness; his slanted blue eyes bright and guileless. His bumpy nose was flattened like a boxer's.

In the shop's dusty mirror, Turbidy examined the script written in blue ink on his upper right arm. Outside, brilliant sunshine replaced the rain, as if to signal approbation for his decision. Filled with a rush of delight—a curious burst of energy at the accomplishment of his "gift"—he went skipping down the rain-washed street like a child. . . .

Returning to Los Angeles, Turbidy packed the camper; in milky, smog-veiled dawn, he embarked on the cross-country journey back to Rhode Island.

3

Turbidy regretted leaving California. The two-month sojourn had been his first taste of freedom since working his way through Providence College, three years as a navy legal officer and a semester of graduate studies in political science. With his brother he had founded a thriving landscape business and, at Thanksgiving, purchased the camper from Pat Walsh's older sister, Maureen, intending to visit Mexico City.

Turbidy never made it over the border. Instead, he had pursued the counterculture lifestyle—natural foods and handicrafts—of friends in Los Angeles and San Francisco. With borrowed tools he fashioned a crude but artfully made shoulder bag from a single piece of suede, with a branding scar in its center, laced with thongs into an attractive pouch. The handbag held a wallet, decorated with a peace-sign medallion, and a drawstring coin purse—given to Pat Walsh as a gift when she had come out for the Christmas holidays.

They had spent twelve memorable days touring the California coast from Big Sur to Mount Tamalpais just over the Golden Gate bridge, visiting Rhode Island friends who lived in San Francisco, and camping out in the Sierras. Then Pat flew back to Providence to resume teaching the second grade at the Laurel Hill Avenue School.

On the road, Turbidy stopped to call the Providence apartment he and Pat Walsh had shared since September. There was no answer. Turbidy dialed the number again at dusk. He was puzzled that Pat had not returned from the weekend in Provincetown he remembered her talking about before their last telephone conversation was interrupted. (The "emergency" had been a ruse, perpetrated by a friend of his "just for the hell of it.")

In the camper, Turbidy listened to the portable AM/FM radio Pat had given him with a hand-lettered Christmas card. Inscribed to "Bob" with the words, "Peace, Gladness and Joy," she wrote:

> I have bought bread
> I have been given roses
> How happy I am
> To hold both in my hands

4

Turbidy looked forward to their reunion. He had met her in March at a student hangout near the campus of Rhode Island College. In fact, he had been sitting next to Pat when they were introduced. She had recognized his name; her parents knew his grandmother. Turbidy was at once taken with the shy, dark-skinned girl with long brown hair. She was tall, long-legged, statuesque, with Turbidy's habit of slurring her s's. When he asked her to a Jefferson Airplane concert, she promptly accepted.

Turbidy was not especially good at picking up women; it was the first time he had enjoyed such success. He had fallen in love with her that night, just thinking about her after their date.

Pat had her own apartment on Branch Avenue in the north end of Providence, but she had spent most of the summer with Turbidy at a cottage he and his brother rented in northern Rhode Island. By September, he and Pat were looking for a place to share. Pat had to be careful, being a schoolteacher. They had found a nice apartment on Prospect Street, in a pleasant neighborhood near Brown University.

The romance was approved by Maureen and Ken Meyers, Pat's older sister and her husband, who went with the couple on camping trips that summer to Cape Cod and New Hampshire. When Maureen and Ken decided to sell their camper, Turbidy bought it; for a lark he and Pat had hitchhiked to Washington, D.C., stayed overnight and driven the camper back to Providence.

Turbidy had saved over two thousand dollars from landscaping when he decided to take time off until March. Pat had encouraged him to visit the West Coast; she said it would do him good to learn to enjoy himself, not be so work-oriented. Turbidy thought she was really unselfish about it.

Turbidy called the apartment again on Monday afternoon. He calculated the time-zone difference to coincide with the hour Pat usually returned home from school. His uneasiness at the unanswered telephone turned to concern. That night he called Pat's father.

Walsh had not heard from his daughter since Thursday, when he had cashed her check for twenty dollars and Pat had mentioned going away for the weekend with Mary Anne Wysocki.

Pat had not showed up at school on Monday morning. She had called in sick Friday morning, but the principal, Ronald Karnes, had not been notified of her continued absence. Karnes was puzzled when he was told. Pat had a near-perfect attendance record and had never failed to let him know in advance when she was not coming to school.

Mr. Walsh learned from Mrs. Martha Wysocki that her daughter had left with Pat Walsh on Friday morning for a winter weekend in Provincetown, a resort community at the tip of Cape Cod. Mary Anne had told her mother that if they were a day late coming home, not to worry—Russell Norton, a boy her daughter had become friendly with the last several months, was going to meet the girls on Saturday, then ride back with them.

Walsh spoke with the Massachusetts State Police at the Rehoboth barracks, just over the Rhode Island line. Police had no record of an accident involving Pat's light blue 1968 Volkswagen.

The next morning Walsh telephoned a missing persons report to the central precinct of the Providence police. He described his daughter as five feet nine, weighing 138 pounds, with dark complexion, hazel eyes and dark brown, shoulder-length hair. He gave the registration number of her car as KV-978. Walsh, a diffident, quiet-spoken clerk at the downtown Providence postal annex, went on his lunch hour to the Bureau of Missing Persons at police headquarters to talk to Detective Sergeant Edward Perry.

"I don't like the looks of *this* one," said Sergeant Horace Craig after reading Perry's report. An APB was teletyped to all Rhode Island police stations before Craig called Provincetown police. He explained to Provincetown Patrolman James Cook that Patricia Walsh and Mary Anne Wysocki were supposed to be in town, and gave their description and the car's registration. Cook entered the report in the daily log in red ink, "so everyone was sure to see it."

Cook left the station for lunch at 1 P.M. After school-crossing duty, he went to the Provincetown Inn to check if the girls were registered; then he patrolled the narrow streets of Provincetown, deserted in the off-season. He did not locate the VW. Going off-duty at 4:45, Cook passed along the missing persons complaint from Providence to oncoming Patrolman George Baker. Baker said he would look around during his night tour of duty. He found no trace of the missing girls either.

2

Bob Turbidy arrived at 135 Prospect Street on Thursday afternoon, half-expecting to be greeted by Pat Walsh with an explanation for her absence. He found the door unlocked; the apartment was silent and empty. On the kitchen counter was forty-seven dollars—the bimonthly rent Pat scrupulously paid on time—a grocery list and a "15 Cents Off" detergent coupon.

The one-bedroom apartment was in good order. Pat had taken little with her for the weekend. Missing from her closet was the army fatigue jacket on which Turbidy had written his name in blue ink on the inside label. Pat often wore his clothes; they were nearly the same size. She was, perhaps, an inch taller. . . .

Turbidy called Russell Norton, a senior at Rhode Island College. Norton had last seen the girls on Wednesday, January 22, when he invited them to spend the evening with him and a friend at Armando's Bar and Grill. They had a few beers and talked about a holiday in Provincetown planned for the weekend.

"I understood Pat was going to call in sick at the Laurel Hill school so she could leave on Friday," Norton told Turbidy. "We'd talked about the trip a few weeks earlier and at that time I planned on going with them, but I'd just changed jobs and couldn't take Friday off: I told the girls I'd take a bus to Hyannis on Saturday morning and then hitchhike to Provincetown. I was going to ride back with them Sunday."

Norton said he had arrived in Provincetown around two o'clock in the afternoon. "I walked around town looking for the girls. I went to the Foc's'le bar and later to the Pilgrim Club. I was surprised I couldn't find them because in the middle of winter it's easy to locate someone in Provincetown. I thought they might have met up with some people and gone out of town for the day."

Norton did meet Donna Cummings, a friend employed at the Provincetown Inn. She let him sleep on the floor of her apartment overnight. "On Sunday morning I walked around town looking for Mary Anne and Pat," Norton said. "I still couldn't find them.

I didn't check any guesthouses or motels because I thought I would come upon the girls any minute."

Norton left Provincetown on Sunday afternoon and returned to Providence. When he called Mary Anne's house that evening, "Her mother told me she hadn't heard from her since Friday."

The next morning Turbidy drove out to Cape Cod. At the police station in the basement of Provincetown's town hall, Turbidy spoke with Patrolman Cook. Cook explained that he had checked around town; neither the girls nor the Volkswagen had been seen by anyone. Cook was pleasant and friendly; he seemed to see no particular significance in the disappearance of Pat Walsh and Mary Anne Wysocki. There were more than four thousand runaway girls listed as missing in New England.

Dissatisfied, Turbidy decided to look around himself. Provincetown was desolate and shabby in winter, without the spirit of summer carnival Turbidy remembered from a day-trip there last August.

He entered the Town House, a bar on Commercial Street; the bartender denied seeing the girls. Turbidy tried the Mayflower Cafe, a restaurant smelling of fried fish and decorated with pencil caricatures of local characters. A hairy-armed counterman eyed him with suspicion, barely glancing at the photographs Turbidy showed before shaking his head.

The color snapshots Turbidy brought with him had been taken during a camping trip. They showed a tall, tanned girl bustling around a picnic table. She was wearing a striped fisherman's shirt; cut-off dungarees exposed her slender thighs.

Turbidy spent the night at a parking lot beside MacMillen Wharf, the harbor a vast flatness of blue-gray like hammered steel. Unable to sleep, he listened to the wind send beach sand scratching at the windows of his camper.

He ate breakfast at Wally's luncheonette. Summoning his resolve, he showed the photographs to the waitress, a pretty blonde in a miniskirt and knee boots. She did not remember seeing Pat Walsh.

Turbidy tried the Portuguese bakery across the street, and three guesthouses. His inquiries met with indifference.

When he returned to Providence, Turbidy looked up Gerry Magnan. "Some people didn't even look at the pictures, or bother to check their registers," Turbidy told him.

8

He had met Magnan once, to move a refrigerator from the basement of Mary Anne Wysocki's house to a third-floor attic she was fixing over for herself. He knew from Pat that Gerry and Mary Anne had gone together off and on for about six years.

Thin, handsome, reserved, Magnan said he had last seen Mary Anne Wysocki on January 18. Mary Anne told him she and Pat Walsh were going to Provincetown the following weekend to relax after semester exams and would be coming back on Sunday night.

Close for years, Pat and Mary Anne had only lately resumed their friendship. They had started Rhode Island College together; but Mary Anne had dropped out after one semester, going to work for the telephone company to save for her education. Pat had gone on to graduate, get a teaching job and move into her own apartment. Their lives had gone off in different directions.

Taking comfort in each other's concern, Turbidy and Magnan spent the night drinking beer and trying to figure out where the girls had gone, and why they hadn't let anyone know where they were. Turbidy was bothered by the indifference of Provincetown police, especially Patrolman Cook's breezy assumption that Pat and Mary Anne had run off.

They agreed on a course of action. Turbidy looked up in the Providence directory of Yellow Pages the listings for "Private Investigators."

At eleven o'clock on Sunday morning, February 2, Carl Benson was driving his jeep on Old Proprietor's Road deep in the South Truro woods on the bay side of Cape Cod, six miles from the Provincetown line, accompanied by his two children, Penny and Richard. Benson often took this route to fetch the Sunday paper.

As Benson later reported to Police Chief Harold Berrio at Truro's tiny station, he approached a sharp bend in the dirt road. "I saw this Volkswagen parked about thirty feet back up in a clearing—up in the woods like."

He had stopped the jeep and opened the door. "I was going to look at the car to see what was wrong. I started to get out and something told me—I don't know why—but something told me to get out of that place." Benson had the feeling he was being watched. "I thought I heard somebody in back running up the hill," he told Berrio. "I just felt there was something wrong. So I got out of the road real quick."

9

His daughter had said to him, "Daddy, don't go so fast."

Benson led the chief back to the woods and pulled his jeep alongside Berrio's police cruiser. A note had been placed under the wiper blade on the right-hand side of the locked Volkswagen's windshield.

"That sign wasn't there when I was here before," Benson said.

Written in red Magic Marker on a torn piece of brown-bag paper was the message:

ENGINE TROUBLE
WILL RETURN

Berrio copied down the Rhode Island license plate number; at the police station, he got a Signal 10 through Barnstable County police radio, returning a no-stolen-auto record.

At 7 P.M., Berrio received another call from someone who had seen the VW abandoned in the woods. He explained that the vehicle had been checked out. Then he went home and watched the Smothers Brothers on television.

3

Magnan and Turbidy contributed one hundred dollars each to retain the private detective seated behind the desk of the grubby office off Trinity Square in Providence. The detective, a flashy fast-talker who had registered his wife's car out of state "for under-cover work," hinted that he paid off police for information.

It sounded underhanded to Magnan, who doubted the detective's investigative skills despite his declaration: "If those girls were in Provincetown, I'll find out!" Nevertheless, by the time they left, Magnan agreed to bring pictures of both girls to a rendezvous the detective chose, a drugstore in the suburb of Warwick.

Magnan had grown fearful for Mary Anne's safety as the days of her unexplained absence lengthened beyond a week. It was not like her to be gone so long without calling home. They had grown up together in the west end of Providence, a working-class neighborhood of dusty tenements and triple-deckers, but had not met until Magnan—a nineteen-year-old sophomore at Rhode Island College—started working at a corner variety store where Mary Anne Wysocki was a steady customer. A pretty, graceful girl of sixteen, she had asked him to the senior prom at Classical High, a secondary school for above-average students with exacting entrance requirements which she and Pat Walsh attended.

The romance had foundered on his ambitiousness. Magnan, the son of a French-Canadian fireman who had died of a heart attack at the scene of a fire, was driven to overcome the straitened circumstances of a poor childhood. Struggling to prepare himself for a teaching career, he confessed to Mary Anne an incapacity to express his emotions very well, although he cared deeply for her. Magnan stopped seeing her periodically, trying to back out of the relationship, but except for one six month period the breakups hadn't lasted very long. During one such estrangement, Mary Anne had dyed her hair blonde. Magnan had not liked the change; she had restored her hair to its natural light brown.

Magnan had taught high school for two years, then returned to Rhode Island College for a master's in math education. He had driven Mary Anne, who had enrolled in September, 1966, to classes and tutored her in calculus. A math major, Mary Anne played an active part in the campaign for a relaxed dress code, a "revolt" that won students the right to wear jeans to class.

In September of 1968, when Magnan secured a position as a math instructor at Bristol Community College in Fall River, Massachusetts, he and Mary Anne started talking about getting married. Like Bob Turbidy and Pat Walsh, they became "sort of engaged."

Turbidy was also pressing Providence police for information about their investigation, but no progress had been made on the case. Turbidy filled his unemployed days with the uneasy awareness of Pat's absence and the hours when he could not sleep learning to master leatherwork, taking instruction from Russell Norton, an

11

experienced craftsman with whom a friendship had sprung up. Norton had been attracted to Mary Anne Wysocki, telling Turbidy, "I knew I didn't have a chance because she was in love with Gerry Magnan." Norton had settled for being "just friends."

The private detective had warned Turbidy it could take a while before he would have any information. Having gone to Provincetown and checked every possible place the girls could have stayed, the detective said, "There's no way those girls were in Provincetown."

The report threw Turbidy into a greater turmoil of apprehension. He had questioned Pat's friends, all of whom concurred that she was headed for Cape Cod on the weekend she disappeared. The night before she left, Pat had told close friends, John and Linda McNally, that she was leaving for Provincetown in the morning. The McNallys still had in their camera a photograph taken of Pat the weekend before she left for Provincetown.

Turbidy had the roll of film developed; he found a dazzling picture of Pat. Standing beside a barren rose arbor, she had struck a stylish pose to model a new dress made for her by Linda McNally from material bought in a Provincetown boutique the previous summer. The dress had balloon-shaped sleeves and the skirt stopped inches above her knees. Pat's long legs were clad in close-fitting boots.

She looked slim, hard-eyed, beautiful—the hollows of her cheeks having lost a vestigial plumpness. Her face smoldered with uncharacteristic defiance, as if daring the camera to pass judgment on her metamorphosis. Turbidy had not seen the new hairstyle before: eyebrow-length bangs and a piquant flip of hair falling to her shoulders.

Turbidy gave a copy of the picture to the Providence *Journal*, which was starting to publish stories about the girls' disappearance and the efforts of their boyfriends to find them. The paper had the photograph cropped so that only Pat's face showed. Her mother did not care for the picture.

"She thinks it makes Pat look tough," Turbidy told Gerry Magnan when he showed him the photograph. He explained he had drawn closer to Mrs. Walsh since Pat's disappearance by keeping her informed of developments in the investigation.

"The image Pat projected in the picture really bothered her mother—she's a very straitlaced person," Turbidy told Magnan. "Pat told me about one time when she was baby-sitting and came

12

walking down the street holding the child she was taking care of in her arms. Her mother came out on the porch and said to her, 'Get into the house before the neighbors see you and think you've had a baby.'"

Pat had laughed about the incident in retrospect, Turbidy said, but the experience had been painful. While going to college she had lived at home under the strict supervision of her mother, a domineering woman who had refused to attend her oldest son's wedding because he was marrying a Protestant against her wishes. Nor had Mrs. Walsh approved of Ken Meyers, the self-proclaimed atheist whom Pat's sister, Maureen, had fallen in love with while attending Pembroke College in Providence.

Turbidy had met the Walshes for the first time one evening when they had arrived unannounced at the apartment on Prospect Street. Pat had looked out the window and recognized her father's car parked at the curb. Turbidy was wearing a T-shirt and jeans and had rushed to fix himself up to receive guests. Pat's parents did not know he and Pat were living together.

Mrs. Walsh had been a revelation, Turbidy told Magnan. "She was a large woman with broad shoulders; she was like a tank. She had a man's voice and she sounded just like a drill sergeant, very tough-talking. It was hard to look her in the eye, or even be in the same room with her. She took up all the space."

Turbidy had been embarrassed to see how she dominated Leonard Walsh, a quiet, sweet-tempered man Pat adored. After they left, Turbidy had said to Pat, "I feel sorry for your father. Your mother really wears the pants."

4

On February 6, a week after Robert Turbidy had returned to Providence, Russell Norton was having lunch in the cafeteria of Rhode Island College when he overheard a conversation at an adjoining table. John Wilson, a student at Upsala College in East Orange, New Jersey, mentioned that his roommate, Len Mattluck, had seen Mary Anne Wysocki and Pat Walsh a couple of weekends ago at a rooming house in Provincetown.

Norton immediately called Bob Turbidy. Turbidy spent an hour on the telephone tracking Mattluck down in East Orange.

Mattluck, a transfer student from Rhode Island College, had talked to the girls for about three hours in their room in Provincetown on Friday night, January 24. Later that night he had seen Pat and Mary Anne sitting at a table in the Foc's'le bar with two other girls. The next morning he and two friends had thumbed back to New Jersey; that was all he knew.

Turbidy called the Provincetown police. He told Sergeant James Meads that Pat Walsh and Mary Anne Wysocki—subjects of a missing persons report—had stayed at a guesthouse on Standish Street owned by Mrs. Patricia Morton.

Turbidy gave his own address as 75 Sunset Avenue, North Providence—his brother's apartment. If police were going to be investigating, he did not want them to know Pat Walsh was living with him and get the idea she was a loose or promiscuous girl.

Sergeant Meads called Patricia Morton. Yes, Pat Walsh and Mary Anne Wysocki had checked into her guesthouse and signed the register, but no dates were included—an oversight for which she apologized. Mrs. Morton thought the girls had stayed one night, leaving Saturday morning, but she couldn't say for sure. She had seen a note from Antone Costa, another tenant in her house, asking the girls for a ride to Truro. She hadn't seen Costa for three or four days.

Meads knew Tony Costa, having recruited him as a police informer in a narcotics investigation. In fact, when Costa was serving time in the Barnstable House of Correction for nonsupport of his ex-wife and three children, Meads had recommended early parole. "Only through his efforts were we able to apprehend the drug pushers and get a court conviction on these people," Meads had written, urging Costa's release "at the earliest possible time."

Costa had been granted parole on November 8, 1968, shortening a term of imprisonment that would not have expired until March 22, 1969. A model prisoner, with a construction job awaiting his release, Costa pointed out in his letter of application that he had never been in jail before. If paroled, the burden of supporting his ex-wife and children would not entirely rest on the state. He wrote, "All I want is to start new and keep out of trouble." . . .

Meads called Costa's mother, Mrs. Cecelia Bonaviri, at 9 Conant Street in Provincetown. She asked, "Is my Tony in trouble?"

Meads explained that two girls from Providence were missing. He hoped Tony would know where the girls had gone after they left Provincetown.

Mrs. Bonaviri did not know where her son was. "If Tony calls, I'll tell him you were asking for him."

5

On February 7, a missing persons report was filed by Martha Wysocki with Detective Sergeant Edward Perry of the Providence police. She described her daughter Mary Anne as 23 years old with brown hair, blue eyes, light complexion, 5'8", 135 pounds, last seen wearing blue slacks and a dark green coat. Mrs. Wysocki had assumed the missing persons report on Pat Walsh had covered her daughter too, since they were traveling together, and she had delayed reporting Mary Anne missing for two weeks.

Perry had taken a personal interest in the case, talking often with Bob Turbidy and repeatedly telephoning Provincetown police for progress reports on their investigation. On February 3, Perry had broadcast over the police teletype a "Try to Locate" on Pat Walsh's Volkswagen. Nothing had turned up until Turbidy had phoned in the tip about the guesthouse in Provincetown where the girls had stayed.

Perry called the Provincetown police again, urging them to locate Antone Costa for questioning; then he called the Yarmouth barracks of the Massachusetts State Police on Cape Cod and requested assistance in the investigation of two girls missing since January 24.

The station chief, Sergeant Robert Bolduc assigned Trooper Robert Sylvia to drive out to Provincetown for a routine check and sent a copy of Perry's request to Detective Lieutenant George Killen of the district attorney's office at Barnstable courthouse.

As the senior officer responsible for the investigation and prosecution of all criminal activity on Cape Cod, Killen had achieved near-legendary status. Tall and dapper, with great dignity in his bearing, Killen had monumental reserve matched by a toughness which, along with the respect and admiration won from colleagues, had earned him the behind-his-back nickname, "Old Stoneface."

Wreathed in cigarette smoke from one of the Parliaments usually smoldering between his fingers, Killen was deep in the preparation of cases for the criminal session of superior court in April. It was a busy Friday at the end of a long week and he had given the missing persons report scant notice; Cape Cod was a magnet for runaway youths from all over the country. But when he got a call from Sergeant Perry of the Providence police with a description of the girls and a summary of their backgrounds, Killen sensed, "Something's wrong here."

Killen called Francis Marshall, Provincetown police chief, a friend since boyhood when Killen was a deckhand on the ferry *Dorothy Brand* and Marshall was one of a crowd of youths hustling tips by carrying tourists' luggage down the pier in Provincetown. Marshall said he would personally look into the missing persons complaint, although he was surprised Killen was bothering with so minor a matter. There was no evidence that a crime had been committed, Marshall thought as he hung up . . . unless Killen wasn't telling him everything he knew about the case . . .

In fact, a minor coincidence had arrested Killen's attention and kept him from putting the report aside: his mother's maiden name had been Mary Walsh.

In Provincetown, Sergeant Meads was reading the teletype on Mary Anne Wysocki when Patricia Morton called the station. She had talked to Bob Turbidy the previous evening and been convinced of the urgency of his concern over the disappearance of Pat Walsh. Checking Tony Costa's room, she had discovered a torn-up letter in his wastebasket that she wanted to give to the police.

16

Meads called Patrolman Cook into his office to ask him what progress had been made in the investigation of the missing Providence girls. Cook remembered talking to Bob Turbidy. He told Meads that Turbidy was "bullshit"—angry—because his girlfriend had taken off.

Nevertheless, Cook went to the small Victorian house on Standish Street, a white-shingled structure set close to the sidewalk behind an unsteady picket fence. He was met at the door of the basement office by a dark-haired woman in her late forties with hyperthyroid eyes and a distracted, nervous manner.

Pat Walsh and Mary Anne Wysocki had arrived at her guesthouse sometime in the early afternoon on Friday, January 24, she said. Mrs. Morton had checked her receipt book; the girls had paid twenty-four dollars for two nights' accommodation.

She had taken the girls through the house to show them the communal arrangement of the bathrooms and, in passing, had introduced them to Tony Costa. On Saturday morning, she had seen a note written by Tony on a torn piece of brown-bag paper asking the girls for a ride to Truro.

"I'm not sure what the note said, exactly. Something like, 'I hate to impose on you, but I could use a ride to Truro in the morning.' " She did not know where in Truro Tony wanted to be taken, or if the girls had given him a ride.

Mrs. Morton then gave Cook the letter she had found in the wastebasket. She had reconstructed it with cellophane tape. "I had no idea Tony was doing such things in his room," she said, "I always tell my tenants: I don't care what your scene is, don't try to fool me. If you want to do your thing—and it's against the law —don't do it in my house."

The letter was written on Museum of Modern Art stationery, a reproduction of a microdot painting by Joseph Levi.

Greetings people:

I've been sitting here stoned on hash and downs, drawing plans for my houseboat for this summer. I really intend to build it soon. I want to share it with one or two people. It will be a complete home on the water. I will show you the plans as soon as I complete them. Three chicks have been staying here and they are super nice, super groovy head people. But Christine is still on my mind.

17

I'm making a collage for you all. Will present it to you soon. I may come up to Hyannis for a couple of days. Ok, Ron?

Until then, go in peace always,

"Anthony of Rome"

Beneath the signature was a drawing of a hypodermic needle leaking a drop of liquid and the legend, "There's No Hope Without Dope!"

The envelope, also torn in four pieces, was addressed to Georgia Panesis and "Romulus," 61 Barnstable Road, Hyannis, Massachusetts.

"I know the 'chicks' he's referring to," Mrs. Morton said when Cook finished reading the letter. Three girls had driven to Provincetown from New York in a "very snappy" car. "And so, incidentally, were *they."* The girls had worn false eyelashes and fur coats; one of them had a Sassoon haircut. Tony Costa had registered the girls at the guesthouse while she was out. "They put a little note on my door saying, 'We hope you don't mind; and that we can stay.' I *didn't* mind, but this is an old house and I like to explain about the heat, and things like not putting Tampax down the toilet—just to prevent mishaps.

"The girls had been very impressed by Tony Costa. He just sort of bowled them over. They sat wide-eyed on the edge of their chairs when he was telling a story."

Costa was a very good tenant. "He was so very neat and tidy about everything—and that's more than I can say for some of the people I've had here. And I didn't have to chase him for his room rent, either." Costa shared a bath with a room on the other side. "He always left it spotless."

Like Sergeant Meads, Patrolman Cook knew Tony Costa well; he had busted him on a nonsupport charge and for driving after his license had been suspended in September, 1968. Costa, he recalled, had been given a six months term in the Barnstable House of Correction on the nonsupport charge. Cook had thought then that he'd gotten a raw deal.

Cook drove over to Truro to see if he could find Tony Costa or the missing Volkswagen. He spotted Chief Berrio's cruiser pulled onto the highway's sandy shoulder. Cook asked him if Truro police had seen a vehicle answering the description of the missing persons complaint from Providence.

Berrio remembered the VW abandoned in the South Truro woods. He said, "Christ! I can take you right to the car."

Berrio resented the fact that Provincetown police had received information on the missing girls as early as January 28 and had kept it to themselves. A lot of funny stuff went on in Provincetown. Berrio occasionally had problems with the "floozies," as he called the homosexuals who flocked to gaudy, free-living Provincetown in summer.

Berrio was aware, too, of the disdain with which his small police force was viewed. Stocky, stolid, a peaceable man, Berrio had been born in Wellfleet and sent to the Westborough State School for Boys as a state ward. Returning to Cape Cod at seventeen, he had worked at odd jobs before becoming town constable; in 1947 he had organized Truro's first two-man police department and been made chief.

As Berrio and Cook were talking, State Trooper Robert Sylvia drove up to the cruiser. Sylvia also asked Berrio about the missing Volkswagen.

Berrio led the way to the South Truro woods, past somber rolling hillsides, a considerable portion of which was under the protection of the Cape Cod National Seashore Park. He stopped the cruiser in the place he had last seen the VW—a popular lovers' lane. The car was gone. Deep tire tracks leaving the area had been imprinted in the ground cover of pine needles.

In a stand of scrub bush nearby Berrio found a five-gallon aluminum lacquer can smelling of gasoline and gave it to Sylvia for a fingerprint check. He checked with the Truro police station by radio; the log confirmed that the car reported on February 2 by Carl Benson matched the registration of the vehicle Cook and Sylvia were looking for.

Berrio and Cook went back into the woods to search the adjacent area. After twenty minutes scanning the woods, Cook walked down a dirt road surrounded by scrub oak. He followed a path to a cul de sac of pines. In a small clearing among the trees, a scattering of paper was strewn along dead ground leaves and caught in tangles of underbrush.

Torn in half was a yellow sales slip from Kent County Motors of West Warwick, Rhode Island, made out to Patricia H. Walsh of 241 California Avenue, Providence; a 1967 Rhode Island registration card; and two Aetna Casualty insurance receipts in Patricia Walsh's name for a "Speed Claim" providing "Complete On-the-Spot Proof of Your Insurance Coverage."

Cook turned the papers over to Trooper Sylvia at Provincetown's police station. Sylvia had talked with Mrs. Cecelia Bonaviri. She told him that her son, Tony Costa, had gone to Boston to look for work and was staying at his half brother Vincent's apartment at 415 Beacon Street.

Sylvia had also questioned Costa's ex-wife, Avis. She had not seen Tony in three or four days.

Sylvia called the barracks. He was ordered back to Truro to await the arrival of State Police Detective Lieutenant John Dunn, just assigned to the case by George Killen.

Dunn, a tall, lumbering man in his late forties with craggy features and a doleful expression of forbearance, was writing a report in the district attorney's office and looking forward to a quiet weekend with his three children and seriously ill wife when he got the word to drive to Truro. A former motorcycle cop assigned traffic control for twelve of his twenty years with the Boston police—dubbed "All Dunn" by his associates—he had one year of Boston College law school before joining Killen's staff in Barnstable in June, 1968, following service with the fire marshal's office in Springfield.

Dunn drove to the Yarmouth barracks to pick up Trooper Edgar "Tom" Gunnery, assigned temporary duty to Killen's office; then he met Patrolman Cook and Trooper Sylvia at the Pamet Road exit off the Mid-Cape Highway. Cook guided the two state police officers into the woods.

In the lowering dusk, Gunnery found the front cover from a Volkswagen owner's manual with Patricia Walsh's name, address and car-key number written on it, a Rhode Island Automobile Club membership, and a spiral-bound "Memo and Datebook Reminder" pad.

Torn in two pieces was a "Purchaser's Tax Return," signed by Pat Walsh, and a quantity of yellow and blue "Notice to Parents" attendance record cards, published by the Providence School Department.

Partially covered over by twigs and leaf mold was a gray driving glove with leather palm and finger insets.

20

* * *

Dunn and Gunnery went to the Provincetown police station to collect the papers found earlier in the woods and the letter written by Tony Costa taped together by Patricia Morton, who received the two officers in her basement office-living room.

Pat Walsh and Mary Anne Wysocki had checked into her guesthouse sometime during the early afternoon of Friday, January 24, she explained for the second time that day. Both girls had been well-dressed, attractive, quite tall. Mary Anne had carried a blue Pan Am flight bag, and a travel case of some sort; Pat Walsh had brought a shoulder bag and some clothes on hangers. "I'm very careful about luggage," Mrs. Morton told Dunn. "No one without luggage gets into my house."

She had inquired how long the girls were staying.

"I was aware of midsemester break—I thought they might be staying on into the week. They said they had come to meet someone on Saturday," Mrs. Morton said, "I was terribly busy. A lot of other guests had come before them." Her establishment was filled that weekend; twenty people occupying eight rooms. "There wasn't much choice left—just a small double on the second floor. I told the girls they would have to take that or nothing. We went into the 'register room'—the room with the large heat register in the floor—on the first floor. I showed them how the doors between the bathroom and bedrooms opened and latched on both sides." The bathroom was next to Tony Costa's room. Costa had been sitting on his bed, reading. "I think it was a copy of one of Hermann Hesse's books—*Demian*—that belongs to me. I don't care for Hesse, but I don't tell these kids that."

She introduced the girls to Tony Costa.

"I think he repeated their names. The girls seemed pleasant and composed. We went downstairs to wind up the details of paying and registering. I asked if they had been in Provincetown before and I got the impression that they had not so I gave them a street map. They were very pleased and thanked me . . . and off they went."

Mrs. Morton had seen the girls that evening, shortly before nine o'clock.

"The weather was frightfully cold. I went upstairs because I was worried. This is the first time I've had winter guests and I was concerned how warm they would be on the top floor." Pat and Mary Anne had both been in the room, "very cheerful and jolly,"

21

Mrs. Morton said. "The Walsh girl was sitting on top of the bed with one of the spare blankets draped across her shoulders like a shawl. I asked them, 'Are you sure you're warm?' I thought if they were not I would put the thermostat up." She had cautioned her guests to leave the door of their room open so the heat could circulate from the register in the hallway directly in front of their door. "They said they were fine and not to worry about it." She offered the use of a Scrabble set, and other games she kept in the office for the amusement of her guests and was politely refused. "The girls told me they were getting ready to go out."

The next morning she had seen a note in the girls' room. "It was hanging by a common pin in the dovetail woodwork on their closet door. It was just on a piece of paper bag—I think it was written in pencil. It said something like, 'I don't want to bother you. Could you possibly give me a ride to Truro?' I think he signed it 'Tony'."

Mrs. Morton took Dunn and Gunnery upstairs to show them Costa's room.

He had moved in on January 18. "I remember that exactly because Tony was my first roomer after I came back from the Virgin Islands. The place had been closed more or less all winter. I had had my sign repainted before I formally opened—I wanted whatever business I could scratch up for the rest of the winter. The sign was lit up outside the night Tony came by to inquire about a room. He knocked on my door; I asked who it was. When he said Tony Costa, I told him I didn't take townspeople, just transients; but he had such a nice voice I let him in and showed him around the available rooms. I had to ask a lot of questions about where he worked and what his habits were and so on. I live alone, and I didn't want him or anyone else to think I was going to be flirtatious."

Costa told her he had worked at the Crown and Anchor Hotel last summer as house carpenter and was now doing construction work.

"He said he had been sleeping on the sofa in the apartment of a young couple in the neighborhood who were expecting a baby, and he had to leave." Costa had spent several nights at his mother's, but couldn't stay there. He told her, "She's getting old and I like to go out nights, and it disturbs her rest."

"I asked for twenty dollars a week," Mrs. Morton said. "Tony said he'd let me know."

A week later Costa moved in, offering to pay a month in advance. "He stayed in the 'register room' two nights, but it was too hot for him. He didn't like to sleep with the windows open. He asked if he could move to the room on the other side of the bath, I call it the bay window room." She had agreed—temporarily. "I didn't want what I think is the best room in the house permanently rented for just twenty dollars a week."

Costa had helped her get the house ready for winter occupancy, turning on the water system and doing odd chores about the house. "He was a very good electrician," she said. "I paid him two-fifty an hour to repair three lamps and he fixed them up just like new."

After Costa moved in, she had had a good run of business; the last three weekends her guesthouse had been full—

"Do you know where Tony Costa is?" Dunn asked patiently.

Mrs. Morton had not seen him for three or four days. "Sometimes he'd be out overnight," she said. "There was a night or two on Sunday, February second, when he was not in his room at night, although he might have come in prior to sunrise for all I know." The last time Tony had stayed in the house was Tuesday night, February fifth. It was apparent he was either moving out or in the process of moving. "There seem to be quite a few things gone from his room, like a small record player with two little speakers—sort of a portable affair—and his records. There was also a drawing board and a T-square thing—a protractor. *That's* gone . . ."

Dunn had listened carefully; Mrs. Morton spoke with such nervous urgency and haste he found it difficult to stem the torrent of words with a question. He had brought along a small tape recorder that he wanted to test for use during interrogations. He couldn't get the machine to work.

That night in Killen's office, Dunn suggested that a search be organized the next morning to look for the missing girls.

Killen knew what Dunn was thinking. There was little likelihood the girls could have survived exposure in the frigid cold Cape Cod had endured the past several weeks if they had wandered away from their disabled automobile and gotten lost in the woods.

Chief Berrio was to provide members of the Truro Rescue Squad and volunteer firemen; and arrangements were already being made to secure volunteers from the Air Force radar station at North Truro. Aerial surveillance would be conducted by the Barnstable County airplane for the wide-ranging search of woodlands looking for Patricia Walsh and Mary Anne Wysocki.

Killen didn't expect to find them alive.

6

About seventy-five men were gathered at nine-thirty the next morning at the same place where the VW was last seen, some woods not far from the Old Truro cemetery. From there the search party would fan out into the cold, snow-dusted woods crossed by slippery trails and leaf-packed hollows.

Chief Berrio led half of the searchers to one side of the dirt road; Dunn took the other side. An hour later, Berrio announced, "My side's clear" and prepared to leave.

Around eleven-thirty, on an embankment twenty feet from Old Proprietor's road, two members of the Truro Rescue Squad came upon a depression some four feet long and two feet wide which had sunk eight inches below the surrounding ground; a piece of olive green cloth was protruding from the bottom of the hollow.

Gunnery used a pick to break open the crust of frost to a depth where the soil softened, turning sandy. When Dunn pulled the cloth free, he discovered it was the strap of a standard army duffel bag, with the initials "U.S." stamped on one side. An odor emanated from the empty bag and the broken ground at Dunn's feet—"like something rotten," Gunnery observed, noticing a red spot on a hook connected to one end of the duffel bag's strap.

Gunnery dug deeper into the ground. At a depth of twelve inches, he uncovered a white object with the appearance of bone, which he suspected could be the portion of a deer buried in the

24

woods by a hunter. Loosening the damp, clinging soil, Gunnery pried the bone free. Connected to its terminus was a human foot.

Dunn stopped the search and ordered radio calls made to George Killen at the district attorney's office, to medical examiner Dr. Daniel Hiebert and to the airplane flying over the search area, one of whose observers was Corporal Roy Nightingale, the official police photographer.

The radio signal to the airplane in Truro came crackling over the Yarmouth barracks radio, and was overheard by Bob Turbidy. Standing at the barracks' front desk, Turbidy froze with dread. The search party had obviously found something.

Turbidy had come to the barracks with Gerry Magnan and John McNally to deliver photographs of Pat Walsh and Mary Anne Wysocki at the request of Detective Lieutenant Bernie Flynn, an investigator attached to Killen's office. Flynn had encouraged Turbidy to join in the search that was to take place in the Truro woods, telling him, "We can use all the help we can get."

Turbidy had no intention of looking for bodies. He and Magnan hadn't been able to get any information out of the police for a week.

Given directions to Hatch Road in Truro by the barracks desk officer, Turbidy, Mangan and McNally clambered into the camper for the half hour's drive down the Mid-Cape Highway. They arrived at Hatch Road's dead-end turnaround at the same time that a funeral home ambulance and a police cruiser converged at the scene.

To the left of the turnaround was a space between a stand of stunted pines hardly wider than a path—the beginning of a dirt road into the woods. When Turbidy explained he and his companions were looking for Bernie Flynn, they were allowed to ride in the back of a panel truck taking the medical examiner into the woods.

Tall, stooped, with watery blue eyes behind thick spectacles, Dr. Daniel Hiebert, at seventy-nine, had practised medicine for over fifty years in Provincetown. "Why do they always have to find bodies on Saturday?" Hiebert grumbled to the driver. He had left an officeful of waiting patients.

The truck bounced along the dirt track that twisted through a tunnellike arcade of overreaching pine boughs that scraped its sides, then came to a stop before a circle of warmly bundled men. Only Dr. Hiebert was allowed to leave; Turbidy and the others would have to wait until an identification was made of the contents of the hole dug in an area close by.

Dr. Hiebert pronounced the object Gunnery had unearthed to be a human foot.

Digging again, Gunnery uncovered a second leg, then two arms severed at their sockets. On the third finger of the left hand clenched into a fist was a ring, clotted with sand. Gunnery brushed the fingers clean. A dull shine of diamonds was embedded in a gold band.

Scraping at the grave with a shovel, Gunnery saw through a layer of dirt the edge of a plastic bag, brittle with cold. Printed across the bag were the words "Horizon Electric Blanket." Through the semi-clear surface, Gunnery discerned a face. He lifted the bag free, untied the knot at its opening and removed a severed head.

The face was shrunken, the skin soft as melting candle wax; blue discolorations marked a swollen cheek and the collapsed chin, as if it had been repeatedly struck by blows which had also smashed the nose nearly flat. The mouth gaped, fixed in unvoiced protest, revealing four missing upper teeth. Sunk in their orbits, the eyes were vacant, colorless, giving the face the empty stare of a ruined doll.

The head had been severed just below the jawbone, the line of separation irregular, but sharply cut. The missing teeth indicated, Dr. Hiebert said, that the victim was past middle age; he judged the head to be that of a white female between fifty and sixty years old.

A white cotton laundry bag had been wrapped around the armless, headless torso Gunnery uncovered when he began digging again. Stuffed in the chest cavity was a pair of blood-soaked panties, size small, with the monogram "Thursday" embroidered on the left leg. Numerous stab wounds had penetrated the chest. Beneath the torso Gunnery found a stubby portion of flesh, covered with sand. Clearing it off, he recognized human buttocks and hip joints, from which the skin had been flayed.

Sifting through clumps of sand and frozen moss, Gunnery found flesh parts and bone, and a large flap of skin, like the hide of some skinned animal.

The eight dismembered parts of the body—separated by a

sharp instrument, possibly a hatchet or an ax, Dr. Hiebert thought —were put into a black body bag and delivered to the funeral home ambulance.

When Dr. Hiebert returned to the truck, Turbidy, Magnan and McNally were allowed to leave. For Turbidy it had been the hardest half hour he had ever waited through. Magnan was pale and silent, certain that the police had found Pat and Mary Anne.

Turbidy was directed to Lieutenant Bernie Flynn. A compact, good-looking man with straight, back-combed blond hair and an air of tense authority about him, Flynn explained that the badly decomposed body found in the grave was neither Pat Walsh nor Mary Anne Wysocki.

Turbidy's relief was short-lived. The discovery of the body, Flynn said, had sinister implications for the safety of the missing girls. Pat Walsh's Volkswagen had last been seen in a clearing less than half a mile from the grave.

From the Truro woods, Turbidy drove with Magnan to Provincetown, going directly to 5 Standish Street. Before leaving Providence that morning, Turbidy had spoken to Patricia Morton on the telephone, telling Magnan and McNally, "She's kind of a scatterbrained lady, very nice and all, but she talks your ear off." Mrs. Morton had confided to Turbidy, "I'd make a *terrible* witness!"

Mrs. Morton greeted the three young men warmly. The police had been there twice the day before, she said, first Officer Cook, and then two state police. She asked them into her basement office and showed the register page Pat and Mary Anne had signed. She had not seen the girls on Sunday morning before they checked out.

"I was rather surprised they left so early. I'd gone upstairs to

27

apologize. I was embarrassed," she said. "I had rented a room to three men, all house painters. And they got dreadfully drunk and made a lot of noise and bothered everyone. I try to keep a nice place, I work so hard at it! You can't imagine how careful you must be in this business. And then these noisy, drunken men made such a terrible mess."

The girls had left her a "sweet" note. The note said, "We're checking out. We had a nice time," she said, "or something like that, I don't remember too clearly. Also, 'Thank you for your many kindnesses'—this was plural." The note was written on a piece of brown-bag paper. She wasn't sure if it was pinned to the door of the room, like Costa's earlier note about a ride, or left on the bureau with the room keys. "The house rule is when you check out, you leave the room locked, and the keys on the bureau. I have a passkey, of course." Checkout time was 10:45, "But I'm not legalistic about it; the sign is on the wall to protect myself." The girls had left much earlier. She had noticed their car gone from across the street first thing when she got up in the morning to start checking rooms. "I thought they might be off having breakfast somewhere; but they didn't come back. When I looked in their room all their things were gone."

Turbidy asked to see the room Pat and Mary Anne had occupied. Mrs. Morton led the way to the front door and a small foyer confronting a steep staircase. At the top of the stairs was a small, shabby room with limp curtains at two high windows and slanted walls of coarse plaster painted a dull ivory.

Mrs. Morton watched in bafflement as Turbidy and Magnan lifted the mattress from the double bed, opened the drawers of an old oak bureau and peered into the half closet wedged under the sharp slant of a dormer wall. The closet disclosed a rack of wire hangers and the faded floral pattern of the room's former wallpaper.

"What on *earth* are you looking for?" she said. She had cleaned the room herself. Little escaped her notice, including the note from Tony Costa asking the girls for a ride to Truro on Saturday morning. She had thrown the note out in the trash. "I didn't realize it had any significance—just like the note your girlfriends left."

Costa had not given notice, nor returned his room keys when he moved out. He had left personal belongings in his room.

"Tony's mother called me," Mrs. Morton said. "She said

Tony had left his hair dryer in the room. I was *rather* annoyed being treated this way, but I didn't want to be disagreeable. I told her, 'Your son is like everybody else.' I said I would give her the things Tony left here when my keys were returned."

Costa had also left a pair of muddy work boots, a length of rope, a half bottle of English Leather aftershave, a "Laugh-In" joke magazine and several overdue library books. There was also a quantity of Riszla papers—"cigarette wrappers that come in a red package," Mrs. Morton explained, "for people who roll their own cigarettes"—a mustard-colored turtleneck she had often seen him wear, a golf shirt and a cheap green and white V-neck crocheted pullover. "But all Tony's mother was interested in was the hair dryer."

At the mention of a hair dryer, Turbidy exchanged a look with Magnan. He asked if he could look at Costa's room.

Mrs. Morton led them downstairs. She unlocked room number 6 off the foyer—the "register room." Costa had occupied a room on the opposite side of an adjoining bathroom.

Large, spacious, with a bay window overlooking Standish Street, the room had been swept clean, the bed made and the wastebasket emptied. When Magnan opened the double closet, the left door stuck. An aluminum cot was turned sideways, wedged into a corner. In the shadow of the cot on the floor beside a neat coil of rope was a round hat box of simulated alligator skin, zippered all around and with a loop handle. Magnan pounced on it. "This is Mary Anne's hair dryer," he said.

Turbidy asked to see Costa's other belongings. Mrs. Morton had put them in the closet of the register room. Turbidy saw a white turtleneck sweater of imitation Irish knit. He held the sweater up to examine the double rows of cable stitching that alternated with a design of linked diamonds—identical to a sweater Pat Walsh owned. The sweater had a feminine scent to it. The label said, "Rosanna—100% Wool—Made in British Hong Kong—Size 40."

In the basement office, Magnan called Mrs. Wysocki—collect —in Providence. He had her describe the hair dryer over the telephone. Opening the case, he found a small mirror on the inside. He lifted out a white plastic bonnet with elasticized edges which attached to a corrugated hose. Magnan asked her to confirm the five settings on the face of the dryer—a "Bettina" model made by Universal.

"That's it!" Magnan said when he hung up. "This is definitely Mary Anne's."

Mrs. Morton had monitored the conversation carefully; Magnan had given no hint of the dryer's appearance. She said to Turbidy, "I was hoping it was all a ghastly mistake."

Mrs. Morton called the Provincetown police. Turbidy recognized Patrolman Cook when he came to the door as the young police officer he had spoken to at the station. Turbidy was disgusted that the police had come to the guesthouse several times and had overlooked such obvious evidence.

Mrs. Morton turned over to Cook the sweater and hair dryer identified as the property of the missing girls found in Tony Costa's room.

"I know Tony," Cook said cheerfully. "He owes me a couple favors. I'll talk to him and find out where the girls are."

Turbidy was incensed by Cook's offhandedness, his assumption that Pat and Mary Anne, now missing for two weeks, were off somewhere with Tony Costa. Shy, introspective, Pat tended to be cautious with people she did not know. At the start of their romance, it had been difficult for Turbidy to keep a conversation going with her. Pat Walsh was not the kind of girl to take off with somebody she'd just met.

Magnan, too, was bothered by Cook's casual response to evidence linking Antone Costa to the girls. Mary Anne might seem a chatterbox, approachable and friendly on the surface, but she was a conservative girl, not likely to take up with a stranger.

Turbidy called the Yarmouth barracks to report the evidence found in Tony Costa's room, now in the hands of the Provincetown police. He was told to stop by the barracks on his trip off-Cape.

As he was getting ready to leave, Turbidy learned from Mrs. Morton that Costa's ex-wife, Avis, had an apartment nearby on Commercial Street.

Turbidy went to the shabby house, mounting the back stairs to the second floor. No one was home, but on his way out he encountered a slender young woman coming up the walk, tending three small children.

Avis Costa was friendly when Turbidy introduced himself and asked about her ex-husband. She had not seen Tony for a while.

"He's been talking for months about splitting town, but no-

30

body really believed he'd do it," she said. "Tony's awful hung up on Provincetown." Her ex-husband had, apparently, finally up and left; nobody had seen him around. She had no idea where he could be reached.

8

When Turbidy entered the Yarmouth barracks that Saturday evening, Sergeant Bolduc led him to a row of cells. Spread on a cell bunk were the torn papers found by Dunn and Gunnery the day before in the South Truro woods.

Turbidy examined the papers with a dread welling up in his chest. His attention was focused on the "Memo and Datebook," whose cover showed a child raptly playing with blocks. It was an annual publication of the Anti-Defamation League, a gift "Compliments of B'Nai B'Rith." Flipping through the stuck-together pages stained from their exposure to the outdoors, Turbidy discovered that Pat had made "Rent Due" entries in the diary every two weeks up to Monday, April 7, 1969. He turned the pages to the listing for Friday, January 24; there was a single notation: "Ptown." At the bottom of the page was printed a quotation from Mark Twain: "When in doubt, tell the truth."

Seeing her personal papers torn to pieces, Turbidy thought, was like seeing a part of Pat herself violated. Some of the papers having to do with her car were out of date, Bolduc pointed out—the kind of things that accumulated in the glove compartment.

"But there's stuff here Pat wouldn't have any reason to throw away," Turbidy said. He was stricken with fear when it occurred to him that someone other than Pat had disposed of her papers.

Bolduc told him there was no evidence of foul play involved in the disappearance. "They're both over twenty-one. "It's no crime if they took off." The files of the barracks were filled with such cases . . .

Despite Turbidy's protests, Bolduc was disinclined to take the case seriously. He seemed more intent on questioning Turbidy's relationship with Pat Walsh when, shortly after 7 P.M. Bolduc excused himself to take a telephone call.

In the conference room to which he had been brought with John McNally and Gerry Magnan, Turbidy puzzled over the indifference of the police, sensing a growing antagonism in the tenor of their questions. As he continued to press the urgency of the situation, it began to occur to him that *he* was being treated as a suspect in the disappearance.

John McNally was amused by Turbidy's growing agitation, that he was letting the negative reaction of the police get to him. Since returning from California, Turbidy had grown a short beard and mustache; "Bobby," McNally told him, "the cops think you're a hippie."

Magnan too had no doubt they were being questioned as suspects; but hippiedom could hardly be applied to him. Short-haired and clean-shaven, he was wearing a striped oxford cloth shirt and crew neck sweater Mary Anne had given him last Christmas.

The call for Bolduc was from Sergeant Meads in Provincetown.

Meads told Bolduc he had just received a phone call from Tony Costa in Vermont. "Tony mentioned that his mother had contacted him about the phone call I made about the missing girls he'd met at Mrs. Morton's, and the note pinned to their door asking for a ride." Meads had told him the girls were missing and asked if Costa had any information as to where they went after leaving Provincetown; the girls' parents were very worried.

Costa said he had met Pat and Mary Anne at the Foc's'le bar about two weeks ago. He had a couple of drinks with them, after which they had gotten friendly. During the conversation Pat told him she needed an abortion and had come to Provincetown to get money for it. "She had a date the next morning with a dude by the name of Russell who was hitchhiking to Provincetown," Costa said. "The three of them were going to Los Angeles to see a guy named Bob who was going to help get the abortion."

Costa had seen the girls the next morning when they drove him to a construction site to pick up a payroll check that was due him; they had dropped him off and headed toward Hyannis.

Costa was now waiting for a ride connection to New York

32

City. He had asked if Meads wanted him to come back to Provincetown to be questioned. Meads said no, but to keep him informed if he heard anything more about the girls. . . .

Bolduc came back into the conference room. "I know where the girls are," he said. "They've gone to pick the lock."

Turbidy failed to comprehend Bolduc's meaning.

"They've gone to get an abortion," Bolduc said bluntly.

Turbidy was stunned—too surprised to say anything.

Tony Costa had just called Provincetown police, offering to come back to Cape Cod, if necessary, to be questioned, Bolduc explained. The girls were friends of his; they had sought his help in obtaining an abortion in Provincetown. "Costa said he couldn't help them, so they went out to California to find a guy by the name of Bob."

"That's *me*," Turbidy said. "But Pat knew I was coming back to Providence. I spoke to her the day before she left for Provincetown."

Bolduc shrugged. "Well, the girls are on their way out there to see you."

Turbidy was deeply disturbed. Tony Costa must have talked to Pat and Mary Anne long enough to have information to lie persuasively. It was clear that Bolduc believed his story. Costa was, apparently, as buddy-buddy with the cops at the barracks as he was with Patrolman Cook in Provincetown.

"Pat Walsh is your girlfriend, isn't she?" Bolduc said.

"Yes," Turbidy said. He was wary of police now.

"Well, you're sleeping with her, aren't you?"

Turbidy flushed. "Hell, we're in love. We're planning on getting married."

Bolduc smiled suggestively and Turbidy felt a rush of anger. The abortion story was preposterous. Pat was on the pill; more than anything she adored babies, she desperately wanted children. Further, Pat was a good Catholic; abortion was anathema to her . . .

Magnan was furious with the police. He said to Turbidy, "Let's get the hell out of here, I've had enough of this bullshit."

Turbidy, however, didn't want to leave the barracks until somebody had gotten the message that the girls could be in serious trouble. He didn't believe Costa's story for a minute; nevertheless, he gave the officers the names and addresses of friends in California Pat Walsh might contact if she was, indeed, on her way to the West Coast. Turbidy was told police would wait several days to give the girls a chance to get to California; then they would have Los Angeles police check their whereabouts.

Turbidy was tense with frustration in the camper. When Russell Norton called to learn the results of the trip to Cape Cod, Turbidy told him only Bernie Flynn among the police was taking the case seriously.

An hour after Turbidy left the barracks, Bolduc transmitted a teletype on the missing persons complaint:

> INFORMATION NOW IS THAT SUBJECTS ARE BOTH POSSIBLY HEADED FOR LOS ANGELES, CALIFORNIA. SUPPOSEDLY TO SEE SUBJECT BOB TURBIDY. UNKNOWN TO BOTH FEMALE SUBJECTS IS THE FACT THAT TURBIDY HAS JUST RETURNED TO THIS COAST FROM LA.

The message was picked up in Providence by Sergeant Perry. When Perry called the barracks, Bolduc told him his station had learned Pat Walsh was pregnant and looking for an abortion; her boyfriend Robert Turbidy was involved in the pregnancy. The missing girls were headed for Los Angeles to see Turbidy after an unsuccessful attempt to secure an abortion in Provincetown.

Bolduc tried to reach Killen to tell him of Turbidy's visit to the barracks, but Killen was not in his office.

9

George Killen was standing in a shed attached to Carlson's Funeral Home in Wellfleet, fuming. Breath plumes showed in the unheated room whose single light bulb was strung on a cord over a chipped enamel table. With Killen was state pathologist Dr. George Katsas, brought out to Cape Cod from the department of

34

legal medicine at Harvard to do an autopsy on the body found in the Truro woods.

"I won't perform," Dr. Katsas said with finality.

Killen confronted Dr. Hiebert. "Why in hell did you have the body brought to *this* place?"

The undertaking establishment did not do very much business, Hiebert explained. "I was only trying to help the guy out."

"I got a murder on my hands!" Killen exploded. "I don't give a goddamn about business."

Killen arranged to have the body transferred to the mortuary of Boston City Hospital. He was also angered by Hiebert's misidentification of the body as that of a fifty- to sixty-year-old woman, information now being broadcast by teletype from the Yarmouth barracks. Examination by Dr. Katsas had revealed the body's missing teeth had been knocked out by the force of a blow, those remaining in good condition without cavities. Katsas put the age of the victim as being between seventeen and nineteen years old.

On Sunday morning, February 9, Chief Harold Berrio called George Killen to suggest that the body found in the woods could be Sydney Lee Monzon, a girl missing from Provincetown since May, 1968.

Killen called Sergeant Meads to check out Berrio's lead. Meads said he had taken the missing persons complaint on June 14, 1968 describing Sydney Monzon as an eighteen-year-old, white female, 105 pounds, with long brown hair, last seen wearing bell-bottom jeans, a tan jersey and sandals.

Meads also told Killen that Provincetown police had traced the aluminum paint lacquer can found on Friday in the woods to Watts's Amoco garage in North Truro.

Russell Watts had sold Tony Costa five gallons of gas about midnight on Sunday, February 2, telling Dunn and Gunnery when they came to his station the following noon: "Tony said he was stuck up near the package store on Route 6, and was headed for Boston." Several days later, Costa had called Watts's brother, Bill to get an estimate on painting a Volkswagen "some exotic color."

Watts quoted one hundred dollars to do the job. "Tony said he'd stop by, but he never did."

Costa already owed the garage money for repairs made on a '59 Oldsmobile he'd junked in January. "He talked about the money he owed, and how he'd pay something on it soon." Tony was good for it, Bill Watts said, he always paid eventually. Costa was a friend of his son, Gary, and often left his tools in a storage room back of the garage when he was working in Truro. "Tony's all right when he isn't goofed up on dope, like these kids today," Watts said, recalling the day last September when he'd gone with Tony to the Truro woods.

"I went in a pickup truck to get Tony's car started. We'd gone about an eighth of a mile into the woods and there was Tony's blue Olds, clear off the side of the road. He said he'd rolled down the hill trying to start the car. I got the booster cables out of the truck and put them on his car and got him started. But I couldn't back out—that hill was too steep. I asked him if he could back up until I found a place to turn around in. Tony backed up and I got out and waited for him to come through the woods. He came real fast, I thought he was showing off, playing around. Tony was stopped right in the middle of the road where I first started him. He came running up the hill by some oak trees. He had two, three little envelopes he was waving in the air. They looked like pay envelopes, buff-colored. I figured it was marijuana or something like that he had hidden out there and I just laughed at him."

Dunn and Gunnery talked with contractor Frank Diego, for whom Tony Costa had done plumbing. Costa had worked until 1 P.M. on a day when he was sent from the job for supplies. He had never returned. His mother had called asking Diego to bring Tony's tools and paycheck to her house. He had refused. "I wanted Tony to finish the job," he explained. "He's a terrific worker when he isn't on dope."

Dunn and Gunnery next spoke to Cecelia Bonaviri in her second-floor apartment on Conant Street. A small, neat woman, with deep circles under large, baleful eyes, she had not seen her son since Tuesday, January 28, when he was rushed by taxi to Cape Cod Hospital in Hyannis suffering severe abdominal pains. Tony had called her from Vermont on Friday night, February 7, to ask her to pick up his belongings from 5 Standish Street. But Mrs. Morton wouldn't give her anything until Tony returned his room keys.

                        * * *

"I thought I would be a bit of a Sherlock Holmes," Patricia Morton told Dunn in her basement office. "I called Mrs. Bonaviri to inquire about my keys again, but what I was *really* trying to find out was where this half brother lived. Young Turbidy and I thought if we could find him we could get in touch with Tony."

Mrs. Bonaviri was immediately suspicious and had asked, "Who wants to know?"

"She said she didn't want her Tony to get into any trouble," Mrs. Morton said. "She promised I'd get my keys back."

Three of Tony Costa's "little friends" had come to the guest-house looking for him. "They hadn't seen Tony anywhere," Mrs. Morton said. "They asked if they could leave a note for him. It said, 'Tony, where are you? We miss you. Where have you been?'"

The high school-age girls had returned a few days later with a ceramic bank in the shape of a lion—Costa was born under the sign of Leo—and a note written on the back of a page of guitar chords. The note said, "In an effort to save for your houseboat," and was signed, "Robin, Paula and Patty."

Gunnery noticed on the sofa in the office a coil of rope with red stains on it. Mrs. Morton said the rope had come from the closet of Costa's room. "I thought it was a clothesline—that diameter—but it's really a bit thick for hanging clothes." She let Gunnery take the rope with him when he left.

Since Tony Costa had moved, Mrs. Morton wanted his things out of her house. Dunn told Provincetown police to pick up a grocery bag containing a turtleneck shirt and a pair of work boots with dirt between the treads of the soles. Then he and Gunnery went to the Foc's'le bar and the Pilgrim Club to show pictures of Pat Walsh and Mary Anne Wysocki to the bartenders. As Turbidy had been told the weekend before, no one remembered seeing the girls.

It was not until 9 P.M. that Gunnery turned the coil of rope over to George Killen at the Barnstable courthouse. Then he made his way to the split-level house on Autumn Lane in Centerville he shared with his wife and three daughters.

Handsome and sturdily built, Gunnery was years younger-looking than thirty-six. A trooper for ten years, he was eager to prove himself and pleased with his temporary assignment to Killen's office, a change from the regular hours and routine patrols of

                          37

the barracks. Gunnery was worried, though. The change to plain-clothes was putting an unexpected burden on his limited civilian wardrobe. He owned a brown suit, and one sport jacket—and that was about it . . .

Around 9:30 P.M. that same Sunday, bus driver George Davis dropped Tony Costa off at the corner of Conant and Bradford streets in Provincetown. A short, spunky man, Davis regularly drove the Hyannis-to-Provincetown route for Cape Cod Bus Lines. Costa told him he was coming from Burlington, Vermont; he was going home because of "family problems."

A half hour later, Sergeant Meads received a telephone call at Provincetown police station. Tony Costa wanted an appointment set up the next day to talk to Chief Francis Marshall about the missing girls from Providence. Costa had come back to Province-town "to straighten things out in my behalf."

Meads was puzzled about Costa's abrupt return, and told him so.

Costa said, "Jim, I've got their car."

Suzanne "Sandy" Carter, a petite, pretty girl of nineteen, lived with her parents at 9 Conant Street, next door to the house in which Cecelia Bonaviri rented an apartment. When her telephone rang on Monday morning, February 10, it was Tony Costa asking, "Where's Pat and Mary Anne?"

"Who?" Sandy said.

"Pat and Mary Anne," Costa said. "You know who I mean."

"Tony, I don't know anyone by that name."

"Sure you do," Costa said. "You know where they are."

"Gee, Tony . . . Pat and Mary Anne? What are you talking

about? I don't know them." When he remained silent, Sandy said, "Tony, are you stoned?"

She heard Costa laugh, then admit he had just shot up four match heads of speed.

Costa had called almost every day he was in town during the past two months asking her to borrow her father's car in order to take him to the woods in Truro where he kept a cache of drugs. Most of the time she had put him off with an excuse, but she had gone to the woods with Costa once. He had kept staring at her. It had been raining, and she had said, "Tony, I don't want to get out of the car." Costa had driven from a parking space off a dirt road and taken her home. The next day he hadn't remembered the incident.

Costa had also asked her to go with him when he left Provincetown at five o'clock on Thursday morning, February 6; he was going to pick up a car in Boston he'd bought for four hundred dollars and head for the West Coast. Before he left town, however, Costa told her he had to find two girls he knew to give them their clothes.

"What are you doing back in town?" Sandy said. "I thought you were splitting for California?"

Costa had come back to talk to police about the disappearance of two girls from Providence he had met several weekends ago, he said. "The state police came to my mother's house looking for me."

"Do you know where those girls are?" Sandy said.

"They're far away," Costa said, "They're in Canada; they took a plane. Right now they're in Montreal."

"The day after you left—it was really funny—they found a body out in the woods all cut up." Teasingly, she added, "What did you do with those girls, Tony? You didn't cut them up, too, did you?"

"Of course I didn't!" Costa said. He had heard about the body found in the woods near the old Truro cemetery. "What probably happened is somebody dug her up to rob her of her jewels. Then, they just chopped her up and threw her in a hole. Maybe that's what happened."

Costa was nervous about his interview with Chief Marshall. He had shot up to give himself "energy" for the encounter.

"What'll you do if you get busted?" Sandy said.

Costa said, "What would *you* do if you sold three pounds of

39

hashish? Would you stick around and let them put you in jail or would you leave the country?"

Sergeant Meads came to 9 Conant Street at eleven o'clock to tell Tony Costa that Chief Marshall was in his office, waiting to talk to him; he offered a ride downtown in the police cruiser.

"OK, Jim," Costa said, "I'll be right down."

Standing at the top of the stairs, Tony Costa looked down at Meads through gold-rimmed spectacles with large, gentle brown eyes. His thick dark hair was parted on the side, worn low on his brow; he had a full mustache and long sideburns. A strong nose, too wide for the rest of his face, gave his handsomeness a compelling, off-center expression of vulnerability, an imperfection that accented the near-delicacy of his regular features. A dark sensuality smoldered under his light skin, like the shadow of his freshly shaven beard. Costa was wearing a turtleneck shirt that hugged his muscular torso, flaring to wide shoulders and tapering to a slender waist, and neatly pressed white denim pants; his dress boots were highly polished. Meads had known him as a schoolboy from Somerville spending the summer with relatives in Province-town. The trouble with Tony Costa was he had married too young and loaded himself down with the responsibility of a wife and three kids before he was mature enough to handle it.

Meads admired the courage it had taken for Tony Costa to turn in a pusher, Jay Von Utter, going to police with information obtained from Avis about a large shipment of drugs Von Utter was bringing to her house. Costa was afraid police would bust Avis as a junkie and he would lose his children.

Costa had proved to be a reliable source of information, giving police the make, model and color of Von Utter's car and the approximate time of his arrival. Police had picked Von Utter up entering Provincetown; dismantling his Volkswagen, they had found drugs concealed behind the wheel covers and under the rear seats—one of the biggest drug busts on Cape Cod.

It was not long after the Von Utter bust that word got around that Tony had snitched. Costa blamed Chief Marshall for spreading it all over town that he was an informer. . . .

Costa reappeared on the landing of his mother's apartment wearing a navy blue warm-up jacket. When his mother came to the doorway, he bent to kiss her goodbye.

In the cruiser, Meads said, "Remember when you came to me about your kids, when Avis got mixed up with narcotics and Jay Von Utter?"

"Yes, I remember." Costa said.

"Well, the parents of the missing girls are asking for help concerning their daughters. And they're every bit as concerned about their children as you were about your children, Tony."

Meads noticed Costa could hardly sit still, twisting around in the front seat of the cruiser, giving off energy like a space heater. Costa seemed on the verge of an outburst by the time Meads got him into the station. Costa was tightly reined in, struggling to control himself. Meads was sure Tony was getting ready to confess something about the girls.

Meads said, "Tony, if you know where these girls are, tell me, so we can find them and relieve their parents' worry."

There were tears in Costa's eyes when he lowered his head in his hands.

"Whatever it is, Tony," Meads said gently. "You know you can tell me."

Here it comes, Meads thought.

When Costa straightened, he was composed. "Jim, if I could help you, I would," he said. "The only thing I know is the girls told me they needed money for an abortion for Pat Walsh. I bought their Volkswagen for nine hundred dollars to help them out. I told them they could use the car a few days and they said they would contact me where to pick it up. I thought it would be on the Cape someplace, but they called and said the car was at the airport in Burlington, Vermont."

Meads was disappointed. He said, "What were the girls doing in Vermont?"

"I don't know," Costa said. "All I can tell you is they were headed for Montreal."

Meads wanted to continue questioning Costa, but Marshall had arranged for the state police to interrogate him, and Detective Lieutenant John Dunn was waiting in the outer office. It wasn't a Provincetown case any more; the DA's office was now running things. Reluctantly, Meads left the station, turning Tony Costa over to Chief Francis Cheney—pronounced "Cheeny"—Marshall.

Marshall's father, a man weighing in excess of three hundred fifty pounds, had been called "Big Cheney" and as a boy Marshall was named "Little Cheney." The name just stuck. Square-jawed

41

and broad-shouldered, a tough, shrewd and coarse man whose steel-gray crew cut fit like a cap tight against his skull, Cheney Marshall was an exceptional police officer in a community that would have daunted a lesser man. Invaded in summer by a population of artists, tourists, young toughs, day-trippers and flocks of homosexuals attracted to the town's freewheeling, good-times atmosphere, Provincetown was a law-enforcement nightmare, lately complicated by a gathering of vagrant hippie youths and a massive drug problem. Feared and respected, Marshall had headed the extraordinarily busy police station for ten years with an iron hand, dispensing—in the words of his detractors—"Marshall Law."

Marshall asked Tony Costa where he had gotten Pat Walsh's car. He said he didn't care about drugs this time. "I won't press dope. Just tell me."

Costa said some hashish was involved and a little bit of heroin. "The girls are dealing," he said. "They bought some shit off me last summer and didn't pay. So I grabbed their car when I saw them in town again. One of them is pregnant—she's gone to Montreal to get an abortion."

Marshall glared across the desk. Costa's superior air, the cultivated, almost lofty tone of his voice was enough to enrage him. He knew Tony Costa as "a pig on drugs—he'd take anything" and as a pusher, too smart to get busted. Only reluctantly had Marshall given permission for Meads to use him on the Von Utter case.

Marshall's raspy voice was ragged with dislike, "I'll give you some advice, Tony," he said, taking Costa in to see the state police. "If I were you, I'd get myself a good lawyer."

As John Dunn began his interview, he found Costa a well-mannered and soft-spoken young man, articulate in rendering the events leading up to his meeting the girls in the Foc's'le bar.

"Pat told me they were supposed to pick up a guy in Hyannis. They were looking for fake ID's," Costa said. "When Mary Anne mentioned a guy named Russ, Pat gave her a real dirty look. Pat wanted to sell her 1968 VW because she needed money."

Costa had seen Pat and Mary Anne the next morning when they drove him to a construction site in Truro to pick up a paycheck due him. The girls had brought him back to Provincetown and he had gotten out of the car. Costa said, "At this time I said goodbye to the girls and they headed out of town for Hyannis . . ."

11

When Bernie Flynn entered the district attorney's office on that Monday morning he said to Killen, "Where's Dunn?"

Killen told him Dunn was in Provincetown questioning Antone Costa about the missing Providence girls. Marshall had already called to say Costa had bought the girls' car as part of a dope deal they were all involved in.

Flynn's contact with Bob Turbidy at the grave site, however, had convinced him of the sincerity of the young man's apprehensions for Patricia Walsh. Flynn also found it odd that the girls would go all the way to Provincetown to sell their car when they could have sold it in Providence.

"How were they going to get home after the weekend?" Flynn said to Killen, "Walk?" The whole deal didn't sound right to him. A car was a major item in the life of a girl Pat Walsh's age. "They'd sooner get rid of their boyfriend than their car." Flynn was intrigued. "George, do you mind if I talk to this guy?"

Killen was pleased to have Flynn volunteer. He was having second thoughts about giving the case to Dunn—a pleasant and dutiful police officer but a little shy on experience dealing with Cape Codders.

Killen called Provincetown police to have them hold Antone Costa at the station. "If Dunn gives you any trouble," he told Flynn, "tell him I've put you in charge of the case."

At forty-five, Bernie Flynn could not remember a time when he had not wanted to be a cop. Good looking, blonde, blue-eyed and cocky, Flynn had joined the New Bedford, Massachusetts,

43

police force in 1947. He had worked himself up to captain of the uniformed branch before taking the state police exam and placing first. Offered his choice of the district attorney's office in New Bedford or Barnstable courthouse, Flynn had jumped at the chance to work with George Killen.

A superb street cop with reflexes as quick as his tongue, Flynn was a tenacious investigator, describing himself "like a dog in heat" once he sank his teeth into a case. Not averse to throwing a punch or kicking in a door once his Irish temper got the better of him, Flynn relished the role of "villain" when interrogating suspects. He had once told the rookie cops coming onto the New Bedford force, "If you want to be a nice guy, maybe you should get into some other line of work."

The asphalt tile and knotty pine of Provincetown's police station reminded Flynn of a VFW lodge. The station was filled with milling police officers. Flynn spotted Dunn standing in a corridor, looking unhappy.

Costa had told him pretty much everything he knew about the girls, Dunn explained to Flynn. "I don't think you'll get much more out of him."

"Let *me* talk to him," Flynn said, with just enough emphasis to tell Dunn where he stood.

Dunn pointed out Tony Costa standing by an entrance counter talking to Patrolman Cook.

Flynn gave an appraising look to the tall young man and was impressed. Costa was a good-looking kid, well set-up; not at all the sleazy Provincetown type he had been expecting.

"This is Lieutenant Bernie Flynn," Marshall said when he introduced Tony Costa in his office. "He wants to ask you a few questions."

Marshall had been surprised to have Killen call to tell him he was sending Flynn to question Tony Costa. Dunn had already interrogated him. What was going on? Killen ran too tight a ship ever to waste time on duplication of effort. But Marshall liked Flynn's style; he stayed in his office to listen.

Flynn began formally, telling Tony Costa he was interested in locating Patricia Walsh and Mary Anne Wysocki to relieve the anxiety of their parents who had reported them missing.

"You are not a suspect in any crime," Flynn said. "If the girls did leave home, this is their right as they are both over twenty-one and are free to come and go as they please . . ."

Costa could stop the interview and leave the station anytime he wished. If he was about to make any statements about the girls, Flynn would inform him of his rights under the Miranda rulings of the Supreme Court.

Marshall said Costa had already been given his rights and was very cooperative.

"Are you willing to give us information about the whereabouts of Patricia Walsh and Mary Anne Wysocki?" Flynn said.

Costa said he had returned from Burlington, Vermont, with the intention of helping police find the girls. "I'll be glad to answer any questions I can," he said politely. "And tell you what I know about the girls."

Costa gave his name, and his age as twenty-four. He was divorced, the father of three children. Presently unemployed, he was going to work for Frank Diego doing carpentry, electrical wiring and plumbing. He would be living in the rear of the former electric company building on Bradford Street, a block from the police station. He had previously lived at 5 Standish Street. On Friday, January 24, around noontime, he was in his room reading when the landlady walked by the open door and introduced him to two girls. He remembered their names as Pat and Mary Anne from Providence, Rhode Island.

"Had you ever met these girls before?" Flynn said.

"No," Costa said.

"Did you see them again that day?"

"I met them that evening at a bar in town called the Foc's'le, around eight or eight-thirty. We drank and talked until midnight. Pat told me she needed money and wanted to sell her car for nine hundred dollars."

Flynn was puzzled by Costa's voice—a soft, high baritone articulated with a precise, almost effete accent, out of character for a Provincetown handyman. It was obvious to Flynn that Costa had a much higher opinion of himself than that.

"What kind of a car was it?" Flynn said.

"A light blue Volkswagen."

"Did you buy the car?"

"Yes, I did," Costa said. Pat Walsh had taken a piece of paper from her handbag and written out a sales slip. "I have the bill of sale right here."

Flynn examined the folded sheet of lined yellow paper Costa took from his wallet:

Sold to Anthony Costa for the sum of $900, my blue 1968 V.W., model #118088538, type 117, engine #H5036528, January 27, 1969.

Patricia Walsh

Anthony C. Costa

Flynn handed back the bill of sale.

"Oh, you can keep it if you like," Costa said. "I just wanted it to show I owned the car."

"Did you give Pat Walsh nine hundred dollars after you received this bill of sale?"

"No, I didn't," Costa said.

"You want me to believe a girl you just met signed over her 1968 Volkswagen to you without getting any payment for it?"

Costa said, "I told the Walsh girl I would pay her in the morning."

"Where did you have the money?"

"In my room. I had six hundred dollars saved and my brother loaned me three hundred."

"Did you see Pat and Mary Anne the next morning?"

"Yes. I pinned a note on the door of their room asking them for a ride to Truro. I wanted to go to the Royal Coachman motel to pick up a paycheck I had coming to me. Around eleven o'clock the girls came to my room and said they had seen the note. They told me they were going to Hyannis to pick up a friend of Mary Anne's—a guy named Russ.

"Did you get a ride to Truro?"

"Yes, I did." In the car Costa had given Pat Walsh nine hundred dollars; then she had driven into the Truro woods and parked in a clearing. "Pat told me she would like to use the car for one more week. When she brought it back she would leave the car in the woods where I could pick it up."

Tony Costa was intelligent and unexcitable. His story had sounded plausible until now. Flynn paused over the steno pad he kept in a leather case on which he was taking notes. "Why didn't they park the car in front of the rooming house where it would have been more convenient for you to pick up?" Flynn said.

"I don't know."

Flynn pressed him. "Didn't you find it *strange* these girls would put the car in the middle of the woods in Truro?"

"No," Costa said. "I just went along with them."

46

"Had you ever been to the woods prior to this time?"

"No," Costa said evenly. "This was the first time."

"I thought you told me you bought the car at the Foc's'le bar on Friday night? Why didn't you take possession of it then?"

"I didn't need the car right away," Costa said. "And I wanted to be a good guy to the girls."

"You're telling me you gave nine hundred dollars for a car and allowed two strangers to keep it for a week on their word they would return it?"

"Yeah, I wasn't worried," Costa said. "I trusted them. I believe they'd bring the car back within a week, like they said."

"What did you do after the girls took you into the woods and showed you where they were going to leave the car?"

"We drove back to Provincetown. I wanted my check, and I had to find Zack—Jimmy Zacharias, a guy I used to work with on the job."

"Did you find him?"

"We were driving down Bradford Street and I saw him on a motorcycle. I told Pat to stop the car. I got out to talk to Zack and the girls drove off toward Hyannis."

"I don't know, Tony," Flynn said. "It seems pretty strange to me these girls told you they needed nine hundred dollars for a VW, then kept it for a week. Don't you think they could have sold the car in Providence and gotten more money for it? Isn't nine hundred dollars a small amount to pay for a '68 Volkswagen?"

"Yes," Costa said. "But I told you, the girls needed money."

"If they needed money so badly and they still had the car all the next week," Flynn said, "why couldn't they have sold the car to a dealer for more money than you gave them?"

Costa looked off, hesitated, then hung his head. "Lieutenant, I'm going to be honest with you," he said. "That wasn't a true story. I didn't give the girls nine hundred dollars. I met them last August. I sold them a pound of hashish for seven hundred bucks —only the girls didn't have any money. They took the hash, and I didn't see them again. When I spotted them in Provincetown again, I took the car in payment for the pound of hash they owed me for, and I gave them three hundred more."

"Wait a minute," Flynn's voice was a cutting edge. *"Now* you're saying the first statement is false, that you *didn't* give them nine hundred dollars for the car. Now you're telling me you paid a

47

thousand dollars for the car—seven hundred they owed you for the hashish and three hundred in cash. Is that right?"

"Yes," Costa said earnestly. His eyes moved briefly to Chief Marshall. "I was covering up for myself. I didn't want you to know I was selling drugs."

"What were the girls going to do with the hashish?"

"I believe they told me they were going to Canada and sell it up there. They were leaving home."

"You previously said you borrowed three hundred dollars from your brother so you could buy the car," Flynn said. "Is that true?"

"Yes."

"When did you contact your brother about buying the car?"

"I borrowed the money a week earlier and—"

"At that time the girls weren't in Provincetown," Flynn cut in. "You couldn't have had any knowledge of the car at that time."

"I was going to use the money for construction work," Costa said, "but I used it for the car instead."

"Did you ever take possession of the car after you let the girls have it for a week?"

"Yes, I went out to the woods one night—it was Sunday, February second. The car was in the same spot Pat Walsh said it would be left."

"How did the girls get out of the woods after leaving the car out there?"

"I don't know," Costa said.

Flynn glared across the desk. "Tony, you've told me one story—now you tell me this story. *Clear your mind.* I want you to tell me what happened after you took possession of the car. I want you to think about this very carefully, so we can have the truth. Do you want to tell me about it?"

"I'll tell you what happened," Costa said agreeably. "I was covering up for the girls because I thought they might get in trouble with the police. The story about the hashish is not true. The girls told me they were both pregnant and they were looking for an abortion and needed money. That's why I bought their car —they were taking off for California to get an abortion."

Flynn barely contained his exasperation. "How were they going to get to California without a car?"

"I don't know. I went out to the woods with two guys named Steve and Timmy and found the car was there."

"How did you know the car would be there?"

"I didn't," Costa said. "I was just taking a chance."

"I assume the girls locked the car when they left it in the woods." Flynn said. "How did you get the key?"

"The key was left under the front wheel of the car."

"How did you know it would be there?"

"The girls told me they would put it there," Costa said. He had driven the car out of the woods to the highway; then Steve had driven to 415 Beacon Street in Boston. "We got there around three o'clock in the morning."

"What did you do with the car?"

"The car was parked in front of my brother's apartment."

"What happened after that?"

"Steve left us on Monday and went back to Provincetown," Costa said. "Timmy and I stayed until Tuesday and returned to Provincetown by bus."

"Why didn't you bring the car back to Provincetown with you?" Flynn said. "You're telling me this is *your* car. Why did you leave it in Boston?"

"I had told the girls I was going to be in Boston that weekend, and if they were on Beacon Street they might see the car and they could use it."

Flynn's face was tense with incredulity; he wasn't bothering to take notes any more. "And *did* they use the car again?"

"I learned later that the girls picked up the car and took off."

"Did anyone see them take the car?"

"No, but my brother told me the car wasn't in front of the house the day after I came back to Provincetown when I called him. He said the car was gone."

"How did they start the car if you had the keys?"

"I don't know," Costa said. "But I'm sure they took it. I got a telephone call from a guy named Russ. He told me the girls had left the car at the airport in Burlington, Vermont."

"Did Russ identify himself any further?"

"No, he just said he was a friend of the girls."

"Did you then go to Burlington?"

"Yes, I took a bus from Provincetown to Boston and then got a bus to Burlington. I went to the airport and the car was parked there."

"How did you have the keys if the girls took the car from Beacon Street?"

"The keys were left in the car."

Costa had driven from the airport into downtown Burlington. He had spotted Pat and Mary Anne on the sidewalk. "I picked them up, and we went to a place to eat. They told me they were going to Canada to run away from home. I drove them to the airport and they took a plane to Montreal. It was about six o'clock at night."

"You said before you never saw them after they left Provincetown on Saturday, January twenty-fifth," Flynn said sharply. "Now you tell me you saw them in Vermont . . ."

"That was the last time I saw them," Costa explained. "At the airport in Burlington."

Flynn unfolded the bill of sale. "Tony, you said this was made out at the Foc's'le bar. Was that true? Or was it made out later? It seems strange Pat would sell you her car, then keep it for another week."

"Well, I'll tell you the truth on that," Costa said. "When I bought the car, I didn't get a bill of sale. I later thought about it and decided I should have one to show ownership. So when I met Pat and Mary Anne in Burlington, I wrote out the bill of sale and Pat signed it."

"Where did this take place?"

"At the restaurant where we ate."

Flynn looked up from the bill of sale. "Tony, it seems to me that Pat's signature and the writing on the bill of sale are the same."

"All right," Costa said, impatiently. For the first time he seemed ruffled by Flynn's questions, "Pat wrote it while we were driving to the airport and I signed it. *That's* the truth!"

"What did you do after the girls left?"

"I got a room," Costa said. "The next day I started looking for a job."

"You didn't plan on coming back to Provincetown?"

"No, I was tired of the town. Things were uptight, I wanted to travel. I decided to take off."

"Why did you come back?"

"I telephoned my mother and she told me about the big commotion over the girls being missing. I thought it would be a good idea for me to come back and clear things up. After all, I had their car. I didn't want any trouble."

"Did she tell you about the body of a dead girl we found in the woods, near where the car was parked?"

"Yes."

"Have you any idea who she is?"

"No, I don't."

Flynn stared fixedly at Tony Costa. "Tony, do you know where these girls are?"

"I told you," Costa said. "They're in Canada."

"Yes, but you've changed your story so many times, you have me confused."

Costa leaped to his feet. He stood, trembling with anger, over the desk. "Are you trying to say I *killed* them?"

Surprised at the outburst, Flynn said, "No, Tony. I didn't say anything about these girls being dead. I said the girls are *missing*. All I'm doing down here today is to try and find them." When Costa resumed his seat, Flynn added, quietly, "I think you know where they are."

Costa's eyes wavered. "Well, they may be a long way off." He smiled slightly. "You're not going to find them."

Flynn was disquieted by the conviction in Costa's voice, soft-spoken, but positive.

Marshall picked up a pair of brown work boots from the floor beside the desk. "Are these yours?"

"Yes, but I don't want them," Costa said. "You can keep them, or throw them away."

Flynn showed Costa the bill of sale. "What about this?" he said. "Don't you want it back?"

"No, you can have it. I don't think I'll need it now. I'm going to hang around town for a while, then decide what I'm going to do."

"Aren't you going back to Burlington?" Flynn said. "Don't you have any interest in the car you left up there?"

"I guess that's gone," Costa said brightly. "It doesn't bother me. One time I gave a girl in California my car to use and she never returned it."

"All right, Tony," Flynn said. "This concludes your interview. I want to thank you for coming in and helping us out. If you think of anything, I'd appreciate it if you would let me know."

"OK," Costa said. "I'll be talking to you if I remember anything."

Outside Marshall's office, Costa said to Dunn, "Jesus, that guy in there accused me of killing those girls!"

Dunn had heard raised voices behind the closed door and was wondering what was going on. "Flynn's all right," Dunn said. "He gets a little excited sometimes, it's just his way. Don't let it bother you." Dunn commended Costa's cooperation. He had been very helpful—particularly with regard to the location of the car.

"Well, to tell you the truth about that," Costa said, "the car isn't at the airport." He took a white sales slip from his wallet. "It's at this place."

Dunn read the letterhead. "Forman Bourdeau's Gulf Service Station, Pearl and North Winooski Avenue, Burlington, Vermont."

"You were pretty rough on the kid, weren't you?" Dunn said when Flynn came out of Marshall's office. Costa struck Dunn as a mild young man, a harmless hippie type.

Flynn was furious. "That guy's a fucking liar," he said. Costa was a cute bastard on top of it, making out by changing his stories that Flynn had "broken him down," making him confess the real truth. Costa was guilty as hell—of what, Flynn wasn't sure.

"The next time I talk to that son of a bitch," Flynn vowed, "is the day I tell him he's under arrest."

12

An hour later, Steve Grund came into the Provincetown police station in an extraordinary state of nervousness. A tall, slender young man in his mid-twenties, with blue eyes and medium-blond hair tied behind his head in a ponytail, Grund was a cook at

Mother Marion's restaurant where police had him picked up after Tony Costa was questioned by Bernie Flynn.

Grund related the events of Sunday, February 2 to Flynn. Grund and Timothy "Weed" Atkins were walking down Commercial Street around ten-thirty at night. "We saw a bicycle parked beside two telephone booths." One of the booths had been occupied by Tony Costa, who greeted them, "Hey, Steve! Hi, Weed. Wait a minute, I want to talk to you." Costa was on the phone with his half brother. "Hold on, Vinnie," he said. Cupping the mouthpiece, Costa said, "You guys want to go to Boston? I have a car."

"How can you have a car?" Grund said, "when you don't have a license? It must be hot."

"It's *not* hot," Costa said. "Don't worry about it."

Grund agreed to drive to Boston if Costa could get him back the next morning.

Costa shut the phone booth door, but Grund heard him say, "Vinnie, Steve is going to drive me up. We'll be there early in the morning, it's nearly eleven o'clock now."

"Where's the car?" Grund said when Costa hung up.

"In Truro," Costa said. "I'm going to call a cab to take us out there, but first I have to go home and get some change."

Grund was suspicious. "How come the car isn't in town?"

"I had to park it someplace the fuzz wouldn't tag it," Costa said. "I'll tell you all about it on the way to Boston."

Sprawled on the bed in Costa's room on Standish Street, Grund and Atkins debated whether or not they should go to Boston while Costa went out to call a cab. When Costa returned to report that nobody was answering the phone, Grund was relieved. "Great!" he said. "Now we don't have to go!"

Costa was going to ask four Columbia University students staying upstairs in the guesthouse if they would give him a ride. Costa came back with one of them, Donald Obers, who had volunteered to drive them to Watts's Amoco garage in North Truro. Costa bought five gallons of gas from Russell Watts; then Costa directed Obers off the highway to Hatch Road, a short dead-end road, culminating in a circular turnaround.

Grund asked Obers if he was going to stick around in case the car's battery was dead. Obers assured him, "I'll stay right here."

Atkins and Grund got out of the car. They were walking to

the left side of the circle, through a space between the trees at the start of a dirt road into the woods when Grund looked over his shoulder and saw the car speed away.

"Hey, where's he going?" Grund said. "There goes our ride back if the car doesn't start!"

"Don't worry," Costa said, "I was out here a week ago, the car started all right."

"I hope so," Grund said, "I don't want to have to walk back to Provincetown in the middle of the night."

They had walked briskly because it was cold. About fifteen minutes later they came upon a car backed into a small clearing in the woods.

"Hey, not bad!" Grund said. "How did you manage to get this?"

"I'll tell you on the way to Boston," Costa said.

"You sure this isn't a hot car?" Grund said.

"Yeah," Costa said. "I'm *positive.*"

"I just hope it starts," Grund said.

Costa took a single key out of his pocket. He unlocked the car door and put the key in the ignition. He tapped it a little to see if there was any juice in the battery. He put the parking lights on, then opened the hood to look for the gas cap.

Atkins called out, "Hey, Tony! The gas cap's over here, on the outside."

While Atkins poured the gas, Costa got behind the wheel of the car and turned on the ignition. The engine turned over at once. "There you go!" Costa said.

Atkins asked what he was supposed to do with the gas can.

"Just throw it over in the bushes," Costa said. "We'll get it later."

"You want me to drive?" Grund said.

"I'll drive out," Costa said. "I know this area really well— I've been out here quite a few times. I guess I know just about everyplace in Truro and Wellfleet."

Headlights illuminated the dark masses of trees. The slender ribbon of dirt road seemed to plunge the car straight into the woods. Costa had turned left from the parking place, driving the car in a direction different from the one by which they had entered the woods.

Bouncing over the deep ruts in the road, Grund said, "Hey, this is the first time I've been jungle cruising at night!" When

Costa steered the car onto a paved road, Grund said, "Jesus, Tony! Where the hell are we?"

Costa stopped at the Pamet Road entrance to Route 6 to change places and Grund drove back to Standish Street. Costa picked up a bottle of Wild Irish Rose wine and the Vitamin B-12 pills he claimed would help Grund stay awake for the drive to Boston.

Grund drove to his apartment on Winthrop Street to pick up a joint. Leaving the apartment, Costa said, "Let's go to the dump."

"Why do you want to go to the dump this time of night?" Grund said.

"I have to pick up something," Costa said. He told Grund to park a short distance inside the town dump. "I'll be right back," Costa said. He disappeared into the darkness, returning crouched over a new Admiral portable color television set with two tags dangling from its handle.

"If that isn't hot," Grund said, "I'll buy it off you right now."

Costa put the television in the backseat beside Timmy Atkins. "I'm taking it up to my brother's," Costa said.

Turning off the dump road, Grund stiffened. A Provincetown police cruiser was pulling out near the VFW post.

If they were stopped and searched, Grund could probably figure out what to do about the television, but he was carrying a joint and could be busted for transporting narcotics.

"Be cool!" Costa said. "Nobody knows I have the TV. They won't know until tomorrow."

To Grund's relief, the cruiser drove off in the opposite direction. He noticed the gas gauge was only a quarter filled.

They stopped at the all-night Tri-S station in Hyannis. After gassing up, Grund drove to the Mid-Cape Highway. As soon as they were over the Sagamore bridge, Costa lit up the joint and passed it to Grund. Atkins had fallen asleep in the backseat.

"OK, what is it about the car?" Grund said.

Costa had bought the car from two Providence girls he knew that owed him money, he said. "I fronted the girls a pound of hashish last summer and they ripped me off—they didn't pay for the smoke." Costa had spotted the girls in Provincetown last weekend and figured they owed him seven hundred dollars, so they made a trade. The car, plus he gave them a couple hundred dollars. The girls had split town; they were going to Canada. Costa was leaving town, too. He was going to meet the girls. From there, they were going to continue to do their thing.

Costa was taking the car to Boston to try to get it registered. He said, "I got to get my license back, now that I have a car." His license had been suspended after he defaulted on a speeding summons in Maine the previous April.

Having run out of cigarettes, Grund helped himself to a nearly full pack of Benson and Hedges 100's he found in the car. At the approach of Boston, he said, "I hope you know this town, because I don't."

"I know it like the back of my hand," Costa said. He directed Grund to an apartment building at 415 Beacon Street.

It was 3:30 A.M. when they made their way up the back stairs, climbing three flights to the top floor. The apartment belonged to Robert "The Deacon" Alves, formerly of Provincetown, who was sharing the premises temporarily with Vinnie Bonaviri and his girlfriend, Cathy Roche. . . .

At eight-thirty, Grund was shaken awake.

"Come on, Steve, let's go," Costa said. He had verified flight space to Provincetown on a plane leaving Logan Airport at 9:10.

Grund was surprised that Costa drove to the airport. "Don't you want *me* to drive?"

"I'm a big boy now," Costa grinned. "Nobody knows me in this town."

Costa gave him fifteen dollars for the one-way fare to Provincetown.

All Monday night Grund wondered, "Where in heck is Weed, did he decide to stay over or what?" Grund had finally seen Atkins on Tuesday afternoon.

"Hey, guess what?" Atkins said, "I might buy a gun." Costa had offered to sell him a .22 caliber automatic for twenty dollars.

Grund advised Atkins not to buy the weapon. "It might be hot. Besides, you're on probation. You get caught with a gun, it's bad news."

The next day Grund and Atkins were sitting at the soda fountain of Adams Pharmacy when Tony Costa rode by on his bicycle. They went outside to talk to him. Grund asked Costa where he was going with the duffel bags hung on the handlebars.

"Tony said, 'I got all my stuff from my mom's,' " Grund told Flynn. "He said, 'I'm leaving in the morning for good.' He said, 'I

56

have to get out of this town, the cops have been hassling me too much. I can't stand it any more.' "

Grund was escorted out of the police station to show police the clearing in the woods where the VW had been parked and the dump area where Tony Costa had picked up the television. He exchanged a furtive glance with Timmy Atkins, seated in the corridor, waiting to be questioned.

Tall, heavy-set, dough-faced and ungainly, Atkins was a twenty-year-old unemployed laborer who had been arrested the previous April and charged with "falsely reporting the location of an explosive by telephone" to Provincetown High School. He was given six months' work probation, Atkins explained to Flynn. "I had to paint all kinds of stuff around town."

Atkins had known Tony Costa for about a year. "I don't know him real well, just to say 'hi' to."

Haltingly, Atkins corroborated Grund's version of the night ride to Boston. When Costa returned from taking Grund to Logan Airport that next morning, he had parked the car behind the apartment building, "but the guy whose apartment it was told Tony he had to move the car because the landlord had rented the parking space to someone else." Costa and Atkins spent the day listening to records and watching television. The next morning they had returned to Provincetown by bus.

13

Under the pitiless glare of a vivid fluorescence, George Killen watched a terrible reconstruction take place: the putting together of eight distinct portions of the body found in the South Truro woods, during an autopsy conducted at the mortuary of the northern district in Boston, on Wednesday, February 12, at two-thirty in the afternoon.

"A white female . . . five feet tall, with light brown shoulder-length hair, weighing approximately one hundred five pounds," Dr. Katsas was saying. The body had suffered a staggering violence, as if torn to pieces by a frenzied animal. The chest had been split open and emptied of its contents, including the heart. The breasts were not found; the liver and upper abdominal organs were missing. The diaphragm had been repeatedly slashed.

The stubby portion of pelvis was bare of skin. The labia and vulva had been extracted, the uterus, ovaries and intestines were missing. Dr. Katsas was astonished to find the heart jammed into the space that had been created by the removal of all interior genitalia.

Both legs had been amputated below the neck of the femur, the line of separation cutting right through the bone, consistent with chopping by a sharp instrument—a dislocation requiring extraordinary strength. The surfaces of both legs were covered with deep slash wounds similar to those which had been inflicted upon the torso and arms.

Dr. Katsas found particularly bizarre the irregular flap of skin which had been peeled off the chest and abdomen; matched to the body at the shoulders, the skin was intact, except for the breast nipples, which had been cut out.

Killen stood in silence beside Cheney Marshall and police photographer Roy Nightingale while Katsas dictated his findings into a microphone suspended above the examination table's metal grillwork. Katsas gave the cause of death as multiple stab wounds to the abdomen. The length of time the body had been buried was difficult to estimate—anywhere from six months to two years.

The hands, clenched into tight fists, were surgically removed at the wrist and given to Detective Sergeant James Sharkey of the Bureau of Photography and Fingerprinting at Massachusetts State Police headquarters.

Sharkey removed the wedding band before he put the hands in the freezer unit of the state police chemical lab to prevent further decomposition. The ring was fourteen-karat gold with five diamond chips. The letters "LB" were engraved inside the band. Sharkey estimated the ring's worth at sixty to seventy-five dollars; from its worn surfaces he thought the ring was from five to seven years old. He found a residue of soap on the setting of the diamonds.

Precise and fussy, Sharkey took exquisite pains lifting fingerprints from difficult sources. These hands were intact but in advanced stages of decomposition, the fingers soft and shriveled, devoid of epidermis.

To obtain satisfactory results, Sharkey amputated the fingers below the second distal joint, tying off the edges with catgut. Under the bulb area on both sides of the fingers, he injected Hydrol tissue builder, a liquid that dried to a firm, spongelike consistency, used by morticians to fill in collapsed tissue. Sharkey's examination revealed a pattern discernible on the dermis—the deeper layer of skin within which were the structures that determined the characteristics of fingerprint patterns—every line on the epidermis represented by two broken lines in the dermis.

When the Hydrol was set, the fingers were inked and rolled repeatedly onto fingerprint cards. Sharkey photographed the best two or three impressions and had eight-by-ten enlargements made. The fingers were placed in individual screw-cap baby-food jars with a description written on a label, and put back in the freezer unit.

Sharkey assured George Killen that a usable print could be lifted from the unidentified body.

Killen also talked to Detective Lieutenant William Broderick at headquarters.

A self-described "knock 'em down, drag 'em out son of a bitch" who never hit a man until he was hit first, Broderick had been shot at, stabbed and hit over the head as a Boston police sergeant assigned to District 4's roving wagon to pick up drunks and other street miscreants. A tall, weary man with a head of curly black hair and the flavor of South Boston in his speech, Broderick had called headquarters around five o'clock on Tuesday, February 4, from Costello's, a bar in Jamaica Plain. Detective Lieutenant Richard Cass had received a "Try to Locate" from Providence on a '68 light blue VW with Rhode Island plates—thought to be somewhere in the Back Bay. Cass wanted Broderick to find the car and keep it under surveillance pending further instructions. "Jesus *Christ,*" Broderick complained, "there's gotta be ten thousand Volkswagens in that area."

Broderick called his wife in Roslindale before going down the block for a six-pack of Budweiser. He started traversing the streets of Boston, peering at the solid lines of cars parked at the curbstone through a veil of hurricanelike rain. Sipping beer as he drove one-handed, sure he was on a fool's hopeless errand, Broderick was astonished, two hours later, to spot the VW parked in front of an apartment building on Beacon Street.

Broderick noticed a lot of activity in the first-floor apartment. Knocking on the door, he held up his badge at the same moment an attractive young woman appeared. Over her head Broderick observed a haze of smoke, the acrid smell of marijuana, and people running from the room and jumping out of windows.

"I'm not interested in your little pot party, folks," Broderick announced. "Just tell me who belongs to that VW with Rhode Island plates parked out front."

The young woman thought the car belonged to one of the tenants on the building's top floor.

Broderick climbed three flights to a dim hallway. Two doors were set into a corner; one door was slightly ajar, spilling a slanting bar of light into the hall. Broderick pushed on the door and found himself looking at a naked young couple making love on the sofa.

"That's all right," Broderick said to the startled young woman who snatched up a robe fallen to the carpet when she saw him in the doorway holding his badge. "I'll wait until you're finished."

Broderick was told the Volkswagen belonged to Antone Costa of Provincetown. Costa's half brother, Vincent Bonaviri, was temporarily sharing the apartment; Bonaviri wasn't home.

When Broderick went back downstairs, the young woman was standing at her apartment door. She said, "You ruined my party."

"I'm sorry," Broderick said.

"Do you smoke?" she said, inclining her head backward, an invitation.

"Only cigarettes," Broderick said. He felt like "Joe Jerk" when he called in and discovered that everybody at the station had gone home.

The VW was still parked on Beacon Street when Broderick staked it out at noon the next day. Around three o'clock a young man with a mustache and glasses walked briskly out of the apartment house, got into the car and drove off. Broderick kept half a block behind the car as it went about the streets of Boston with no apparent destination, returning to Beacon Street at nightfall. Broderick waited several hours before the driver came out again, and drove to the Punchbowl, a gay bar on Stuart Street, near the Hotel Statler.

Broderick was well acquainted with the place. As a Boston policeman, he had hired himself out as an off-hours security officer to keep order there. Greeted by the manager, Broderick was set up with a drink and the information that the butch number with the mustache seated halfway down the bar was a stranger.

Broderick figured Costa was "playing the fags," but observed him leaving the bar alone to return to Beacon Street an hour later.

The next morning the car was gone.

Broderick talked to Vincent Bonaviri, a slight young man with evasive dark eyes. Bonaviri said his brother had brought the car to Boston and left it overnight. He had no idea where his brother was. Bonaviri was getting ready to move to a new apartment. He did not know when he would see Tony Costa again.

Broderick now reported to Lieutenant Cass on the "Try to Locate," usually a routine matter not involving a crime. Since no stolen-vehicle report had come through on the car, Broderick figured it to be some personal matter to trace the whereabouts of the car's owner.

A day later a teletype came through with the information that the VW belonged to one of two girls missing from Providence.

While at headquarters, Killen received a teletype from the Massachusetts probation office in Cambridge, giving Antone Costa's previous police record. Among a list of minor traffic violations, two items caught Killen's attention: in January, 1962, Costa had been convicted of breaking and entering in the nighttime with intent to commit a felony; and assault and battery.

14

While Tony Costa was being interrogated by Bernie Flynn at Provincetown police station on Monday, February 10, George Killen had been on the phone to the police in Burlington, Vermont, making a stolen-vehicle complaint on a blue 1968 Volkswagen bearing Rhode Island registration KV-978. He told Detective Lieutenant Richard Beaulieu that the car was last seen in an area where a dismembered body had been recovered and that it belonged to two missing young women, believed to have been murdered. The car was reported by Tony Costa, a suspect in the case, to have been parked at the Burlington airport. Killen wanted the car located and impounded, but not processed.

On his way to the airport, Beaulieu learned via police radio that Tony Costa had just changed his story: the VW was at Bourdeau's Gulf Station on the corner of Pearl and North Winooski Avenue.

Beaulieu found the VW covered with six inches of snow. The car had not been moved since a storm the night before. The license plates were missing.

According to station attendant Wayne Blanchard, the car belonged "to some hippie" who had identified himself as "Anthony Costa" and rented overnight parking space on Friday, February 7. Costa had left the car, and walked up the street.

Beaulieu started checking rooming houses along North Winooski Avenue. At number 30, Mrs. Stella Smith told him "Anthony Costa" had checked into her house on Thursday, February 6, paying fifteen dollars for one week's rent for a second-floor bedroom.

A matronly woman wearing glasses, Mrs. Smith said, "He was a sort of hippie-type young fellow, but he had very nice manners and a pleasant personality."

Costa received no visitors during his tenancy. Mrs. Smith had seen him pull up in front of her house in a small blue car on Friday afternoon with two girls and a young man as passengers.

He had gone to his room, returned a short time later to the car, and driven off. He had slept most of the day, coming in late both nights he spent in her house. On Sunday morning she had found a note from him:

Saturday evening

Dear Mrs. Smith,
I have to return home because of illness in the family. I will return as soon as possible. Please hold onto the things in the top drawer for me. Thank you so much.

Anthony Costa

Please hold any mail that comes for me.

Thanks again.

Beaulieu asked to see Costa's room. The door was unlocked. He found an army-type duffel bag in the closet, and clothes on hangers. The wastebasket contained torn pieces of yellow lined paper upon which a bill of sale for a Volkswagen had been written; an application for a post office box in the name of "Anthony Costa and Josiah Shannon" and a smashed peace-sign pendant on a broken chain.

Beaulieu had the VW towed to police headquarters by Fairview Wreckers. The next day he obtained a key from a local VW dealer and opened the trunk. He found the license plates under a rubber floor mat and a Rhode Island registration card dated March 11, 1968 in the name of P.H. Walsh. In the glove compartment were a red Magic Marker, a quantity of book matches and two road maps.

Beaulieu got a call from Lieutenant Dunn. Dunn wanted a check made of information received from Tony Costa that Pat Walsh and Mary Anne Wysocki were in Burlington with him on February 7, and had gone to the airport to take a plane to Montreal. Dunn gave a description of the girls.

Beaulieu talked to a clerk for Mohawk Airlines. Neither Pat Walsh nor Mary Anne Wysocki appeared on passenger lists from February 6 through 8; nor did their descriptions fit any of the passengers that had booked tickets for the only daily flights scheduled from Burlington to Montreal living at 12:15 P.M.

Burlington was only a hundred miles from Montreal; it wouldn't have taken much effort on Tony Costa's part to drive the girls across the border. Beaulieu pointed this out to Dunn and Gunnery when they came to his office on Thursday, February 13, sent by Killen to return the impounded VW to Cape Cod and gather the results of Beaulieu's investigation. Dunn had been told emphatically to send no communications on the case through police teletype.

Dunn and Gunnery went to Mrs. Smith's rooming house. She had received a telephone call from Tony Costa on Monday, February 10 around 9 P.M. She said, "He wanted me to put his duffel bag of clothes on a bus for Provincetown." In the closet of his room Costa left a corduroy sport jacket, a navy CPO shirt, a plaid lumber jacket and a pair of new work shoes and zippered dress boots.

Mrs. Smith could not identify the girls she had seen in a car with Costa on the afternoon of Friday, February 7 from photographs Dunn showed her. Neither could Lawrence Messier, a retired man who lived next door to the Smith house. Messier had been walking his dog when Costa drove up to the house.

Two girls in a blue VW with Rhode Island plates had asked Leroy Griffin for directions to Maple Street around 1:30 P.M. the same day, but Griffin couldn't identify them from photographs as being Pat Walsh and Mary Anne Wysocki.

Dunn and Gunnery went to the Burlington post office. The clerk did not remember if Tony Costa had been alone when he picked up the application for a post office box.

Dunn called Montreal police. He gave a description of Pat Walsh and Mary Anne Wysocki, then he sent a teletype to Yarmouth barracks addressed to George Killen's attention:

WILL RETURN FROM BURLINGTON EARLY AM 2-14-69. SHOULD ARRIVE BARRACKS 1600 HRS 2-15-69. MISSING GIRLS WERE PROBABLY IN BURLINGTON WEEKEND OF 2-8-69 TO 2-9-69.

Killen hit the ceiling when Bolduc read him the message. Through the state police in Montpelier where the teletype had originated, Killen tracked Dunn down to a motel in Burlington where he and Gunnery were staying.

Killen ordered Dunn to stop sending information "verifying" that the missing girls were alive. The teletype he'd sent could be exculpatory should Costa hire an attorney and the contents of the message become known. The girls seen in the company of Antone Costa had *not* been identified as Pat Walsh and Mary Anne Wysocki.

"Those girls are dead," Killen said flatly.

When Dunn hung up the phone his ears were red. He complained to Gunnery that Killen liked to control things too much, so there would be only one boss running the case.

Gunnery was eager to pursue the investigation further, but Dunn was convinced—despite Killen's call—that the girls seen with Tony Costa were Pat Walsh and Mary Anne Wysocki. The "evidence" was at best sketchy, but Gunnery didn't think it was his place to tell Dunn how to run the investigation. He was just a trooper; he kept his thoughts to himself.

Killen was thoroughly disgusted. He told Bolduc to write a postscript onto the offending teletype message in red ink:

The contents of this message to be kept *absolutely confidential*. No unauthorized person to be given contents of this message.

Killen was still fuming about Dunn the next morning, complaining to Marshall, "That goddamned dopey son of a bitch. The guy's in a trance!"

Marshall had taken a missing persons report that morning from Mrs. Helen Andrews, mother of Susan Ellsworth Perry, eighteen. Susan had dropped out of high school in September. She had been bored living with her father, a fisherman who had won custody of five children after the divorce. Susan was reported to have gone to Mexico with some hippie friends she met last summer in Boston, but she had not been heard from since the Labor Day weekend.

Marshall wanted to know why Mrs. Andrews had waited six months to report her daughter missing. She told him, "The way kids are today, you don't know where they are most of the time."

Killen and Marshall went to the Truro woods. Sifting very carefully through the open grave, Killen found pieces of body parts, bone and skin tissue, and a human liver cut in half. Two masses of muscle and fatty tissue were "consistent with the region of the breasts, including the mammary glands," according to Dr.

65

Arthur McBay of the state police chemical lab who received it the following day; but the exact nature of the material could not be determined because of the degree of decomposition.

15

Truro Police Chief Harold Berrio had raised the possibility that the unidentified body could be that of an Eastham girl who had disappeared the previous year around Memorial Day in Provincetown. Sydney Lee Monzon's description perfectly matched the nude, dismembered body whose autopsy Killen had witnessed.

Killen was introduced to Sydney's sister, Linda Monzon, at Provincetown police station. A slight young woman with long hair, she was accompanied by her boyfriend, David Salvador. Linda had last seen her sister around five o'clock on Friday, May 24, 1968.

"I was living at 25 Watson Court and I was coming out of the gate. Sydney was standing on top of the hill beside a car, calling me. She was terribly upset and she wanted me to go up there and talk to her. I was in a hurry, and I said I'd see her later. Sydney got into the car." Linda had gone in search of her sister an hour later. "People said she had been looking for me, but nobody knew where she was. I looked for her about a week, then I finally called my mother in Eastham. My mother reported her missing."

"Was there anybody in the car?" Killen said.

"I believe it was Tony Costa," Linda said, as if thinking of it for the first time. Sydney had often been in his company for about a month before she disappeared, she recalled.

"Did Sydney ever indicate to you that she wanted to leave Provincetown or run away?" Killens said.

"She mentioned it a couple of times," Linda said. "One thing

66

she wanted to do was go to California and start a new life—just leave all her old identity behind her."

Her sister had left all her belongings. "She left her pocketbook and her cosmetics and all her clothes, except what she was wearing. Sydney had a special prescription for chronic palpitation —she left those pills." There was only ten dollars missing from a pay envelope she'd received for her first week working as a produce clerk at the A & P where her bicycle was found parked.

"Did Tony Costa have any knowledge of Sydney's whereabouts?" Killen said.

"I saw him about three weeks or a month later on the street and I asked him if he knew where Sydney was, because I figured if anybody knew he would know. Tony said he had no idea—he couldn't imagine where she was."

David Salvador spoke up. Sydney had lived with his brother Roland, he said. "I told Roland to keep Sydney away from Tony Costa. She was too young to be hanging out with a shady character like him, real heavy into drugs and everything, but every now and then I'd see Sydney out bike riding with Tony again."

After the interview, Marshall said to Killen, "Funny how that name keeps turning up, isn't it?"

Killen was getting ready to leave Marshall's office when he was told Tony Costa was in the station again. Costa wanted to talk to him.

Marshall asked Costa into his office and introduced him to Killen.

"What do you want, Tony?" Killen said.

"I want to talk to you about the missing girls, Pat and Mary Anne."

"Tony, you talked to Lieutenant Flynn the other day," Killen said. "As far as I'm concerned, you're in serious trouble. You're a suspect in the disappearance of these girls."

"I want to help the police find them," Costa said, "so I can clear my name."

"The best thing you can do now is get in touch with a lawyer," Killen said.

Costa said Frank Diego was going to take him to see Maurice Goldman that afternoon.

Killen knew Goldman, former Massachusetts assistant attorney general. He was a tough, skilled criminal lawyer. "You go see

67

Goldman," Killen said. "If Goldman tells you to talk to me, all right. In the meantime, I do not want to discuss the disappearance of Pat Walsh or Mary Anne Wysocki with you. I think you'd better leave."

"I don't want to leave until I've talked to you," Costa insisted. "I want to help find the girls. Some people in town are getting suspicious and the cops are asking all kinds of questions about me. I want to get this over with."

Killen's caution was founded on misgivings over the recent landmark ruling of the Supreme Court dealing with the questioning of suspects. The Miranda card of rights police were now obliged to read was ridiculous, in Killen's view.

Killen said, "All right, Tony. I'll listen to what you have to say, but before you say anything let me tell you something. You are a suspect in the disappearance of these girls and in the larceny of their car. You have a right to remain silent. Anything you say may be used for or against you in a court of law. You have the right to have an attorney present at any questioning. You will be provided with a lawyer, if you are unable to afford one. Anytime you want to stop talking you may do so. Do you understand these rights which I have told you?"

"I was told the same thing the other day," Costa said, "I know my rights."

"OK," Killen said, "go ahead and talk."

"First I did *not* steal the car. I bought it from Pat Walsh and paid her nine hundred dollars for it. She needed the money for an abortion."

"When did you pay Pat Walsh for the car?"

"While I was riding with the girls to Truro."

"Did you pay cash or by check?"

"Cash," Costa said.

"Do you remember the denomination of the bills?"

"They were all small bills—twenties or less."

"Where did you get the money?"

"I had three hundred saved," Costa said, "and my brother loaned me six hundred so I could buy the car."

Killen was impassive. "You say you bought the car on Saturday, January twenty-fifth and used six hundred dollars your brother loaned you?"

"Yes, that's true."

Broderick had checked with Vincent Bonaviri about the purchase of the Volkswagen, "Your brother told us he lent you three hundred dollars on February third at seven-thirty in the morning," Killen said. "You told him the car cost you seven hundred dollars."

"He must have made a mistake," Costa said.

"I don't think anybody who loans out that kind of money makes a mistake about it," Killen said. "All right, Tony. What else do you want to tell me?"

"The girls are all mixed up in drugs. They're heavy users of heroin and hashish. I sold them seven hundred dollars worth of heroin last August."

"We have not found anything in the background of these girls that indicates they were drug users," Killen said.

Costa was silent.

"Why did you try to register the car in Vermont?" Killen said. A Burlington police check of the records of the Vermont Department of Motor Vehicles in Montpelier had revealed an application to register a 1968 blue VW made out by "Anthony Costa" on February 8, accompanied by a check for thirty-two dollars issued by the Burlington Savings Bank. Costa had also applied for a Vermont driver's license. He had checked the "No" box following the question: "Is your operating privilege restricted, suspended, revoked or refused in any state?"

"I found Burlington to be a nice town," Costa said. "I thought I'd stay there."

"When did you last see Pat and Mary Anne?"

"When they dropped me off in Provincetown on Saturday, January twenty-fifth."

"How was it that Pat Walsh's sweater and Mary Anne's hair dryer were found in your room?"

"They were in the room when I rented it."

"They *couldn't* have been in the room when you rented it," Killen said.

"There must be some mistake," Costa said. "The hair dryer was *definitely* there when I rented the room."

"What about Pat Walsh's sweater?"

"I'm not sure about the sweater," Costa said.

"Well, how did it get into your room?"

"Pat must have left it there when she was in my room."

"When was she in your room?"

"On Saturday, when I went to Truro with the girls."

69

Killen sighed. Costa was a good-looking young man, with a pleasant, well-modulated voice. Listening to him, Killen could understand a voice like that influencing young women. He said, "Tony, you're getting deeper and deeper in trouble. You were the last person to see Pat and Mary Anne alive—they've been missing since the day they took you to Truro. You have Pat's car in your possession, and personal property belonging to the girls was found in your room. I suggest you stop talking to me and see Maurice Goldman."

"I have told you the *truth*," Costa protested. "And time will prove what I have told you is true!"

"Tony, I want you to leave this office right now," Killen said.

"The last time I saw the girls they were going to fly to Canada."

"That's *enough*," Killen said. "I think you better leave."

Killen was astonished when Costa suddenly reached across the desk to shake his hand. "Thank you for hearing me out, Mr. Killen," he said politely, and left the office.

On his way out of the station, Costa stopped to talk to Sergeant Meads. Meads asked him if he had talked to a lawyer yet.

"Jesus, Jim," Costa said, "you know what a lawyer costs?"

"If we bust you," Meads said evenly, "you're going to need one."

Tony Costa walked across Bradford Street to the construction site where he was employed converting four garages into apartments.

Joe Beaudry observed Costa's arrival from under the lowered brim of a plaid cap. Foreman on the job, Beaudry had hired Costa in January to do carpentry, electrical work and plumbing. Because he was self-taught, non-union and unlicensed, Costa worked cheap. Beaudry was only paying him three dollars an hour.

"Tony would come to work carrying a paper bag with four, five different-colored pills he would put together in a plastic capsule he'd take with a glass of water," Beaudry explained later to Bernie Flynn. "He worked two, three hours, then took off." Beaudry wouldn't see him for a day or two days later—Costa never put in a full week at one time.

"Tony would come in the morning, work a while, then sort of slow down, get to laughing and talking to himself and make foolish mistakes. Like he'd put up a partition and sheetrock it, put the electrical boxes in and leave the wire for the boxes outside on the floor, so a lot of times we had to rip the partitions apart to put the wires in for the boxes. When he was doing plumbing, sometimes he was fast and did a good job—other times he would sand pipe and put the flux on it, and then forget to solder it. Water would go all over the floor—that's happened more than once."

But Beaudry never fired him. He couldn't get anybody else to work because the man who owned the building had a bad reputation for not paying his help.

Brought to the construction site by Frank Diego was a portly man with slicked-back brown hair and a commanding presence; Maurice Goldman maintained law offices in Brewster and on Bradford Street in Provincetown where he was town counsel. Goldman had been retained by Frank Bent, longtime Provincetown town treasurer, to represent his nephew, Antone Costa.

As soon as Costa was introduced to Goldman he complained that police had accused him of killing two girls missing from Providence after he had returned voluntarily to Provincetown to help find them. "We were *friends,*" Costa protested. "We all lived in the same house." To Costa's knowledge, the girls had returned to Providence.

"Did the police give you your rights when they questioned you?" Goldman said in a penetrating voice.

"I know my rights," Costa said. He had studied law books at the Provincetown library. Costa had memorized the Miranda warnings.

Goldman was amused. "Then for God's sakes stop talking to police, young fellow. You don't have to answer any questions without a lawyer being present. If the police bother you again, you just refer them to Goldman."

Costa impressed Goldman as well-spoken and intelligent. Tall, broad-shouldered and muscular, Costa was surprisingly young-looking for a 24-year-old. A callowness lingered about his pale, almost delicate skin, in contrast to the heavy brows, thick brown hair worn low across his forehead and dark, almost brooding eyes behind gold-rimmed spectacles. According to his uncle, Tony Costa was something of a ladies' man in town, and Goldman could understand the allure that such good looks—and the air of sensuality Costa gave off like fragrance—could have for young women.

When Goldman left the construction site, he dismissed the

matter as nothing more than a coincidence that Costa had met the missing girls at Mrs. Morton's rooming house.

Costa had said nothing about the car.

16

Bernie Flynn was at the Providence police station on February 14, interviewing Russell Norton. Long-haired, mustached, wearing a leather jacket and worn jeans, Norton blamed himself for the disappearance of Pat Walsh and Mary Anne Wysocki.

"If I had gone to Provincetown with them on Friday, like we originally planned, they wouldn't be missing."

Norton told Flynn how he had met Mary Anne Wysocki at Rhode Island College about three months before and became friendly with her. They had dated on a few occasions—nothing serious, just a friendship. Through Mary Anne, he met Pat Walsh. They had talked about the weekend in Provincetown at Armando's Bar and Grill on Wednesday night, January 22nd—two days before the girls left. "I told them I couldn't go with them on Friday because of my new job, but that I would leave on Saturday by bus and get into Hyannis around noon and hitch to Provincetown."

Norton had searched all weekend for the girls and couldn't find them. On Sunday afternoon he returned to Providence alone.

"Did you ever hear from the girls after you got back to Providence?" Flynn said.

"No, I never saw them again."

"Did Patricia or Mary Anne at any time indicate to you during your conversation with them at Armando's they were not returning home?"

"No, they were definitely coming back to Providence," Norton said, "I was supposed to ride back with them on Sunday. If they were going to leave home for any reason, Mary Anne would have told me."

Norton had worked last summer at a Provincetown leather shop on Commercial Street but he had never heard of anyone by the name of Antone Costa.

"Did you ever call a person by the name of Costa in Provincetown during the past month?" Flynn said.

"No," Norton said.

"Was there any conversation at any time between you and Mary Anne or Pat about an abortion, or about the selling of narcotics?"

Norton sent Flynn a scathing look of incredulity. "No," he said, emphatically. "Never."

Mary Anne Wysocki had never used drugs of any kind, to Gerry Magnan's knowledge, nor could he think of any reason for her to leave home, he told Flynn at his mother's house on Parade Street. Before Mary Anne left for Provincetown, she had talked about the courses she was planning on taking when she registered for her senior year at Rhode Island College in February.

"She *definitely* planned on coming back to Providence," Magnan said, insisting on the importance of his having found her hair dryer in Tony Costa's room. "Mary Anne washed her hair every day. She would never leave her hair dryer behind."

The trip to Provincetown had been Mary Anne's first vacation in a long time, Magnan said. "She had very little money to spend on herself." Working to pay off his student loans, Magnan didn't have much himself. "But I had a bit more than she did." Before Mary Anne left for the weekend, they had gone shopping. Mary Anne had admired a pair of brown plaid slacks in a store window. On impulse, Magnan had bought them for her.

Magnan had told the Wysocki family to expect the worst. "But I didn't keep them up on every detail of the investigation that made it look bad for Mary Anne," he said. Magnan cautioned Flynn to "take it easy," when he brought him to the three-story frame tenement on Superior Street. Martha and Walter Wysocki were simple, hard-working people. Magnan had tried to shield them from the publicity surrounding their daughter's disappearance by acting as spokesman for the family to the press.

The Wysockis struck Flynn as an elderly couple—more like

grandparents than parents of Mary Anne, the youngest of their three children.

Walter Wysocki, a bulky, taciturn man, with large hands calloused from years of working for the railroad, had little to say. Martha Wysocki was sweet-faced, her nearly white hair a soft halo about her head—the kind of woman, Flynn observed, who still wore aprons and kept a sewing basket. She had a cup of coffee and a dish of pastries on the kitchen table's worn oilcloth in front of Flynn the moment he sat down.

With her arthritic hands folded in her lap, Martha Wysocki told him about Mary Anne leaving home on Thursday night to sleep at Pat Walsh's apartment. She had returned the next morning to pick up a green, waist-length leather jacket with sheepskin lining and three pairs of slacks. In a blue Pan Am flight bag Mary Anne had owned since a 1966 group charter flight to Bermuda taken with fellow telephone company employees, she put several changes of underwear and a set of hair rollers. She had taken her hair dryer, and about thirty dollars in cash. Before she left, Mary Anne said, "Don't worry if I'm not back until Monday, Pat will drop me off."

Flynn was taken to the attic apartment, three small rooms under a slanting roof. Mary Anne had given up her bedroom downstairs so her grandfather—to whom she was devoted—could get the nursing care he needed following the amputation of a leg. The apartment was cold; the space heater turned off. Flynn was shown the ruffled curtains Mary Anne had sewn herself, and the desk and chair she had refinished. Magnan told Flynn he had helped her paint the place.

Flynn glanced at the row of books—mostly physics and math texts on a single bookshelf over the desk. The Wysockis were terribly proud of her, Magnan explained, the only member of the family who had ever gone to college. Mary Anne had worked part-time in a "Progress for Providence" program tutoring ghetto children to improve their learning skills. She had wanted to be a teacher.

Flynn was moved by Mrs. Wysocki's humility, the strength of her stoicism. The fear in her eyes was more eloquent than any appeal she could have voiced. Flynn volunteered no information about Mary Anne's possible whereabouts.

74

Flynn found the Walsh house more prosperous but less hospitable. He was at once challenged by Catherine Walsh.

A large woman, forthright and voluble, she demanded that police find her daughter, indignant at the rumors stemming from the investigation that Pat had been involved in drugs and was seeking an abortion. Fastening a hard eye on Flynn, she said, "My daughter would *never* have an abortion." Pat loved children; she would not sleep with a man before she was married. A good girl of the highest morals, her upbringing had been strictly supervised. While Pat had her own apartment, Mrs. Walsh said, she stayed at her parents' house as often as two or three nights a week.

Flynn liked her. He recognized she was covering up a great deal of fear with her anger, sounding as concerned about protecting Pat's reputation as she was for her safety.

Mrs. Walsh disliked the photograph of Pat appearing in all the newspapers. She gave Flynn a framed studio portrait of her daughter, and he was amazed at the difference between this portrait and the informal and more recent photographs Bob Turbidy had given him. In the studio portrait, Pat appeared a big-boned, matronly girl who strongly resembled her mother with thick eyebrows and short "sensible" hair. She wore cameo earrings; a small circle pin was attached to the cowl-neck collar of a short-sleeved black dress. Pat looked a good thirty-five, Flynn thought.

Flynn went to the Laurel Hill Avenue School. A bland and pale-skinned Principal Ronald Karnes told him, "It's been a pretty hard three weeks. We all miss her. Miss Walsh was liked by all the faculty and loved by the children. She was a wonderful teacher, very dedicated to her job. She stayed after school to give the children extra help." Pat had always consulted him if she wanted to be relieved of her duties for any reason.

Pat was still making payments on the Volkswagen through the Providence Teachers Credit Union—ninety dollars a month being deducted from her salary.

"She was really fond of that car," Katherine Perriera, a fellow teacher, told Flynn. "Pat was always having something or other done to it." Miss Perriera had not known Pat Walsh well. "She was a very private person, well-liked by everyone here, but no one had any social dealings with her outside of school." Miss Perriera was surprised that Pat went to Provincetown to spend a weekend. "It didn't strike me as the kind of place that would have appealed to Pat at all."

Flynn was shown the classroom in which Pat Walsh had taught the second grade, a brightly lit place, furnished with small tables and chairs. The walls had been decorated with displays of children's artwork. Through the windows Flynn heard the shouts of children in the schoolyard at recess.

Bob Turbidy welcomed Flynn into the apartment at 135 Prospect Street. He was grateful to Flynn as "the most human" of all the cops he'd talked to, a man who had taken the case seriously and the first one to question Costa's story about his involvement with the girls.

Turbidy confided that he and Pat had lived together for six months. He had concealed the information from the police because of his fear of injuring Pat's teaching career.

Turbidy took Flynn through the apartment. Stopping before a large bookshelf in the living room, he said, "Most of these are Pat's—she was the intellectual in the family." He paused over a paperback copy of *Cannery Row* by John Steinbeck; he and Pat had read the novel out loud to each other. Pat's reading of *The Second Sex* by Simone de Beauvoir had catalyzed her interest in women's rights. But her favorite book was *Summerhill,* about a school in England with unorthodox teaching methods.

"Pat was very interested in alternative kinds of education," Turbidy said. She had taken a class in children's theater as a means of improving her teaching skills, a method that involved no book learning. Pat had written him about the class: "Everything is *doing.* We're always acting things out and improvising, it's really amazing what you can do—it gives you the greatest feeling."

At the end of the letter Pat wrote, "You have a beautiful face and I'd like to see it."

Turbidy refused to relinquish the few love letters he had received in California from Pat Walsh when Flynn asked for samples of her handwriting.

Flynn looked over her record collection, mostly Bob Dylan, Jesse Colin Young and Richie Havens. Turbidy had given her a copy of *The White Album* by the Beatles, along with a leather handbag he had made her as a Christmas present. When Flynn examined Pat's closet in the bedroom, Turbidy explained about his army fatigue jacket Pat had taken with her to Provincetown for the weekend.

Flynn was puzzled why the girls would get into a car with a virtual stranger and go to an isolated area in the woods with him. He said, "Would Pat have gone if Tony Costa promised to sell her drugs?"

"Maybe, because Mary Anne was with her, she might have felt safe." But Turbidy doubted drugs were the reason. Pat had smoked grass with him on several occasions. "But she wasn't a big pothead. Drugs are pretty easy to get in Providence. She wouldn't have to go to Provincetown to score drugs." The apartment was not far from Benefit Street, a notorious hippie colony near the Rhode Island School of Design.

That the area of the woods where the VW was last seen was close to an old cemetery would be more reason for Pat to visit the place. "She collected tombstone inscriptions," Turbidy said. "And she'd done gravestone rubbings."

Turbidy showed Flynn the odd-shaped stone in the living room Pat had found on a camping trip to New Hampshire. "We were hiking in the mountains and just stumbled across it in the middle of nowhere—what must have been an old family burial plot." Gray slate, with interesting erosion markings obscuring the name that had been carved upon the crumbling stone, it had an angel of death—skull-faced and winged—lightly etched into one brittle corner. Pat had been charmed by her discovery; she had taken the stone back to the apartment as a decoration.

"Could there be a possible lesbian relationship between Pat and Mary Anne?" Flynn said.

Turbidy was astonished. "Pat is a normal, heterosexual girl as far as I know, and so is Mary Anne." After a moment's reflection, however, Turbidy was gratified that Flynn had thought seriously enough about the case to come up with even so farfetched an idea; Turbidy was ready to believe anything so long as it meant there was a chance Pat—and Mary Anne, of course—were still alive.

But when Turbidy identified the broken peace medallion found in the wastebasket of Costa's room in Vermont as the same type as one he had bought and given to Pat in Provincetown last August, Flynn told him it was only a matter of time before the searches in the Truro woods turned up more bodies. Flynn was convinced Tony Costa was a psychopath and had murdered the girls.

"I knew it was all over when they told me they'd found Pat's VW in Burlington. She'd never sell that car," Turbidy said. He had tried to find Tony Costa himself. He and Magnan had even hired a private detective for a time, without result. "Costa kept jumping around all over the place and I never could catch up with him. I wanted to get my hands on him—not to hurt him or anything, but to get the truth out of him about the girls. I wanted to shake him by the shoulders and say, 'Tell me. *Tell me.*' "

Flynn said, "I know the feeling."

Before he left Providence, Flynn asked Sergeant Perry to secure dental charts for both girls and samples of their fingerprints. When the searches uncovered more bodies, Flynn wanted to be ready to make an identification.

Returning to Cape Cod, Flynn felt a surge of renewed determination to break the case. He had come away from Providence with a picture of two nice girls, from good families and solid backgrounds, a picture that had put the case into a different perspective for him.

Flynn liked to solve all his cases, he told George Killen at the courthouse. "Although sometimes you can't help think some people deserve what happens to them, hanging around with the wrong people and getting mixed up in things they shouldn't." Pat Walsh and Mary Anne Wysocki were different. For all their education they were innocent girls, too trusting for their own good perhaps, but undeserving of their fate. Flynn felt sorry for them.

"The poor bastards," Flynn said to Killen. "They couldn't even take a lousy weekend vacation without a son of a bitch like Tony Costa has to kill them."

On February 14, at three-thirty in the afternoon, Dunn and Gunnery delivered Pat Walsh's Volkswagen to the Bourne barracks of the state police on Cape Cod. The two had taken turns driving the car over the slippery heights and swooping mountain curves of Vermont's Route 69.

The next morning at eleven o'clock—a Saturday—state police chemist Melvin Topjian examined the car. He found no evidence of a struggle having occurred inside the car, or that its interior surfaces had been recently washed. Using benzidine tests to detect the presence of "occult blood"—blood not visible to the eye—Topjian got positive reactions from the steering wheel, the right-hand door panel, the right front seat belt bracket and the rear seat and window trim. The strongest reaction came from the back of the right front seat.

Scattered reddish brown smears on the wooden handle and plastic bristles of a snow brush found in the car's trunk gave positive reactions to the test. No blood was detected on an air mattress, two cans of de-icer or a green and white bedspread.

Topjian examined the rope Gunnery had taken from Mrs. Morton's living room. Approximately twenty-three feet in length and five-eighths of an inch thick, and made from three strands of cordage with a leftward twist, the rope disclosed a number of brown female hairs, and a fuchsia-color stain suggestive of lipstick; its surface indicated the presence of blood.

The work boots Tony Costa had given to Flynn's disposal revealed the presence of blood on the surface of both shoes and the bottom cleats of the soles; the clothing taken from Costa's room in Vermont, however, was clean.

Gunnery drove the Volkswagen to Wellfleet, meeting Bernie Flynn at the town pier. Before he went to Providence, Flynn had questioned a local man named Finley Christians. Christians had seen a VW with Rhode Island license plates and a blue duffel bag on the backseat off nearby Griffin Island Road on Saturday, February 1. A police search of the area had been hampered by bad weather.

While Pat Walsh's car was "very similar" to the one he had seen, Christians couldn't definitely say for sure it was the same car. He showed Flynn the road where he'd seen the car in an area off Duck Harbor. Another search was conducted by Killen, Dunn, Marshall and three rangers from the Cape Cod National Seashore.

Flynn left the search site in Wellfleet to go to Provincetown to speak with Steve Grund at Mother Marion's restaurant. Flynn was trying to find out more about the peace-sign pendant found in the wastebasket of Tony Costa's room in Burlington. Grund had never seen the jewelry before; he couldn't identify it as belonging to Tony Costa.

Grund was unnerved by his interrogation by police. He and Atkins had stayed clear of Tony Costa ever since. "I kept thinking —all these things going through my head, like the car was hot, and the TV."

Tony had come into the restaurant a few days ago with Sandy Carter, Grund said, pointing her out to Flynn at a table talking with two other girls.

"Tony told me he bought the car from the missing girls for four hundred dollars," Sandy said to Flynn after he had introduced himself. She thought it was a small amount to pay for a new VW. Costa had stopped calling her for rides out to his drug cache in Truro.

"Do you know if anyone else took him out to his drug cache in the Truro woods?" Flynn said.

Sandy thought that David Nicholson might have.

A handsome young man, home from Stowe Prep on mid-February school vacation, Nicholson surprised Flynn by blandly admitting he had taken Costa to the Truro woods two days before. Flynn calculated it to be a day when police had been searching an area in Wellfleet.

"He asked me to drive him out there to get a stash of pills that he had," Nicholson said, "Tony went into the woods for a couple of minutes and then he came back." Costa had used a long, bayonet-type knife to dig up his stash—an army surplus ammunition canister, about a foot and half high with a screw-on cover.

"What did he have in the can?" Flynn said.

"Pills—prescription drugs—like sleeping pills."

"What kind of a container were they in?"

"Just bottles, I guess—the kind that you get from the drug-store."

"Did he take the ammunition can with him?"

"Yes, he did."

"*And* the knife?"

"I think he had it under his coat. I'm not sure."

"Did you have any conversation regarding two girls missing from Providence?"

"Yes."

"What did Tony tell you?"

"I had heard all the gossip so I asked Tony about them. He said it was ridiculous—that the girls had left for Canada."

"Did he tell you why they left?"

"He said they left with a lot of drugs to sell."

Flynn was returning to the police station when Tony Costa appeared in front of Malchman's Shoe Port. It was not the first time Flynn had encountered Costa on the street in Provincetown.

Costa lifted his hand in greeting and smiled.

Flynn waved back. *You son of a bitch,* he thought.

Tony Costa had been to the police station to demand the return of clothes taken "illegally and without a search warrant" from his room in Burlington, Vermont.

Costa called at the police station again the next afternoon and asked to speak with Sergeant Meads. Meads was off duty, so Costa demanded to see Chief Marshall.

Marshall was amazed at Costa's effrontery. "Christ," Marshall told Patrolman Cook, "he's in here every ten minutes for one reason or another. You can't walk into the place without falling over the guy." When Costa stepped into his office Marshall said, "I don't know anything about your clothes. The DA's office would have that information."

Costa told him his attorney was coming down from Boston to see him, and gave Marshall a slip of paper upon which was written the name of a lawyer: "Hector Cicchetti, 342 Hanover Street, Boston."

Marshall was puzzled. Town hall gossip had it that Costa had retained Maurice Goldman. Marshall said he would only talk to a lawyer if Costa wanted to talk.

Costa objected to the state police—especially Bernie Flynn—

81

ruining his good name by asking questions about him all over town. He said he was considering an injunction from the courts to put a stop to the investigation.

Marshall said to him, "Tony, one of these days we're going to find those bodies."

Costa said, "I don't know what you're talking about."

The next day Meads delivered a message to Tony Costa at his mother's apartment. It was from Bernie Flynn, telling him to pick up the clothes taken in Vermont. Costa was with Peter, his oldest son, a lively five-year-old who had entered kindergarten in the fall.

"Boy, Jim," Costa said. "This case is certainly getting a lot of publicity. I read in the Boston *Record-American* yesterday where the police think Pat Walsh and Mary Anne Wysocki killed that girl that was dug up in the woods."

Meads hadn't read the story.

"That really surprises me," Costa went on. "Knowing those girls for the time I was with them, I didn't think they were capable of committing such a crime."

Meads found a copy of the newspaper. It carried a recapitulation of the case with no new information in it. The story speculated that a link might exist between the missing Providence girls and the body exhumed in the woods, but no suggestion was made that Pat and Mary Anne were responsible for the death of the unidentified girl.

Newspaper accounts of the disappearance of Pat Walsh and Mary Anne Wysocki had accelerated from the time the dead body was found in the woods. Police had been closemouthed about their investigation. "We have no suspects, although we have questioned many persons," Bernie Flynn told reporters. "It has been established who has the car and drove it to Burlington, Vermont." Police were continuing their searches for the missing girls because "certain circumstances about the departure of the girls necessitated an investigation."

Chief Harold Berrio was even vaguer. He told the Provincetown *Advocate* that there was "no evidence that the missing girls were victims of foul play." The police had no suspects regarding their disappearance, or the dismembered body of an "unknown" young woman found in the Truro woods.

Berrio was virtually under siege at his small station where every morning he gave out "progress reports" on the searches being conducted in the woods. He had received a number of telephone calls from parents, anxious for their missing daughters, from as far away as Pennsylvania.

Berrio's attitude reflected the detached view prevailing in Truro about the case. Townspeople, certain that the body buried in the woods had been killed elsewhere and "dumped," were outraged at having their unspoiled landscape thus "violated." Berrio was glad the state police had taken over the case. He had neither the training nor the stomach for work like this. He was expected to account for virtually every paper clip in the annual police department budget at town meeting, and he tended to be conservative when it came to using police resources on cases involving "outsiders." Truro, with the lowest crime rate of all the towns on Cape Cod, hadn't reported a missing person for over three years. If the Massachusetts State Police wanted to spend time and money looking for two girls from Providence, Rhode Island, it was all right with him.

George Killen maintained a stony silence with the press, refusing to talk to reporters. He was under pressure from the FBI to arrest Tony Costa for the larceny of the Volkswagen and transporting a stolen vehicle across state lines. Killen told the resident FBI agent in Hyannis, "We've *got* the goddamned car. To hell with the car."

If Tony Costa was picked up for car theft, police could not hold him very long; the arrest was likely to provoke him into running. Killen wanted to do nothing to panic Costa into leaving Cape Cod.

Killen was prepared for pressure from the FBI; it was he who had sought their assistance, submitting for examination by the bureau's Washington laboratory the bill of sale Tony Costa had given to Bernie Flynn. The package of evidence Killen mailed off also included Costa's application for a Burlington post office box and Vermont driver's license, the torn bill of sale found in the wastebasket of Mrs. Smith's rooming house in Burlington, and the note Costa had written to her. Costa's handwriting was to be compared with Pat Walsh's signature on the torn Auto Club of Rhode Island membership card, the cover of the Volkswagen owner's manual and her "Memo and Datebook" found in the woods.

Killen wanted fingerprint cards for Pat Walsh and Mary Anne Wysocki, if any existed, compared to any latent prints developed on the evidence submitted.

Killen asked that the FBI's examination be expedited and an early reply furnished, "since the missing girls may be homicide victims."

Killen's decision to resist FBI pressure to arrest Tony Costa was fully supported by District Attorney Edmund Dinis when Killen went to his office in New Bedford to brief him on the progress of the investigation. Dinis was going to be interviewed by a reporter from station WPRO-TV in Providence.

Dinis gave Killen sanction to continue the searches in the Truro woods and to follow up on all leads.

Killen returned to Cape Cod on Thursday, February 20, and held a conference in this office with Flynn, Gunnery and Dunn to review where they stood on the case.

Flynn was convinced Tony Costa had killed the girls, stolen their car, and was getting ready to run. "It's all over Provincetown that Tony's leaving," Flynn said. "Christ, he's told *everybody.*" The only thing Costa hadn't done was taken an ad in the *Advocate* to say goodbye.

Killen too thought the girls were dead, but whether Tony Costa had anything to do with killing them, he wasn't so sure. Los Angeles police had now checked and found no trace of Pat Walsh and Mary Anne Wysocki. "So you can cross off the abortion story," Killen said. He thought Costa had either stolen the car or gotten it from someone else who had.

Dunn was subdued. It was clear to him that the case had passed into Bernie Flynn's hands. Privately, Dunn thought they were chasing phantoms. Still smarting over the tongue-lashing

Killen had given him for sending the teletype, Dunn cautiously put forward the idea that *if* the girls were dead—and he wasn't positive that they were—he didn't think Tony Costa had anything to do with their murder. Costa had no motive for killing the girls. "How long did he know them?" Dunn said. "A day and a half?" Granted, Costa was lying; he probably knew more about the girls' disappearance than he was telling, perhaps to protect the person from whom he had gotten their car. "But it doesn't make sense to me for somebody to kill two girls for a lousy Volkswagen," Dunn said.

Gunnery, as a participant in a conference with three state police detective lieutenants, kept a respectful silence. He tended to agree with Flynn's idea that Costa was a conscienceless psychopath, a wily and cunning killer who had murdered both girls, disposed of their bodies somewhere in the woods and made off with their car. Gunnery enjoyed working with Bernie Flynn. In his view Flynn was "a sharp guy and one helluva cop." Even when nothing was happening, Flynn created a velocity of his own by the force of his restless energy.

Flynn was incensed by the provocative game of catch-me-if-you-can Tony Costa appeared to be playing with police, threatening openly to leave town and complaining of police harassment. "The guy's a fucking *actor,*" Flynn said.

"What we gotta do," Killen said quietly, "is break up his act."

Flynn left the conference to go to the Colonial candle factory on Main Street in Hyannis where Georgia Panesis and Ronald Enos were employed.

Georgia, a pretty girl with a thick mass of dark hair down her back, had briefly shared an apartment with Tony Costa at the White Wind apartments in Provincetown. Tony had invited her and Enos to stay with him last December when he heard they had no money for rent; Enos had gone to live with his mother because Tony's place was too small.

Georgia had seen all kinds of narcotics in the apartment. By counting the pills he kept hidden in the shower, she calculated that Tony Costa had taken twenty 100-mg tablets of Nembutal in a single day. "I told Tony he shouldn't be taking so many pills," she said. " 'When you run out,' I told him, 'what will you do?' "

85

Costa had laughed at her: "I have a lot of pills, and I won't run out."

"Tony was so regular when he was stoned it was really hard to tell," Georgia told Flynn. "Tony talked to me one night about dying, and committing suicide. He was terribly upset over the death of a girl in New York, Christine Gallant. He told me he loved her, that they were supposed to get married." The next day Tony had remembered nothing of the conversation. Moody, extremely anxious whenever he did not have drugs, Tony had never been menacing to her. "He was always very good to me, very considerate. I was never worried about him hurting me." She and Enos had moved to Hyannis after Christmas.

"Did he ever make a pass at you when you were living together?" Flynn said.

"No, Tony never did," Georgia said, looking over at Ronnie Enos. "Tony and Ronnie are very good friends. Tony would never do a thing like that."

Costa visited her at work on January 28 after being treated at Cape Cod Hospital for severe abdominal pains. He said he had been diagnosed as suffering from a minor virus infection and had been given a prescription for Vistral. Tony had stayed at her house from four-thirty to seven-thirty that night, waiting for a bus to take him back to Provincetown. She had not heard from him again for two weeks.

"Then Tony called me at home around four o'clock from the bus station in Hyannis on February ninth . . . a Sunday. He said he had come back to Cape Cod because the police wanted to talk to him about the missing girls from Providence. He said he had met the girls at the Foc's'le and bought their car for nine hundred dollars."

Ronnie Enos spoke up; he had gone to the Hyannis bus station to visit with Costa. "He told me the girls' car had freaked out on the way back from Vermont and he had taken the bus home." Enos was tall, long-haired and swarthy, an ex-member of the Barbarians, a rock band that had enjoyed a modest success. He had worked for Tony Costa as a carpenter's helper and had accompanied Costa to California in January, 1968. They had spent several weeks in the Haight-Ashbury section of San Francisco. "Tony had a super-bad trip on speed out there—he almost died. He had to be taken to the hospital." Enos had seen Costa take fourteen Nembutal capsules in one day. "He was in the bathroom taking a shower and you could hear him falling against the walls and making all kinds of noises in there. He could hardly walk."

Enos knew of the drug stashes Costa had kept in the Truro woods. "Tony liked to go out there to take pictures when he was high. He said he saw things he didn't see in a normal state of mind. He got some real good pictures. Slides mostly."

Costa had told him before they left for California that the "straight life" wasn't for him. "When he took off, Tony left Avis like eighty dollars," Enos said. Avis told him Tony had once raped her on the kitchen floor in front of their children, "because he wasn't getting anything from her."

Costa considered his children a burden, Georgia said. "Last summer, Tony would come to Avis's house and the kids would be hanging on him—like hugging him and everything—and Tony would more or less be trying to talk through them. He kept pushing them away. He said he didn't even feel like they were his kids because he never saw them."

Costa had written from Burlington about getting a job in a furniture factory, and that Vermonters were friendly and the girls very pretty, Enos said. "Some of the words he wrote, I don't even know what they mean. We had to look them up in a dictionary, like a puzzle. You had to figure out—what is he saying?"

The letter had been signed, "Josiah Shannon."

On Friday, February 21, Flynn returned to the Truro woods to join Killen, Chief Marshall and Trooper Gunnery for another search. Beginning at the clearing where the VW was last seen, Flynn went down the dirt road running through scrub bush and ragged uplands to the Old Truro Cemetery which occupied the top of a hill—an acre of cleared space fenced by granite posts and iron railings. Many of the leaning gravestones dated back to the early eighteenth century and were covered with lichen. Flynn peered into an unlocked brick mausoleum built into the side of an incline, and examined a small pond close by. The search party found nothing.

George Killen had secured the fingerprints of Sydney Lee Monzon from the county sheriff's office, but not without a struggle. As part of a civil defense project initiated by Deputy Sheriff Donald Doane, in 1963, Cape Cod schoolchildren had been fingerprinted for identification in the event of a national disaster. The sheriff's office did not want their files to be disturbed. At Killen's insistence, fingerprint charts were secured from Deputy Sheriff Louis Cataldo, and sent to Sergeant Sharkey at state police headquarters in Boston.

The prints did not match those taken from the unidentified body.

Killen had better news from the FBI, whose examination revealed that the "Anthony Costa" signature on the bill of sale was genuine, matching his handwriting on the fingerprint cards in Costa's identification record. The signature of Pat Walsh "was not prepared by Patricia Walsh."

"Characteristics" also indicated that Costa had signed the torn bill of sale found in the wastebasket in Burlington, but the disarrangement of the writing caused by the paper's being torn precluded a definite opinion—handwriting samples were not sufficient for a satisfactory evaluation. The evidence Killen had submitted was being treated for latent fingerprints, the results of which would follow in a separate report.

Flynn, however, was annoyed at the cautionary nature of the bureau's report. He called Washington for a stronger indication that the bill of sale was a forgery. The FBI, he was told, required additional writing samples in order to make such a qualification.

Flynn called Mrs. Walsh for additional specimens of her daughter's handwriting. Mrs. Walsh delivered to the Rehoboth barracks of the Massachusetts State Police a blue examination book, dated March 31, 1965 containing an exam Pat Walsh had taken for a Western Literature course, and a seven-page paper, "Psychological Research Methods," which she had written as a student at Rhode Island College.

Flynn also received from Provincetown police files, as an additional handwriting sample, a one-page letter Antone Costa had sent to Sergeant Meads on October 15, 1968 from Barnstable County House of Correction, asking Meads to send the parole board a recommendation for his early release.

Dear Jim:

I have a special favor to ask of you. I would appreciate it greatly if you would send me, or the parole board, a recommendation for my release on parole as soon as possible. In here I am only wasting my time, and am of no use to anyone. The state holds the entire burden.

Jim, although I was wrong in not paying the welfare people, I realize it now. But I complained to the Welfare Dept. so many times and they did nothing. So, I refused to pay, hoping that some action would be taken against Avis and all her friends, and their various *habits*. She used the money to support them all, and my kids went without. I feared that whatever I did would hurt my children eventually. I would have asked for your help, but I recall doing that before and Mr. Marshall let the whole town know what was happening. I can never trust him again. What I do now I must do alone, until such time when I can anonymously drop it in your hands, if that time ever comes.

Please reply and let me know if you can return this favor for me.

Sincerely,
Anthony C. Costa

Flynn, in Provincetown to talk with James "Zack" Zacharias, was losing patience with the sluggish progress in the case.

Zacharias had met Tony Costa at the construction site of the Royal Coachman motel. "He was just one of the guys I was working with I was getting to know," he said. "I thought he was an OK guy."

The job had been disagreeable—digging the frozen ground to set the footings for a new motel, the site exposed to blasts of wind coming off the waterfront at Beach Point.

After missing four days of work, Costa had been fired on January 23. "The foreman told the crew if any of us saw Tony to tell him not to bother to come back. He gave me Tony's check because I was riding in a car pool every morning with him and John Anthony."

Zack had not seen Costa until two days later, a Saturday morning when he was on his way to do some grocery shopping. "I was riding on my friend Shirley Sill's motorcycle," he told Flynn. "As we crossed Bradford Street, heading for the A & P, I saw Tony go by in a car heading out of town. He waved to me. I got off the bike and walked across the street. Tony said he'd just been to my house looking for me—he'd heard I had a check for him."

Costa was sitting on the passenger side of a light blue VW, wearing a white sweater. A girl was driving; another girl was in the backseat.

Zack had handed Costa a check through the window and said, "I'll see you later." He got back on the motorcycle and went to the A&P; Costa had taken off with the girls in the car. "I think he said they were going to Wellfleet or Hyannis."

"What time of day was this?" Flynn said.

"I would say it was around noontime . . . between noon and two o'clock."

"Tony told me he was with two girls, and that he got out of the Volkswagen and went with you," Flynn said. "Is that true?"

"No," Zack said. "He never got out of the car."

19

At nine o'clock in the morning of Saturday, February 22, George Davis of Cape Cod Bus Lines called Gunnery at the Yarmouth barracks to report he had driven Tony Costa to Provincetown on the seven-thirty bus from Boston the previous evening. Costa told him he had been visiting his brother for a couple of days.

Flynn blew up when he got the news that Costa had left Provincetown unobserved. Costa was supposed to be under constant police surveillance. Flynn found out that Patrolman Cook had checked on Costa at work on the morning of Thursday, February 20. According to Joe Beaudry, Tony had then gone to his mother's for lunch and not returned. He was gone two days.

Chief Marshall had Tony Costa brought to the police station. Costa said he had gone to Boston to help paint an apartment his brother just rented. Transportation had been provided by Robert

Lee Hedrick, owner of the White Dory Inn, who had met Costa when he was working for Joe Beaudry.

"I liked what I saw of his work," Hedrick told Flynn. Hedrick had asked Tony if he was interested in part-time work, some odd jobs of interior carpentry he needed done on the cottages he rented in the summer. "Tony came over and I showed him what I wanted. He said he thought he could do the work in one day and told me what materials to order." Then Hedrick mentioned going to Boston the next day. "Tony called me up that night and asked for a ride. I picked him up around noon at his mother's." Costa had a trunk tied all around with rope and carried a green duffel bag. "He said he had his laundry in it." Hedrick had no idea that police were investigating Costa's possible involvement with missing girls. "Tony told me he had driven two girls he met at Pat Morton's house to Burlington, Vermont. They were going to take a plane to Montreal."

"Did he tell you how he got their car?" Flynn said.

"They owed him money—like six or seven hundred dollars from last summer. He said the girls were going to Canada because they were involved in some big dope ring. It all hinged on dope," Hedrick said. "That's how Tony bought the car."

Costa had told him about a bad experience he'd had with LSD. "He said he only smoked pot now." When Hedrick mentioned he was tired of driving, Costa said, "I wish I could drive for you, but I lost my license about a year ago. I can't drive in the state of Massachusetts."

Hedrick let Costa off at the Prudential Center in Boston. "He was going to take a Checker cab to the office because his brother's girlfriend worked there as a bookkeeper. Tony was going to get the key to an apartment from her."

Hedrick told Costa if he wanted a ride back to Provincetown to call his hotel after ten o'clock the next morning. Costa had called, but they had somehow missed connecting.

At one o'clock, Flynn went to the building site of the Royal Coachman to talk to John Anthony who had occasionally picked up Tony Costa at Mrs. Morton's to take him to work. Anthony had parked his father's Chevy Malibu in front of Adams Pharmacy the previous evening and was talking with Gary Watts and another boy, Larry Andresen, when Tony came by and got in the car.

"We got to rapping about some photographic equipment

91

Tony wanted to sell—a couple of developing pans and some paper he had," Anthony said. "Tony asked Larry if he wanted to buy the stuff to let him know by Sunday night. Tony said he wasn't going to be around on Monday, he was splitting town."

Flynn went straight to the Provincetown police station to report to Killen that Tony Costa was getting ready to run.

Killen wanted a warrant prepared for Costa's arrest for the larceny of an automobile, but both he and Flynn were hesitant about serving it, deciding instead to keep Costa under tight surveillance over the weekend. At the first sign Costa was leaving Cape Cod, he'd be picked up.

Killen was at the station to talk to Mrs. Mary Roderick, owner of the house at 9 Conant Street where Costa's mother rented an upstairs apartment. Mrs. Bonaviri was a nice woman, Mrs. Roderick said, but she was afraid of Tony Costa and didn't like him hanging around her house. She was having problems with the plumbing; the toilet in the apartment upstairs had run all night long. She suspected Tony Costa was flushing things down the toilet.

Killen ordered the cesspool pumped and its contents examined at the town dump. Marshall found photographs of young women, torn into unrecognizable fragments. He said to Flynn, "Not the kind of police work they show you on television, is it Bernie? Sticking your hands in shit."

20

It was snowing heavily on the afternoon of Monday, February 24, when George Davis called the Yarmouth barracks again, this time to report Tony Costa on board his bus, bound for Hyannis from Provincetown.

Flynn was en route with Gunnery to the Samurai Motor Inn

on Route 132 in Hyannis with the book of matches found in the glove compartment of the Volkswagen, to see if either Pat Walsh or Mary Anne Wysocki had ever registered there. When he got the radio call, Flynn drove through the snow as fast as he dared, getting to the Almeida bus terminal in time to see Costa get off a bus carrying a portable phonograph and a duffel bag. He watched Costa enter the terminal and head for the ticket counter.

Shouldering his way through the crowd of travelers, Flynn flashed his badge and said, "State police." He put a restraining hand on Costa's arm. Flynn could feel the nerves jump under his grip. He said, "Can I talk to you a minute, Tony?"

Costa looked frightened. "I've got to catch the bus to Boston right now," he said.

"This won't take long," Flynn said. He tightened his hold on Costa's arm and propelled him out of the terminal to his car in the parking lot.

"I don't want to get into the car," Costa said.

"Well, you just come along anyway," Flynn said. "We've got a few questions."

Flynn took a place in the front seat. He turned to face Costa seated in back with Gunnery. Costa's eyes blazed with anger.

"Tony, at this time, the very least you are a suspect of is the larceny of the Volkswagen," Flynn said. As a result of the FBI's examination, Flynn was of the opinion that the bill of sale was a fake; the car was stolen. Costa was not under arrest at this time, "But I'll repeat the Miranda warnings before I ask you any questions."

Costa was tired of hearing Miranda. "I know my rights," he said coldly. He was impatient to end the interview. "I don't want to miss my bus."

Flynn asked if he had permission from his probation officer to leave town.

"I called Jimmy Cordeiro a few days ago," Costa said. "He told me I could go anywhere as long as I didn't leave the state. You can check with him if you want."

"We'll do that," Flynn said. He was stalling for time, waiting for the Boston bus to pull out of the terminal. "Are you leaving the area, Tony?"

Costa was going to 364 Marlborough Street in Boston, his brother's new apartment; he was going to help paint the place.

"How long will you be in Boston?" Flynn said.

93

"A few days, maybe a week, I'm not sure." Costa didn't know where he was going afterward.

"Aren't you coming back to Provincetown?" Flynn said.

"No," Costa said, "I don't want to go back to Provincetown. I don't like the place any more—I'm losing all my friends. You're asking a lot of questions about me and now, when I walk down the street, people I used to know don't speak to me anymore. They're afraid to have anything to do with me." He had been continuously hassled by police coming to his place of work to take him to the station just to answer the same questions over and over. "I've told the cops everything I know about the girls."

Flynn decided to change tactics. Costa was running, there was no doubt about that. Flynn had pondered springing the warrant, slapping the cuffs on him and taking him in. Costa was a cool bastard, telling him boldly that he was taking off, almost daring Flynn to arrest him.

Instead, Flynn turned conciliatory. "If it's true, what you've told us, that these girls sold you their car, don't you think you might hear from them?" Flynn said. He saw a bus roll out of the terminal.

"I think I might," Costa said. "I'm surprised I haven't heard from them because I helped them out and we parted company the best of friends."

"Did you give the girls an address or telephone number where you could be reached?" Flynn said.

Costa said he had told Pat Walsh to contact him at his mother's. He had been at his mother's house the past few nights hoping the girls would call.

"Tony, if you hear from the girls—whether by phone or by letter—for God's sake let me know immediately," Flynn said. "If I can have an assurance that these girls are alive, I won't bother you any more. I don't want to be in Provincetown every day questioning people about you if I don't have to. I've got other cases to work on."

Flynn watched Costa walk from the car into the bus station. It was a calculated risk to let him go.

Gunnery was baffled. He assumed they had raced to the bus station to put Tony Costa under arrest.

Flynn had something else in mind. "Did you see how his eyes lit up when I mentioned him hearing from the girls? You could see

94

the wheels turn in his head and him thinking, 'Oh, boy. I got me a sucker here.' ''

Flynn had set the trap; now, all Tony Costa had to do was fall into it.

Tony Costa was shaken by his unexpected interview with Bernie Flynn and incensed that the interrogation had been deliberately prolonged for him to miss the last bus to Boston. Because of the increasing severity of the storm, all remaining scheduled buses had been canceled.

Costa reclaimed his luggage from inside of the terminal and trudged unhappily through the blinding snow to the Mayflower Restaurant, a block from the bus station. He did not want to be stranded overnight in Hyannis and give Bernie Flynn the satisfaction of spoiling his plans.

Costa counted over eighty dollars in cash in his wallet—more than enough to get him to Boston.

Vincent Keavy of the Hyannis Taxi Company was dubious about driving to Boston in the snowstorm as soon as he was dispatched to the telephone booths on the corner of Main and Ocean streets to pick up a fare. By the time Keavy reached Route 6 in Sandwich, he was ready to give up. Snow, driven by fierce wind, was sending blinding traceries against the windshield, making the road ahead an unnavigable white space. Keavy could feel the wheels shudder for traction under him as the battered cab made its way slowly through the dark afternoon.

"Are you sure you got to go to Boston today?" Keavy asked his passenger.

Tony Costa said, "Well, I'm more or less committed."

Keavy couldn't promise to make it all the way to Boston in the storm; he offered to charge only the fare to the point where he let his passenger off.

Route 3 was empty of traffic, a pristine stretch of highway. The sound of the windshield wipers and the wheezing of the heater's fan were the only accompaniment as the cab slid uncertainly over thick tracks of snow. It was hours before the glow of Boston, misty and indistinct, showed in the sky ahead. As Keavy drew near the outskirts he asked whether he should take the Kneeland Street exit in order to reach Marlborough Street, the destination he was given.

Tony Costa changed his mind, telling Keavy to let him out at Park Square. Costa paid him thirty-five dollars and got out across the street from the bus station.

Three boys from Provincetown were riding in the back of a New York-to-Boston Greyhound bus, idling at the Natick-Framingham stop. Paul Campbell saw a figure running out of the snowstorm to board their bus. He said to his companions, Matt Russe and Joey "Fluff" Adams, "You won't believe who I just saw. Tony Costa!" Since two buses were coming from New York, Campbell wasn't sure Costa hadn't gotten off the other bus.

Costa boarded the bus, looked straight at Campbell and the others but didn't say anything; he took a seat in front.

Matt Russe, a husky young man with dark, curly hair, had left Provincetown on January 28 with Adams and Campbell, bound for Mexico. Running out of money in California, Russe sold his car for their return air fare, arriving in New York to find Boston's airport closed because of the snowstorm.

Tony had wanted to go with him, Russe told the others. "He wanted me to go to Canada with him—on some fishing ventures, and things like that. He kept saying, 'Man, I got to get out of this town and go to Canada, we *both* should go.' Tony said things were real bad in Provincetown, he had no money or anything."

Costa had suggested they rob a bank in Boston; Russe hadn't taken him seriously. Tony had a vivid imagination. "Once Tony said he was driving down Route 6 and picked up two girls hitchhiking and they both died of an overdose of heroin and he had to bury them."

Russe had talked to his mother from California. "She told me about the body the cops dug up in Truro and the two other girls disappearing. She heard Tony had something to do with it. I don't know if he's crazy or what."

When the bus pulled into Boston, Costa said, "Hi, how are you?"

Paul Campbell asked him where he was headed.

"North," Costa said. The bus was going to Portland, Maine. "I'd really appreciate it if you guys didn't tell anybody you saw me. Things are real bad in Provincetown."

Costa addressed his remarks to Campbell and Thomas.

"Tony's mad at me," Russe told them later.

Tony Costa arrived at 364 Marlborough Street around nine o'clock. He explained to Vinnie he had taken a cab from Hyannis because he missed the Boston bus, and a circuitous route to the apartment because he thought detectives were following him.

Vinnie was suspicious about his brother's story—that he had gotten the Volkswagen from Pat Walsh. He later recalled, "All during that week in the newspapers they were showing pictures of the girls from Rhode Island that were missing and the registration and make of the car. I kept asking Tony to tell me the truth, and all the time, I get the same story."

"Don't worry about the car," Costa said. "The cops have the car—they took it away from me." Vinnie was hardly reassured.

The next morning, Costa boarded a bus for Burlington, Vermont; in Burlington, he took a bus to Montreal.

At the Canadian border, a gray-haired customs inspector examined Costa's luggage and asked him how long he was planning to stay in Canada. Costa said he was visiting friends for about two weeks; he had fifty-five dollars. The inspector gave him a border-crossing card good for two days.

21

Flynn joined another search of the South Truro woods, a mile-square area from Old Proprietor's Road branching off along snow-covered trails that wound through the trees. After several fruitless hours he was chilled in the lung-aching cold, and very discouraged. He went to Provincetown to talk with Donna Cummings and her boyfriend, Richard Oldenquist.

Donna had met Russell Norton at the Foc's'le. He told her he was looking for two chicks with long hair from Rhode Island. Later, she'd seen him at the Pilgrim Club. "I asked him if he had found his friends yet and he said he hadn't." She let Norton sleep on the floor of her apartment that night. The next day when she asked him about the girls, Norton said he was going to meet them at noon at the benches in front of town hall.

Oldenquist had been in the Foc's'le on Friday night. He had seen Pat and Mary Anne sitting with two other girls. One of the girls was a hairdresser—a blonde chick with black-rimmed glasses who drove a white MG; the other girl was also blonde, but taller and hung out in Provincetown a lot on weekends. She was the girlfriend of a young fisherman in town, a kid named Davey Joseph.

That evening at 6 o'clock, Flynn and Gunnery talked to Irene Hare and Brenda Dreyer at Justin's beauty shop on Route 28 in Centerville. Irene, a plain-faced, vivacious girl of 21, had recently moved to Hyannis and was sharing an apartment with Brenda, who called herself "Bunny."

On Friday, January 24, around 9 P.M., Irene and Brenda had gone into the Foc's'le, a bar occupying a clapboard storefront on Commercial Street furnished with thick tables and benches and lit by ceiling-strung lanterns. By Provincetown standards, the decor was authentic: paint-peeled buoys in clusters and drapes of rotting fishnet; a portion of a dory was nailed to the side of the wall. Lobster pots served as containers for bags of potato chips.

The bar was crowded, Irene said. "Two girls were sitting at a table by themselves on the side and there were four empty seats. We went to the table and asked if we could sit down. They said sure."

"I asked Irene if we should talk to them," Brenda Dreyer said. A secretary-bookkeeper, she had straight blonde hair and a long, oval face. "Irene said no, because the girls were involved in a conversation. I said, 'Oh, let's talk to them!' I looked across the table and said, 'Hi, my name's Bunny—and this is Irene . . .' "

"Pat Walsh was wearing knee boots, a skirt and vest and a real grungy khaki army jacket," Irene said. "Her hair was pulled back. She was a real pretty girl, distinctive looking." Mary Anne Wysocki had on leather riding boots, a green and blue plaid jumper and a dark green sweater coat. Both of them were drinking Schaefer beer.

"I asked them why they'd come to Provincetown," Bunny said. "Pat told us she hadn't been down since last summer and they wanted to get away from Providence for a few days. Mary Anne was a junior in college. She'd just finished her midterm exams and was real tired on account of she had studied so hard. They were staying at Pat Morton's and were leaving early on Sunday because Mary Anne had a lot of things she had to do at home. Pat said she had papers to correct for her second-graders."

Irene had asked Pat if the kids ever gave her a bad time.

"Pat said she loved the children, but had reservations about the teaching methods she had to use, and all the paperwork and stuff you had to do and lesson plans. It was her second year teaching; she was really enjoying it. 'Nobody likes their first year of teaching,' I think that's what she said."

"Then Stevie Joseph came in and sat with us for a little bit," Bunny said. "I like David, his brother." She had shown David's picture to Pat Walsh. " 'David's a Libra,' I told her, 'I get along well with Libras. What sign are you?' Pat said, 'I'm a Taurus.' I told her, 'Hey, that's my sign! I don't think I ever met a Taurus girl before.' And she said 'I don't get along with Taurus girls,' just like that."

Pat was a very smart person, Bunny thought, who would say funny things and show no expression; no one could tell if she was serious or not. Pat confided that she enjoyed drawing, writing poetry, the Beatles and Bob Dylan. She liked folk music better than rock.

Irene had asked if they had ever been to the Blues Bag, a Provincetown nightclub that was closed in winter. Bunny had gone there to see Tom Rush.

Mary Anne had replied that she liked Tim Hardin. "She was a real quiet person, she didn't say very much," Irene said. "She smiled a lot and let Pat do most of the talking." Pat was more hip than Mary Anne. "You could tell from the way she talked, her whole attitude. Pat said she'd smoked marijuana a couple of times and she had smelled hashish once, though she never tried it. Mary Anne had never done anything in the drug line."

"They didn't know their way around Provincetown, or what places to go," Bunny said. "Pat asked us what there was to do on Saturday—something inexpensive."

Bunny suggested some beaches in Truro she went to with her boyfriend. The beaches were cold in winter, but the breakers were beautiful—better than in summer. She gave them directions to Highland Light Road off the highway.

Around 11 o'clock, Irene and Bunny said they were going to the Pilgrim Club. Mary Anne and Pat had never been there. "They asked us if it was within walking distance," Irene said. "Bunny suggested we all go in my car, but Pat said no, she had her own car. She didn't want to inconvenience us if she and Mary Anne wanted to leave before we did." Irene was parked across the street from the Foc's'le. "I said, 'We'll race you.' Pat and Mary Anne walked back to Standish Street and we drove around the block; they followed us out to Shank Painter Road."

At the Pilgrim Club "Pat was really hassled by the guy at the door about her ID, so she just had a Coke. They wouldn't serve her." Neither Pat or Mary Anne were big drinkers, Irene said. "They couldn't have had more than three drinks all night."

"Then this fisherman—an older guy in his thirties—came over and bought us all a beer. He took a liking to Pat and started talking to her," Bunny said. "They rapped until the bartender started yelling at all of us to get out." They left the Pilgrim Club at 1:15 A.M.

Pat and Mary Anne said they would like to come back to Provincetown again before summer, maybe during the next six weeks. Bunny suggested they come down in March for a weekend. Mary Anne was enthusiastic about the idea. Irene gave them her mother's address and the address at the shop where she worked. "I was in the process of moving and I didn't know where I'd be," Irene said. "They said they'd write to let us know when they were coming down, and we could all stay together, it would be fun."

Because it was late and Pat did not know the area, Irene led the way back to Standish Street to make sure she wouldn't get lost. As the VW pulled into a parking space across from the guest-house, Irene rolled down the car window. She and Bunny were returning to their home in western Massachusetts in the morning.

Irene remembered calling out, "See you in March."

Bunny and Irene knew Tony Costa by sight, but they had never been formally introduced. They had not seen him at the Foc's'le or the Pilgrim Club the evening they spent with Pat Walsh and Mary Anne Wysocki.

"Tony Costa didn't come to your table at all?" Flynn said.

"No," Irene said. Neither Pat nor Mary Anne mentioned they knew Tony; Pat hadn't said anything about wanting to sell her car.

Bunny had seen Tony last week while having lunch with Davey Joseph at Mother Marion's. Jimmy Steele had come over to their table. It was all over town about the body that the police had found in the Truro woods and the disappearance of the girls from Providence. Costa had told Steele he'd traded hashish for the VW, and the girls had taken off with two guys and gone to Montreal.

"Jimmy said the cops were trying to blame his friend Tony for the disappearance of the two missing girls who probably got murdered," Bunny said.

"I been into his head a long time," Steele told them, "Tony could never do a thing like that."

22

Bernie Flynn groaned when he reached Pilgrim Heights in Truro on Tuesday morning, February 25. Provincetown was spread out before him like a withered arm cradling the dead-gray harbor, the magnificent space of water and sky punctuated by the gray Florentine bell tower that served as a monument to the first landing of the Pilgrims. Flynn had come to hate the place.

Hostile to outsiders, enclosed within itself, distinct, separate from the prim and orderly charm of the rest of Cape Cod, Provincetown was an outpost of singularity, a frontier unconnected with the rest of Cape Cod. Flynn thought the canal and the bridges that separated the Cape from the mainland belonged at the town line of Truro.

With most of the leads drying up and the investigation getting nowhere, Flynn was digging at the underside of the case, buttonholing anyone who had any association with Tony Costa.

Flynn found it hard going. As the centerpiece of a coterie of young people deeply involved in Provincetown's drug scene, Tony Costa was vigorously defended. "They all love the guy," Flynn complained to Meads at the police station. Flynn figured Meads as the likeliest police officer to know who Costa's friends were.

Meads warned him that town kids were streetwise—old for their years. "You can say anything you want to them, use any kind of language and they'll understand you," Meads said. Exposed to the free-living, sybaritic lifestyle of a summer resort of artists and tourists, kids grew up fast in Provincetown.

The first name on the list of Tony Costa's friends Meads gave Flynn was Larry Andresen.

Flynn went to Provincetown High School, a shabby brick building beside a municipal parking lot on a hill overlooking Bradford Street.

A skinny seventeen-year-old, with long hair tied in a ponytail behind his back, Andresen lived with his grandmother. Despite a severe stammer, Andresen managed to be, in Flynn's view, "a fresh little bastard."

Andresen had bought a Tower-57 camera from Tony Costa for twenty dollars the day after talking to him in John Anthony's car; Tony told him he was splitting town.

Tony had befriended a lot of young kids in town, Andresen said. "Tony liked to rap about his philosophy of life—about peace and love and all kinds of things like that." He said, "Tony was real nice to me."

There was a bunch of young girls who hung around Tony—mostly for friendship. One girl, however, Tony had told him he was in love with.

Twenty minutes later, Flynn was being introduced in principal George Leyden's office to a slender, delicately pretty girl with an exquisite complexion and clear blue eyes. Marsha Mowery was shy, holding her schoolbooks against her sweater for protection. She had known Tony Costa about three years and had gone to the Truro woods with him many times.

"The first time I went with him was in 1967. Tony wanted to take care of his marijuana plants—to water them or something. It wasn't a field or anything, just a few plants, maybe fifteen or so." Costa did not want to go to his garden alone. "He liked to have someone with him, because he said he was afraid."

One day when she was in the woods with him, Costa brought a bow and two target arrows with him. "Everybody said he was an excellent marksman with a bow and arrow," Marsha said. She and Costa had harvested some plants from his garden. "We were walking back through the woods when Tony said he was going to shoot the arrows off into the trees. He wanted to get rid of them. I said I'd meet him back at the car. I started walking—I was halfway between him and the car—and all of a sudden I felt a heavy jolt in my back, under the left shoulder. An arrow hit me in the back."

Tony came running over. He said, "Are you all right? Should I take you to the doctor's?"

"He was *really* concerned," Marsha said. "I had on this heavy army coat that took some of the force out of the arrow. I insisted I wasn't hurt—it just felt like a hard blow on the back. Tony said he was trying to wing the arrow past me and hit a tree, just to scare me—all in fun. We got in the car and drove back to Provincetown. I was getting ready for bed when I noticed this big hole in my back. My mother took me to Dr. Hiebert. He said the bottom of the puncture wound was only a quarter of an inch from my left lung."

The accident had to be reported to the police. Tony had called her to find out if she was all right and told her he had gone to the Truro police station and made out an accident report.

Flynn had remained silent throughout the recitation, not wanting to interrupt. "This clearing where Tony had his garden," Flynn finally said, "was it in the area where he parked his car?"

"It was further down the road, through a trail in the woods, in this big open space in a kind of a valley-like." At the edge of the clearing was Tony Costa's garden.

Flynn felt a quickening of excitement. The woods were dense with trees; there was no clearing where a garden could be cultivated that he remembered from police searches. "Did you ever go back to the woods with Tony after the accident?"

"I drove out there with him a couple of times last summer, not as often as the summer before. I didn't see much of Tony last summer," Marsha said, "I think he was working in Boston."

"Do you know of any so-called stashes of drugs and pills Tony had hidden out in the woods?" Flynn said.

Marsha hesitated. "Well, he had places along the same side of the road where his garden was." Tony always behaved very peculiarly when he got to where he kept his drugs. "He'd jump out of the car and dash back and forth through the woods—not even following a path or anything, just running around like a crazy Indian. Then he'd come back with some drugs from his stash. He never showed me where the drugs were hidden."

103

"Did he have a shovel out there, do you know?" Flynn said.

"He might have had one in his car. He had all kinds of tools and things like that in the trunk."

Marsha had also been friendly with Avis Costa. "She told me all about how Tony used to do really perverted things to her when they were married. She almost died one time. I asked her about it. She had taken some sort of medicine Tony used to put animals to sleep with from his taxidermy kit—she took some to knock herself out because Tony liked to make love to her when she was unconscious. She also used plastic bags to try to pass out—he used to tell her that's what he wanted. This one time she took the medicine by herself, but she took too much and she almost died. Avis told me—we got into this big discussion—she told me about all the other things he did to her, and she would do to him."

"Such as what?" Flynn said.

"One time he had her beat him with a belt," Marsha said, flushing. "He used to hang himself up by his feet from a hook in the ceiling of their bedroom and have a sexual relationship that way. But mostly he would hang *her* from the hook."

Avis had gotten uptight when Tony started taking her places, Marsha said. "After Avis explained a letter Tony wrote about me I understood what was bothering her. In the letter Tony said he loved me and wanted to marry me. I was really surprised. Tony never said anything like that to me. I told Avis I only wanted Tony for a friend. She was OK after that."

The letter, written in New York where Tony Costa had worked for an air express company, was dated December 21, 1967 . . .

I sit here looking through the window studying the scene. Marsha is now on my mind. It makes me extremely happy to be around her. She has a beautiful creative atmosphere about her. I love it. I would adore being hers. I recall all the good times we shared this past year. She is the girl I would do all for! But I realize also that she may be too young to understand all this yet. But, again, she may be quite mature. She is a woman.

Through the few years which I have "turned on" I have analyzed my every thought. I have picked apart every fault, every one. I have been *totally* honest in analyzation. The knowledge I have gained is incredible. I am not who I was three years ago. I have matured, learned much of myself. A great deal of this knowledge has buried the old me. I buried myself deep, never to reopen the grave.

When I look back at myself, I can't see me. I picture another, totally separate individual whom I detest immensely. I analyze my being more and deeper every day. In doing this I will eventually form of myself a greater person. I want everyone to love me, but I want to love only one, if she will love me in return, always . . .

"Tony was probably stoned when he wrote it," Avis Costa said to Flynn. Costa had gotten heavy into the East Village drug scene while living in New York. "He was so tripped out on LSD once, he wore out a pair of shoes walking the streets." Tony had worked three months in New York, then had been fired.

Avis was a tall girl, with limp, stringy hair; her face was pinched and pallid with hollows like scars under high cheekbones —a face from which all the juices of youth seemed to have dried up. Flynn found it hard to believe she was only twenty years old.

Flynn stood in the second-floor apartment appalled at the squalor he found—a real hippie setup, he thought. There were dog droppings on the floor and two small children running around naked. Sprawled on a studio couch was a scroungy-looking kid with a beard and long hair, wearing jeans and playing the guitar. Flynn kept moving. He didn't want the colony of cockroaches exploring the kitchenette to crawl up his pants leg.

Avis corroborated Marsha Mowry's story about her sex life. She told Flynn she had last seen Tony a week and a half ago; he had come over to say goodbye—he was splitting town.

Marsha Mowery had refused to show Bernie Flynn the location of Tony's garden, telling him, "I don't think Tony had anything to do with what happened to those girls." Costa had never done any harm to anyone she knew about; the police were persecuting him because of dope.

George Killen did not hesitate to call Marsha Mowery's parents. That did the trick. The next morning, Killen and Flynn picked up Marsha and her father and drove to Truro.

A freezing rain was falling when Marsha got out of the cruiser to show the police the space where Tony Costa parked his car. Flynn was excited. The place was in a small clearing off the road about a mile from the place where the VW was last seen—the area of the most intense searches. Costa's parking space was not far from the grave where the unidentified body had been found. Passing the grave site, Flynn saw a shovel stuck in the center of the excavation.

Marsha pointed out a trail, obscured by brambles, on the opposite side of the road, making a twisting course through the trees. Some three hundred yards into the woods, down a gentle slope, was a large, open area, a natural clearing in the woods, rising to a slight knoll where the trees began again. At the extreme end of the clearing was the location of Tony Costa's garden.

Flynn felt a surge of elation. The place had not, he was sure, been explored by police. An arena of privacy, protected by a circle of woods, it was, Flynn suggested to Killen, the place Tony Costa had taken Pat Walsh and Mary Anne Wysocki the morning they had driven him to Truro—the place they must have been killed.

If Flynn was right that the scene of Costa's "accident" with Marsha Mowery was also the murder scene, Killen conceded it was the biggest break in the case so far. The discovery had occurred on the one-month anniversary of the disappearance of Pat Walsh and Mary Anne Wysocki.

Killen was dismayed that Truro police had an accident report on Tony Costa in their files and had forgotten about it. Chief Berrio could have led search parties to the clearing weeks ago.

Berrio had showed up most mornings to join the search party with Killen and Marshall, but it seemed to both men that he usually didn't stay around very long. On one occasion, Berrio had disappeared, then returned in uniform and carrying a shovel, accompanied by a newspaper photographer.

Watching Berrio pose, pretending to dig the earth, Marshall told Killen, "That guy's as useless as a tit on a bull."

Killen had another reason to hope the breaks in the case were coming faster. A further comparison of the handwriting of Tony Costa and Pat Walsh had now emboldened the FBI to suggest that Pat Walsh had not signed the torn bill of sale found in the wastebasket. "Characteristics" indicated the writing may not have been prepared by her, but the disarrangement of the torn paper still precluded a definite opinion. The writing of both bills of sale contained evidence of "disguise," the FBI said. "Anthony Charles

Costa should not be eliminated as a suspect in the preparation of these documents."

The FBI's laboratory was not so hesitant when it came to the identification of latent fingerprints developed on the torn cover of the Volkswagen owner's manual found in the woods, and on the Vermont Department of Motor Vehicles application.

Both prints had been identified as "finger impressions" of Antone Costa.

23

On Sunday, March 2, Mrs. Cecelia Bonaviri called Province-town police and asked to speak with Chief Marshall, who was not in his office. When he returned her call, she told him Western Union in Wellfleet had just telephoned. They had a telegram for her son, Tony, sent collect from New York City.

Marshall asked her to read the telegram over the phone:

WHAT HAPPENED WE WAITED AS PLANNED IS EVERY-THING ALLRIGHT WILL MEET YOU AS SCHEDULED NEW YORK CITY CALL CHUCK FIRST LOVE PAT AND MARYANN

Mrs. Bonaviri promised to bring the telegram to the station when she received a copy of it in the mail.

Killen and Flynn were together when Mrs. Bonaviri arrived at the police station on Monday morning. "Now, maybe you'll believe my Tony!" she said. Killen was finding her a high-strung woman, arrogant in her conviction that police were unreasonably harassing her son.

Flynn called Mrs. Wysocki in Providence. She had never heard her daughter speak of anyone by the name of "Chuck."

Mrs. Walsh was not so sure when Flynn called her. "Patricia knows a lot of people," she said suspiciously. Mrs. Walsh questioned Flynn relentlessly about what police were doing to find her daughter, complaining that statements police were issuing to the press speculating about drug use were ruining Patricia's reputation.

Flynn was sure Tony Costa had sent himself the telegram to "prove" to police the girls were still alive. Killen thought the telegram was a "dandy" piece of evidence if it checked out that Costa had anything to do with it. Killen was assigning Dunn to go to New York to verify the sender.

A half hour later, Marshall accepted a collect call from Tony Costa.

Costa was at his brother's apartment in Boston where he expected to be staying for a week. He asked if his mother had brought the telegram to the police station.

"I have it right here," Marshall said. He read the message to Costa.

"I hope you're satisfied now that these girls are all right," Costa said.

"Will you go to New York and meet these girls as arranged?" Marshall said.

Costa said he would.

"When you do," Marshall said, "have Pat and Mary Anne call me here at the station."

Bernie Flynn returned with a new sense of urgency to the clearing in the woods which Marsha Mowery had shown to police. Snow was forecast for the afternoon. Using long metal prods to probe ground slushy with dirty snow and very slippery, Flynn and Gunnery came upon a high mound of sand protected by a grove of dwarf oaks not far from Tony Costa's garden.

Flynn and Gunnery took turns digging a trench to a depth of nearly six feet before giving up.

Flynn had examined an ammunition can found in the woods by a hunter, Alfred Souza, who had turned it over to Chief Berrio. It was a tall, green metal canister, rectangular shaped with a screw-type handle, empty except for the wrappings from several physician-sample drug packets. Flynn threw the canister away as having no evidenciary value. Also found in the woods and discarded was a torn man's shirt, neck size 15½.

Snow began to fall. Flynn was chilled and discouraged. The area of Costa's garden he had thought so promising had yielded nothing after four days' search.

With more snow predicted, it might be days before the search could be resumed.

Chief Cheney Marshall was also glad to be leaving the woods. He had spent the better part of three weeks with George Killen, tramping the wilderness from Wellfleet to Truro and visiting construction sites and new foundations—anyplace where a body could be concealed. Marshall figured he had samples of every category of vegetation to be found on Cape Cod embedded in his clothes.

Marshall was no outdoorsman. He admired Park Ranger Raymond Kimple, a clever naturalist who could identify animal tracks and foliage, and comprehend any unnatural phenomenon not customary to the season. Kimple was able to find his way out of the densest woods, without a trail.

Marshall had been nervous in the Truro woods, afraid of losing his bearings. George Killen had carried a Boy Scout compass, telling Marshall that if he kept the sun over his left shoulder he would never get lost. Marshall accused Killen of pulling his leg; sunshine had been scarce the past several weeks of cloudy gloom, icy rain and snow.

"George, let's go to the liquor store," Marshall said, eager to leave after another day in the cold. He knew he could entice Killen with his favorite, Early Times bourbon, and he promised to take Killen home for some of the good kale soup made by his wife, Kay.

Waiting in Killen's office that evening was a teletype sent from the Rehoboth barracks of the Massachusetts State Police:

TWO MEN ARE TO BE ARRAIGNED IN NEWPORT R.I.
DIST. COURT ON MONDAY AND BOTH ARE CHARGED
WITH CUTTING UP A GIRL IN ROGER WILLIAMS PARK
IN PROVIDENCE R.I. AND PUTTING PARTS OF HER BODY
IN PLASTIC BAGS AND BURYING SAME IN PARK.

Middletown, Rhode Island, police had requested the information be passed along to Killen "as a possibility regarding the case in Truro."

Killen was shaken by the similarity in the condition of the body in the Providence park murder to that of the body found in the Truro woods. According to Mrs. Morton, Pat Walsh and Mary Anne Wysocki had come to Provincetown to meet a person Flynn had identified as Russell Norton. If the girls *had* returned to Providence after leaving the car behind, it would confirm Costa's farfetched story about a drug deal, and explain his lies to the police—particularly if Costa knew the girls had been murdered. Should the identity of the body found in Rhode Island prove to be one of the missing girls, Tony Costa's alibi would verify he was not the killer. . . .

Killen said nothing about the message he'd received to the search party gathered in the Truro woods the next morning.

The woods were covered with several inches of snow. In a spray of bushes beside the parking area, Park Ranger Raymond Kimple found a pint-size plastic jug with bits of soil clinging to its sides.

Kimple showed the jug to Killen. In late winter it was unusual to find soil on the surface of the ground; Kimple suggested the jug had been buried and recently unearthed.

Killen put the jug on the hood of a police cruiser before proceeding to the area of Tony Costa's garden to start the tedious, yard-by-yard search of the clearing.

Joining the search party along with Sergeant Meads was State Trooper William Waterhouse. A large, jovial young man, Waterhouse had brought along his dog, Cookie. Claiming the dog was part-bloodhound, Waterhouse said, "If there's anything around here, this dog'll find it."

Killen was skeptical. The moment Waterhouse unleashed the dog it began lifting its leg to every tree at the edge of the clearing. Flynn was amused by the antics of the "hunting dog." He warned Tom Gunnery, "If you stop moving that stupid mutt will piss on your leg."

Resting from the back-breaking, bent-over posture required for the search of the wet, leaf-strewn ground, Flynn watched the dog gambol, playful as a puppy, tearing up a slope, then dashing full speed across the clearing. Flynn saw the dog trip over something under the snow, sending it flying behind his racing hind legs.

"What the hell was *that*?" Killen called over to where Flynn and Kimple were standing.

Kimple picked up the object, dusted it off and gave it to Flynn.

A pouch of suede, artfully constructed with laced sides and a shoulder strap made from two long strips of twisted leather, the handbag was almost the same color as the russet ground leaves. Before he opened it, Flynn knew it had belonged to one of the missing girls. He found a wallet, decorated with an enamel peace-sign medallion; inside was a quantity of credit cards and other identification in the name of Patricia Walsh.

"Bingo!" Flynn shouted.

He brought the handbag over to Killen.

From the wallet, Killen withdrew a Rhode Island driver's license issued to P.H. Walsh, a Blue Cross group membership card, Social Security card number 036-30-1433, a membership card for local 958 Providence Teachers Union of the American Federation of Teachers, AFL-CIO, a green Dymo label in the name of Pat Walsh and a 1966–67 student identification for Rhode Island College. There was a ticket to a Judy Collins concert at Alumnae Hall, December 2, 1967, an appointment notice from the office of Dr. Michael E. Scala for "March," a business card from "Kent County Motors, Inc.—Helmut K. Krein, Service Manager," and a green ticket stub from the Janus 2 theater for a December 26 performance of *Bonnie and Clyde*.

A small-change purse contained four tightly wrapped one-dollar bills and sixty-five cents in change. The handbag also held an eyebrow tweezer, a blue comb, a tube of Maybelline "Velvet Black" mascara, an eyebrow pencil, a plastic tube of Cover Girl medicated makeup and a compact of pressed powder—brunette. On a metal curtain hanger were two keys; one marked "ILCO" had been stamped "2"; a brass "Yale" key was marked "D."

"What'd I tell you guys?" Waterhouse said, patting the dog panting at his feet.

Raymond Kimple was still looking for a place where the plastic jug could have been buried when the search party returned to the parking area to unload equipment from a pickup truck that had been brought into the woods. Kimple noticed sand and clay on the top of the leaves at the base of a tree some thirty feet from the road.

He uncovered a shallow hole. Just under the surface of earth he found pieces of brown leather embossed in a crocodile pattern, then a shoulder strap of looped leather alternating with brass rings, sliced cleanly by a sharp-edged instrument. Digging further, he came upon two yellow Juicy Fruit gum wrappers, then an empty French purse of tan cowhide marked "Baronet" in gold letters.

Torn in half were two plastic student identification cards from Rhode Island College with photographs of Mary Anne Wysocki, a charge plate for Shepard's, a Providence department store, and Wilbar's "Beautiful Shoes." Torn in four pieces was a state of Rhode Island Division of Vital Statistics certificate of birth with Mary Anne Wysocki's date of birth given as December 3, 1945. There were three pens, two pencils and a pair of silver pendant earrings with a fringe of silver balls, a Dermetics lipstick in "Gold Mocha" and a Cosmetically Yours lipstick tube in "Frosted Look Alive—Slic Pink," and a plastic compact with four panels of eyeshadow, and a bottle of Dream-Glo liquid makeup base. Kimple unearthed a small green plastic pencil sharpener, a rubber eraser and a torn "Rhode Runner" bus schedule, a nickel, a leather hair barrette, and a crinkled snapshot of a handsome little blond boy posed against a fence. An identification card listed Martha Wysocki of 157 Superior Street, Providence, as the person to notify "in case of accident or serious illness."

Kimple also found a Providence Library card and a quantity of papers with Rhode Island College letterheads: a bill from the Office of the Bursar for general fees and student activity charges—including insurance—amounting to $163.75, due January 27, 1969; a semester student schedule for fall '68–'69 for sixteen credit hours, and report card for fall '67 giving a cumulative index of 2.86.

Torn in half was a business card in the name of Gerald Magnan—"Instructor, Mathematics, Division III, Engineering Technologies, Bristol Community College."

Kimple found a receipt for $24.00—Fri. & Sat." signed by Patricia Morton, and a blue business card:

5 STANDISH STREET
Guest House
Charming * Clean * Comfortable
ROOMS
Center of Provincetown, Mass.
MRS. PATRICIA MORTON   Phone 487-1319

112

Flynn could scarcely contain his excitement; he sensed they were close to the place where the bodies of Pat Walsh and Mary Anne Wysocki were buried. But the fading light made further search impossible.

24

Before he left Provincetown police station the next morning, Wednesday, March 5, Chief Marshall said to Meads, "We're going to find those bodies today."

"Did you get a tip?" Meads said.

"No tip," Marshall said. "Every time I go into that valley and look up the hill, I get this feeling *something's* there."

Marshall met George Killen in the woods. Tony Costa had probably killed two girls at one time, Marshall said. "That means one of them had a chance to run. She would have gone up that hill for sure—people always feel safer on heights, for some reason."

Marshall's eyes were drawn to a large tree at the edge of the clearing with a split-off branch dragging to the ground. About six feet up the side of the tree was a knob where a limb had broken off. He saw strands of rope adhering to the bark.

Gunnery also noticed hemp fibers clinging to the tree—a tall pine surrounded by an open space bedded with moss, a place one might spread a picnic.

At the base of the tree, Gunnery found two small pieces of paper; then several bits of darkly stained rope. Probing further, he came upon a piece of cotton material, a glass vial, a gold-foil tablet container and a quantity of screw-type bottle caps. In the leaf mold was a single-edged razor blade with the imprint "Accuracy Blade—Warner" stamped on a stainless steel edge. Gunnery showed the blade to Killen.

"Keep going," Killen said.

Four feet from the base of the tree, Gunnery found some solidified, pinkish matter that crumbled in his fingers; he could not identify it. The light caught something glittering in the dirt; Gunnery fished out a single earring. Made of gold, with a curved prong for pierced ears, it was a dangling square of black onyx in a delicate setting.

The cold air painful in his lungs, Gunnery felt a tightening in his chest; tension pulled at the muscles of his stomach.

He cleared aside leaves and turf. The outline of a recently dug hole began to emerge.

Gunnery asked for a shovel and started digging. The earth began to soften when he reached a depth of three feet. The roots of the tree had not been cut, and they caught the shovel's edge, making the work difficult.

Gunnery put the shovel aside. He started taking earth from the hole with his hands. Kneeling beside him at the edge of the excavation, Bernie Flynn felt the cold of the bare ground penetrate the trouser material at his knees.

Killen came over to the edge of the hole with Marshall. An area so close to a tree was, in Killen's view, the worst place to dig a grave. He was about to call a halt to the digging. Gunnery was still taking earth from the hole with his hands. When his fingers touched something cold and yielding he recoiled, withdrawing his hand as if he'd been stung. "There's something down there," he said.

Marshall peered into the hole; he saw something white, under a layer of earth.

Killen squatted down on his haunches. He reached into the hole and brushed aside the sandy soil.

"Jesus *Christ*," Marshall said.

An arm was projecting from the ground. Exposed was a wrist and a hand. On the little finger was a ring made of alternating turquoise and iridescent-orange beads.

Gunnery stared at the discovery. The woods seemed enclosed in absolute silence. Flynn kept taking handfuls of earth from the grave. He saw a matting of brown hair. He stretched his hand down and grasped the hair and pulled; the hair came away from the scalp.

Flynn dropped into the hole up to his waist. Carefully, he loosened the dirt surrounding the hair. He cupped his hands

114

around the head and lifted up; a severed head came out of the ground.

Flynn cradled the head in his arm. He brushed sand and gravel clinging to the open eyes and took dirt from the gaping mouth. The face was a mask of terror, lips drawn back in a grimace of surprise and pain. The face was bluish, the left cheek discolored and swollen. The nose had been broken by the force of a powerful blow. Flynn thought he recognized Mary Anne Wysocki.

Killen fired off a shot from his police revolver to alert the other members of the search party.

"Goddamn it, George," Marshall said excitedly, "I think I'm entitled to a shot, too!" Marshall unholstered and fired off.

Flynn placed the head on a mound of earth beside the grave to be photographed by Roy Nightingale, alerted by Killen's signal. The search party arriving from other parts of the woods were gathered around the grave Gunnery had found.

Working beside Flynn, Gunnery dug further into the grave. Starting with the exposed arm, he deepened a trench around the outline of the body. Reaching his hands under the armpits, he pulled up the headless torso with arms attached of a female body which had been severed at mid-abdomen. With Flynn's help, he struggled to lift the torso, covered with sand and soil, from its burial place. The chest had been opened, the skin cut down the center and peeled back to the shoulders.

Flynn found a pair of tan suede two-eyelet ankle boots, lined in white pile, a green dress sleeve whose snap closure had been fortified with a small safety pin and the foot and waist portion of torn black panty hose with a label "Tall—100% Nylon." There was a quantity of empty physician-sample drug packages and many screw caps—several maroon-colored ones were marked "Wallace" in silver letters. There was a plastic jug similar in size and shape to the one Kimple had found, a yellow plastic Murine bottle and several rubber stoppers. Slashed into pieces was a pair of dark brown suede Capezio knee boots with pink nylon lining, and shattered bits of brown bottle glass. At the bottom of the grave, Flynn uncovered a coil of three-stranded, coarse oiled rope about twenty feet long, stained with blood.

After weeks of frustration, Flynn was elated at the discovery of the bodies, but he was worried that Tony Costa would run to Canada before he could be picked up, and he told Killen so.

It was 1:30 P.M. Killen and Marshall left Flynn in the woods. At Provincetown's police station, Killen called state police head-quarters at 1010 Commonwealth Avenue in Boston, telling Detective Lieutenant Richard Cass to arrest Antone Costa on a warrant for the felony of larceny of an automobile.

Killen said, "Grab the son of a bitch."

Bernie Flynn pulled on a pair of white canvas work gloves with blue knitted cuffs. Sifting through the dirt at the bottom of the grave he found a green cotton smock with elaborate embroidery ripped up the side labeled "India Imports," the sleeve of a white jersey and more pieces of panty hose and cardboard pill holders—but no further body parts. Flynn realized there must be another grave.

Raymond Kimple was examining a sandy area up a slight rise about two hundred feet away from the first grave. Kimple had been attracted to the place because of the soil sprinkled on the surface of the leaves. He called over to Bernie Flynn.

Digging through two feet of frost crust, Gunnery saw what seemed to be human flesh. Flynn stepped into the hole to uncover a tangle of body parts. There was the lower portion of a white female body severed just above the hips. The legs had been deeply slashed, exposing pink strips of flesh under the skin.

Flynn tried to pull out the body, but it was too heavy. Loosening the earth with a shovel, he raised the lower portion of the body and, with Gunnery's help, placed it at the edge of the grave.

Flynn continued digging. There appeared the upper portion of a body—the abdomen, chest, arms and head of a white female with long brown hair. The skin of the chest had been cut open and pulled back. The face was swollen and badly mauled. Grimly, without pausing for reflection, Flynn saw that it was Pat Walsh.

Beneath the upper body portion was a pelvis severed at both hip joints and two severed legs, deeply slashed down the front and back. Between the layers of body parts Flynn found a white cable-knit sweater, darkly stained with blood. There was a pair of brown plaid slacks with an ILGWU label attached to its black lining, and a new-looking pair of bell-bottom dungarees slashed down the legs, marked "Male Jeans."

Flynn uncovered an army jacket with the name "Turbidy" printed in faded blue ink on an inside label, a Sears bra edged in lace, two torn pair of panty hose and a beige-lined glove. There

116

was another bra—Exquisite Form 36-B; at the bottom of the grave was a length of rope.

Flynn was puzzled. The bodies taken from the grave were in a good state of preservation because of the cold and their recent burial, yet the grave was giving off a terrible odor—one that he knew all too well from the nearby site where the unidentified body had been found nearly a month before.

Taking turns digging with Gunnery, standing side by side in the opened grave, Flynn came upon another body. Blackened by decay and badly deteriorated, the body's parts had been placed in a recumbent position, as if care had been taken to fit the pieces together to effect a natural state of repose.

Flynn finally gagged on the stench. The face of the long-haired corpse was frozen into a ghastly smile, clenched teeth exposed in a grimace.

Gasping, able to breath only through his mouth, Flynn forced himself to empty the grave. The stench of decomposing flesh was unbearable. Despite the cold, Flynn was sweating; his jacket of knitted wool and leather was stained by grave-soil and reeked of putrefaction.

Flynn found a pair of sandals, a bloodstained jersey and a pair of bell-bottom dungarees with a belt laced in the loops.

In one pocket of the dungarees was a neatly-folded ten-dollar bill.

When Killen returned to the woods, he brought two large cartons of sandwiches and some coffee. Flynn was glad for the rest. His arms and shoulders ached from the exertion of lifting and digging.

Gunnery was tired, too, but satisfied. He had done a good day's work, discovering the grave of Mary Anne Wysocki that had led to finding the other grave. He was glad for the hot coffee; he used the plastic container to warm his hands.

During the investigation in Provincetown, Killen had always picked up the tab for lunch. One day, Gunnery had started to buy Killen a cup of coffee; but Killen wouldn't hear of it. "On a trooper's pay," he had said, "you got no business treating anybody."

The extra hours Gunnery worked on the case had put a strain on his homelife; Gunnery's wife had teasingly threatened divorce on grounds of desertion, naming Bernie Flynn as co-respondent. One rare night off, Gunnery had taken her to the movies to get his mind off the Costa case. The film was *Three in an Attic* and showed scenes of Provincetown. Gunnery groaned when he saw the familiar landscape passing before his eyes.

Killen returned to Provincetown police station to call District Attorney Edmund Dinis in New Bedford.

"Does anyone else have this information?" Dinis asked him.

"No, Eddie," Killen said, knowing that Dinis would be giving the press the story as soon as he hung up. "It's all in your little hands."

Killen then called Providence police, instructing Sergeant Perry to notify the families of Pat Walsh and Mary Anne Wysocki. Killen made arrangements with the Nickerson Funeral Home in Provincetown to have their hearse take the bodies from the woods. Only then was Dr. Hiebert told a police cruiser was on its way to his office to pick him up. Killen wanted no repetition of the fiasco that had occurred at Carlson's Funeral Home.

It was getting dark when Hiebert was brought to the grave sites. He was astonished at the savagery that had been inflicted upon the bodies he examined. The legs of the third, badly decomposed body had been severed at the hip. Rather, one leg had been found in the grave—the left was missing.

25

Following Killen's telephone call to state police headquarters in Boston, Lieutenant Broderick went to 415 Beacon Street, accompanied by detective lieutenants William White and James DeFuria. They were told Vincent Bonaviri had moved.

Broderick then went to Macey's liquor store on Canal Street where Vinnie was working. Vinnie told him he was now living at 364 Marlborough Street; he hadn't seen his brother for ten days.

Broderick called him a fucking liar.

"Tony's in Provincetown!" Vinnie insisted. "I'll call my mother and he'll come up."

Broderick had a hunch. Taking White and DeFuria to a four-story red brick building on Marlborough Street, he punched the buzzer for apartment 3. A young man with a mustache, sideburns and gold-rimmed spectacles came down the stairs to answer the door. He was neatly dressed in a blue turtleneck shirt and white denim pants.

Broderick's hand moved under his raincoat to touch his gun. He said, "Say, aren't you—"

"Vincent Bonaviri," the young man said.

"You're *kidding* me," Broderick said. "We just talked to Vinnie at the liquor store."

"All right, I'm Tony Costa."

Broderick placed him under arrest for the felony theft of an automobile and read from a Miranda card.

Costa offered no struggle; this time he listened to his rights in silence.

Lieutenant White thought Tony Costa was the cleanest hippie he'd ever seen.

Tony Costa had spent one night in Montreal, renting a five-dollar room across from the bus station. Then he had taken a bus to Toronto, staying overnight in a large downtown hotel. The next day he had taken a bus to Buffalo, crossing the border at Niagara Falls. Costa got a room, a block from the bus station, at a derelict place called the Hotel Villanova, registering as "Jonathan Cabot." He visited several downtown Buffalo discotheques and bought a poster for Vinnie and Cathy at a head shop. The poster showed a field of marijuana under the banner: "This Is Marijuana Country."

Then he ran out of money.

On Sunday morning, March 2, he had called Vinnie to wire him seventy-five dollars. Around noon he walked into a telephone booth on Franklin Street with a pocketful of change. The phone booth's number was 852-9859. Costa hung around the LaFayette Square office of Western Union until the money order arrived. That night he took a bus to Boston, arriving at eleven o'clock on Monday morning, after having spent eleven hours on the bus.

When Cathy Roche got home from work at five-thirty, Costa

told her, "Gee, I had some nice news. I called my mother; she got a telegram from the missing girls. They're in New York City."

Costa slept on the hi-riser in the living room. On Wednesday morning, he told his brother, "Vin, I'm going to go out and get a job."

He had breakfast at the Newbury Delicatessen on Massachusetts Avenue and bought a Boston *Globe* to read the want ads. He got a haircut, then applied for a food preparation position at Massachusetts General Hospital.

On his application, Costa listed his employment from 1965 to 1969 as "self-employed builder," his special skills as typing and fluency in Spanish, his hobbies photography, swimming and "outdoor recreation." Under comments, he wrote, "I would like to pursue a medical career. It has always been of major importance and interest to me."

The interviewer scribbled on the application: "Very fishy. Lousy job record."

Costa found an ad for a liquor store clerk, called the number, and was told to report for work the next morning.

Elated, he bought an ounce of marijuana on Charles Street. After a walk in the Public Gardens, he returned to his brother's apartment. He was reading when the buzzer sounded. He went downstairs to open the front door. Through the glass he saw three men wearing raincoats standing on the stoop.

At 4 P.M., Lieutenant Cass called George Killen at Provincetown police station to say that Antone Costa was in custody. Killen told him Costa was now a suspect in the killing of two young Providence women and to book him for murder.

Broderick was furious. On a major pinch, Boston police were customarily alerted to come in and share the glory. Broderick was disgusted with George Killen. "That egotistical bastard," he told Cass, "he wants all the credit for himself."

Costa was printed and photographed by Sergeant James Sharkey. Costa impressed him as "a big, strapping kid, with a pair of shoulders on him he could pick you up and throw you across the room."

Costa was docile, assisting Sharkey in the ritual of fingerprinting like an obedient child. While an arrest form was typed up, he was given a mimeographed Massachusetts State Police interrogation form containing a breakdown of Miranda rights.

Costa wrote an emphatic "Yes!" to those paragraphs which questioned his understanding. In the space reserved for comments, he wrote, "I do not wish to answer any questions at this time."

Broderick asked him, "Tony, did you kill those girls?"

"No, I didn't," Costa said. He didn't want to say any more.

Costa was brought to a third-floor office by two plainclothes detectives. No further attempt was made to interrogate him. He was allowed to call a lawyer. He called Hector Cicchetti, the lawyer he had retained for his divorce. Cicchetti declined to represent him; he did not take criminal cases. Costa tried to reach Maurice Goldman on Cape Cod; Goldman was not available. Costa called Vinnie at the liquor store. He told him to try to get hold of Goldman.

Costa overheard Broderick on a telephone tell somebody to have reporters present when Cape Cod police picked him up around six-thirty that evening.

The quiet room was invaded by the sounds of traffic from busy Commonwealth Avenue. Costa sat with his hands folded in his lap and realized what special significance the day had: it was his son Michael's fourth birthday.

Assigned by Killen to pick up Tony Costa in Boston and return him to Cape Cod, Flynn and Gunnery stopped at the Yarmouth barracks. Flynn was hungry after a day spent in the out-of-doors. The barrack's kitchen was open; a resident cook had prepared roast beef, rare and bloody. Flynn and Gunnery took one look and couldn't eat.

Sergeant Bolduc drove the cruiser to Boston. The Commonwealth Avenue station was swarming with reporters, photographers and parked television mobile units.

Flynn advised Tony Costa of his rights. Then he said, "Tony, why don't you tell us about those girls?"

Costa was silent.

Flynn said if Costa told him how he had gotten the car, he would do all he could to have the charges reduced. "Tony, you've got four murder charges against you."

Costa said, "Well, that's where it's at, then."

Flynn searched Costa's wallet. He found the address and telephone number for Hector Cicchetti; a classified ad for a liquor clerk's job, "$100—No Experience"; and a receipt for a personal

121

money order for thirty-two dollars from the Burlington Savings Bank, payable to the Vermont Department of Motor Vehicles.

Folded in quarters was a clipping from the New York *Daily News* of November 26, 1968, nearly four months earlier. The headline read:

CHRISTINE'S TRIP TO THE MORGUE:
WHAT A WASTE AT 19

The story was an account of the death of Christine Gallant, whose nude body had been found by her roommate in a partly-filled bathtub. There were three burn marks on her chest. Christine had spent the previous weekend in Provincetown tripping on LSD. An autopsy revealed a quantity of barbiturates in her brain and stomach. The medical examiner had called the death "a possible suicide."

On a piece of magenta paper, Flynn found the telephone numbers for Christine Gallant, "Vinnie," and Georgia Panesis. The last number listed was, "Primo, 417 East 9th Street—982-5763."

Flynn put the paper in his pocket.

Among the police gathered at state police headquarters in Boston was Lieutenant John Dunn. Dunn had come back from New York to find Jimmy Lino, of the Falmouth police, at the door of his house on Clinton Street with a message from George Killen: Killen wanted Dunn to assist in the arrest of Antone Costa.

As Dunn drove to Boston in his own Volkswagen, he reviewed the previous day spent in New York, checking on the telegram and interviewing Donald Obers at Columbia University.

122

Obers confirmed he had driven Tony Costa and two of his friends to Hatch Road in Truro on February 2. Tony told him his car was located about a mile away in the woods and was out of gas. Obers had dropped his passengers off near a rotary—a traffic circle—and they had gone into the woods. At no time had he seen the car.

Dunn had also talked with Assistant Superintendent Jules Mattaschian at the Western Union Building on Hudson Street. A photostat of the original telephone message sheet identified the receiving operator of a telegram sent at noon on Sunday, March 2, collect to Tony Costa, as Margaret Procino.

"I asked for the name and address and a male voice gave me, 'Pat Walsh, 9 Conant Street, Provincetown,' " Miss Procino told Dunn. "It's routine to ask for a name and address when anyone calls collect from a coin box in case the person to receive the message refuses to pay."

Miss Procino could not accept an out-of-state address. "I needed something in New York, so he gave me a telephone number where he could be reached," she said. The number was written in the lower left-hand corner of the original message sheet—212-982-5763.

A second telephone number was written in the upper right-hand corner. The number 852-9859 was from a telephone booth and had been given to her either by the caller or an assisting long distance operator. The number's accuracy could not be verified by either Western Union or the telephone company. New York Telephone Company security agents told Dunn it was not possible to check on the time or frequency of the use of a public telephone.

Dunn traced the first telephone number, 982-5763, to portrait artist Primitivo Africa, residing at 417 East Ninth Street. A very tall black man with a towering Afro, Africa told Dunn he knew Tony Costa slightly, having been introduced to him in November by a friend, Christine Gallant—two weeks before she was found dead in her bathtub.

Dominating the wall of Africa's studio-living room, Dunn observed, was a painting of enormous female genitalia gaping like an arch of triumph, under which columns of uniformed servicemen marched.

Dunn arrived at state police headquarters in Boston in time to watch Bernie Flynn take Antone Costa into custody. Wearily, Dunn wondered why Killen should want him present since it was clear Flynn was in charge of the case and had been given the better part of the credit for solving the murders, although many other police officers had worked on the case. Relegated to the background, Dunn stifled his resentment at Killen's favoritism as he watched Flynn lead Costa out of the building into an explosion of flashbulbs from a waiting crowd of reporters.

Flynn announced, "Antone Costa is a suspect in a double murder involving two girls missing from Providence, Rhode Island, since January twenty-fifth." He gave no further comment. Posing for photographers with Flynn, Costa peered quizzically into the cameras, his manacled hands attached to a restraining belt at his waist. Costa made no attempt to cover his face.

Costa was silent during the trip from Boston to the Yarmouth barracks on Cape Cod. In the warmth of the heated car, Flynn became aware of the sickening odor emanating from his own jacket.

Brought into the barracks around nine o'clock, Costa posed almost nonchalantly for photographers, at one point folding his arms and yawning.

Flynn was met by District Attorney Edmund Dinis. Dinis had called a press conference the next morning. Dinis said to Costa, "We've got the evidence you killed those girls, Tony. We *know* you did it. You might as well tell us now."

"I didn't do anything," Costa said. He asked for an attorney. He had not been able to contact a criminal lawyer, explaining, "I haven't had the chance to do anything because my lawyer doesn't take capital cases."

Dinis said his office would take care of it.

Costa was led to a cell by Bernie Flynn, who asked him again if he had killed the girls.

Costa said, "No, I didn't. I *liked* those girls. I had nothing to do with killing them."

"Where did you get the car?" Flynn said.

"I don't want to talk about it anymore," Costa said. "I'm innocent, and that's where I'll stand."

Dunn came by the cell. "Well, Tony," he said. "What do you think of all this?"

"I think," Costa said, "that there's a maniac loose somewhere out there."

124

* * *

Flynn examined the contents of the square-shaped, blue Pan Am flight bag Broderick had confiscated when he arrested Tony Costa in Boston.

There was a paperback copy of *The Science of Being and Art of Living,* by His Holiness Maharishi Mahesh Yogi, setting forth the techniques of transcendental meditation, a hard-leather case containing prescription granny-type sunglasses, eighteen pictures of a tall, slender girl with long brown hair, an application for permanent residency in Canada, a spiral ring notebook with drawings and diagrams of electrical work, and a yellow binder of scuba instruction with a certificate from Divemaster Skin and Lung Diving School of Chicago, Illinois, certifying that Anthony C. Costa had satisfactorily completed the prescribed course of instruction dated August 28, 1964. There was a Hohner "Blues Harp" harmonica, a diploma from the Greer Technical Institute—heavy equipment operators division—of Braidwood, Illinois, a package of white envelopes, a leather wrist bracelet, two lock sets, a green candle and six handwritten pages of vocabulary drills and five pages torn from a paperback dictionary listing "The most common synonyms and antonyms."

At the bottom of the flight bag Flynn found an order blank and envelope from the Northwestern School of Taxidermy & J.W. Elwood Supply Company of Omaha, Nebraska.

Flynn and Gunnery stopped off at Mildred's Chowder House, a popular restaurant and bar on Iyanough Road in Hyannis, and each ordered a bourbon old-fashioned. They were on their first drink when the eleven o'clock news came on Boston's channel 5.

The bar's patrons were silently attentive to the evening's lead story: the arrest of Antone Costa of Provincetown, a suspect in a series of grisly murders on Cape Cod.

Flynn winced when the cameras flashed to him leading Costa out of 1010 Commonwealth Avenue: hair tousled, his face sagging with exhaustion, his jacket smeared with grime from unearthing three bodies that morning. Flynn murmured to Gunnery, "Jesus, I look like hell." Tony Costa, in contrast, looked like he just stepped out of the shower, and Flynn overheard one of the patrons at the bar explain to his drinking companion that "the guy on the right, the dirty-looking one," was the killer. Flynn was too

125

tired to argue. He finished his drink, said good-night to Gunnery and drove to Scranton Avenue in Falmouth.

Flynn was met at the door by his fiancée Jacqueline Buzzee. A tall, stately looking girl with lustrous dark hair, she had watched the news of the arrest on television. She was so proud, she wanted to give Flynn a big hug.

Flynn backed away, "Don't touch me!" he said. "I smell of death."

Bob Turbidy was baby-sitting for John and Linda McNally when the telephone rang.

It was his brother, Dave, asking him, "Is your radio on?"

"No," Turbidy said. He clenched his fingers tightly around the telephone receiver.

"I'm sorry to be the one to tell you," Dave said. "They found their bodies; it just came on the news."

"OK," Turbidy said.

He was not shocked; he had been expecting word. The newspapers and what little information he had gotten from Bernie Flynn had all tended to confirm the girls were dead. After the agony of waiting weeks with the last edge of hope growing dull, it was almost a relief.

Turbidy called the McNallys and asked them to return home. He went to the apartment on Prospect Street and called Bernie Flynn at the Yarmouth barracks. Turbidy had talked to him several days earlier, but Flynn then hadn't been able to tell him anything.

Flynn said he was very sorry about Pat Walsh, but would give no details of the murders except to say, "It was pretty bad." Flynn thought the girls had been killed around one o'clock in the afternoon on Saturday, January 25.

Turbidy called Gerry Magnan.

Air Force Sergeant Magnan was at a desk at the Warwick airport. He had signed up for six years with the reserves to discharge his military obligation and had been scheduled for duty in Arizona. Not wanting to leave Providence as long as Mary Anne Wysocki was missing, he had persuaded officials to let him serve his time at the Warwick airport doing clerical work. Turbidy's call came too late; Magnan had been typing a report when a voice down the hall had called out, "Hey, Gerry, turn your radio on."

Magnan joined Turbidy at his apartment. Together they went

to the Wysocki house on Superior Street. The block was crowded with press cars, photographers and the curious from the neighborhood.

Martha Wysocki had learned of her daughter's death when a neighbor called to express sympathy, having just heard the news on the radio. She embraced Magnan when he entered the house, entrusting to him the task of giving a statement for the family to the press waiting outside.

Turbidy envied Magnan his closeness to the Wysockis, who had always seemed aware of Magnan's feelings and had never interfered with his relationship with Mary Anne.

Turbidy found a different atmosphere at the Walsh house. The living room was tense with anger. Providence police had come to the house to tell the family of Pat Walsh's death.

Turbidy was surprised to see Pat's oldest brother, Joe, and his Protestant wife, along with Maureen and Ken Meyers and Pat's younger brother, Dennis—the whole Walsh family united. He found it ironic that Pat's death had made possible the reconciliation she was unable to accomplish during her lifetime.

Turbidy felt like an outsider. Mrs. Walsh had found out that he and Pat had been living together.

"She wouldn't talk to me," Turbidy told Magnan outside. "She just gave me cold stares."

Turbidy spoke briefly with Maureen and Ken Meyers. Maureen told him she was coming to the apartment the next morning to pack up Pat's belongings.

Disconsolate, Turbidy went home alone.

Undressing for bed, he noticed the tattoo on his upper right arm, all but forgotten in the weeks of anxiety over Pat's disappearance.

He stared at Pat's name written in blue ink on his skin, remembering the inexplicable rush of elation in San Diego, the puzzling high he had experienced when his "nice present" had been finished.

Only then did it occur to Turbidy that, according to Bernie Flynn's calculations, he was being tattooed at the same hour that Pat Walsh was being murdered.

PART TWO

Susan and Sydney

———

1

Bernie Flynn awoke on Thursday morning with a numb ache in his shoulders. He had not slept well. Nightmares of partially buried, dismembered bodies, their hands reaching from the grave demanding recognition, plagued his dreams. Twice he had awakened to find himself standing beside his bed, shivering.

Flynn jettisoned the stained jacket he had worn the previous day, certain that no dry cleaner could remove the smell of putrefaction from it. Then he drove to the South Yarmouth state police barracks for the press conference District Attorney Edmund Dinis had scheduled for eight o'clock.

Flynn recognized Evelyn Lawson among a gathering of reporters awaiting Dinis's arrival. A vivacious blonde in her midsixties, she had heard the early morning radio reports of Tony Costa's arrest and hastened to the barracks to cover the story for the weekly Dennis-Yarmouth *Register* which published her column of chat, "Dateline: Cape Cod."

An eruption of flashbulbs greeted Edmund Dinis's appearance at the doorway of the barracks' conference room. Impeccably dressed in a blue suit and a regimental striped tie, Dinis accommodated photographers by pausing to speak with George Killen. At forty-four, Dinis was a tall, theatrically handsome man, his black wavy hair streaked with gray. Mercurial and unpredictable, he was considered "good copy" by the press. Dinis had attacked the probate courts as "the most corrupt" because judges served for life and exercised personal prejudice daily. Dinis had labeled the jury selection system in Massachusetts in general and Cape Cod in particular as "absolutely discriminatory" and "a systematic denial of justice." Dinis had caused a furor in 1967 by his successful prosecution of a Christian Scientist for involuntary manslaughter in the death by pneumonia of her six-year-old daughter.

Flynn had known Edmund Dinis for years. As a young patrolman directing traffic in downtown New Bedford, Flynn had received a complaint that a blaring sound truck parked in front of a clothing store was making the orderly conduct of business impossible. Flynn had approached the vehicle, whose loudspeakers were exhorting the reelection of Jacinto Dinis, Edmund's father. The elder Dinis, a fiery politician, had once shown up at the statehouse in Boston wrapped in the Portuguese flag. The son, a law student and his father's campaign manager at the time, had balked when Flynn ordered the sound truck moved, citing a city ordinance. Flynn had arrested both the candidate and his son on charges of disorderly conduct, taking them and the sound truck to the police station, where Flynn was advised by the chief of police to "reconsider" his complaint. Police were seeking a pay raise in a few months; the elder Dinis wielded considerable political influence in New Bedford.

Something of a political *wunderkind*, Dinis had taken over his father's seat in the legislature at twenty-four and developed a flourishing insurance and real estate business. A maverick Democrat, he had failed in three campaigns for mayor of New Bedford, and unsuccessfully sought a seat in the U.S. Congress. Elected district attorney in 1958, he had twice been returned to office. . . .

Flynn watched Dinis stride confidently to the microphone behind a makeshift lectern. Dubious about the press conference and mistrustful of Dinis's penchant for publicity, Flynn had a sinking feeling of impending disaster.

In a mellifluous baritone, Dinis formally announced the discovery of the dismembered, nude bodies of Patricia Walsh, Mary Anne Wysocki of Providence and an unidentified teenager in an area of woods a mile and a half from Old Truro Cemetery where, on February 8, another mutilated corpse had been recovered.

"The hearts of each girl had been removed from the bodies and were not in the graves, nor were they found," Dinis said. "A razorlike device was found near the graves. Each body was cut into as many parts as there are joints. There was some instances in which it appeared that an ax or cleaver was used, a definite pattern repeated in all four cases of dismemberment. Whatever method was used, the evidence points to an extreme degree of abnormality. It was purely maniacal, insane." Parts of the bodies bore teeth marks and other evidence of having been chewed, Dinis added in describing "the most bizarre murders in the history of Cape Cod."

"A Cape Cod vampire?" a reporter interrupted.

Dinis nodded assent. Police had been attracted to the grave sites by pieces of rope found at the base of a tree. "The rope might indicate the girls had been tied up before they were butchered, since one of them had a rope around her face." Asked if the victims could have been drugged before being murdered, Dinis said, "The autopsy should determine that, but preliminary examination does not indicate that drugs were used."

Stunned by the inaccuracy of Dinis's remarks, Flynn muttered to Tom Gunnery who was standing beside him, "There goes the case." He shot a look across the room to George Killen, standing impassively behind Dinis. Since the Escobedo-Miranda Supreme Court rulings, Killen had maintained tight security on the release to the press of anything but minimal details of crimes.

Charged with the murders, Dinis announced, was Antone Charles Costa, twenty-four, "a handyman-carpenter and taxidermist." Costa had made no statements at the time of his arrest and had refused to take a lie detector test. Police were checking to ascertain whether a quantity of photographs of young women found in Costa's possession at the time of his arrest were of any missing young girls. Discovery of the graves had prompted "hundreds" of calls to his office from parents of missing children, Dinis said, estimating there were from two thousand to three thousand young women missing in the United States, several from Cape Cod. Police searches of the woods were to continue indefinitely, Dinis announced. "In view of what has already happened, we are apprehensive about finding other bodies. There may be more, we don't know."

Dinis ruled out robbery as a motive for the murders. The bodies had been discovered shortly after 5 P.M. on Tuesday, March 4; handbags containing money and other valuables were found with them near the graves.

"The evidence indicates that the Walsh girl was attacked first. Her companion ran for her life, only to be caught, dragged back and killed."

Dinis praised the work of police search teams which had

combed the woods for twenty-five straight days, despite bad weather. He singled out George Killen, Bernie Flynn, Tom Gunnery and the assistance provided the investigation by police chiefs Francis Marshall and Harold Berrio.

Leaving the conference for the convoy of police cruisers to escort Antone Costa to Provincetown for arraignment, Detective Lieutenant John Dunn was first out the front entrance of the barracks, blundering into a blaze of flashbulbs that greeted the first public appearance of Antone Costa since his arrest. Dunn had forgotten the protocol which required Killen, by order of rank, to lead the escort, with Flynn, Dunn and Gunnery following.

Amused by Dunn's gaffe, Flynn told him, "Boy, is Killen pissed off at you!"

Dunn had already ruffled Killen's feathers. Before leaving his office that morning, Killen had questioned Dunn about his trip to New York to investigate the telegram allegedly sent to Tony Costa by Pat Walsh and Mary Anne Wysocki.

The telephone number given to the Western Union operator belonged to black portrait artist Primitivo Africa, Dunn reported. Africa had met Tony Costa through a mutual friend, Christine Gallant.

"How did Costa get Africa's telephone number?" Killen said.

"In the usual way," Dunn said.

"And what way is that?"

"In general conversation."

Killen was exasperated. This was the elementary stuff of investigation. "Did Africa *give* Costa his telephone number or did Costa *ask* him for it?"

Dunn assumed Costa had received the number from Christine Gallant, but he wasn't sure.

Killen wasn't satisfied. Dunn was going to have to go back to New York City to question Africa again. Killen also wanted Dunn to check out the telephone booth from which he suspected Costa had called Western Union himself, and question any witnesses who might have seen Costa in the area. Furious at his dressing-down, Dunn kept his irritation about Killen's obvious favoritism toward Bernie Flynn to himself.

Killen spoke briefly with Flynn in the barracks parking lot. He had no idea where Dinis had received the information given

134

reporters at his press conference. Killen called it "the goddamnest stuff I ever heard!"

Killen was disturbed about the effect such highly inflammatory and prejudicial statements might have on the prosecution of the case, particularly when it was rumored that Tony Costa had retained Maurice Goldman as his lawyer.

"If that's true," Killen said, "we could be in a lot of trouble."

2

Antone Costa was not represented by Maurice Goldman nor anyone else insofar as he knew upon waking in one of three barracks cells. A trooper, posted all night to guard against a possible suicide attempt, reported that Costa had slept peacefully through the night.

Costa was given a glass of water and two slices of cold toast for breakfast. He was allowed to shave. A trooper stood at his elbow while Costa scraped at his heavy beard and carefully combed his hair.

Costa was not interrogated. Silent in the cruiser taking him to Provincetown, he was placed in a cell at Provincetown police station to await his arraignment in the Second District Court upstairs in the town hall.

Costa ignored the crowd milling about the corridor outside his cell and peering with curiosity at the prisoner. Finally the area was cleared by Patrolman Jimmy Cook, who called out jauntily, "Hey, Tony! How're you doing?"

Costa did not reply. Nor did he respond when Chief Marshall told him public defender Frederick Long was available if he wanted to speak to him.

Costa was not even aware of the arrival of attorney Justin Cavanaugh until the tall, hearty man with a mane of wavy gray

135

hair and a rosy complexion appeared at his cell. Cavanaugh observed a broad-shouldered young man with a bush of lustrous dark hair seated at the edge of the cell's cot, hands folded in his lap, staring at his shoes. A light bulb cast his figure in a halo of shadows, providing a perceptible ring of isolation.

Cavanaugh introduced himself. "Maurice Goldman sent me to represent you at the arraignment." Costa stared back in suspicious silence.

Cavanaugh found it difficult to talk privately with his client with police close by. He learned, however, that Costa had made no admissions during his interrogation and told him to keep his mouth shut. "I'll instruct you what to say in the courtroom," he said.

Costa was taken from the station up the front steps of town hall. Built in 1886, the large wooden structure of white clapboard and corner columns with an incongruous brown-painted clock tower loomed over the adjacent Provincetown Cinema, a former Congregational church.

A police escort cleared a passage in the overheated antechamber of darkly varnished wood thronged with silent, watchful spectators. Costa's eyes looked unfocused behind wire-rimmed glasses, failing to connect with the intense stares of those observing his progress toward a wide corridor. Costa looked up at the large canvas done in vivid oils hanging on a wall beside the courtroom's doorway. "Provincetown Fisherman" portrayed a group of yellow-slickered fisherman carrying baskets of mackerel. The gift of the artist, Charles W. Hawthorne in 1899, it was a painting Costa had long admired.

Peering over the heads of the curious milling about the corridor who were unable to find accommodation in the courtroom, Costa caught sight of the stricken face of his uncle, Frank Bent, who stood outside the town treasurer's office. Costa ducked his head and entered the shabby courtroom partially paneled with varnished laths, its plastered walls painted a dingy beige.

A limp flag stood beside a raised dais. Seated on the bench was special part-time judge, Gershom D. Hall, also known as "G.D." or "God Damn Hall" by lawyers and prosecutors who had struggled to penetrate what often seemed a willful obtuseness. A bulky man in his mid-seventies, Hall stubbornly guarded his judicial discretion, tolerating no interference in the frequently capricious conduct of business in his court.

136

Hall ignored Antone Costa's entrance and the expectant stirring of more than one hundred of Provincetown's year-round population of thirty-five hundred who were seated on the courtroom's creaky folding chairs. Probation officer James Cordeiro warned that no photographs would be allowed taken in the courtroom per Judge Hall's order. The routine schedule of a civil list of cases resumed—the arguments involving an unpaid laundry bill.

Observing the proceedings from the rear of the packed courtroom, Bernie Flynn was incensed. Judge Hall was going to let everybody wait to arraign Antone Costa.

No delay occurred in the basement embalming room at the Nickerson Funeral Home, several blocks from Provincetown's town hall. Promptly at 9:30 A.M., Dr. George Katsas, state pathologist from the department of legal medicine at Harvard, assisted by Dr. Daniel Hiebert, began the pathological examination of the mutilated body of a nineteen-year-old, brown-haired white female, whose living stature Katsas estimated to have been fifty-nine inches.

Separated into four portions, the body had suffered postmortem degeneration more advanced than the two bodies found with it and now contained in black, zippered plastic bags on the cement floor awaiting examination.

The face of the corpse was badly lacerated. The tip of the nose was missing, exposing the sinuses. The skin of the chest had been cut, opened and peeled back in the manner Katsas had observed on the body exhumed on February 8. The breasts were present on the skin flaps and were free of injury. The heart was of normal size; the kidneys were not found. The skin of the separated pelvis was essentially missing, stripped off. Internal genitalia had been eviscerated. The left hip bone was almost detached, the stump of the upper thigh bone irregularly chopped where the left leg had been amputated. The leg, in advanced decomposition, had lost flesh in the toes and about the knee which was disjointed. The right leg was not found in the grave.

Katsas worked swiftly against the stench of rotting flesh. Death had occurred as the result of "traumatic injuries"—the exact nature and extent of which could not be determined because of mutilation and decomposition.

The left hand had completely deteriorated, the bones held together by remnant tendons. Katsas removed the right hand at

137

the wrist. The hand was intact but dessicated. There was a rusted ring on the middle finger. The hand would be taken to Sergeant Sharkey at state police headquarters in Boston for possible identification. Katsas did not think there was much chance any fingerprints could be lifted from it.

3

Antone Costa stood at his place in the courtroom following an hour of routine court business. He listened attentively but without expression to the charges of murder read out by the clerk of the court John Agna in an aggrieved and strident voice. Truro Chief Harold Berrio had signed the complaint alleging that Antone Costa "did assault and beat" Patricia H. Walsh with intent to murder her by stabbing her several times with a knife, "and by such assault and beating did kill and murder Patricia H. Walsh." Killen had signed an identical complaint on behalf of Mary Anne Wysocki.

Costa stood mute. Cavanaugh asked that a plea of not guilty be entered on his behalf.

Peering over the rims of his glasses, Judge Hall studied the defendant briefly before ordering him taken to Bridgewater State Hospital for thirty-five days of psychiatric observation. Many of the spectators packed into the small courtroom had waited upward of two hours for a procedure that took no more than five minutes.

An escort of state troopers, closely followed by Flynn and Gunnery, led Costa from the courtroom. Flynn was startled to hear cheers and applause when Costa appeared at the top of the town hall steps. Voices called out, "We're with you, Tony!"

A relay race of photographers followed Costa's progress to a police cruiser parked at the curb. Ensconced in the backseat,

Costa permitted himself a faint smile. As the cruiser pulled away, he raised his right hand in a peace sign.

"It makes me so mad," a long-haired youth muttered. "Look at all those guys; they're making a circus out of this."

A young man with a curly beard leaning over the handlebars of his bicycle told reporters, circulating among spectators, "Tony was a friendly person, very soft-spoken. He seemed very mild. As far as I'm concerned, it isn't so much of a big deal. I don't know about the rest of the people."

"It's a sad commentary on the times that a person charged with such crimes could receive so much cheering," said Joseph Macara, a local merchant. "It's the worst kind of publicity for Provincetown. I'm sorry they used the name so prominently in the newspapers. Actually, the bodies were found in Truro."

"I imagine we'll be in the news for a while," retired fish dealer Alfred Cabral said. "I don't think it's good; it won't help."

Appearances did not appear to concern one elderly man who observed the occasion wearing a sardonic smile, a cigarette dangling from his mouth. "It could happen to anyone, anytime, anywhere," he told an inquiring reporter. "Insanity, that's all it is. Nothing anyone can do about it."

Seated on the town hall steps surrounded by friends and well-wishers was Avis Costa, a waiflike, gaunt young woman wearing corduroy slacks and white canvas boating shoes. Her pale eyes obscured by hair that fell to the shoulders of a navy pea jacket, she told reporters, "Tony was much too passive a person to have committed any murder. I can think of nothing he has done in the past that would lead me to think he was a killer."

Bernie Flynn accompanied Edmund Dinis to the Truro woods to show Justin Cavanaugh the site of the graves, and the location of Antone Costa's former marijuana garden.

Police were "very cooperative" in giving details of the crimes, Cavanaugh acknowledged in a memo he left on Maurice Goldman's desk. A Volkswagen belonging to one of the Providence girls had been seen in the area with an "Engine Trouble" sign on the windshield. As a result of an investigation, four bodies were found. Antone Costa had produced a bill of sale containing his signature and that of Pat Walsh for the purchase of the car police had located in Burlington, Vermont.

"Costa is known in Provincetown as a drug pusher," Cavanaugh concluded. "Many people indicated they knew he would be picked up for these slayings. This is something we should investigate further."

4

Bernie Flynn entered the Nickerson Funeral Home while the autopsy of Patricia Walsh was in progress. Washed clean of sand and gravel from the grave, her body, separated at mid-abdomen, gleamed whitely under the harsh fluorescence above the examination table. Identification had been made through dental charts Flynn had procured from her parents.

A bruiselike discoloration marked the skin of her forehead; there was a large swelling on the left cheek. Small bruises were scattered about the larynx. An inconspicuous halo of blue discoloration surrounded a small hole at the back of the neck with the appearance of an entrance gunshot wound—something Flynn had seen before. When Katsas cut through the skin, he found profuse hemorrhaging; the track of a bullet led to the inside of the left cheek. Another incision revealed hemorrhaging on the floor of the mouth and the root of the tongue. The left carotid artery had been perforated—the cause of death.

"This girl's been shot!" Katsas told Killen. "You've got a gun here!"

Katsas could not locate the bullet. Killen approached the table. Peering into the mouth, he discovered, lodged at the gum line behind an upper front tooth, a metal pellet the size of a beach pebble.

Katsas found an identical cutting-open of the chest as in the first corpse he had examined: a large T-shaped incision extending from the breast-bone to the edge of the body's separation had split the skin of the abdominal wall. The skin of the chest, including the breasts, had been pulled back on both sides of the incision and

140

was attached at the shoulders. Three deep stab wounds had penetrated the entire thickness of the chest; the eighth right rib had been fractured. A wound on the left side of the spine had severed an artery close to the heart, which was of normal size and showed no evidence of disease.

The liver had been stabbed twice; but Katsas could not determine whether the wounds had been inflicted through the skin or after dismemberment, when the liver was exposed.

Scattered across the buttocks and the front and back of both thighs and legs were multiple, deep slash wounds measuring up to eight inches. The wounds bore no surrounding hemorrhage, suggesting they had been inflicted after death.

Genitalia were present with no evidence of injury. The vagina was intact and contained a small amount of viscous fluid.

Katsas followed the same procedure after the five separate portions of Mary Anne Wysocki's body were placed together on the examination table.

A slight deformity at the junction of bone and cartilage had resulted from the nose being broken. There was no other injury to the face.

Bullet fragments were lodged just under the skin against the occipital bone at the back of the head. A second gunshot wound, above and slightly behind the left ear, showed a hole approximately one centimeter in diameter. Removing the top of the crown, Katsas tracked the downward path the bullet had taken from the entrance wound through the skull, traversing the brain from left to right. Katsas found a bullet lodged at the base of the skull on the right side of the head.

Presenting the bullet and two fragments to George Killen, Katsas speculated that the first bullet had only wounded the victim, flattening against bone, and penetrating the skin. He suggested that Mary Anne Wysocki may have been running from her killer when she was shot. She had been in a sitting or kneeling position when the second bullet was discharged, the bullet's path indicating that the killer had stood over her before firing into her head.

The skinning operation of the chest had been performed on the headless torso, just as with the two other bodies Katsas had examined. The upper end of a long incision, three inches below the line of amputation of the neck, was irregular and ragged. The skin that had been pulled away from the underlying chest wall was attached about the shoulders and lower neck, a phenomenon Katsas called "a sweater effect."

The breasts were present and showed no injury. The heart was normal. On the right side of the chest, Katsas found five deep stab wounds. Below the left shoulder blade was a puncture hole. There was a shallow stab wound in the liver, which had been "independently attacked." None of the stab wounds had been necessary for the process of dismemberment.

The pelvis had been separated through the vertebrae of the spine, several bones of which had been broken by the terrific force of separation—a process which had required tremendous strength. The skin of the pelvis had been carefully removed, cut in a pattern corresponding to the outline of a pair of panties.

Both legs, separated at the hip joints, exhibited multiple slash-type wounds measuring up to ten inches, involving the skin, muscles and soft tissues, with flesh exposed to the bone. The arms had not been injured. The fingers were ornamented by two bead rings and a silver "friendship" ring.

Mary Anne Wysocki's death had resulted from a gunshot wound on the left side of her head. Katsas speculated that some of the stab wounds might have been inflicted during the "agonal" period, when she was alive, but dying.

Katsas found no evidence of pregnancy or injuries consistent with abortion in either body.

Microscopic examination of rectal and vaginal smears taken from the bodies of Pat Walsh and Mary Anne Wysocki disclosed the presence in large numbers of human spermatozoa.

5

The identification of gunshot wounds as the cause of death of Pat Walsh and Mary Anne Wysocki altered the course of the investigation for Bernie Flynn, to whom Killen assigned the task of finding the murder weapon. Recalling that Tony Costa had offered to sell Timmy Atkins a gun, Flynn immediately had Atkins

142

picked up at Mother Marion's—where he was sometimes employed as a dishwasher—and brought to Provincetown police station for questioning.

Atkins was nervous, pale and scared. "Tony asked me if I wanted to buy a .22 pistol. I asked him how much did he want for it. He said twenty dollars. I thought about it and said 'No, I can't. It's against the law. I don't want to buy it.' He said if I *did* want to buy the gun it was buried in the woods someplace. I never heard anything more about the gun or saw it or anything."

"Have you ever been out to Tony's garden in Truro?" Gunnery said.

"I never knew he had one until recently. I never knew he had *anything* out in the woods," Atkins said.

Flynn grimaced with impatience. Atkins, slow-witted and cautious, wasn't going to give him any straight answers about his friendship with Tony Costa. According to Chief Marshall, Atkins had called in a bomb scare to Provincetown High School—only to have his voice recognized by the principal who had often talked to the boy about his chronic truancy. Last year, Atkins had run off to Connecticut with Susan Perry, a local girl reported missing by her mother after the first body had been uncovered by police in the Truro woods.

"Did Tony Costa know Susan Perry?" Flynn said, suddenly.

Caught off-guard by the switch in questioning, Atkins was evasive. "I guess he must have known her."

"Don't *guess!*"

"Well, I couldn't say for sure whether he knew her to talk to, or knew her real well."

Flynn was about to dismiss Atkins, along with the question about Susan Perry he had asked off the top of his head, a net cast into unknown waters.

"Susan left Provincetown around Labor Day, or the day after," Atkins went on. Hesitantly, he added, "I heard she went to Dedham . . . to stay with Tony."

Flynn nearly jumped out of his chair. "How do you know *that?*"

"Because people told me," Atkins said. "She went up to Tony's apartment with Jimmy Steele and Davey Joseph."

"Did you see Susan anytime after she left to go to Dedham?"

Atkins blinked, and wet his lips. "No. Nobody did."

Flynn telephoned state police headquarters in Boston to report that an autopsy had disclosed that a gun, most likely a .22 caliber pistol, had been used in the commission of two murders. There was reason to believe the gun might be found at the Marlborough Street apartment of Vincent Bonaviri, the only place in Boston Antone Costa was known to have stayed. Flynn also described the knife Timmy Atkins had told him Costa had owned, a 12″ dagger kept in a wooden sheath he called his 'pig stabber.' Lieutenant William Broderick applied to the Municipal Court of the City of Boston for Criminal Business for a warrant to search the second floor apartment for a "a certain firearm." Accompanied by lieutenants DeFuria and White, the same officers he had taken with him to arrest Costa, Broderick went to Marlborough Street but could not gain entrance.

Broderick was told at Macey's liquor store that Vincent Bonaviri had "stepped out." Figuring it to be a stall, Broderick went to the offices of the Checker Cab Company on St. Botolph's street where Catherine Roche was employed as a billing clerk. He told her to come with him and to bring her key to the apartment.

Dark-eyed and petite, Cathy Roche secured permission from Broderick to telephone Vincent Bonaviri before she left the office to open the apartment to a police inspection. When she reported that Bonaviri had told her not to make any statements to police until he got there, Broderick threatened to press charges against the both of them if Bonaviri did not immediately come to the apartment.

Broderick seized a small quantity of marijuana wrapped in aluminum foil he had found in the apartment the day of Costa's arrest. Not having a search warrant at the time, he had concealed the package behind a window shade. Broderick also confiscated a pair of brown-striped trousers that appeared bloodstained, a leather vest, a blue sweat shirt and three coils of window cord tied into knots. Opening a rope-tied trunk belonging to Antone Costa, Broderick found a quantity of Skil-saws, sanders and electric drills; he was told Costa had purchased them in Provincetown. Broderick copied down the serial numbers of the tools in order to make a stolen-property check before bringing Cathy Roche and Vincent Bonaviri to state police headquarters for questioning.

Cathy Roche had lived in Provincetown from the end of May to September, 1968. She had known Tony Costa for about a year.

"Did you ever see a gun in his possession?" Broderick asked.

"Tony kept some clothes at my cottage in Provincetown this summer," Cathy said. "The gun was with his belongings and things; he showed it to me. I was shocked. He said it wasn't loaded or anything. He said he used it for protection and target practice. I only saw it once."

"Did he have any shells for the gun?"

"I saw them in a plastic box in his suitcase."

At the end of summer she had returned to her parents' house in Philadelphia. In January she had moved to Massachusetts to live with Vincent Bonaviri and friends at 415 Beacon Street. Sometime in February, Tony Costa had brought a blue Volkswagen to the apartment. "It was at night, so I didn't get a good look at the car."

"Did Tony say where he got it?"

"He told Vincent and me he bought it from a girl from Rhode Island and had a bill of sale." Costa did not have the car with him when he came back to Boston several weeks later to help paint the apartment on Marlborough Street.

On Monday, March 3, Costa had again visited Boston. "I don't know exactly what time he got there. I was at work. Tony was there when I got home at five-thirty. He said he was on the bus all night." Costa had slept on the couch in the living room.

On Wednesday morning, Cathy had observed Costa put a small aspirin bottle in a Kleenex box on the fireplace mantle. "I didn't think about it at the time, although it seemed funny Tony would put anything in a Kleenex box. When Vincent came home that night and told me Tony had been arrested, I took the bottle out and showed it to him. There were pills in it, little black capsules and a couple of yellow ones."

Vincent Bonaviri was brought into a conference room for questioning after Broderick warned Detective Lieutenant Richard Cass, acting captain of detectives: "Vinnie's a little shithead. He's not too bright, except when it comes to lying; then he's got a real gift."

Reluctantly, Vinnie admitted his brother had owned a gun.

145

"A real small snub-nosed .22. I saw the gun last summer on the dresser of Tony's room at my mother's house."

"Did you ask him where he got it or anything?" Broderick said.

"I didn't question him about it because I never saw him again after that. I was in Boston looking for an apartment. I just happened to call my mother. She said the police had locked him up for non-support and not to worry about it."

"Did you ever see any type of knife in his possession?"

"He had a hunting knife, a light brown handle with sort of pink or reddish stripes, a regular cutting knife."

"Did you ever see a dagger, about twelve inches long in a wooden case?"

"Yeah, I saw that quite often. His dad made it for him. It was a souvenir Tony had from his dad."

"Did you know your brother took LSD?"

"I guess so, yeah."

"Did he ever take any other stuff?"

"Marijuana, hash of all sorts, tranquilizers for backaches and nerve pills."

"If your brother did these killings, would you want to see him free on the street?" Broderick said.

"I just couldn't believe he did it," Vinnie said. "Tony was a pleasant, easygoing guy. He never got mad."

"You have come here and talked voluntarily? There has been no coercion or pressure to make you answer any questions?"

Vinnie, recalling Broderick's threat to throw the book at him, smiled in acknowledgment of the irony of the question, aware that a police stenographer was taking down his answer. "My father told me to cooperate. There's no protection now; it's over and done with."

Vincent Bonaviri and Cathy Roche returned to their apartment on Marlborough Street to find the place had been thoroughly searched. The painted-shut frame of a louvered sliding door had been knocked down; power tools were scattered across the living room floor.

Vinnie turned on the television to watch the WNAC channel 7 news which, in its coverage of the "Truro murder case," featured the appearance of Boston psychiatrist, Dr. Robert Mezer.

Mezer was asked, "Is it possible for a sane person to commit a crime where the bodies are dismembered, and things like that?"

"I would doubt it greatly," Mezer said. "This type of crime is much too bizarre to have been done by a normal individual."

"A person who dismembers his murder victims, does this have a sexual connotation?"

"I think in this case we will probably find that hostility and sexuality have been joined," Mezer said. "In normal people we see that sex follows love. In people who commit this type of crime, we see that sex follows violence, or violence follows sex. And I am quite sure that this is what we are going to find in this particular case."

Reiterating that "Mr. Costa is only a suspect and we are talking in generalities about this type of case," the interviewer said, "From your experience, are there any behavioral patterns that are typical in this type of criminally insane murderer?"

"Not specifically," Mezer said. "Each individual criminal has a certain method of operation. So that if this individual, for example, has been picking up young girls and giving them rides and then killing them after sexually assaulting them, then that is probably the type of thing he would continue to do."

"You say in all probability whoever did these murders—there are at least four, apparently—is insane? Under the laws in this country, an insane person cannot really be convicted and sent to the penitentiary for knowledgeable commission of a murder like this—murder in the first degree. Do you feel the laws are adequate to cover what we have learned in the area of psychiatry?"

"I do not think the laws are adequate," Mezer said. "The way they are set up now, the jury is asked to find a person not guilty but insane. For many people who sit on these juries to find the murderer not guilty is not possible. I think that the fairer thing, which is closer to reality, would be that the finding should be guilty—which is true, he *did* do it—but insane. If that were done, I think we would have a better carrying-out of justice."

"Do you favor a man committed as insane having a minimum period of time to spend in a mental institution rather than the probability of parole or rehabilitation within a short period of time?"

"This is another point the public does not seem to understand," Mezer said. "A person sent to prison for a determined number of years is released when his sentence ends, regardless of

147

his mental condition at the time. On the other hand, if you have committed him as insane, he cannot be released until he is no longer dangerous. As a matter of fact, he could stay there for the rest of his life." Mezer added, "But this business of these individuals getting into institutions and serving three years after committing a murder, then getting out to commit it again, just isn't right."

6

Around 1:30 P.M., Antone Costa arrived in Bridgewater, a slumberous, elm-lined town south of Boston, following a pleasant two-hour drive from Provincetown. A discreet, all but unnoticeable sign directed the state police cruiser to a winding road at the end of which was a cluster of red brick buildings of Victorian factory-style architecture erected in the 1880's by inmate labor.

No high walls or electrified fence protected the snow-covered grounds crossed by residential streets. Under the Massachusetts Department of Corrections, the Bridgewater facility harbored inmates judged criminally insane or sexually dangerous, including confessed "Boston Strangler," Albert DiSalvo. The hospital also provided facilities for the state Department of Mental Health, whose policies overlapped and sometimes conflicted with the institution's corrections function. Lately, a drug addiction treatment center had been established.

Costa was turned over to Superintendent Charles Gaughan. A small, frail-appearing man wearing shirtsleeves and bow tie, Gaughan had assumed charge of the institution in 1959. A pioneer in the treatment and rehabilitation of alcoholics and with a background in education and social work, Gaughan had no experience in corrections. He had sought to "humanize" the institution by keeping the aged buildings clean and in good repair and replacing

148

drab interior colors with bright pastels. Gaughan's innovations were, however, insufficient against a rising tide of public outrage against the "cruel and inhuman treatment" of inmates most graphically portrayed in the controversial documentary, *Titicut Follies*, filmed at the hospital, which had doomed several of the facility's older buildings.

Stripped and body searched, Costa was given a complete physical examination. He was six feet tall, 175 pounds, light complexion and of medium stature, with no scars or tattoos. Costa said his health was "good."

Costa's arms were checked for needle marks; his eyes closely scrutinized during a retinal examination. There was nothing in the examination which led to the conclusion that Costa was addicted to anything. The examination also assured Gaughan that Costa had not "ingested any poisonous substances during his transfer from the district court in Provincetown." Gaughan had a horror of inmate suicide. In highly publicized cases, he knew, the public felt "cheated" if a prisoner took his own life before he could be brought to justice.

Costa was introduced to the assistant medical director, Dr. Lawrence Barrows. A brilliant diagnostician, once listed among ten outstanding young neurologists in the country, Barrows was, in Gaughan's view, "a tragic case." Barrows had come to Bridgewater after his discharge as a patient at Brockton Veterans' Hospital where he had undergone treatment for severe depression and acute alcoholism. Gaughan had hired him in the hope that Barrows would "hold up," as a superb addition to a staff that only rarely could afford so high a degree of expertise.

Barrows examined every prisoner brought to the hospital accused of a capital crime to ascertain how best to work up a psychiatric evaluation to determine his mental competence to stand trial for eventual report to the courts. Competency was based on three criteria: knowledge of the offense charged, comprehension of the consequences if convicted, and the ability of the inmate to cooperate with counsel in his own defense.

Short, balding, sad-eyed, Barrows found Costa friendly, cooperative and in no way resentful of the interview. Barrows observed no disturbance of psychomotor activity or odd mannerisms, disturbance in the organization or progression of his thought processes or dissociation. Barrows was impressed with Costa's coolness, considering the charges against him. An inmate was usu-

149

ally somewhat upset or apprehensive for a period of time until he adjusted to hospital routine.

Costa, giving a brief history of his life, spoke in a monotone, showing a degree of passivity so marked, Gaughan observed, that "you could tell he had mental problems."

Costa's father had been born in the Azores. A carpenter's mate in the navy, he had drowned at sea trying to save the life of a shipmate who had been swept overboard. Costa described his father's death in minute detail, having committed to memory a letter of commendation for bravery his father had received posthumously from the navy.

Costa's mother had remarried; there was a half brother twenty-two months younger with whom Costa claimed he got along well after some initial difficulty. Disagreements and quarrels had brought about a separation between his mother and stepfather, following an argument in which neither would give in. The separation had led to a divorce in 1962, when the family moved from Somerville to Provincetown where Costa graduated from high school. Costa had married at eighteen, and fathered three children. Divorced in August, 1968, Costa explained, "My wife was interested in other men." Yes, he had minded the breakup of his marriage. "But I was glad my wife was happy."

Costa had served a sentence for nonsupport at the Barnstable House of Correction and been paroled, resuming employment as a carpenter from which, in good times, he earned from one hundred twenty-five to one hundred fifty dollars per week.

He had no history of epilepsy, head injuries or previous psychiatric study or treatment. He had never been admitted to a general hospital as a patient. He did not drink alcohol. A year prior to his divorce Costa had smoked marijuana regularly, but did not use other drugs, he said.

At the conclusion of the "admission interview," Barrows noted that Costa's consciousness was clear. He was free of delusions, hallucinations, overvalued ideas and defects in judgment. Insight was not impaired; he was neither obsessive, compulsive nor hypochondriacal. He exhibited no sign of psychiatric illness or suicidal tendencies.

Gaughan was not taking any chances. For a period of forty-eight hours, Costa would be closely watched. As a precaution against attempted suicide, Costa's glasses were removed; his clothes were replaced by a sacklike paper gown. He was taken to Admission Ward F, a maximum security section he would not be allowed to leave except for psychiatric examination and conferences with his attorneys. His meals would be dispensed from a food wagon that plied the corridors, passed on a tray through a hinged panel in the metal door of the eight-by-ten-foot room whose cement floor felt cold against the paper slippers he wore.

Three layers of wire mesh blocked most of the light from the single window that overlooked a brick smokestack. Costa's eyes passed over the view of snow-covered fields stretching to a stand of pines beyond the hospital's outbuildings.

The paper gown tore up the back when he settled onto the bare mattress on the floor—the room's only furniture. He drew a single coarse blanket up to his shoulders against the cold.

Several days later, Costa memorialized the occasion "as I looked through my window and witnessed such beauty—may it come again when I am free":

Sundown

Fleece-lined lavender clouds
Suspended in a turquoise sea of milk.
The chirping of the birds outside,
Their voices made of fine silk.
All God's colors before my eyes,
An artist's brush cannot duplicate.
"Free me Lord from unjust hands,
Don't make these prison walls my fate."

George Killen presented a stony silence to reporters waiting outside his office at Barnstable courthouse on Friday morning. Already deeply concerned about the sensational news coverage generated by Dinis's press conference, Killen had been appalled

151

by statements attributed to the medical examiner, Dr. Daniel Hiebert.

Hiebert had told the *Boston Herald Traveler* that bullets had been fired into the brains of Pat Walsh and Mary Anne Wysocki before their bodies were mutilated and dismembered by a sharp instrument, probably an ax or a cleaver. According to Hiebert, both girls had been repeatedly slashed "in the pelvic region" by the same knife used to cut off their legs and arms. Hiebert had managed to confuse the victims, telling reporters that Pat Walsh, not Mary Anne Wysocki, had been decapitated.

Killen suspected that the somewhat doddering medical examiner had been in part responsible for the misinformation Dinis had delivered to reporters at his press conference. When Hiebert called his office, Killen was in no mood to be charitable, advising him to make no further statements about the Costa case to the press.

Hiebert was apologetic. Dr. Katsas had told him to be very careful about what he said, and to check with Killen first. Dr. Hiebert said, "My wife told me I shouldn't say anything to reporters, but I wanted to allay the fears of the people of Provincetown."

Killen reminded Hiebert that such assurances were not "his field." Hiebert had already made statements highly prejudicial to the case.

Hiebert had just given an interview to Neil Nickerson, Provincetown correspondent for the Cape Cod *Standard-Times*.

"What did you tell him?" Killen said.

"I just said that no major parts of the bodies were missing, and that reports of the hearts having been removed were erroneous." Hiebert also told of having treated Tony Costa with sedatives "to quiet his nerves" after he was questioned by police.

Killen had received another missing persons report regarding a young woman, Margo Failing, who had disappeared in December after delivering a car to the Falmouth office of National Auto Rental. Employed as a part-time nurse's aide at Cape End Manor, a medical facility for the aged in Provincetown, she had lived at 215 Bradford Street.

"This might be another one of Costa's," Bernie Flynn said when Killen gave him the complaint.

Flynn was on his way to Provincetown. Chief Cheney Marshall had received an anonymous telephone tip that Mrs. Joanne Watts had loaned Tony Costa a car and a shovel last spring.

"Tony borrowed my Rambler in May or June," Mrs. Watts told Flynn when he questioned her. "When he returned the car, it was covered with sand." She had known Costa for the past year. He had known her sons, Gary and Billy, and had on occasion dated her daughter, Bonnie. "Tony was very friendly; you couldn't help liking him. He was such a polite person. Everybody feels bad it had to be a Provincetown boy."

"What kind of a shovel did Tony borrow from you?" Flynn said.

Mrs. Watts wasn't sure. She suggested that Flynn talk to her husband who operated the Amoco garage on Route 6A in Truro.

"It was a German army combat shovel. It opened up to about three feet. It had a ring lock to undo it with. You could make the shovel into a hoe. When it's compact it's only like two feet long." William Watts stood talking to Flynn in his garage. "My wife was hollering at Gary for losing it. My brother Russell said Tony came by the garage one morning in a pickup truck with a lot of sand in back and asked to borrow a shovel, a board, and a length of rope. We never got the shovel back."

Garrulous and friendly, Watts added, "I was talking to my daughter-in-law. She said something about a knife police were looking for. When she described it, I told her I had one just like that. It's a real dangerous weapon with a point, for cutting brush. You hit anyone with it, you'd kill them. I was nervous leaving it around the house, so I stuck it in a workbench with a collection of bayonets and Japanese guns I keep locked out of the way in a back room—this is in the garage. I went to show her the knife, and it was gone!"

Tony Costa had also used the back room. "He would leave his tools there at night when he got through work, rather than carry them back and forth," Watts said. "Maybe that's the knife he used to chop the girls up with . . ."

Billy Watts thought his father was mistaken. He had seen a knife belonging to Tony Costa at the White Wind apartments. "It was a homemade knife with a funny-looking blade, made out of a file; a real sharp knife with a black wooden handle." Costa had also owned a .22 revolver with black-and-white grips. "I never saw that; I only heard about it from others."

A married, twenty-year-old laborer, living with his grandmother, Billy Watts had known Tony Costa a long time. "When I

153

first met Tony he was dissecting a fish. He said he wanted to be a doctor and go to medical school. He used to read medical books about abortions and operations, how easy it was to do. I can't remember which one he said, abortion or appendix, but one of them operations was relatively easy."

"Did he ever tell you he had performed such an operation on a person?" Flynn asked.

"No, he never said that."

"Did you ever see Tony do any taxidermist work?"

"I never seen him do any, but I'm pretty sure he was teaching a friend of his how to do it."

Watts had not been as friendly with Costa as his younger brother, Gary. A junior at Provincetown High School, Gary Watts had worked for Costa the previous spring, getting the Crown and Anchor Motor Inn ready for the tourist season.

"Did you ever see him on drugs?" Flynn asked.

"Once at Adams's pharmacy, he was sitting on one of the stools. He said, 'I'm having a bad trip, have you got any smoke?' " Costa had smoked pot and shot speed in his presence, but was never violent.

The previous September, Watts had seen Tony Costa with Susan Perry on the Boston Common, shortly before her disappearance. "Susan was living with Tony in Dedham," Gary said. "Later I asked him where Susan was, and he told me she'd had a bad trip on LSD. He said she'd gone to Mexico with two guys and another girl."

Flynn and Gunnery did not take part in the seventy-five-man posse that entered the Truro woods at dawn to conduct a search for additional bodies in an area close to Costa's former marijuana garden. Interrupted for several hours by a snowstorm, the search uncovered a partially buried bone, believed to be a human leg with the foot missing, protruding from the ground not far from the graves.

There was some "material" on the bone, but no flesh, Flynn told reporters at a press conference held at Provincetown police station. Flynn decided that until the bone was examined by pathologist Dr. George Katsas, he would not confirm it as being a human leg.

8

Truro chief Harold Berrio held his own briefing for reporters crowded into his small station. Berrio had not heard from District Attorney Edmund Dinis since his press conference. "He's talking about the possibility of finding more bodies, but I don't see him going through the underbrush looking for them," he said. "I don't expect to see him on Cape Cod again."

Berrio's telephone had been ringing all night. "A woman would call up and say, 'My sixteen-year-old daughter is missing and she used to go to Provincetown.' I'm getting calls from all over New England. People read something like this and they all get panicky."

Berrio had no reports of any missing Truro women, but police were stepping up their investigation into the disappearance of two local girls—Susan Perry of Provincetown and Sydney Monzon of Eastham.

Tony Costa, it turned out, had lived at several rented apartments in Truro. A quiet type, he had not drawn attention to himself, Berrio said. "We knew he was a drug user, but we could never catch him. Otherwise, he never gave us any trouble."

Privately, Berrio had confided to Killen an occasion when Avis Costa had called Truro police because her husband had threatened her. Berrio had gone to an apartment on Hughes Road himself. "It was just a family squabble. Costa said she was spending too much money and he wasn't making that much." Berrio had heard rumors that Avis had been rushed by ambulance to a doctor seriously ill. "I heard that Tony had fed her embalming fluid."

Convinced the murders had occurred in Provincetown and the bodies brought to Truro for burial, Berro suggested that the duffel bag found in the first grave had been used to carry body parts to a grave hastily dug on top of a road bank.

Plagued by the press who wanted sensational details about the murders, Berrio had lost his temper when one particularly insistent reporter had demanded "exclusive" information. "I got

155

to tell you *nothing!*" Berrio thundered, and had the reporter ejected from the police station.

"The press is bad," Berrio told Killen afterward, "but the tourists are even worse."

Despite Berrio's complaint, most of the curious people roaming the scrub pine woods to stare at the open graves that had held the murdered girls were year-rounders, some with small children. Others rode on horseback along the narrow one-track cart roads leading to desolate Old Truro Cemetery. A busload of Golden Agers on an excursion to Cape Cod stopped to inquire of a passerby: "Is this the road to the graveyard?"

One visitor brought his own shovel and commenced digging for other victims of "a sadistic murderer," dissuaded from his self-appointed task by park rangers who cordoned off a square mile of woods, blocking access roads with chains and posting the area where police searches had been discontinued because of wet weather and throngs of sightseers overrunning the scene.

Masses celebrated at Our Lady of Lourdes Roman Catholic Church in Wellfleet included prayers for the departed, Patricia Walsh and Mary Anne Wysocki, whose holiday on Cape Cod "had ended in terror on a lonely road in Truro."

"Foremost of Cape towns concerned with intangible values, not sacrificed in the race for financial exploitation of a resort area," according to a town spokesman, Truro had been "blanketed in dismay" since the first body was discovered, then horrified when three more corpses were exhumed.

"It shouldn't have happened in Truro," an official observed. "The town didn't deserve it."

People were stunned "by this encounter with a strangeness of which the town had no previous experience," according to Grace Deschamps, Truro correspondent for the Provincetown *Advocate*. Filled with sorrow and pity at the deaths of four young women, Truro was moved as well with indignation. "Shock and bewilderment" were the first reactions. "Next comes resentment, and a rising anger that the town's remote and quiet places have been desecrated and defiled, made the scene of some Witches' Sabbath."

"Drugs, death, horror moved upon a little town beloved by inhabitants to make it a focus of an evil pictured in the news media," Deschamps complained. It was an article of faith that nothing really bad could ever happen in Truro, where children gathered blueberries along the old cart roads through the woods without fear—an unspoiled loveliness now being represented on television as a place "where horror struck." The town's simplicity and innocence had been infected by "some dreadful malignancy from outside its borders."

The area of woods where the bodies were found fell within the boundaries of the Cape Cod National Seashore Park, a reservation which had, however, provided no protection against "human outrage . . ."

9

Maurice Goldman was outraged to read in the Cape Cod *Standard-Times* a report that Tony Costa had, on occasion, burned parts of his wife's body severely enough to require medical treatment. The newspaper had also given an account of an "accident" in the Truro woods during which Costa had shot an arrow into the back of a teenage girl. Goldman was preparing to protest such "inflammatory and prejudicial" statements emanating from the district attorney when Justin Cavanaugh entered the offices of Thomason, Goldman & Cavanaugh, a single-story white bungalow on Route 6A in Brewster.

Two years before, Cavanaugh had successfully represented a client in a gas explosion case in Springfield, Massachusetts, and when Goldman was retained for a similar case on Cape Cod, he had written Cavanaugh's law firm asking for the pleadings—a standard practice among lawyers. Cavanaugh had delivered the papers in person, the two men had struck up a friendship, and Goldman suggested that Cavanaugh associate himself with his office. Cavanaugh had commuted from Springfield, where he had been a city councilman for twelve years, until he built up a sufficient law practice on Cape Cod to relocate.

A portly man with pale, hooded eyes, Goldman's strong, thrusting profile dominated a dark, Levantine face. Born on July 4, 1900, while his parents vacationed in Toronto, Canada, Goldman carried a scar near his right eye from a fight at age six with a rival newspaper boy over a favored street corner. Scrappy and ambitious, he had attended Boston English High School, writing news of scholastic events for the Boston *Record*. As a cub reporter, Goldman covered fires and police blotters. After two years of law school at Northeastern University, he had joined the Franklin Syndicate to write a series of muckraking articles, which had appeared in two hundred newspapers, about the hoarding and profiteering prevalent during a serious wheat shortage. Goldman had returned to law school, earned his degree and was admitted to the bar in 1925.

Goldman enjoyed regaling associates with tales of his early years as a brash and lusty young lawyer who had regularly represented prostitutes, following periodic police raids around Boston's notorious Scollay Square. "Sometimes as many as thirty girls would be rounded up in one night," Goldman recalled. "At two dollars a head, that was a real bonanza for me. If I got the girls out of court after they paid a substantial ten-dollar fine, and without them losing too much trade, I'd even get a tip."

Plunging into Boston's rough-and-tumble political arena, Goldman's scramble up the political ranks had been accomplished as an unabashed ward heeler, banging on doors to wheedle votes from his constituents. Goldman was elected a Boston city councillor from Ward 4; then a state senator, commended in 1944 for a 100 percent pro-labor voting record and his fight against discrimination in employment on grounds of race, color and creed.

As assistant attorney general for ten years under four governors, Goldman had been hailed as "another Brandeis" by the Boston *Post*. A pioneer consumer advocate, Goldman had made headlines for his prosecutions of small-loan frauds, auto purchase trickery and the traffic in fake proprietary drugs. Suave, dapper, with a beautiful wife on his arm, Goldman cut a singular swath through Boston's buttoned down legal community, handling in excess of ten thousand cases as a government trial lawyer and in private practice, four hundred of them before the Massachusetts Supreme Judicial Court. Goldman had also been admitted to

158

practice before the United States Supreme Court. Practicing law for the past twelve years in Brewster, where he owned a trailer park and campgrounds, Goldman had quickly established himself as the premier criminal lawyer on Cape Cod.

Goldman disclaimed any exceptional ability, telling Cavanaugh, "I just work a little harder than the other guy." Amused by the myths that had sprung up about the "secret" of his success, Goldman complained, "They say, 'Goldman bribes the judge; Goldman bribes the jury; Goldman bribes witnesses.' Where in hell is all this money coming from?" He was a "poor man's lawyer," Goldman said, warning Cavanaugh there were no million-dollar clients on Cape Cod.

Despite his reputation, Goldman was easily bored with standard criminal work unless a particular point of law was at issue. He disliked divorce cases involving child custody, regarding the conference rooms off the second-floor gallery of Barnstable's probate court as "a real chamber of horrors" where the lives of children torn from their parents were routinely destroyed "by a piece of paper."

Nearly sixty-nine years old, Goldman had lost none of his zest for practicing law, complaining that he had spent at least thirty of his more than forty years as a lawyer "waiting around in corridors for something to happen." A courtly man, with a sprightly step, he was known to spear antagonists with a shriveling wit, administered in a dry, crisp voice whose commanding sonorities made him sound like a radio actor. Tough and shrewd though he was, Goldman's warmth and charm had endeared him to colleagues and clients, one of whom recalled, "Goldman doesn't defend his clients, he *fortifies* them."

Goldman had not heard from Tony Costa since their first meeting in Provincetown. He had been annoyed to learn that his client had, on a number of occasions, gone voluntarily to the Provincetown station to talk to police. Goldman was surprised to hear the news of Costa's arrest when Frank Bent called his office late Wednesday afternoon. Goldman didn't think the softspoken, gentlemanly young man could possibly be involved in such matters. Because he had a deposition hearing the next morning, Goldman had sent Cavanaugh to the arraignment.

The case against Costa appeared, at first blush, to be totally circumstantial, Cavanaugh said, when he discussed the memo left on Goldman's desk. Then he and Goldman left the office to meet with Tony Costa on Saturday, March 8, in a small conference room off a visitor's area at Bridgewater State Hospital.

Costa reported he had spoken earlier that morning with Superintendent Gaughan. "It was basically to ask him for certain restrictions to be removed, such as my glasses, and permission to have certain magazines and reading material," Costa said. "He wanted to know how I was getting along—how I felt about being here in Bridgewater, and if I had any complaints about how I was being treated. I told him that I had none. The care has been rather decent."

Cavanaugh was disconcerted by Costa's voice. His locution was curiously stilted, almost prissy in its precise articulation and so lofty-sounding as to be effete—totally out of character with his rugged appearance. Cavanaugh asked Goldman later if this was a Provincetown accent. Goldman replied, "No, this is just something he's picked up along the way."

Seated across the scarred table in the bare conference room, Goldman fastened his baleful eyes on Tony Costa. "I'll say it bluntly, Tony. Did you kill those girls?"

"I had nothing to do with it." Costa said, emphatically. "I have killed no one!"

The charges against his client being for two murders—not four as reported in the press—Goldman first asked Costa to describe Patricia Walsh and Mary Anne Wysocki. "Tell us about their physical makeup—weight and height and so forth. Start with Pat first, give us your best judgment."

"Pat was roughly about five feet nine inches tall, and perhaps one hundred twenty pounds," Costa said. "She had black hair, shoulder-length. I don't know the color of her eyes. I think they may have been brown. She was quiet when I first met her; but after a while her personality opened up. She became sort of open and quite friendly. She seemed to be a nice girl."

"Would you call her attractive?" Cavanaugh said.

"She wasn't ugly; she was a nice-looking girl," Costa said. "But she is not the kind of girl I would be attracted to. Pat came on super-strong as the all-out hippie chick. She was dressed in a heavy army-type jacket, an old green thing. And she wore bell-bottoms and boots—the regular hippie attire. She had some beads and things she wore around her neck."

"What about Mary Anne?"

"Mary Anne had sort of blonde hair. I don't know the color of her eyes. She stood about five eight, a little shorter than Pat and I guess about the same weight. They looked to be about the same in bodily structure. She was plain, simple; she was a quiet-type girl. I did notice she wore makeup. She might be attractive to someone else, but for me, I don't like a girl with makeup. It turns me off."

"Were they both straight?" Goldman said. "Or was there anything between the two of them?"

"In what essence?" Costa said.

"In the essence of whether they were lesbians in any way," Goldman said. "Were you able to gather that?"

"I don't know. I don't think they were. They hung around together all the time during the days that I knew them. It could very well have been, but to me it wasn't totally obvious."

"For purposes of the case, I think we ought to have your own statement as to events starting with that Friday, the twenty-fourth of January, so we can pick up exactly what went on from that day up until sometime in the first week in February," Goldman said. "Now, Tony, tell us from the moment you first met these two girls, what you said and what they said, so I can get it exactly word for word what went on, giving days, times and places up until the time you last saw the girls. Would you like to try a statement on that?"

"This is the most important, these two days," Costa said, "because this evidence shows that I was not the last one with these two girls."

"That's right," Goldman said, "that's very important."

"The first time I saw them was when I was introduced by the landlady, Mrs. Morton. I was relaxing in my room; I was reading *Steppenwolf* by Hermann Hesse. They simply said, 'hi', and turned around and went downstairs, evidently to sign the register, and I continued reading. A few minutes later Pat and Mary Anne both came back upstairs and asked if they could use the bathroom which served as a passageway to my room—someone was using the one upstairs. I told them the bathroom belonged to anyone in the house, that it was not a private bath. It was a house bath and anybody could use it. They said they had some things in the car to bring in, so I helped them."

"Could I interrupt to ask exactly what they had in the way of bags and clothes, to the best of your memory," Goldman said.

"The entire backseat of their Volkswagen was filled with bags, such as shopping bags and big grocery-type bags, filled with clothes. And they had a small suitcase. In the trunk was a rather large blanket and some kind of plastic mat—and there were clothes, regular dresses and coats and things all on hangers, just lying there."

"How many pieces of luggage would you say?"

"I don't know really. They had a big bunch of stuff, it was incredible! They had enough stuff to go away for a month. It took three of us two trips to bring in all the stuff they had, although I went out only once with them. I brought in the blankets and the clothing that was in the trunk on hangers. Outside, they told me to bring some of the stuff to my room, which I did. On the second trip they brought some things to my room, toiletries, shampoos, deodorant and makeup. Then they came down and separated some of the clothes."

"Wasn't it unusual for two girls you just met to take over your room like that?" Cavanaugh said.

"It's a pretty normal thing, because everybody in the house used the same bathrooms; it was a communal kind of house."

"What happened next?" Goldman said.

"Mary Anne took a shower first. While she was in there I talked to Pat concerning the general scene in Provincetown, such as what was going on and what there was to do. She wanted to know where there was a good place where people gathered, where they could talk to different people. I asked her at the time exactly what they were doing in Provincetown, whether they were on school vacation, or whether they had come down for the winter or what they were going to do. She was rather vague about the whole thing. But in conversation she kept hinting around at various things concerning narcotics, and sort of waiting to see what I had to say. And in this conversation we got to a point where I told her that I had quite a few friends around town that were interested in narcotics traffic and whatever she had to offer. At which time she came out and bluntly said that this friend she was going to meet was bringing in some stuff and she wanted to know if I could line her up with anyone interested in purchasing anything."

"Did you know what she was going to bring in?" Cavanaugh said.

"She stated the guy was bringing in junk—which is heroin. I asked her how much it would be. She said this guy was selling in gross amounts—not in small quantities—and that he would be in either sometime that day or the next day, but they were to wait there and if he didn't show up, they were to pick him up."

"About what time on Friday did this conversation take place?" Goldman said.

"Roughly around . . . I'd say two o'clock. They checked in around one-thirty," Costa said. "I was still talking to Pat when Mary Anne came out of the shower. She had some kind of long dress-type thing on and she took some of her things and went up to her room and got dressed. Then she came down and started drying her hair. At which time Pat went into the bathroom and took her shower. I said a few things to Mary Anne . . ."

"What did you say?" Goldman said.

"I just asked her how she felt after her shower and she said she felt good. I told her I had been talking to Pat and wanted to know just exactly what was going on. She told me I had better talk to Pat, because it was Pat's friend that was coming in and she didn't really know much about it. She was more or less hanging around with Pat and I would have to go through her on anything. She picked up a "Laugh-In" magazine I had in the room and started commenting on some of the jokes. And we got into a conversation and had a rather nice time laughing concerning these jokes. At this time the conversation stopped because she had this thing on her head—the hair dryer—and couldn't hear anything. When Pat came out of the shower I asked her more questions concerning who was coming in. She said that it was a guy named 'Buddy' Hansen she knew. She said his actual name was Chuck, but they called him 'Buddy,' and that he was coming in the next day. They were supposed to meet him."

"Did she say where?" Goldman said.

"This is what I asked her," Costa said. "I asked her how soon I could have this stuff. She said it would be there tomorrow afternoon—that would be Saturday. She said I could have a quarter of what Chuck had—which was a pound of heroin. I could buy it for nine hundred dollars. I told her I would try to get the money, nine hundred dollars, and have it for her the next day. She said OK. Then, another guy came into the room."

"Who was this other guy?" Goldman said.

"He evidently was a friend of theirs. I didn't know him at all; I wasn't introduced. I told the girls that I had to go out and take care of some errands if I were going to complete my part of the bargain. I had to call my brother to try to borrow some money. At this time I put my coat on and told them to make themselves at home, to take care of the place and not leave anything messy."

"Were they drinking or eating?" Goldman said.

"They had these bags of Mexican potato chips similar to Fritos. Some of them were spilled on the floor. I didn't really care, but I didn't want the place a mess either. So I explained to them to leave the place clean. I reached into my pocket to get out my key, but it was not there; so I told them to leave the porch entrance open. I went out at that time and left them there."

"Where did you go?" Goldman said.

"I went to visit Woody—that's Paul Candish, he's a good friend of mine. We just chatted for maybe a half an hour. I didn't mention dope to him because Woody's never used drugs. He is very strong concerning the Buddhist religion," Costa explained. "After I left Woody's. I was just sort of trotting around town thinking as to who would want anything. I went downtown to Adams Pharmacy to see if there might be someone there who would want some heroin, as there aren't many people in town who do use it. I talked to the counterwoman, I think it was Loretta; and I bought a glass of milk and a package of Lorna Doone cookies. From there I proceeded on up to my mom's for supper. We had hot dogs and beans."

"About what time was this?" Goldman said.

"It was five o'clock; my mom always has supper ready at five. I stayed there and watched TV. About seven-thirty or so I went over to Frankie Rosa's—nicknamed "Sheiky." We watched TV, listened to records and we talked about Tommy Russe, a friend of mine who had come from California to visit his mother. Tommy's brother Matt was there. We all sat around and drank wine. Around eleven o'clock, me and Sheiky decided to go to the Foc's'le. Wolf Fissler, a friend of mine who is a bartender at the Crown and Anchor was there. We stayed until closing, almost one o'clock; then we got the idea to go to the Pilgrim Club before they closed to see who was there."

"As I understand it," Cavanaugh said, "you were waiting for night when some of your friends would be around so you could make contact with anybody that might be interested in the stuff you were going to buy from the girls?"

"Right." Costa said.

"Had you reached your brother for money during this time?" Goldman asked.

"I called him about eight o'clock. And at that time, 'The Deacon,' that's Bobby Alves, answered the phone. He said Vinnie and Cathy were out having dinner. It wasn't really important because I had borrowed three hundred dollars from my brother the Monday before; and I had six hundred that was supposed to be for my support payments—"

"Let's finish the rest of Friday night," Goldman said.

"Wolf and I stayed at the Pilgrim Club until closing, about one-thirty in the morning. Then Wolf drove me to Mrs. Morton's. While I was getting myself ready for bed, I heard some noises upstairs, like a bunch of people. I thought it was guys' voices I heard. I went upstairs to ask the girls or someone for a ride the next day to get my paycheck; but when I went up and listened, there was no noise, so I figured they were asleep. I went to my room and wrote a note asking the two girls if they would be kind enough to give me a ride in the morning. I just tacked it on the doorcase of their room—this was about two o'clock in the morning. Then I came down to my room and proceeded to pick up and put away a hair dryer, towels, boots, loafers and stuff from the floor; they had left everything strewn all over the room. A marijuana cigarette was left partially burned in an ashtray with many cigarette butts on my night table. I cleaned everything up, flushed the pot down the toilet and got myself ready for bed. I slept well through the night."

"What time did you wake up Saturday morning?" Goldman said.

"I was still sleeping when I felt somebody tugging at my blankets. I sort of got up and rolled over. It was Pat and Mary Anne, standing there with their coats on. They had received my note and Pat said she would be glad to give me a ride. She wanted to know how soon I could be ready. I told her I would get up right away and take a shower, that I would be ready in half an hour. She said OK and asked me where they could get some breakfast. I told her to go to Wally's, because that was the only place I knew that was open where they could get a decent breakfast."

"Any talk about the heroin?" Cavanaugh asked.

"Pat said they were in a hurry because they had to meet this guy, Chuck. She said we had a lot of things to discuss when they came back. They returned around ten-thirty or so. They both came into my room and we got into a conversation again and— oh, I know what it was! I mentioned that everything, like the hair dryer and towels, was just left where it wasn't supposed to be. I told Pat I put them away, and where the stuff was if she wanted it. She just said OK, and apologized for leaving the room a mess. At this time we got discussing the matter of the heroin."

"What was said about it?" Cavanaugh said.

"I simply told her that I had gotten the money, but that I wanted some guarantee as to this guy showing up and what he was going to do. At this time Pat said she could give me collateral. I figured as long as she could do that, it was OK."

"Tell us what she said," Goldman said, "rather than conclusions, if you know what I mean. What *she* said and what *you* said, in a conversation—as best you can remember."

"I told her I had the money and if she could give me some form of collateral, She told me she could and not to worry, that everything would be exactly as she said."

"Did she say what the collateral was?"

"Not at this time. I didn't exactly ask her what it was; but I *did* give her the money."

"Right then and there?" Cavanaugh said.

"Yeah," Costa said. "She said they were going up-Cape to pick up this guy Chuck; she was going to leave at approximately one o'clock. She said Chuck would be hitchhiking, or he would take the bus, so if they didn't find him on the highway, they would stop at the bus terminal in Hyannis and wait."

"Tony, didn't it occur to you that Chuck wouldn't be hitchhiking carrying a pound of heroin?" Goldman said. "That represents a lot of money, doesn't it?"

"Yes, definitely. It represents a *tremendous* amount of money."

"Now, would he be walking along the highway bumming a ride, Tony?"

"It seemed strange to me . . . but I felt they were using this as a cover or something. Pat said Chuck had a car, and I figured perhaps he *was* using his car, but I wasn't supposed to know. I let it go at that—I didn't care how he was getting in," Costa said, putting the question to rest once again, apparently. "Right after Pat took my money she asked if I knew where she could get credentials for this guy."

"What did she mean by 'credentials'?" Goldman asked. "Did she say what he wanted?"

"He wanted a driver's license, he wanted a draft card, and he wanted a birth certificate," Costa said. "I don't know what he was going to do. My first assumption was that he was dodging the draft, that he wanted to go to Mexico or someplace and just bide his time there for some reason. I told her I had a friend who lived on the Lower East Side in New York. And in that section you can get anything you want—false identification papers or dope, anything that's illegal you can find there. I gave her his name, address and telephone number."

"What name did you give her?" Goldman said.

"His name is Primo, and he lives on East Ninth Street. She took down the address and they just sort of walked off. They thanked me for everything and said they had things to do. I heard them get into the car and drive off. The thing was, they didn't take anything with them. I didn't see them take any of their belongings. They just had their coats on and off they went."

"Isn't it strange that a schoolteacher would be engaged in this type of activity?" Goldman said.

"Pat told me she was a schoolteacher, but I didn't really believe it," Costa said. "She didn't seem to have a vocation of any kind."

"What about the other one," Goldman said, "the college girl."

"Not really," Costa said. "They said they were twenty-three years old, and that didn't appear to me to be much of a college age."

"When was the next time you saw the girls?" Goldman said.

"The girls returned about ten minutes later. I had straightened things out in my room and we simply passed greetings. I sort of sat around doing nothing really. They did go up to their room; then they came down and we all went out to the Royal Coachman —that's right on the Provincetown-Truro line."

From his talk with Bernie Flynn, Cavanaugh had learned that the girls had been killed around one o'clock on Saturday afternoon. "What time was this?" Cavanaugh said.

"Just before noon."

"Who drove the car?" Goldman said.

"Pat did," Costa said. "First we went out to a wooded area in Truro where she explained this deal that was coming in; for some reason her car was going to be left there. She said she would call me in a day or two and let me know when to take the car to Boston so I could pick up my merchandise. She would call me at my mother's, she said. And I couldn't see any reason for going out to this particular area; it came as a total bewilderment to me. And I simply asked her what the purpose to this was. She said if I didn't mind, she would rather not say, except that I would be able to pick up my stuff when I brought the car to Boston. So I didn't really think much of it, except why would she put the car out there."

Goldman was startled at the ease with which Costa placed himself at the scene of the murders.

"Then she knew the area?" Goldman said.

"I asked Pat what brought her to this area, how she knew about it," Costa said. "She said she had been there before, she said she liked the appearance of the road and what formed like a tunnel in the summer. She said quite a few of her friends from Providence had camped out there. She said she had spent a lot of time writing the inscriptions on the gravestones out there; she kept these sort of things in books."

"Weren't you surprised she went out to that area, because you had at one time a marijuana patch there?" Goldman said.

"I was quite surprised. This is why I asked her, because it sort of shocked me," Costa said. "My marijuana patch was there two years ago; I haven't been out to that place for a long time. Where she parked the car wasn't exactly where I had it. She did mention the cemetery, and that was very close to it, like halfway between both points. I didn't really think much of it."

"How long did you stay there?" Cavanaugh said.

"We just drove into this little area off the side of the dirt road and she said this spot is where we'll park the car. So I was bewildered and just said OK. She backed the car out again, and away we went."

"Where did you go?" Goldman said.

"We went to the Royal Coachman," Costa said. "I got out of the car and knocked on the trailer door where the main boss, John Taylor was, and asked him for my check."

"Did he see the girls in the car?"

"If he looked out the trailer window he did," Costa said. "He told me that the foreman, Roger Nunes, had my check; he was down in the excavation. Roger told me he had given my paycheck to Jimmy Zacharias who is one of the construction workers. So we drove back into town and went to Zack's house. His girlfriend said Zack was out riding a motorcycle. And at that very instant we both happened to look out the window and Zack was going around the corner. So I ran downstairs and jumped into the car and asked the girls if they minded if we chased him. And they were all for it. They said, 'Good, it's OK with us.' So we went around the corner and followed him down Bradford Street to the intersection of Conwell where we hailed him. I asked him for my check at that time."

"Did you introduce him to the girls?" Goldman said.

"Yes, I believe I did. I usually introduce people I'm with. I asked him for my check and he took it out of his wallet and gave it to me; it was for the large amount of thirty-six dollars. At that time I bid him adieu. He got back on his motorcycle and drove off. The girls and I drove to Center Street, right by the Chrysler Art Museum and down Commercial Street. I got out at Adams Pharmacy. And the girls drove off; they just went on their way.

"I waved to them and went into Adams and had a vanilla frappe. I left Adams after talking to Ethel Ross, who was working there, and walked up to my mom's for lunch. My oldest boy, Peter, was there. I stayed most of the day with him. We made puzzles, colored pictures in his coloring books and watched bowling on TV. About three o'clock Peter and I went to the Laundromat for my mother and came back about four o'clock. I stayed there with my little boy until roughly seven o'clock; then I left. I met Sandy Carter and Tommy Russe on their bicycles heading downtown. We spent the rest of the night at the Foc's'le bar until it closed. There was a tremendous crowd there, it seemed just like summertime. After a while I noticed Pat and Mary Anne sitting with two other girls at a table directly across from us."

"Did you go over and see Pat?" Goldman said.

"No, there was a table down the center of the Foc's'le which divided us; there were too many people in between. I don't think they noticed me at all. Pat and Mary Anne left roughly around eleven o'clock, or maybe shortly before."

"They didn't say goodbye to you?" Goldman said.

"No, they didn't even look my way."

"They had your nine hundred dollars though," Goldman said.

"Right," Costa said. "They went out into the street. I saw

them waving to someone. I think they might have hollered, but I couldn't see to who, or hear what they said."

"Where was their car, as far as you know?"

"I didn't see their automobile at all. It was not in sight. They just started walking toward the center of town."

"Was that the last time you saw them that night?" Goldman said.

"That was the last time I saw them *ever,*" Costa said. "Tommy, Sandy and I stayed at the Foc's'le until closing time at midnight. Then we went to Sheiky's and watched TV and listened to some Dylan records until approximately two in the morning."

"When you left there, did you leave alone?" Cavanaugh asked.

"Sandy came with me. She rode her bike to her house on Conant Street."

"So we can confirm this with Sandy Carter, that you were with her to about 2 A.M. ?"

"Yeah," Costa said.

"Tell us how you acquired the automobile," Goldman said.

"Well, I hadn't heard from the girls since Saturday night," Costa said. "I was wondering if they had met who they were going to meet, what they had done or what was happening. I was waiting the next few days for some word from them."

"Weren't you *surprised?*" Goldman said. "Here they had your money, two perfect strangers, and you hadn't heard from them."

"Surprised?" Costa said, "I was *shocked.* I didn't really know what to think."

"And their car," Goldman said. "You didn't know where their car was?"

"They said they were going to leave the car out at Hatch Road, but I hadn't been out there because I had no transportation. The next thing I know—it was either on a Tuesday or Wednesday night—someone called my mother's while I was there after suppertime. She gave me the phone and said it was some guy."

"Who was the guy on the phone?" Cavanaugh said.

"It was Chuck—'Buddy' Hansen. He seemed very tense. He said he had to have the car, that he needed it desperately. He wanted me to bring the car to Boston that night. I told him I was tired, that I didn't really feel like it; but he begged and said please, so I said, 'OK, I'll try.' It was about nine o'clock. I went downtown to see if I could find anyone who could drive the car to Boston, because I didn't have a license. I stayed downtown until eleven or so looking for a ride. I was in a phone booth calling my brother to ask him if anyone had been there—"

"How did Chuck know your brother?" Cavanaugh said.

"He had Vinnie's address. The girls, I reckon, had given it to him. I was told this was where I was supposed to bring the car, to 415 Beacon Street."

"Did you know where the car was at the time you talked to Chuck?" Cavanaugh said.

"He told me it was where it was preplanned to be at Hatch Road, so I just supposed it would be there. He informed me I had better get some gas," Costa said. "I met Steve Grund and Timmy Atkins on the street. I asked Steve if he would drive to Boston and he accepted. We all went to my room and I asked one of the guys living upstairs if they could give us a ride to where the car was. Before we left I called Russell Watts and asked him if he could sell me a can of gas."

"Was it the girls' intention to leave the car at Hatch Road for Chuck or for you?" Cavanaugh said.

"I don't really know if it was their intention. They had definitely made plans with *someone,* and it wasn't with *me* they made the plans for the purpose of leaving the car there. I was simply to take the car to Boston when they called me so I could pick up my stuff."

"The reason I ask, Tony, is that Hatch Road is quite a bit out of the way. If the girls left the car there, they would have to have some mode of transportation back," Cavanaugh pointed out. "They never indicated what their reason was?"

"I found out when I got to Boston what the reason was," Costa said. "It was that this Hansen, or someone, had left a great amount of dope in the car."

"Doesn't it seem strange to leave a car out in the middle of nowhere with heroin in it?" Cavanaugh said. "Wouldn't that attract attention?"

"Yes, it would attract attention. This is why I couldn't understand it."

"Isn't it rather unusual to give a girl whom you have never met before nine hundred dollars upon her representation there was going to be delivered to you a quarter pound of heroin?" Goldman said.

171

"It wasn't strange for me to give out that much money, because this summer in Boston this was the usual thing," Costa said. "I was always giving out money for hashish to sell, where you really didn't know who anybody was. And in getting the merchandise I would give out five or six hundred dollars at a time—this was in cash."

"It seems like a strange way of doing business to me," Cavanaugh said.

"Except, I suppose, in dealing with this type of merchandise," Goldman said.

"I would think you have the stuff, I give you the money and you hand me the stuff right then and there," Cavanaugh persisted.

"The thing is, I am a *stranger,*" Costa said. "Like this fellow Dan . . . my hash connection—I never got his last name. I saw him on three occasions. But if you approach a stranger who is dealing in some illegal thing such as this, he doesn't know if you are working for the police or something. So the chances are he will never hand anything directly to you at that time. Instead, he will take your money, and tell you to come to this place where you can pick up your stuff. That way it's out of his hands; you don't even see him."

"Don't you agree that this Chuck Hansen plays an important part in this case as it affects you?" Goldman said.

"Yes, he does," Costa said. "If I could find Chuck Hansen, I wouldn't be in this place at all."

"Why do you say that, Tony?" Cavanaugh said.

"Because right now he's out there evidently running around with my money. This whole thing is *his* fault! I mean, I know I've done things wrong, I admit to that, but—"

"What have you done wrong, other than dealing with the subject matter of this heroin?" Goldman said, a little sharply. "You told us emphatically that you had nothing to do with killing these girls; that you had nothing to do with these girls' being injured in any way—"

"No, nothing whatsoever!" Costa said. "I don't have anything to do with that. But I feel that I have done wrong in . . . getting myself into this dope thing. Because if I didn't get myself into that, then perhaps the girls would not have had anything to do with this other fellow."

"Well, if you didn't kill them, you have nothing to be fearful of," Goldman said. "Am I correct in that?"

"True," Costa said.

"Suppose—for the record—you give us a description of Chuck Hansen."

"He's got blondish-red curly hair," Costa said. "I don't know if you're familiar with Bob Dylan, but it's long, curly hair and sticks out like so. I don't recall the color of his eyes, but he's got sort of a madly freckled complexion. He stands about five feet ten, he's only a little bit shorter than I am. He appeared a bit chubby to me. When I saw him he had on dungarees and a maroon jacket that came down to his waist. It had an insignia on it; I thought it might be a college jacket of some kind. I don't know where he lives. I do know this much: he made runs from Providence to New York. This was told me by the girls. He got the stuff in New York and from there he went different places doing different things. He has spent some time on the Lower East Side of New York, which is down in Greenwich Village. I know he was there; he spoke of it. And he spoke of his car. He had some kind of car he called, 'Baby Blue.' He talked about it three or four times, how it could lick anything on Cape Cod. And to me this became boring, because to me a car is a machine, with four wheels and an engine and that's all."

"When were your conversations with Chuck?" Goldman said.

"I spoke to him in Boston, and on the telephone."

"You never saw him in Provincetown?" Cavanaugh said.

"No, I didn't ever see him myself in Provincetown. I'm pretty sure Herbie Dam might have seen him. I think it was Herbie or someone, came up to me and said Chuck was looking for me."

"Well, we've gotten pretty far off the subject," Goldman said, shifting in his chair. "I still don't have it clear in my mind how you ended up with a car out of this heroin deal." Goldman had brought along two "Attorney's Daybooks" for the years 1968 and 1969 in which he wanted Costa to record, as accurately as he could remember, the events which had led up to his arrest.

Cavanaugh added, "In the next few days, Tony, will you see if you can set down in sequence those events that led to the car being left in the woods you eventually picked up? See if you can reflect a little bit more on that. You can appreciate that the one thing the district attorney can tie you in with is that car. Now we want a reasonable explanation, something we will be able to sell to a jury, so that the facts will be clear the next time we visit."

Before Goldman left, he tore a page from a memo pad upon which he had scrawled a statement for Antone Costa to sign:

> I desire to retain as my attorney Maurice Goldman to be assisted by Justin Cavanaugh, both of Brewster, Mass. I do not have sufficient funds and need the help of others. In fact, I have no money except $15 which is at the bank of the hospital.
> I don't want the public defender. I want an experienced lawyer, and I want attorney Goldman.

The two lawyers did not discuss the interview until they had been escorted out of the prison ward. Antone Costa had impressed Cavanaugh as a personable and articulate young man. Despite his arrest and incarceration, he appeared to be in command of himself. Costa tended to become entangled in unnecessary details while relating his puzzling story to the point of being downright confusing, Cavanaugh said, "But then, I suppose, he's pretty scared."

"Of *course,* he's scared," Goldman said agreeably. "You'd be scared, too, if you'd killed four people."

10

Goldman rose early on Sunday morning. Glancing through the *New York Times,* he was disquieted by a brief news story reporting that associate medical examiner Dr. Michael Baden had called on New York City police to reopen their investigation into the suicide the previous November of Christine Gallant, on the basis of her "possible involvement" with Antone Costa, charged with the murders of two young women on Cape Cod. Costa had exchanged visits with the nineteen-year-old library clerk at Columbia University before she was found in a partly-filled bathtub, dead from an overdose of barbiturates.

Joined by Cavanaugh, Goldman drove to Provincetown to talk to Steve Grund, who had already been questioned by police.

A slender young man, with a red headband tied across his forehead to keep his shoulder-length hair out of his eyes, Grund was respectful and friendly. He and Timmy Atkins had met Tony Costa on a Sunday evening around eleven o'clock and had agreed to drive a blue Volkswagen to Boston. Costa had assured them the car was "legally mine," but Grund had had his doubts about the car being "hot." Grund didn't touch the car until Tony Costa had his fingerprints all over it.

"Timmy and I asked him, 'Do you have the keys?' Tony said, 'Yeah, I got them right here,' and slapped his pocket. He put the key in the door lock and it opened. After Tony tested the ignition, we started looking for the gas tank. We thought it might be in the trunk."

"What was in the trunk?" Goldman said.

"There was a quilt and a package in a brown paper bag up toward the right-hand corner."

"What was in the bag?" Goldman said. Grund appeared to be corroborating a crucial point in Costa's story.

"I haven't any idea. We didn't look in the bag."

"Was there a note on the windshield of the car?" Cavanaugh said.

"No, I didn't see anything like that."

"Did you have any further conversation with Tony about the automobile?" Goldman said.

"When I asked him how he gained possession of the car, Tony said he had sold two girls from Providence a pound of hashish, but they couldn't come up with the bread right then. He said they had to split town suddenly, so he paid them two or three hundred dollars in addition to the price of the hash, and they gave him a bill of sale for the car. A little later he told me he had paid five hundred dollars for the pound of hash he sold to them for seven hundred."

"Did Tony mention a 'Chuck' or 'Buddy' Hansen?"

"Not that I remember."

"Was anybody waiting for Tony when you arrived in Boston?"

"I don't recall seeing anyone."

"What about the package in the trunk? What did you do with that? Did you take the package up to the apartment?"

"Tony asked Vinnie if he wanted him to bring in a TV set he'd picked up at the dump. Whether Tony brought the TV or the package upstairs, I don't know. We didn't carry nothing in. It was between three or four A.M.—we were tired."

Grund had returned to Provincetown by air the next morning. "The plan was, if Tony could get the car registered, he and Timmy would drive back. I saw Timmy on Tuesday. He said he had taken the bus. He said, 'Tony's back, too.' Tony had called the registry. He couldn't get the car registered, so they left it in Boston."

"What did Timmy and Tony do in Boston, do you know?"

"Weed said they got a bunch of speed and spent the whole night—it was the night of a storm—riding around in the car. Weed said, 'I might buy a gun from Tony, a .22 caliber.' I told him not to, that it might be hot."

"When was this?" Cavanaugh said.

"A couple days after I drove to Boston."

"Did you ever hear anything more about the gun?" Goldman said.

"The next day Tony said he was going to split town. He asked *me*, 'Hey Steve, do you want to buy a gun?' I said, 'Is that the gun you were going to sell Weed?' Tony said it was; he said he buried it in the woods in Truro. I told him 'That's a good place for it.' "

Costa had left town again the next morning, Grund recalled. "Apparently he went back to Boston and drove the car to Vermont. The next I heard from him was after he talked to the police. Tony came over on his bike, real friendly-like."

"What did he say, if you remember?"

"Tony knocked at my door. Man, was he scared! He said he had been talking to the cops for six hours straight. He'd called his mother from Burlington and she told him the cops were looking for him. He called Jimmy Meads—that's a cop he knows—and agreed to come in voluntarily to talk about what he knew about two missing girls. Tony said the cops started hassling him real bad. Like putting words in his mouth and asking the same questions over and over. Tony said he was going to meet the girls in Canada, but he'd gone to Burlington first."

Costa had said, "Well, guys, I have to run outside. I got a bag of stuff I don't want anybody to take." He had returned with a paper bag from which he took a new pair of pliers and three screwdrivers, explaining, "I've been collecting all new tools to replace the ones that got stolen." When Costa removed a plastic pillbox, he said, "This is my suicide kit."

"What was that again?" Goldman said.

"Tony showed us his 'suicide kit,'" Grund said. "There were twelve pills for him to take all at once—four Nembutals, four Tuinals and four something else—definitely an overdose. Tony said, 'All these hassles with the cops I'm getting, this is just in case they try to pick me up for something. If they hassle me too much, I don't have to worry. I just drop these and it will be all over.' He said the cops had told him he was under suspicion of murder."

"Did you ever hear anything more about the gun?"

"The day before yesterday some detectives came by. They said, 'You bought a gun, where did you hide it?' I told them, 'I didn't buy any gun!' They really threatened to bust me. Two or three days they've come and knocked at my door and just walked in whether they were invited or not. Like yesterday, I was taken down to the police station and they started in about the gun again."

Grund had also been followed by investigators. "I think they were federal men. I went to Wellfleet to pick up five tabs of acid and the guy I was with said, 'Do you know you're being followed?' And it was a couple of agents in a green Ford."

"Did Tony ever show you his stash places in the woods?" Cavanaugh said.

"No, I was never out there; I knew about it, though. He talked about how he had hidden some stuff out there."

"Did you ever observe anything about Tony that would indicate mental illness?" Goldman said.

"He could be schizoid," Grund said, thoughtfully. "Three or four weeks before we went to Boston, Tony came to me and said, 'Steve, I'm really screwed up. I've got to get off these downs, man. I'm so strung out I don't know what I'm doing any more. What day is it?'" When Grund told him, "It's Friday," Costa had said, "Oh, no, it *can't* be! Tomorrow's Tuesday!"

"He'd lost a whole week," Grund said.

Grund recalled another occasion, when Timmy Atkins had visited Tony Costa several days after the trip to Boston. "Weed told me he went over to Tony's house to turn him on to some pot and there was mud all over Tony's clothes and everything. Tony said, 'I got hung up and walked all the way to Wellfleet.' " The night Grund had driven the Volkswagen to Boston, he had observed a book on the night table beside Costa's bed. "It was called *Psychology and Psychoneurosis*—something like that. Tony was always reading psychology and medical books."

"Did you ever see Tony violent or aggressive?" Cavanaugh said.

"The only time I ever saw Tony violent was when he had some liquid morphine stashed and somebody emptied the morphine out and replaced it with water. He asked me if I knew anything about it. He was real upset because, he said, 'You just don't *do* that to people!' Tony said if he found the guy who did it, he'd kill him."

"You say Tony was using morphine?" Goldman said.

"Yeah, he was punching morphine."

"He's denied that," Goldman said. "They checked his arms at Bridgewater—no needle marks anywhere."

"Well, check his legs," Grund said. "I'm almost positive he was using a syringe."

"How long have you known Tony?" Cavanaugh said.

"Three months."

"What do you really know about a person you have known for only three months?"

"I know he wouldn't lift anything from me," Grund said. "I heard Tony had forged some checks, but I know he wouldn't steal anything of mine."

On the evening Costa had come to Grund's apartment after talking with police, he had admired a knife from Grund's collection.

"Where did you get this?" Costa had said.

"I got it when I was in California," Grund had told him. "It was under the front seat of my car; the cops found it the day I got busted."

Costa had turned the knife over in his hand. "How much do you want for it?"

"I don't want to sell it," Grund said. "Too many memories."

"I have a real thing about knives lately," Costa had told

178

Grund. "There's something about them that's fascinating. Just beautiful."

Grund excused himself to answer the door. He brought Timmy Atkins into the room.

Goldman asked Atkins, "Did Tony leave the apartment at any time the day you were in Boston with him?"

"When he took Steve to the airport, that was in the morning; then he came back. We just sat in the apartment all day and watched TV." Vinnie Bonaviri had sold the television set, giving Tony one hundred dollars that afternoon and another fifty dollars more that night. "Then Tony and his brother and his brother's girlfriend, we all went down to get something to eat at the Cross-roads restaurant; then we came back to the apartment and watched TV."

"Did Tony try to sell you a gun?" Goldman said.

"Yeah, he did," Atkins said. "He asked me did I want to buy a .22 automatic pistol."

"Did you tell the police this?" Goldman said.

"Yeah."

"What did they ask you about specifically?"

"All's they've been bugging me about is that gun," Atkins said. "They keep on trying to make me say that I bought it. But I never got the gun. I didn't even *see* the gun. I don't know where it is."

"Can you think of anything else that might be useful in Tony's defense?" Cavanaugh said.

"All I know is that he is a darned good guy," Grund said. "And this is really a botched-up thing, all the rumors."

Getting up to leave, Goldman asked Grund, "Do you know Tony's former wife?"

"Yeah, I've met her."

"How would would you evaluate her?"

"Well, I worked as a part-time private detective in Holly-wood before I came east," Grund said. "I think I have a fair estimate of her. She's a very defensive person. Whether Tony is right or wrong, she will still defend him. Their friends say she was afraid of him, but I don't think so."

179

11

Avis Costa did not appear to Goldman to be the kind of young woman who was afraid of anything. He interviewed her in his car, parked in front of a large, shabby house converted to apartments at 364 Commercial Street. She was a tall young woman, almost wraithlike, pale and worn, her fine, transparent skin hollowed and pinched beneath sharp cheekbones. Born in Fall River, Massachusetts, on October 15, 1948, she had lived in Provincetown all her life. Her parents had separated when she was two years old.

"It was funny," Avis said. "I met my father in 1967. It was a day when Tony had packed up and left. My father just stayed a couple of days. He died two weeks after he visited me."

She had known Antone Costa from the time when he had come to Provincetown summers as a youth. "Tony was a senior at Provincetown High School when I started going around with him. I was thirteen years old," Avis said. "Yes, that's right," she added with a crooked-toothed grin at Goldman's startled expression.

"Who signed for you when you got married?" Goldman said.

"My mother signed."

"Were you pregnant?"

"Yeah, but it wasn't quite that way," Avis said. "I got pregnant because we wanted to get married. We started going together in April, and all that summer and into the winter we stayed together. When we asked my mother's consent to marry, she said no. So we decided I was going to get pregnant. We went out every day before I went to school and every day after school . . . every chance we got. Sometimes we'd go down below the dump and sometimes out to Pilgrim Spring. I didn't know anything; Tony taught me everything I know about sex. Like he told me about the rhythm system; that's how I got pregnant."

Avis had been fourteen, a high honors freshman at Provincetown High School when she had married on April 20, 1963. Five months later a first child, Peter, was born.

180

"What kind of a person was Tony when you got married?" Goldman said.

"He was different than he is now. He was quiet, but interesting. We didn't argue very much the first year. I'd say we got along just fine. I think he was very fond of the children. My feeling is that he cared—everything Tony felt was *deep*, but he didn't put on a show. Except for the baby; he cares about the baby mostly. He wanted a girl, so he is especially fond of the baby." Tony had chosen the name, Nico; Avis registered the child as Nicole.

"Tell us something about his disposition." Goldman said. "How he behaved, his moods, things like that."

"You mean at first, or later?" Avis said. "Tony changed after he started on drugs. I think he's schizophrenic, because when he got mad—*really* mad—and showed any kind of violence, he was like a different person. But he got over it fast; then, he wouldn't admit that he had ever been sore."

"What was likely to make him mad?" Cavanaugh said.

"Like if he was picked on or aggravated; like if anyone persisted in bothering him. If Tony thought he was right in an argument and someone disagreed, he'd flip. He never admitted he was ever wrong about anything. He was the sole judge himself of everything. But when he was being nice—and I think he was nice most of the time—he was like a different person. He wrote things, he played the harmonica, and he painted—I should say, sketched. Mostly psychological sketches. The titles were always really deep. It wasn't professional work, you know."

"Since you're divorced, you must have fallen out of love with him." Cavanaugh said gently.

"It wasn't like that," Avis said. "I still feel pretty deeply for him. I would say we were better friends than mates. Tony liked to do his own thing. He would go out by himself and walk around. He didn't like to answer questions about what he did."

"Didn't you find that upsetting?" Cavanaugh said. "Did you quarrel a lot about that?"

"No, I don't think so. Tony would leave, then come back later. We separated lots of times. Last January, when he left to go to California, we decided we wouldn't go back together."

"Is that when he started using drugs?" Goldman said.

"Tony didn't use drugs until the summer of 1965. We had some friends who were using drugs before that and Tony was against it. He kept warning them it was dangerous. The first time he used drugs that I remember was when he went to Dr. Callis who gave him pills that were getting him stoned. Like the first time he used them we were eating dessert, and he didn't have enough strength to pick up a spoon. He nearly fell out of his chair."

"Why did Tony go to Dr. Callis?" Goldman said.

"He was getting very nervous, he had trouble sleeping, he couldn't sit still—and we weren't getting along."

"Could you tell when Tony was using drugs?"

"It was very hard to tell with Tony. He looked straight even when he wasn't. On acid sometimes you could spot it; but he wasn't much on acid. The only thing was, when he didn't take drugs he would sit squeezing one hand with the other, really nervous. And he would bite his fingernails. He could bite his toenails, too. He could put his feet up to his mouth. When he wasn't stoned he was just impossible! I don't think he could stand to be around himself when he was straight. Like I'd say to him, 'Jesus Christ, Tony, will you go get stoned, smoke or do something!' When Tony was stoned he was always in a good mood; he was jovial, people could be around him. Toward the end when we weren't together any more, I just never saw him straight. Every time I saw him he was stoned on something."

"Did you know Christine Gallant?" Goldman said.

"Yes, I knew Chris when she worked on the cosmetics counter at Adams Pharmacy. She was a pretty girl, very mature-looking for her age; she looked around twenty-three or twenty-four. She would call Tony up, and I used to say, 'He's not here,' or 'I'll give you a number where you can reach him,' and we'd talk and she'd say, 'It's really strange; you're just so nice about the whole thing.'"

"Didn't it bother you, a girl calling up Tony?" Cavanaugh said. "You were still married."

"No, we were just living together then," Avis said. "I didn't care what he was doing."

"Did Christine use drugs?" Goldman said.

"Pills mostly, whatever the group was using. She was pretty messed up. She was going with Raul Matta; and I guess she loved him. But she was going with Tony, too; and she loved Tony. He used to call her up and sometimes Raul would be there and they wouldn't meet. Sometimes Tony would be there and Raul would show up and Tony would have to leave.

"One time Tony went to see her when she was living in Hyannis and working at King's department store. And he got back at three o'clock in the morning. I asked him why he didn't stay over. He said that Raul had showed up and Chris thought it would be better if Tony left. Like, Chris lived with Raul sometimes; then he'd leave her. He always left her hanging. Tony told me Raul used to beat her up. He was always afraid Raul was going to beat her up."

"Tony was in love with her?" Cavanaugh said. "He was emotionally involved?"

"Oh, yes," Avis said, "Very much so."

"Was Tony in Provincetown when Christine died in New York?" Goldman said.

"Yes, he was. The night before Chris died, Tony came to my apartment and he was very calm and seemed happy. The next day he came over, all upset. I looked at him and said, 'What's wrong.' And he completely broke down. He was crying and shaking. I guess it was her roommate told him Chris was dead; she drowned in her bathtub. It threw him. He was almost out of his mind with grief. He kept saying he wished he had stayed with her; that if he had stayed with her it would never have happened. He had said right along he was going to marry her. I told him, 'You know you can't be married until February, because our divorce isn't final until then.' And he said he didn't care. He wanted to marry her anyway. They were supposed to have gotten married at Christmas. He asked if we'd drive him to Fall River to go to her funeral, because he had lost his license."

Goldman hesitated, silently appraising the young woman half-turned to face him in the front seat of the car. "We need your best recollection concerning what may be a delicate subject with you," Goldman said. "The area of sexual abnormalities . . . Tony's sexual hang-ups, so to speak. Can you tell us anything about that?"

"Those things happened way back—I'm trying to remember —back in 1964," Avis said. "Tony used to tell me when he lived in Somerville, the crowd he went around with. He said at parties everyone ran around naked and the boys would make the girls pass out, so the boys could do certain things. He said it was a normal kind of thing and he wanted me to try that with him. Once, he held my face in a pillow because he wanted me to pass out. I'd just about get to the point where I'd pass out and I couldn't do it. We argued a lot about it; we'd have big fights about it and everything. Once or twice he held a plastic bag over my face. He didn't pull it over my head, he just held it on my face so I couldn't breathe. I'd get to the point where I'd start to fight for air and I'd rip it off and he'd get really mad. But he never *forced* me . . . it was always with my consent. Like every night he'd want to do it because we never really were successful at it. So if he'd fall asleep early, I was so uptight, I'd set all the clocks ahead to early-morning hours. I'd wake him up and tell him it was really late and maybe we should save it for the next night. Then I'd get up in the morning before him and set all the clocks back again. Finally, I got so disgusted fighting about it, I went into the bathroom and took some chloral hydrate to make myself pass out."

"Knockout drops!" Goldman said. "Where did you get them?"

"Tony had some from a taxidermy kit; the stuff was supposed to knock out animals. Tony found me and took me to Dr. Hiebert. They tried to say it was a suicide attempt. I was fifteen years old."

"How did *you* explain it?" Cavanaugh said.

"The only thing I told my family was that I was really tired, that I hadn't been getting any sleep and I knew it was something to make me sleep; I just didn't know how much to take," Avis said. "Tony said the police came and took fingerprints from the bottle and pictures of the place and everything. I don't know how true it is. I guess if I had died, Tony would have been charged with manslaughter."

"When did he start experimenting in the sexual area?" Goldman said.

"When we were first married he was still pretty interested in sex. It was just conventional, just very brief foreplay; then the act itself—it never lasted very long, and nothing after that. We'd just go to sleep. It was just touch, stimulation that way. No oral stimulation; because I don't really like the idea of that. I don't mind a chick doing it to a guy; but a guy doing it to a chick really turns me off. Because it's kind of a messy situation. I think Tony probably felt the same way.

"It was after Peter was born that he started these diversions, or whatever you call them. Like he found a wooden phallus, I don't know where. We talked over how it looked and everything; so then he decided he wanted to do it to me. I thought it was crazy; I thought it was really stupid. But I let him do it anyway. I

184

don't know what pleasure he got out of that, unless probably it was bigger than him. *I* didn't get very much pleasure out of it."

"There are stories around that he used to burn you with lighted cigarettes . . ." Goldman said.

"That's not true, it never happened! Tony never used cigarettes to burn me at any time," Avis said. "There was a story around town that he tied me to the bed—that's not true either.

"There was something similar to that. There was a hook in the ceiling of our bedroom and Tony said that if he hung me head downward, the blood would rush to my head and I would feel high. I let him do that. He tied my feet with a rope and then hung me from the hook by a chain. And he would masturbate himself just on to me, or have me masturbate him. I did it to get it over with; it didn't excite me. I didn't feel anything one way or the other. Tony would hang himself up that way, too. We did this three or four times; then I refused to do it any more. It seemed foolish. I really didn't know much about sex, but from what I did know it seemed like a very abnormal thing to do. I thought it was perverse. For a while it seemed that's all we ever did. We never had actual relations; all I did was masturbate him. Or he'd kneel down by the side of the bed and like rub my body while I was lying there. When he felt like he was almost ready to come, then I would do it. I just got more and more turned off to him all the time. I just didn't want anything to do with him."

"He did not have an active sex life, then?" Goldman said.

"It was kind of like that all the time we were married. Except once in a while he'd get really demanding and say, 'You're my wife and I want to fuck you'—like that. And in between there was nothing. I didn't know if he had any sexual desire at all, or whether he just had a very perverse sexual desire and didn't know how to *do* anything. Like he seemed to avoid touching me for some reason. It was like, I don't know, sometimes I felt he saw me way above him, like he just couldn't approach me. Like on the surface he would say I was very loose and promiscuous, but actually feeling that I was very pure, and that he shouldn't kiss me at all."

"*Were* you promiscuous?" Goldman ventured.

"Yeah . . . I suppose. I dig people a lot easier than he does. Like while he was in California that winter, there were guys coming over all the time. That was when I was going out with Jay Von Utter."

"Was Tony jealous?" Goldman said. "You were apparently interested in other men."

"When we were first married he was jealous, but when he started taking drugs, he became unusually passive. Tony had very strong feelings about girls that ran around and just gave themselves to anybody. He talked a lot about his feelings about women. He thought that a woman should be a woman and that she was degrading herself by going to bed with guys. He wanted me to feel ashamed for whatever I was doing, like my promiscuity. I think he was trying to degrade me in his own way, trying to make me think I was doing wrong."

"Did he ever threaten to harm you, or to kill you?" Goldman said.

"No, I don't ever remember any time he threatened that. If he got mad he would go out and walk on the beach or in the woods. One time I wasn't having intercourse with him, and he threw me down on the bed and took me forcibly—but I *was* his wife," she explained. "The only threat he ever made was that he would talk to my social worker and have the Division of Child Guardianship watch me and take the kids away if I wasn't behaving in a proper manner to suit him. He *did* hit me once, from behind, the back of the head. I was really shocked."

"Can you remember anything about Tony's attitude toward violence?" Cavanaugh said.

"He didn't like violence, or the sight of blood—anything like that. We went to see a move called *Two Thousand Maniacs*. We thought it was going to be a comedy, but it turned out to be a very gruesome horror story—and it was in color. There was one scene where these guys tied a girl down on a table and chopped her arms off. And like you could see the whole thing, the veins and everything. It really nauseated him. We had to leave the theater; he couldn't stand it. Tony went outside to the car and was really sick. He thought he was going to have a heart attack."

"You have not during this time referred to Tony's mother," Goldman said. "How did he get along with her? How did *you* get along with her?"

"Tony loves his mother, but he always felt that she interfered in his life too much," Avis said. "I got along with her very well. I still do; I see her all the time."

"Would you like to go to see her today with us?" Goldman said.

"Yes, very much," Avis said. "I'll take the baby along."

Avis got out of the car, started to walk away, returned and, with her hand on the door, leaned forward and said, "One thing I wish you would do when you see Tony. Tell him I had the newspapers spread out on the bed and the baby went over and saw his picture in the paper. She put her finger on the picture and said, 'Daddy! Daddy! Daddy!'"

12

Gray-haired and frail, with dark circles under her eyes, Cecelia Bonaviri was under sedation prescribed for her by Dr. Hiebert. Presently on welfare, she worked as a chambermaid and cleaning lady during the summer tourist season, when she was physically able.

Mrs. Bonaviri had refused to talk to the press about her son. "I have no comments," she said. "I'm not feeling good and I don't want to be bothered." She had also refused to speak to Bernie Flynn when he had come to her apartment the previous day.

"My sister Lucy was here," Mrs. Bonaviri told Goldman when he took a place on the sofa of a small, cluttered but immaculate living room. "The detective starting asking all kinds of questions. I told him Tony had done nothing wrong. The police, they've been after my Tony since he worked for them. All he wanted to do was to fix up this dope business; and from then on they've been after him. They haven't left him alone. I told the lieutenant I didn't want to say anything, that my lawyer advised me not to talk to the police. I brought a telegram Tony got from the girls to Chief Marshall. He said Tony sent it to himself; he asked me where Tony was. I told him he was in Boston with his brother. And Mr. Marshall didn't believe me."

She had been married to Antone Costa, Sr., a handsome carpenter's mate in the navy, for sixteen years before Tony was born. "Tony always said he remembered his father's funeral, the casket, the flowers, being carried by his Uncle Manuel . . . everything. When he was seven he told me a man would visit him at night and talk to him. I showed him a picture of his father and Tony said that was the man." Costa had treasured the navy letter of commendation for bravery his father had been awarded posthumously and used to carry it with him to show school friends. He had kept a trunk of his father's uniforms and war souvenirs in his room. "Tony grew a mustache because his father had one. He wanted to learn carpentry because that was his father's trade. I think he missed his father very much." When Tony married, she had turned over to him four hundred fifty dollars worth of savings bonds, and two thousand dollars saved from his father's ten-thousand-dollar government insurance policy.

Raised a Catholic, she told Goldman, Tony had attended catechism classes, taken first communion and been confirmed in the church. He had done well in school, receiving a commendation "for splendid cooperation and honesty" from the headmaster of Western Junior High School in Somerville. From the age of twelve, he had handled all the bookkeeping, correspondence and tax returns for his stepfather's masonry business. Tony had worked at odd jobs to earn money to maintain his first car—a red-and-white Pontiac Bonneville she had indulged him by buying when he was sixteen. Following the breakup of her second marriage, she had moved back to Provincetown to be near her family.

Mrs. Bonaviri's eyes filled when she brought out an album of photographs, showing Goldman a bright-eyed, handsome boy of ten, wearing a cowboy shirt with a necktie knotted at his throat.

Yet Costa did not look very happy standing in the back row of the stage crew for the senior class play—the only photograph of him to appear in the *Long Pointer* yearbook. He was one of forty graduates of the class of 1962, whose graduation had been held in the town hall's second floor auditorium, above the courtroom where Costa had been arraigned. A snapshot showed the tassle of a tilted mortar board falling into Tony's eyes as he accepted a diploma with a shy smile. Mrs. Bonaviri had also saved the yellow commencement program that had appeared in the Provincetown *Advocate,* along with coverage of the event by Kathy Reise, PHS correspondent: "Without exception, we know that every graduate will have a happy and successful future."

When Mrs. Bonaviri was joined by her son Vincent, Cathy Roche and Matt Russe, Goldman said, "Do you know anything about a bow and arrow incident that occurred several years ago with a young girl?"

"I don't know where the newspapers get all the crap they print," Vinnie said angrily. "This was just a target arrow with a round point Tony was using. He went out there to practice target shooting; he had a hunting bow with a forty-pound pull. If he had been using hunting arrows the thing would have stuck in her back and killed her. The day after it happened the girl went to Doc Hiebert and there was a little scratch on her back that he covered up with a Band-Aid." Costa had sold the bow along with some skin-diving equipment. "He got rid of a lot of his stuff."

"Let's clear up this taxidermy business if we can," Goldman said.

"Ah, that's a lot of baloney!" Vinnie said. "He's no taxidermist—not amateur, not professional. He couldn't stuff a sausage."

"Tony sent away ten dollars for a mail order, but he didn't like it," Mrs. Bonaviri said. "It must have been ten years ago."

Dandling two-year-old Nicole on her lap, Avis recalled a stack of thin paperbound books on taxidermy Tony had owned when they were married. "And there was some tools, like a little scalpel to work on the heads of birds, to pick out the eyes or something. Tony lost interest in it before we met."

Goldman was especially concerned about police questioning Vinnie and Cathy in Boston. "What did you say to them with regard to the gun?"

"I told them I saw the gun once," Vinnie said. "Then later on I remembered that me and Matt went out to target-shoot, that was last November when I was living here at home. I bought a pack of fifty bullets, both shorts and longs. We went out to the place everyone goes to shoot, across from the Pilgrim Club on Shank Painter Road. There are empty packs all over the place. We fired the pistol and we also had a BB gun, and we plinked with that." Tony had once owned a single-shot rifle but had sold it. "We had a lot of guns. We'd buy them from a catalog."

"What happened to Tony's gun?"

"I heard he sold it to Gary Watts," Matt Russe said, "but Gary says no."

The police had already asked them about Tony's knife, Vinnie said. "Tony's father got the knife as a souvenir during the war and made a case for it. He either made the knife or the case, I'm not sure which."

"Did the police take anything that belonged to Tony from your apartment?" Goldman said.

"They took some pants I had given him, brownish with pink stripes. There was a rip in the leg my mother sewed. There was paint stains on them, but no bloodstains. And they took a leather vest and a sweater. The cops, I guess, have all the clothes he owned," Vinnie said. Police had also taken some rope. "Tony brought it with him to my place, window cord, I'd say it was, brand new."

The police had found a package of marijuana, Cathy added. "They said there was about a nickel in it."

On the day of Costa's arrest, three state police officers had come to Macey's liquor store on Canal Street near North Station. "They told me there was no trouble," Vinnie said. "They said, 'We're sick and tired of the car; we want to get it out of the compound.' They wanted to see Tony. I said I hadn't seen him. But the Monday before that when I got home from work Tony was there. He'd called me from Buffalo to ask for bus fare home. I sent seventy-five dollars on Sunday, March second to the LaFayette Square office from the main Western Union place in Boston. I asked the man how long it would take and he said Tony would get it at three-thirty."

"Did you ever give him any more money?" Goldman said.

"I gave him three hundred dollars so he could buy the car from two girls in Provincetown." The car had stayed in Boston for two days. "Then I think Tony drove it to Vermont. I'm not sure," Vinnie said. "After the cops came to my place and asked me if I had seen Tony, and I said no. Lieutenant Broderick called me up. He said, real sarcastic-like, 'Thanks a lot for the information about Tony.' I asked him what he meant. He said, 'We just picked him up at your apartment.' I said, 'What for?' And he said, 'Murder.'"

"Did you ever go out to the woods in Truro with Tony, to his so-called drug caches?" Goldman said.

"Never," Vinnie said. "I'll tell you the truth. I don't even know where his place in the woods is. A lot of people Tony knows, that he used to sell drugs to, like his good customers and his friends, know where that place is, a lot of bad people."

Avis knew the area. "We used to go parking there before we were married."

When Goldman and Cavanaugh left the apartment, Bernie Flynn was waiting to talk to Vincent Bonaviri and Matt Russe.

13

Flynn took Vincent Bonaviri's statement, then brought Matt Russe to the Provincetown police station for questioning. Then he and Gunnery were called to the Truro police station. Patrolman Harold Veara had received an anonymous telephone call from a young male, giving information about a white pillowcase containing, possibly, the murder weapon, to be found in the Truro woods.

Veara had gone into the woods. Under an oak tree within ten feet of the graves he found a Cannon-brand white pillowcase with "Kalmar Village," a cottage colony at Beach Point in Truro imprinted on its border. The pillowcase contained a fifty-seven inch length of chain with swivel snap hooks at each end and an "S" hook on the middle link for hanging a sign when used as a barrier. There was an empty physician's sample package of Triavil 2-10 tablets, and a fruit jar containing seven Remington .22 caliber short shells of the "Golden Bullet" variety.

Detective Lieutenant John Dunn returned to Cape Cod late Sunday night after a frustrating second journey to New York City to check on the telegram sent by "Pat Walsh." Primitivo Africa had not been home when Dunn called at his apartment. Dunn had gone to Bellion's Bar and Grill at 137 Court Street, Brooklyn—the location of a wall-mounted public telephone, number 852-9859. The number had been given to receiving Western Union operator Margaret Procino by either an assisting long-distance operator or the sender of a telegram to Antone Costa on Sunday, March 2, at 12:05 P.M.

Bellion's did not open until 1 P.M. on Sunday, according to the proprietor, Louis Bellion, who did not recognize Tony Costa from photographs Dunn showed him. On the day the telegram was sent, Bellion had opened his establishment for business at 12:30 P.M. However, he employed a part-time cleaningman who worked from nine to one o'clock. The forty-four-year-old Syrian resident alien, Mohamed Ben Laidi Aboulhouda, told Dunn he had not opened the bar for anyone on the day in question until he unlocked the door for the proprietor. Dunn was baffled at how Costa could have used the telephone at 12:05 when the bar had not opened until twenty-five minutes later.

Dunn did not find out until Monday morning that Tony Costa had been in Buffalo, not in New York City on March 2. Bernie Flynn had confirmed with the Buffalo office of the New York Telephone Company the location of "call booth" number 852-9859 on Franklin Street, a short distance from the Western Union office on LaFayette Square.

On Monday morning, Justin Cavanaugh revealed to reporters that Antone Costa's family had indicated their unshaken faith in his innocence at a conference on Sunday. Cavanaugh objected to references to Costa being a taxidermist made by District Attorney Edmund Dinis. "Costa only dabbled in taxidermy in an amateur way."

Maurice Goldman told the Cape Cod *Standard-Times* that Tony Costa's constitutional rights may have been infringed by "inflammatory remarks" made by Dinis at his press conference. Goldman was filing "appropriate pleadings" to stop further prejudicial statements from the district attorney's office.

While Goldman privately questioned Costa's innocence, he was not entirely convinced of Costa's guilt. Goldman suspected his client knew a great deal about the murders he wasn't telling. At this stage of the case, however, Goldman was more concerned with Costa being able to get a fair trial because of an avalanche of publicity being generated from the district attorney's office. In Goldman's view, it was outrageous for Dinis to persist in discussing the case publicly when Costa was only being held on a complaint from the district court. Costa had not been indicted by a grand jury who had heard whatever evidence police had gathered against him.

Whether he was guilty or not, Tony Costa was still entitled to a fair trial, Goldman told Cavanaugh. "We've got to shut up Dinis and try this case in court and not in the newspapers!"

Exhausted after a day spent in Provincetown checking Costa's story, Goldman realized the case was going to require considerably more investigation. Goldman called Lester Allen, a retired Boston police reporter who had done some minor investigations for Goldman's office. Allen jumped at the chance to earn ten dollars an hour and six cents a mile as "chief investigator" on the Costa case.

More than the amateur investigative skills of Lester Allen were required for the Costa case, however. Goldman retained the services of private investigators Kervin, Delaney and Wilhite, Inc. of Boston. Anna Wilhite Dunbar and Stephen Delaney had worked with the "Boston Strangler" bureau in the office of Massachusetts Attorney General Edward Brooke; Ernest Kervin, like his partners, was an experienced former police officer.

"In fairness to the defendant, and in view of the extraordinary complexity of the charges against the accused, top-notch investigation talent has become necessary," Goldman explained in a press release from his office. "We feel the prosecutor and the police are entitled to be informed of this step we have taken."

Private detective Phillip DiNatale had been keeping abreast of the Costa case since it first appeared in the newspapers. He wrote to Goldman: "I believe that it would be to Mr. Costa's and to your advantage if you would consider me for this investigation."

DiNatale, a member of the Boston Police Department for twenty-one years and cited with many commendations and awards "for outstanding police work and dedication to duty," had for four years been assigned as special investigator on the Boston Strangler case.

"Some of my experiences while investigating this case are portrayed in the movie. The Academy Award-winning George Kennedy plays Phillip DiNatale, whose perseverance and work in the investigation resulted in the assumption that DiSalvo was the strangler." DiNatale had served as technical adviser to Twentieth Century-Fox during the filming of *The Boston Strangler* and had just completed a promotional tour on behalf of the film, he explained. "One of my most interesting television appearances occurred on the 'Joey Bishop Show,' when the planned four-minute interview developed into a forty-five-minute period."

Goldman was not impressed. One thing the Costa case didn't need was more publicity. He gave his secretary DiNatale's letter to file, then had her place an order to the Harvard Co-op bookstore in Cambridge for paperback copies of *Psychopathia Sexualis* by Richard von Krafft-Ebing, and volumes one and two of *Sexual Aberrations* by Wilhelm Stekel.

At 9 A.M. on Monday morning, March 10, a high requiem mass was celebrated in St. Mary's Church in Providence for Mary Anne Wysocki. Bob Turbidy sat with Gerry Magnan and the Wysocki family during the services for which he and Magnan had helped make arrangements. Turbidy left the graveside rites at St. Ann's Cemetery in nearby Cranston, Rhode Island, to attend the mass said for Patricia Walsh at ten o'clock—the funerals staggered to allow friends of the girls to attend both services. Turbidy sat in the back of St. Paul's Church, telling Magnan afterward, "I felt like a complete outsider."

Turbidy had read with horror the newspaper accounts of the mutilation of the corpses found in Truro. Having endured police indifference to his initial inquiries following Pat Walsh's disappearance and the preposterous questions asked by state police at the Yarmouth barracks regarding Pat's search for an abortion, Turbidy reacted bitterly to the front-page story in the Providence *Journal* which quoted District Attorney Edmund Dinis as having suspected foul play from the beginning of the girls' disappearance: "The backgrounds of the girls indicated they would not just simply up and leave," Dinis had said. "Both came from very fine families."

An hour after the funeral services, Tony Costa was being interviewed by psychiatric social worker Charles Fitzsimmons at Bridgewater State Hospital. Fitzsimmons, a pleasant young man, recently graduated from Holy Cross, found Costa cooperative, articulate and oriented.

Costa painted a picture of a homelife filled with superlative "goodness," yet he was a loner, "because people didn't understand." Costa claimed close relationships with his family. His mother was "a beautiful person," super-clean, and a perfectionist who had allowed animals only in the basement of the apartment in Somerville where they lived. She worried too much about others, and not enough about herself and tended to poor health. "She has

194

high blood pressure. I practically had to force her to see a doctor about it," Costa said. "My mother's quite a woman. She's not conventional in any sense, really. Like, I've actually smoked pot in her house; and she's not against it. She's only uptight that I might get caught. She really saw nothing wrong with it. Because I'm sitting in front of her and she's known me all my life and she didn't see any drastic change except that I became tired and sluggish."

Costa's father had died a hero in the navy during World War II. "He was the love of my mother's life," Costa said. "My mother used to tell me that all the time; that he was the love of her life."

His mother had then married Joseph Bonaviri, a stonemason, "a jolly type person," a hard-working man who had tried to provide well for his family. Costa had not been legally adopted and had encountered some difficulty getting along with his half brother, but by adolescence they had become friends. Costa felt that Vincent was his mother's favorite, that she would not hesitate to help him in any way, including emotional and financial support. Costa had suffered economic reverses without his mother's assistance. When his brother had gotten into trouble at fourteen, when he and a friend dumped ice from a bridge onto a moving train and almost caused an accident, "My stepfather was very angry and punished Vinnie too severely," Costa said. "But my mother wasn't angry enough; she just wanted to forget the whole thing."

Both parents had been warm, loving, permissive. When Costa started taking an interest in girls, he had been allowed to have them in the house. He had learned the facts of life from his stepfather first, then from his mother. He had felt "good" about it and never had any hangups about sex, he told Fitzsimmons. He had commenced masturbation at twelve, and experienced intercourse for the first time when he was fourteen and had enjoyed it ever since. He felt no diminution of his sex drive.

Costa had attended the first through sixth grades at the Proctor School in Somerville, with no repeats; and the seventh through ninth grades at Western Junior High. He had been a member of the Future Teachers of America at Somerville High School. A devout Catholic, he had attended Mass every Sunday until he was twelve years old, when he had ceased believing in the literalness of the Bible, particularly the story of the Garden of Eden and "Christ as God," but continued to believe in "Christ the man."

When he was seventeen, Costa was convicted of assault and attempted rape of a fourteen-year-old neighborhood girl and placed on probation. He felt this was unjust; the girl had attempted to seduce him, he said. As a result of the scandal, he had moved to Provincetown to live with his aunt, Mary Perkins. Costa did not feel that Provincetown High School was as good as Somerville, a class-A school, but Costa had come to love the town.

"Provincetown to me holds beauty," Costa said. "To me, it's God's country. It's small, it's confined, and you know everybody. I walk the beach a lot there. I would start out at the center of town and walk all the way out to Race Point. It takes hours, but it's a nice walk. Once you get past the breakwater, you're on the ocean side. And it's a beautiful thing, because you start out in surroundings that are familiar, and you go to total, almost oblivion. There's nothing but peace and quiet and tranquillity. You can be alone with God there. You can be alone with your own mind and your own peace."

Around the time of the rape incident, a number of relatives he was close to died: his Uncle Manuel, then his maternal grandmother for whom he was a pallbearer. "Her funeral was an ugly scene," Costa told Fitzsimmons, recollecting his grandmother's face in her coffin. "She had no color. She was ugly and looked horrible." The deaths had convinced him he would die young, probably of cancer.

Costa learned stonemasonry from his stepfather, carpentry and other building skills from his uncles during summers spent in Provincetown. He had taught himself "basic engineering." After high school he had taken a correspondence school course in heavy construction equipment from the Greer Technological Institute in Chicago. At eighteen, he married Avis Johnson; she had deliberately become pregnant to force her mother's consent. The marriage had suffered difficulties, due to his wife's mother, whom Costa described as "the town tramp."

"Basically her mother didn't like me for some reason from the beginning, she didn't want us to get married. I guess she held that against me all through the years. She felt I was taking her daughter away. Marian was the type of woman that is extremely domineering. Like, she expected to have Avis live with her, and be her manservant, sort of. She wanted Avis to do the housework, because Carol—Avis's sister—couldn't do anything, she was crippled. Avis had to take over the chores and duties of the house so

Marian could go off flitting with all kinds of guys. Like that Chinese guy named Lee something Marian was dating—this was during the early years of our marriage. Then Marian got off on this kick with Joe Sance, who she's still with. . . ."

At nineteen, Costa had gone into the construction business, finding the pressures of work combined with his responsibilities as husband and father too difficult to bear. He had sought the help of a marriage counselor when his wife became involved in an affair with another man. Costa had confronted her and the man involved and they had reached an agreement that it would be best for all concerned for a separation, and eventually divorce. Costa and his ex-wife were on very friendly terms now, Costa explained. Possibly, at a later date, the marriage might be "reconciliated."

Costa had no military record. "It's not that I wouldn't go if I was drafted. I would go; I just wouldn't touch a gun. I'm dead set against the military. To me it resembles a gestapo movement, and I don't want anything to do with the army or with killing. I have a very strict ethical code of my own."

As the interview came to a close, Costa denied the murder charges against him. Police had constantly watched him with the aid of detectives prior to his arrest, he knew. They would not listen when he tried to tell them they should question a "Buddy Hansen," a heroin addict who had come to the rooming house where the girls were staying.

Costa had never suffered serious head injuries, epileptic seizures, blackouts or dizzy spells. He denied using addictive drugs. He had tried marijuana "on a few occasions," but never took any of the more serious drugs, he told his interviewer. He drank beer on occasion. Costa denied having hallucinations or delusions. He did not appear severely depressed.

"He understands the nature and object of the charges against him," Fitzsimmons reported, "and the possible consequences of what can happen to him."

14

On that same Monday, March 10, at 10:30 A.M., as Costa was being interviewed, the hand taken from the body found in the grave with Mary Anne Wysocki and Pat Walsh was delivered to state police headquarters. When the hand was defrosted, Sergeant James Sharkey observed it to be intact, but soft, shriveled and devoid of epidermis. From the middle finger, Sharkey removed a silver ring with roughly scalloped edges, welded into a circlet. Microscopic examination proved the ring to have been made from a five-cent piece.

Sharkey amputated all four fingers and thumb. He carefully washed and tied off the digits with fishing line before injecting the bulb area with Hydrol tissue builder—an operation requiring great delicacy so as not to further damage the remaining surface of skin.

Two fingers had decomposed through the dermal layer, eliminating any possibility of lifting prints from them. Sharkey inked the remaining two fingers and thumb, rolling fifty to sixty impressions onto print cards for each finger. The middle, or number 3 finger, gave the most significant partial print. Sharkey rerolled the finger again and again until he was satisfied the best possible impression had been obtained. Using a photomicrograph camera, he photographed the print. An enlargement gave an even finer impression. Given comparison fingerprint charts, Sharkey was certain he could make an identification, but young women of the corpse's estimated age were rarely fingerprinted. Sharkey doubted a set of charts for the unidentified woman existed.

In another area of the state police laboratory, Dr. Arthur McBay was able to match the leg bone found in the Truro woods with the femoral stump on the pelvis of the unidentified body exhumed on March 7. Except for the missing foot, internal genitalia and the liver, the body was now complete.

Detective Lieutenant Richard Cass received a telephone call at state police headquarters from a Richard Whyman, the sales manager at Alewife Motors in Arlington, a suburb of Boston. Whyman had recognized newspaper photographs of Antone Costa as the young man who had come to his dealership the previous August and put a $50 deposit on a 1968 dark blue, used Triumph Spitfire convertible costing $2,497.00. Costa had been accompanied by a young woman whom Whyman described as five feet six, 115 pounds, with long blond hair parted in the middle and worn in a "mod" style.

As a result of a check through the Beneficial Finance Company, Costa had been rejected as a poor credit risk, but the attempted purchase gave Whyman the information he now passed to Lieutenant Cass—Costa had been employed as a carpenter for Starline Structures, a dormer-installation, home-improvement company in Walpole, Massachusetts.

From Mrs. Norma Donlan, a secretary at Starline, State Police Detective Lieutenant John O'Donovan learned that Costa had been employed as a carpenter from July 15 through September 5, 1968. Costa had been an average worker with no complaints against him. Mrs. Donlan also confided that Costa had lived in an apartment in Dedham and had dated a local girl, Sandra Kropoff.

Pretty, slender, soft-spoken Sandy Kropoff submitted to questioning by O'Donovan with her parents seated in an adjoining room in the neat frame house at 291 Central Avenue, Dedham. Employed as a secretary at the Rust Craft Greeting Card Company since high school graduation, she had met Tony Costa while on vacation in Provincetown last June. Costa had been working and living at the Crown and Anchor Motor Inn where she had seen a black gun with a white handle he took from a closet.

"Tony called it his 'pistola,'" Sandy said.

Costa had smoked marijuana in her presence, and used other drugs, too. "One time Tony had a backache and he went to the Norwood Hospital clinic and they gave him Darvon, I think— little gray and red capsules. But they didn't help. After that, Tony went to a doctor in Dedham who gave him a prescription, but I don't know what it was for."

She had never observed any unusual or abnormal behavior when Costa was high or straight.

She had never gone to the Truro woods with him, "but when

I saw the place on television, I recognized it from what Tony had told me."

She had lost interest in Costa around September 5, and started dating another boy. She had heard from Costa in January when he wrote her a letter in which he enclosed a photograph taken of them at Herring Cove Beach in Provincetown:

> Hi "Croakie":
>
> How's things? I was looking through my files and I came upon the enclosed. Thought you might dig it. Write when you can, ok? Would like to hear from you.
>
> Until then, go in peace always,

The letter was signed with a peace symbol.

"Tony, do you know anything about a pistol with a white handle?" Justin Cavanaugh asked when he and Maurice Goldman returned to Bridgewater on March 11 to interview Costa.

"I used to have a Colt like that," Costa said. "I purchased the pistol from Cory Devereau for twenty dollars, due to the threats I had received after the Von Utter thing. I kept it for protection only. I fired it once and the noise scared me, so I put it away. After I got out of Barnstable House of Correction, I decided I had better get rid of it. My girlfriend Christine knew a guy named Mark—I don't know his last name. He wanted to buy it. I sold it to him for thirty dollars."

"You *definitely* got rid of the gun some time last November?" Cavanaugh said.

"Definitely!" Costa said.

Goldman was skeptical. Both Atkins and Grund had said that Costa had a .22 caliber revolver he was trying to sell in February.

"The car situation is still disturbing Mr. Cavanaugh and myself," Goldman said. "You see, Pat's got your nine hundred dollars, all you've got is a car. We just don't get it clear in our mind how the car supplants a quarter pound of heroin."

"You were talking about the car being left on Hatch Road," Cavanaugh added, "but you don't really know how it got there."

"No, I don't," Costa said.

"Now, you went out to Truro with Atkins and Grund," Goldman said. "When you got there, you saw the car?"

"Right, it was left in the place where it should have been."

"Where was the key to the car?"

"It was under the left front tire."

Goldman frowned. Grund and Atkins had told him the key was in Costa's pocket. "Was that arranged?"

"That had been arranged, yes," Costa said. "There was a note on the windshield indicating 'Engine Trouble.' It was written in red Magic Marker on some envelope. I became a little bit nervous, because here we were in the middle of the woods to pick up a car that was broken down, and it came to be it wasn't broken down at all. It started right up."

"Who wrote the note indicating the car was out of commission?" Cavanaugh said.

"That I don't know."

Goldman, recalling his interviews with Atkins and Grund, realized that neither of them had observed a sign on the windshield. He asked Costa, "Did you look to see if any package was left in the trunk of the car for you?"

"I opened the trunk, but I didn't see any package or anything," Costa said. "I drove through the dirt roads, then Steve Grund took over and we headed for Boston. We stopped for gas in Hyannis. When we arrived in Boston we left the car in front of my brother's house at 415 Beacon Street. Steve, Timmy and I went up to my brother's and bedded down for some sleep after saying hello to Vinnie."

"What time did you next see the car?" Goldman said.

"Steve had to get back to Provincetown early the next morning. He had some speed coming in and he was going to do some acid, so I drove him to the airport."

"You had no license, but you drove the car to the airport yourself just the same." Goldman said. "You took the chance?"

"Right," Costa said.

"Now, where did you park the car again?"

"In front of the apartment on Beacon Street, almost the exact same place. I went upstairs and went back to bed. Timmy was still sleeping. We woke up around noontime, roughly. I was expecting a visit from Pat, Mary Anne and Chuck that day. We were watching TV when suddenly I heard the Volkswagen—or *a* Volkswagen, I should say, it sounded like a foreign engine—in the back of the building. So I looked out the window and saw Pat's car backing into a parking space. I wanted to see who was getting out of it, and it was this guy Chuck. I had seen him in Boston once and I recognized him."

"The time you saw Chuck before was when?" Goldman said.

"A day when I had seen some friends up there," Costa said. His brow was wrinkled with concentration. "When was it I had seen Chuck before? Damn! I can't remember!"

"All right," Goldman said, "you saw the automobile and Chuck. Did you go downstairs?"

"I quickly ran down there to see who else was with him. At this time the trunk of the car was open and Chuck was pulling out —I don't know exactly what it was—a plastic Baggie filled with white powder which I had reason to believe was heroin. That's all it *could* have been."

"He took the Baggie out of the *car?*" Goldman said. "How did it get *in* the car? Because when you left Provincetown it wasn't in there."

"This I don't know," Costa said. "I didn't see it when I opened the trunk at Hatch Road, but I didn't look for it either; it was pretty dark. But it *must* have been there."

"What did you say to Chuck?" Goldman said.

"At this time we exchanged greetings. I asked Chuck where the girls were. He said they were at a friend's house and he motioned down Beacon Street. He was becoming tense; he was extremely nervous. He reached into his wallet which was bulging with money and handed me a hundred dollars and said, 'This is for your troubles.' "

"Did he say anything to you at that time about your quarter pound of heroin?" Cavanaugh said.

"I started questioning him about where my stuff was, and he said not to worry, that he would take care of it. He stuck the bag of stuff in his pocket and said I would be taken care of."

"He stuck a *pound* of heroin in his pocket?" Cavanaugh said. "How big a package would that be?"

"It amounted to the size approximately of Baggie, a good full Baggie. This is apothecary measure, or something, in reality it would be . . . maybe nine ounces. This is a bit confusing to straight people because when you speak of a pound, it's not sixteen ounces. It's quite a bit less; but still it's a lot of heroin. He said he was going to take it to some friends' house to divide it and weight it out. I said okay and invited him up to the apartment. He said he and the girls would all come over later."

"What girls did he mean?" Goldman said.

"Pat and Mary Anne," Costa said.

"What happened to the car?"

"The car itself stayed there," Costa said. "Because Chuck had the key at that time. The key was in the glove compartment, I left it there because he told me on the phone when he called to do that."

"What did he drive the car in back for?" Cavanaugh said.

"This I don't know," Costa said. "He's really a weird guy; he's all screwed up."

Goldman was impatient with the ethics of dope-dealing, determined not to be thrown off the line of questioning. According to Atkins, Costa had only left the apartment to take Grund to the airport. Goldman said, "All right, the car is in back now. What happened to the car? When did you next see the car?"

"I didn't really notice the car after that," Costa said. "The next time I saw the car was in Burlington."

Costa made no mention of trying to register the car in Boston. Goldman asked him, "Who drove the car to Vermont?"

"That I don't know," Costa said.

Goldman studied Costa levelly. Vincent Bonaviri and Steve Grund had told him they thought Costa had driven the car to Burlington himself.

"Who told you the car was going to be in Vermont?" Goldman said.

"Chuck called my mother's a second time. It was about two days after I got back to Provincetown from Boston, a Thursday or Friday. He simply said he was at the airport in Burlington and that if I wanted the car, I could pick it up there . . ."

Impatient with what he suspected was another of Costa's elaborate lies, Goldman cut him off.

"How did you get to Burlington?"

"I took the early bus from Provincetown to Boston; then from Boston to Burlington. I got there in the middle of the afternoon, about three-thirty or so."

"Had you ever been to Burlington before?" Goldman said.

"No, I had never been there before in my life."

"How did you find the car?"

"From the bus terminal, I hitched out to the airport. I didn't have any idea where it was. When I got out there I walked around for an hour, looking for the car. There were a lot of Volkswagens. I walked around and finally I had made a complete circle. The car was at the entrance of the airport itself."

"Where was the key?"

"In the glove compartment."

"What else was in the glove compartment?" Cavanaugh said. "Was the note saying the car had engine trouble in there?"

"I took most things out of the car; there wasn't much there. I took a pad of yellow paper that was on the back seat, and a pen that was in the glove compartment with a red Magic Marker, and a flashlight. There was a pendant of some kind, a gold thing, all smashed up. It was a peace sign—a hippie symbol. And the registration to the car was there at that time and, oh!—the bill of sale for the car!" Costa added, his voice rising with excitement. Costa shifted in his chair. "It *shocked* me. I took it out and read it. It signed the car over to me; and I didn't know what to make of it."

"Have you any idea what happened to all the girls' luggage?" Cavanaugh said.

"No, I don't. There wasn't anything in the car by way of luggage when I got it. There wasn't a thing in it."

"What did you do next?" Goldman said.

"I got a room."

"You have no idea who wrote the bill of sale?" Cavanaugh said.

"I have *no* idea," Costa said firmly. "I was completely shocked."

"So for your nine hundred dollars all you got—or were to get —was an automobile?" Goldman asked.

"I hadn't expected the car," Costa said. "I didn't really *want* the car; The car to me was not worth half as much as what I had paid the money for. The heroin thing would have been worth roughly forty-five hundred to five thousand dollars. I could have mixed one pound of quinine and a quarter pound of heroin and sold it in Boston for five times what I paid for it. So I knew I had gotten the shaft or something."

"Well, they say truth is stranger than fiction," Goldman said.

"I believe it," Costa said.

"It's the strangest story, because nothing seems to dub in," Goldman said. "That's the unfortunate part about this case."

"It makes no sense whatsoever," Costa concurred agreeably.

"Now you see why we're faced with so much work, Tony, in picking up details," Goldman said carefully. "I think we've got the car situation straightened out now. At least it's straightened out in *my* mind," Goldman added with a glance at Cavanaugh. "I was confused before."

"You didn't write the bill of sale yourself, did you, Tony?" Cavanaugh said.

"No, I didn't want the car; I had nothing to do with the car."

"Was your name mentioned in the bill of sale?" Cavanaugh said.

"Yeah, it was."

"And it was signed by who?"

"It was signed by Pat Walsh."

"Your signature appears on the bottom of the bill of sale, does it not?" Goldman said.

"Yeah, I signed it," Costa said. "I don't know, an impulse came over me to sign it. I thought it was more or less a joke."

"I would say it's been a very beneficial visit," Goldman said benignly. "And I know, Tony, if you have anything else to say, that you trust Mr. Cavanaugh and myself to tell us."

"Right," Costa said. "Definitely."

"Even if you want it kept in strict confidence, we are going to keep it that way," Goldman said. "If anything occurs to you, please don't hesitate to tell us. What we want to do is the very best for one person and one person alone: Tony Costa."

Cavanaugh was still curious about Costa's accent, so out of character for a Provincetown carpenter, and he asked him about it.

"This isn't something I was aware of until about the past two years or so," Costa said. "People have constantly been coming to me with the comment, 'Where did you get that voice?' I just abhor to a great extent these people who go around and say, 'Oh, that's nuttin', and this sort of thing; to me to speak correctly is as important as anything else. It shows your capabilities to some extent. It's kind of ridiculous to be ignorant."

Cavanaugh changed the subject, explaining that he and Goldman had met Steve Grund on Sunday. "He seems a very nice fellow," Cavanaugh said. "Now, Tony, did you ever have any blackouts from using drugs?"

"No, I've never had any blackouts whatsoever," Costa said. "Like these occasions, like my joking and things, it's just a common thing. I go up to a lot of people and I have certain phrases that I use, and this is one of them: 'I've lost from Monday through Friday.' It just touches off a little bit of laughter. When people get to know me, they realize that this is part of my metabolism. I like to create laughter in people."

Cavanaugh had brought a letter for Costa that Steve Grund had given him on Sunday:

Dear Sire:
Say sport, what's up? Everyone here says 'hi', and be cool. Everyone sends their love and Peace, and God's will to pull through this God-awful mess.
We've talked to your lawyer and told him everything we could think of that could possibly help you out. The cops are hasseling us as usual and we can't turn on anymore, but it's cool in a way, I guess.
 'Weed' is sitting here with me now, and he says he would like you to come through this, too. We're all with you, Tony.

District Attorney Edmund Dinis told the Boston *Record-American* that police searches in the Truro woods were continuing. "Thus far, we've come up with four bodies and a fourteen-by-sixteen-inch mortar ammunition box that apparently once contained a considerable amount of drugs but had only one package of marijuana when found. Obviously this area was used not only as a burial ground but also for hiding things."

Dinis's office had received more than three hundred and fifty calls from parents reporting a missing child, he said. Inquiries about the case had come from South Africa, Australia, and other parts of the world. "It has stirred up international interest."

Led by George Killen, a search party entered the snow-dusted woods. Police used metal detectors in a foot-by-foot search of a hundred-square-yard area adjacent to the grave sites looking for a gun, knife and an army combat shovel.

Sifting through the sandy soil of the grave where he had found the head and torso of Mary Anne Wysocki, Tom Gunnery came upon two expended .22 short shell casings. Bernie Flynn located a third casing in the same grave.

A pair of "Blue Swan" size 5, white bikini panties stained with excrement was found under a tree by Park Ranger Raymond Kimple. The search failed to turn up more bodies—or the murder weapon.

Coming out of the woods at noon, Killen made a rare statement-for-attribution to waiting reporters: "We have found all we are going to find. We have searched thoroughly the last six weeks. We don't expect to find any further bodies. When we leave today, this will be the end."

A metal detector was also being used in the search for a .22 caliber revolver believed to be concealed in a ceiling light fixture in Boston. Lieutenant Broderick had returned to 364 Marlborough Street with explosive technician Joseph Sainato. Broderick received a "consent to search" from Vincent Bonaviri.

207

Sainato made two sweeps of the apartment, but found nothing. Broderick had twice searched the place, seizing a Stanley "Jobmaster" circular saw with attached yellow electric cord, valued at seventy-nine dollars. A check at headquarters revealed the saw had been stolen on February 21 from the lumberyard of the N.T. Fox Company in Westbrook, Maine.

An anonymous letter to Chief Cheney Marshall of Provincetown was turned over to Broderick, naming "Jack Condon" as a person with information "regarding the recent murders you are investigating."

This young man is an addict and a dealer and spends the summer in your town. He has a cottage on Shank Painter Road. He is a hippie. He worked as a carpenter two years ago and drives a truck painted with the usual hippie motif of flowers, etc. He could prove useful. I cannot sign my name for obvious reasons.

Following up the lead, Broderick went to the Boston Tea Party, a rock music nightclub, where Condon was employed as a ticket collector. Long-haired and bearded, Condon was baffled to be questioned in connection with Antone Costa.

Broderick also investigated an inquiry received from Mr. and Mrs. Earl Taggart of Beachlake, Pennsylvania. Taggart had read about Antone Costa in the Scranton *Tribune*.

"We fear our daughter might be one of his victims," Taggart wrote of his daughter, Meryl Joan, twenty-four years old, five feet one, weighing 120 pounds and missing for several months. Meryl Joan had not contacted her parents since the previous August when she was working at the Jordan Marsh department store in Boston. A letter written to her on September 8 had been returned: "Address Unknown." Broderick spoke with Brenda Morell at 463 Beacon Street, Meryl Joan Taggart's last known address.

"I saw Meryl last week and she's fine," Miss Morell said, explaining to Broderick that Meryl Joan Taggart had given birth to a baby girl the previous November and was now living at 129 Endicott Street. "The reason she never contacted her family was her father has a bad heart, and she didn't want to upset him."

Leaving the Truro woods, Flynn and Gunnery went to 5 Standish Street to secure as evidence the register pages Pat Walsh, Mary

Anne Wysocki and Antone Costa had signed. Mrs. Morton verified the room receipt found in Mary Ann Wysocki's handbag.

"If we show you a Pan American flight bag, could you identify it as similar to the one the girls were carrying?" Flynn said.

"Well, I presume they are all pretty similar," Mrs. Morton said. Wearing a blue housecoat whose gaping decolletage exposed a considerable portion of her breasts, Mrs. Morton was giddy with nerves and appeared to Flynn more coquettish than became a woman of her years—or the occasion. Unable to contain the information any longer, she blurted out "the real reason" Pat Walsh and Mary Anne Wysocki had come to Provincetown.

"The girls were involved in the sale of $10,000 worth of drugs. Tony paid them $900 for a pound of hashish and was given the car as security; but the deal went sour and he wanted his money back. That's how the car deal began."

Flynn was astonished. "Where did you hear *this?*"

"Jerry Murphy of the Boston *Globe* invited me to the Pilgrim Springs motel for cocktails," Mrs. Morton said. "Oh, there's nothing about *dating.* He's married and has children! We have mutual friends in Rockport we wanted to talk about. While we were sitting there, Dr. Hiebert and his wife came toddling out of the dining room. He said Tony had been in his office and explained that his relationship with the two girls from Providence had involved the sale of a pound of hashish. I almost fell off my chair!"

Costa's "little friends," Robin Nicholson, Paula Hoernig and Patty Avila, had visited her house. "They came over on their bicycles, giggling and chattering away while I was talking to Julia Brody of the *Record-American.* They said, 'You've got a nerve saying Tony was a skinny young man.' They said they would 'fix me' for talking about Tony to reporters, and tried to bully me into denying things I actually saw," Mrs. Morton said indignantly. "I'm positive they were using drugs, and so would you be if you had talked to them. They chattered on about the 'six steps to Nirvana,' and a lot of other hippie stuff. They said they knew Susan Perry was alive and living in Boston. They were thoroughly obnoxious and kept threatening me. I was going to call the police."

Flynn recommended that Mrs. Morton not discuss the case with anyone. She would be called to testify at Tony Costa's trial. She could do all the talking she wanted—from the witness stand.

* * *

"I don't want to talk about the girls," Mrs. Morton told bearded, long-haired defense investigator Steve Delaney the next day. "Lieutenant Flynn said for me not to talk to anyone until he says I can. I'm only a housewife; I don't know what I should do."

When she called the Provincetown police for guidance, Mrs. Morton was referred to the district attorney's office at Barnstable courthouse. Asking for Flynn, she got George Killen. Killen told her to use her own judgment.

Mrs. Morton showed investigators Tony Costa's room. "He was as quiet and calm as any other person. He helped me a lot, too; he was a very good electrician. He was so very neat and clean about everything; and that's more than I can say for some of the people I've had."

"What about smoking pot—did he, so far as you know?"

"Not that I knew about. Some of the kids who stay here leave seeds in the drawers, but he didn't."

"Do you think it's possible that Tony and the girls—Pat and Mary Anne—knew one another?"

"They seemed distant enough when they were introduced," Mrs. Morton said. "But they got on a friendly basis very rapidly for people who had just met."

Dr. Daniel Hiebert was prickly and uncooperative when Flynn went to his office. Hiebert dismissed the account given by Patricia Morton.

"Tony was just telling me stories," Hiebert said. He had treated Costa for "nerves" following his interrogation by police.

Hiebert had known the Costa family for years; Cecelia Bonaviri was a patient and his former cleaning lady. Flynn was entitled to know the cause of death of the girls from Hiebert in his capacity as medical examiner; but Hiebert refused to disclose anything about Tony Costa's use of drugs as his patient. Critical of the police investigation which had created an uproar in Provincetown, Hiebert said, "The police would never have arrested a summer resident, given the evidence they have against Tony."

Flynn did not press the old man. Whatever his present infirmities, Hiebert was something of a legend in Provincetown where he had practiced medicine since 1919. Named "General Practitioner of the Year," in 1960 by the Massachusetts Medical Society, and honored with a "Dr. Daniel Hiebert Day" in Provincetown,

210

he was nearly eighty years old. Hiebert continued to minister to a large number of patients crowded into the waiting room of his office.

Hiebert had posed for press photographers peering with curiosity at the bone of the leg found in the Truro woods. The photograph appeared on the front page of the Cape Cod *Standard-Times,* and Hiebert's contradictory statements given to the press were sufficient provocation for Maurice Goldman to dispatch Justin Cavanaugh to the white clapboard house on Commercial Street where Hiebert conducted his medical practice.

"I don't want to know anything that you feel you should hold back," Cavanaugh assured him, "only what the defendant—or at least his counsel—is entitled to know."

Hiebert greeted Cavanaugh with a long silence, during which he looked at him through thick spectacles that blurred and enlarged the staring pupils of his eyes. In a soft, breathy voice, Hiebert said, finally, "The cause of death is shown in the death certificates on file at the Truro town hall."

"Was it possible to determine the time of death of the last two girls?"

"Sometime between January twenty-fifth and the day the bodies were found."

"That leaves the time of death wide open, doesn't it?" Cavanaugh said.

"I would say so," Hiebert said.

"There seem to be quite a few discrepancies between what you found in the autopsies and the official announcement as to the cause of death."

"I am a public official," Hiebert said. "And I am not going to get into a dispute over statements made by another public official. I want to help Tony Costa all I can. I've known the family for years. I personally would never believe he was capable of such a crime."

"Would you say the dissection of the bodies was done by someone with a knowledge of anatomy?"

"No, I would not. The second two were done more skillfully than the first two; the first two were simply cut across and hacked. The second two were not that well done, but there seemed to be a greater familiarity with the area to disjoint a body; they were cut at the pelvic region, near the hip socket. And a different instrument was used; sharper."

"You mean an ax, or something like that?"

"I wouldn't say," Hiebert said. "I merely certify the cause of death. The interpretation of the medico-legal evidence is up to Dr. Katsas."

"Do you think the last two bodies were dissected at the grave site?"

"No, I do not," Hiebert said. "If they had been, there would have been blood around there, and there wasn't any. Not in the quantity that would result from a dissection."

"What reason would there be for dismembering the bodies other than to disguise the nature of what was being transported?" Cavanaugh said.

"Well, the *weight,* for one thing," Hiebert said. "I tell you, we were tuckered out carrying the torsos from the graves to the road. One of the girls weighed around a hundred and fifty pounds—*that* would be reason enough why they were dismembered, I'd say."

"But you won't say whether the hearts were missing, or whether there were teeth marks on the bodies?" Cavanaugh said. "It was stated when the bodies were found that the girls had been stabbed. Later, that was changed to gunshot wounds in the head."

"There were cuts on the bodies, but those were not the cause of death," Hiebert said. "I have certified the cause of death as gunshot wounds."

"Did you ever observe any psychotic tendencies in Tony Costa?" Cavanaugh said.

As Hiebert was answering, his wife entered the room. She said, "I do not believe he did it!"

"Did you ever find him to be hostile and vicious?" Cavanaugh said.

"No, he used to bring his wife and children here for treatment," Hiebert said. "He would sit there in the waiting room holding the baby, and he was very tender and gentle with them."

"When is the last time you saw him as a patient?"

"It was right after he had talked to police about taking the car to Vermont. He had a cold and he said he hadn't been sleeping. He wanted some medication. He told me all about his talks with the police. And I said to him, 'For God's sake, Tony, go see a lawyer.'"

"Did he tell you anything else at that time?"

"He said that he wanted to be reunited with his wife and children, that he loved them and wanted to resume living with

212

them. He asked me if I would use my good offices and talk to his wife about it."

"You said you do not believe Tony Costa was capable of a crime like that?" Cavanaugh said.

"No, what I said was, I would never have believed him capable of a crime like that."

Before Cavanaugh left, Hiebert confided information that District Attorney Dinis had not disclosed at his press conference: The bodies of Pat Walsh and Mary Anne Wysocki had been sexually abused; but it could not be determined whether the girls were alive or dead when intercourse had taken place.

Hiebert was one of three recipients of a letter in which Maurice Goldman gave notice of a motion he was filing with the Second District Court. The motion was required, Goldman explained, "so that the rights of our client, Antone Costa, be protected by prosecuting authorities in connection with the complaints presently pending against him." Goldman cited "false, misleading and highly inflammatory prejudicial information" had been given out by prosecuting authorities at various press conferences. To illustrate the "kind and nature" of such publicity released for public consumption, Goldman cited the March 14 issue of *Time* magazine, "a summation of similar erroneous information given by authorities to national, regional and local news media."

Time's report indicated "trial by newspaper, the effect of which deprived the defendant of his constitutional rights to a fair trial." *Time* had published "a disorganized rehash of details reported in the daily press across the nation which distorted the story and placed events in the development of the case out of sequence."

Reporting that four nude bodies had been "similarly butchered" by an ax or cleaver during "grotesque operations," *Time* repeated Dinis's allegations that teeth marks were found on the bodies, concluding, "In none of the random graves could they find any of the four girls' hearts."

Goldman wanted the autopsy reports not made public "until counsel for the defense have been apprised of their contents and consulted as to the propriety of any pretrial disclosure of medico-legal evidence."

Goldman included a copy of his motion with the letter sent by certified mail to Hiebert, Dr. George Katsas and District Attorney Edmund Dinis.

At his next conference with Tony Costa at Bridgewater, Goldman explained, "We've got four investigators out checking for you. We have a former expert police officer who is now running an independent detective agency. One of his partners is a genuine beatnik in style, dress and manner of speech."

Costa laughed. "Really?"

"He spent Sunday night in the Foc's'le bar in Provincetown and nobody recognized him. The head of our investigation staff was a former crime reporter who ended up an editor of the Boston *Post*. His name is Lester Allen, and he's writing up all the material as we take it from you and checking each detail so we come out with a good story. We are doing everything we possibly can, getting people like this to see if we can't arrive at some conclusions here. We want to make sure that every bit of defense is afforded you, Tony."

Determined to get the truth out of his client one way or the other, Goldman wanted to be absolutely satisfied about Costa's guilt. By adopting a nonjudgmental, paternal and—despite his natural impatience—benign attitude during his conferences, Goldman was seeking to build Costa's confidence to the point where he felt secure enough to tell the truth. Goldman had only rarely challenged Costa's story, not wanting to scare him off by pressing too hard or too soon in those areas where Costa's account was weak. Because the murders were so gruesome, difficult for anyone to confess to, Goldman was prepared to give Costa plenty of time and space to work up enough courage to admit the crimes. Goldman wanted no surprises once he stepped into the courtroom.

Goldman wanted to know more about Jay Von Utter. "He's the fellow you helped the police with, is he not?"

"Yeah," Costa said. "I knew that Jay was headed for my wife's house with a tremendous amount of LSD and methedrine. I felt I simply could not let these drugs go there because of the fact that Avis would get in trouble, the children would get in trouble. I *had* to do something!"

"It seems pretty much everybody in town knew you had informed," Cavanaugh said.

"Well, that was Mr. Marshall," Costa said. "The cops did nothing whatsoever about protecting me. He went around telling everybody in bars that I was working for him. Then, he'd go out when he was completely sober and say I was the biggest pusher in town. I lost a lot of friends after Jay was busted. The older people wouldn't associate with me that much. In fact, it became hard for me to find work in town because they would think I was going to bust them."

"You *were* dealing, weren't you?" Cavanaugh said.

"Could you clarify 'dealing'?" Costa said coolly.

"You were selling drugs to people."

"No, that's erroneous," Costa said. "To me a big dope pusher is someone who comes into town and supplies a lot of people with a lot of stuff. And all I had at times were a few choice little things. I didn't push anything much. In fact, it was just this past summer that I got into dealing, because I met a few people in Boston around the Common. Drugs were flying around there like the birds were dropping them out of the air. I had the chance to pick up some gross quantities and make some money. So I took the chance. Basically, it was just hashish."

"In our investigation there has been some indication that a guy named Eddie Silva once threatened to kill you."

"Yeah, he did."

"Can you tell us a little about that?"

"Eddie Silva was a very good friend of Jay Von Utter's, the man who was bringing drugs to my wife and children. He came out and told many people, including myself, that he threatened to shoot me or kill me or some other thing, because I was working for the police. This was in front of the fire station next to Adams's pharmacy." Costa smiled disarmingly. "I just took it all in my stride. It even went to the extent that a car I had—which was an Oldsmobile—at one time someone put two bullet holes in the passenger-side door."

"Were you in the car when it was shot at?" Cavanaugh said.

"Fortunately, I was out of the car. The car itself was parked out on a parking strip near the New Beach. It was a sunset evening and I went off and walked down to the lighthouse, which was approximately one and a half miles away. When I returned there were two bullet holes, or what appeared to be bullet holes, in the car."

"What did this mean to you when you saw the bullet holes?" Cavanaugh said, "Was this some type of warning that Silva meant what he said?"

"I felt at that time it was some type of warning by a group of people in town, friends of Jay's. These people kept coming to me and there were threats. There was at one time a bunch of threatening notes left at my door, like, 'Don't walk in the dark alone,' and 'I saw you on the beach this afternoon, too bad other people were around.'"

"Tony, at one time you expressed a willingness to take a lie detector test," Goldman said. "Are you still of the same opinion?"

"Yeah, I am," Costa said.

"The last time you were pretty upset," Goldman said. "I think I told you it is not a good idea to take a lie detector test when you are upset. Are you still upset to the point where you don't want to do it?"

"I *do* want to take the lie detector test," Costa said. "I'm not in any great rush at the moment; it depends on you. As soon as you need it, I will go ahead. Whatever will benefit the cause."

Goldman had brought Cecelia Bonaviri and Avis Costa to Bridgewater, the first time Tony Costa had been allowed visitors other than his lawyers.

Avis had told the Boston *Record-American* she wanted to tell Costa to his face of her faith in him: "I would like very much to see him and tell him someone cares. I will never be convinced he could do the things which he is charged with."

Costa told her it was important to find a guy named "Chuck," twenty-four years old, five feet ten, curly Bob Dylan-type hair, wearing a campus varsity jacket.

"Tony was uptight about finding him," Avis reported to Goldman after her visit. "I asked him several times about the description but it was always the same."

Avis's visit was cut short by Costa's schedule of psychological tests with clinical psychologist Dr. Mildred Clifford.

216

Costa appeared pressed for time, aware of the stopwatch and straining to work rapidly. He was guarded, his answers to test questions often evasive and indistinct. Costa tried to suppress his snickering at some of the test materials, Clifford observed. "He sat with his arms folded as if holding himself together and spoke in a quiet manner, ever-conscious of his actions and what he said, only occasionally dropping the facade of calm and control in which he seemed to engulf himself. His voice was well controlled except when he spoke of a girl he used to visit in New York with whom he had 'truly communicated.' As he was explaining that she had died accidentally in the bathtub, a perceptible tremor appeared in his voice." The other instance in which Costa showed emotion was with regard to a dog that had been run over on a day his stepfather had taken him out unleashed.

Costa scored in the "bright-normal" range in the Wechsler Adult Intelligence Scale, a test also used to detect psychotic tendencies by measuring vocabulary, general knowledge, mathematical ability and other nonverbal skills. Discrepancies between the verbal and performance portion of the test indicated to Clifford some confused thinking. "He may be scoring lower than his capacity because of sporadic, basically disorganized thinking, arbitrary perceptual organization and suspicious overcautiousness," she wrote. Interference with Costa's new learning processes suggested the disturbance could be a functional one, involving anxiety and feelings of frustration and tension.

Clifford gave Costa the Bender-Gestalt test in which he was asked to copy a series of nine dot or line drawings. Costa could evaluate past experiences, but always showed himself as the central figure in events. "His controls tend to break down at times allowing him to respond in terms of immediate needs and may interfere with his ability to function up to his capacity," Clifford observed. "His good intellectual energies generally compensate effectively for his impulsivity, as he is able to almost immediately recover from aggressive, acting-out behavior showing poor judgment." For the most part, Costa was able to utilize his constructive energies fairly effectively to maintain behavioral controls.

Socially, Costa appeared to be "a narcissistic, inadequate, somewhat depressed man who showed a great deal of anxiety and had difficulty maintaining reality contact, tending to become superficially and unjustifiably optimistic in his general outlook," Clifford reported. "He pictures men as aggressive and manipulative, but probably relates to them in a comparatively warmer manner than to the emptier, more superficial relationships he seems to have developed with women, who are viewed as immature and ungiving."

Costa denied sexualized attraction, showing signs of aggressive feelings toward seductive females. Despite his confinement in maximum security, he admitted no discomfort, and expressed concern for other patients who were unable to control their outbursts—particularly those he thought were undergoing drug withdrawal. Costa denied taking drugs himself.

Costa was reading the New Testament; he saw parallels in his own life with that of Jesus Christ, who was, according to Costa, "a passive man who attacked others only verbally."

Following the tests, Costa asked Clifford her opinion of "a person who had really killed somebody," and was curious about her knowledge concerning the feelings of patients committed to the hospital accused of capital crimes. Costa wanted to know, "how they felt and what they had to say."

Clifford reported, "The use of the commode in his cell has been substituted for by paper cups, as he apparently could not bring himself to use it."

After returning to Cape Cod from Bridgewater, Goldman posed for photographer John Kerr of the Cape Cod *Standard-Times* with Cavanaugh, Avis and Mrs. Bonaviri during a "conference" in his office to discuss the defense's case. The picture appeared the following day in the Cape Cod *Standard-Times* with the letter Sergeant James Meads of the Provincetown Police Department had written recommending parole for Antone Costa "at the earliest possible time," because of the assistance he had provided as an informer during a drug investigation.

Goldman told the Boston *Globe* that Costa was giving day-to-day details of his activities and had made emphatic denials that he was involved in the murders. "Tony acknowledged having owned a gun, as many young men in rural areas do. But he disposed of the weapon long before police claim he killed the two girls." Costa said he wanted his freedom and was willing to take a lie detector test if it would in any way aid in establishing his innocence. His client could undergo two tests, Goldman explained, one with an independent Boston organization with whom arrangements for the test were being made, and a standard examination administered by a state police polygraphist.

Reporting Goldman's comments, the *Globe* speculated that both motive and murder weapon were still missing in the "macabre mystery" of four murdered and dismembered girls. "What motivated the killer not only to fire bullets but to sever the bodies at the waist and the limbs of his victims? What evoked a madness to remove vital organs, then dig two four-foot graves?"

When Goldman opened the daybook journal he had brought from Bridgewater, he found Tony Costa's exposition of the bow and arrow incident involving Marsha Mowery.

The Marsha Mowery Incident
1967

It was a brilliant warm day in August. I had just gone to visit Joey Thomas at his small apartment in the east end of Provincetown. No one was home. I was hoping he would be there so that he could go with me to get my plants in the woods. I had harvested them two weeks previously. After harvesting they require two weeks of drying time.

I went back to my car, and was heading out of town when I saw Marsha Mowery, a long-time acquaintance of mine. I greeted her and told her where I was going and asked if she'd like to come along. She anxiously and gladly accepted and we were on our way.

When we arrived in Truro, I stopped the car, got out and looked for my weeds. I found them and brought them back to the car, and presented them to Marsha.

I then told Marsha that I was going to take my bow out of the back seat and shoot my one last 29-cent target arrow, just to get rid of it since I was going to sell the bow and had no other arrows or equipment. She wanted to come along, and so it was.

Marsha walked ahead about ten feet then waited for me. I called to Marsha that I was going to shoot the arrow into the bushes. Upon releasing it, I saw it ricochet off a tree and turn at such an angle so as to strike poor Marsha and bounce off!

I became extremely concerned and ran to her to assist her if she were in need of it. I insisted that we drive immediately to Dr. Hiebert for medical attention. But Marsha said it was only "mildly uncomfortable" and assured me that all was well. I took the arrow which lay on the ground and broke it in half, throwing it in the road again! I put the bow in the trunk. I cared not to even look at it again, ever!

Then I took Marsha home and telephoned Truro Police Chief Harold Berrio to tell him of what had happened. He told me to go to the station at 7 P.M. that night and fill out an accident form. I did. Patrolman Veara was at the station at the time. Then I returned home and called Marsha to ask how she felt. She said she had finally gone to the doctor so I told her it was the right thing to do, and that I would pay the expenses. But she declined my offer. Now, I felt tremendous relief because she had obtained the proper medical care. Of course, it was altogether possible that Marsha could not have been hurt at all, but it is always best to be sure! One's health is a priceless gift.

Marsha Mowery had grown hostile to Tony Costa since his arrest, telling Stephen Delaney that Costa was changed when he got back from California the winter of 1968. "I'd always enjoyed talking to him before he changed from the easygoing likable Tony," Marsha said. "I liked him for his quiet ways. After I found out how he felt about me I was always fearful of being alone with him. I think now that he wanted to kill me, and the bow and arrow accident was intentional."

Marsha and Sandy Carter accompanied Delaney to Truro

220

Woods, showing him the location of Costa's garden, and at least a dozen places where Costa had, at one time or another, kept a store of drugs.

Sandy Carter had also observed the change that had occurred in Tony Costa after he returned to Provincetown from California. "He was real moody and strung-out. A lot of times he would scratch himself with a comb when he was uptight."

Costa had started taking his nickname "Sire" seriously, Sandy recalled. "It was something that started in high school as a joke. Tony would give out sticks of gum to the kids, but you had to call him 'Sire' first." Last summer Costa had taken to referring to the group of teenagers who hung around him as "my disciples," and calling himself "Anthony of Rome" or "Lord Anton, the Bringer of All That Is True."

Sandy Carter was impatient to terminate her interview with Bernie Flynn, who saw her after her talk with Delaney.

Flynn was still in pursuit of the murder weapon. He said, "Did you ever see Tony with a gun?"

"Yes, at his mother's house, in a gray metal box, some kind of a filing thing about a foot long. He had bullets too, little ones, that he showed me."

"Did Tony ever use drugs in your presence?" Flynn said.

"I saw him shoot Methedrine in California," Sandy said. "I saw him once in the mountains with that girl Barbara. I happened to be going the other way and we passed each other. Tony didn't even notice me." After returning to Provincetown last April, she had met Costa on Commercial Street. "Tony didn't recognize me; he was staring into space. I asked him about Barbara. He told me 'she wanted to come to Provincetown.' He said he had borrowed money from his mother to send to her. Later I saw him on the street again. He said, 'My mind is going blank.' He hadn't heard from Barbara after all. She was missing; he was real upset about it. I asked him where Barbara was. Tony didn't know. He said, 'She probably died.'

"Her sister had Barbara's baby," Sandy continued. "She didn't know where Barbara was. I don't think they ever found out if Barbara is dead or not. Nobody knows."

"Did you ever see Tony wearing a white fisherman-knit sweater?" Flynn said. Flynn had checked stores in Provincetown and Hyannis, but had been unable to trace the bloody sweater found in one of the graves.

"It was a very pretty sweater," Sandy said. "What does that have to do with anything?" When Flynn remained silent, she said, "You can't tell me?"

"Could you identify the sweater, if you saw it again?"

"I don't know," Sandy said. "I don't like saying things about Tony; he was really nice to me. I don't believe Tony would do these things."

"That's your privilege," Flynn said curtly. He told her she might be called as a witness at Tony Costa's trial.

"Oh, I *couldn't* do that," Sandy said.

Flynn was outraged. "We saved your *life,*" he said angrily. "Why do you think Tony kept calling you up all the time, wanting you to drive him out to the woods? *You* were next on his list."

Sandy Carter sent Flynn a look of disbelief, the first time she had met his eyes during the interview.

"I'd rather go to jail than testify against Tony," she said.

Around the end of January, Sandy Carter had met Cecelia Bonaviri, in front of Provincetown's post office. "She told me Tony had gone off to Rhode Island with two girls," Sandy said—a statement Mrs. Bonaviri refused to corroborate when Flynn and Gunnery went to her apartment to search for a .22 caliber revolver and a knife approximately two and a half inches wide with a wooden handle. They found nothing.

Flynn and Gunnery had no better luck searching for the gun at the basement of a cottage at 18 Shank Painter Road, rented to Tony and Avis Costa in 1968 by David Raboy. A professor of sociology at Rhode Island College, Raboy had found "a weird and frightening" collage made up of cut-up portions of nude women's body parts taken from "girlie" magazines hidden behind a workbench Tony Costa had built in the cellar.

Raboy had destroyed the collage.

Edmund Silva, a twenty-year-old laborer at Provincetown Cooperative Fisheries Industries, told Flynn that Tony Costa had asked where he could get a fake driver's license and registration and have someone write up a bill of sale for a Volkswagen. The conversation had occurred in early February at the apartment Robert

Alves was sharing with Vinnie in Boston. Silva figured the car was stolen. Costa had stopped Silva on the stairs to say goodbye and shake hands. "Well, I'll see you," Costa said. "I'm leaving for good."

Silva's cousin fished on the *Three-in-One* scallop boat with a Davey Joseph. Joseph had mentioned seeing a pearl-handled revolver in Tony Costa's apartment in Dedham.

A good-looking youth of eighteen, Joseph had become friendly with Tony Costa the previous summer and had visited him in Dedham around Labor Day with Jimmy Steele and Susan Perry. Joseph had dated Susan in the past but their relationship prior to her disappearance had been platonic.

"One morning when Tony was at work Susan showed me a black .22 pistol with a white handle," Joseph told Bernie Flynn. "Susan was always a snooping chick; she'd gone through Tony's stuff. She said she found the gun in the dresser. When Tony came home I asked him if he could get me a gun like that. He said he could, that it wasn't a hard thing, if I could wait a while. After that, Tony kept the gun on a night table beside his bed."

Joseph had returned to Provincetown leaving Costa and Susan Perry in Dedham. A week later he had bumped into Costa in front of the First National Bank in Provincetown. "Tony told me Susan had left a note saying she was splitting with two guys she met and thanks for letting her stay there and give this ring to Davey."

Costa had produced a yellow gold class ring with a blue stone from Mt. Everett High School. Joseph had seen no significance in the ring. "I told Tony I didn't want it; but he kept insisting. He got real uptight. He said Susan wanted me to have it, 'So take it!' " Several days later Joseph had given the ring to a cousin visiting from Kentucky, but he remained puzzled by Susan Perry's abrupt departure. "She never said anything to me about going anyplace," he told Flynn. "She didn't even want to go to Boston, but she did; she was afraid of being alone. She had like ten or fifteen dollars with her when she went to stay with Tony."

Joseph had been stoned most of his five-day visit to Costa's apartment. "Tony was on downs, and he was smoking pot; but he was working steady doing carpentry." Joseph had slept on cushions on the floor of the living room; Susan Perry and Costa had slept in the bedroom. "While I was falling asleep, I overheard certain noises."

Joseph had no doubt that Tony Costa and Susan Perry were having sex.

19

James Leslie Steele had quit his job as a stockroom clerk at Peter Bent Brigham Hospital in Boston and was employed as a laborer at a Provincetown fish processing plant at the end of Mac-Millan Wharf. He told Flynn and Gunnery, "I hope to get something better."

A slender, wiry young man in his early twenties, Steele had known Tony Costa a long time. "But I never really started talking to him until last summer."

"Did your conversations center around marijuana and drugs?" Flynn said bluntly.

Steele looked surprised. "At different times, yeah."

"Did you ever see a gun in Tony's possession?"

"The gun was in a green duffel bag in Tony's room at the Crown and Anchor," Steele said. "It was a .22 pistol, short black barrel with a white pearl handle, a Colt. I asked Tony where he got it because I wanted to buy it. I think he said it was 'hot' at the time, and we more or less dropped it at that. The last time I saw Tony was the last week in February. I was sitting in Mother Marion's with a girl I know. I told him I still would like to buy the gun. He said, 'No, I have it buried.' "

"Did you ever go to Tony's marijuana garden?" Gunnery said.

"Yeah, we went there one time," Steele said. "We were just riding around, killing the afternoon."

Steele later revealed to defense investigators that he had taken part with Tony Costa in the robbery of Murray's drugstore in Wellfleet the previous July. "I drove Tony's old blue Oldsmobile. We stopped in the parking lot near a church. Butch Gaspar started a brushfire and set off an alarm to distract the police. Tony took an empty laundry bag in there. When we picked him up the bag was full." Steele had been given drugs as his share of the robbery.

Steele had seen Tony Costa with a syringe at the end of January, he said. "Tony was dropping acid, too. I saw him swallow a tab of LSD outside the Boatslip motel. And he was doing downs, especially Nembutal. Tony really liked Nembutal."

Convinced that Susan Perry was one of the victims whose unidentified remains had been found in the Truro woods, Bernie Flynn sought out Paula Hoernig for questioning. A serious, plump-faced girl with a mass of thick brown hair tumbling to her shoulders, she looked to Flynn to be younger than fifteen. She had met Tony Costa on March 22, 1968.

"I remember the date exactly because I was going out with David Salvador and I liked him. I was with David and Susan Perry. We had all gone to some gas station in Truro. We were walking back to town and Tony picked us up.

"I don't think Susan knew him any better until the end of summer. She got friendly with him between August and September. She was going with Tony when he was living in Dedham. She told me she wanted to go up there to live with Tony because she didn't have enough money for a place of her own."

"When did she leave?"

"On September fourth, the day I went back to school."

"Did you see her after September fourth?"

"We met on the Common in Boston the Saturday after she left. I was with Gary Watts; Susan was with Tony and Davey Joseph. I brought her clothes in a duffel bag. Jimmy Steele had asked me to get Susan's clothes and withdraw some money from her Provincetown bank account."

"Did you have a conversation with Susan about her going off with anybody?"

"We walked around the Common for a while," Paula said. "We were going down the street to a restaurant when these two strange guys came along. Although we didn't know them, one of the guys called out to Susan and asked her if she would like to go to Mexico. We just kept on walking. Tony was with us and he heard it; he just laughed.

"Susan went back to Dedham with Tony. When I came back to Provincetown I wrote her a letter. I saw Tony the next weekend in Provincetown—I think it was Saturday, September seventh or eighth—and I asked him if Susan got my letter. He said, 'No, I don't think she got it; it didn't come to the house'—something like that. He said Susan had dyed her hair black and had gone to Mexico with a girl and two other guys; that's what he told everybody. He said Susan left a note with a ring she wanted him to give to Davey Joseph. Davey didn't want to take it; but Tony kept insisting, telling him that Susan wanted him to have it."

"Did you ever hear from Susan after this?" Flynn said.

"I never heard from her at all," Paula said.

Around the beginning of January, Paula had gone to the Truro woods with Costa, riding around the back roads, "jungle cruising." She had seen a green army-type cannister covered with sand and dirt. "Tony unscrewed the top of the can and showed me a bunch of pills," she said. Costa had also asked her to accompany him to a cement house on the dunes, "But I didn't go. Every time I was alone with Tony, he would be uptight, as if he was afraid he might do something. He wouldn't even put a hand on my arm or anything."

On the inside of a waterproof coat Paula owned Costa had drawn three "grotesque things, like something you might get in a head shop," Paula said. "He drew a weird-looking head, and a hash pipe."

"What was the third thing?" Flynn said.

"A female body without arms or legs," Paula said.

Before he terminated the interview, Flynn asked, "Can you think of anything else regarding Susan Perry you haven't told us?"

Paula hesitated. Her pale face colored. "That time I met Susan on the Common, she told me she had stayed at Tony's place . . . that she had slept with him. Susan said, 'I hope he will like me now.' "

Paula Hoernig was far more candid when she spoke to defense investigators. "When Davey Joseph told me how Tony tried to make him take the ring, saying Susan wanted him to have it, I made up my mind that Tony had done something to Susan," Paula said. "Tony gave something to Susan once that made her awful sick. She stayed at my house to recover from whatever it was."

Paula was convinced Tony Costa had also killed Pat Walsh and Mary Anne Wysocki. "The reason I think he killed the last two girls is that I was riding to Provincetown on Sunday morning, January twenty-sixth, with a boy named Dave Tankle. Tony was thumbing in Truro and we picked him up and gave him a lift back to town. David said Tony had a very bad odor about him. My sense of smell isn't too good, so I didn't notice anything. But I knew from Avis that Tony took two and three showers a day. I thought it was odd that Tony would smell," Paula said. "David said the smell was like rotten fish."

Julia Ann Kelly had bought a second-hand army duffel bag for two dollars at Marine Specialties, telling Flynn, "It wasn't brand new, nothing really grand. It had been washed and felt pretty stiff." She had gone to Susan Perry's house to collect her clothes. "I took a couple of white blouses, some skirts, shifts, shoes and underclothes."

Recalling the briefs marked "Thursday" found in the first grave on February 8, Flynn said, "Were there any panties there with the days of the week embroidered on them?"

"I seem to remember there were," Julia said. She had given the duffel bag to Paula Hoernig to take to Boston on the bus. "Paula told me she met Susan on the Common."

Julia had known Tony Costa since he was paroled from jail in November. He had taken photographs of traffic signs, "One Way," "Do Not Enter," "Detour" and "Exit," Julia explained. "Tony said each of the pictures had a symbolic significance toward your relationship with him. If he gave you an 'Exit' sign, it meant you could not longer enter his life—it was one of Tony's little games."

Costa had given Julia an "Exit" sign once. "I felt a little uncomfortable getting it; but he took it back and I was glad not to be ostracized from the group."

Costa had spoken to her about the two missing Providence girls. "He was really angry because the police were accusing him of having something to do with their disappearance after he had come back to Provincetown of his own accord to help find them.

Tony told me he had driven the girls to Vermont, that they were going to Canada."

On every occasion Julia had seen him, Costa had been stoned. "Tony had lost touch with reality; he was apart from the world."

20

On Monday, March 17, at 10 A.M., a motion to order prosecuting authorities to refrain from making public pretrial prejudicial information about the Costa case was heard by the Massachusetts Second District Court.

Goldman's motion was unprecedented, never before attempted at the district court level in Massachusetts, which did not have restraining power. In Goldman's view, however, "The inherent power of this court grants you the authority to control the issuance of such inflammatory publicity, and to order the protection of the defendant's constitutional rights" by ordering Dinis, Hiebert and Katsas not to discuss with the press any extra-judicial statements.

Goldman was seeking court-ordered "guidelines" for the future handling of publicity in the Costa case, following "some of the most sordid pretrial publicity ever released to the press by investigating agencies."

Reporters had descended upon Cape Cod to cover the story that, by its very nature, had become national in scope, "hitting the newswires with an impact comparable to that of the Boston Strangler case." Even foreign newspapers had mentioned the murders, describing in sensational detail evidence of doubtful admissibility that tended to incriminate Antone Costa and imply his guilt.

"Neither the press, nor the public have the right to be contemporaneously informed by police or prosecuting authorities of

228

the details of evidence being accumulated against the defendant," Goldman said. "Ever since March fifth, up to and including last Saturday, venemous and incriminating publicity about this defendant and the murder of two, three, four or possibly more girls has made this case notorious. Statements by the district attorney and his staff, as well as the medical examiner in Provincetown have been fraught with images of sexual perversion, mutilation, diabolic mischief and suggestions of occultism involving descriptions of murdered nude females, drugs, so-called 'beatniks,' combined in such a manner as to intrigue, captivate and sway the public to a degree unparalleled on Cape Cod." Such massive, pervasive and prejudicial publicity would prevent Antone Costa from receiving a fair trial.

"As officers of the court, and as counsel for Costa, Mr. Cavanaugh and myself deem it our duty to direct this sordid appeal to public prejudice to the attention of this court and to seek relief from continuance of highly inflammatory prejudicial publicity."

Goldman vowed to take the issue to the Supreme Court, if he did not get satisfaction.

Edmund Dinis sent his protégé, First Assistant District Attorney Armand Fernandes, to defend the motion. Colorless, serious, bespectacled, Fernandes was a skilled and hard-working lawyer. He denied all allegations, then challenged the district court's jurisdiction in the matter.

Judge Gershom Hall fairly bristled from the bench, "I'll decide whether this court has jurisdiction or not, Mr. Fernandes!"

Taking up his position in front of Hall's bench, Goldman launched his argument on behalf of the motion, listing seventeen specific instances of factual pretrial publicity detrimental to the defendant.

"At his first press conference, District Attorney Dinis gave an account of the case for direct attribution during which he said, 'The hearts had been removed from their bodies and were not in the graves, nor were they found.' He said that each body had been cut into as many parts as there were joints, and that teeth marks and other evidence of mutilation were on various pieces"—such information reported by the New York *Daily News* which had, on March 7, displayed a front-page photograph of Antone Costa at his arraignment alongside the headline:

Dinis had used the word "mutilated" repeatedly to character-ize the murders as "most bizarre," declaring there could be more bodies in the Truro area where the bodies were found.

The Boston *Globe* had focused coverage of the press confer-ence around a photograph of Costa, captioned on page 1:

SUSPECT ANTONE COSTA HELD IN CAPE MURDERS
POLICE DESCRIBE HIM AS AN AMATEUR TAXIDERMIST

The story quoted Dinis that the discovery of the graves had led to widespread talk on Cape Cod of a "Provincetown Vam-pire."

The *Boston Herald Traveler* reported, "Costa stood mute, al-most trancelike" at his arraignment.

"Thus in the first twenty-four hours of public discussion of the case, Costa was labeled the 'Provincetown Vampire' and had been officially described as a taxidermist for the sole purpose of giving substance to the authorities' charge of dismemberment and mutilation," Goldman said. "All of which constitute prejudicial publicity!"

The New Bedford *Standard-Times* of March 7 had published Dinis's opinion that, "All indications point to identical dismem-bering of the four bodies found." There was no doubt in the minds of detectives that the same pattern of cutting was used in all four cases. Goldman said, "I wish to point out that Antone Costa has been charged with only *two* of the slayings, not four!" The same account had quoted a woman employed in a Provincetown drug-store: "To think that such a demon lived among us! Even though they have arrested a man for those awful things, I know I won't be able to sleep nights. It's worse than the Boston Strangler." A second reaction had been published: "It makes us believe that some of us can be possessed of the devil." Wondering why she had come to the courtroom to witness Tony Costa's arraignment, a pretty young woman had confided to reporters, "I couldn't eat my breakfast this morning just thinking about those cut-up bodies. And yet, I couldn't stay away from the courthouse. I *had* to see him!"

"In this sampling of public reaction, the defendant was equated with the Boston Strangler, a demon and a convicted murderer and cutter-up of bodies!" Goldman said indignantly. "And he had only been under arrest for a few days, with prejudicial information supplied by official sources arousing the public against him!"

The March 7 edition of Boston's tabloid *Record-American* had repeated Dinis's theory that the murder victims had been tied with rope before being dismembered. "This, we submit, is a fanciful and certainly misleading statement from a responsible public official!" Goldman said. The same article had reported, "A modern-day Bluebeard was on the loose," along with the "horrifying belief" that more dismembered and mutilated bodies were buried in Truro, quoting Dinis's expectation that more bodies might be unearthed, and his estimate that upwards of three thousand young women were missing in the United States, several of them from Cape Cod.

"Apparently the district attorney sought publicity nationwide by suggesting that Truro had become a vast burial ground for missing girls, thus contaminating the entire Commonwealth—the effect of which would be to deny Costa a fair trial." Goldman added acidly, "Mr. Dinis is well aware that such an allegation as three thousand missing girls cannot be introduced under *any* circumstances as evidence against this defendant."

The following day, the *Record-American* had published the information that a dozen photographs of young girls found among Costa's effects were being checked against lists of missing persons by detectives from the office of the district attorney. Police had found the Polaroid pictures along with a blank application for permanent residency in Canada among items taken from Costa at the time of his arrest.

"This information emanated from the office of the district attorney, the intent plainly to suggest that a dozen girls may have been killed and that Costa intended to flee the country," Goldman said. The same edition of the newspaper "had attempted to construe an accident as a deliberate attempt to kill a young girl" by reciting the bow and arrow incident involving Marsha Mowery. Goldman said, "An even more farfetched statement—again, emanating from investigators for the district attorney's office, was that Costa had on occasion burned his wife with a lighted cigarette, requiring medical treatment. This distortion, misinformation and prejudicial publicity has continued up to the present."

The Associated Press distributed a report that police had

found three .22 caliber cartridge casings and a piece of blood-stained feminine underwear close to the area where the bodies of four girls had been uncovered, Goldman said. "And this, without the slightest reference to the undisputed fact that the area is a so-called 'Lover's Lane,' and also where hunters frequently go."

The accumulated result of such prejudicial publicity was best illustrated by *Time* and *Newsweek* magazines, which had provided summaries of reports appearing in other news media concerning the case. *Time*'s report repeated the district attorney's allegations that the bodies bore stab wounds made by an ax or a cleaver. "*Time* did not get around to the medical examiner's report that the girls had died of bullet wounds, not stab wounds," Goldman said.

Newsweek's coverage carried the ironic headline:

A WEEKEND ON CAPE COD

It dwelled on the "fiendishly mutilated and dismembered bodies of victims apparently tied to trees and killed with shots from a .22 caliber rifle."

Newsweek reported, "Both girls had been slashed around the pelvic region before their murderer severed their arms and legs at the joints with what a coroner indicated was almost professional skill."

References to Costa as an amateur taxidermist had reached a climax in *Newsweek,* which had quoted a Provincetown woman: "He got a kick out of it; one of his favorites was rabbits."

"We do not suggest any invasion of the rights of the press as an appropriate remedy to insure a fair trial," Goldman said. "But we do assert only that which transpires in the courtroom is public property. What we seek today is effective control over the prosecuting authorities' premature disclosure of clues they are investigating and evidence not yet verified under oath and subject to cross-examination in court. We are asking that the district attorney be ordered *not* to release any factual findings as pretrial publicity," Goldman said. "This court must take steps that will protect judicial process from prejudicial outside interference. Neither the prosecutor, counsel for the defense, the accused, witnesses, court staff, nor law enforcement officers coming under the jurisdiction of the court should be permitted to frustrate its function."

"With Tony Costa's life at stake," Goldman concluded, "it is not too much to ask this court to order the district attorney to try the defendant in an atmosphere undisturbed by so huge a wave of public passion."

Goldman sat down to stunned silence in the courtroom packed with spectators.

Judge Hall promised a ruling in ten days.

"We are trying to stop the district attorney from this constant issuance of wild statements concerning your doings," Goldman explained to Tony Costa when he went to Bridgewater following his appearance in court. Goldman brought a newspaper clipping of Dinis's press conference for Costa to read.

"This is a lot of trash," Costa said angrily, "It's no good. All it is is trash."

"By 'trash,' do you mean the prejudicial statements that are emanating from the district attorney's office?" Goldman said.

"It seems to be just a lot of bull. He has this circumstantial evidence, and he has nothing else. Mr. Dinis must really be desperate, saying the hearts are missing and the bodies were chewed. That guy's really sick. To even *say* anything like that, he's *got* to be sick. Because it's so gory, it's unreal."

Costa had written in the daybook his recollections of the Friday and Saturday that Cavanaugh had come to refer to as "the eventful weekend." Reading it over, Cavanaugh recognized the account closely conformed to what Costa had already told them about those days in previous conferences.

"You've obviously done a lot of hard work in that book." Cavanaugh said. "We ran over Sunday in a perfunctory manner before. Can you tell us any more about Sunday now? You said that Saturday night was the last time you saw these two girls. Do you know of anyone who saw them on Sunday?"

"No," Costa said. "No one."

"How about Mrs. Morton?"

"I don't know; perhaps she did. She can verify the fact that I was there all morning. She was around the house cleaning the place up after a rather heavy weekend. She was cleaning the room next to mine and she would come in and we had some insignificant conversation."

"She seems worried that people are going to say you were sleeping with her," Cavanaugh said. "She says you were very clean and minded your own business; then she says, 'There was nothing between us . . .' "

Costa laughed. "She said that? Jeez, she was always bopping around the room in just a housecoat; I don't exactly know what her hang-up is. There was never anything between Mrs. Morton and myself. She wasn't my type."

Goldman had secured permission from Bridgewater officials for Costa to receive a book and a letter from Vincent Bonaviri and Cathy Roche:

Dear Tony:

I hope you're fine and not worrying overly about this mess. Vinnie and I have the utmost confidence in you and your judgment, and so far things haven't been too bad on this end. The usual hassles, but nothing we can't handle.

We were in Provincetown this weekend and your mother is taking things extremely well. The doctor has been to see her a couple of times and has given her sedatives which she only took a few of. We also spoke with your lawyers, who seem to be really cool people, and they too were very confident. Please confide in them because they really know what they're doing.

That's all for now, so keep your cool, confidence and faith.

We'll be up to see you soon!

Love

Vinnie and Cat

The letter had been delivered with a copy of "The Sayings of Buddha."

21

Flynn's search for the murder weapon took an abrupt and puzzling turn when he talked with Mike Andrews. A handsome and athletic youth, Andrews had seen a small, pearl-handled revolver at Cory Devereau's house last July. "It was on the bureau of Cory's room," Andrews said. "He got it from his grandmother."

Andrews thought Devereau had sold the gun to Tony Costa last summer, but he wasn't sure. Andrews hadn't been friendly with Cory Devereau since last August.

Mrs. Nora Welch claimed that Pat Walsh and Mary Anne Wysocki had purchased nine dollars' worth of cosmetics at a variety store she operated in the A&P shopping plaza in Provincetown around five o'clock on Saturday, January 25. Mrs. Welch had not been able to describe the girls or identify them from photographs Flynn showed her at Provincetown's police station. Flynn believed her to be well-intentioned, but mistaken—until Chief Marshall informed him that she was Cory Devereau's mother.

Marshall filled Flynn in on Devereau. A thief and a drug user, Devereau had once admitted breaking into Adams's pharmacy.

"What did you take out of there?" Marshall asked.

"Flea powder," Devereau said.

"Are you *kidding* me?" Marshall said.

"No," Devereau said. "It was all I wanted."

Four days from his seventeenth birthday, Devereau was a thin, unprepossessing youth with shoulder-length hair. Wiry, but well built, he was, Flynn judged, the toughest, most street-wise of all Tony Costa's young friends.

Devereau coolly denied the story Mike Andrews had told about the origins of Tony Costa's gun. He had seen a revolver in Costa's room at the White Wind sometime last fall. "It was a black, short-barrel, .22 caliber revolver with a vanilla-colored handle; Tony was trying to sell it."

"Do you know the make?" Flynn said.

"I think it was a West German make."

"Did you ever see Tony with any type of a machete knife?"

"Yeah, a real long knife, razor sharp; sharp enough that if you held it an inch above your finger and it fell, it would cut you."

Devereau had become friendly with Costa last March. "Tony told me he had been shooting up a lot of speed, that he had been in the hospital in San Francisco. He told us—myself and a lot of my friends—that he had a girlfriend out there he was in love with. He said she was going to come down here and live with him. About two weeks later he said he thought she died."

"Do you know the girl's name?"

"Barbara," Devereau said. "Her last name was Spaulding. She lived in Sausalito."

"Did he ever take you out to the woods in Truro to his drug stashes?"

Devereau shifted his gaze; a muscle in his jaw tensed. "He took me out there last December to show me where he had his stash. We went in his blue Olds—it was all battered up. He said to look for a strange-looking tree and to watch out for a big hole. I walked behind the tree and there was this metal can buried there, full of pills. He had a bunch of like white plastic bottles stuck next to tree trunks, under leaves, all over the place. I saw two of them that he dug up; they held about a thousand pills each."

"Is this just off the road?"

"Yeah, you can stand on the road and reach over and just grab them."

Devereau agreed to accompany Flynn and Gunnery to the drug stashes in the Truro woods. He located them without difficulty, pointing out the hole wherein two ammunition canisters had been buried. Flynn had already examined one of the cans, found near the graves and turned over to Truro police by a hunter —the one Flynn had disposed of at the Yarmouth barracks because it was empty and had no evidenciary value.

On his return to Provincetown, Devereau confided that he had lately not been as friendly with Tony Costa. "Once in a while he'd come over to my house; but my father didn't like him. He didn't think somebody Tony's age should be hanging out with a sixteen-year-old kid."

What relationship Devereau could have had with Tony

Costa, given the difference in their ages, also puzzled Gunnery. "He's like a little kid trying to hang out with the big kids."

Despite Devereau's reluctance to volunteer any information he didn't have to—and it was obvious he wasn't telling everything he knew about Tony Costa—Flynn liked him. A tough, stalwart kind of boy, more loyal than Costa probably deserved, Devereau wasn't spilling his guts like Costa's other friends now that the heat was on. Flynn told Gunnery, "Cory reminds me a little bit of myself at that age."

Increasingly frustrated in his search for the murder weapon, Flynn told Gunnery, "There aren't three people in this town that haven't seen that fucking gun!"

Flynn was dismayed when he talked to Warren Johnson. A twenty-one-year-old fisherman, Johnson had been formerly employed at Marine Supply in Provincetown.

"Tony came into the store one time and bought two nonmagnetic, watertight containers, red and aluminum in color," Johnson recalled. "He asked me whether they could be weighted, so they would sink."

On his way back to the Provincetown police station, Flynn's eyes were drawn down the broad concrete pier jutting into the sweep of Provincetown's vast, gray, rippling harbor, a stone's throw from Commercial Street.

If Tony Costa had wanted to get rid of a gun and a knife in a hurry, he wouldn't have had very far to go. . . .

At Provincetown police station Flynn learned from Chief Marshall that Albert Perry had identified the fourteen-karat yellow gold wedding band with five small diamonds taken from the hand of the body found on February 8 as a ring identical to one belonging to his daughter, Susan. Perry had purchased the wedding band from the Olympia jewelry store in New Bedford for fifty dollars. The ring had been returned to him by his former wife, following a divorce.

The second eldest of six children, Susan Ellsworth Perry had lived with her father for the past two years. "She was a typical girl who wanted to go places and see things," Albert Perry said. "She wanted to go to Mexico for the Olympics; she was trying to save money for the trip with a group of friends." After a summer job as a chambermaid, Susan had chosen not to return for her senior year at Provincetown High School, expressing the wish to be on her own and go to Boston to live. Perry said, "She never caused us any trouble."

Librarian Alice Joseph had known Susan Perry since she was a little girl, Bernie Flynn learned when he went to the tall, white Victorian structure across Commercial Street from the Foc's'le, to check on the books Tony Costa had taken out.

A plump, motherly woman, Mrs. Joseph recalled that Costa often came into the library to look up books on taxidermy and law. "Tony would come in with two or three of his friends; they were all much younger than him. He was obviously the leader of the group. Tony was always polite and well-spoken, but there was something about him, whether he was on dope or his hippie style of dress, that made me a little apprehensive in his presence."

Mrs. Joseph had heard rumors that Susan Perry was thought to be one of the unidentified victims found in the Truro graves.

"I know Susan's family well," Mrs. Joseph said. "She was a very sweet girl. I always associate Susan with doing the dishes; she always seemed to be doing dishes when I saw her. She craved affection and attention, but for some reason she never seemed to make much of an impression. Susan reminded me of the saying—I think it's Robert Browning, or one of the poets—'A maid for whom there were few to love and very few to praise.' It's terribly sad about Susan, isn't it?"

Flynn agreed. It was sad, all right.

22

George Killen was annoyed about the delay in procuring fingerprint charts of Susan Perry.

Killen had received a letter from Dana Hathaway, a ski instructor and safety patrolman in Aspen, Colorado. A lifeguard at the Cape Cod National Seashore for five years, Hathaway had worked as supervisor of Head of the Meadow Beach in Truro last summer. Hathaway's work habits and personal behavior had been "outstanding" according to Park Ranger Richard Strange. Hathaway had called Strange following Tony Costa's arrest, with information about a possible connection between one of the unidentified bodies and Sydney Monzon, a young woman he had dated. Having followed the case in the newspapers, Hathaway cited certain physical similarities between Sydney and the first body found on February 8, as well as the length of time of burial as reported in the press.

"I feel my principal contribution might be the exact date of Sydney's disappearance, which might be difficult to recall now, but which I happened to record in an occasionally-kept journal," Hathaway wrote Killen. "The date was Friday, May 24."

Hathaway had met Sydney on April 5, 1968. The last time he had seen her was on Tuesday, May 21, in the company of her sister, Linda.

During the period April 5th through May 21, I saw Sydney sporadically and informally, usually meeting her by chance on Commercial Street, at a laundromat or at the Pilgrim Club (where we sometimes played pool). She never mentioned any long-range plans, nor did she express any intention of leaving Provincetown soon; she seemed to be mildly excited over her new job at the Provincetown A&P, not having worked for a long time.

She mentioned "Tony" Costa's name often, always favorably, and sometimes sympathetically because she said he was being snubbed and rejected by his acquaintances for having been falsely rumored a narcotics informer. On the other hand, she said it was being maliciously rumored that he was "shooting speed." She introduced me to him at the Pilgrim Club pool table one night, at which time I seem to recall him inviting her to his house the next morning for breakfast or coffee. Thereafter, we often stopped to talk to him on Commercial Street. My contact with him from then on through the summer was limited to chance meetings on the street. He always seemed to me to be especially mild, polite, friendly, with nothing ominous about him.

Hathaway was reluctant to mention that Sydney Monzon was "staying" with Roland Salvador, "because of the additional discomfort it might cause, but one of which you are probably aware:"

At one time Sydney said she was going to move (because of unhappiness with where she was living) and asked if she could rent a room in the house I was living in alone. This idea, however, was immediately vetoed by the owner in May, something I never had occasion to tell Sydney because she never raised the question again. When I saw her last she seemed relatively content.

On Tuesday, May 28, Linda Monzon stopped Hathaway on Shank Painter Road to tell him Sydney had disappeared, leaving all her belongings behind.

Having received from George Killen fingerprint charts of Susan Perry taken on March 27, 1963 by Deputy Sheriff Richard Doane of Barnstable County when she was in the fifth grade, Sergeant James Sharkey quickly matched them to a partial print of the dermal layer of the right little finger which had circulated as identification bulletin 2-29—the first body police had found in the Truro woods on February 8.

Sharkey had received fingerprint charts for Sydney Monzon on February 14 to compare with the same unidentified body. Sharkey compared the record copy of the number three finger with the photomacrographic enlargement he had made of the middle finger of the decomposed hand he had received on March 10 taken from the body found with Pat Walsh and Mary Anne Wysocki. He found them to be identical. The chart gave a description of Sydney Monzon as being four feet eleven, weighing 95 pounds, with green eyes and long hair. Having identified both bodies within an hour, Sharkey telephoned Killen's office.

While District Attorney Edmund Dinis was announcing the news from his New Bedford office, Chief Cheney Marshall told Albert Perry his daughter had been identified as a murder victim. Perry had just bought the trawler, *Jennie B.*, and had planned a weekend of fishing. Recollecting that his daughter's eighteenth birthday was October 15, Perry said, "I wonder if she ever made it."

Florence Edwards was shocked when Bernie Flynn told her of Susan Perry's identification. An attractive seventeen-year-old with a head of tight curls, lively and well-spoken, she apologized for not having identified the wedding band Sergeant Meads had come to her mother's house on Court Street to show her.

"I'd seen that ring on Susan a hundred times, but I couldn't admit to it; I blanked out. I couldn't accept it emotionally that Susan was dead and Tony had probably killed her."

She and Susan had been "like sisters." They had shared a "special attention" class in Household Arts at Provincetown High School. "That was the class for the dummies, I guess. Susan wasn't too bright, but she was a very sweet girl, the kind that collects recipes for peanut butter cookies and stuff. Her family life was pretty awful; like her mother would sit in the living room bombed-out all day, drinking one beer after another and chain-smoking Pall Malls—that used to bother Susan a lot, especially after her dad took the kids and left."

"When was the last time you saw Susan Perry?" Flynn said.

"It was at Tony's apartment in Dedham. Susan was up there living with him. I didn't think she should be there, Tony being so much older and freaked out all the time. I told her she could move in with me and my brother in Boston if she wanted to. Susan wouldn't hear of it! She was in love with Tony and really excited about living with him. She had never lived away from home before and she was really digging it."

Costa had shown Florence around the apartment. "Tony was painting the place. He took me into the bathroom and showed me some blinds he had put up at the window. He said, 'Nobody can see through *these.*' I thought it was a pretty weird thing for him to be proud of." In the fall she had seen Tony in Provincetown and asked him, "Where's Susan?" Tony seemed very nervous and changed the subject. "I thought, 'Oh-oh, a broken romance'; so I didn't say anything else."

The last time she saw Tony Costa was in December. "We were riding around in Tony's old car when he decided his mother needed a Christmas tree. We went out to Route 6, and pulled over to the side of the road. Tony went into the woods with an ax and a saw he had in the car."

Florence had contributed to a collection being taken by friends of Susan Perry to buy a gravestone, but she could not bring herself to go to the funeral.

Flynn and Gunnery went to the A&P in Orleans, a town about twenty miles up the Cape from Provincetown, to inform Dorothy Monzon of the identification of her daughter, Sydney.

A small, inoffensive-looking woman in a nylon smock, Mrs. Monzon was brought into the manager's office. A stricken expression crossed her face when she saw Flynn and Gunnery. Before Flynn finished telling her of her daughter's identification as the last body found in the Truro graves, her eyes had filled with tears.

Born in Cape Cod Hospital in Hyannis on July 20, 1949, Sydney Lee Monzon had a particular love of the outdoors. Like her sister Linda, she had been an active Girl Scout. In elementary school she took a special interest in art. Called "Snyd" by classmates at Nauset Regional High School in Orleans, she had graduated in the middle of the class of 1967, listing her hobbies in the *Tides* yearbook as "reading and weekend trips."

Unhappy with living on Cape Cod, Sydney had talked of becoming an airline stewardess or joining the Peace Corps. During her senior year she had waited tables after school until 8 P.M. at Nonnie's Country Kitchen in Orleans operated by Jim and Nonnie Degnan.

"Sydney was petite, with a beautiful smile," Jim Degnan told Flynn. "She had lovely shoulder-length hair she wore up when she worked. She was very quick; she got around like a cricket. She scarcely ate anything. Sydney didn't seem to have any friends her own age, no boy or girl to chat with or fetch her after work. She always went home with her mother who came to pick her up."

A month before graduation, Sydney had quit her job. With money saved, she bought a small sports car and, accompanied by a girlfriend, set out for California in August, excited and happy at the start of the journey, bundled up in "rough-weather clothes" because of the open car. She had returned to Cape Cod in January, 1968, moved to Provincetown to live in a Bradford Street rooming house, before sharing an apartment with Roland Salvador. Employed for two weeks at the A&P in Provincetown, she

242

had failed to report for work one Monday morning in late May. Her bicycle was found parked and locked at the rear of the supermarket.

"Sydney was a good kid, a good worker and very likable," according to a co-worker. "She was a lovely little thing; a very pretty girl." Tony Costa had become friendly with Sydney the last two or three weeks prior to her disappearance. They had been seen walking along Commercial Street, holding hands.

A former bartender, presently employed in the Provincetown collector's office, Roland Louis Salvador was thirty-four years old and looked, to Bernie Flynn, as though he had been crying.

Salvador had known Sydney Monzon about a year. She had lived with him for two months. "I didn't know she was seeing Tony Costa when he was living at the Crown and Anchor last summer," Salvador said. "My brother David told me to keep Sydney away from him. He didn't give me a reason, but I trusted my brother's opinion and I asked Sydney to sever her relationship with Tony. Occasionally my brother would drop in and tell me Sydney was out bike riding with Tony again. I kept telling her 'no.' The week before she disappeared, Tony dropped up to the apartment with her one evening and we sat around and talked. He was quite an intelligent person, self-learning or otherwise, as far as I was concerned."

"After she disappeared, did you ask anybody in town where she was? What had happened to her?"

Salvador was on the verge of tears. "I asked her sister Linda; but she didn't know where Sydney was. I had Linda come over to the apartment and look over Sydney's things. And there was nothing . . . not even an overnight bag was missing."

23

Maurice Goldman brought his long-time secretary, Edith Thomas, to Bridgewater the following day to notarize the signing of a contract granting him exclusive dramatic and book rights to the life story of Antone Costa in lieu of the payment of a retainer. Goldman had already discharged considerable out-of-pocket expenses to provide for investigators, travel expenses, legal filing fees, to say nothing of the time and effort he had put on the case, and he was not likely to realize any compensation for his efforts for some time. No book could appear on the Costa case until after his trial.

Another book about Tony Costa was already being prepared. Through the good offices of her friend Norman Mailer, whose agent Scott Meredith had negotiated a contract with World Publishers, Evelyn Lawson had received a five-thousand-dollar advance for a work tentatively titled *The Deadly Charm.*

Lawson had reported in her column on the press conference held at Yarmouth barracks:

> As Dinis talked, I felt my skin prickle in dread and disgust. The place where the bodies had been found was near an old cemetery, not far from a dirt crossroads— the traditional site for witches sabbath ceremonies. Dinis indicated evidence of cannibalism.

Lawson had some unusual theories about the case, telling Kevin Kelly of the Boston *Globe:* "Look, sweetie, I firmly believe two things about the murders: first, they're the work of a coven of witches and—don't laugh, I *mean* it! And second, the coven is a front for a large narcotics group." Lawson suspected that Tony Costa was supplying drugs to the coven to whom he had applied for membership and been refused as too unstable and "a security risk." Costa's amateur dabbling in the occult had materialized an "elemental," his use of drugs having weakened his resistance to demonic possession. "Without exorcism," Lawson explained, " 'elementals' don't let go of their victims. Eddie Dinis doesn't want to hear any of this. He thinks, rightly or wrongly, that Costa's his pigeon, and he doesn't want to cloud the issue. Believe me, there's a lot of evidence he's overlooking."

Lawson had once done considerable research at UCLA's library on witchcraft and demonology. "I used to do monster stuff for Vincent Price at American-International. The more I thought about the Costa case, the more certain I became that there were—and *are*—other forces at work. There's evidence the bodies were hung upside down. The mutilation implies ritualistic murder."

Once called "Storm Hill," the area of the graves had a long history of violence, having been, in colonial times, the locale for a gallows, stocks and whipping post. "Provincetown was once called Helltown," Lawson said. "It has always been a gathering place for strange people. Even before the American Revolution, people drifted there from Salem and there were pirates."

Tony Costa had been born at 12:33 A.M. on August 2, 1944, the day after Lammas (August Eve), one of four major annual festivals representing a distinct phase in the tide cycle of the witches' calendar. Once celebrated as a harvest festival in England when bread baked from the first crop of wheat was consecrated, Lammas was also a Roman Catholic festival observed to commemorate St. Peter's deliverance from prison.

Lawson was having problems getting a story line for her book. She had read Truman Capote's bestseller *In Cold Blood* and wanted to take the same approach. She was interested in Costa's behavior patterns and wanted to understand why the murders were committed; but neither the police, Maurice Goldman nor defense investigators would talk to her.

"If we get some money out of this thing and there's anything left over—which we don't want or would belong to you, we would like to make some arrangement to give some to you or your family," Goldman explained while Costa read over the contract. "We want to set up a percentage which I'll prepare as a separate instrument with respect to how you want this money distributed, if we should get it—and we don't know whether we will or not. But if we do, I want you to tell me what you want to do with this money."

"Just give any money that comes along to my mother and she can divide it between my children and herself as she sees fit,"

Costa said. "My freedom is really all I want; and you can't get that with money."

Goldman was deeply disturbed about the identification of the two other bodies found in Truro graves. Costa's links with Pat Walsh and Mary Anne Wysocki were, at best, coincidental—a chance meeting at Mrs. Morton's, a Saturday afternoon ride in Pat Walsh's Volkswagen, and possession of the car in Vermont. So tenuous and brief a relationship presented police with a considerable challenge to put together a prosecutable case.

Costa's association with Susan Perry and Sydney Monzon within the small-town precincts of Provincetown would be much easier for police to pinpoint, providing a local element to the case more dangerous to Costa's defense.

"Today, I want to concentrate on Sydney Monzon and Susan Perry," Goldman said.

"Susan Perry?" Costa said.

"Did you know her, Tony?" Cavanaugh said.

"She was a local girl," Costa said.

"They were both local town girls, weren't they?" Goldman said.

"Well, Sydney was in town for a little while," Costa said. She was from Orleans, I think. I used to hang around with Sydney at the Pilgrim Club and talk with her once in a while; or ride with her through town on our bikes."

"Did Sydney use dope of any kind?" Cavanaugh said.

"Sydney was a speed person," Costa said. "She was always using speed. She used a tremendous amount."

"What about Susan?" Goldman said. "Was she on dope of any kind?"

"Susan, as far as I know, was just getting into LSD. She wasn't using a needle or anything. She was using speed also."

"Did you know that an accident happened to her—she was found dead? That she was buried in Truro?"

"I just found it out tonight when you told me."

"When did you first meet the Perry girl?" Goldman said.

"I knew her for a while, not as friends but as an acquaintance during the summer. She was hanging out with some other people through town, in the center. We would all gather together, all my friends and everybody; and Susan was among the crowd."

"Did you ever take her out?" Goldman said.

"No, sir."

"Did you ever sleep with her?"

"No," Costa said, then hesitated. "Well . . . uh, yeah."

"Don't be ashamed to tell us," Goldman said.

"Yeah, I did," Costa said. "I *did* sleep with her."

"How many times?" Goldman said.

"Approximately two nights, I'd say. She was at my place in Dedham. She and Davey Joseph came up for dinner and stayed two nights. Then she went over to Charles Street in Boston with some friends."

"After you had sexual relations with her . . ."

"Oh no, *no!*" Costa interrupted. "Not with Susan."

"Didn't you just say you *slept* with her?" Cavanaugh said.

"I *slept* with her, yeah," Costa said. "But we didn't . . . you know, have any sexual relations."

"When we say 'sleep' with a woman, we mean having sexual relations with her," Goldman said. "Now, I will ask the question again: Did you ever sleep with Susan Perry?"

"No," Costa said, and laughed. "Her boyfriend Davey Joseph was right there in the next room; he slept on the floor of the living room. There was only a thin wall separating us. We gave Susan the bed. I, of course, slept in the bed because I had to get up to go to work the next morning," Costa said, "Susan and I never had relations or anything. She was a bit too young for me. She was small; she only stood about yea high."

"Were you ever with Sydney Monzon?" Goldman said. "Did you ever sleep with *her?*"

"No, I never did. I was always thinking of Sydney being Roland Salvador's girl. She was, at that time, very dedicated to Roland. I never got into bed with Sydney; I never got *near* Sydney."

"Was it necessarily because she was someone else's girl?" Cavanaugh said.

"No, it's a funny thing. I am not the type of guy who will get into bed unless a girl will meet me there. I prefer knowing a girl for a while before I crawl into bed with her." Costa said. "Sex with me is a thing where I can take it or leave it, really."

"It sounds to me like you took it quite often!" Cavanaugh said. "And I don't *blame* you. What kind of a fellow is this Roland?"

"Roland, from what I know, was a homosexual at one time and I believe he still is; but he was at that time going with Syd-

247

ney," Costa said. "He was super-wasted on speed. He was working two jobs, having a hard time staying awake."

"Did Roland ever make a pass at you?" Goldman said.

"No, Roland's the kind of guy, like he's extremely insecure; he's afraid I might come out and belt him or something."

"Was he a violent-type fellow?" Goldman said.

"I know he became violent with Sydney, because one time I saw him either slap her or pull her hair or something. He just hauled off and smashed her. He was always bopping her around because he was extremely jealous."

"Isn't it unusual for a homosexual to be jealous over a girl?" Cavanaugh said.

"Yeah, it is." Costa said. "The homos that I know—I've worked for most of them in town, usually they don't want anything to do with a girl."

"Was Sydney a pretty girl?" Cavanaugh said.

"Yeah, she was. She was short but not skinny. She was well-built for a little girl. She was spunky, carefree; she liked living. The hang-up with Sydney is that she'd go with anybody, anytime, as long as they offered her speed, or some other good drug that she could get super-high on."

"You had no sexual relationship at all with the Perry girl and the Monzon girl?" Goldman said.

"No, I didn't."

"What about Pat and Mary Anne?"

"No," Costa said.

"No sexual relations of any kind with any one of them?" Goldman said. "Is that a fact?"

"That is a fact," Costa said.

"I don't know, Tony," Cavanaugh said. "It seems to me a fellow has to have pretty good control if he sleeps with a girl all night and he doesn't have any relations with her. It's possible, I suppose."

"If you get to be *my* age," Goldman said ruefully, "But Tony says he has no particular strong sex urge."

"Susan isn't the first girl I've slept with and never had relations with," Costa said. "I know to some people it sounds strange; even some of my friends don't believe it. I don't take particular zest in sex, really. I like a girl for the intelligence she has, and how she can put her thoughts across, not for the pleasure she can give me."

"So we can rule out the Perry girl," Goldman said. "You never went out with her socially, sexually or otherwise?"

"No," Costa said. "Susan I don't really know that much about before this past summer. I met her through Jimmy Steele."

"Will he talk to us?" Cavanaugh said.

"I think so."

"Well, we've ruled out two girls now," Goldman said. "You had no real connection with them."

"Offhand, I would say no," Costa said.

"What do you mean *offhand?*" Cavanaugh said.

"Not unless the district attorney tries to say that I did, or something else."

"Well, you've already said that you didn't, and I assume we can confirm this," Cavanaugh said. "We try to confirm everything you tell us, Tony."

"This can be confirmed, I have no doubt about that," Costa said. "It's just that I get a little edgy when people try to say things that aren't true."

Goldman observed that the conference had gone past Costa's supper hour.

"It doesn't matter," Costa said, "It'll be there when I go upstairs."

"Do they bring your meals to your room?" Goldman said.

"To my *room?*" Costa said, and cocked his head with an ironic shrug. "It's what you would call a *cell.* It's all concrete and there's a mattress on the floor with a blanket. And I am kind of, more or less, at home."

"Comfortable, huh?" Cavanaugh said.

"The place I had in San Francisco had a mattress on the floor," Costa said. "A lot of places I've lived it's been mattresses on the floor."

"Typical of your so-called life?" Goldman said.

"Right," Costa said. "There's no toilet in the room; there's half a plastic bleach bottle and a roll of paper. The bottle is stuck in a vent like, so it doesn't smell or anything. They don't give you anything that you could commit suicide with—this is the way they put it. It's more or less comfortable. And you have the cockroaches to keep you company. There's about ten or twelve local roaches that visit you every night."

Goldman was amused. "Can you set them up in sort of a racetrack? Have you got them trained?"

"Oh, yeah," Costa said with a mocking smile. "I give two knocks on the wall and they go. It's fun watching them."

Avis Costa did not think Tony had known Susan Perry or Sydney Monzon well enough to have killed them. "There was only one girl Tony cared about," she said, "and that was Christine Gallant."

PART THREE

Christine

——————

1

Christine Gallant led a very tragic life, in my eyes," Costa said to Maurice Goldman. "She was very psychologically unstable at times. For one thing, she was deeply in love with Raul Matta. Then all of a sudden she found out that her sister Charlene was having an affair with Raul. And the result of that affair was a baby; and Charlene just gave it up for adoption. This is what caused so much commotion, because Raul was supposed to be going with Chrissie.

"Chrissie got pregnant by Raul also; but she had an abortion to prevent having the baby. Chrissie wouldn't tell me who did it, but she often spoke about how ugly and horrible it was," Costa said. "I believe we should learn exactly who did this to her, since it contributed to her destruction both physically and psychologically and may have great bearing on the case. It just might come to pass that the abortionist is none other than Roland Salvador. All Chrissie would ever tell me was that Raul made the arrangements.

"Chrissie finally stopped seeing Raul. She and I had an affair going for about two years; not what you would call a love affair, but more or less she would confide in me about anything. She respected me; she *did* love me and I loved her, but we never really got into a *real* love affair until a year ago; after she left Raul. She finally came to the conclusion that her and I had a lot of love for everyone, for doing whatever we could for our fellow man. If we had something to give, we would give it. I stayed with her the entire Labor Day weekend. We talked about marriage. She wanted to have a baby, and I did, too. And we made our attempts at it. I thought things were pretty much settled; I thought her mind was rested. She seemed more calm and secure than she had ever been before. She was going back to Fall River, and from there to New York to work at Columbia University. She was going to take classes there."

"Wait a minute," Goldman said. "Weren't you going with this 'Croakie' girl at the time? And the Perry girl was living at your place?"

"Yeah, well I told her Susan was there with these other people. Croakie asked me where Susan was sleeping; so I told her she was sleeping in my bed because that was the only place there," Costa said. "Croakie and I broke up around that time."

"Was it because Susan was staying at your apartment?" Goldman said.

"This is what Croakie took it to be. She was already starting to go out with this other guy," Costa said. "I was breaking up with her because I found her to be dumb; she was very immature for her age."

"Well, you were having sex relations with her all summer," Goldman said, losing his patience. "She wasn't too immature for *that.*"

"For the first month or so that I knew Croakie, we didn't have any relations," Costa said. "We slept at the Crown and Anchor together and everything. Later in our relationship we did; when we started going steadily. This was part of the relationship. We broke up on mutual terms. She didn't want me smoking pot or doing drugs.

"Croakie was straight; she tried a little hash once and it didn't really do anything for her; she went back to liquor. She was a juicehead. She was the type of girl that was more or less a boozehound; she liked her drinks. I've been thinking of writing to her, but her parents are sort of super-strict people. And with all the publicity in the papers, I don't know whether they would like it. I don't want to get her into any hassle with them."

"Let me see if I can get this straight," Goldman said. "It was three girls you were involved with around Labor Day. Susan Perry at your apartment; you just broke up with Croakie, and then you picked up with this other one, Christine."

"I didn't have anything to do with Susan," Costa said. "It was a situation where Chrissie would all of a sudden disappear and go somewhere and she would contact me. She called me one night when she was living in Hyannis and working at King's department store and said, 'I'm at the Bradford motel; come over and see me.' So I did. We had our little romance going there; and we continued our thing. We had an understanding, her and I.

"We were sneaking around because she was afraid of Raul. On many occasions he went to the extent of beating her up. One time he pulled her by the hair and dragged her down a flight of stairs and threw her out on a freezing cold January night with nothing on but a pair of panties. And she came running to me. She was pretty much black and blue; she was all bruised up, her hair was pulled out of her head. And I couldn't take that. I wanted her to pack her bags. I insisted we were going over there to get her clothes; we were getting to hell out of town and not coming back. She went over to a friend of hers; I told her to stay there because I didn't want her to face Raul. She was afraid, she said something about Raul having a gun and he'd shoot me, kill me, some ridiculous thing! And my mind was so blank all I wanted to do was to get her clothes and get to hell out of there. On my way over to Raul's, I decided I'd better forget it and think for a while before I got myself involved. If I got shot or something, it wasn't going to help her any."

"Did that finish her with Raul?" Goldman asked.

"No, they patched it up or something, I don't know. Raul beat her up on other occasions. One time she just mentioned my name because of something I had written in a poetry book I gave her. She said, 'Oh, here's something Tony wrote,' and Raul came over and started beating the hell out of her, and she came running to me."

"Where's Raul now?"

"To my knowledge, he's in Florida at the present time."

"Was he ever arrested for assault?" Goldman asked.

"I don't think she really complained that much about it," Costa said. "Raul's a rough character; he's sort of a big, husky guy, he weighs about two hundred pounds. For some reason Chief Marshall has always condoned Raul Matta. I don't know what the reason is, but Raul has gotten into things which Marshall had evidence to—he taps numbers on car engines and things, he's got half a dozen other rackets going—but the police have done nothing. Chrissie told me Jimmy Meads came to Raul's cottage one time. Someone had complained of a cohabitation charge. It was the night after Raul had beaten Chrissie and thrown her out into the freezing cold. Jimmy Meads went up there and simply told

Raul that they couldn't be living together. And Chrissie went and lived with this girl, Mary. I was up at Mary's with Chrissie one time and Raul came in there and caused one hell of a scene. It finally ended up by Chrissie telling him that it was all over, that she didn't want nothing more to do with him, and if he tried to do anything she would go to the police. And Raul became furious."

"Well she *did* have something to do with him after that, didn't she? If she had an abortion."

"Yeah, I guess so," Costa said. "The time of her abortion was after she left Hyannis to move back to Provincetown."

"How did you know the baby wasn't *yours?*" Goldman said, "if you were seeing her at the same time Raul was."

"The thing is, Chrissie and I didn't have any relations previous to that time. Every time we'd get together, Raul would step in, or something else would happen cutting the whole thing off. Chrissie was really bothered by the abortion bit. She kept thinking of the child she had just given up, the child she had lost. Like she didn't even tell me she was pregnant until after the abortion; I'd say it was around May. I hadn't seen her for a couple of months and I met her in Provincetown by the town hall. She came walking over to me and I noticed she was awful thin; she looked like a skeleton. She had no color or anything. I just asked her what had happened; what she was doing. If she was on a diet or something. She asked if we could go down to the beach. She told me that she had had an abortion, that she had almost died from the thing. She didn't know if she was going to make it even yet; she was just hoping so."

"She wasn't treated by a doctor?" Goldman said. "She didn't go to Hiebert or anybody?"

"Oh, no! Hiebert's super-straight," Costa said. "He would never do abortions or anything."

"Were you in love with her?"

"Very much so," Costa said. "I've gotten to the point where there won't be anyone else. There was always this thing about Chrissie on my mind. She was the most beautiful thing I ever saw. She had light brown wavy hair and a beautiful body, like a model. I shot a lot of pictures of her in the nude while we were balling. We were going to produce a book of art studies, but when she died I tore them up and flushed them down the toilet at my mother's house."

"How old was Christine when she . . . committed suicide?"

"She was nineteen," Costa said. "Chrissie looked much older, though. She was really mature-looking. She was tall, about five nine, her eyes were brown . . . It's a funny thing to say about her eyes because at times they gave a reddish glow. If the light struck them properly, her eyes looked extremely red; they burned with a deep fire."

Goldman was confused about the sequence of events from the time Susan Perry stayed at Costa's apartment in Dedham and the resumption of his romance with Christine Gallant to the time of his arrest for nonsupport on September 9. Goldman wanted Costa to write out a narrative of his doings over that period of time, leaving him a fresh date-book.

Goldman was also uneasy about the reopening of a police investigation in the "suicide" of Christine Gallant. It did not appear to matter whether Tony Costa was seriously involved with a girl or not. Death had followed in his wake.

2

Three days later, the date-book was delivered to Goldman's office, with an attached note:

Mr. Goldman:
I can now guarantee the dates and occurrences since I have related them all to Labor Day weekend. This was the most joyful weekend I've ever had in my life. I spent the entire weekend with Christine and her sister, Charlene at 69 Bradford Street. With this in mind I have put every date and happening in its proper sequence.
You may now turn the page and witness a portion of the 'free life,' with all its confusion! Ready? Go . . .

Saturday, August 24, 1968

I reckon I had worked the usual half day today. I had just showered and dressed when someone pounded on my door. I opened it, and behold! There was an entire regiment of Provincetown people. Jimmy Steele, Sue Perry and Davy Joseph.

I, of course, invited them all to remain overnight, to feel free to eat, sleep or do anything they so desired, but to keep the place clean. That evening I was in the kitchen putting peanut butter on Ritz crackers when Susan came in and sat down. She said quite seriously that she wanted to discuss her staying there. The conversation is similar to what follows:

"I don't really know you well. I feel uptight and funny barging in on you like this but everyone said you wouldn't mind. I'm only going to be here for another day because I met some friends today and I'm going to live with them near the Common."
"You mustn't feel funny, Sue," I said. "While you are here consider it as you would your own home."
She looked sad and replied, "I have no home any more. My father said if I left home to never return, and he meant it!"
"Sue, he would not throw you out if you went home. You parents love you even if you do not believe so now. Don't you think it hurt your dad to see you leave?"
She sat silent and I almost cried as I saw a tear in her eyes. Then she replied, "I think I'll go to bed now."

Friday, August 30, 1968

After work I drove to Provincetown and arrived at 8:30 A.M. I walked to the town hall area. As I stood around looking for friends, Jimmy Steele approached me. He was excited and said, "Christine is looking for you. She's leaving this weekend and want to see you." Jimmy and I agreed to go our separate ways to locate Chrissie. I loved her and would not rest until I found her. I had no idea that she was in town. Through some unexplainable force of nature we have not communicated recently. Later she explained it was because she had heard of my affair with Sandy Kropoff and did not desire to disrupt it.

I was walking along Commercial Street and was directly in front of Robinson's clothing store when Chrissie and her sister, Charlene hailed me. I sensed a rush of joy come over me, particularly when she grabbed me and we kissed openly right in the center of the street. After our excitement subsided, we proceeded to Charl's apartment. It rained that early morning around 5 A.M. and Chrissie and I got out of bed to go to a window to watch it. It was beautiful, so powerful! We returned to bed and slept holding each other. I will never forget this night— so full of life, and love and joy! Since we hadn't been together for so long, Chrissie and I spent the entire weekend together. On Sunday, Chrissie and I went for a walk to the Sea View beach and issued our temporary goodbyes passionately and lovingly. I was sad to see her go, but I was going to visit Chrissie in ten days in New York—that helped ease the pain of departure.

Week of September 2 through 9, 1968.

On Monday, September 9, Joey Thomas and I were on our way to work when Jimmy Cook approached us at the Corner Gift Shop and arrested me for non-support. I spent the rest of the day in jail. On Tuesday, I went to court in front of Judge Hall. From there I was taken to Barnstable House of Correction. I had made arrangements to go to New York to see Chrissie, but instead I was in jail. It really made me sad. I cried for a long time in my cell.

Costa explained to Goldman the "running battles" with the Provincetown welfare department that had led to his arrest. "I told them that my kids needed more than they were getting, that Avis was having a hard time with all the people living there—they were eating my kids' food and everything else. I was furious and said, 'Well, if you don't get off your fat ass and do something, then I'm not going to do anything either.' When the welfare issued the papers for my arrest, Jimmy Meads realized what was going on.

259

He wanted me for investigations because I told him I would give him a hand again after the Von Utter thing. He knew the scene with the welfare, so he got me out."

Avis Costa's recollections of her ex-husband's time in jail differed markedly. She showed Goldman the letters Costa had written from the Barnstable County House of Correction, blaming *her* for his incarceration.

"I gave you freedom last January, a divorce in August, gave you happy pills when you wanted them and went to jail—how much more do you want?" Costa wrote. He reminded Avis that he could have made "trouble" because of her lifestyle:

It would have been easy to bust you for cohabitation, violations of welfare rules, etc. Yet it was not in my heart to do so. Because I *do* understand your head. You have one great hangup: you are completely self-centered. You'll have your good times at anyone's expense—even your own. If you want the love of a man as you say, then look for a man, not boys, hippies, acid freaks, etc. You must realize you are a mother. You should be a woman. My children are without a home. Many nights I have shed tears for them. They need you as I did once. Don't let them down, too. You could be a truly beautiful person if you could but try. Become beautiful in the eyes of those who still love you.

Costa also sent a scathing letter to the probation office:

I want to thank you for what little consideration you gave to my last request of you. But I must also emphasize how ignorant you, welfare and other law enforcement authorities are to the solemn truth! Try walking in on that house, almost every night, and observe an acid party. Everyone so high that they can't even spell their own names; my kids being abused physically, sexually and mentally! Ask a few of her neighbors on Conant Street how much exaggeration there is in this. They have eyes.
What was half the high school doing at her place every night this past winter, spring and summer? And what's

even more degrading is the fact that welfare is supporting all this debasement, degeneracy, without asking a
single question.
Venereal disease has been rampant through that household! Yet with all these facts facing you, welfare and the
police, you have the colossal gall to tell me *I* need
straightening out! It only demonstrates to me how blind
and biased the town officials really are.

Goldman was appalled by Costa's efforts to manipulate Avis
in order to secure his release from jail by suggesting she drop nonsupport charges against him. Costa reminded her, "If you were off
welfare, I wouldn't be here. Do me one favor and I will love you
for it—get off welfare."

Avis had denied having anything to do with Costa's arrest.
"It would have been inhuman to me to have done such a thing,
knowing you depend so much for tranquillity on freedom and
your close contact with nature." Nor did Avis think she deserved
"the rancorous things you wrote in your letter."

Despite the divorce, I can honestly say that I love the
man who was the father of my children, and want you
for a friend. Believe that I want you to be happy and I
will make such sacrifices as I must to provide for the
children.
I join with Peter, Michael and Nico in sending my love,

Always,

Avis

"Do you really love me?" Costa wrote back. "What happened to all your lovers? Wasn't one of them supposed to stay
around, or did he take you for everything he could steal? Was I
such a bad mate? How much would you give to start anew, or
better yet, a second chance?"

Even as he sought a reconciliation with Avis, Costa was not
able to conceal his feelings for Christine Gallant. "I think I have
lost Chris," he wrote, "that's why I'm so uptight about jail. She
hasn't written to me; I don't know if she will."

Ever forbearing, Avis managed to get a message to Christine
telling her that Tony would like to hear from her. He was
overjoyed when he received a letter from Christine, but was disap-

pointed when she failed to show up for a promised visit to Barnstable. He told Avis, "I do love her, but my situation prompts me to expect the worst. What girl would wait for a guy? Should it fall apart, I won't be hurt."

Costa enjoyed working in the jail's garden harvesting vegetables, and he had been exercising to keep in shape, boasting that his waistline was still thirty-two inches. "I have been thoroughly rehabilitated in jail. I have now found peace of mind; my spirit rests harmoniously. When I get out on parole, can I stay at your place until I get myself settled? Floor space is enough. It will only be a two or three night affair. I shall treat you well (if I can)."

A week later, however, Costa had rejected Avis's offer of accommodations. He had petitioned Jimmy Meads for help in securing parole and was impatiently waiting for word of his release. In the abrupt moodswings that characterized his letters from prison, Costa wrote Avis:

> When I first came to BCHC I disliked society. Now, I abhor society. I no longer think they are wrong, I *know* they are! I have little or no respect for the law and have lost all pride in the United States government. I have been confined totally unjustifiably, and have wasted one and a half months of my life needlessly. The law seems to be crucifying innocent, righteous men these days. There is no justice in America!

Costa asked Avis to visit, "So I can rap to you, put you down and ask you about your recent LSD trips. Have you given any to the kids yet?"

Furious, Avis replied, "Who are you trying to convince that I'm into drugs such as LSD, me or the jail censor?"

Granted parole, Costa returned to Provincetown, but stayed clear of Avis and his children. Anxious to contact Christine Gallant, but unable to remember her telephone number he had sent her a telegram:

> I'M FREE. CALL COLLECT 487-9118. LOVE YA!

Christine called him an hour and a half later. "It was a joyous occasion," Costa recalled in a daybook entry. "We talked for almost an hour. We spoke of marriage . . ."

262

Costa went looking for work and a place to live. On November 9, 1968, he had moved into the White Wind apartments, paying one hundred twenty dollars for two months' rent. He had spent a week enjoying his freedom, walking the beach to the west end breakwater and Long Point.

Avis and her current lover, Jon Dorringer, had driven Costa to Hyannis to catch a bus for New York City. In his daybook, Costa observed, "I stayed at Chrissie's place all night. We talked, loved, slept. Christine was overjoyed. So was I."

The apartment at 545 W. 111th Street was shared with Cynthia Savidge, a thirty-two-year-old schoolteacher. "I think Chrissie mentioned that Cynthia was a lesbian she had met in Provincetown; a friend of somebody Chrissie knew. Cynthia invited her to live there, I guess."

The next day, Costa had toured the Lower East Side with Christine. Then: "We went home and cooked up some food, and listened to records until 3 A.M. And we read the Kama Sutra together and *The Lord of the Rings*. These are fantasies about little elves; we went in for things like that. We read a lot of English literature, such as poetry. Chrissie was super-intelligent. She read nothing but clean, good, decent literature that was put out by the best authors. It was all intellectual; there was very little of any trash. She had a book of Sara Teasdale's poetry; she really dug that."

On Sunday morning, Costa went to the Port Authority Bus Terminal to return to Cape Cod. "I got on the bus after our farewell kiss. I really didn't want to leave, but another weekend was ahead."

Christine came to Provincetown, on November 16.

"She was on Nembutal. She was getting them constantly from a doctor at St. Vincent's Hospital, she was addicted to those things."

Costa and Christine had visited Avis that weekend. "They were both stoned on LSD," Avis recalled for the defense investigators. "She wanted to get out of it, to come down from the acid. She was going to go back to Tony's apartment to take something to bring her down. And Tony, I guess, gave her something like downs. And she passed out; Tony couldn't wake her up. And he came to us looking for speed to bring her out of the downs, but we didn't

263

have any. So he went back and walked her around. And she finally came out of it."

The next day Christine had been taken to Hyannis to catch a bus, Avis recalled. "Tony was continuously asking her whether or not she would be all right in New York alone. And Chris told him she would call if she needed him. She was really mentally tired and very confused; even *I* was worried about her. She was really confused between Raul and Tony; she couldn't make up her mind. I think in a way she thrived on being fucked up. She kept saying she wanted to 'shed the flesh.' She mentioned suicide, but she said she thought she was too much of a coward to take her own life. . . ."

Costa recalled in the daybooks, "Chrissie confided in Avis because she knew there was no hatred between Avis and me, that there was only love. Chrissie said she couldn't live in this world, because there was no love in this world, that if anything did happen to her she wanted me to carry on. And I got really uptight. I told her, 'Don't be talking so ridiculously. We have enough love between us, so what more did we need?' On the way to Hyannis, I made her promise not to do this Nembutal thing, and she said, 'No, I won't.' "

"It was the next day—either Chris called or Tony was worried, so he went to New York to see her." Avis recalled. "I think it was the night before she died."

"A week before she died, I went down to New York for three days," Costa's version said. "We went to see one of those French movies where you have to read the dialogue and try to keep up with the action of the picture. We weren't exactly digging it; we didn't care for that. Then we walked around Times Square for a while, had supper and went back to the apartment; it was like one-thirty in the morning. The next day we went to a place called the Cloisters. From there I went back to the apartment and got my things. Chrissie had finally gotten off this kick that she wanted to 'shed the flesh,' that she couldn't bear to live in this world, but that with me it was possible. When I left, I gave her some Nembutal. I didn't give her many. She had a little pill container and I put some in that; they were hundred-milligram."

The night after Costa returned to Provincetown, his brother

Vinnie had come to the White Wind apartments. "He said Chris had called Mom's and wanted me to call her right back. So I went to the Boatslip motel and called her. She told me Raul had called and threatened her because of me. He said he would kill the both of us if she kept seeing me. I just told her that there was nothing to it, to relax. She was crying and everything; she wanted to know if I could go right down there. And I told her I'd be down in a couple of days because I had some work to do."

Costa telephoned New York the following day to see how Christine was because he was worried about her condition. "I called her . . . and she wasn't there. I talked to Cynthia. And she told me then that Chrissie was dead, that she had drowned in the bathtub; but she didn't say anything about suicide."

Avis and Jon Dorringer had driven Costa to Fall River for the funeral. Matt Russe had gone along for the ride. En route, Costa smoked a joint. "I was a pallbearer, at her mother's request. Her mother asked me because that's the way Chrissie would have wanted it." Costa had observed Raul Matta at the funeral. "He was there all dry-eyed and everything."

After Christine's death, Costa invited Georgia Panesis and Ronald Enos to live with him. "Ronnie and Georgia had no money for rent or anything. Georgia lived with me for a while, but Ronnie decided to live at his mother's because of the food and the accommodations there."

Costa had discussed Christine with him, Enos told defense investigators. "Right after Chris died, Tony came over to my mother's house and said he was going to church to pray for her. He started getting on a religious thing." Costa had indulged in "weird poetry and weird pictures," putting together a book of drawings that was supposed to be the story of a man looking for a goal in life. "The last picture was of a graveyard," Enos recalled. "Tony thought a lot about the next world. He used to say strange things like, 'Chris is gone. I'll see her in the hereafter.' "

"After Chris died, Tony was really upset," Georgia Panesis told investigators. "He talked a lot about dying, said he didn't have anything to live for. He cried a lot when he talked to me about her. He just said that he loved her, that they were supposed to get married soon."

Costa now conceded his drug use to Goldman. "Because of Chrissie's death, I was on Nembutal for about a week. After that I

265

called it quits, just before I moved out of the White Wind. I went on a strong health diet."

In Costa's diary for December 5, 1968, he marked Christine Gallant's birthday with the note; "Chrissie's birthday, if the Lord had willed it. So young, yet He must have had his reasons! May she rest in peace under His tender guidance."

Costa also commemorated the occasion with a poem:

(To Love)
The happy times we knew,
    have all turned to tears;
But the love that we once shared,
    will last throughout the years.
For you were called and chosen
    and I, well, I must remain.
To fulfill my purpose here on earth,
    until we meet again!
(From Love)

Costa had walked the winter beach in mourning. "It's just an area that's so peaceful and calm. I got a lot of peace, a lot of tranquillity there, a lot of memories of Christine, of us together, of things that happened. I did a lot of reflecting. At times, I would meditate on God and divine personalities."

On Christmas Eve, Vincent Bonaviri and Cathy Roche had come to Provincetown to spend the holidays with Vincent's mother. He had not seen Tony for a long time. Vinnie found him changed when he visited the White Wind, finding Costa sprawled on the bed, reading. Obviously stoned, he had not seemed to react when Vinnie and Cathy greeted him.

"Tony was like a different person, all hopped up. He was carrying a needle with him and shooting speed; or crushing up pills, mixing them with a little water and shooting them into his arm."

During the week Vinnie had walked downtown with Tony to get something to eat. Costa had ordered swordfish two days in a row for lunch, Vinnie recalled. "I said to Tony, 'You are always ordering the same thing; you must really like that fish.' And Tony didn't know what he'd eaten the previous day—he had no memory of it at all."

Costa spent Christmas Day at his mother's. "No one was

there yet; they were out visiting. I opened my gifts alone. I thought of how much I had looked forward to Christmas with Chris. I prayed and cried for Christine and all those I loved. I asked the Lord to forgive me for being so weak; and to forgive Chrissie if she had intentionally passed away."

Costa had breakfast at Adams's pharmacy on New Year's Eve, spending the rest of the day at his mother's watching television. After supper he went to the Foc's'le, then attended a New Year's Eve party given by Woody and Donna Candish, friends who had provided a temporary place for him to stay.

Costa had four or five drinks of whiskey, then came into the kitchen and began talking to Donna about death and reincarnation; he started crying. He spoke about "having friends who stuck by you, no matter what."

Avis came into the kitchen and saw Costa's watery eyes.

"Are you stoned?" Avis said. "Because you sound like it."

"Yeah, I'm stoned, but not on drugs."

Avis told Donna she had seen Tony drunk three times before. "And every time he was crying about something. Tony got drunk when we were first married. He was sitting on the couch crying because he thought his feet were staring at him. He made me go get a towel to cover his feet." Avis turned to Costa. "What's the matter?"

"What would you do if you had sold your soul to the devil and you wanted it back?" Costa said. "And nothing you can do will ever get back?"

Avis was tripping on LSD and wanted to be happy. "What are you talking such nonsense for? This is really stupid; you're just scaring yourself."

"You don't understand," Costa said. Tears coursed down his face. "Nobody understands. I try to tell people, and they just don't understand."

"What's there to understand?" Avis said.

"Some things I have done that I can never be forgiven for."

"Don't be ridiculous!" Avis said blithely. "God forgives you for everything you have done."

"No, this is three things I have done that I can't be forgiven for; I just know it. The only way I can be forgiven is to die."

"What are you talking about?" Avis said. "Christine's death, I suppose?"

"Yeah, that's one thing."

267

"What else? Is Barbara Spaulding one of the other things?"

Costa nodded. He was rocking in his chair, holding his arms, crying.

"What's the third thing?"

"I can't talk about it," Costa said. "It's just three things that I've done I can't be forgiven for."

Costa had found employment at the Royal Coachman motel as a day laborer on a construction project. One day on the job he had been using a pick when it deflected from the icy crust of earth and tore through the rubber boots he wore, breaking the skin of his arch. Costa was still recuperating at the Candishes when a baby boy was born on January 15 to Donna, forcing him to find another place to stay.

Costa moved to 5 Standish Street. He spent a lonely week at Mrs. Morton's, reading, listening to records, and favoring his foot. He had been living there only eight days when, on Friday afternoon, January 24, Mrs. Morton had knocked on his partially opened door to introduce him to two strangers. . . .

3

At his next conference with Costa, Cavanaugh wanted to know the address and telephone number of Cynthia Savidge, the woman who had been Christine Gallant's roommate.

Cynthia Savidge did not wish to discuss the death of Christine Gallant with defense investigators. She had last seen her roommate alive at 2 P.M., Friday, November 22.

"I was away that weekend. When I came home on Sunday I found Chris dead in the bathtub." There had been three burn marks on her chest and a bruise on her shoulder. Cynthia had accompanied Mrs. Evelyn Gallant to the morgue to identify the body. Mrs. Gallant had looked in disbelief at her daughter's face, and fainted.

Miss Savidge informed New York City police that her telephone bill revealed that Christine had called Florida three times in one hour the last day of her life, presumably to Raul Matta. Christine left no suicide note. Beside an empty pill bottle on a table in her bedroom was a volume of poetry by Sara Teasdale, opened to a page containing one of Christine's favorite poems:

I Shall Not Care

When I am dead and over me bright April
Shakes out her rain-drenched hair,
Tho' you should lean above me broken-hearted,
I shall not care.

I shall have peace, as leafy trees are peaceful,
When rain bends down the bough,
And I shall be more silent and cold-hearted
Than you are now.

Sara Teasdale had committed suicide on January 29, 1933, in her New York apartment by drowning in her bath after taking an overdose of sleeping pills.

When Detective Lieutenant John Ferguson of the New York City Police Department spoke to Jimmy Meads about the death of Christine Gallant, Meads explained that on Saturday morning, November 23—the day before she was found dead—Tony Costa had been observed by a local woman, Alice Fratus, leaving town on a bus. Costa had carried a paper bag, but no suitcase.

On that same day, Christine Gallant had written to a Mrs. Martha Henrique of Provincetown, announcing she and Raul Matta were planning to be married. "I was real surprised," Mrs. Henrique told Meads. "The last time Christine was in town, she and Tony Costa were saying *they* were going to married." The letter had been delivered the day after Christine's body was found.

In an earlier letter to Martha, Christine Gallant had told of going on several LSD trips with Tony Costa. "She said Tony was very strange; that he overpowered her with his talk. Mostly about peace and love."

Milton Silva wanted Assistant District Attorney Armand Fernandes to tell him whether there had been any findings by the medical examiner's office regarding Christine Gallant's death as having been either accidental or the result of suicide. Silva, partner in the A.T. and M.R. Silva, Inc., Funeral Home of Fall River, was trying to collect under the double indemnity clause of an insurance policy issued on her life.

"You suspected that possibly Tony Costa had something to do with her death," Silva said, referring to an earlier inquiry he had made to the district attorney's office in New Bedford. "Do you have anything on her in your files that would assist me in establishing accidental death in my negotiations with the insurance company?"

The death of Christine Gallant was still under investigation by the New York police, Fernandes replied. "Tony Costa was a suspect in the death, but the case is circumstantial and would be very difficult to prove."

4

On March 24, Bernie Flynn talked to Woody Candish. Bearded and ascetic, Candish was puzzled by police interest in a dented green ammunition can tossed beside the walkway leading to his apartment building's rear door.

Costa had lived with Candish and his wife Donna for about a month. "Tony was aware the shelter we provided was temporary, because my wife was expecting a child," Candish told Flynn. "I talked with Tony many times about Oriental sectaries, but mainly about karma, its achievement and the peace of mind and composure I had derived from this discipline." Candish and his wife had experimented with "mind-blowing drugs," but had abstained for more than a year before Tony Costa was their guest. "It was my observation that during the time Tony stayed with us, he was using speed regularly in one form or another, even though he assured us he would not keep drugs in our home."

"Tony made a great pretense that he was not using speed or LSD," Donna Candish said, "but I believe he was using such drugs every day. Each night I would hear him raise the window very quietly and lower it again, then repeat the same procedure in the morning."

Candish had observed Tony Costa closely on several occasions. "Tony was not communicative about himself or his thoughts; he seemed to spend a great deal of time walking alone. He was the kind of person who, if 'freaked out,' remained self-contained insofar as external evidence goes; but who are inwardly in turmoil. Tony strove to present a cool exterior. He talked from the back of his head, every response calculated and delivered after some thought, rarely giving an impulsive answer."

Another friend, Herbie Dam, concurred with Woody Candish's characterization of Tony Costa, telling defense investigators that "Tony would think first before offering any opinions on anything. If you asked him the time, Tony's answer would be slow in coming. In the hip society, this is considered a cool thing."

5

Agreeing that that publicity in the Costa case had been harmful, Judge Gershom Hall ordered Edmund Dinis, Dr. Daniel Hiebert and Dr. George Katsas "not to impart information in connection with their respective findings to the press" prejudicial to Antone Costa's defense—the first time such an order for restraint had been brought at the district court level in Massachusetts.

271

Calling the Second District Court "nothing more than a kangaroo court," Dinis responded that "part-time special justice Gershom D. Hall has exceeded his jurisdiction. I charge that many irregularities are taking place and the rights of defendants and citizens of the commonwealth are totally ignored." Dinis called for Hall's resignation.

On his way to Bridgewater to tell Costa the news personally, Justin Cavanaugh told reporters, "The district courts do not have restraining powers; but this is the only court at this time that has jurisdiction over Costa. We felt we had to exhaust all possible areas to preserve our client's rights."

Costa was happy with the ruling, and pleased that the court had acted so promptly. He had information he wanted checked out by defense investigators.

"These are basically questions I am going to see if we can answer," Costa said. "The supposed boyfriends of these girls—a fellow named Magnan, I believe it was, and Bob Turbidy—appeared in Provincetown less than two days after this weekend; or it might have been that exact weekend, I don't know. I *do* know the girls met someone on Saturday night. The question I have is: Who did they meet? I believe the boyfriends were in town that Saturday."

"Do you know anyone else who saw these fellows in town we could check with?" Cavanaugh said, listening carefully.

"I'm not sure they were in town Saturday, but I do know this, which is puzzling me even more: these two guys, from the moment they stepped into town, *they knew me by name.* Now, how could they possibly know me since I had never met them once in my life?" Costa said. "And this guy Hansen showed up at the same time; they all showed up at the same time exactly."

"Were they together?"

"This is what I don't know," Costa said. "This is what I'm trying to find out."

Cavanaugh was intrigued. "Is there anything else you know about these two fellows?"

"This fellow Turbidy came all the way from Los Angeles. Now why was he coming all that way, on this particular weekend, just to join the girls in Provincetown? Could he have been carrying dope for Chuck Hansen? This what came into my mind: could he have been Chuck Hansen's *carrier?*"

"That sure is a possibility," Cavanaugh said. "Your mention

of Magnan and Turbidy is extremely important, because until this minute we've had no indication that they were in Provincetown."

"The other thing is this," Costa said. "All during the time I've lived in Provincetown, certain groups of people have been terribly annoyed, and actually frightened of the fact that I was working for the police. They even went to the extent of shooting those bullet holes in my car and sending me threatening notes and threatening me openly on the street. Now why were these people so afraid that I was working for the police, unless I was coming close to something? Do you see what I mean?

"The thing I can't understand is, why would they go to the extent of wanting me eliminated? Would they go to the extent of putting a car in the woods to get me out there?"

Costa had recalled another point concerning the girls. He had written it in his notebook and wished to bring to Cavanaugh's attention:

"It was the fact that while we were riding to get my paycheck, the discussion came up about my children; Pat asked me how old they were. And I couldn't understand it because I had never before brought out that I had children, that I had been married. Yet, she knew this! Pat and Mary Anne had a *lot* of information about me; and so did their boyfriends. And I had never seen or associated with them. And to me, all I see is one picture: It's a setup. It *has* to be. How else can you explain it?"

"I can't explain it any other way," Cavanaugh said, truthfully.

"I know for a fact, Mr. Cavanaugh," said Costa, "that I am being totally framed in this whole thing. I have dealt with narcotics people before. I lived with these people, I know how they operate. I have given information to Sergeant Meads in the Von Utter case, and this is the same exact thing. I even wrote a letter to Sergeant Meads when I was in the Barnstable House of Correction last September—that's how he got me out early. I told him I would work for him again, help him apprehend dope pushers. But I had to do it my own way, and he understood this. I didn't want any police assistance until the actual time when everything was tied up together.

"This thing with the girls would have been the biggest raid that Cape Cod has ever seen. At one time I saw an ounce. Now an ounce of heroin is considered a tremendous amount—but to see a *pound* of heroin! This is more than New England has ever seen.

This was the whole thing: I could have turned this over to Sergeant Meads."

"Well, you didn't have any intention of turning it over to Meads, did you?" Cavanaugh said, pushing a little.

"Not directly I didn't; not at this time anyway. Not until I could lure them all into Provincetown, which I did have the chance to do," Costa said.

"But it doesn't *look* that way, Tony," Cavanaugh said. "Especially since you told us you drove the car from Truro to Boston and the dope was in it. Let me ask you something. Assume for the moment that you had this in mind and you started to carry it out. What possible benefit would you have derived?"

"I would derive the benefit from the fact that my friends—who are high school people, fifteen and sixteen years old—I *know* have used heroin. They would grab anything they could. And if this stuff were in town and they had access to it, they would use it and ruin their lives."

"Is there a possibility some of these friends of yours who were heroin users could have been in touch with Chuck Hansen, separate and distinct from you?"

"The only one I know who could have been in touch with him is Cory Devereau, the same person I bought the gun from. Cory's a hard-drug user. His arm is really screwed up, if anybody cares to look at it; his vein looks like a disaster area. He's gone to the point of using drugs until he passes out completely. He'll pass out with the *needle* in his arm—"

"Is there a possibility that Cory could have been in touch with Hansen?"

"He could have been. Since Hansen was dealing heroin he may be someone Cory knew. Cory has been involved in really hard drugs."

"You started to tell me if this big raid were pulled off and the police grabbed the heroin it would benefit you by protecting some of your young friends," Cavanaugh said. "Is there any other benefit that *you* might derive?"

"The benefit that I felt I might derive specifically rests in the fact that Pat and Mary Anne said they wanted to try heroin. Pat was all for it; she was all anxious and everything. Mary Anne was very naive. I don't believe she had tried much of anything. I knew they were running from something, because of what they said about this Hansen wanting credentials so he could hide out some-

274

where or just disappear, and because of their apparent nervousness, or you might call it anxiety. And they appeared in Provincetown for a weekend with three shopping bags, three or four suitcases and clothes on hangers and everything else."

"We have been thinking exactly the same thing. This is why we checked with Mrs. Morton that they had all the luggage you indicated. We believe you," Cavanaugh added quickly, "but we wanted verification on it. What benefit would *that* give you? That's what I don't quite get yet."

"Because, in talking with Sergeant Meads, I would have been able to entirely eliminate the girls from this thing they were involved in. In other words, it wouldn't ruin their future careers. I could have left them out of it," Costa said. "It would have benefited me by my doing something good, by doing what I thought was right."

"If you were about to become helpful to the police in this matter of a pound of heroin, you'd really be dealing with the so-called big-timers in dope traffic, wouldn't you?"

"That's true."

"Did you give any thought to the possibility of retribution against you by these big-timers?" Cavanaugh said. "They don't fool around."

"I realize that fact," Costa said, "but as I said, I'd been threatened before. And I believe God is my father and the Lord protects me."

"You have a sincere desire to help eliminate the hard stuff?"

"I don't want to *see* hard stuff in Provincetown," Costa said fiercely. "I don't want to see it anywhere. I'll do anything I can to destroy it. That would include anything I had to do, even concerning my life. It doesn't matter to me because we're all going to die someday."

"Do I gather from what you're saying that you really don't care about your life?"

"I *do* care about it, in the sense that as long as I do something good for mankind; because, like I say, there's no telling how long I'm going to be here. As my figure for identity, I have the figure of Jesus. The Lord is watching you, he's with you all the time. As long as you look at it this way, it doesn't matter whether He takes you today or tomorrow or ten years from now; because He's *there!* As long as you're doing good, something that's clean and pure and decent, you don't ever have to worry about a thing."

275

"Would you say that you're a fairly religious person, Tony?"

"Yes, I would say so. I don't openly profess my faith. I don't try to push it on anyone. But it is said in the Bible when you pray or do anything in the name of God, that you should do it in private. The Lord will hear your prayers which are said in secret."

"Would it be fair to say that your religious convictions are in your heart and soul, and not on your sleeve?" Cavanaugh said. "Even though, as I understand it, you don't necessarily attend church services regularly?"

"I don't attend Sunday mass because of the fact that I have built up a horrible picture of a bunch of hypocrites going to church on Sunday and then coming out and going to their chores and using vulgar language, cursing their fellow man, slandering everybody and doing vicious things—this is less than an hour after they got out of church! I will go to church—and it's generally on Sunday afternoons or during the week when there's nobody there. I will go in and do my piece in private. I'm not saying it's as good as a Mass; but I would rather go and be at peace with myself and my God, rather than to go in and witness this scene that these awful hypocrites are in there ruining everything. Just doing what they want other people to see them do. I don't want other people to see what I'm doing."

"How would you account for the fact that the bodies of Mary Anne and Pat were found in the same grave as Sydney Monzon?" Cavanaugh said. "Is that pure coincidence?"

"To me, it doesn't really seem to be coincidence," Costa said. "It *can't* be."

"I don't think so either, Tony," Cavanaugh said. "It seems quite significant."

"There has to be one or more people in Provincetown that knows what's going on and is responsible for this," Costa said, "and in turn has brushed this whole thing on me, because of my behavior in the past concerning the police and what have you. Like you say, I was getting too damn close to the big-timers for them to start messing around."

Costa promised to write in his daybook a narrative dealing with the "setup" to give to Cavanaugh the next time he came to Bridgewater.

Before he left, Cavanaugh had one more question: "Tony, our investigation indicates that at one time you worked for the A&P."

"Yeah, I did."

"What did you do for them?"

"I worked at the deli counter, putting out the frozen pizzas, the linguicas and the hot dogs."

"Did you ever work at the meat counter?"

"I worked a little bit out in back helping Art Ventura, who was head of the meat department. I just gave him a hand whenever he requested it."

"Was this cutting up meat, preparing it for packages?"

"No, it was taking chickens out of boxes that were already prepared and putting them in packages and wrapping the cellophane on the packages," Costa said. "I don't have any meat-cutting experience at all."

"Well, that's really what I wanted to know," Cavanaugh said. "Whether at that time you were studying to be a meat cutter . . ."

Costa smiled. "No, it's not my type of job."

When Cavanaugh left, Costa met with Dr. Lawrence Barrows in the guard room. Barrows had been impressed with Costa's self-possession, taking into account the serious charges against him. Costa was unconcerned during the battery of psychological tests.

Barrows was seeking additional information about Costa's day-to-day habits in Provincetown. Costa said he only visited bars to socialize with his friends. He drank an occasional beer, but usually had soft drinks. Hard liquor upset his stomach. He disclaimed the use of drugs except for occasional and "experimental" smoking of marijuana. When Barrows mentioned the murders of which he was charged, Costa emphatically denied he was involved.

Barrows found Costa's ambivalence about his religion puzzling. Claiming to have "always been a Catholic," Costa manifested a significant interest in yoga and Zoroastrianism—as an interpretation of what he called meditation, and the 'Eight Steps to Nirvana.' "

"Nirvana signifies heaven in the Buddhist religion," Costa explained. "All that means is ways of getting to heaven, such as love one's neighbor, and the virtues of patience, peace and everything like that. The philosophy is part of the hip movement—what young people are involved in today. It's more or less a thing, because the past society, my mother's generation, has been raised on the theory of war, of violence. This has been the whole theory of America. It's something that they have been trying to impress upon us. We do not want it; we do not want war. We do not want any part of violence. It's just something we're completely sick of. We want to lead a good life, a pure life; something that isn't going to lead to war, that isn't going to cause us to go out there and kill our fellow man for reasons that someone else believes in. What we believe in is being right, being just, and being pure."

In a diary entry, Costa wrote:

I fear for what my attorneys will think. I am innocent! But *scared.*

George Killen wrote to the chief of police in Omaha, Nebraska, regarding Antone Costa, a part-time taxidermist who had done business with the Northwestern School of Taxidermy and the J.W. Elwood Supply Company. Killen wanted both establishments checked out with reference to any supplies or equipment Costa may have purchased that would assist in an investigation of four murders for which Costa was under arrest.

"Parts of these bodies are missing," Killen explained. "And may have been used in experiments in taxidermy."

Killen had sent Bernie Flynn and Tom Gunnery to Burlington, Vermont, to collect new evidence given Lieutenant Richard Beaulieu by Mrs. Stella Smith. Cleaning the second-floor bedroom formerly occupied by Tony Costa in preparation for a new tenant, Mrs. Smith had become frightened when she saw something in the back of a high shelf in the room's closet and asked Beaulieu to investigate.

"She thought it was a gun," Beaulieu explained to Flynn. Beaulieu found a red-bound, dictionary-sized 1968 *Physicians' Desk Reference of Pharmaceutical Specialties,* listing every known soft and hard drug manufactured in the United States, with color plates and descriptions of functions and responses. Beaulieu also found a torn green and blue Jantzen T-shirt, size medium, and the February 26, 1969, issue of *Hush Hush News,* a tabloid whose front-page headline Flynn observed:

EATS RAW FLESH AT VIRGIN SACRIFICE

Returning to the Yarmouth barracks the following morning, Flynn found a letter addressed to "Lt. Bearnard Flynn," waiting for him:

March 22, 1969

Dearest Lt. Flynn:

I have done much thinking concerning this ugly crime I am accused of. I believe I may have brought forth some information which will be of *utmost* importance to both of us.

If you would have the kindness to come and see me here at your earliest convenience, I would appreciate it greatly. We may both benefit since you want the correct man and I want my freedom.

Thank you so much and may God bless. Go in peace,

Tony Costa
10910 F-Ward

Costa had circled the daily visiting hours printed on the stationery of Bridgewater State Hospital.

"We were in for quite a shock when the telephone rang this morning," Maurice Goldman told Costa when he came to Bridgewater the following day. "I think you should know I got a call from the district attorney's office regarding a letter you have written to Detective Flynn."

Costa shifted uncomfortably in his chair. A three-day growth of beard gave his pale face a shadowed, furtive look. Costa had complained to hospital authorities that he was allowed to shave and shower just once a week. Looking away from Goldman's hard and angry stare, Costa said: "Well, this is what I decided on; that I've got to do as much as I can."

Costa's precise and lofty accent was never more in evidence, Goldman observed, than when he was under stress.

"When did you write the letter?" Goldman said sharply.

"I think it was Saturday. Either Saturday or Monday."

Goldman tried to control his exasperation. "Would you tell us what you *said* in the letter?"

"I sent a request that Mr. Flynn come up and visit, to give me a chance to chat. Because I wanted to find out if he, you know, had been investigating some of these other people, or if he was just dropping the whole thing in my lap. And I would refer him to you people, of course, so he could get information to continue this thing, rather than just calling it quits, as that is not the right thing to do. They should continue. Because there's someone else out there that is a maniac or something. This crime thing has happened many times. What's to say it isn't going to happen again if they don't do a damn thing about it? And that bothered me; that got to me."

"Your inquiry was to determine what the district attorney's office was doing with respect to finding out who is committing these horrible crimes? Or if they are just going to rest because they think *you* are the one that did it?" Goldman said. "Is that the *sole* purpose of your letter?"

"Yeah, that is the *only* purpose," Costa said. "Just to see if they were doing anything so that this terrible thing won't happen again. Because *I* didn't do it; and I know for a fact that someone else is out there that *did* do it. And, God forbid, if anything should happen again. I just don't want to see it."

"When you say 'this terrible thing,' " Goldman said, "do you mean the selling of dope, or do you mean the death of these girls?"

"The death of these girls," Costa said, "and, of course, the selling of dope which is connected with it."

"Is there any other reason you can possibly think of you might want to see the police about, Tony?" Goldman said.

"Only to find out if I can assist them in any way possible. I mean all of us, you and Mr. Cavanaugh and myself. Because I feel we should do something if possible to try and track down who is at the bottom of this whole thing."

"Do you feel I should reveal some of the information that I have in my files to them?" Goldman said.

"That, Mr. Goldman, depends on yourself," Costa said. "You are my attorney. You just do what you think is right for the case."

"As your attorney, Tony, I have certain obligations to you first," Goldman said patiently. "I must know your feelings and your entire doings in this matter—exactly what you want done, before I do anything in that direction. I am certainly not going to the district attorney with any information you have given me until I have your express permission to do so. And then I have to be satisfied in my own judgment—and Mr. Cavanaugh joins me I'm sure—that what we are doing is in the best interests of one person only, namely Tony Costa. *That* is where our loyalty lies. Our oath of office is dedicated to *you,* Tony!"

Costa said, "I feel that if you do come up with anything that would help in any way, then you have my permission to reveal it, using your own judgment. Because I am not capable of judging such matters. I've gotten about six letters this week, and everyone says you are out there working hard. I'm glad to hear it; it really boosts my spirits."

"Now, Mr. Cavanaugh had a very interesting conference with you the day before yesterday," Goldman said. "I was disturbed that you didn't tell him you had written to the district attorney's office. I wish you had."

"At that time I didn't really think of it because of all these notes I have concerning these three fellows—Chuck Hansen, Turbidy and Magnan, and how they arrived in Provincetown, and this sort of thing. I was really concerned about getting that; so I didn't really think about the letter until now."

"You've *got* to level with us, Tony," Cavanaugh said. "If you don't level with us, you will tie our hands."

"Don't talk to *anyone,*" Goldman said. "You never know who you're talking to, if he's a guard or an inmate. Tell them, if they want to know anything, to see your lawyers. That goes for everyone, unless we're with them or we introduce them; like we might introduce Lester Allen or one of our other investigators."

"Right. Definitely," Costa said. "I don't say anything to them. I keep it quiet. When they refer to the case I just tell them it's 'classified information.' There's one guy here—maybe it's just a delusion or something—he keeps looking at me all the time. He sort of wallows around and every once in a while he'll ask a question about the case. And I just say I can't say anything about it; that I'm sorry, I don't want to be rude or anything, but I can't. I seem to have seen him before. I sort of associate him with the police somewhere, but I can't place him."

"The papers in our office concerning this case, all your records, are in the vault. I don't want any of this information to get outside our office," Goldman said. "I think you ought to write to the district attorney. You might say there is no need for him to come to see you, that he should just tell Mr. Goldman or Mr. Cavanaugh what he is doing in connection with your case. I think that should be added, don't you? Otherwise, they'll be down to see you. Just tell them to talk with either Goldman or Cavanaugh about what they are doing in the direction of locating the person or persons who may have committed this horrible crime, or are you resting on your laurels, trying to convict me for something I never did. Is that what you would like to do?"

"Yeah, that is *exactly* what I would like to have done," Costa said. "Just let them know exactly how I feel."

Goldman fastened his eyes on Costa, securing his attention. Leaning forward, he lowered his voice, as if there was someone in the room he did not want to overhear what he was about to say. "Now, Tony. Whatever you did, if you did anything at all of any kind, name or nature, just tell us so we know what to do and how to act. We'll judge what the proper thing is to do."

"Right," Costa said. "Definitely."

Goldman expressed his thanks to Killen for having called him regarding Costa's letter to Bernie Flynn. Still, Goldman was taking no chances. He had Costa himself write Flynn:

282

Dearest Lt. Flynn:

My letter to you concerned the purpose of attempting to ascertain exactly what your office is doing about further investigation of this crime. There is a maniac still running around loose out there somewhere. What are you doing about it or are you doing nothing? It is my desire to assist in any way I can, so please consult with my attorneys to let them know what you are doing concerning the above.

Sincerely,
A. Costa

P.S. Please do not visit since it is now unnecessary but consult my attorneys instead.

A.C.

Flynn was grimly amused at the letter, received on the morning Leonard Walsh came to the Yarmouth barracks to sign a "property recovery sheet" for Tom Gunnery for a 1968 Volkswagen.

The district attorney's office had received notice from the Providence Teacher's Credit Union that an account under the name of Patricia Helena Walsh for a two-door 1968 Volkswagen contained a chattel-lien filing with the Employees Mutual Insurance Company of Wausau. According to treasurer Paul Mirante, "There is an outstanding balance in the account which will be paid in full by our loan protection insurance. This means that the car is free and clear for the proper beneficiary of her estate."

Pat Walsh's brother, Dennis, drove the car back to Providence.

Gunnery was bothered by the vague and elusive memory of having met Tony Costa before. Checking through state police files, he came upon his own record of having stopped a blue Oldsmobile near the Truro-Provincetown line on September 6, 1968, while on traffic patrol. The car had a bad muffler and "was going like hell." Gunnery had not ticketed Costa, warning him instead about his rate of speed. Costa apologized for the noisy exhaust, explaining he had an appointment to have a new muffler installed at Watts's garage the next morning.

Costa had gotten out of the car and walked toward the cruiser—always a sign that the driver did not want police near the car. Gunnery wondered what Costa did not want police to find. Since the incident had occurred close to the time of Susan Perry's disappearance, Gunnery now wondered if Costa had her body in the car, brought down from Dedham for burial in the Truro woods. . . .

Gunnery did not share Flynn's conviction that Costa's gun was lying at the bottom of Provincetown harbor in a watertight aluminum container. Instead, Gunnery led a small search team made up of state police troopers, park rangers and volunteers into the Truro woods to concentrate his searches at the base of trees— a pattern Costa appeared to have used for all his hiding places.

Three feet from the parking space where, on March 4, Mary Anne Wysocki's handbag had been found buried, Gunnery came upon a rusted lock assembly and a carpenter's apron imprinted "Nickerson Lumber Company" with a quantity of galvanized nails in the pocket.

At the base of a pine tree close by, Gunnery found a small cardboard pillbox, sodden with moisture. Park Ranger Raymond Kimple joined Gunnery to uncover turf and leaf mold. A foot from the pillbox, under a mound of pine needles, Gunnery and Kimple came upon a cellophane bag containing a small, .22 caliber, six-chamber revolver with off-white grips.

Gunnery was jubilant, thrilled at making another important

discovery in the Costa case. After taking the gun from its hiding place and laying it out on a cleared space to enable Corporal Roy Nightingale to photograph it, Gunnery sifted through the soil in an adjacent area. Several feet from the tree, he uncovered a hunting knife with a red-striped handle enclosed in a leather snap sheath.

Gunnery took both weapons to George Killen's office in triumph, accompanying Killen the next morning to state police headquarters in Boston where the gun was examined by Chester Hallice of the firearms identification bureau.

No malfunctions were noted during test firings of the gun. The three cartridge cases Gunnery and Flynn found at the grave site had been discharged from the gun, Hallice decided after microscopic comparison. The gun was submitted to police chemist Melvin Topjian, who restored the obliterated serial number 549086.

Reddish-brown material Topjian extracted from the crevice of the hunting knife's guard tested positively, indicating the presence of blood. Topjian also got strong positive reactions from a razor blade recovered near the graves. The blade was supplied with a tool used for cutting heavy fabrics and trimming wallpaper —a tool suggestive in its design of a surgeon's scalpel. Other positive blood tests were obtained from one of two brown-handled paring knives Broderick had taken from the apartment at 364 Marlborough Street and a badly stained man's fisherman's knit sweater found in one of the graves.

No blood or seminal stains were detected on any of the clothing removed from the graves. The matted hair found buried with the bodies by Bernie Flynn had once been dyed a lighter shade and probably was that of Mary Anne Wysocki.

Rinsings of an empty white plastic capsule bottle disclosed a residual mixture of rapid-acting and slow-acting barbiturates. The empty physician's sample package, similar to those found in a pillowcase discovered near the murder scene, had contained Triavil 2-10, a tranquilizer prescribed for the management of psychotic patients with mixtures of anxiety and agitation. A prescription product, Triavil was extremely dangerous when not administered by a doctor.

George Killen thought there was a good possibility that Susan Perry had been murdered elsewhere and her body transported for burial to Truro. Killen wanted an investigation made of Costa's former apartment at 205 Bussey Street, Dedham, and other tenants in the building questioned in order to identify a large laundry bag found wrapped about Susan Perry's torso, and the plastic blanket bag which contained her head.

Landlord Michael Putignano told Lieutenant Robert Masuret of the state police detective bureau that Tony Costa had come to him as a result of an advertisement. Costa had paid seventy-five dollars in advance for one month's rent around the first of August. Putignano had collected another seventy-five dollars from Costa on September 1. He had rarely seen his tenant in or about the apartment. Putignano could not identify the photographs of Susan Perry which Masuret showed him.

Accompanied by the Dedham police chief and Detective Allan Hoban, Masuret took Melvin Topjian to the second-floor apartment consisting of three small rooms and bath. With the permission of James MacKenzie, the apartment's present occupant, Topjian tested the interior and exterior surfaces and the claw legs of the bathtub, the bathroom floor and window shade. If Susan Perry had been dismembered in the bathtub, a positive reaction would still be indicated despite numerous washings.

Topjian's tests of the kitchen sink, headboard of the bed, various doorknobs and light switches were negative.

All tenants in the building were questioned. No one could identify pictures of Susan Perry or Antone Costa, or offer any information as to parties, noises or disturbances which had occurred in the apartment.

In his report to George Killen, Masuret concluded, "There is no possibility to secure sufficient evidence to indicate that the girl was slain in the apartment or surrounding area."

Killen took Topjian to the woods in Truro to conduct benzidine tests on a tree located near one of the graves. Topjian found the presence of blood on a denuded branch stump some six feet from the ground, and on an area of bark close to the base of the tree.

9

On March 31, Antone Costa appeared before a diagnostic staff meeting of personnel at Bridgewater. He had shown no signs of overt psychosis during his period of observation, was in contact with his surroundings and knew the nature and object of the charges against him. Costa was diagnosed as a "schizoid personality," a standard diagnosis listed in the nomenclature of the American Psychiatric Association among 285 categories of mental illness. "Schizoid" in conjunction with "personality" represented an individual whose makeup was such that he made only marginal adjustments to life in reality. Such persons had spotty work records, did poorly in school and were predisposed to drug and alcohol addiction. Acting medical director Dr. Samuel Allen explained this to Justin Cavanaugh when he arrived at Bridgewater.

Costa, Cavanaugh found, was recovered from a brief illness. "It was sort of a head cold; it had my sinuses bound up. The doctor here gave me some stuff for it. I had antibiotics of some kind."

Freshly shaved, looking fit, Costa said, cheerfully, "What have the police been doing out there? I'm hoping they would come up with something on the boyfriends or Chuck Hansen."

"They've been quiet since the restraining order," Cavanaugh said. "There have been reports in the papers that the police are still looking for the gun, but nothing much else."

"How are things looking so far in the case?" Costa said evenly.

"Things haven't changed that much," Cavanaugh said. "We've been investigating, talking to everybody we can." Cavanaugh was awaiting a report from defense investigators who had gone to Providence to find out everything they could about Pat Walsh and Mary Anne Wysocki by talking with their parents, friends, associates and boyfriends. "We are trying to run down every possible aspect, Tony."

"Any word on Hansen?" Costa said.

"Nothing yet," Cavanaugh said. "He's a very elusive character. We want to catch up with him if we can."

"I myself came quite close to finding him at one time," Costa said.

"When was this, Tony?"

"It was a situation in which I now realize the police were closing in on me, trying to get me for this whole thing. And at this time I decided I was on a seesaw, with the police on one end, Hansen on the other end and I was in the middle. I went to Burlington at that time. I went to a local bar at which I saw a guy that was with Hansen when I met him on the Boston Common. This guy said, "Chuck is supposed to be in Montreal, and then is going to Buffalo. So I went looking for him, but my efforts were futile."

"I thought you might be interested to know that I have talked to Dr. Allen and he told me they were sending a report back to the court tomorrow that you would be returned to stand trial," Cavanaugh said, gathering up Costa's notebooks. Police would be moving his belongings to the Barnstable House of Correction in a week's time and Cavanaugh did not want the material falling into their hands.

"Can you tell me a little about these court things," Costa said. "What exactly is going to happen after I leave here?"

"I assume we will have a hearing on probable cause," Cavanaugh said. "That means that we go into the district court, and the district attorney has to tell enough about the case to connect you with it. If he connects you with the case in the judge's mind, then the judge will bind you over to the grand jury. Then the grand jury will return the indictment."

"What will he have to have to connect me with this?" Costa said coolly.

"All he has to have on a probable cause hearing is to show that you knew the girls, that you had their car up in Burlington and that the girls were murdered; that their bodies were found and properly identified."

"When does the trial itself come up?" Costa asked. "This summer, or in the fall?"

Cavanaugh could only guess. "If the trial is scheduled before we feel we are quite ready, in case we want to do further investigating, we'll then have it postponed."

"Do I have to be there all during this thing?" Costa said.

"You have to appear at everything that happens in the courtroom, at every stage of the proceedings; and you have to be represented by counsel at that time."

"Is there anything the police have done that could reflect on my case?" Costa said. "Like when Flynn at the bus station just dragged me by the arms and forced me into his car and started questioning me? I wasn't arrested or anything, and he deliberately held me there until I missed my bus. Is that going to have any bearing on my case?"

"It's not proper police procedure, I'll tell you that; he had no right to do it," Cavanaugh said. "But it won't make any difference in your case. If you made any admissions to Flynn, those admissions would not be admissible in court. We would be able to suppress those."

"So whatever I told them before would have no bearing?" Costa said.

"Oh, *that* can be brought up. You walked into the police station in Provincetown voluntarily, so that whole conversation can be related; because at the time you were not even a suspect," Cavanaugh said. "What difference does that make? You didn't tell them anything, did you?"

"In talking to them I was really beating around the bush," Costa said, and smiled. "I gave them a lot of misleading information. I was covering up for the girls and for Chuck. I was concerned because Mr. Marshall was sitting right there beside me; I believed firmly at that time he had followed the girls all the way to Provincetown and was trying to bind us all together as to one big dope ring, which was to my mind what he was doing. Marshall wasn't tough, but he was sleazy. He was trying to insinuate certain things; he was trying to squeeze certain things out. But you can't squeeze anything out of something that isn't there. So I just covered up as much as I could."

"Since you didn't trust Marshall," Cavanaugh said, "why didn't you talk to your friend, Jimmy Meads?"

"I *wanted* to talk to Jimmy. When I called him and he said, 'I'll pick you up in the morning and we'll go down to the station and I'll talk to you,' I thought, 'Here it is, I'm going to let him know what I'm doing.' So we get to the station and he runs out; he just left me there with Marshall, Lieutenant Flynn and Lieutenant Dunn. And I didn't like this scene at all! I wanted to tell the whole story to Jimmy; but when I got there all the state cops were waiting and they wouldn't let Jimmy stay in the room. They started persecuting me, like saying, 'We know you killed the girls,' and this turned me right off. It was presented to me as being a gestapo interrogation. And Flynn came out and started being idiotically ridiculous. He started accusing me of being doped up at the time. He said, 'You're in a trance.' And I just sat tranquil in my chair and said, 'Oh, for God's sake, don't be so ridiculous! What are you trying to say?' "

"Did Flynn mention Susan Perry or Sydney Monzon at that time?"

"He asked me about a bunch of people in town that were missing. He had a list of about maybe sixty names and he just rambled on through it. At that time I didn't even know they had found a body in the woods. It was the next day it was in the paper. The police thought I was a fool! They thought I had never been into this. And I knew all these things they were doing; so they weren't beating me around the bush. I knew police tactics, because I had studied them."

Costa was amused that a report on his mental faculties should be written on April Fool's Day. "Dr. Barrows came up and said they could find nothing," Costa said. "He said just a little bit of schizoid personality. And I said, 'Geez, what does that mean?' And he said, 'It just means that you cannot judge things properly at times.' And I guess he meant something about this mess that I got myself into."

Dr. Allen's two-page report was contained in a letter with a warrant authorizing Tony Costa's return to the district court in Provincetown as competent to stand trial. The diagnosis had been arrived at as a result of tests and "other information." Details of the crimes Costa was accused of had been obtained from newspaper accounts, not from the patient himself. Costa had denied drinking alcohol excessively. "For one year prior to his divorce, patient smoked marijuana regularly, but denies all other drugs."

Costa had spent six weeks at the Barnstable House of Correction for nonsupport. "His only other arrests were for breaking and entering in the nighttime with intent to commit a felony, and assault and battery."

> During his current period of observation, patient has been cooperative and oriented in all spheres. He appears to be of average intelligence with a Full Scale I.Q. of 121. The EEG performed here was evaluated as "normal." He appeared apprehensive but exhibited very little anxiety. His thought content showed no overvalued ideas and he did not evidence severe depression or suicidal material. His memory for recent and remote events showed no impairment.
>
> It is the opinion of the staff that patient shows no sign of an overt psychosis, is certainly in contact with his surroundings, knows the nature and objects of his charges and the possible consequences and appears to be able to assist counsel in his own defense.

Goldman didn't think much of the report. "They say that he's got a personality, or whatever the hell that is. Doesn't mean a thing. *Everybody's* got that." Goldman was talking to Lawrence Shubow, a lawyer with the Boston firm of Allen, Hemingway, Morse and Shubow, whom he wanted to bring into the case to handle the psychiatric aspects of the defense. That Costa was both apprehensive and had displayed very little anxiety was, to Goldman's way of thinking, completely inconsistent. "A person who is apprehensive means that he is frightened." Goldman said. "A person who displays very little anxiety means he is not concerned." The examination had taken place sometime after March 5, but the report was issued a month later, Goldman explained. "During the intervening time, Tony has probably been recovering from drug use, or certainly didn't know what he was talking about when he denied use of all other drugs than marijuana."

Having served as president of the Massachusetts Mental

Health Center area board, Shubow was in touch with the best psychiatric talent in the state— "If that should prove useful," Shubow added dryly after accepting Goldman's invitation be co-counsel on the Costa case.

Goldman was astonished at Costa's reaction to the report.

"Those fabulous psychotic doctors and psychologists decided to endow me with the term 'schizoid,' since they felt it their duty to make some finding."

Costa complained the living conditions at Bridgewater had been intolerable with cockroaches "crawling about in throngs," mice running across the floor, and freezing cold temperatures in his cell. "I was allowed to leave my room only once or twice a week for an hour or so to speak with the doctors or an occasional visitor. I was deprived of all my clothes and eyeglasses, without which I am blind. I was completely restrained from reality and life —no radio, TV, newspapers. I was given my prayer book and rosary beads. This was my greatest consolation and was all I needed. I was denied church privileges. Thus, for a total of thirty-six days I remained under these conditions and still have managed to possess my mental faculties intact." Costa said. "Finally, I had to divulge my entire private life to these doctors. So they can call me schizoid, or any other name, but my proper title is 'man.' "

In his daybook, Costa wrote;

Unless one can experience the pain and torment of my imprisonment, false accusations and persecutions, then one is definitely ignorant of the actual sensations involved. You are made to feel less than human, less than animal. I ask: When were these doctors ever made to experience this? They have observed it in others, but never in themselves.

So, you doctors of the mind, to judge others is fine theory but you lack the most necessary ingredient: experience.

Goldman was interested in the report's reference to Costa's breaking and entering and assault record as given in his history.

"That was a strange thing," Costa said. "This girl Donna, she kept more or less harassing me. She was quite loose morally; and for some reason she had this big hang-up about me. Like I

292

had just gotten my first car and I rented a garage from her mother. I was doing work for her parents, like digging up the lawn and replanting. Every time I would get a chance to sneak away to the garage, like man, in she comes! And she was telling me all this bull and it got to the point where I just couldn't bear it anymore, and I told her to leave me alone. She came to the point of inviting me up to her room; she gave me a key to the house and everything. I didn't really know what to make of it, and I told her to stop bothering me or I would have to go to her parents. And then, lo and behold, she comes up to my front porch. I was just going in the door and she's following me in. And I turned around, and the next thing I know she's like clawing me and grabbing me; she's pulling at my shirt. And I pushed her away. I guess I used a little bit of force or something and she didn't dig the idea. I told her to get lost; I wanted nothing to do with her. And she went home crying and invented this big spiel about how I had tried to attack her or some other thing."

"Did you ever go to her house?" Goldman said.

"Previous to this occasion I did. I don't remember exactly what the circumstances were, but it was in the daytime and we discussed matters. The next thing I know she's giving me all this bull. It was ridiculous! The police came and got me. I didn't know exactly what to say; I was confused. I was kind of lost. Like this whole thing came up all at once. I can't really recall now what I said. I looked for the easiest way out."

"You never had sex relations with her of any kind?" Goldman said.

"No, not at all. She was just a little squirt; she was a little, skinny thing," Costa said with a grimace. "She was nothing."

George Killen had also looked into Tony Costa's previous criminal record, receiving the details from Captain John Powers of the Somerville Police Department.

Around 4 A.M. on November 18, 1961, Tony Costa had entered a second-floor apartment at 150 Hudson Street in Somerville and made his way to the room where fourteen-year-old Donna Welch was sleeping. A flashlight Costa turned on had wakened the girl; her head struck Costa's elbow as he was bending over her. Costa had fled when Donna screamed. She did not see who was in her room.

Three days later, Costa sent a child to the Welch apartment

with a message that a neighbor wanted to see Donna after school. When Donna visited the neighbor that afternoon she was told that no message had been sent. Returning home, she was on a first-floor landing when Costa came out of a basement door, grabbed her by the arm and tried to drag her down the stairs. Her screams brought some of the building's tenants into the hallway. Costa let Donna go, then disappeared into the basement.

After his arrest, Costa had given Powers a statement;

I met Donna Welch on Thursday afternoon, November 16. She gave me a key to her house and told me to come to her bedroom the next night after the dance. About 7 P.M. that evening I met Michael Grant. He told me Donna told him to tell me she hated my guts. I asked him why and he said he didn't know.

On Friday night I went to the dance at the high school. The dance was over at 11:30. I took a bus back and walked to Hudson Street and stood outside Donna's house for about an hour, then went into the back yard at Welch's and up the back stairs. I used the key Donna had given me and closed the kitchen door quietly. I walked to the front of the house and saw a girl on a bed. I was not sure it was Donna. I had a flashlight and I flicked it on for a second to make sure it was her. I tapped her on the shoulder and she jumped up real quick. Her head hit my elbow. I told her it was me and she said, "I'm glad you came." I told her, "We shouldn't be doing this, we will get into trouble." She said she didn't care. I told her I was going home and she started to scream. I got scared and ran out of the house. . . .

On Tuesday, November 21, I sent Sandra Sprague who lives on the first floor in my house over to say that Mrs. Williams, who lives on the second floor of my house, wanted to see Donna after school. Around 2:20, I heard someone going up to the second floor I thought was Donna. I waited until she came down the stairs. As she reached the landing, I grabbed her by the shoulder and the coat. I wanted to ask her why she hated my guts. She screamed and I let her go. I did not punch her or try to choke her.

Costa had also admitted that two years earlier he ..
table in the basement of the triple-decker where he lived with ..
mother and half brother. "Donna came over a lot. One time I tied
her up with rope and she did not holler and I took her underpants
down and looked at her. I did not do anything else. Another time
I had her in my house and no one else was home and I tied her
hands in the bathroom and took her pants down and just looked
at her."

Costa was found guilty of assault and battery and breaking
and entering in the nighttime with intent to commit a felony on
January 4, 1962. Given a suspended one-year sentence in the
house of correction, he was put on probation for three years.

Cecelia Bonaviri, separated from her husband for two
months and planning to initiate divorce proceedings, had no explanation for her son's abnormal behavior. Tony did not use narcotics or intoxicants and had never been a discipline problem at
home. He attended church regularly. In order to remove him from
"neighborhood influences," she sent him to live with her married
sister, Mrs. Mary Perkins, in Provincetown.

Costa had regularly reported to Thomas McGovern, chief
probation officer at Barnstable courthouse. A senior at Provincetown High School, Costa was "getting along well," according to
principal George Leyden. "The boy seems to be a gentleman, and
seems to have settled down."

After graduation Costa had been employed as a grocery
clerk, a part-time mechanic and a gas company deliveryman.
Costa told McGovern he would like to move to California because
employment prospects in Provincetown were "not too favorable,"
but decided to wait until he was discharged from probation on
January 28, 1965.

Mrs. Martha Wysocki flinched when Bernie Flynn showed her a bloodstained white fisherman's-knit sweater. She shook her head silently when Flynn asked her if it had belonged to Mary Anne. Nor had Catherine Walsh ever seen the sweater before, although she positively identified a sweater of similar design, found in Tony Costa's room, as having belonged to her daughter.

Flynn showed Gerry Magnan a pair of brown plaid slacks retrieved from the grave.

"Mary Anne owned a pair of slacks just like that; she wore them in my presence," Magnan said. "In fact, I bought them for her."

Flynn found Bob Turbidy changed. Bearded, his hair grown long, Turbidy had put up seven hundred dollars for the rental of a shop on Commercial Street in Provincetown for the coming season, as a partner with Russell Norton in a leathercraft business. Turbidy was planning a trip to Provincetown to build workbenches and shelving for the new enterprise.

Turbidy and Magnan spent three hours giving defense investigator Stephen Delaney the details of the weekend trip to Provincetown from which both Pat and Mary Anne had made definite plans to return, Turbidy explaining his conversation with Pat had occurred the night before she left Providence. Police had placed no significance in the girls' disappearance until Bernie Flynn entered the case.

Turbidy solved the "mystery" of the man the girls had told Mrs. Norton they were going to meet. "They invited Russ Norton to ride to Provincetown with them, but he had a conflict," Turbidy said. "He did go there on Saturday, but he couldn't find the girls."

Neither Turbidy nor Magnan knew anyone by the name of Chuck Hansen ever having associated with either of the girls.

"Pat was the least outgoing," Turbidy said. "I'd say she was rather shy; she didn't make friends very easily. Mary Anne was much more talkative, but more conservative in her views—very straight, Pat liked the informality and the ideals of the hippie generation. Her parents didn't understand or approve of that scene at all; they were pretty much a hindrance because they wanted her to live conventionally. They were very possessive. They wanted to run her life. That's why she got her own place, so she could live like she wanted to live." The Walshes had objected to Turbidy. "They thought I was part of Pat's hippie life," he told Delaney.

Turbidy had not been in contact with Walsh family since the funeral.

"From what they have told others, they're hoping Costa is executed," Turbidy said. "I think that would be as great a crime as the one he's charged with. He had to be insane to do what they say he did. The way he was running around when I was trying to find him, and the statements he's made . . . I'd say only an insane person could act that way. There's a chance if he remains alive and under study in a mental institution, society may learn something about mental illness like his. I'm against capital punishment anyway. I think this is a chance to learn something, or the girls' deaths will have been to no purpose at all."

"Can you think of any reason Pat and Mary Anne would go with Tony to the Truro woods after just meeting him?" Delaney asked. "Would Pat have gone with Tony if he offered to sell her some good pot?"

"I think so," Turbidy said, "but only if Mary Anne was with her. Is that what Costa says?"

"He's talked about a sale of hard drugs involving the girls. Did Pat ever use heroin?"

"Hell, *no*," Turbidy said. "She smoked pot once in a while with me, but that's all. And Mary Anne didn't even smoke. Pat and I offered her a chance, but she wasn't even interested in trying it."

Delaney left the interview with the opinion that both young men had been candid and cooperative. Turbidy had loaned Delaney a photograph of Pat Walsh with a request that it be returned. "Both young men have been assured that police have evidence to prove beyond a doubt that Tony Costa killed the girls," Delaney reported to Goldman. "It was no consolation to them."

12

When Flynn returned to Cape Cod he spoke with Brenda Dryer and Irene Hare in the district attorney's office. The girls had moved to Cape Cod and were sharing an apartment at 146 South Street in Hyannis. Scheduled to be called as witnesses for the prosecution, they reviewed with Bernie Flynn the evening they had spent at the Foc's'le in the company of Pat Walsh and Mary Anne Wysocki. "Bunny" Dryer had finished her statement and was preparing to leave the office when she mentioned having visited her boyfriend, Davey Joseph, several weeks ago in Provincetown.

"It was the day his mother called Kentucky about a blue stone ring Tony Costa said Susan Perry wanted Davey to have. Davey gave the ring to his cousin."

"Had Davey given the ring to Susan?" Flynn asked.

"Oh, no! He'd gone out with Susan about four years ago, when they were in school," Bunny said. "Davey was upstairs waiting for the phone call; I was downstairs talking to Cory Devereau. Cory was drunk. He said to me, 'Do you think Tony did it?' I told him I did. He told me, 'I do, too.' And he told me about the night he and Tony had broken into the Crown and Anchor when the place was closed: 'There were rugs rolled up all over the place and Tony kept saying, "There's dead bodies on the floor." He was running in and out of the rooms, yelling, "Ha, ha, death is after you!" He always talked about death; how wonderful it was.' "

Devereau had told her, "Nobody knows this, but I was the one that sold Tony the gun. I don't know what he did with it, but he hid the knives, too."

Devereau went voluntarily to the Provincetown police station to speak with Chief Marshall a week after Susan Perry's body had been identified, telling Marshall, "We were close friends; I went out with her. It was all teenagers in our group, except for Tony."

Flynn confronted Devereau in Marshall's office. "We have

received information you had a certain gun in your possession in the summer of 1968."

Devereau readily admitted he had. "I was uptight before, that's why I didn't tell you. I got the gun when I left town with Mike Andrews, last April sometime. We went to Boston; from Boston to Washington and by bus to Bluefield, West Virginia. We visited my grandmother. She had a drugstore called Taylor's—it's closed now. We stayed there one day. While we were at my grandmother's, she told me to get some towels and razor blades and get cleaned up. When I was looking around the room I found the gun on the floor near the headrest of her bed. Mike said for me to take it; I put it in my suitcase."

"Describe the gun," Flynn said.

"It was a .22 caliber, six-shot revolver with a pearl handle, made in Western Germany. A short barrel with a black finish."

"After putting the gun in your suitcase, what did you do?"

"We got cleaned up and walked around Bluefield. We eventually returned to Provincetown."

"After you came back to Provincetown, did you have a conversation with Tony Costa regarding his searching around to buy a gun?"

"Sometime in July, Tony asked me if I knew where he could get a gun. Tony said he was dealing and he wanted a gun for protection. He asked me and several of my friends if we knew of anyone that had a pistol; I said no. I kept the gun for a while in my house. I fired the gun out at the old dump into a yellow chair or sofa. I figured if I kept the gun I would get in trouble. I saw Tony outside the parking lot of the Crown and Anchor. He asked me if I had heard of anyplace he could get a gun. I said, 'I have one, if you want to buy it you can.' I took the gun to his room at night. He paid me twenty dollars. He asked me if I had any shells for it. I said 'no.' At the beginning of September I asked Tony if he still had the gun. Tony said he did."

"This statement we just received is a true statement, given of your own free will?" Flynn said. It was the fifth time in as many weeks he had interrogated Cory Devereau. Flynn wondered how much more information there was in that tough little skull.

"Yeah, it is," Devereau, said, evenly. *"Completely."*

Flynn and Gunnery flew from Boston to Washington where they boarded a Piedmont Airlines plane that to Flynn resembled something out of World War I. The low-flying plane seemed to skim precipitously over the West Virginia mountaintops. Flynn was shaky-legged at the end of the harrowing ride, hailing a taxicab at the airport. When Flynn gave the Bluefield Hotel as his destination, the driver swiveled about in his seat and said, "Are you *sure* you want to go there?"

Flynn was sure; arrangements for accommodations had been made by a travel agent on Cape Cod who told him the hotel was comfortable and centrally located. When the cab drew up to the Bluefield Hotel, however, Flynn saw that the place was in an advanced stage of dilapidation, most of its residents hanging out of windows to appraise the new arrivals with curiosity. Flynn asked to be taken to a motel outside of town.

Still unsettled from the plane ride, Flynn asked the desk clerk for the bar and was told the county was "dry" by local option. They could get a drink in the next county, twenty miles away.

A cab took Flynn and Gunnery to a single-story cement-block building squatting in the center of barren flatlands, a private club. When Flynn pushed the buzzer, an eye appeared in the peephole set in the door.

"Are you a member?" a thickly accented female voice asked.

Flynn assured her that he was.

The door was opened by a pretty young woman holding a ledger. She asked Flynn his name. He could only think of "Ferreira," a common Portuguese name in New Bedford. Looking over the young woman's shoulder as she slowly went down the club's roster, Flynn spotted a listing for "Ferrago."

"There I am," Flynn said. "That's me!"

Flynn and Gunnery enjoyed several rounds of drinks, and a superb dinner. Flynn signed the tab with a flourish, using the name he had "borrowed" and left a very generous tip. He had the young woman at the door fetch him a cab.

Gunnery thought he would die laughing during the drive back to Bluefield.

The next morning Flynn spoke to Lester Shrader, manager of the sporting goods department of the Bluefield Supply Company, a wholesale outlet store selling sporting goods and camping equipment. Records revealed that gun number 549086, a Model E1, six-chambered .22 caliber revolver with white grips, had been received from the EIG Cutlery Company of Miami, Florida in January 1962. On April 24, 1967, the gun had been sold to pharmacist John B. Taylor, proprietor of Taylor's drugstore in Bluefield.

Her late husband had kept the gun in its original box under the counter of the drugstore, Mrs. Viola Taylor told Flynn. She had brought the gun home when she heard prowlers about the house, and had kept the gun in her bedroom, sometimes in a closet and on occasion by the side of her bed. Last spring, her grandson Cory, had visited, staying overnight. When Cory left, she discovered the gun was missing. She had not reported the theft to local police.

Mrs. Taylor was afraid the two Massachusetts policemen were going to ask her why she hadn't, but they just thanked her and left.

Flynn returned to Cape Cod to give testimony before the grand jury. Killen had given the responsibility for presenting the case to Flynn because of his glibness, presence and total conviction of Costa's guilt.

Killen had allotted Flynn a large measure of credit for breaking the case by discovering the locale of Costa's marijuana garden. His tireless interrogations of Costa's young friends had led police to the scene of the murders, Killen conceded, "We could have been wandering around those woods for months."

Flynn was confident that there was sufficient evidence to find indictments in the murders of Pat Walsh and Mary Anne Wysocki. He was less sure that Costa's links with Susan Perry and Sydney Monzon—other than the location of their graves and the similar mutilations—were strong enough to convince a grand jury that Costa had killed them, and he resolved to supply the missing connections if he could. As the prosecution's only witness, he spoke for five straight hours, giving a step-by-step recital of all known evidence. During his testimony he relied on notebooks and various reports, including his own, which would eventually amount to 132 double-spaced legal-size pages, perfectly typed for him by his fiancée, Jacqueline Buzzee.

13

Goldman was not surprised when the grand jury brought indictments charging his client with the murders of four young women. Goldman went with Cavanaugh to Bridgewater to break the news to Costa himself, taking Avis along to soften the blow.

Goldman had come to admire Avis. A spunky girl, devastatingly candid, she had never flinched from telling investigators the truth. Goldman had arranged for her to move into a three-bedroom apartment above his former law offices in a building he owned on Bradford street, much more comfortable accommodations than the cramped quarters she presently occupied. Goldman was reducing the rent to whatever the welfare office could afford to pay for the place.

Avis had signed a contract with Goldman granting him sole and exclusive "world rights and title" to all dramatic and publishing uses of her "personal narrative and life story" as the former wife of Antone Costa. Goldman was free to draw upon "common source materials" furnished by Avis and on notes of her relationship "with any person concerned in these matters." From such "gross sums" as Goldman might receive from the media, Avis was to be paid an amount equal to 15 percent, but in no event more than fifteen thousand dollars.

Costa took the news of his indictment well, expressing surprise that the grand jurors should find him involved in any of the murders. Goldman gave him plenty of time for a private talk with Avis.

Costa showed her a picture he had drawn in blue pencil to illustrate a dream he had, explaining, "I stood on a pier watching two fishermen in a small boat pulling in their net. It contained the largest and most fish I had ever seen. They were extremely close to shore. It impressed me religiously; it could be a vision from God."

Costa had been having other visions, Avis reported to Goldman, "In one vision, Tony saw himself being tested by the Life Force if a verdict of innocent was returned. If he was found guilty, it was a God-spirit force calling him away. He saw himself ascending to heaven. He believes he will return. Tony has always had a firm belief in reincarnation."

Avis herself had had several occult experiences. "One night when we were living on Hughes Road in Truro, we were sleeping. It was around two o'clock in the morning and I heard somebody walk into our bedroom. I thought it was Tony; he usually got up in the middle of the night to go to the bathroom. But when I reached over to see if he was there, he was.

"It was totally dark, but I could see somebody standing at the bottom of the bed. I woke Tony up. I said, 'Tony, there's somebody in the room.' He told me I was dreaming. I got all hysterical and made him get up. Tony kept saying, 'Where is he?' I could see the guy, but Tony couldn't. The guy was standing right at Peter's crib. And Tony kept asking the guy who he was, because he thought it was one of our friends, drunk or something.

"Tony had a rifle he had been cleaning that day. I was totally hysterical; I was up in the corner of the room telling him where to shoot the guy. And Tony took two shots where the guy was, like over his head. And the guy just turned around and walked out of the room. I had curtains hanging at the bedroom doorway and I saw the curtains part. I put the light on and looked through the whole house; but nobody was there. All the doors and windows were locked from the inside.

"All kinds of weird things happened in that house; it was a freaky place. Like you could sit in the living room reading a book and a cat would run across the floor. You'd look up and it would be gone. When we were getting ready to move out after I saw the ghost, I was gone. Like my mind was out to lunch; so I went to Connecticut to rest for a while."

Her visit with Tony had upset her, she told Goldman. "I'm really uptight. Tony told me again he wants me to get someone to say they saw Chuck Hansen. And I'm not going to do that. I hate seeing him in there like that, but I won't lie for him. Tony asked me to get Herbie Dam to say Chuck had come to his door looking for him. He's sore at Herbie, because Herbie won't say it," Avis said. "Tony still wants me to try to get someone to say it." Costa had asked her to propose the idea to Woody Candish, who had also refused.

"Tony hasn't been telling us the truth about a lot of things," Goldman said.

"Well, like Tony's funny. He will tell you one thing, and then forget what he told you and change it. Tony told me he had known the Providence girls from last summer, that they had beaten him out of some money or something. Then another time he told me he never knew them before he met them at Mrs. Morton's. Like when we started getting into drugs—when we went through the transformation or whatever it was—I would say, 'Remember the time . . . ?' And Tony used to say, 'No, I don't want to talk about that, that was somebody else.' We never really talked about the perversion things, but anytime we did, he would refer to it as being another self, somebody he had no connection with. He saw himself, the person that he is now, as totally removed from the person he was."

"Do you know anything about Davey Joseph and Susan Perry going out together?" Goldman said.

"They used to go together for a while," Avis said. "I saw Davey several days ago. He didn't want to talk about Susan; he didn't want to get into it. Nobody wants to get involved now."

"Well, they are going to be involved whether they want to or not, if they are called as witnesses," Goldman told her.

"It doesn't matter to these people," Avis said. "They aren't afraid to lie in court. If I was caught up in something this big and asked to put my hand on the Bible, it wouldn't matter to me. You can find justification for lying. I would do anything for Tony, but I wouldn't lie. If there's a crisis I wouldn't just say, 'Well, Tony, fuck you; I can't be bothered.' You know, my family wants me to drop him. My mother said, 'I don't see why you should be involved after all the shit he put you through in the past.' But I don't think that way."

"Tony told us he had Jay Von Utter busted to protect you and the children," Cavanaugh said. "He was afraid Jay would put the children on LSD."

"Oh, *Jesus*. He's told me and friends of mine these stories, too. There's no truth at all to the story of Jay giving LSD to the kids. At that time I was down on acid anyway. All Jay ever gave me was smoke, pot. The reason Tony had Jay busted was that Cheney Marshall said he knew Jay was bringing drugs into town and that if Tony didn't tell him where he could pick up Jay, he would wait until Jay got to my house and bust *me*. And the kids would be taken away. Tony said he was protecting me and saving the kids from being put into a home."

"Tony said you were sleeping with Jay," Cavanaugh said.

"Tony said that about everybody," Avis said. "Everybody that I had been *seen* with he said that about; he had a very low opinion of me. You'd think I was jumping into bed with everyone. I only saw Jay one weekend."

"*Did* you sleep with him?" Cavanaugh said.

"Yeah," Avis said. "I wasn't totally aware of it. I was stoned and I fell asleep. When I woke up someone's arm was around me; I couldn't understand it. And Jay was lying there. It was a thing like he needed a place to sleep and there was the bed. Nothing happened that night; it was the next . . . I don't remember exactly. Jay called me up and said he'd be coming back next weekend with the dope."

"When did Tony start stealing things?" Goldman said.

"It must have been like late '67. I think he might have broken into a few places while he was still with me. One time he came home with a big bunch of change he had gotten someplace or other. I said, 'Wow! What did you do; it's really insane!' He said, 'Don't worry about it, honey. I know what I'm doing.' I think that was the first time I knew. There was something about a stereo once, too . . . I can't remember the circumstances, but it must have been stolen."

The police had questioned her on two occasions, both times asking her if Tony was prone to violence. "They mentioned the hook incident; I wasn't surprised. I'd discussed it with friends. I was surprised the police knew about the pictures Tony took of me hanging from the hook in our bedroom. Tony thought I might have shown them to someone. I *did* show them to Sandy Carter, I think. She was at my house one time and she said something about the pictures and Tony was really furious with me. He kept saying, 'Did you show somebody those pictures?' And I kept saying, 'No! No!' He was really upset about it, so he burned them. It was almost like he was ashamed to have anyone know that he had taken them," Avis said. "In the beginning I think I liked the idea of seeing the pictures, of looking at them; but I think after a while they started getting on Tony's nerves. So he destroyed them."

On the way back to Cape Cod, Avis asked Goldman, "Can I tell you something about Sydney? I haven't said anything about this up until now because I didn't feel it was necessary; but something has been said to me that the cops have this information, and I think you ought to have it, just in case. I don't remember when it was, like the beginning of the summer, April or May of last year, Tony broke into Dr. Callis's office in Wellfleet and stole five thousand dollars' worth of dope; and Sydney Monzon drove the car. Callis knew Tony did it and he wanted to prosecute; but Cheney Marshall said, 'No, he's working for us and we don't want you to touch him.' The police went to Tony's room at the Crown and Anchor and searched, but they didn't find anything—the stuff was buried at Truro. That's where Tony got all his speed from."

Costa was a former patient of Dr. Callis's, Avis said. "He got Tony started on pills. I went to talk to Callis a couple of times myself. I guess Tony was telling him I was screaming all the time. I *wasn't* screaming all the time, but I was upset. One of our biggest hassles was money; money to pay bills. Callis said, 'I'll give you something to calm you down.' And he gave me pills; he gave me shit pills. I wouldn't take them. They didn't *do* anything; they didn't help. I was still irritated and uptight all the time. He was giving Tony these orange football jobs that really zonked him out. When he first started taking them they just knocked him out. Most of the time he just fell asleep."

"What were the orange pills?"

"It was Solacen."

14

On Thursday, April 10, Antone Costa was brought to Barnstable courthouse by Tom Gunnery and two other state troopers. Heavily manacled, wearing a long-sleeved blue turtleneck and immaculate white duck slacks, Costa sat in the front row of the spectator's section behind the bar in a courtroom packed with spectators eager for their first look at the most publicized killer in Cape Cod history. Two rows behind Costa were his mother and Avis.

Presiding was Judge Wilfred Paquet, a florid man who liked to indulge his bad temper from the bench.

Before Costa was brought into the courtroom, Paquet had delivered himself of a choleric lecture on the problem of drug abuse on Cape Cod. A recent report by the Barnstable County Narcotics officer, he said, had revealed that drug use on Cape Cod was "a seventy-five percent middle-class phenomenon." Heroin addicts on Cape Cod were "white, middle-class kids," according to the report. "They have money, wheels and can go where the action is."

Vowing a crackdown on dope peddlers, Paquet announced: "This area is *infested* with these people. It's lethal and we are going to stop them. I am going to clean up this mess on Cape Cod. Anyone convicted for the sale of narcotic drugs is going to jail."

Costa stood up when the clerk of the court, Barbara Holmes Neil, called his case.

Paquet asked Mrs. Neil to read the first of four indictments, charging that on or about the tenth day of September, Costa "did assault and beat Susan E. Perry with intent to murder her and by such assault and beating did kill and murder Susan E. Perry."

"What say you to this indictment?" Mrs. Neil said. "Are you guilty or not guilty?"

"I stand mute," Costa said, as he had been instructed by Goldman, refusing to plead on the ground that the indictment had been obtained in violation of his constitutional rights, there being insufficient legal evidence presented before the grand jury. Further, Costa had had conversations with and was subject to questioning by prosecution officials while not represented by counsel.

"Enter a not guilty plea by order of the court," Paquet said.

The same procedure was followed with the indictments for Sydney Lee Monzon, Patricia Walsh and Mary Anne Wysocki.

"The commonwealth recommends that the defendant be held without bail." Edmund Dinis said.

"I never intended to ask bail in this type of case!" Goldman said.

"We are prepared to go forward for trial whenever the defendant is prepared." Dinis said.

Paquet wanted the report from Bridgewater on Costa's psychiatric examination. "Do we have it here?"

Dinis had a copy in his office.

"How come the newspapers get it before the court?" Paquet said. "Who is responsible for that?"

"Not *our* office," Dinis said.

"I would like to find out why and how a report from Bridgewater State Hospital is made a matter of newspaper publicity before it is presented to the court!" Paquet's voice boomed across the courtroom.

"It didn't come from the defense's office," Goldman said.

"It appears from the Bridgewater report that this man has no mental deficiency and is competent to stand trial," Paquet said, moving on. "There is a question by defense counsel for a change of venue."

"We would welcome that action," Dinis said.

"Well, ordinarily any change of venue would be a matter for the trial justice to decide," Paquet said.

"I am contemplating such a move," Goldman said, "but at this moment I am simply going to ask the court for thirty days to file a series of motions."

Paquet granted Goldman's request.

"There is considerable publicity and many statements made about this matter, which in my judgment as a member of the court, have been most inappropriate," Paquet said, with a scathing glance at the district attorney's table. "I now direct that there be no further extra-judicial statements concerning this case by any of the parties involved; meaning, the district attorney's office and his staff, the police and defense counsel. I will require that all whom I have mentioned comply with the regulations with respect to pretrial publicity. This case will eventually be tried in the courtroom and *not* through the media of communications outside the courtroom." Paquet glared at the crowded press section on his left. "A word to the wise is sufficient, I think."

Escorted out of the courthouse in a blaze of flashbulbs, Antone Costa was taken up the broad green hill behind the courthouse, passing the white colonial house occupied by Sheriff Donald F. Tulloch, to an elevation from which a magnificent view of Barnstable village stretched to marshes and beyond to the flat and gray-blue water of Barnstable harbor.

Chambray-clad young men tended the steep slope of greensward, the flower beds set about the brick building that, without the barred windows, gave the appearance of a high school in an

308

affluent neighborhood. A sylvan quiet surrounded the Barnstable House of Correction, a pastoral jail.

From the front entrance, Costa was taken through the "gates," a series of grilled enclosures leading to a brightly lit guardroom. Passing a removable wooden banister attached to a railing that separated the visitor's area—a double row of mismatched chairs on either side of the barrier—Costa was taken to the first cell of a corridor off the guardroom. After the narrow cubicle at Bridgewater, cell number 1 was fairly commodious. A steel shelf hinged into the cement wall contained a thin, foam-rubber mattress. There was a stainless steel commode, a chipped enamel washbasin and a single window overlooking a grove of stunted pines.

Goldman expressed his appreciation for Sheriff Tulloch's having arranged visiting schedules for his client and facilities for interviewing and recording background material for a "a difficult and complex case." Goldman promised to limit his visits outside of regular-scheduled jail hours to a necessary minimum.

Established in his new quarters, Costa was finding it difficult writing in his daybooks because his cell was unlighted. Goldman hoped Tulloch could provide some illumination. "Other than that, Tony is quite happy and content." Goldman left the Spanish-English dictionary, a Webster's and a Roget's Thesaurus Costa had requested, along with a fresh supply of daybooks into which Costa recorded his return to Cape Cod:

Reflections of a Golden Past

Once upon a time, not so long ago, I cherished the Cape Cod area with a love so precious it was but a dream! Each and every shore, hill and every living creature of God's making was then a joy, a true elation! I sensed beauty indefinable. Love was constantly present and emanated from within this land of wonder. It was truly God's country! Today as a I scrutinized this same area, my only sensation of this land I adored became one of alienation; a land I did not know. I searched every possibility in an attempt to locate any prospect of love and warmth emitting from this land; there was no acceptance. This land no longer knew me, nor I it.

For His own reasons my Father above has forsaken this land, as He did Sodom and Gommorrah. Perhaps this was done only for my cause and benefit. For what purpose is there for one to love a people who will not love in return. A people who possess no love! I have been enlightened!

A.C.

15

Judge Paquet's ban on information emanating from "official sources" did not stem the flow of publicity regarding the Costa case. With access to official sources closed off, news accounts were filled with speculation and rumor. Reporters cornered anyone with even remote connections with Tony Costa or the murder victims. While Goldman was happy to have official statements stanched, he recognized that the ban would perpetuate the misinformation already given by Edmund Dinis at his press conference.

Goldman learned from *Front Page Detective* magazine that the Costa case "has already been covered for us by our New England staff writer." *True Detective* had followed "the Cape Cod cemetery case" since it first broke. *Startling Detective* was already on press with its version of the Costa murders, destined to appear on newsstands on April 24. An editor explained, "We try to give our readers the most current crime cases as soon as possible. Therefore, we rushed to print with our story the minute it was legally safe to do so."

With Costa in Barnstable, Goldman turned the interrogation of his client for background over to Lester Allen. Allen found Costa attractive and personable, but difficult to pin down, vague on details, likely to go off on tangents at the slightest provocation —particularly when the subject under discussion connected him with any of the murdered girls or the area of the Truro woods where the graves had been uncovered. Costa denied having hidden drugs where he once cultivated a marijuana garden.

"The drugs I had were hidden in back of the old dump road in Provincetown. I might have told people I hid them in Truro so they wouldn't go looking for them. The canister right now is at Woody's house," Costa said. Then he suddenly conceded, "At one time there *was* a canister in Truro. I believe it's still there."

"Can you tell us where it is so we can go look for it?" Allen said. "We'd rather find it than have somebody else find it. Do you know what I mean?"

"It would be kind of difficult to explain, unless I took you out there," Costa said. "Because you have to go through some bushes—"

"Has anyone else been out there with you at all?"

"No," Costa said. "I think I could draw a map."

"If there's anything else out there, we want to get it before the police do." Allen said. "We have to be very careful because as officers of the court, Mr. Goldman and Mr. Cavanaugh have certain obligations. I'll have to try to make some sort of search not involving them, because they would have to report any findings of evidence which might be pertinent to the case."

Costa had been familiar with the Truro woods for a long time. "I guess it was years ago when I was still in my teens. I used to go out there with some friends from Provincetown and do some peashooting and this sort of thing. We'd just go out hunting or practice with our bows and things, just putting around. That was always a great place because the trees form like a big tunnel. It's nice because it's always shady. The sun can really be hot but it's still cool under there. The other places, like all those back roads and everything, they're more or less dumpy; it's not too good. But this is a nice, clean, decent area."

Costa was writing a "satire" based on his experiences of raising a crop of marijuana in the woods, the result from which had been only three joints. "Everything in it is going to be factual, just the way I did it. It will be a complete satire on one plantation; everything I went through, and I just got three little things out of it. It was funny. You can give it to the *Evergreen Review,* or somebody like that; they'll probably accept it for publication. You may get a pretty good profit out of it."

311

Allen promised to "edit" the manuscript before Costa submitted it for publication.

With the juices of creative writing apparently flowing, Costa dashed off a poem for the amusement of his attorneys:

WEED #37

That fateful night, I mounted my steed
And travelled far to find some weed.
When suddenly, upon a field came I,
Of marijuana ten feet high!
'Twas no illusion, 'twas not unreal!
I jumped off my horse, my pipe to fill.
When in its bowl I found a pill,
The pill I ate, the pipe I did light,
My eyes soon beheld a groovy sight.
The stars they danced; the moon did sigh,
So many colors passed on by,
And in my heart I held a hope,
For people on earth and lots more dope
When all at once to my surprise,
Heaven's gates appeared before my eyes.
In I went to eternally dwell,
That's my story; no more to tell.

Goldman wrote a letter to Dr. Sidney Callis, requesting assistance in the preparation of the defense of Tony Costa. "It is important for us to determine facts of treatment which you gave him and, particularly, advice as to the various drugs which he had been using." Goldman urged Callis to discuss the matter freely with Lester Allen. Goldman's letter carried a postscript authorization, signed by Costa, asking Callis to furnish his attorney with "all the information he requests in connection with my treatments."

Costa doubted Callis would cooperate. "He has this strange idea that I broke into his office and took a lot of things," Costa said. "He confronted me directly, right in front of Adams pharmacy shortly after someone broke in his place. He wanted to know if I knew anything about it. I told him I didn't; I just commented on it as being a terrible thing. I asked him how much damage was done. He said no damage was done, but there was quite a bit of stuff missing. And he just toddled on down the street. Mr. Marshall and a narcotics agent came up to my room at the Crown and Anchor. This agent asked me if I would go to the pharmacy to check on the prescriptions I had for Solacen. While I was gone, Mr. Marshall stayed in my room. One of the chambermaids said he opened drawers and was looking for something." Costa grinned broadly. "All he found was a bottle of One-a-Day vitamins."

"How did you happen to go to Callis in the first place?" Goldman said.

"I was going to Dr. Hiebert when I felt physically ill. Dr. Hiebert's treated my grandmother, my uncles, my mother; he's been the family physician for as long as I can remember. But this was more a psychological strain; I was having rough times marriage-wise. My wife had gone to bed or something with another guy—he was just wrecking the marriage. I had been thinking of going to a doctor, more or less a counselor, and I heard Callis was a good counselor.

"It was a freaky visit. Callis invited me in and I sat down and he looked at me and said, 'You're here for a nervous thing.' So I said, 'Yeah, that's right.' And he said, 'You've built up some nervous tension.' And so I said, 'Yeah, how did you know?' And he said, 'Well, for one thing you're sitting there and you're more or less playing with your hands. And you reached up and scratched behind your ear, and these are indications of nervousness.' So I said, 'Yeah, but it's not a giveaway as to my being here or anything; I'm here for some consultation.' And he said, 'Well, you've come to the right place; I've been at Bridgewater for twelve years. I've got all kinds of degrees. I'm a psychiatrist; this is my primary profession. I'm a psychiatrist first and physician second.' And he said, 'We can take care of any little problem that you have.' I figured, well, I'm here for marriage counseling, and he said he was a marriage counselor, so I said, 'Great!'

"He gave me Solacen. They were big yellow-orange things. And some other things, too, some yellow-and-white ones called Nembutal."

Costa had recommended Callis to David Salvador. "I sent Joey Thomas to him, too. Joey was going to Dr. Callis for draft counseling. Joey went up there shortly after someone, I guess, broke into Dr. Callis's office. And Callis told Joey that if I ever went back to see him again, he'd give me poison or something in a pill that would kill me. So I didn't want anything more to do with the guy after he accused me of breaking into his office. Because I felt it was a very ugly way of doing things."

Goldman decided it was time for Lester Allen to have a talk with Dr. Callis.

Dr. Sidney Callis had practiced medicine in Wellfleet since 1950. Balding, with a round, open face and a potbelly, Callis was a garrulous and friendly man, likely to call his patients by their first names. Something of a police buff, he was proud of his close friendship with George Killen. As a carryover from twelve years at Bridgewater where he had often worked in dangerous areas, Callis packed a gun in a holster strapped to his side. Among his patients were critic Edmund Wilson and novelist Edwin O'Connor, both members of a literary colony that frequented Wellfleet in the summer.

Callis conducted his practice from the Wellfleet Medical Offices, a single-story business block he owned on Route 6. The name was something of a misnomer, since Callis's was the only medical facility among a package store, a fish market and a gift shop.

Callis asked Lester Allen into a consulting room in the rear of his suite of offices where they could be "more comfortable."

"Why don't you have a seat over there?" Callis said pleasantly from behind a desk cluttered with medical magazines and physicians' samples. "I received a letter, as you are perhaps aware, written by attorney Goldman with Mr. Costa's authorization to release the information in connection with my treatment," Callis said. "I feel that any time spent in this should be reimbursed. By that I mean if I'm going to have to go through a lot of stuff—"

"Oh, no. *No,*" Allen interrupted. His high-pitched voice was already edged with impatience. "I don't think you have to worry about that now. You can talk that over with Goldman when we get into that phase of the case. Right now, all we're trying to establish is whether was Costa using certain drugs."

"How would I know that, when I haven't seen him since April 19, 1968?"

"That's one of the things we need to know," Allen said. "April 19, 1968?"

"That was the last time I saw him," Callis said. "I hadn't seen him regularly for some time. Anything I gave him prescriptions for—which he legally purchased through drug channels— would be nothing which would be conducive to doing anything but acting as a mild tranquilizer."

"We don't suggest anything to the contrary," Allen said. "Now on his first visit there was some marriage counseling involved? This is another thing that he tells us."

Callis consulted the file on his desk. "He had an emotional problem with his wife, that's correct."

"And what date was that?"

"The date of his first visit was . . . December 8, 1965."

"He was then living over in North Truro, on Hughes Road?"

"No, he told me he was living at Route 6A, North Truro. He gave me several addresses. He later moved to Hughes Road."

"He told us what you prescribed for him was an orange-colored pill. He had the name of it . . . I've forgotten what he told me."

"It was Solacen," Callis said. "S-o-l-a-c-e-n. It's a tranquilizer."

"You never prescribed thorazine or any of that sort of thing?"

"Never."

"Methedrine?"

"Never, *never.*"

"Now, let's get to the time when your office was broken into."

"What's he got to do with that?"

"Well, this is what we want to know," Allen said querulously. "Whether he *did* have anything to do with it. Was there a break-in at your office and some drugs stolen?"

"Oh, yes. That's a matter of official record. You can get that from the Wellfleet police."

"Did you talk to the Provincetown police about the break-in?"

"Did I talk with *Provincetown* police?" Callis clearly found Allen's inquisition insufferable. "What are you doing, interrogating me?"

"I'm just trying to find out how and where it was reported. We're told that the Provincetown police were called in."

"By whom?"

"I don't know."

"Well, I'm telling you that I reported it to the Wellfleet Police Department," Callis said.

"The federal agent searched Costa's room at the Crown and Anchor Inn looking for drugs which he thought were stolen from your office."

"I would have no knowledge of that. When my office was entered and drugs stolen, I reported it to the proper authorities; that would be the Wellfleet police."

"And you won't give me the date of that?"

"I don't really remember it."

"I mean approximately."

"Oh, you can ask the Wellfleet police anything about that you care to."

"You know, doctor, we're trying to cooperate," Allen said irritably. "We just want to get some facts. We're not trying to put you in any kind of a bind."

"I'm not suggesting you are," Callis said. "I'm giving you all the facts."

"We've got a guy whose charged with four murders. We just want to know whether or not he was so badly hooked that he was running around stealing drugs."

"Well, how would *I* know that? I couldn't help you there. I can tell you that in my professional attendance I prescribed a drug, and that's all. And my office was broken into. As to the date, I can't off the top of my head tell you. As to what was done, or what wasn't done, or to whom it was reported, my suggestion is that if you wish to pursue this—"

"All we've got to do is subpoena it in, you know," Allen interrupted.

"Then *subpoena* it. I can't tell you if a federal man went down there or he didn't, because I don't have knowledge of it."

"I assume that if they did they would come and talk to you."

316

"No, I talked with the local chief of police."

"You haven't seen Costa since April of 1968?"

"That's right."

"What did he come to you for the last time?"

"Same thing."

"He was tense, nervous?"

"Yes."

"Do you think he's a schizoid personality?"

"I'm not going to give any opinion on that."

"But you're *not* a psychiatrist, are you, doctor?"

"I'm not going to give any opinions on anything."

"Are you also a marriage counselor? Do you have a diploma in marriage counseling?"

"I don't see where that has anything to do with the matter you are investigating." Callis rose from his desk.

"Well, I guess that's it," Allen said. "That's all I need to know."

"Good," Callis said, holding open the office door.

"One other thing," Allen said. "Have you given a statement to the police recently?"

"Have *I* given a statement to police recently? In regard to what?"

"In connection with this case."

"Of course not. Nobody's asked me anything."

"That's all I wanted to know."

"I don't think I'm of much value to you," Callis said, leading Allen from the office. "Or to the police, either."

"Well, I hope not," Allen said. "It's difficult enough as it is."

Callis returned to the office to retrieve the cassette from a tape recorder on top of a filing cabinet he had turned on before inviting Lester Allen into his office.

Callis opened the medical file on his desk. Rereading his records, he remembered Tony Costa very well. Costa had appeared in his office without an appointment one very cold December afternoon. An attractive young man with clear skin, good teeth—a fine physical specimen—Costa had talked in a low, soft voice and been very polite. Callis had immediately noticed that Costa had severely bitten his finger nails.

Costa had been treated for four years by Dr. Hiebert and been given phenobarbital for "nervous tension." Costa's chief complaint was a gnawing pain over the stomach area so intense it would wake him out of a sound sleep. X rays had revealed no ulcer, the condition diagnosed as "gastritis." Costa also complained to Callis of a burning sensation during urination. Costa was having difficulty sleeping; his two children were troublesome and drove him crazy with their incessant crying. Costa confessed to "an emotional problem with my wife." He had married her only because he had gotten her pregnant, Costa said. His wife was too young and immature to understand him, was a terrible mother and a dirty housekeeper. Costa was being abused at home because of lack of money.

After a physical examination and review of Costa's medical history, Callis had noted in his file that Costa was "a psychoneurotic with anxiety." For Costa's gastritis, Callis prescribed Kolantyl wafers and gave him thirty Solacen, a mild tranquilizer he dispensed from his office.

Callis took particular pride in Solacen. As one of the original investigators of the drug for the Wallace Pharmaceutical Company, he had written a paper on the new tranquilizer for the *International Journal of Neuropsychiatry*, reporting on a double-blind study in which the nonaddictive tranquilizer, generically known as tybamate, was shown to be beneficial in the treatment of depression, particularly in those patients whose anxiety states were manifested physically. In Callis's view, Costa's stomach distress had a mental origin: the result of his domestic problems.

Costa had brought a urine sample on his next visit, the file recorded. Diagnosed as suffering from urethritis, Costa was started on sulpha drugs. His nervousness was "much improved"; Callis gave him another thirty Solacen from his office supply.

In March of 1966, Costa disclosed that his marital problems had deteriorated to such an extent he was considering a separation. "My wife's only seventeen and she wants to get rid of it all," Costa said. Disagreements had centered around their children and her general unhappiness with him. Callis changed Costa's medication to Aventyl, a mild antidepressant for the treatment of mental depression "with psychophysiological gastrointestinal disorders." Callis encouraged Costa to bring his wife to the office for consultation.

When Avis Costa came in, she complained that her husband had a violent temper and was unbearable to live with. He was sullen and moody, could not tolerate any noise and had struck her and the children. According to Avis, Costa was fine when he was taking Solacen, "very calm and really pleasant, an affectionate, passive nice person," but was increasingly nervous and irritable when he was not on medication.

Callis gave Avis Meprospan, a mild tranquilizer—twenty pills to take, as necessary, once every twelve hours. Callis counseled Costa not to fight with his wife or be harsh with his children.

Costa was "much improved" by May. With many construction jobs lined up, he was looking forward to a busy summer building season, and Callis did not see him again until late August. Costa told him he had suffered a motorcycle accident and had been treated by Dr. Hiebert. A cut on the bridge of his nose had required a butterfly stitch. While X rays had shown no internal injuries, Costa complained about shortness of breath and pains in his chest.

By March of 1967, Costa was again suffering "gnawing pain" in his stomach and nausea; he was depressed. Costa and his wife were "fighting all the time." Callis gave him Aventyl. Costa returned to the office a month later in high spirits to announce the birth of a daughter, Nicole Lynne. Several weeks later, Costa told Callis he had separated "amicably" from his wife. "We just realized we had married too young," Costa said. He was having trouble sleeping, so Callis kept him on Aventyl.

Costa suggested that he work off an accumulated one-hundred-forty-dollar medical bill by painting the trim and gutters of Callis's building. While working about the office, Costa observed a pretty, dark-haired girl at the reception desk.

"Who's the chick in your office?" Costa asked.

"That's my daughter," Callis said. "You stay away from her."

Callis need not have been concerned. An athletic sixteen-year-old, Bonnie Callis was not interested in her father's good-looking patient; she did not care for boys with long hair.

Costa continued to suffer a mild depression throughout the summer because of "home problems." His stomach was upset, he was not eating regularly and felt weak. By July, his weight had dropped to 175 pounds. Callis kept him on the Aventyl and prescribed Mylanta, an over-the-counter antacid.

In October, Avis Costa came to Callis's office for a pregnancy test; the test was negative. She and Tony were living together again, but the marriage was not going well. A month later, Costa was complaining he was having trouble seeing. When Callis examined Costa's eyes he found him to be "terrifically myopic"; without glasses, Costa was virtually blind. Callis wrote a prescription for fifty 350-milligram Solacen capsules with two refills instead of dispensing medication from his office. Costa got a second prescription shortly before he left for California in January, 1968.

Callis was not to see Costa until April. Costa returned filled with tales of the hippie drug culture he had seen in the Haight-Ashbury district of San Francisco. He was still suffering from nervousness and an upset stomach. Concerned that Costa might have himself sampled the California pharmacopoeia, Callis gave him a single, unrefillable prescription—for fifty more Solacen.

On Monday morning, May 17, Callis discovered his office had been broken into. Entry had been gained by the removal of a screen from a window in the emergency treatment room in the rear of the building. Callis found the screen on the flat roof of an adjacent ambulance entrance, a fact suggesting that the burglar was a person of some height. The burglar had burned paper towels to provide light while he inspected an unlocked cabinet containing bandages, antiseptics and sutures, scorching the floor tiles of the emergency treatment room. Access to a locked drug closet had been achieved by the removal of hinge pins from the door. Callis also found the doors of several consulting rooms resting against their frames.

Because Tony Costa was a carpenter-handyman, familiar with the setup of the offices from more than thirty visits as a patient, he was an immediate suspect. Callis calculated that Costa's last prescription for Solacen would have taken him up to the time of the robbery.

Callis was furious at the burglary and the damage to his premises. Patrolman Patrick Padden of the Wellfleet police came to Callis's office with Barnstable Deputy Sheriff Richard Doane to investigate.

"Callis stated he was aware that Costa was a pothead and pill user," Padden noted in his report of the burglary. "However, Callis stated he is a doctor and felt justified in treating him this way." Costa had painted and worked on the office and had knowledge of the building's layout.

Padden found footprints at the rear of the building, but was unable to lift them because of an early-morning rain. Callis asked him to dust the window, screen and doors for fingerprints while he took inventory of the drugs which had been stolen. Various drugs and syringes had been bypassed. Missing were:

1	30 cc vial of amphetamine sulfate
900	Solacen capsules
875	phenobarbital pink tablets, $1/2$ grain
1,480	amphetamine sulfate, 10 milligrams white tablets, otherwise known as Benzedrine, in a white tin container
4	one-ounce bottles of Robitussin A-C cough syrup

A number of physician sample packages of Triavil 2-10 were also missing. Callis calculated the stolen drugs to be worth $385.69.

None of the missing drugs were narcotics, except for the sample bottles of cough syrup, which had each contained less than half a grain of codeine—an "empty narcotic" exempt from drug control laws. Drugs having more than one grain of codeine to the ounce had to be prescribed and records kept of their distribution. The only drugs Callis had in his office were exempt narcotics, he explained—"and damn few of those."

Padden and Doane went to Provincetown to look for Tony Costa. Returning to Callis's office several days later, Padden reported that Costa had moved recently and Provincetown police did not know his exact whereabouts.

Additional photographs of the scene were taken and some partial prints lifted from the emergency treatment room's cabinet; but other evidence-gathering in the case had not proven fruitful. Costa was the only suspect.

Angry at the ineptitude of the Wellfleet police, Callis went to Provincetown himself the following Sunday to search for Tony Costa. Callis stationed his wife Jean, a pretty woman with chestnut brown hair and vivid Scottish coloring, at the town hall benches with a description of Costa to compare with passersby. In the police station, Callis was told by Patrolman Robert Silva, "Tony's not around; I haven't seen him for a while."

Walking down Commercial Street, Callis spotted Costa in front of Adams Pharmacy talking to a group of long-haired youths. Beautifully turned out in new clothes, Costa tried to turn his back when he saw Callis approach.

Callis felt his suspicions confirmed. Costa had always been respectful, courteous and glad to see him. "I'd like to talk to you privately, Tony," Callis said.

Costa refused to step away from the group. Keeping his hands in his pockets, he said, "I've got an appointment; I don't have much time." He expressed his sympathy when Callis told him of the break-in at his office. Callis wanted to know where Costa was living. Costa told him he had a room at the Crown and Anchor Motor Inn across the street.

Callis returned to the police station to demand a search be made at once of Costa's room. He was told that police could not conduct a search without a warrant. To secure a search warrant required evidence of "probable cause" that drugs were likely to be found in Costa's room—evidence more substantial than Callis's suspicions.

Callis appealed to his friend, George Killen, during an occasion when Killen and his wife, Helen, were dinner guests. Callis complained that Wellfleet police officer, Padden, who was conducting the investigation "couldn't find his ass in a phone booth with both hands."

Killen asked Cheney Marshall to look into the matter "unofficially." Marshall went to Costa's room with a narcotics agent but found nothing but some power tools he suspected had been stolen.

In June, Callis had cooled down and asked Tony Costa to give him an estimate for remodeling a barn on his property into a studio, as a surprise birthday present for his wife, Jean, a talented painter. Costa never followed through on the estimate.

Callis did not hear from Tony Costa for the rest of the summer, although Costa recommended several of his friends as patients. One of them was Raul Matta, a very good-looking house painter. Matta wanted to be checked out for the possible recurrence of syphilis he had contracted "extramaritally," then given to his wife.

Callis sent Matta to a urologist.

Callis, despite his suspicions about the break-in, was astonished when Tony Costa was arrested for murder. His years at Bridgewater, he told Killen, had prepared him to detect any signs of a mental disorder of a psychotic nature. Costa had never manifested such symptoms. More puzzling to Callis was his failure to recognize in his patient any indication of drug abuse, since pharmacology was something of his specialty. "Tony was always quiet-spoken and totally in control of himself during his office visits."

Callis was saddened to learn of Sydney Monzon's identification as a murder victim, recalling the pretty girl as a frequent dinner guest who had once been friendly with his daughter, Bonnie. The friendship had faded, Bonnie told him, "because Sydney started hanging around with the wrong bunch." The girls had seen little of each other while attending Nauset Regional High School in Orleans. Bonnie Callis had often ridden horseback in the area of the Truro woods where Sydney's body was recovered.

Sydney Monzon had disappeared one week after the break-in at his office, Callis pointed out to Killen. "If the police had properly investigated the robbery at my office, and Tony Costa had been arrested, those four girls would still be alive."

Maurice Goldman was a spectator in Boston's Suffolk Superior Court for the sensational murder trial of Richard Quillen, charged with killing and mutilating former state representative William F. Otis and his wife. According to defense attorney Herb Abrams, Quillen had been legally insane when he fatally stabbed the couple in their Back Bay home, having suffered an "amphetamine psychosis."

Abrams claimed his client had consumed from seven to fourteen biphetamine pills and a quart of vodka every day for two months prior to the murders. The day before the killings, Quillen had taken thirty-four antidepressants known as "black beauties" and suffered a "psychotic reaction." Quillen had bloodstains on the turtleneck shirt, pants and shoes he was wearing when he was arrested the day after the murders attempting to use Otis's credit card in Philadelphia.

"He did not comprehend what was taking place; he was a mentally sick young man," Abrams said, asking the jury to convict his client of second-degree murder, or to acquit him on grounds of insanity based upon his use of drugs. "In either case, it will mean a life sentence, instead of death."

A brilliant courtroom tactician and Northeastern University lecturer on "criminal law, evidence and procedure," Abrams was a handsome and aggressive lawyer. He suspected that Maurice Goldman's presence in the courtroom showed more than a general professional interest in his innovative plea of insanity based upon the use of mind-altering drugs.

Goldman suggested to Abrams that he come into the Costa case to deal with the medical aspects of the most publicized murder trial in Massachusetts since the Boston Strangler. Goldman explained that Costa was indigent. Fees, if any, were speculative, depending entirely on the expectation of possible revenues accruing from the sale of book and dramatic rights to Costa's life. All concerned with the defense had been similarly made aware that they must serve without compensation. Costa was dependent on Goldman for the expenses of the preparation of his trial, funds for which were severely limited and all of which Goldman had himself provided so far.

Abrams agreed to Goldman's terms. His present client, Richard Quillen, was bankrupt and abandoned by family and friends, none of whom had appeared in the courtroom to support him. Abrams had taken the Quillen case for the modest fifteen-hundred-dollar fee set by the court—considerably less than his formidable skills could command in the legal marketplace. Before Abrams came into the Costa case, however, he had another murder trial to defend; a patricide by a teenager named Richard Valois.

Abrams promised Goldman he would bring Dr. Harold Williams with him when he came to Cape Cod to discuss the Costa case. A brilliant young psychiatrist, Williams was scheduled to testify after Quillen collapsed on the witness stand and had to be taken from the courtroom, kicking and screaming.

Quillen was found guilty of second-degree murder; he received a sentence of forty-five years. Given the extraordinary violence of the murders, and the terrible mutilation of the bodies, the verdict was a triumph for Abrams.

When Goldman returned to Cape Cod, he was disturbed by rumors circulating in the corridors of Barnstable courthouse that a police search of the Truro woods had uncovered important new evidence in the Costa case. Goldman feared the worst. Taking the map Costa had drawn for Lester Allen, he and Cavanaugh went immediately to the house of correction. Their conference with Costa was held in a small, windowless room whose cement blocks had been painted a bilious yellow.

"Tony," Goldman began, "we have a strong suspicion the gun is already in the possession of the police. We believe they got it within the last three or four days prior to your coming to Barnstable."

Costa was silent. His locked fingers flexed in his lap; his eyes slid away from Goldman's hard stare. "Are you sure they have it?" he said coolly.

"No, we're not sure," Goldman said. "The reason we have a strong suspicion is that up until that time their faces looked very depressed. Then their expression changed to—well, I'll say it bluntly—'We've got the bastard good now!' Did they find a gun? We don't know. But they *did* find something." According to press reports, police had been using metal detectors in their searches of the woods. "It'll pick up anything metal; that's how sensitive it is." Goldman fastened his eyes on Costa. "I say this again, Tony, as your *friend*. For God's sake, tell us everything you can. We have faith in you. Now, did you put a gun out there?"

"Yeah."

"Where did you put it?"

"The gun itself is right at the base of the biggest tree by the parking space. I intended putting it in the can I spoke of the last time to Mr. Allen, but I was more or less in a state of uptightness and panic-thinking about what could have happened. I knew there was a body discovered on that road. I put the gun beside the tree because it was given to me and I didn't know what to do with it. This was on my return from Boston, the day before I went to Burlington."

"Who gave you the gun?" Goldman said.

"It was given to me by Hansen when I went to Boston,"

Costa said. "I think this was part of the reason for my getting the hundred dollars."

"What did he say when he gave you the gun?" Cavanaugh said.

"Well, this is the thing—and oh!—I got that other information on Hansen; where he is. And that other guy, Mark, who I sold the gun to . . . I have his address. I got it from one of the guys here that knows him. Mark's last name is McClusky. He was living in the East Village." Extremely agitated, Costa spoke very rapidly, as if he feared to be interrupted. "And I got that other information, too," Costa said, twisting in his chair, his face flushed and tense. "Chuck and Mark are buddy-buddy. I don't know how Hansen got the gun—I'm just surmising. That's why I think we should go see Mark and find out just what the story is there, how Chuck got the gun from him . . ."

Goldman was tired of hearing about Chuck Hansen, whose existence he was beginning to doubt. Investigators had spent countless hours trying to track Hansen down; thus far, Hansen remained a phantom.

"Let's stay with the gun, so I can get that clear in my mind," Goldman said sharply. "Will the gun contain your fingerprints?"

"Yeah, I'm pretty sure it will," Costa said. "It wasn't wrapped in anything; it's just in the ground, in a plastic bag."

"What type of gun is it?"

"It's a .22 revolver with a white handle; it's got a barrel that turns. As far as I can remember, I believe it to be a Colt product, I'm not sure. I'm not hip on guns."

"What about bullets?" Goldman said. "How many were in there?"

"There should be none. I never carried it with anything in it. I don't believe in it. When it was given to me by Chuck there was nothing in it."

"Will the gun reveal any recent firings, if the police have it already?"

"I don't know."

Goldman's voice was ragged with exasperation. "Had you told us about this, it would have been of greater help some time ago." He took from his briefcase the map Costa had drawn and spread it open on the table. "Now, where is the gun, exactly?"

"The gun is in the other direction from the canister in the woods, in an area beside the parking space." Costa indicated a spot on the map. "Beside this big tree, right there," Costa drew a large X, "is where I put the gun and a knife."

Goldman rose out of his chair. "The gun and a *what?*"

"A knife," Costa said.

"There's a *knife* there, too?"

"Yeah, there's like a bowie knife with a five-inch blade; it's got a reddish-type handle on it and everything. The handle is made out of some kind of imitation material; I think it's plastic."

"Could it pregnate a fingerprint?"

"Yeah, I suppose it could."

"So if the police were successful they would find a .22 caliber revolver and a knife—both implements they could tie in as belonging to you?"

"The gun, yes," Costa said. "The knife they couldn't really tie in to me, property-wise."

"Where did the knife come from, Tony?" Cavanaugh asked.

"I got it from Chuck in Boston together with the gun. He said, 'There's a package in the glove compartment for you.'"

"The police have talked to Cory Devereau," Goldman said. "They probably have his statement on the sale of the gun to you."

"Well, I've admitted that anyway," Costa said.

Mrs. Nora Welch, Devereau's mother, had told defense investigators she had opened a store at the A&P shopping plaza the weekend the Providence girls were in Provincetown and they had bought nine dollars' worth of cosmetics. Goldman now suspected Mrs. Welch's interest in "helping" the defense had another motive. "What other things could Cory be involved in that his mother would be so anxious about?" Goldman said. "Other than selling you the gun?"

"Well, Cory's a hard-drug user. Since this guy Hansen was dealing heroin, it may be somebody Cory knew. Cory has a very sleazy habit of stealing things. He's on probation right now for breaking and entering. Cory brought this gun over to the Crown and Anchor and said I could buy it for twenty dollars. He said he brought the gun back from Virginia, together with a load of cough syrup. And he had pills from Adams's pharmacy. Gary Watts, Peter Cordeiro and Larry Andresen were in on that job with Cory."

"They broke into Adams's pharmacy?"

"Yeah," Costa said. "Cory had a key to Adams. They copped

a bottle of twenty-five milligram Librium. I gave that to my brother; he was eating them like candy."

"Where did Cory get a key?"

"They were putting in a sidewalk out front of Adams. It was a thing where the workmen went off for lunch or something and left the key in the door. And Cory noticed it; he grabbed the key and ran into one of the hardware stores and had a duplicate made and then stuck the original key back in the lock again."

"Let's have a talk about Dr. Callis. First of all, I'm going to put it very bluntly: did you take any drugs out of his place?"

Costa hesitated, looked away and said, "Uh, yeah."

"You don't have to be afraid to tell us," Goldman said. "How much did you take, quantity-wise?"

"There was quite a few jars of the speed drugs," Costa said.

"Try to help us a little bit more, because we have something cooking in the back of our minds that we know will be to your benefit on Dr. Callis," Goldman said, thinking of the Richard Quillen case. "You've been treated by Callis for a long time, haven't you? Practically four years?"

"Right," Costa said. "He gave me prescriptions for Solacen, but mostly he used to give me stuff out of the office directly. He showed me a paper that had his name on top; he said he had something to do with coming up with the drug, these Solacen things he gave me. He told me to come back if I liked them. His exact words were, 'When you need more medication, come back and see me.' The first time I took Solacen they really knocked me for a loop. We were eating supper and I got to the point where I couldn't even pick up the spoon to finish dessert."

"Getting back to the drug situation, the approximate date and quantity . . ." Goldman prompted, "who was with you?"

"It was, I guess, the early part of June last year, in the night-time," Costa said. "I myself did it alone. I walked away from the building and stored the things up in the woods in back of his building until I could get a ride to town. I went back there, I guess, a couple of days later . . . I think it was with Butch Gaspar in a jeep."

"What did you take out of there?"

"I had about five bottles of amphetamine-type drugs—Dexedrine, bennies, things like that. And some barbiturates that I could recognize: phenobarbital, some Nembutal, Tuinal, and a few other small things."

"Did you get any drugs that deal with trips of any kind—LSD for example?"

"No, there were a lot of white powders in small bottles but they were unlabeled, so I didn't touch them at all. I have this hang-up: I won't take anything unless I've had it before from a doctor. Even if it comes from a doctor, I like to look it up and see exactly what it does before I take it."

"The reference book on drugs you left in Burlington," Cavanaugh said, "did that come from Dr. Callis's office, too?"

"I got that from Dr. Hiebert," Costa said. "I went in there one day when the office was open. Mrs. Hiebert was there. I had just come from the library, and I had a bunch of books with me. And this book was lying there. And I just sort of scoffed it up when she turned around."

"What was the dollar-and-cents market value of what you took out of Callis's place," Goldman said.

"On the black market, what I took out of there totaled about roughly four hundred fifty to five hundred dollars; that's the total amount I profited from it."

Goldman could not conceal his disappointment. "That's a very insignificant amount; so the statement about five thousand dollars' worth of drugs is highly exaggerated."

"I stole five thousand dollars?" Costa said incredulously, and laughed.

"We've been giving you just strict gossip, Tony, and maybe worth nothing," Goldman said. "We just don't want a lead to get away from us, so we thought we'd tell you about that."

"Did you keep this stuff you took from Callis's office out in the woods in your drug cache?" Cavanaugh said.

"I put it in two places. One was a canister in Provincetown, right off the highway. That can is down at Woody's, around the yard somewhere. The other place was a similar canister in the woods where I drew the map, where my marijuana patch was two years ago; I haven't been out there to that place for a long time."

"So there's a reasonable likelihood if police are in that area they'd find a gun, they'd find a knife, and they could very well have gotten possession of the drugs, too, by virtue of being in the canister."

"The can itself was empty when I left it," Costa said. "I hope it's empty now."

"Did you have anything to do with breaking into a drugstore

in Wellfleet?" Cavanaugh said. "Or was it just Dr. Callis's office you broke into."

"No, it was just the doctor's office, I believe," Costa said evenly.

"Well, that takes care of the drug situation," Goldman said. "Now, Tony, you told us there were some other people working with you in this drug business. Could you tell us who they are? We've got Hansen's name, and the lad you just gave us, Mark, in New York. What I'm getting at is, who do *you* think—in your judgment—killed these girls?"

Unhesitatingly, Costa said, "My personal belief is Roland Salvador; and I have strong reason to believe that their boyfriends, this Magnan and Turbidy, knew of this . . ."

Cavanaugh had quietly been observing Costa. Like Goldman, he had been struck by the Richard Quillen case as a possible defense plan. Cavanaugh said, "With a fellow using speed, Tony, would he completely forget what happened on any trip he took, or would he keep that straight?"

"From my knowledge of it, a person using speed doesn't completely lose his memory. If he has taken LSD before, the speed can bring back his whole trip. The same is true of alcohol. You can't take speed with alcohol because it will mess your head up so bad."

Goldman took his cue from Cavanaugh. "Is there any history of *your* using a combination of speed together with alcohol?"

"No, I drink very little," Costa said. "The only speed I've ever used was that one time in San Francisco. I had no more use for it."

"Could you be able to say under oath that you were a victim of drugs?" Goldman said.

"No, I wouldn't say I'm a victim of drugs, because I have will power. I have a rational mind," Costa said. "If I used as many drugs as people say, I would be a physical wreck. I would have experienced symptoms of withdrawal at Bridgewater. My body was checked for drug use!" Costa's voice rose indignantly. "I am not a drug user!"

"You couldn't say that these acts of alleged murder could have been committed by you when you were under the influence of any kind from any source?" Goldman said.

"No *sir,*" Costa said, flatly. "There's no way I could have committed that crime whatsoever. Not even under drugs of any kind. No way whatsoever!"

Goldman backed down, for the time being. "Well, that wasn't in anybody's mind here," he told his client.

Before Goldman left, Costa said, "Last night I had a bad night's sleep. It's going to be my daughter Nico's birthday next week, and it's kind of rough on me because I want to be there so badly. I've got this birthday card; I propositioned one of the guards into bringing me a card I'm sending her. I'd really appreciate it if you could ask Avis to bring her up or something." Costa's visitors were limited to members of his family. Avis had to get special permission, since she was his ex-wife. "She's really uptight about that," Costa said. "In her last letter she said, 'I'm really not any relation to you.'"

"Well, she's doing everything she can to be helpful," Cavanaugh said. "She's been very cooperative with our investigators."

"She's a good kid," Costa said. "That's one good thing we have in common. Neither one of us has grudges; it's just not our way of life. It's unrealistic. You've got to treat others the way you want to be treated yourself," Costa said as the prison guard took him by the arm. "If you don't do that, you're disobeying the greatest law there ever was."

18

It had not been difficult for Costa to arrange with his guards for so small a matter as a birthday card for his little girl. Costa was popular with the correction officers, on a first-name basis with most of them. Every guard had his favorite Costa story to take home. Costa was an "interesting" inmate—voluble, literate, always scribbling in a notebook or sketching. A paint tray was set up to catch the light from his cell window.

Costa's favorite officer was Donald Parker. Wiry, muscular,

with a short crew cut and a tense, lean face, Parker found Costa a likable inmate, with a good sense of humor who responded well to correction officers and was willing to communicate. Costa was sometimes depressed, Parker thought, but had resigned himself to his trial and adapted well to prison life.

Costa kept his cell immaculate. He had volunteered to wash and wax the corridor outside his cell. Costa had been especially pleased to be given a part-time job in the prison's library, a dungeonlike room in the basement whose ceiling-high barred windows filtered pale and shadowy light. The place was usually empty. Costa enjoyed tidying the shelves, which held more than thirty-five thousand books, and spent hours reading behind the library's barred gates.

Costa had embarked on a daily program of weight lifting. The abundant and tasty prison fare, combined with his enforced idleness, had brought his weight up from 175 to 192 pounds.

Costa had taken to attending Mass celebrated by the prison's Catholic chaplain every Sunday, telling Goldman: "I haven't been to confession; I don't believe in confession as such. I mean, I talk to the Man directly. I don't go through other channels."

Goldman had told Costa's brother Vinnie, "When you come down, I think it would be advisable that you bring along Tony's tools, since they are stolen." Goldman was furious when Vinnie brought the tools to his mother's house in Provincetown, and said so to Tony. "He was told to bring those things to my office! If the police find stolen tools at your mother's house, it isn't going to help you any." Goldman was annoyed that Vinnie had spoken so freely to police about the gun, without realizing the significance of what he was saying.

"Well, Vinnie's just a screwed-up guy," Costa said. "He's exactly like his father. Like his head is not ready to face what's happening. He's sort of way out and doesn't realize what he's saying. He's more or less for himself; that's the way his father was. He doesn't really mean any harm."

"The road to hell is paved with good intentions," Goldman said, "don't you know that, Tony?"

"I don't know it," Costa said. "I may find out."

At a conference in Goldman's office on Monday, April 21, Vinnie confessed he had not loaned his brother any money to buy Pat Walsh's Volkswagen. "Tony said he didn't buy the car; he told me

332

the car was stolen." Vinnie and his girlfriend Cathy Roche had tried to see Tony the day before. "We had little Peter with us; he wanted to see his dad. But we couldn't get in."

In his excitement, the five-year-old boy had run into the side of a car door being opened on the passenger side and had split open his forehead. It had taken ten stitches at the emergency room at Cape Cod Hospital to close the wound. The driver of the car had offered to pay all damages, Vinnie reported. "Peter's going to have that scar for the rest of his life."

19

Avis denied to Goldman Costa's story that she had been offered Pat Walsh's clothes by Bob Turbidy. "All he did was come to the house once looking for Tony; he didn't say anything to me about any clothes," Avis said. "I also heard that after all this began to happen—these death things of the girls—that Tony was sitting in the Foc's'le talking to somebody, I think it was Dickie Oldenquist, and Tony said to him, 'You know sometimes I have a feeling I'd like to do horrible things.' And Dickie, kiddingly—because Dickie's a funny person—said, 'Yeah, I know what you mean, Tony. We all go through that; we all like to do horrible things sometimes.' And Tony said, 'No, I mean *really* horrible, horrible things.' And Dickie said, 'Yeah, yeah, I know what you mean.' And Tony got really upset and said, 'Oh, you don't understand either! *Nobody* understands.' And he got up and walked out."

Lester Allen brought Avis to the Barnstable House of Correction to help record the sexual history of her marriage for the benefit of the psychiatrists that were due to examine Tony. Avis continued to be more candid with defense investigators regarding her sex life than her ex-husband, sitting beside her.

"Sex didn't really enter into our relationship that much," Tony Costa began. "It was more or less a totally normal relationship with no aberrations, no weird fantasies or anything that much. Like Avis didn't remind me of another girl or anything. It was more a companionship thing than a strong sex thing."

"A teacher-pupil relationship," Avis said. "Like, I didn't know anything at all; I was a virgin."

The experimental phase of their sex lives had been inspired, Costa said, by his reading of the Kama Sutra. "This was the basis for the suspension from the ceiling, and the idea for reaching a semiconscious state," Costa said. "It was played up to be a big gracious thing and it didn't turn out to be anything; it turned out to be horrible."

"It turned out to be a drag," Avis said, recalling that the sexual aspect of the marriage had soured almost from the beginning. "We went to a lawyer the first year we were married . . . Henson and Doyle, remember, Tony? He told us we didn't have grounds for a divorce. He said, 'You just can't walk into this office because you don't like each other anymore and get a divorce.'"

The marriage had crumbled when Avis was unfaithful with Bob Arthur, while Costa was in Illinois fulfilling a resident requirement of a correspondence school course in heavy construction equipment.

"Someone had written to me while I was in Chicago saying my wife was going around with another guy," Costa said, "so I came home. I tried to patch things up and it left me rather nervous. We consulted Dr. Callis as a counselor; he gave us both tranquilizers."

"Bob used to come over every night almost," Avis said. "I used to like Bob Dylan and nobody else did; he would bring some of his records over and we'd listen to records . . . and stuff. I never admitted this to Tony, though. I told him I loved Bob, but I never said I went to bed with him."

"Bob admitted to me what was going on; he told me everything they had done. So we all came to an agreement. I proposed the idea of letting me and Avis stay together for six months more and after that, if they still felt the same way, then they could have their own thing, and I'd go my way. The only request I made was they didn't see each other during that time. So we all agreed and

334

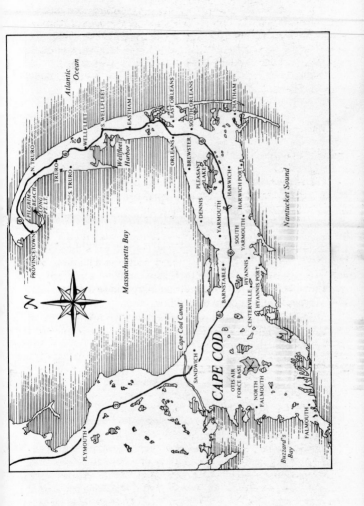

Friendly and outgoing, Mary Anne Wysocki dropped out of college to earn money to continue her education. She once bleached her hair blond, but her boyfriend Gerry Magnan had her dye it back to her natural light brown. *(Courtesy of George Killen)*

Patricia Walsh and Mary Anne Wysocki arrived at Mrs. Morton's guesthouse on Friday, January 24, 1969 around 1:30 p.m. and paid $24.00 for two nights' accommodation. *(Ted Polumbaum, Life Magazine © 1969 Time Inc.)*

The South Truro woods. In this cul de sac of pines, police found a scattering of papers belonging to Pat Walsh. *(Photo: Roy Nightingale. Courtesy of George Killen)*

After disappearing from the Truro woods, Pat Walsh's Volkswagen was found by police and impounded at a Gulf station in Burlington, Vermont. *(Photo: Burlington, Vermont, Police Department. Courtesy of George Killen)*

Bernie Flynn leads Costa from the Yarmouth barracks to a police cruiser that will take him to Provincetown for arraignment. *(Cape Cod Times)*

Costa has a subtle message for photographers. *(Photograph by P. M. Koch. All rights reserved)*

A last photograph of Sydney Monzon, from her high school yearbook. She wanted to hitchhike cross-country "and just leave her old identity behind." *(Cape Cod Times)*

Maurice Goldman and Tony Costa in the South Truro woods during a "view" of the murder scene, during the third day of the trial. Costa said, "That was an enjoyable experience." *(Provincetown Advocate)*

Edmund Dinis (far left) shows one of the graves to members of the jury, while Costa and Goldman look on. *(Cape Cod Times)*

The formal portrait of Pat Walsh identified by her father on the witness stand. Bernie Flynn thought it made her look middle-aged. *(Courtesy of George Killen)*

Costa runs through a rain shower pursued by press photographers following a session of his trial. *(Cape Cod Times)*

Avis Costa greets photographers with a peace sign and a flower. On the witness stand she objected to questions about her sex life with Tony. *(Cape Cod Times)* went along with the thing. Bob respected my wishes and I respected him for doing it. It worked out rather well. He said he was leaving town; and I was trying to show her he was not coming back. Six months later, he couldn't have cared less for her."

"I wanted to run away with Bob. I used to say, 'Take me away from all this,' just like in the movies," Avis said with an ironic smile. "I didn't really love him; he was such an asshole. Tony said for us to wait a couple of weeks and see if we still felt the same way about each other. Then Tony decided it was going to end, and that's all there was to it; he didn't want me to see Bob anymore. So then we split and Bob went to Boston. I really resented it; I was heartbroken. I was getting drunk all the time."

"She got involved with her guys and I got involved with others," Costa said. "I don't mean there was any big affair going on, I mean we became interested in different people until finally I came to the judgment a year ago January that the best thing to do would be to call it quits."

"The fact is you were upset," Avis said. "You were always like that, running around being the big man, and saying 'I don't care,' and inside it was like eating you away. Of course you had justification for leaving; you had justification for everything you did—like I wasn't as good a housekeeper as your mother."

"I wouldn't *want* anyone to be as good as my mother," Costa said, "because then you wouldn't even be able to sit and relax comfortably. The thing that bugged me the most, to give an example, is that whenever I wanted to take a shower, I would have to go in and bale out half a showerful of dirty clothes."

On one occasion Costa had thrown Avis into the shower fully dressed and turned on the water. Costa grinned, and said, "That's the only way you'd get her in there!"

"And you made a spectacle of yourself, too!" Avis said. "He was taking girls home," she said to Lester Allen, "taking them out to a movie, riding his bike with them, taking them out to see the houses he was building."

"That was more a psychological war thing, you could say," Costa said. "I was trying to get her back into the situation again. In other words, I would present her with another girl and I figured it would touch her off a little bit and she might kick back in." Costa had been close friends with one girl, but had never gotten involved sexually with her. "She was very seductive, but my resistance is very strong."

"What about Susan Porter?" Avis said.

"Oh, forget Susan Porter—"

"And Lee was before her."

"No, not with Susan Porter and not with Lee Harris. Like I slept with these two girls, but I didn't have sex relations . . . except for the Linell Morris thing. That was the first occasion—"

"Oh, I just *knew* it!" Avis said. "And that kid with the black hair is yours, too. She looks just like Nico. She's the only cute one Linell's got. I knew it had to be yours."

"Now that you've found out something, are you happy?" Costa sneered.

Costa said he had been closer in temperament to Christine Gallant. "Like Chrissie was clean. She was always in the shower, always changing her clothes. This was a very good thing I liked about her. She didn't use makeup; I can't *stand* lipstick! Christine was everything I was looking for in a woman; to put it bluntly, she was *me*. She liked the same things I liked. The only disagreement we had was about her use of drugs. And we came to an agreement where she wouldn't do this to any extent . . . and . . . that gradually she would not do certain things . . ." Costa's voice had developed a tremor.

"When you came over to tell us Christine was dead," Avis said, "I've never seen you like that."

"Her death didn't destroy my mind," Costa said. "I did rationalize the thing finally." His eyes had filled with tears.

"He gets that way when he talks about Chris," Avis explained to Lester Allen.

"He doesn't get that way when he talks about *you*," Allen said.

"Well, I don't get that way when I talk about *him* either," she said.

"I don't like to see anybody die or dead," Costa said, wiping his eyes. "I can't stand things like that."

Tony Costa wrote to Sergeant James Meads:

Dear Jim:
As you may well recall, this is the second occasion I am writing to you for assistance you may or can offer. I fully understand that you will and must consult with Mr.

336

Marshall, Mr. Killen, Lt. Flynn, etc. It is my hope that they will understand my situation and attempt to consider all possibilities of a reciprocal agreement.

When I last corresponded with you I explained that I would help you but I would have to do it *my own way!*

I did not deceive you, Jim. It involved a few months to gain the trust of "a certain group of people." They had surmised that I was working for the police, but after a length of time, I had dissuaded them.

Unfortunately, I discovered "too much." I had been threatened on numerous occasions. Fear possessed me. That is why I lost the courage to disclose any information to you. Please consider what I have written here and discuss it thoroughly with the proper authorities.

When Meads showed the letter to Cheney Marshall, the chief told him, "Put it in the round file."

20

In late April, Herbert Abrams defended Richard Valois III, the teenager charged with murdering his sixty-three-year-old father in Foxborough, Massachusetts, on August 22, 1968. The senior Valois's partially decomposed body had been found more than a month after the killing. He had been shot twice in the head and three times in the back. Police found two torn-up suicide notes. Valois pleaded not guilty by reason of insanity.

At the close of the three-day trial, Abrams was as eloquent in his twenty-minute summation as he had been in the Richard Quillen case. Abrams contended that the Valois boy was insane at the time of the murder, and that psychiatric treatment for him had been denied by his father, who had confined him to the house from May 1967 to the time of the killing and had not allowed him to attend his mother's funeral or visit his grandmother in a nursing home.

Dr. Harold Williams—the psychiatrist Abrams had used in the Quillen case—testified that the Valois youth had suffered from mental illness prior to the murders and had amnesia of events surrounding the killing.

"Dr. Williams was magnificent," Abrams said when he told Goldman of the "nice result" he had in the case—Valois was acquitted of second-degree murder by reason of insanity and was committed to Bridgewater State Hospital for life.

Goldman offered his congratulations: "This is an exceptionally good win."

Abrams had spoken to Williams about examining Antone Costa. "I feel it would be a great imposition if he were not compensated," Abrams said. Williams anticipated a two-hour interview, figuring a minimum of six hours with travel time from Dover, Massachusetts. "As a favor to me," Abrams said, "his fee will be one hundred fifty dollars."

Abrams assumed that if an advance on publication of a book on Costa had not already been received, one would be forthcoming and requested that Goldman pay him a retainer of fifteen hundred dollars in view of anticipated legal research required before the argument of motions for which Abrams was planning to appear at Barnstable Superior Court with Goldman on July 9. Abrams expected *Life* magazine to be contacted, since his appearance in the case would be filed prior to the publication of a story on the Costa case. "I think that under the circumstances you would be extending a courtesy to me, at no expense, to have my name included in the *Life* article as co-counsel. This, of course, is one of the prime considerations in my agreeing to assist in the trial and I sincerely trust you will honor and respect my wishes."

Abrams enclosed a half dozen six-by-eight glossy prints of "a fairly recent photograph," and a short biography listing him as a former assistant district attorney for Norfolk County and a special assistant attorney general, for use in any further publicity given out to the press. "You might wish to add my successful defense of insanity due to 'drug induced psychosis' in the Quillen case," Abrams said. "It may be a subtle way of apprising those interested that we are pursuing a different line."

21

Maurice Goldman had been in touch with writer Bard Lindeman who was working on an article for possible development into a book about "the dashing Tony C." Lindeman had discussed the project with his agent, who had been noncommittal.

"You should learn, if you don't already know it, that the book business is unlike any other you've encountered," Lindeman explained. "Frustration is its hallmark." Busy with several magazine assignments, Lindeman was holding off on the piece he planned to call "Ladykiller."

Goldman was horrified. The title seemed to him to be "exactly what the court has directed should *not* be done by the communications media, since it suggests that Costa did in fact kill these women, and explores the very subject matter which we were forbidden to discuss." Goldman had expressed his willingness to cooperate in an article communicating "community attitudes" as a theme of Lindeman's article, but had no desire to be cited for contempt of court, adding, "We are primarily concerned with getting a fair trial for Costa."

Goldman had reason to be concerned about continuing publicity about the Costa case. The June issue of *Inside Detective* was already on the newsstands. The cover featured pictures of Mary Anne Wysocki and Pat Walsh and two blank photographs with question marks for faces:

HOW MANY MORE GIRLS IN THE DUNES?
Four Dismembered Bodies Found on Cape Cod!

Written in racy, breathless prose, the article described the "macabre landscape" of Truro, and the "ghostly atmosphere" of the woods, the setting for "the most morbid investigation" in Cape Cod's history, an "incredible story of brutal murder and sadistic mutilations"—the work of a psychopath.

Tony Costa was portrayed as a high school dropout who had been initially identified in the case when a parking lot owner in Burlington, Vermont, called police to say a man had just driven a Volkswagen into his lot and paid a month's storage. *Inside Detective* had Captain of Detectives Daniel I. Murphy, supervisor of the detective bureau at state police headquarters in Boston, going to Vermont to learn the name and address of the driver of the Volkswagen, questioning the missing girls' boyfriends and accepting a bill of sale during his interrogation of Costa. The searches had located Mary Anne's handbag in some underbrush, while Pat Walsh's bag had been hastily buried, her decomposed, decapitated and mutilated body found in a shallow, sandy grave.

If *Inside Detective* had made a shambles of the facts in the Costa case, it was a model of journalism compared with the July issue of *Startling Detective,* whose cover advertised:

Shocking Facts!

NEW ENGLAND'S
CHOPPED-UP GIRLS
IN CAPE COD GRAVES!
The Knifer Had Sex-and-Slay on His Mind!

Written by Jonas Bayer, "Sand Dune Graves for Dismembered Girls" reported that Chief Harold Berrio had come upon the Volkswagen in the Truro woods at night "in the beams of a flashlight." The "Randell Guest House," operated by a Mary Randell, was the place in Provincetown where Pat Walsh and Mary Anne Wysocki stayed, their boyfriends given as "Henry Tomsen and Gordon Blanding." Antone Costa was referred to as a "hirsute taxidermist," described as "short and slight in build with wavy black hair." The bodies had been located with bloodhounds "baying wildly" as police officers "feverishly began digging for graves." The autopsy of Susan Perry had occurred at the "Harvard School of Legal Medicine." Repeating Dinis's comments on the dismemberment of the bodies, *Startling Detective* added that a "demented sadist" had staked out part of the woods as his own private graveyard. The girls had "clearly been tied to trees and tortured before being killed by a sadistic killer who had cut off his victims' legs and arms," having carried on his "demonical activities" for hours.

The article closed with belated sanctimony:

Under the laws of our land, Antone Costa is entitled to a fair and impartial hearing. If he is indicted, he must be presumed innocent of all allegations made against him, unless proved otherwise beyond a reasonable doubt.

Goldman had terminated the services of Kervin, Delaney and Wilhite. Despite their excellent work, investigators had found it virtually impossible to corroborate much of what Costa said.

In his tapes with Lester Allen, Costa had woven tales of a "syndicate" involved in a conspiracy to sell drugs, murder young women and set him up as a fall guy because he was a police informer. He had not accounted for his whereabouts at the time of Christine Gallant's death, and his responses when questioned about her were anything but reassuring. Costa had reported on the sexual and drug proclivities of his "enemies," of whom there seemed to be an ever-growing number, delivered philosophical ruminations on the subject of peace, love and brotherhood, and postured as a self-appointed vigilante dedicated to keeping Province-town "pure"—for pot. Goldman himself had checked police, school and telephone records in Boston, Providence and New York and had yet to locate "Chuck Hansen." Costa had lied about selling his gun, the use of drugs, the purchase of the Volkswagen from Pat Walsh and the burglary of Dr. Callis's office. With the trial coming up, Goldman was determined to find out what else Costa was lying about.

Goldman had secured the services of Charles Zimmerman of Security Services, a division of Raymond August, Inc., of Boston. One of the foremost exponents of polygraph examination in the world, Zimmerman had been granted clearance by Sheriff Tulloch to conduct a lie detector test of Antone Costa, on May 31, at the Barnstable House of Correction.

PART FOUR

Barbara and
the Diggers

———

1

Short and stocky, his cherubic face animated by penetrating and small shrewd eyes, Charlie Zimmerman had been trained as a polygraphist by the Department of Defense crime lab in Frankfurt, Germany, in 1949 and made adviser for lie detection in all cases dealing with Interpol-level intelligence matters. Since emigrating to the United States in 1958, Zimmerman had conducted more than ten thousand polygraph examinations, lectured on lie detection at various law schools, including Harvard's, and looked to the time when polygraph evidence would become admissible in the courtroom. While the hardware of "truth verification" had remained virtually unchanged, techniques of examination had made great advances in the previous decade—a growing professionalism which the American Polygraph Association sought to secure by requiring a degree and the successful completion of an examination before certification. Standardization was making it possible for one examiner to "read" another examiner's polygram.

Zimmerman had tested all of the suspects in the Boston Strangler case, often working with law enforcement agencies. A tenacious and devastating interrogator, he was increasingly being sought out by defense lawyers as well, as a means of reinforcing the denials of their clients with validity and reliability. In Zimmerman's opinion, "informed counsel is brilliant counsel."

Zimmerman was introduced to Antone Costa in the medical suite off the guardroom at the Barnstable House of Correction—two adjoining rooms thought more suitable for polygraph testing than the claustrophobic conference room in which Costa met with his lawyers. Zimmerman had explained to Goldman that the polygraph technique was based on physiological responses beyond the control of the subject being examined. Such involuntary behavior was reflected by the reaction of the autonomic nervous system to acute stress.

An information-gathering preexamination interview measured an individual's suitability as a candidate for the polygraph. By gathering data such as hours of sleep, drug use, medical and mental history and observing responses to simple personal questions, the examiner determined whether a thought disorder was present. If faulty organization of speech, incoherent or rambling answers that were not responsive to the questions appeared, no test was run.

Zimmerman always asked several stress questions to test a subject's "cool," to ascertain if he became upset at the mere mention of the crime about which he was going to be examined or had a more rational outlook. No test was ever conducted following extensive, accusatory examination, however.

The interview confirmed that adequate "case information" was available to conduct a test, and that the "strength and distinctness of issue" was sufficient to prompt a significant response —if the subject was attempting deception. "If we know that the subject pulled the trigger of a gun, causing death, then we have a high distinctness of issue," Zimmerman had explained.

The pretest interview permitted the subject to tell his story uninterruptedly, covering his knowledge, awareness and participation in the crime of which he was accused—information Zimmerman used for the formulation of test questions.

Zimmerman was unmoved by the criticism directed at his profession, the most persistent being that a subject could "beat" the polygraph. Zimmerman knew of cases where the tests had been inconclusive, but none in which a polygraph test, administered by a qualified examiner, had verified a subject to be telling the truth when subsequent events showed him to have lied. "Innocence leaves no traces," he said.

Zimmerman had listened to several of Costa's tapes and read a portion of his daybook recollections to familiarize himself with the crimes.

"You realize, Tony, the delicate position this case has in the eyes of the public due to the gruesome aspects, which will not create sympathy with the general public," Zimmerman said, in a lightly German-accented voice.

"Whatever I've told in the past is not true," Costa said quietly. "I am about to give the true facts, because I want the test to be as accurate as possible."

Zimmerman was not surprised. The prospect of a polygraph test was frequently so intimidating that subjects confessed to their crimes rather than suffer the humiliation of having the instrument respond in such a way as to point to their guilt.

"Do you know who killed these girls, Tony?" Zimmerman said.

"Yes," Costa said. "It is one person who is responsible for the deaths of all four girls."

"Who is responsible, Tony?" Zimmerman said.

"Cory Devereau is responsible. He's a good friend of mine. What happened was this: Cory broke into Billy Smith's house with two other kids. They were supposed to stand guard and watch outside; when Billy showed up, they just ran off without saying anything. Cory got caught in the house and he ran off to Chicago. Cory told me he had needles and dope of all kinds on him when he was arrested out there. And Chief Marshall flew out personally to take him back. Cory was brought in here. In fact, I was in cell number one in B section and Cory was in cell number two. He was uptight because he thought the police were after him for something else he had done, for a horrible crime concerning two girls. He said it blew his mind completely when they only charged him with breaking and entering. He was elated; he was overjoyed. Somebody came and bailed him out the same day. And this is how it came to be he came to my apartment at the White Wind after I was paroled. It was November, I'd say. I was just sitting there reading. I heard somebody stumbling on the stairs, and lo and behold there's Cory, all groggy-eyed. He was pretty much shot and stoned. He asked me if I had any stuff. All I had was a couple of Tuinals I had gotten from Dr. Hiebert. He wanted to do those. And he took out his works and things—he doesn't eat anything, he shoots everything. He was sitting there doing it all up, and he said he had something he wanted to get off his mind. And he told me he had done in Susan; and he started speaking of Sydney; that he had gone and killed these girls."

"Did he tell you why he killed the girls?"

"I don't know why. I didn't question him on it because he didn't really make much sense. He was incoherent. And he started crying. He said he needed help, that he didn't know where to go and what to do, that he was in fear of what he had done, and a complete line of this sort of news.

"And what does he do? He passes out right there on the couch! His eyes started flipping back in his head and he passed out with a needle sticking in his arm. Larry Andresen came by later and stayed a couple of hours. Cory was on the couch; off and on he came to for a few minutes, but basically he was out."

"Was Cory familiar with the area in the woods where the girls were buried?"

"Yeah, he was. I took him out there with quite a few other people. Cory knew where the can was. He used it."

"Why didn't you tell anybody about this?" Zimmerman said.

"I kept it to myself because of the fact at the time I didn't have any reason to believe him. Like, Cory's strange. He's into a lot of weird things. He's a great doctor's office robber of books— and doctors' bags. He boasted of two I know of—Dr. Hiebert's is one. The reason he takes doctors' bags is to look for hard drugs, such as heroin and morphine. I know he's had surgical instruments, but he never told me what he did with them."

"What about the other girls?" Zimmerman said. "Patricia and Mary Anne."

"I met Pat and Mary Anne around two o'clock at the Mayflower Cafe," Costa said. "I knew Pat from the summer before, by sight and by her first name. Pat and Mary Anne were involved in a syndicate of narcotics traffic dealing in dope. They would come ahead of time, make a phone call and the drop would follow. Pat was a user. She and Mary Anne were runners for a guy named Chuck Hansen."

"Tony, thus far Hansen has not been located; there is no trace of him to be found."

"Well, yeah, I've been thinking about that. I think maybe Sandy Kropoff might have his right name. He's my hash connection in Boston. Usually I met him on the Common or the Charles Street area. I ordered hard stuff through him. The guy's name is Dan; but as far as his last name, I don't know."

"This is the name of the man you've been calling Chuck Hansen?" Zimmerman said.

"Yeah," Costa said. "There was a raid in Providence; Danny and the two girls were making their travels up this way. He was a major supplier through Providence, Greenwich Village and Boston. Pat had called Chuck—rather, Danny—at 509 Beacon Street on Saturday morning about the stuff. It was coming in. After I gave Pat nine hundred dollars at Mrs. Morton's we went out to Hatch Road to check the hold; but nothing was there. After that we went to the Royal Coachman to get my paycheck. The girls dropped me off at Adams Pharmacy. From there I went to my mom's for lunch. I was at my mom's when I got a call from Danny saying he had delivered the stuff. He wanted to know where the money was, why he hadn't gotten it. I told him I gave it to Pat."

"Did you go out to the woods to see if the stuff was there?" Zimmerman said.

"I didn't go out there until Tuesday, to see what the hell the story was. Pat's car was there, maybe four hundred feet into the woods. I went to the hold and there was nothing there. No dope, nothing. So I went home. Around seven o'clock, Cory came over, all flipped out. He said he had again killed somebody. Cory told me he had met the girls out at the hold. He discussed buying drugs with them—heroin—but Pat wouldn't give him anything, because the stuff was mine to dole out. And Cory totally flipped over that and killed them. He said he had taken my gun from the can and used it."

"How did Cory know the gun was there?" Zimmerman said.

"Cory knew since I got out of jail in October where I was keeping the gun," Costa said. "I didn't want a gun at my place because I was on parole. So I decided I'd better go out there and find out what's going on. When I got to the hold, I took the gun from the can. The gun had been used; it was pretty well fouled. I put the gun beside a tree. There was a knife out there, too."

"Whose knife was it?"

"It must have been Cory's."

"Is that when you took the car?"

"No, I had Steve Grund drive the car to Boston at a later date. From there, Danny drove it to Burlington."

"To the airport?"

"Forget the airport," Costa said. "It has nothing to do with anything. We left the car at the Gulf station. Danny took a bus. To Montreal, I believe."

"What about the bill of sale?"

"The bill of sale is a phony. Pat's name was copied from some written matter that was in the car."

"Who wrote the bill of sale?"

"The bill of sale was written by Danny."

"You're *sure* Danny is the name?"

"Yeah, this is a positive fact," Costa said. "My girlfriend Sandy Kropoff can verify that."

"Well, she can't verify that Danny forged the bill of sale, can she?"

"No, but she can verify that Danny does exist. Because I know Mr. Goldman has been uptight about that."

"Did you tell Danny that Cory had killed the girls?"

"Yeah, I explained the situation to him. He wasn't overly upset about it. *I* was more upset than he was; I guess because I was involved. He said we should get the car out of there. Danny told me where Pat usually put the car key, so I went out there hoping it would be there. The spare key was under the engine—a magnetic tin-can type thing," Costa said. "I might have told Steve Grund the key was underneath a tire because I didn't want to let him in on what was going on. All I wanted was somebody to drive the car."

In constructing the actual test questions, Zimmerman took the most intense issue first to construct "relevant" questions—direct and nonambiguous questions relating to the "target" of the test involving some degree of stigma on the part of the subject being tested. "Control" questions, similar to the relevant questions, but without the intensity of response in case the subject attempted deception, provided a factor in the test structure to detract from natural nervousness, the stigma of the issue and the subject's resentment to the accusatory nature of the test. Control questions carried some appropriate emotional involvement for the subject and enough stigma to override the "artificial" one presented by the test itself. Zimmerman sought reactions to either relevant or control questions, which were placed near each other in the test. When a subject answered a relevant question and there was no reaction, reliability was established. With two relevant questions, accompanied by two control questions before and after, Zimmerman had six opportunities to interpret and evaluate each test chart with regard to truth or deception.

In constructing test questions, Zimmerman used no legal or police terms, sticking instead to the language of the person being examined who actually collaborated in creating all questions. Zimmerman then read back the questions to the subject for verification. The exact wording was agreed upon in advance; under no circumstances was a question injected into the test that had not previously been asked and approved, nor did Zimmerman change a word in the question without talking it over with the subject. Surprise could artificially intensify the degree of reaction; Zimmerman wanted no reactions except to the questions themselves.

All questions were short, unambiguous and, if possible, not emotion-creating, and answerable with a "yes" or "no," rather than a narrative statement. Extensive talking distorted test readings. The test would be very concentrated: ten questions to be asked at twenty-second intervals.

Zimmerman attached a pneumatic cuff to Costa's arm to record blood pressure and pulsation during the test. A second pneumatic component was a respiratory harness made of corrugated rubber tubing operating as a sealed unit strapped across Costa's chest to measure breathing patterns and changes. Any attempt to force a breathing pattern was immediately recognizable by a trained examiner.

The galvanic skin response lead placed on the top of Costa's hand measured minute changes in the electrical outputs of the body. Zimmerman balanced the polygraph to Costa's output, then locked it in. Any changes that occurred during the test would now be caused by the subject under examination and not by the instrument itself. The device had been validated by years of psychological testing and was in wide use in psychology departments for classroom instruction to indicate relative changes of resistance when a subject was under emotional stress. Fear, in particular, was an emotion recognizable by a rise in blood pressure, then recovery, and the slowing of pulse rate immediately after the question. Breathing suppression was often present, as well.

The use of drugs was not a significant problem to polygraph testing unless the subject was so heavily under the influence that it was obvious to the eye. Subjects on tranquilizers were in a more relaxed condition for responding to the polygraph; stimulants only exaggerated reactions. Conscience, feelings of guilt or lack of them, remorse or shame were not factors in lie detection. The reactions measured by the polygraph were not under the conscious control of the mind. Creating reactions in no way fooled an examiner. To "beat" the polygraph, a subject would have to prevent any reactions from occurring at all.

* * *

Zimmerman took a position behind the desk so that Costa could not observe the progress of the test as recorded on chart paper. Zimmerman rarely ran more than five charts, each from three to five minutes in duration. He ran two consecutive tests. "Reactions" were almost continuous, indicating considerable heightened involvement—an unusually high degree of reactibility.

Zimmerman wanted a second opinion. He stepped outside and sent William LaParl, an associate polygraphist, into the medical offices to test Costa.

When LaParl was finished, Zimmerman asked him, "What do you think, Bill?"

LaParl said, "I'd say he's got problems."

Zimmerman showed Costa the polygraph charts, pointing out "the rather outstanding reactions" even a layman could recognize. "The tests do not support your story, Tony," he said. "I can't recommend your answers to your attorney."

Zimmerman reported the news to Goldman.

"If all I said was that Costa had run a bad test, I would be nothing more than a mechanic, and not be providing any service." Zimmerman had not wanted to get involved in too many details of what Costa told him. "I just wanted to have a rough idea of his change of story. Not being totally familiar with all the facts, I had to concentrate on what he was saying."

At no time did Costa admit he was present when the girls were killed or their bodies cut up. His story was loaded with inconsistencies: Why would Costa give Pat Walsh nine hundred dollars when he went to the woods with her? Why should Costa get a call on Saturday afternoon that the heroin had been delivered and wait until Tuesday to go out to the hold in Truro?

"These matters need to be tied down into facts with a very methodical approach, especially where Costa has changed the story from what he told before—the first time he has made a statement which is crime-connecting." Zimmerman had to follow through by "isolation techniques" in areas where there had been reactions on the polygraph. "Our aim will be to break down which crime Costa had actual participation in or knowledge of."

2

Zimmerman's task was to eliminate all alternatives of Costa's involvement in the murders before talking about guilt. He cautioned Goldman, "A suspect can be deceptive and still be telling the truth. Every lie has some element of truth in it; whether it's one percent or fifty percent.

"The general trend of the tests clearly indicates that Costa is still not telling the complete truth, and that he is aware of more details in the cause of death of the girls than he is telling," Zimmerman continued. "Our object is not to prove that he is a liar. Our object is to find a course of action to take in the defense of this case."

Zimmerman's second polygraph test of Tony Costa took place on the following Saturday, June 7. Steadfastly denying any direct involvement in the murders, Costa said, "On reflection, I've decided to tell the entire truth."

"Cory came to me on Sunday night around eleven or eleven-thirty. He showed me a lot of money. He must have had at least three hundred dollars, I'd say—all twenties. Cory said he had killed Pat and Mary Anne and left them both near the hidden can. Cory started shaking violently when he was talking about it. He was crying. So we hitchhiked out to the area. A car with New York license plates picked us up. We were dropped off at the underpass on Route 6. We climbed down the embankment and went to Hatch Road. Pat's car was still there. We walked from the car into the woods. I had brought a flashlight along."

Costa hesitated, looked away, shifted in his chair and brushed his hands through his hair, "There was a pile of cut-up bodies, maybe one hundred yards behind the can," Costa said coldly. "I basically recognized who they were. I became sick and vomited right there. It was something like I've never seen before in my life; and I've got a weak stomach to begin with."

"Were the bodies all mixed up, or were the remains of one in one section and the remains of the other in another section?" Zimmerman said.

"There was more or less two piles; they were generally together. It didn't appear to me there were two bodies in one pile, they were like, I would say, parts of one someplace else. I didn't really stop to check. I assumed this was the gross part of it. Cory was doing something in the bushes; I didn't know what he had up there. He dragged something along, but I don't know what it was. It must have been part of something. I didn't inquire because I was sick. I couldn't take it; I couldn't stomach it."

"Did you ask Cory what the reason was for cutting up the bodies?"

"At the time I didn't really think of it. I was just so shocked that my basic thought was just to eliminate the sight, to bury the poor things. Nothing came to my mind except to cover them up. We both started digging holes. I used a white cap—a round white metal bottle cap about three inches in diameter—to dig with. The ground wasn't that hard. Under the layers of leaves and pine needles it was basically sand. I dug one hole in the lower section there —like a little clearing, almost; Cory was digging another one up in some bushes somewhere. He was using what looked like maybe part of a plastic bottle or something, brownish color. It was a hurry job; Cory came back in a big rush. I didn't even think he had had time to really *do* anything, that he hadn't dug a hole yet. It took me around half an hour to dig my hole. When the hole was deep enough I started putting things in. I used a stick to push them into the hole with. I definitely recall putting one head into the hole. The one I did had more or less short hair; I think it probably would have been Mary Anne. I put the cap in the hole; I just threw it in there. I covered the hole with sand. There was a little bit left over and I spread it on top. It didn't form a clump or anything; it was pretty level. It seems to me it was spongy when I stepped on it, packing down some of the earth. And I just thrashed some leaves over it, just spread them over with a stick. We got out of there, it was maybe between two or three o'clock in the morning. We went off the area and thumbed a ride back to town. We got picked up by, like a Cape Cod *Standard-Times* truck, except it was white. I assumed it was making restaurant deliveries or something. Cory was quite high. He was in a daze. He didn't talk to the driver at all."

"You never asked him why he cut up the bodies?" Zimmerman said.

"I think I may have out at the site. I know I questioned the reason why. I asked him what happened, what had gone on. He didn't say anything."

"Did Cory tell you what he used to dismember the girls with?"

"No, he simply said that there was a knife out there. I know that I had none out there, so I questioned him as to where it came from. He just said that it was his knife."

"Did Cory tell you he had cut up Susan and Sydney the same way?"

"No, he didn't. This is what shocked me even more. Because I didn't even believe Cory when he told me about Susan and Sydney. But when I called my mother and she said the police had found a body in the woods, then I began to get uptight."

"Did Cory ever speak to you about this incident later on?"

"Yeah, he was always chasing me around town. He came looking for me the day after I talked to Jimmy Meads. He came over to where I was working for Frank Diego to ask me about being questioned by the police. He was really shook up about that. He wanted to know if I had said anything. I told him, 'Hey, they're onto this!' And Cory just brushed it off and said, 'Keep quiet about it.'"

"What did you tell the police?"

"When I got to the station, I became so uptight. I wanted to tell the whole story to Jimmy because I had confidence in him. He had come through for me before and he would have come through again," Costa said. "But I couldn't get my courage up to say, 'I went out there and helped bury these people.' Because I felt that I was involved. And when I got there all the state cops were waiting; they wouldn't let Jimmy stay in the room."

Zimmerman could not run another test on Costa, explaining to Goldman, "The recollection of the events—visualizing these activities and reliving the facts—created an unfavorable condition for testing."

Zimmerman asked Costa to write down "every outstanding thing" he could remember about Cory Devereau, his relationship with the girls from Providence and the events of the night of the murders. Zimmerman was coming back the following Saturday to run another test. To Maurice Goldman, Costa wrote:

It is now my pleasure to inform you that I have spoken the entire truth concerning my implications in the demise of the girls from Providence.

It took a tremendous load off my mind and has left me barren, desolate. I truly regret not disclosing this information sooner, but I regret even more my attempt to cover up this hideous crime.

Please give me your opinion on the following: Would it be rational to confront Mr. Dinis with the knowledge I possess and possibly have him allow me to "testify for the State?"

I must impress upon you that I am *not* intent upon reducing any sentence I may receive. I am simply concerned with the fact that Cory may never reach trial; then our case is lost. Cory said he is guilty of all 4 deaths.

Please advise me as to whether you believe this would be a wise idea.

Always,
Tony

3

Costa was bothered about lying to his attorneys, he told Cavanaugh. "I know it took a long time, but I got there finally. I didn't really trust you people that much. Because I figured if I let you know the involvement that I had and everything, you might say, 'goodbye,' or something. Either consciously or subconsciously I wanted the lie detector test because I knew once the machine was there it would bring it out."

"Tony, why did you sit quiet for three months with four murder charges hanging over you?" Cavanaugh said. "Why protect Cory when you didn't have to? You never brought Cory into this until you talked to Charlie Zimmerman. What was the reason you were covering up for him?"

"I don't know what the motive is," Costa said. "In the beginning I figured the police didn't have that much, that I could get us both out of it."

Cavanaugh was astonished. "Tony, how could you believe that, after you were arrested, after you had been arraigned in court and sent to Bridgewater and indicted for four murders. That's three months ago! And during that time you kept quiet about Cory. How could you believe you could get out of it?"

"Because I was *there,*" Costa said. "I can't offer any explanation other than that! And I think a very strong thing with me is, I don't believe in judging others. I don't believe in it whatsoever."

"Did you put one complete body in the grave you dug?" Cavanaugh said.

"I don't think it was complete," Costa said. "I think it was the big bulk of it; it was a big section. I just more or less shoved it in with a stick. I prodded it along the ground and it went into the hole. The head, I remember went in almost last. I don't remember putting any arms in there. I think there might have been one leg . . . I'm not sure as to two."

"Then an arm and a leg of that body went into the grave Cory dug?" Cavanaugh said.

"Yeah, I believe so; whatever was left over. It was kind of dark. I heard Cory thrashing through the bushes. It sounded like he might have been dragging something along."

"Did you move the gun from the can that night?"

"I had the gun out of the can already. When we went in, we stopped at the can first. I wanted to check that out. I really didn't believe what Cory was saying, but I was a little bit uptight. I took the gun out of the can because I wanted to have it in my possession. I didn't want to leave it hanging around because of Cory."

"Was the gun loaded?"

"No, I emptied the gun myself. All the shells were spent. It was all dirty. There was like sand ground in where you turn the thing to check to see if bullets are in it."

"How about the knife?"

"That I couldn't see. It didn't seem to be utterly messy; it didn't appear to me in the darkness to be very dirty or anything. It seemed to be fairly clean."

"Did you question Cory about the girls' being killed?"

"I just asked like a few minor questions, such as why it was done and if anyone else was involved with him and this sort of thing. I didn't really get any answers from him. He wouldn't comment on much of anything."

"What's your opinion, Tony, as to why the bodies were cut up?" Cavanaugh said.

"This I don't know. The only opinion I have is that it could very well have been a drug-induced thing."

"If the girls were killed on the spot, what would be the necessity of dismembering their bodies?"

"This I can't understand," Costa said. "The only thing I can see is that Cory is a very strange guy. It must have been something in his mind; it must have been something that triggered him to do this. Cory's been totally wasted for a long time. He shoots anything he can get his hands on. Like he'll shoot LSD, and if he doesn't have LSD, he'll shoot heroin. If he doesn't have heroin, he would shoot things like Nembutal, Tuinal—any of these barbiturates that come in a capsule. Most of it is in powdered form and you can put in a little bit of water in the needle and stick it in your arm. And this is what Cory did. Without even stopping to think there's stuff like buffers which you don't know what it's going to do to you. He'd take any pill apart, just like a guinea pig. He took a capsule one time, like Contac—and those are incredible, I wouldn't even think of doing it—and he crushed those things up, put in a little bit of water, heated it and drew it up into a syringe and shot it into himself. And he went into this big flair; he got all red and started grabbing his heart and almost keeling over. And I was saying to myself, 'God, that's the end of Cory'—he really had me uptight. But he went over to the bed as usual and lied down. He came out of it about four hours later."

"When do you think Cory killed Susan Perry?"

"It would have to be after Susan visited me in Dedham. There was a pile of them that came up, three or four guys—Jimmy Steele, Timmy Atkins, Davey Joseph. Cory, in fact, left a note in my mailbox telling me that he'd be back at seven, but he never showed up."

"Davey Joseph said you had sexual relations with Susan," Cavanaugh said.

"That's impossible! I never had relations with Susan!" Costa said hotly.

"Well, she jumped into bed with you, didn't she?"

"She jumped into bed with any guy that came along."

"How did Cory know Susan?"

"Cory knew Susan from having gone to school with her—Davey and Timmy, that crowd. Cory also knew Sydney. He used to buy speed from Sydney and he used to sell her speed when he had it; there was a thing going on. He had many connections with big people. In other words, he had his hands in everything; he was like a big octopus."

"Did he say *how* he killed Susan?"

"Cory never said what happened to her. He couldn't really remember. What he said was a certain argumentation and discrepancy came up and he flipped out. All I know is it had something to do with stabbing. He told me he had help, but he didn't say who or how."

"What happened to Susan's clothes that Paula brought to Boston in a duffel bag?"

"As far as I know they were picked up," Costa said. "She didn't leave nothing at my place."

"Did Cory tell you why Susan was buried in a different place from Sydney?"

"No, he didn't."

"Why not bury Susan and Sydney together rather than put Pat in there, since Sydney was the first one to disappear?"

"I don't know, unless someone was with him and influenced him," Costa said. "I don't know where Susan's grave is, so I can't exactly place it with the other ones, if you know what I mean."

"Did he bury Susan and Sydney by himself?"

"I have a lot of reason to believe that someone else was involved. The only people I can think of is Roland and Eddie."

"*You* didn't have anything to do with that, did you?" Cavanaugh said.

"No, I didn't."

"You helped him with Pat and Mary Anne, but not with Susan or Sydney?"

"I had nothing to do with Susan or Sydney."

"Did Cory ever admit this to anybody else other than you?"

"The only people I could say would be Larry Andresen and David Nicholson. He would admit it to David, because David is a guy I would call perverted anyway. He takes relish in these kinds of things. He's Cory's best friend. Like on two occasions, I was invited by Cory and David to go for a ride and we ended up at the cemetery in Truro. Once we took the Cadillac that belongs to David's mother. And who in their right mind is going to ride through the woods like that in a Cadillac? One time Cory and David were talking about having sexual intercourse with dead bodies. They took me into a crypt. It had a wooden door and there was a hasp on it with some kind of a little stick in it. They just pulled out the stick and walked in. I never thought about it until now, but this would be the place where Cory put the bodies. It's altogether possible, now that I think of it."

Cavanaugh didn't think the motivation for Cory killing the girls was very clear. "Unless there's some very far out sex hang-up that Cory has," he suggested.

"The only thing I know of is I guess a fetish to do with clothing," Costa said. "Cory had a pair of underwear belonging to his girlfriend he used to carry around in his pocket all the time, for some strange reason, a pair of panties, black lace things. See, with Cory, nobody realizes it, but he's very sick."

"Well, I still don't know why you protected Cory when you didn't have to," Cavanaugh said.

"I had no reason to believe anything," Costa said. "Or let's say I didn't really want to believe. Because my mind is strange. I don't like to believe anyone is hurt or anything unless I find it to be true."

"You said Cory ran away to Chicago after he was caught housebreaking," Cavanaugh said. "Did he ever talk about leaving town after killing these girls?"

"Yeah, he wanted to, but he didn't have any money. Cory was always talking about going to the West Coast. He didn't have any particular destination, he said he just wanted to get away from everything."

Costa had drawn a map of Cory Devereau's room he showed to Cavanaugh, explaining: "Cory liked to show off using the gun he sold me. He'd show off with maybe a fast draw or something, just goofing off. And he fired, I don't know how many, anywhere from three to four bullets in his room. There's one in the wall about halfway up as you walk in the door—the wall directly in front of you. And on the same side as the door there's a big chunk that was taken out of the plaster. The bullets are evidently still lodged there."

* * *

On Saturday, June 14, George Killen received a telephone call at his home in Chatham from Lester Allen. Allen had information from Tony Costa's polygraph tests which Maurice Goldman wanted brought to the attention of police. Costa had given permission for the release of evidence, and Killen dutifully recorded it in a spiral-ring notebook, when Allen came to his office on Monday morning:

> Costa had been in his room on the night of Sunday, January 26, when Cory Devereau came to see him. Cory was using speed and was very high. Cory said, "Where is the heroin? I was out to the drop, the two girls said it would be there; it wasn't there." Cory had blown his top and killed the girls. Costa said they should go to the police, that he would call Sgt. Meads. Cory said, "No, you can't, because I shot them with your gun." Costa and Cory had thumbed a ride to Truro and gone into the woods with a flashlight. They had come upon a pile of bodies on top of an embankment. Costa was horrified at what he saw. Cory told him he had to help bury the bodies. There was a plastic gallon container there. Costa took the top of the container and Cory took the bottom; they both dug graves. There was only a crust of frost on the ground; it took only ¾ of an hour. Costa packed two arms, two legs, a torso and head into his hole, covering the grave with brush, leaves and sticks. Cory put the rest into the grave he dug. There was no conversation as to why the bodies had been cut up. Costa was revolted. While in the woods, Costa checked a metal canister where he kept his gun. The gun was there; also a knife with red stripes on the handle he had never seen before. Costa took the gun and knife, wrapped them in some cellophane he had with him and dug a hole near a dead tree and buried them before he left the woods, sometime around 2:30 A.M. He and Cory had thumbed a ride back to Provincetown in a brown-and-white vehicle, similar to a milk delivery truck.
> Last October, while Cory was in cell number 2 at Barnstable jail, he told Costa he was glad to have been arrested for B&E, because he thought he was in for mur-

der. Cory had confessed to having killed Susan Perry and Sydney Monzon and was going out of his mind with worry.

According to Costa, Cory had a key to Adams Pharmacy, had broken into the community building and stolen hi-fi equipment and band instruments. Cory had also stolen two doctors' bags, looking for morphine.

Killen wanted to know if he could question Tony Costa. Allen didn't know; he'd have to ask Goldman. Killen put no credence in the story. Nevertheless, he called Cheney Marshall to ask Provincetown police to keep an eye on Cory Devereau, in case he tried to leave town.

4

On June 20, Costa wrote to Georgia Panesis and Ronnie Enos:

Greetings Aries, Georgette:
Your latest correspondence was delivered to me today. It sure feels good to have you people remember me. I have at last encountered who my true friends are. May it always be so.
I am going to court between July 7 and 15 just to hear "motions," etc. There may be a rapid change of events soon, but it all depends on the police. If they get off of their ignorant, prejudiced asses and commence some apprehending of the proper people. They have all the information. Now all they have to do is their job. If they'd approach me properly, I would give them all the help

they need. But I need their protection due to certain uptight people.

I've never been in such a horrible situation in all my life! It's ugly! It weighs heavily upon my heart. Is Cory still in town? How's his head? Is he messed up? Is he still using much stuff? Please let me know. How's Larry?

Ron, please trust in my law people if they interrogate you. Tell them all you know about Adams' key, the Center, etc. The facts involved in these matters are vitally important to my case. The lawyers shall not disclose where the information came from. *I need it,* Ron. Tell them all you know about that whole crowd. I really appreciate it, brother. *It's my life I'm after.* We can no longer hold back any information; and thanx. The Gods shall reward you richly in Nirvana.

In the morning, I have another lie detector test coming up. I reckon this one will be the Grand Finale, since I've said all there is to say. I reckon if I pass this one I'll get my diploma. Then I'll become "The Graduate."

Avis and the three urchins came up yesterday. I dug them all. They are super people. They are growing so fast.

And so, Ron, we come to that hour of the nocturnal season when I must now commence a process of profound meditation. To paraphrase: I'm going to sleep.

So, write again soon. Be cool and take care. Go in peace,

> Love ya's,
> Tony C.

Tall, dark-skinned, with long black hair, once a member of the Barbarians rock band, which had enjoyed a brief vogue, Ronnie Enos was puzzled at Costa's characterization of their friendship.

"I don't really think Tony helped me that much," Enos told Cavanaugh, who compared his statements with Costa's prison daybooks. "He gave me a lot of advice; I enjoyed talking to him, he was intelligent. But he had this attitude like he was much smarter than me, sort of superior. When I first met Tony he wasn't like that, I don't think. He was just an average guy."

Enos had accompanied Costa to California in January, 1968.

"He wanted to check out the Haight-Ashbury district of San Francisco because drugs were pretty cheap out there."

On Friday, January 26, at ten o'clock in the morning Costa had backed his 1959 red-and-white Bonneville out of the short driveway at 18 Shank Painter Road with four hundred fifty dollars in cash in his pocket, the proceeds of a roofing job he had just completed. Costa had just sold his diving equipment, Enos recalled. "Everything was fairly new: a wet suit, spear gun, diving tanks, regulator and face masks. Tony sold the complete thing for eighty dollars to Jimmy Nunes and put the money in a tin can for Avis."

Avis, holding nine-month-old Nicole in her arms with Peter crying beside her, was furious at being abandoned. Costa could hardly contain his eagerness to be off.

He and Enos had driven continuously, spelling each other, stopping only for gas, food and to stretch their legs. Enos observed Costa taking four or five Solacen capsules at a time from a stash in the glove compartment.

Costa had "blissed-out" over the passing landscape. They stopped at a motel in Chapel, Nebraska, for six hours' sleep and arrived at an apartment in San Francisco occupied by Sandy Carter of Provincetown on Monday afternoon, January 29. Costa called Avis to let her know he had arrived safely, but gave her no address or phone number where he could be reached. Anxious to tour the area, Costa went to Golden Gate Park to score hashish. The next day he and Enos went looking for an apartment in Haight-Ashbury.

Costa and Enos had rented a dingy, barely furnished apartment at 1667 Haight Street, across from the Straight Theater, inviting another displaced Provincetownian, Matt Russe, to share the apartment.

"Matt was AWOL from the army," Costa's daybook confirmed. "He had no place to live. He was just bumming around the city. He finally turned himself in." Enos and Costa had looked for work with no results. Costa was running out of money, having spent his last thirty-seven dollars for the rent on the apartment. Enos was planning to visit his mother in Arizona; Costa chose to stay in California, "because nobody in 'Hashbury' was really ever without dope. There was all kinds of drugs available like grass, speed, acid, hash, opium, scag, DMT, STP and THC—anything you could want."

364

Costa met Barbara Spaulding during his second week in California.

"There was a party upstairs one night and this girl came and knocked on our door and that's how we met her," Enos told Cavanaugh. "We invited her in and Tony started talking to her."

Costa's recollection of the incident had been far more vivid:

She came to a party in the apartment upstairs. I think she knocked at our door by mistake. We all went upstairs. We looked inside and there was a big scary painting done in fluorescent paints, so it really stood out set way back in the living room; they had ultraviolet lights on it. A guy came to the door and told us to get out, that it was a private party. So we went back downstairs. Barbara came down later to apologize for the guy. We got talking a little bit and the next thing I know she's leaving; and like she was going out the door and Matt Russe was standing there with his pants down; he's got his ass right toward her. That just cracked everybody up; but for me, it wasn't funny. Because here's this girl and she's going to think we're all nuts. So I pushed Matt aside and went running after her. I called Barbara back in. She was a little reluctant. I apologized for Matt's behavior. We made arrangements to see each other the following day.

Three days later, Costa had moved in with Barbara. "She had a two-year-old little boy named Robert, real cute. He had long blond hair and blue eyes. I loved him," Costa wrote in his daybook.

It was a communal living house. Many people shared the kitchen, but each couple had their own bedroom and privacy—simple but nice. The landlord took us to a supermarket and told Barbara to buy all the food she needed; it was his gift to us, a token of friendship. The bill came to twenty-seven dollars. He paid it and gave us fifty dollars more in cash to help us, since our money was almost gone. He was a super-nice guy; he was young, about twenty-three or twenty-four. He was a mailman who was renting the house. We would sneak into his apartment on the first floor and clean it for him while he was at work.

Costa had also sneaked out mornings to "borrow" milk and other products left on doorsteps. He raided gardens to "prune" vines of fruits and vegetables. He had joined others living in the house to "shop" supermarket dumpsters, sifting through piles of rubbish for lettuce, tomatoes, bread and pastries—a bohemian delight," Costa recalled. "The food was cooked in the second-floor communal kitchen by groovy head chicks."

"Once Tony met Barbara, I hardly saw him anymore," Enos told Cavanaugh. "He was with her all the time." Enos had observed Costa using large amounts of Methedrine and LSD, sometimes mixing them to achieve a trip of greater intensity. "I don't think he'd ever done that until then." Costa and Barbara had gone into convulsions, suffering from a combination Methedrine-acid "bummer" in Golden Gate Park. "Tony almost died," Enos said. "He had to go to the hospital; he spent the night there and everything."

Costa had learned from his mother that a warrant had been issued for his arrest on non-support charges and had borrowed money from Vinnie to fly back to Cape Cod.

"He said he left his car with Barbara in San Francisco, that she signed a bill of sale from the registry out there," Enos explained.

Costa was ordered to pay thirty-five dollars a week child support, and received a suspended sentence and one year probation when he returned to Provincetown—"a changed man," according to Enos. "Tony was badly strung out on dope; he was shooting speed. He'd be irritable and uptight, and then a few minutes later he'd undergo this complete transformation; he'd become elated. Most of the time he was just confused. He didn't know who he was or where he had been. Tony was dropping acid, too. He dug the hallucinations he got on LSD." But Costa had complained that the other side of his high were visions of terror, anguish and unbearable horror.

"Tony loved San Francisco," Enos told Cavanaugh. "He talked about it all the time. He said he learned a lot about life and things by going out there. He told me he had called Barbara's sister in California and she told him, 'Barbara's gone; nothing concerns her anymore.' "

5

"Can you give us the name and address of Barbara in San Francisco?" Cavanaugh asked Costa at their next conference.

"Her name is Barbara Spaulding. Her home, she said, was in San Jose. At the time I knew her she was living at 2743 McAllister Street in San Francisco, but I know she isn't there now."

"Didn't she die?" Cavanaugh said.

"No, she didn't die!" Costa said.

"As far as you know she's still alive?" Cavanaugh said.

"I should hope so, yes," Costa said. "Definitely."

"The reason I ask is . . . the police think you killed Barbara out there," Cavanaugh said.

Costa was indignant. "This is why I told Mr. Goldman I think it's extremely important that we locate her out there. I gave Mr. Goldman a bunch of information, everything I could possibly know about her that I wrote out one time."

Costa described Barbara as "five feet five, 110 pounds, brown hair, a Gemini, intelligent, writes poetry and lives in hippie areas."

"I got a postcard from her," Costa said. "It's in a little blue flight bag the police confiscated when I was arrested; they took it. They have the postcard; that's her writing. You can establish that; it's got a postmark on it and everything."

"Why would the police think you killed her if they have a postcard from her dated after you left California?" Cavanaugh said.

"I don't know. They evidently have the idea I went back out there or something; this is one of their stipulations: that I returned to the West Coast or some ridiculous thing. She can be found; there's no doubt about that! In fact, I'd like to present her right in court, right in front of everybody, just to say, 'Well, here she is.' "

"It's irrelevant to the cases we're now a part of," Cavanaugh said. "Any reference to Barbara is absolutely inadmissible."

"But the fact is she's *there!*" Costa said. "She was a decent chick, sort of super well-built. She had a lot on the ball."

"You were apparently in the hospital in San Francisco?" Cavanaugh said.

"Yeah, I was at the San Francisco General Hospital on Parnassus Avenue. It was in February, around the twentieth, the night of the Haight Street riot. At that time Barbara and I had a little bit of Methedrine that contained alcohol. In other words, it was something we shouldn't have had. I really thought I was going to die."

"The San Francisco police have established that Barbara left her child with her sister and was never seen again; she disappeared."

"Really? When was this?"

"When you left, or right after," Cavanaugh said. "They said the car was never used by her after you left. They said the car was found abandoned on Cole Street and stayed there for five months."

"That's a lie," Costa said. "Because Tommy Russe did see Barbara driving the car around with a bunch of speed freaks. That was long after I was back here. Tommy can verify this. I got a thing from the police out there. I had my plates on the car and this is how they got back to me. They said it was in poor condition and they wanted to know what I was going to do with it, that if I didn't reply they would tow it away for junk. I didn't reply because now the car was Barbara's and I assumed she had registered the car."

"Did Sandy Carter know Barbara?"

"Sandy didn't know her, as far as I know."

"What about Barbara's sister?"

"I didn't know Barbara had a sister," Costa said. "She never mentioned any sister that I know of."

"Sandy told our investigators she'd talked to Barbara's sister. She had Barbara's little boy, and nobody had seen Barbara."

"Who said that, Sandy Carter?" Costa sneered. "You can't go by what Sandy says. Sandy is more screwed up than anybody I know. She's so flipped out it's incredible! She's just naturally insane. Like it runs in her family; none of her people are really on their bean. Her grandmother is taking shock treatments. Right now, Sandy's out on the West Coast doing nothing. She just lives off her friends."

"Well, you know *why* she's out there now, don't you, Tony?"

Cavanaugh said. "She didn't want to testify against you, that's why she took off. She told Avis that."

"When Tony got back from California, I saw a couple of letters he said Barbara had written to him—that's what he said they were anyway," Avis told Cavanaugh. "I didn't read them. I don't know if she's still alive. He got some kind of word that she wasn't around. It didn't actually say she was dead, but that's what we assumed."

The San Francisco police had questioned Costa's former landlord. The apartment Barbara and Costa had shared had been vacant following Costa's abrupt departure for Massachusetts. But a letter had been left addressed to Tony Costa in Provincetown with instructions for the landlord to mail it the following week.

Costa's journey to San Francisco with Ronnie Enos in January 1968 had not been his first trip to the West Coast. In June 1966 Costa had driven two girls, Bonnie Williams and Diane Federoff, to Hayward, California.

"They were from Sarasota, Florida," Costa explained. "They were known as the 'Diggers'—this is a hippie term for someone who's really down and out, dirty and grubby. When they got into town they were a mess. They didn't have any money. They needed a place to stay and they were hungry. And my first instinct was to bring them home and give them some food."

"How did Avis feel about you bringing two strange girls home?" Cavanaugh said.

"Avis was taking it more or less in her usual uptight, but casual stride," Costa said, and laughed. "But the thing was they ate the whole refrigerator! They cleaned it right out. And I didn't particularly care for that part. It was insane! You wouldn't believe it. We'd get through supper and Bonnie would take the scrapings off the plates, like little Peter's plate and Avis's plate and mine. She'd take all the leftovers and her and Diane would divide them. After dinner they'd go looking for cookies and lettuce sandwiches and all kinds of other things. They ate everything but the mouse seed—and I think they started nibbling on that!"

"Were they attractive girls?" Cavanaugh said.

"Yeah . . . I guess they were. I'd call them attractive. Diane had long blonde hair; she was very thin. Bonnie was a bit heavier; she stood about the same height and had sort of reddish hair, sort of curly and fluffy. I wasn't attracted to them because they seemed like pseudo people; you could see they were trying to put something over on you. I got the impression through things they said they had done something and were running from it. They were both in the bedroom and I walked in on them. Diane was weeping; and Bonnie was comforting her. I caught a few words they were saying. It was something about everything would be all right, not to worry about what she had done. I wanted to know what happened, but they never said much about it." The Diggers had stayed for a week. "I got a little sick of it, but I couldn't tell them to go."

"So you drove the girls to California? Cavanaugh said.

"I was planning on leaving before I met them. It was one of the things between Avis and I; we were splitting up. I couldn't leave them there because I was afraid Avis wouldn't have anything to eat, and the kids wouldn't either."

"What were you going to get out of it?" Cavanaugh said.

"All I really wanted out of it was the company of going all the way cross country," Costa said.

On the long drive to California, Tony had only about four hours sleep, using Benzedrine to stay awake. "That was really something, that was a super trip—without LSD! I drove more or less constantly. Bonnie and Diane took over the driving at times. We stopped one night for about six hours in Texas; I forget the town, but the name of the place we stayed was the Bonanza motel, in the northern section of Texas. My car started overheating someplace in New Mexico. A state policeman came by. He took us twelve miles down the road to a restaurant, a little shabby place and bought us breakfast. He gave us a ride back to the car and put water in—he treated us rather well. He checked our identification, but Diana didn't have any. I found out she was only sixteen when I left them out at Hayward, California. They had some really ritzy homes up there, a real high-class section. It was some uncle or friend or something of theirs. They had no money or anything, but they invited me into the house. I stayed overnight. It was incredible! The place was really a mansion. It was unbelievable that they knew people who had money like that."

After dropping off the girls, Costa had gone in search of work. "Everybody told me there was big pay, you could get all kinds of positions and all this garbage. I called a guy in Santa Barbara. He was giving a party and he was all drunk when he came on the phone. He said, 'I don't do business on Saturday night.' He started cursing me out and everything on the phone. So I said, 'Oh, to hell with this!' I hung up, got in my car, and drove home."

The entire trip to California and back took him eight days.

Avis told Cavanaugh that she did not know Costa had driven the Diggers to California. "He told me the chicks were going as far as Pennsylvania; he was going to drop them off. Then he was going straight through to California. I remember him telling me they pulled into a gas station in Pennsylvania and a state cop come over and asked for ID's. And Tony found out one of them was too young to be traveling over state borders—he wouldn't take them any farther because he could be arrested for interstate transportation of minors or something. We never talked about them after that trip. We just assumed they were back in Florida. One of them gave me her address. I think I wrote to her once, but I never got an answer."

Charles Zimmerman was not able to run another test on Costa on June 21. Costa was tense, distracted and concerned about his psychiatric examination by Dr. Harold Williams which Goldman had scheduled for the next morning. Zimmerman thought it would be more productive to concentrate on general interrogation.

Costa said he had something he wanted to tell him. "But I don't want you to look at me," he said.

"All right, Tony," Zimmerman said agreeably. "I'll look out the window."

"But you can still see me in the reflection of the glass," Costa protested.

Zimmerman removed his suit coat jacket, arranged it over the bars in front of the window and resumed his seat, "All right, Tony."

"What I want to say is," Costa said in a small, choked voice, "I helped Cory cut up one of the bodies."

"The dismemberment took place right there at the graves?" Zimmerman said.

"They were partially dismembered when I arrived. They were cut in halves. It seemed to be at the waistline, straight across there."

"Were the bodies stiff, or were they loose?" Zimmerman asked.

"They were cold and stiff," Costa said. "They were bound; like there was no free movement or anything. It was pretty cold out. It wasn't freezing, but it was probably I'd say forty degrees, maybe. I like the cold anyway; I can't stand the heat."

"Which body did you help Cory cut up?"

"Mary Anne," Costa said. "Just the legs and the head—that was it. I didn't touch the arms at all. It was more or less an expression of Cory's to place them so there was just enough room to bury them, so the arms were left, to the best of my knowledge. I didn't touch them myself. They were there when I covered up the grave."

Zimmerman was struck by the cold, pitiless recitation. Costa was unique. Zimmerman had never had a polygraph subject confess to the mutilation of a body—always difficult and painful for a killer to admit—but not the murder. "How did you cut her up?" he said.

"We brought the upper section out; it was in some bushes. We just dragged it out onto the ground. And Cory sort of stood on it to make it more stationary. And we did the leg thing, too—I did that alone. Cory was up on the hill doing something. The legs were more or less attached, but not totally. They had been pretty

372

well bashed up; they had been really destroyed. It was just a matter of a few minor cuts to break it up."

Appalled, Zimmerman nevertheless kept his own voice expressionless. "Why did you cut off the head?"

"Just to get the depth to stick into the hole," Costa said evenly. "The hole was about three feet by two feet or so; about three feet deep, not even three feet deep."

"Did Cory help you dig?"

"No, he didn't. He was more or less doing his own thing. He said he was going to take care of the other part. I heard him moving through the bushes. I didn't really hear him digging that much. I didn't exactly know what he was doing because I couldn't see in the darkness."

"Was that Patricia he was doing?"

"Pat I'm not too familiar with, because I didn't handle all of her. I mean just her upper torso section . . . she was more or less Cory's job. I really didn't do anything with her to the extent of any vicious cutting."

"What did you use for the cutting up?" Zimmerman said.

"We only had one knife; we used it between us. Like I was putting Mary Anne into the hole and he was doing his thing on the hill and vice versa. So I don't know exactly what he did."

"Did Cory mention that Sydney Monzon's body was in the same grave he dug?"

"No, he was more or less quiet," Costa said. "The only thing he did was he told me I'd better keep things quiet, that there was other people involved, and it was not he alone that I had to worry about. He definitely threatened me; he made it very explicit."

"Did he ever threaten you again, after you helped him?"

"Yeah, when I was working at Levy's. It's the big white house directly behind the electric light office. We were putting in the plumbing for five apartments. Cory came over there and put up one hell of a big stink. He said he wanted the car out of there, that it's *got* to be done soon, and that I'm implicated now."

"Did Cory say who put the sign on the car's windshield?" Zimmerman said.

"No, he didn't. That was a surprise to me concerning that sign."

"You didn't write it yourself, did you, Tony?"

"No, I had nothing to do with it!"

"And Cory never told you why he killed these girls?" Zimmerman said.

"No . . . just that he flipped out."

"Well, Cory would have to have a stronger purpose for killing these girls than you've said so far," Zimmerman said. "To kill and cut up from just a momentary thing, from being crazy by drugs. Because they were all cut up the same. He *had* to be more specific than that about his motive . . ."

"It's getting me uptight!" Costa said irritably, "Because I'm telling you *exactly* what went on."

"Tony, you *know* you have been telling lies."

"Yeah, I've told some in the past, but now I've come out with exactly what is going on, and where it's at, and you ask for motives!"

"What did he tell you?" Zimmerman said. "He *must* have explained more to you than that."

"Like Cory's very secretive in the sense of not really letting you know enough," Costa said. "I don't know that much about Cory's comings and goings except what I was told by himself. Like Cory's confided in me for quite a while; that whole group, they've all come to me with their problems, no matter how severe they were. Like Patty Avila used to come to me crying her eyes out because her parents weren't treating her right. And Robin Nicholson has been up there crying and weeping. Gary Watts and Larry Andresen have laid their problems on me. I don't know what it is with that crowd. It's just a thing they feel that I'm someone to go to, that they can confide in. Because I never related anything they told me to anyone else."

"Were they on drugs, Tony?"

"Yeah, every one of them, They kept running over and wanting stuff; so I gave it to them."

"Tony, don't you realize these people were using you, to get dope from?"

"Yeah," Costa said. "I've been taken by them; I've been beaten, I've been threatened. They've stolen from me, they've done everything. And I've just stood by and taken it lightly. Like this thing I'm involved in right now . . . I'm just sick about it," he added with a wan smile. "Because you can only be so good."

374

8

Dr. Harold Williams came to Barnstable for his first interview with Tony Costa on Sunday, June 22, at 11 A.M. Williams had grown up on Cape Cod, graduating from Barnstable High School in 1950. After a year at Exeter, he had majored in chemistry and quantitative biology at MIT. Finding work in the labs "tiresome and lonely," and influenced in part by the illness of his father, a hardworking Hyannis attorney who had suffered a cerebral hemorrhage, Williams entered Harvard Medical School. A residency in surgery at New York's Roosevelt Hospital preceded Williams's decision to specialize in psychiatry as a resident at Massachusetts General Hospital in Boston. Williams was presently in charge of the violent ward at McClean Hospital in Belmont, a suburb of Boston.

A sturdily built, good-looking man who considered himself "a callow youth" at thirty-six, Williams viewed with some uneasiness his growing reputation as a skilled medical witness in two sensational murder trials. Williams had wearied of lawyers and courts, sensing that his abilities were being exploited. He had suffered second thoughts about having supplied Herb Abrams with the information that Richard Quillen could not tolerate the knowledge that his mother was a prostitute, since Abrams's probing questions about this had provoked an uncontrollable outburst, a dramatic demonstration of Quillen's pathology for the jury that, in retrospect, Williams regarded as a cheap trick.

Williams had been warned by Abrams that the Costa case could involve "underworld connections" with narcotics traffic, adding to an atmosphere of melodrama which had prompted Williams to strap a .357 Magnum in a holster concealed under his jacket before leaving his house in Dover that morning.

Williams met Goldman in front the Barnstable courthouse. Seated at a table in the Dolphin restaurant, Goldman struck Williams as irascible and in a bad temper, the pressure of the Costa case obviously getting to him. Furious at Costa's lying, Goldman presented a ruthless summary of Costa's madness, drug addiction and sexual perversity, all of which Williams found offensive since it was delivered in the presence of Avis Costa, about whose feelings Goldman seemed totally insensitive. Williams found Avis a pathetic creature seated in a corner "like a little mouse," afraid to open her mouth while Goldman inveighed against her ex-husband.

Goldman was also engaged in trading insults with Cavanaugh.

"You're a son of a bitch," Cavanaugh said at one point.

"Cav, if I ever change," Goldman said, "I should get out of the law business."

Williams stood in line with other visitors to the Barnstable House of Correction—most of them lawyers—to check weapons at the railing that divided the visitors' area. Then he was escorted down a corridor to a small, windowless conference room where Tony Costa was waiting for him. The room provided closer physical intimacy with Costa than Williams found comfortable.

Mustached, wearing long sideburns, but otherwise clean-cut, Costa looked appealing. He seemed a thoughtful, almost bookish and mannerly young man. But Williams discerned such an aura of corruption, of ruination about Costa's dark good looks that he was physically repelled, feeling his skin prickle in revulsion.

Strangely mannered and emotionless, desperately seeking to control himself, Costa was guarded at first, testing Williams's reaction to him—a normal response. He spoke in a cool, affected voice as if measuring out precise samples of himself for Williams to inspect.

Williams listened "with the third ear," a term Wilhelm Reich had borrowed from Nietzsche's *Beyond Good and Evil* to describe "the extra sense" a psychiatrist used in listening to patients, to hear the hidden meanings of what was said and not said—the ability of one mind to speak to another beyond words and in silence. The capacity of the unconscious for "fine hearing" was, according to Freud, one of the prerequisites for psychoanalysis, a capacity which could also be turned inward to perceive voices within the psychiatrist himself, otherwise inaudible because of the "noise" of conscious thought processes.

Gaining confidence, Costa next spoke of his family history, occasionally sending a sidelong glance across the table to gauge Williams's reaction, but keeping his eyes averted most of the time.

Costa outlined his "happy childhood," of loving parents who "understood." It became obvious to Williams how painful the recitation was for Costa, who was determined to impress him by a picture-book ideal of family life, trying to be controlled like his mother, a perfectionist who had kept an immaculate house and had not allowed pets except in the basement of their apartment building in Somerville.

Costa's family situation was "very pathological," Williams explained later to Goldman. "His father died when Costa was eight months old, presumably a hero's death in World War II. His mother remarried and had a child by her second husband. Costa was barely able to conceal from himself the awareness of being left out of the circle of mother-stepfather-stepbrother. It is likely that there was a great deal of strife in the family, although Costa denies it." Costa subconsciously viewed his mother as degrading herself by being mixed up with this inferior stepfather and stupid stepbrother. "It is possible that his mother may have actually done something to reinforce this degradation."

As Costa began speaking of his ex-wife, Williams observed his composure diminish. He became deeply, intensely involved in what he was saying, to the point of anxiety.

Costa gave a brief résumé of his "disastrous marriage." He had kept count of his ex-wife's lovers.

Costa had not been bothered by his wife's infidelities, he said. He had understood the reason for Avis's promiscuity. "I know the reason for that, or part of the reason anyway," Costa said. "It was because her aunt, Sarah Cook, was living with Avis at the time on Shank Painter Road. Sarah is Avis's aunt, but she's almost as young as Avis; there's just a few years between them. All the young guys who were hanging around the house were all flipped out over Sarah. Avis wasn't getting that much attention and that made her uptight. And all those guys—Gary Watts, Larry Andresen and Peter Cordeiro—came over and Avis would jump into bed with all of them. Like with Peter, Avis I guess devirginized him. And Cory said he went to bed with Avis, too. Like Cory's on probation for breaking and entering. He's very violent, very uptight. He's very sleazy at times; but I consider him a good friend." Costa smiled ruefully. "I guess there's a strong love-hate relationship there, something more than platonic love between the two of us. It's what you would call homosexual but not homogenital. Like, it was almost an inseparable thing between us concerning

377

the drug relationship; it was superstrong. I knew it was wrong for me giving him stuff; but there was something there. I couldn't deprive him of it; I couldn't say no."

"Is Cory an attractive boy?" Williams asked, watching Costa's reaction.

"Actually, there's really not much attractive about him. It's just that—and I've noticed it in others also, but it was stronger in him because of his situation concerning drugs and getting into criminal situations. I mean, he's a very young guy. And I felt I could lead him along a proper path, if I had the time to do something. And like Cory's superclose with Larry Andresen; there's like a trinity between Larry, Cory and myself. It was a type of relationship where there was a tremendous amount of trust. Cory knew if he came to me he could speak in complete confidence about his problems and it would go no further."

Williams asked Costa if he had ever had a homosexual experience.

"Not really. One time I was at the Lechmere station of the MTA in East Cambridge and this guy more or less made a pass; he tried to grab me. It was nothing of any great consequence. I just told him I'm not that kind of person and he went off."

Williams reclaimed his Magnum at the visitors' barrier where Avis Costa was waiting to see her ex-husband. She stood transfixed as Williams reloaded the gun.

Goldman was anxious to hear Williams's first impression of Tony Costa.

Williams was shaken from the two-hour interview but had not lost his sense of humor, telling Goldman, "I was perched on

Tony's ego, peering into his id." What Williams saw had disturbed him.

"He thinks of himself as a superintellectual and local wise man, above the common herd—and above the moral code," Williams said. Costa's actions were not likely to be inhibited by law or ethics. "His megalomania takes on an even more psychopathic tone when he carefully and openly implicates himself in criminal activities such as drug pushing, while avoiding involvement in such things as murder. This, in the vernacular, is called 'copping out' on the lesser crime, a way of dealing with punitive conscience, both his own and society's."

Costa attempted to handle anger, resentment and involvement by withdrawing to lofty levels, by being above all human contact and weakness. Of average intelligence and very afraid of being helpless and vulnerable, especially with women, Costa had married a fourteen-year-old girl to ensure his superiority over her. In a way, Avis had made an ideal mate for Costa. Transfixed by violent men, desperate to be loved, but expecting to get hurt, she always chose the wrong man. In her enslaved status as Costa's wife, she had participated willingly in shadow plays of sadistic acts Costa had practiced, rehearsals for the perversions he would later fulfill in reality. Costa had claimed to have read about such things in books and pictured them as "normal." Naive as she was, Avis had come to recognize Costa's perverse nature. Her final break with him and subsequent promiscuity had represented to Costa a further example of female treachery, like his abandonment as a child by his mother in favor of a hated stepbrother. Costa saw himself as victimized by these circumstances of life, especially by women, and turned a basic feeling of deprivation and helplessness into a kind of "heroic isolation." He saw himself as an omnipotent intellectual, a superior being who could be impervious to these faithless, depriving women—his wife and mother.

"He then can treat his wife's infidelities with patronizing forbearance," Williams said. As long as this position held and Costa was not aware of needing women, he could feel superior, avoiding his terrible vulnerability. When Costa's anger toward women broke through his intellectualized insistence on objectivity, with its attendant fear and rage, a shift occurred.

"He deals with this by the use of multiple sadistic perversions which serve to achieve closeness to these despicable and degraded women while at the same time vents his fury at them. Thus the sexual excitement in torturing and possibly killing women." Costa's megalomania served to rationalize the sadistic act. "Whatever guilt he has is dealt with by psychopathic means."

Costa was not likely to admit committing the murders—or any sadistic acts. The deterioration of his marriage had occurred in the spring of 1968, when his marital problems with Avis had come to a head. Williams said, "Her harboring, nurturing and loving great numbers of homeless hippies in his home was too much for his intellectualized aloofness, and the old fury and fear broke through into sadistic perversions—and, in my opinion, the definite possibility of murdering women."

Costa had gone from his problems with Avis to Cory's confession of the murders to him, becoming caught up in ever stronger emotional involvement as he spoke, until the distinction between Cory and himself became blurred. It was typical for such a man as Costa to experience sadistic acts as done by another self —a Jekyll-Hyde phenomenon, in Williams's opinion. "Yet, because of his megalomania and psychopathy, Costa is much more accepting of Mr. Hyde than Dr. Jekyll was. Costa uses this subtle distinction to 'invent' Cory." When Costa realized he was giving himself away, Williams had terminated the interview without tipping his hand, leaving Costa off guard in case Williams needed to interview him again.

Costa had shown himself to be worn out, empty, afflicted by so dreadful an inner deadness that no amount of activity on the surface had the power to bring him back to life. Costa was "like a man pretending to be a king when all around him, his castle lies in ruins." Williams had been profoundly disturbed by the "vibrations" Costa had given off.

A sense of evil had pervaded the small conference room during his examination, Williams observed. "I felt the devil was watching . . . from Costa's side."

Williams reiterated much of what he told Goldman in a report mailed a week later, which concluded:

> This man suffers from a severe sociopathic personality disturbance. He is a modern-day "Marquis de Sade." He is in my opinion a *sexually dangerous* man and is capable of committing murder.

10

"This is the second time that I have made an effort to run a test on you, and the second time I keep getting reactions," Charlie Zimmerman complained to Tony Costa on June 28. "You must have total confidence in your attorney that legally and evidence-wise, everything will be handled in your interest. Until we have a clear picture of your involvement, we can't hope to determine the degree of involvement of Cory Devereau. If you want to turn the recorder off, I'd be more than willing; because I'm not so much interested in recording as I am in the truth. You tell me to turn the damn thing off and we'll just talk a little."

"Seriously, there isn't much more I can say," Costa said.

"Yes, there *is*, Tony. Were you *there* when any of these girls were killed?" Zimmerman thought for a moment, then explained: "I'm going to suggest that from the indications to the question: 'Did you pull the trigger,' or some question along the line that caused the death of either one of the last two girls, I have a *reaction*. And I cannot overlook it. Now this could mean *you* pulled the trigger; this could mean you were right there when somebody *else* pulled the trigger. The trouble is, you have made up your mind, you have conceded certain things as far as this case is concerned. And Tony, when you reach that degree of conviction, that creates this area of discrepancy between what truly happened and what Tony tells us so far happened."

Costa was silent.

"If you recall, the first time we met, you were talking about not being around. We talked, and for some reason I helped you recognize the situation and you were then crime-involved. The next time we talked you were crime-associated. The last time, I asked you a very important question: 'Why did you not tell the truth from the very beginning?' Do you know what your answer was?"

"I don't know, I guess it's just a lot of things built up inside and my own involvement in the thing. Just coming upon the scene

381

like I did, it was unreal! It was incredible! And it's kind of a—well not kind of, it *was* a shocker!"

"You really want me to believe it was a shock to you Tony?" Zimmerman said gently.

"It was a hell of a shock to come upon something like that! It does something to you. It's not every day I go out into the woods and find something like that right in front of me. It's not part of my metabolism, my makeup; it just isn't there."

"All right, Tony, let me accept that for the sake of talking this thing out," Zimmerman said. "How do you account for turning around and starting to separate parts of the body if it was such a shocking thing to you?"

"Normally I wouldn't have done anything like that. But out of respect for these people, I wanted to bury them—or whatever you have—just to get them out of sight, to discourage this."

Zimmerman knew he needed to try a different tack.

"Tony, how much time is really required to pull the trigger of a gun? It is only fractions of seconds; and you have hours, days and months later to try to explain why within those fractions of a second you did something. Isn't it true, Tony, that this could well be the problem that you and I are having right now?" Zimmerman said. "The last examination I ran, I gave you the charts and you looked them over. I'm sure they were very clear even to a layman such as you. And this is why I told you: Tony, you don't know how to fly a 707 or any other kind of jet, yet you get on that plane and you feel at home because the pilot knows what he is doing. And this is the same here, Tony. You've *got* to have that degree of confidence in your examiner. Do you have that degree of confidence with me?"

"Yeah, I do," Costa said.

"Whatever I have in the last chart comes from *you,* Tony; no one else," Zimmerman said. "These reactions on the polygram are caused by three psychological elements: anticipation, hesitation and association . . . by 'association' I mean an experience you have had that you try to shy away from. In the first examination I ran, you said you had nothing to do with the separation of these bodies. Obviously this telling of a lie was a form of self-defense. Now, my question is, why did you need that moment of self-defense? You were talking to your attorney, somebody who is trying to defend your cause. Obviously this is not to cook up a crime, but to try to marshal all the facts to come up with a defense based on your side of the story. Now, Tony, these recollections are clear. They cause increases in your blood pressure up to twelve millimeters of mercury. I think the problem is not that of lie detection, Tony. I think the problem is you need someone to sit down and talk to, to help you create a moment of confidence, to help you say, 'All right, this is what Tony did.' Because Tony *knows* what he did. You are facing a very serious situation; so if there is any gamble indicated, that gamble should be taken along the lines of your survival. Unless you have given up on life. Have you?"

"No."

"The thing I want to impress you with is, I have reactions which indicate a direct involvement on your part in the cause of death of the last two girls. Now, this could well mean any other girl, because the association is so close. There is no use in my running another test unless I have clarification on this point," Zimmerman said. "The area I think you've got to gain confidence in, first of all, is the total elimination of embarrassment. I know it isn't the easiest thing in the world to say: 'Look, I killed somebody.' But we've got to get over that. We cannot go into that courtroom not knowing what truly happened."

"Yeah, I realize that," Costa said.

"I told you the last time, if you were stupid I wouldn't even talk to you like this," Zimmerman said. "I've got to reason this thing out with you because you are an intelligent man. You should *know* what happened."

"Just being there doing this thing—this to me is involvement," Costa said. "How much more can I go?"

"Tony, I asked that question on the test. I asked you, 'Were you at the grave site?' You said, 'Yes.' And there was *no* emotional involvement connected with just being at the scene, as you now want me to believe there was. So we moved to the next question: 'Did you cause the death of Patricia or Mary Anne.' And then I have this reaction within one, two, three, four, five pulse beats. Do you see what I mean?"

"Yeah," Costa said.

"I asked you about firing a gun, and I got a reaction—so *something's* there. The purpose of this technique is that if a person is telling the truth *the test itself* can establish that beyond a shadow of a doubt. But if a person is crime-involved—however slightly—it requires the total sitting down and saying, 'This is

383

what I did; this is what I did not do.' And Tony, you and I have not reached this point yet."

Costa looked down at his hands.

"Is there anything that you are afraid of?" Zimmerman said. "Any fear that you haven't discussed with me?"

"Not that I can think of," Costa said.

"What do you think your attorneys would do if you said, 'All right, I was there. I did this myself.' What do you think Maurice Goldman would do?"

"I suppose he'd take it and use it in any way he could for the defense, to square things away."

"Well, don't you think, Tony, that if you *did* this, you would need medical attention?"

Costa reared back, his eyes blazing with outrage. "You're damn *right* I would! Because a thing like this . . ." He didn't finish.

"Don't you realize that you can only get that medical attention if you open the door and let people know what makes Tony tick, what *forced* Tony to do these things—if, in fact, you really know."

"I've been into psychology for quite a while," Costa answered. "Why certain people do certain things."

After Costa was served lunch in his cell, Zimmerman had him returned to the medical suite. "Now, I want you to go over the events of Sunday night again," Zimmerman said. "And try to stay with the facts."

"There were four of us. Mary Anne, Pat, myself and Cory," Costa said. "The purpose in our going out there was because the stuff we had ordered was supposed to have come in, the heroin. Pat and Mary Anne had checked out of Mrs. Morton's on Sunday morning. They had put everything into the car and gone. That night they came back."

"What time did you go out there?"

"It was approximately eleven o'clock, Sunday night," Costa said. "We all jumped into the car and took off. Pat was driving and Mary Anne was sitting in front; Cory and I were in back. She drove out to the area. We got out there and parked the car in the place exactly where the police saw it. Cory had a thing of what you call works to shoot some stuff. I took it and put it underneath

384

the car and covered it up with pine needles, just in case someone saw the car there.

"Then we four walked up the road—a good ten-minute walk. I had a flashlight, black with a yellow front, a screw-type thing we took and went up to the area. We got to the place and I opened the can. The stuff was there, a regular sandwich-type Baggie, all rolled up. There was approximately an inch of heroin across the bottom. Cory got all excited and everything; he was on LSD to begin with. He wanted his stuff. And Pat and Mary Anne wanted to try it before they went back to Providence. Pat had done heroin before, she said, she was quite into it. Mary Anne had not. She was quite naive to drug use, but she wanted to try it. And Cory's the type who's out for doing everybody. He was going to do some, too.

"I suggested we all go back to the car and do it there, but Pat didn't want to. She was uptight that someone might come by, so I volunteered to get Cory's works. It took me about ten minutes to go and come back.

"At the time I was heading back I heard gunshots—maybe two or three. There was a series of them, and then they sort of stopped. At this point I quickened my pace, and there were more shots. I went directly to the hold. When I got there this whole scene ensued. Pat was lying on the ground, she was face down, almost on her side. I didn't know what to make of it; I couldn't hear her breathe or anything. I noticed there was like blood on the side of her shoulder. Cory wasn't there; Mary Anne wasn't there. And I didn't know where in hell they were!" Costa's voice rose, then rushed ahead. "There was an argument pertaining to Cory and Pat because she wouldn't give him the stuff he wanted. In fact he grabbed it from her; it was all over the ground. And he had shot both of them—"

"Now, wait a minute," Zimmerman interrupted. "Tony, we've got to be correct on this because only the police know where the bullet entries are; the point of entry and the point of exit has to check out all the way down the line. So you'd better be realistic here. Did Pat say to you, 'He shot me?'

"She didn't say anything. She was just there on the ground near the can."

"Was she dead?"

"I assumed so. She didn't move or anything. She didn't respond. I put my arm like under her and picked her up. And she was, you know, floppy-like. I just let her rest there."

"Where did Cory shoot her?"

"I don't really know. The back of her neck was all blood; it was horrible. You could see it on her coat and everything. I didn't question what had gone on. I was just really freaked out. And I got sick."

"How about Mary Anne?"

"Mary Anne was off somewhere with Cory; they had both disappeared. The next thing I know Cory runs back to the area of the can, all flipped out. He came over and he pointed the gun at me. It was cocked; the thing was back. And he went to the extent of firing. He shot the thing and it clicked, because it was empty. He was really in a pathetic fit. He saw the heroin all over the ground and he crouched down for it; he tried to scoop up some stuff that had spilled. And I went over and kicked him on the side and took the gun away from him. It didn't seem to faze him; he was more or less concerned with the stuff that was on the ground. I grabbed him and shook him. I said, 'What's happening? Where's Mary Anne?' He said she was in the bushes and he got all excited. I wanted him to take me to her and we just took off looking through the woods. It took us nearly fifteen minutes to find her."

"Now, who did you fire a shot into, Pat or Mary Anne?" Zimmerman said.

"I didn't shoot *anybody*. I couldn't!"

"Think it over, Tony."

"I didn't fire a shot into anybody! I just went to try to find Mary Anne with Cory leading me around. It seemed like he led me in a circle. We went tramping through the woods and we finally came upon her lying on the ground. I went down to see if I could help her. She was sort of making these like gurgling, choking-type sounds or something. It just blew my mind!"

"Was she bleeding?" Zimmerman said. "Where was she shot?"

"I don't know where she was shot. I didn't care to look. There was no use doing anything to help her as far as I could see, because she was just nothing, a mess. I felt that she was dead."

"Is this when you shot her?"

"No! No!" Costa protested. "I had honestly nothing to do with killing these people!"

"Are you *sure*, Tony?" Zimmerman said. "It doesn't make any difference if you shot into a dead body."

"No, I'm positive. What I'm trying to get at is, Cory's standing behind me and the next thing I know there's this big thing slashing down right through me. The whole arm to my jacket was ripped wide open when he nudged me aside and started attacking Mary Anne. All I could see was this big silver thing flashing in the night. He is going after this girl like crazy; he is stabbing her for no reason whatsoever. He just cut her dead! And at this point, I just went to pieces, because I couldn't take this whole scene. I just hauled off and let him have it; I smacked him in back of the neck. He just flopped on the ground. And I took the knife away from him and threw it to one side. I was in such a state of shock I just picked her up, I took Mary Anne and I started carrying her out of there over to where Pat was. And I started to think, 'What do I do now?' "

"How could you carry her?"

"I took her from under the arms. I tried picking her up but she was really heavy; I was afraid of hurting her further. So I crouched down and picked her up and kind of dragged her along. Cory was sitting in the bushes holding his head and moaning. I just walked off. About two or three minutes later, Cory came flying behind me, all concerned. He started grabbing me and pushing me and saying, 'What are we going to do?' And I told him, 'I don't know what we're going to do; we've got to just think.' So he comes up with the suggestion that we ought to bury them or something. And in my state of mind this was a logical thing to do."

"Now what is it with this cutting up? How did that happen?" Zimmerman asked. "And Tony, don't change facts. Let a fact be a fact. Who did the cutting up?"

"We both did," Costa said. "We took them out, we dragged them off. We undressed them. We put the clothes all in one pile; Cory scooped them all up and took them away up to an embankment. I started digging my thing and Cory came back so quick from digging his hole I didn't think he had done anything. He was in a pretty psyched-up mood. I asked him how far ahead he was, and he said he had his thing dug and he was just going to stick the things into it and cover it over. And the thing that keeps bugging me is the time limit he had to dig that hole. It was impossible to dig a hole that fast, unless it was open or something; unless it was super-shallow. It was hard digging until you got down to the real soft sand."

"Who did you cut up?"

"I took care of Mary Anne. Cory was up in the bushes handling Pat. The purpose, like I said before, was just for fitting them into the holes. Cory began the thing; he went right across the waist. Then I, sort of, did the rest of it—this is when he took the clothing and stuff and went up the hill."

"The cutting up was exactly as you told me before?"

"Right."

"Did he help you in any of the cutting up?"

"Yeah, he did. He started out—and this is again what I said earlier, the influential thing. It was my idea to go and leave them, to put them in some bushes and stop to think a while as to what I was doing. Then it was his idea to stick them into holes and to go through with what we did. And the thing that baffled me most was the strength that Cory came up with. It was incredible! Like I was trudging along, and to him it was no sweat."

"OK, we've got these two out of the way," Zimmerman said. "Now, how about Susan and Sydney?"

"Susan and Sydney I don't know anything about except what Cory told me. All I know is that it had something to do with Eddie Silva and Roland Salvador. In fact, they had something to do with getting rid of Pat and Mary Anne's possessions; but what they did I don't really know, because he didn't tell me anything about it."

Sensing that Costa was backing away from revealing anything more, Zimmerman contented himself with the significant progress achieved during his interrogation. Costa had gone further than ever before by admitting, for the first time, that he had been present at the murders of Pat Walsh and Mary Anne Wysocki.

Zimmerman wrapped up the interview. "Tony, when I come back next week, I want to run a test on you. Because right now I could not run a test that would do justice to you, Tony, because there's involvement here. Let me ask you one thing: why did you hold back as long as you did?"

"I don't know," Costa said. "That's a hard question."

"Tony, I want you to look at me," Zimmerman said. "I want you to level with me all the way. *Why* did you hold back?"

"Because I'm *involved,*" Costa said. "I know I'm innocent for one thing, to begin with, and—"

"Tony, you are *not* innocent. You are involved in this crime. The extent of your involvement is the point! Each time we've talked, I was on the same wavelength with you; then somewhere along the line there was a relay switch. And that switch was thrown and *boom* we were off into another area. I want to make sure we are not off into that area again."

Costa agreed to give this some thought during the coming week. "You know, Charlie, all these guys in here are telling me how to beat the polygraph, but they never met you," Costa said. "I told them, the lie detector isn't the machine, it's the guy behind the machine. I tried it with yoga breathing and you always catch on. You always say, 'Tony, stop moving, breathe normally.' " Costa grinned. "How the hell can you control your own blood pressure?"

As Zimmerman was leaving, Costa showed him a hand-lettered birthday card for his mother he had made of construction paper. "Her birthday's tomorrow," Costa said. "She'll be sixty-one."

On July 1, George Killen received notice that Justin Cavanaugh was coming to the district attorney's office to talk about the Costa case.

Cavanaugh told Killen that because of the responsibility upon them as officers of the court, he and Goldman felt police should have Costa's latest and changed version of the killings of Pat and Mary Anne. For the second time Killen took out his spiral notebook and scrawled a precis of what Cavanaugh told him Costa had said, amending the version of the murders he had given to Charlie Zimmerman on June 28. Costa had changed the time of the killings to Saturday afternoon, claiming that after Cory shot Pat and Mary Anne, they had fled the area, leaving the bodies in the woods. They had returned that night to dismember and bury the bodies when they were stiff and easier to cut, and there would be less blood.

In return, Cavanaugh wanted to know if police had been able to develop any information about drug use in the backgrounds of Pat Walsh or Mary Anne Wysocki.

"There's nothing in the history of either girl, regarding drugs," Killen said.

"We haven't found anything either," Cavanaugh said. He was concerned about a motive for the murders. "There doesn't seem to have been any reason for the crimes."

Costa had put himself into the case as an "accessory after,"

Killen said, by his first statement reported by Lester Allen in June. "In this second statement, Costa puts himself in as an 'accessory.' That's quite a difference."

It was the second time Costa had fingered Cory Devereau as the murderer, Killen told Bernie Flynn. Flynn gave no credence to the story. Devereau was a petty thief, a drug user, a layabout and a con artist, but no killer. Tom Gunnery agreed: "Tony Costa was just trying to implicate others in his crimes; his story is nothing but a snow job on the part of the defense to try to throw police off the track."

Devereau was shocked and angry to be told that Tony Costa had put him in the picture as the killer of four girls. Devereau denied being in the woods with Costa on Saturday, or even knowing the Providence girls were in town. He had not seen Costa at all that weekend. "We weren't as friendly as we have been in the past," Devereau said. "I was spending more time with my girlfriend those days."

But when Flynn suggested that Devereau take a lie detector test to clear himself, Devereau was evasive. "I'll have to let you guys know on that," he said.

11

Immaculately groomed, wearing a white shirt, a blue necktie and dark slacks, Tony Costa was brought into Barnstable County superior court on July 9.

Prepared to argue nineteen defense motions, Maurice Goldman began to speak. "This case has sustained probably the worst barrage of publicity ever known to Cape Cod—a willful, deliberate and malicious news campaign waged by the media and promoted by the police and prosecuting officials." Goldman mentioned the order to stop pretrial announcements—the first of its kind ever known to have been directed from a district court—which had preceded Judge Paquet's order at the arraignment regarding prejudicial publicity.

Goldman wanted all his motions heard in chambers or in a cleared courtroom, and their determination kept secret except to those specifically authorized to have knowledge. Goldman feared, otherwise, a renewal of publicity about the Costa case.

Appearing for the prosecution was Assistant District Attorney Ernest I. Rotenberg. A good-looking man with a quick and dazzling smile, Rotenberg was an aggressive prosecutor with ambitions for a political career.

The district attorney's office had made no statements since Paquet's order, Rotenberg said. "It has always been my understanding that a trial is a public hearing, unless it offends the morals of the public."

Low-key and deliberate, Judge Robert Beaudreau observed dryly, "This is *not* a trial," reminding Rotenberg that they were arguing motions.

"Well, if I were in a newspaper office and such a motion was made, that in itself would attract publicity," Rotenberg said. Rotenberg had no objection if Beaudreau wanted to hear arguments in chambers. "The fact is, we feel strongly that this is nothing that should be kept from the public eye."

Judge Beaudreau had no desire to dictate what newspapers should print. The argument of the motions would require some disclosure from both sides. "I think it would be in keeping with the guarantees of a fair trial to have these matters aired in camera. But immediately upon my acting on the motions and handing them to the clerk for docketing, they are going to be made public."

Beaudreau asked that those not directly concerned with the Costa case leave the courtroom, which was crowded with spectators eager for a look at the most publicized killer since the Boston Strangler. Left at the prosecutors' desk with Rotenberg was Assistant District Attorney James Smith, George Killen and Bernie Flynn. Beaudreau asked those seated at the defense table to identify themselves. Goldman introduced Cavanaugh, Lester Allen, and Herb Abrams, who was considering entering the case,

Goldman said. "There are certain elements of the case we would like to have him handle for us that have not yet been ironed out."

"Are you court-appointed or not?" Beaudreau said.

"No, I am not, Your Honor," Goldman said. "I have been requested by the defendant to act for him." Goldman asked for a formal appointment. "I'm not asking for any payment from the court."

"You're *not?*" Beaudreau said.

There was an affidavit on file setting forth the state of Costa's finances. "If my brother will read it." Goldman nodded toward the prosecutor's table. Costa's worldly assets consisted of less than three dollars out of seven dollars in borrowed money. "His mother is on welfare in the town of Provincetown; his ex-wife is likewise, and his children are on town welfare. He doesn't possess a single, solitary dollar. He is completely indigent in every sense of the word. He needs help from this court financially." Goldman was seeking funds to continue to engage an investigator. "We can get services, but we haven't got funds to carry on this thing. This is the only money I'm asking for. I am asking nothing for myself."

"I am not convinced there is a substantial showing of evidence that this person is indigent or doesn't have funds for his own investigators. He has private counsel not appointed by the court," Rotenberg said. "It is our understanding that in the last two weeks there are book and movie rights already obtained and other means of funds available. Three counsel have been engaged to represent Mr. Costa at no pay. If counsel is going to get paid later on through some fund, there ought to be some way of reimbursing the county."

Goldman was willing to repay any funds furnished by Barnstable County for the preparation of defense and trial of Tony Costa from monies received from any source.

Goldman wanted copies of all oral statements made to police by the defendant "subsequently reduced to writing."

Beaudreau granted the motion.

Goldman wanted to be furnished with copies of the autopsy and pathological reports. Rotenberg did not have them at the moment, but would be happy to make them available.

"They're being prepared," Killen said.

"The defendant has been under considerable strain and stress through constant interviews," Goldman said. "He has shown many instances of aberration and confusion consistent, in my opinion, with a mental condition." Costa had undergone psychiatric examination at Bridgewater. "I think we are entitled to have a similar examination at the county's expense."

"Is there going to be a plea of insanity here?" Beaudreau asked.

Goldman was wary not to tip his hand. "I don't know what I'm going to do at this stage, Your Honor."

"Unless I know more about the reasons why you want a psychiatric examination," Beaudreau said, "I am going to deny the motion."

Goldman wouldn't tell him. Beaudreau denied the psychiatric examination, as well as Goldman's motion to engage a geneticist to determine whether a classification made by blood testing showed Costa was of a type who commit the alleged crimes by virtue of the so-called "double male" chromosome.

"I think the time has come when the court should order the statements made by all witnesses in the hands of the prosecution be furnished the defendant," Goldman said. "Several courts in the country already allow the practice."

Beaudreau was astonished. "I was not aware that we had reached the stage in Massachusetts where such motions are allowed."

"I think it's time Massachusetts moved forward with the rest of the country," Goldman said.

"I will give you an opportunity to have that determined," Beaudreau said, denying the motion nevertheless. "Do you want an exception?"

"I certainly *do!*" Goldman said jovially.

Next the defense moved for a Discovery and Inspection of Items and Evidence in possession of the commonwealth.

Beaudreau said, "When you tell me such evidence or items, I want you to specify what you want."

"Whatever they've got in their hands," Goldman said.

"You're not going to get anything as broad as that," Beaudreau snapped.

Goldman said he wanted to be furnished with "exculpatory" evidence.

"Tell me what *that* means," Beaudreau said. "What are you looking for?"

"Very plainly it means if there is evidence at all favorable to the defendant, I want it. And I am entitled to it." Goldman cited

Brady v. Maryland: "The suppression by the prosecution of evidence favorable to an accused, upon request, violates due process where the evidence is material either to guilt or punishment, irrespective of good faith or bad faith of the prosecution."

Beaudreau wanted Goldman to say exactly what it was he wanted. "But no broad statement where I don't know if it's exculpatory or not."

"I don't *know* what they have at the moment," Goldman said. "But I am entitled, if Your Honor will give me the statement of their witnesses."

"I have denied that," Beaudreau said.

Rotenberg was on his feet again. He was not going to give Goldman a list of witnesses unless Beaudreau ordered it.

"I am not going to have you disclose all your witnesses," Beaudreau assured the prosecution. "But I think it is only fair at the time of trial to have any record of prior criminal convictions available, so he can impeach witnesses."

"What good is that going to do me as a practical matter?" Goldman said. "If I don't have this a week or two in advance, I can't move."

Beaudreau denied the motion on exculpatory evidence, inasmuch as Goldman had not particularized.

Goldman wanted to be furnished with reports dealing with bullets, handwriting experts and fingerprints.

"Are there ballistics reports?" Beaudreau asked. When Killen said there were, Beaudreau denied ballistics.

"Why can't I have the ballistics report?" Goldman said.

"I am not going to give it to you," Beaudreau said. "Take an exception."

"I will have to do just that, Judge," Goldman said. "I understand there is also a fingerprint report."

Beaudreau denied the fingerprints, too.

"There is a claim that a revolver is involved in this case and the possibility of a knife," Goldman said. "I want to have those examined; and inspect the Volkswagen."

The automobile was no longer in possession of the police, having been returned to Pat Walsh's family, but Rotenberg had no objection to an examination of the gun and knife.

"On the area in Truro, the alleged scene of the alleged crime," Goldman said. "I don't know where it took place."

"Mr. Cavanaugh went to the actual scene with police officers," Rotenberg said.

"I went to an alleged grave," Cavanaugh said. "But I don't know if these decedents were killed in this particular place or somewhere else. We want to know exactly where the crimes took place."

"The best description of the place of the crime is in the indictment," Rotenberg said.

"That doesn't help us in the slightest, Your Honor," Goldman said.

"Well, that's going to be my ruling."

"There is an alleged rope, which was allegedly obtained under a search-and-seizure warrant, that's the tie-in," Goldman said. "This is all by newspaper reports."

"Well, the newspapers *were* helpful to you, then," Beaudreau said, smiling.

"They weren't very helpful to me except to help destroy!" Goldman said tartly. "There were reports that ropes were found on the premises allegedly obtained under a search warrant and tests conducted."

"You will hear that in court," Rotenberg said. "We don't want to disclose it if we don't have to."

Beaudreau denied Goldman's motion.

Goldman wanted the telegram received by Cecelia Bonaviri. "We don't know who sent it."

"Mrs. Bonaviri knows the sender," Rotenberg said. "We will be happy to supply the defense with a copy of the telegram."

Goldman wanted to know the means employed to establish the identification of the corpses.

Beaudreau denied the motion. "If they don't establish that at the trial, they won't get very far."

Goldman wanted a list of objects found in the grave "other than segments of Susan Perry's body."

Rotenberg protested. "That is a matter of evidence that will be presented at the trial!"

Beaudreau denied it.

Goldman's next motion dropped like a bomb on the proceedings. "Did the prosecution allege involvement of individuals other than the defendant to the alleged murders?"

Astonished, Beaudreau said, "Nobody else has been indicted."

"I know that," Goldman said sharply. "But we have furnished information to the police that there *is* someone else involved in this case. We would like to get an answer from them."

Goldman's announcement had an immediate effect at the prosecution table. Rotenberg was in an urgent huddle with Flynn and Killen.

"I want the record to note that I now assert that there *is* someone else involved in these murders," Goldman said. "And I am calling it to the attention of the court and the prosecution staff."

Rotenberg was white with fury after his consultation. "Is it someone else other than Costa—and *with* Costa, the defendant in this case?"

"We don't know that," Goldman said. "We know that someone else is involved in these murders."

"Are you prepared to make a statement before a grand jury that we will specifically convene?" Rotenberg's voice rang angrily through the empty courtroom.

"I am prepared to make a statement that I have already made," Goldman shot back. "Whatever statements I make here, you act upon accordingly!"

"I *can't* act accordingly," Rotenberg said, furious, "unless a further description is given by counsel."

Beaudreau denied the motion.

Goldman got the number of handbags found and an inventory of their contents, but not the identification of women's undergarments found in the graves. "They won't tell us about the wedding ring," Goldman complained. "I think we are entitled to get that. That ring couldn't belong to that girl. It belonged to somebody else entirely."

Beaudreau allowed only the wedding ring taken from the hand of Susan Perry.

"I don't know why I should not be allowed to know what was in the grave, Your Honor," Goldman protested.

"This is still an adversary system," Beaudreau said. "I haven't heard differently from the Supreme Court."

Goldman said he was not finding fault with Beaudreau at all, and expressed his utmost faith in the fairness of the court. "But does the prosecution have the *prima facie* right to have all this information? There is a duty upon the district attorney, too. I think the defendant was deprived of his rights by the police and prosecutors refusing to reveal material evidence to counsel for the defendant, and by restrictions placed on witnesses before they discussed with defense investigators important and relevant information necessary to the defendant's case."

"Are you saying you were prevented from interviewing witnesses?" Beaudreau said.

"I went to Chief Marshall. He said, 'My name is Chief Marshall. I live in Provincetown. Do you want my serial number? Because that's all you are going to get off me in the Costa case.' He said he was so instructed by the district attorney—"

"And by the superior court!" Rotenberg interjected.

"I hadn't finished when you interrupted me," Goldman said sweetly, "so you owe me an apology this time. In that instance, there is a violation. The only one who has given us any help at all in this case is Lieutenant Killen. At least he'll talk to us. The rest of them say they won't. There is no reason why the district attorney should not turn everything over to me. He represents Costa as well as myself; he is a public servant. There shouldn't be this adversary proceeding. This is a crime involving at least four murders. A man's life is at stake here."

Goldman wanted the fingerprint evidence that had been used to identify the bodies of Pat Walsh and Mary Anne Wysocki.

"I don't know why you can't give them that," Beaudreau said. "Do you have any reports on that?"

"We don't have, Your Honor," Rotenberg said.

"There are no fingerprint tests? Is *that* what they say?" Goldman said. "Was there any fingerprinting done with respect to the VW, or reports pertaining to blood in the car?"

Rotenberg was willing to make the blood tests done on the car available.

"I repeat, was there any fingerprinting done with respect to the Volkswagen?" Goldman pressed.

"We are willing to make the blood tests available, Your Honor," Rotenberg said.

"Any fingerprints found on the VW?" Goldman said. *"Three times* I am repeating myself on fingerprints—"

"You can repeat it a *hundred* times, as far as I am concerned," Rotenberg said.

"I pray Your Honor's judgment," Goldman said.

Rotenberg had no objection to inspection of the razor blade found at the scene of the graves. Goldman wanted any report on the book *Demian* by Hermann Hesse, allegedly seized as evidence by police. "Have they got the book or any written reports on that?"

"We do not have it now," Rotenberg said. "That doesn't mean we might not look for it."

"What kind of an answer is that supposed to be?" Cavanaugh put in.

"He doesn't have it now," Beaudreau said. "This is Discovery here and Mr. Goldman is on a rightful—I don't want to use this in a derogatory manner—fishing expedition. He made that remark and he got an answer for it."

"I am *not* on a fishing expedition!"

"Let's cross out those words," Beaudreau told the court stenographer.

Goldman wanted whatever articles had been voluntarily surrendered to police by Costa, his mother, brother or any part in connection with the case where a search warrant was not used, such as clothing and a duffel bag in Vermont.

"At this time, or available to us now?" Rotenberg said. "That doesn't mean our investigation is complete, Your Honor."

"One minute you want to go to trial tomorrow morning," Goldman snapped. "The next minute the investigation isn't complete!"

"No speeches, please!" Beaudreau said. "I have enough problems. Go ahead."

Goldman made a motion to dismiss the indictments on the grounds the indictments stated conclusions rather than facts. Further, he said, the grand jury lacked jurisdiction, because the offenses charged had occurred within the boundaries of a federally controlled national seashore park. A jurisdictional question also arose insofar as Susan Perry was concerned; whether she was killed in Suffolk County and buried in Barnstable County.

Finally, Goldman had a motion for severance. "There is no connection between the four murders which occurred on three different dates, with the exception of Walsh and Wysocki."

Beaudreau refused to rule on severance. "This is the kind of motion that should be taken up with the trial judge." He would, however, entertain Goldman's motion for a change of venue. "That should be determined now, not two days before the trial."

Goldman wanted Herb Abrams to argue the motion, since Abrams had prepared the brief.

Suave and confident, Abrams submitted a volume of news clippings and copies of *Inside Detective* and *Startling Detective,* pointing out the "devastating headlines," and reading out selected portions of the articles to make the court aware of "the virulent, incriminating publicity which has made the Costa case notorious."

"In this atmosphere of a Roman holiday for the news media," Abrams said, "Antone Costa stands trial for his life. Is he not entitled to a change of venue? Is not the buildup of prejudice clear and convincing? I ask this court, could there be a more shocking and repellent crime than that which the defendant stands accused?"

Defense investigators reported that the entire Southern District was eagerly awaiting what had been referred to as "The Trial of the Century." Abrams requested the trial of Antone Costa take place in the westernmost part of Massachusetts.

Rotenberg had no objection. His office had already expressed the view that a change of venue in the Costa case was warranted. As for publicity, Rotenberg couldn't resist pulling Goldman's tail. A representative of *Life* magazine and two Boston reporters had accosted him in the courthouse corridor. Rotenberg said, "They indicated that counsel for the defense had called their office to tell them the case would be heard today."

Goldman sent Herb Abrams a scathing look of accusation.

After the court session, Cavanaugh explained to Costa, "Herb Abrams has joined the defense in case we have to go into medical or mental testimony."

"Mental would be pertaining to what?" Costa asked suspiciously. "My doings at the scene?"

"That's right. We have asked him not to discuss any aspects of that with you. We will provide him with the necessary information."

Costa was delighted that Goldman had accused "someone else" of the murders during the proceedings, gleefully observing, "The prosecutor really got uptight!"

"They're going to have to do something about that," Cavanaugh said.

"Well, they *should!*" Costa said. "They're just letting the thing ride and it's getting nowhere."

Two days later, Costa was in good spirits. He smiled and fixed his hair for the television cameras that were waiting in the courthouse parking lot for his appearance. He had to wait an hour and a half for the arrival of Maurice Goldman.

In the judge's shabby two-room lobby, Costa signed an agreement providing that in the event he should receive money from any source, he would reimburse Barnstable County for expenses that were being furnished for his defense.

Beaudreau wanted to reconsider Goldman's motion for severance. Cavanaugh asked that the matter rest with the trial judge, as Beaudreau had suggested earlier, and did not wish to argue the matter further.

"Well, I am going to act on it!" Beaudreau said. He asked Costa if he consented to his attorney's position.

"Yes, your honor," Costa said. "I trust my counsel in whatever they do."

Beaudreau denied severance. He set the trial of Tony Costa to be heard at Greenfield, in western Massachusetts, starting November 3. Costa would remain in custody at Barnstable so he would continue to be available for consultation in the preparation of his defense until directed by the court to be delivered to the sheriff of Franklin County—the westernmost portion of the state.

Goldman wanted his motion with respect to the appointment of a psychiatrist reconsidered. "Any man charged with dismembering four female bodies, even at first blush cannot be presumed to be of normal tendencies." Goldman had brought Dr. Williams's report to the conference for Beaudreau to read.

Beaudreau appointed Williams and authorized one hundred fifty dollars for the expense of his June 22 interview and report on Costa. "I will authorize two more examinations," he said, "in the event Dr. Williams feels they are required."

"May that read, 'Dr. Williams or some other psychiatrist'?" Goldman asked. "The reason I say that is the defense may properly have the benefit of both views."

Goldman was furious to read in the *Boston Herald Traveler* that Herb Abrams, acting as spokesman for defense counsel in the Costa case, had described the change in venue as "a landmark decision."

Abrams had directed Goldman's attention to the Supreme

Judicial Court's decision of April 9 on *Commonwealth v. John Von Utter, Jr.* Abrams pointed out the unidentified police informer mentioned in the case, as "our boy."

Skeptical about Costa's motive for turning drug informer, Goldman was gratified to read that the details of the case confirmed what Costa had told him. Von Utter's appeal did not dispute the fact that drugs had been found in his car, but rather that Provincetown police, in seeking a search warrant, had relied on information supplied by an informer of questionable reliability.

Upholding conviction, the Supreme Judicial Court ruled that the mere establishment of probable cause for the issuance of a search warrant did not require the kind of evidence necessary to justify criminal conviction.

On July 11, Von Utter was brought to Barnstable House of Correction to serve a one-year sentence for possession of harmful drugs. Concerned to have Von Utter in the same jail as the man who had helped to put him there, Goldman spoke to Sheriff Tulloch about keeping the prisoners separated. Goldman wanted no injury done to his client.

Costa seemed more concerned for Avis, telling Cavanaugh, "She didn't come to see me this week. She sent me a letter; nothing fantastic, just to say hello, and that she's situated in her new house. She's worried, though. She's been straight a long time, but she's been having flashbacks. She isn't the first person this has happened to; that's why I don't like anything but pot. I've seen so many people go down the drain with drugs it's ridiculous! I'm just hoping she stays together, because if she trips out now, it's going to be bad news. She asked me about a shrink. I'm going to tell her if she can wait three weeks maybe we can see Dr. Williams together. It would put my mind to rest and ease her up some. Those drugs really screwed her up. It's really a shame, but that's where it's at."

12

Charles Zimmerman was unable to run a successful test on Tony Costa when he returned to the Barnstable House of Correction on July 12. Costa was again sullen, distracted, not feeling well. Zimmerman had come to recognize all the symptoms: Costa had something he wanted to say, another change in his story.

"I have to tell you. I used the knife on Mary Anne." Costa spoke in a hushed, childish voice, sitting with his head bowed. Tears ran silently down his face.

Zimmerman glanced away. Costa didn't like anyone looking at him when he made any serious admissions about the murders.

"She was unconscious totally except for the gurgling sounds that I heard; I took this to mean she was still alive," Costa said, softly. "I knew we couldn't get her out of there; we couldn't do anything for her, just by the loss of blood itself. It was all over her clothing. She was in a puddle of it. I asked Cory if he had his knife with him and he did; he usually carried it with him. I took it and stabbed her in the breast area, just below the bone." Costa demonstrated the place on his own chest. "A couple of seconds later the noises stopped . . ."

"What was going on in your mind when you stabbed Mary Anne?" Zimmerman said.

"I did a lot of thinking before I actually did anything," Costa said. "I looked her over and tried to talk to her, but there was no reaction. After I had done this, I put the knife down on the ground and I said a prayer for what I had done. While I was going through this, Cory grabbed the knife. He went into this complete frenzy, stabbing her two or three more times."

"Cory did not say any prayers?" Zimmerman said, tongue-in-cheek.

"No, he was completely wasted," Costa said coldly. Talking about Cory Devereau had restored his composure. "He was in a state of just concerning himself with his dope; that's all he spoke about. He was going insane."

Costa had something else he wanted to tell Zimmerman:

"The night before, I had been to bed with Pat. It was a scene that I had mentioned, but I didn't detail it."

"I don't remember you saying this before," Zimmerman said.

"No, I didn't. This is what I'm getting at; I want everything on the table. Mary Anne was expecting this guy. She asked if her boyfriend came in could Pat stay with me in my room. I said, 'Sure.' A guy did come in and stay with Mary Anne on Saturday night and Pat came down to my room. I was lying in my bed at the time and she said, 'Mary Anne's friend is here and I'd like to stay.' I said 'OK.' Then she shut the lights off. She undressed down to her panties and she climbed into my bed. There was another bed beside it, so I expected she'd sleep there; but she crawled into the bed I was in. And it turned out to be a groovy night."

"How many times did you have intercourse with her?" Zimmerman said.

"Just once, that was it. In the morning she got up and went upstairs. I didn't even know, like I was still sleeping when she got up."

"So if the autopsy report finds semen, it's yours?" Zimmerman said.

"Yeah, if it would last that long," Costa said. He and Pat had talked in bed about *Demian* by Hermann Hesse. "Pat wasn't really my type. She was a nice chick, but not somebody that I could become attached to."

Leaving the Barnstable House of Correction, Zimmerman observed considerable activity in the courthouse, unusual for a hot Saturday in July on Cape Cod. Zimmerman caught a glimpse of George Killen getting out of his car, looking rushed. During the past eighteen months, Killen had dealt with a record fifteen murders on Cape Cod. "Every time I picked up the telephone, somebody was telling me, 'We've got a body.'"

That morning, chief of police Dominic Arena of Edgartown, Martha's Vineyard, had reported to Killen that a young woman's body had been recovered from an automobile submerged in Poucha Pond on the island of Chappaquiddick. The automobile was registered to Senator Ted Kennedy.

Killen talked to Dr. Donald R. Mills, an associate county medical examiner. "Are you satisfied as to the cause of death?"

Mills had examined the body for ten minutes and certified

that Mary Jo Kopechne had died by drowning. He didn't think there was any need for an autopsy.

Killen released the body.

13

Kurt Vonnegut, Jr., the writer, lived a mile from Barnstable courthouse. His tall, loping figure was a familiar and popular sight in the streets of Barnstable village. Both Vonnegut and his wife, Jane, were active members of the Barnstable Comedy Club, a community theater. Lately, Vonnegut's house on the corner of Route 6A and Scudder Lane had been overrun by groups of hippie youths come to pay homage to a writer with a huge following on college campuses. Lately celebrated for his best-selling novel *Slaughterhouse-Five*, Vonnegut had accepted a commission from *Life* magazine to probe "the tale of four horrible murders on Cape Cod" in an article entitled, "There's a Maniac Loose Out There."

Vonnegut was miscast as a crime reporter, his laid-back, throwaway style ill-suited to the horrors he recounted, seeming to minimize the events rather than illuminate them. Vonnegut pointed out that he did not have access to much official information. He said of the killings: "Since the victims were cut into so many random chunks, only the murderer could make an intelligent guess as to what the actual causes of death might have been."

Vonnegut was interested in the coincidence of his daughter Edith's having met Tony Costa during a summer she spent in Provincetown studying painting. She had received and declined Costa's invitation to "come out and see my marijuana." During that summer she had mentioned a young man who had repeatedly said he wanted to kill her. When Costa was arrested for murder, Vonnegut had called his daughter in Iowa City to ask her if Costa was the person who had threatened her.

"Tony wouldn't say anything like that," Edith told her father. "If Tony is a murderer, then anybody can be a murderer."

Vonnegut portrayed Tony Costa as "a gentle, quiet, twenty-four-year-old six-foot Provincetown carpenter," a spoiled little boy who, at the age of thirteen, had kept the books for his stepfather's masonry business, adding, "How straight can you be?"

A photograph of Patricia Morton posed in front of 5 Standish Street illustrated Vonnegut's article, along with a gallery of the murder victims and a grainy photograph of an empty grave. Mrs. Morton had told Vonnegut that Costa had helped Pat Walsh and Mary Anne Wysocki with their luggage when the girls registered at her rooming house. "Who says chivalry is dead?" Vonnegut wrote.

Vonnegut learned from Lester Allen that Costa suffered from an ulcer and took three showers a day. Allen was one of two Cape Codders Vonnegut knew who was writing a book about the case; Allen had accumulated more than a thousand pages of transcribed conversation with Costa and his friends, many of whom had some experience with the drug culture in Provincetown.

Evelyn Lawson, the columnist, a witchcraft buff of Vonnegut's acquaintance, was also engaged in writing a book about Tony Costa. She had reported in her column that when Costa was brought outdoors following his arraignment in Provincetown, a long-haired youth rushed to kneel at Costa's feet, kissed his manacled hands, and proclaimed, "Tony, we love you." Vonnegut doubted the incident had occurred, he reported, before suggesting: "Is it possible that Tony was framed?" Costa had done "one of the most suicidal things a young drug dabbler can do" by informing to police on a dope dealer. Nevertheless, Vonnegut wondered, "Who would chop up and bury four nice girls to frame one small canary?"

Vonnegut repeated an admittedly sick joke then circulating on Cape Cod:

Tony Costa walked into a Hyannis Cadillac agency to price an Eldorado.

"It'll cost you an arm and a leg," the salesman said.

"It's a deal!" Costa said.

Vonnegut suggested that young women in America would "continue to look for love and excitement in places that are dangerous as hell." He concluded, "I salute them for their optimism and their nerve."

405

Tony Costa was thrilled that a writer of Vonnegut's prominence had taken an interest in his case. Costa embellished the Cadillac joke with details of his own.

"I went in there with my hippie clothes and looked at an Eldorado and said, 'Oh, what a beautiful car; this is the one I want.' And the salesman said, 'Son, you can't afford it; it'll cost you an arm and a leg.' And I said, 'If you have a shovel handy, I'll be back in ten minutes.'"

"Well, it's a good thing you have a sense of humor, Tony," Charles Zimmerman said. "Otherwise you could go crazy."

Zimmerman didn't mention that on the wall of the laundromat on Shank Painter Road Costa favored for washing his clothes, someone had carefully printed: "Tony Costa Digs Girls."

In his next interview with Charlie Zimmerman, Costa's stories continued to shift and evolve. Susan Perry had died of an overdose of heroin at Cory Devereau's house, Costa said. "Cory simply explained he was turning her onto scag, that he enticed her. And, according to what he said, Susan passed out. She died."

"Why did he cut her up?"

"This I don't know. I have no idea."

"Tony, you *have* an idea!" Zimmerman said, looking at the polygraph tracings. "I have reactions there! If it isn't actual involvement, it has to be a knowledge factor!"

"I can only tell you what he says!" Costa shot back, angrily. "It was just a thing where he considered her dead and wanted to get rid of her. He then proceeded down to the bathroom and did his dirty work there. From what Cory said, his mother would evidently be coming home soon, and he didn't want her to find out what had gone on. He had gone and cut Susan up and was trying to bury her in the back yard or something. But then his mother *did* show up. The body wasn't there, but the bathroom itself was a mess. He didn't have time to clean up anything. He said there was blood all over the place."

"You mean he told his *mother?*" Zimmerman wondered if the scene being described could have actually taken place between Costa and his own mother.

"There was no way he could avoid it," Costa said. "His mother evidently discovered the whole thing and he had no alternative but to explain. And he simply stated that an argument ensued; they were both really uptight. And he went out and con-jured up a ride."

"What did Cory say he did with the body he cut up in the bathroom?"

"He moved it; he took it out of the house."

"How did he carry the parts of the body out of the house? A suitcase, a laundry bag or what?"

"I don't know how he got it out. Cory's mother had a car there. It was either that or David Salvador's station wagon."

"Did he tell you what he did with the body?"

"He took it out to the area in Truro. He knew I had stuff out there; he and I shared this thing—among others people. And this was a way to serve two points: to get rid of Susan and get more stuff out of the can. After he told me this I told him, 'You're not goofing me. You're not pulling my arm. You're just a bunch of horseshit.' I told him if anybody heard him they'd think he was insane. He said he was telling the truth and he could prove it; he would show me."

"He took you out to the scene and dug up the body?" Zim-merman said, incredulously.

"Yeah. An arrangement was made to go out there. The day we went Robin Nicholson, Patty Avila and Larry Andresen were there. What we did was, we said we were going to look for some pills and things I had buried at the side of the road. So I said, 'Everybody look to see if we can find the stuff, because I forgot where I put it.' It was an occasion for me and Cory to sneak off."

"What did you do when you got to the scene?"

"When we got there Cory said, 'This is where it is.' There was an indentation in the ground. I kicked the dirt over a little bit with my foot. I saw what looked like a dirty old bed sheet, or something. And I sort of moved it over with a stick because I didn't know what the hell was there. And I saw it."

"What did you see?"

"I saw a hand. And I saw what appeared to be parts of a body; they were all dirty and messy. And I just looked at him. I was shaking. I couldn't say a word."

During Costa's recitation, Zimmerman had observed a curi-ous change take place. Generally, Costa was subdued, on uncer-tain ground when talking about his involvement in the murders, obviously groping for a memory of the events and very unsure of himself. But whenever Costa talked about Cory, the slow, lofty talk, the monotone voice was replaced by an assured and positive manner, a voice of authority that was definite, positive, factual and emphatic. Even Costa's posture changed: he squared his shoulders and maintained a more direct eye contact. He appeared more manly and straightforward. When Costa talked about Cory, it seemed to Zimmerman, he *became* Cory. Costa avoided using Cory's name, talking about events without putting a label on them. Zimmerman had to ask him often who "he" was. Then Costa would say, "Cory."

Fascinated, Zimmerman said, "How old is Cory?"

"He's only about seventeen or eighteen; he's just a kid," Costa said. "He's a strange guy; he's sleazy. He's gangster number one as far as I'm concerned. He's got a head on him that would put Al Capone to shame."

"Now, Tony, I'm going to insist that you give consideration to Sydney Monzon."

"Cory didn't say too much about Sydney. He didn't exactly say he killed her; he said she died, that's the way he phrased it. He said it had something to do with poisoned drugs. She was using speed, I know. And she used acid quite a bit," Costa said. "I had nothing to do with Sydney whatsoever; nothing at all."

"In other words, the reaction I had on the polygraph was in reference to Susan Perry?"

"It must have been. I didn't even know Sydney to begin with, really."

"Avis told Mr. Goldman that Sydney drove you to Dr. Callis's office the night you broke in there."

"That's completely untrue," Costa said, indignantly. "After the Callis job we had a thing going. I sold some speed to her, both in capsule and liquid form, and that's about all that developed out of it. We had nothing else to do with each other."

"What did Cory say he did with Sydney's body? You must have asked him."

"The thing you don't understand is, Cory only tells you so much. He said it was a drug thing, but he didn't give me any details concerning Sydney."

"I cannot understand why you were holding back this story about Susan Perry that you could have told me before."

Costa squirmed in his chair and looked away. "I don't know why. Like for me it's a hard thing. This is why I want to talk to Dr. Williams again. This whole thing has just got me bound up. I realize my life is at stake, but then again I'm going to have to get up on the stand and crucify this young kid. And this is one thing I don't want to do. What happens if he's locked up in an asylum for years? I'm going to be the guy who put him there. And even what he's done, the fact is these people are dead. There's nothing we can do now to bring them back or correct the situation. What happens to *him?* This is of concern to me; and the fact that I'm afraid for myself because I know these things."

"Tony, I knew from the time we started to talk that there was some extra force. This is why I told you, I think you have conceded; you have given up. You have more or less sold your soul to the devil."

"It isn't so much selling my soul to the devil," Costa said. "It's wanting to do the right thing. It's just the way I'm made. I've never been made to go through anything like this before."

Based on his various interviews with Costa, Charlie Zimmerman felt there was "a possibility of merit" to the claim of Cory Devereau's involvement in the murders, but he cautioned Goldman, "I have no reason to support this position other than the cohesive manner in which Costa talks about Cory, no second lost in thought, and so forth. This is nothing but a feeling, and is not supported by polygram verification."

Zimmerman had conducted a total of seven different polygraph examinations. "Each time I attempted to verify the truthfulness of Costa's statements about Devereau, I found I was unable to do so because the impact of the realization of his own involvement and the lies he had been telling were always stronger than the areas I was interested in clearing up." Three charts were devoted exclusively to this; all were negative.

After each test a new story or addition to previous statements had followed, Zimmerman said, "I find myself chasing the truth with uncertain boundaries." Costa had admitted killing Mary Anne Wysocki. "He tells me that he stabbed her below the breast, but I cannot evaluate that information because I don't know what the autopsy disclosed."

Goldman was still waiting for the autopsy reports; In order to evaluate Costa's accounts of events, Zimmerman desperately needed crime-scene information regarding the position of clothing found at the scene, the number of bullet entries, and the location of stab wounds.

Zimmerman added, "Tony said he feels guilty about Christine Gallant *and is actually the cause of her death.*"

Zimmerman had not pressed the matter; nor had he pursued Costa's inadvertent hints that he might have murdered Barbara Spaulding and the Diggers. Costa had said, tauntingly "One of these times I'll tell you about them, if you really want to hear a story."

14

Dr. Harold Williams spent one hour with Tony Costa when he returned to the Barnstable House of Correction on July 27. Later he joined Goldman for dinner and explained that in jail Costa still harbored the same anxieties that had led him to kill— his anxiety about the dissolution of self from which he had suffered "great psychic pain." He was harboring tremendous pent-up rage against women. The perversions had provided a release, allowing Costa to function as a person.

Costa's personality change, Williams explained, occurred during episodes of "ego-splitting," during which he became the vehicle for a personality not his own—the secret self he had come to identify as "Cory Devereau." What his conscious mind did not allow was then allowed, part of his mind giving way during the ego-splitting to act out the most abhorrent and hideous impulses, usually in a strict ritual form in which everything had to be "right," an altered state of consciousness his other mind did not participate in. "Cory" was the link between both minds, allowing the good Tony to become an innocent bystander, a victim of Cory's evil, thus bearing no responsibility himself for the crimes, having suffered a "brainout" on details.

The perversions became a glorious, singular act, a high, a means of dealing with his anxiety, a safety valve, a way of letting go of his pain and a defense against the intense feelings of infantile deprivation Costa felt when he had been abandoned in favor of his stepbrother.

By killing women and having sexual relations with them after death, Costa was acting out a terrible drama of incest and matricide in which he sought a reunion with his mother in the ideal state of bliss he had enjoyed as a child, seeking to fuse again with the "good woman"—cleansed, punished, purified . . . and always his. Hating what he loved because he could not get from her what he needed, Costa had dared not show his hatred for fear of losing what he already had.

The removal or mutilation of genitalia rendered Costa's victims sexless, pure and perfect in the same way little Antone as a child had lacked sexuality—a "state of grace" Costa remembered as a two-year-old when he had had his mother to himself, before her betrayal of his "heroic" father and himself by her remarriage and by giving birth to another child.

The murders had been foreplay, to release tremendous pent-up sexual energy, a necessary though ghastly experience for him. Sex became a prelude to the grand union with the ideal in death, during which Costa was joined with his victims before they were immortalized, merged forever in this heroic state, a state of Nirvana. The French called orgasm *le petit mort*—the small death; the moment of sexual release was a kind of death for Costa, a relinquishment of the "bad" part of himself that he buried with his victims. Once they had gone through the purification ritual of death, the girls became his forever; they could no longer betray him, cheat on him, belong to another.

Susan Perry and Sydney Monzon were perfect victims for such a ritual of vengeance, punishment and immolation. Homeless, drifting, searching for real connections, they, like Costa, had wished to fuse with something larger than themselves, something immortal—a childlike, romantic dream of fulfillment.

Costa had been out of control by the time Pat Walsh and Mary Anne Wysocki arrived at Mrs. Morton's, and the time lapses between his episodes of "ego-splitting" were beginning to accelerate. Both young women had borne a superficial physical resemblance to Avis. Costa revealed his contempt toward Pat Walsh as a "hippie chick," and toward Mary Anne for having worn makeup. Failing to measure up to Costa's extraordinary ide-

411

als of "goodness and decency," both girls became victims for his ritual.

Williams was sympathetic to Goldman's dilemma in defending the case. A definite psychotic diagnosis could not be properly made of Tony Costa. He was, rather, a psychopath—hedonistic, amoral, caring only to satisfy his immediate wishes and desires—the prolongation of infantile patterns and habits, his fixation of sexuality was stuck at an infantile level of development. Costa was essentially antisocial, conscienceless, with a total disregard for truth. Predatory and inclined to violence, Costa expressed emotion but had no tolerance for it. Psychopaths dealt with enormous quantities of guilt and were willing to take great risks, seeing everything in terms of extreme right and wrong. Such duality could be observed in Costa's "goodness" and manifested in his religiosity, his desire to be "clean and decent," to help "my fellow man," and in the "evil" he exhibited by acting out his rage at women in sadistic acts of murder and necrophilia under the guise of "Cory." (Costa had ascribed a knowledge of necrophilia to Cory in the story about the crypt in Old Truro cemetary, a projection of his own fantasies, as were the crimes he sought to blame on Cory such as the theft of doctors' bags and books.) Costa saw himself above the common herd, omnipotent, godlike. His friendship with Cory and Larry Andresen was a "trinity," three versions of one personality.

The penal code excluded a "psychopathic defense"; Costa's condition did not meet the legal definition of insanity. Nor could a case be made for "drug-induced psychosis." Williams could not in good medical conscience testify that drugs had prompted psychotic episodes. Costa was not physically addicted to drugs, as shown by his examination at Bridgewater as well as his own disclaimers.

Where Richard Quillen had provided specific descriptions of his drug use and their effects—such as seeing everything from the end of a long tunnel, descriptions so graphic that the jury had understood the impairment that had occurred to his mental faculties—Costa was not about to give a step-by-step recitation of having taken large quantities of drugs, his speeded-up reactions to them leading up to the murders, then a blow-by-blow account of the killings in his state of mind at the time of the murders. Costa was wary of self-incrimination of any kind, reluctant to admit any serious drug use except for the smoking of marijuana and hashish.

In his megalomania, Costa thought he could fool everyone into believing he was "normal."

In Williams's opinion there was little correlation between Costa's pathology, his use of drugs and the acts of murder, their only effect being to have released certain "controls" leading to outbursts of violence. Costa's drug use had grown from "recreational" enjoyment to "prescribing" for himself, with the aid of the stolen *Physician's Desk Reference*, to try to deal with his anxiety, to blunt and anesthetize the intense psychic pain he felt. But drugs were not the cause of the episodes.

Costa's use of Dexedrine when he drove the two young women to California had probably contributed to what was likely to have been his first murderous episode of ego-splitting. The two homeless young women, without money or resources, whom Costa had contemptuously referred to as "the Diggers," had probably been his first murder victims—somewhere en route to California. After Costa recovered from the ego-split, "reconstituted" his personality and discovered what had occurred, he had fled in panic, returning at once to Provincetown.

Other "triggers"—not drugs, he explained to Goldman—had prompted succeeding episodes. The warrant for his arrest on a charge of nonsupport was sufficient to provoke an explosion of anger leading to violence with the young woman Costa was living with in San Francisco, Barbara Spaulding. Sydney Monzon's death had occurred when Costa was being rejected and vilified by his friends for being a police informer and for the breakup of his marriage to Avis while she lived with a lover. Despite a tolerant and patronizing attitude on the surface, Costa had suffered great pain and anguish about his wife's infidelities. Susan Perry's death had closely followed Sandy Kropoff's abrupt breaking-off of her romance with Costa. To the psychopath, any rebuff or criticism was regarded as an insult and brought immediate aggressive and hostile feelings. It was almost impossible for Costa to be aggressive without being destructive.

Williams thought the death of Christine Gallant could have been a suicide pact that was aborted, either by design or by a loss of nerve on Costa's part. Clinging to a precarious sanity, desperate to hold his disintegrating self together and frantic to stave off the advent of a madness that was a perpetual threat by treating himself with drugs to control the rage inside him, tormented and desperate in his separateness and despair, Costa might seem a likely candidate for suicide. But psychopaths, because of their egotism and megalomania, almost never committed suicide. If it was true that Christine had expressed plans to marry Raul Matta and Costa's love for her was not reciprocated, he had probably exploded in a fury at this further demonstration of female treachery, preferring to kill her rather than lose her to Matta. For Costa, Christine had become the "bad woman" who had to be punished and purified.

The details of Christine Gallant's death bore indicators of Costa's peculiarities. Far away from his ritual "killing place" in Truro, and without implements for dismemberment, Costa had mutilated Christine symbolically, with three burns on her breast. Not satisfied with the overdose of Nembutals he had given her, he had placed her naked body in a bathtub to "drown"—the purification ritual this time accomplished by water, not by blood.

Goldman was stunned. He asked Dr. Williams how Tony Costa could have become so tortured and twisted.

Beginning when he was eight months old when his father drowned heroically in the South Pacific, the split in Costa's personality was possibly already under way by the time his mother remarried and gave birth to another son.

"You could almost say," Williams said, "that Tony Costa died with his father."

On Tuesday, July 29, George Killen accompanied Cory Devereau to state police headquarters in Boston. Because Devereau was underage, his mother signed a permission slip, allowing him to undergo polygraph testing. Devereau was voluntarily submitting to an examination on the Keeler polygraph instrument; he had agreed to the use of a tape recorder during the test. Devereau had a right to remain silent, if he wished. Anything he said during the test could be used for or against him in court, Killen explained. He had a right to consult an attorney, but no one could be present during the test, since the presence of another person other than the examiner could be the basis for a misleading reaction.

Devereau was nervous when he was introduced to John A. Cahalane, a veteran state police polygraphist. Cahalane ran three polygrams to evaluate Devereau's denial that he was involved in the murders of four young women on Cape Cod.

"Is your first name Cory?" Cahalane said.

"Yes," Devereau said.

"Were you born in West Virginia?"

"Yes."

"Did you tell the police all that you knew about the girls' murder?"

"Yes."

"Did you have any part in killing any of the girls?"

"No."

"Is today Sunday?"

"No."

"Did you ever go out with Susan Perry?"

"Yes."

"Did you go out with Susan Perry in 1968?"

Devereau hesitated. Cahalane saw a reaction. Devereau wasn't sure if he went out with her in 1968. "I might have."

"Do you drink water?"

"Yes."

"Were you present when Susan Perry was killed?"

"No."

"Did you have any part in causing her death?"

"No."

"Have you a mustache?"

"No."

Devereau had a slight, thin line of sparse blonde hair on his upper lip he did not consider to be a mustache. His answer showed a disturbance, but no deception.

"Did you have any part in killing Sydney Monzon?"

"No."

"Did you bury either one of these girls?"

"No."

"Did you assist some other person in burying them?"

"No."

"Do you have a license to drive a car?"

Devereau hesitated, "Well, not really," he said. He had no valid license; but he had owned a phony license for a time.

"On January twenty-fifth did you and Costa double-date the Providence girls?"

"No."

"Do you own a car?"

"No."

"Did you shoot either the Walsh or Wysocki girl?"

"No."

"Did you supply the knife so that Costa could cut them up?"

"No."

"Are you wearing a wristwatch?"

"Yes."

"Did you go into the woods on January twenty-fifth in the Volkswagen to get drugs?"

"No."

"Did you ever ride in the girls' Volkswagen?"

"No."

"Did you assist in burying either one of the Providence girls?"

"No."

"Did you tell the truth to all questions on this test?"

"Yes."

After the test, Devereau said he did not know for certain whether he went out with Susan Perry in 1968, but on reflection felt that he did not.

Devereau had asthma, so his "pneumo" or respiratory responses had been erratic. Devereau had told substantially the truth, Cahalane reported. "He had nothing to do with killing the girls."

When Goldman heard the results of Devereau's polygraph test he went straight to the Barnstable House of Correction to confront Costa.

"I can tell you that Cory has been completely exonerated by the police and lie detector tests in having any connection at all with the deaths of these girls—that's the latest word from Lieutenant Killen. Cory denies having anything to do with Pat and Mary Anne; or even having *met* them."

"Well, you don't think he's going to admit it," Costa said, coldly. "I firmly believe that Cory was super-drugged. He must have been when he went in there. I don't know whether they checked his arms or what, but it would have been evident."

"Well, it *isn't* evident, Tony," Goldman said sharply. "What *is* evident are the four murders you're charged with. I have to know how to deal with them, having in mind the presentation the police are going to make. Now tell me, first of all, about the Perry girl. Did you have sexual relations with her?"

"I didn't have any sexual relations with her whatsoever!" Costa said firmly. "At that time, Davey Joseph was her boyfriend. He and Susan came up to my place because they were having an affair. Susan's father didn't want Davey with her at all; this is why they were there to begin with. Because they couldn't be together in Provincetown—"

"Did you *kill* her, Tony?" Goldman said, cutting Costa short.

"No, I didn't," Costa said mildly, barely responding to Goldman's provocation. "These people that are saying I had relations with Susan, that comes from Davey Joseph, who was jealous due to the fact that Susan desired sleeping in my bed rather than with him on the floor. Susan evidently told Paula Hoernig some stories about what she would *like* to do, expressing that she did."

"What about her clothes that were brought to your place?"

"As far as I know somebody must have picked them up. I know Cory was up there; but I don't know what the hell happened to her clothes."

"How do you account for Susan being cut up in the same fashion as the others?"

"This is simply what the police say. I myself am not totally sure it *is* the same fashion, unless you people have some report or something."

"I merely point out to you that I'm left in the dark on the Perry girl at the moment," Goldman said irritably. "All right, is there anything you want to tell me about the Monzon girl? Did you have anything to do with *her?*"

"I had very little to do with Sydney except in dealings with dope. And that was on a few choice occasions."

"Did you ever screw her?"

417

"No, I didn't. I had nothing to do with her. It was just a completely platonic thing where if we passed each other we said hello, or she'd say a few words in general conversation in front of town hall."

"I'm going to be completely at the mercy of the police in those two cases, then?"

"In those two cases, if they can come up with something to tie me in, then all well and good," Costa said. "But to me it's impossible!"

"Will you write down in your notebook every single detail of the relationship that you had with Sydney, so I'll have something to go on? Will you do the same thing on the Perry girl? I've *got* to have that!"

"Yeah, I'll do it tonight."

"If you had anything to do with these girls, for God's sake Tony, tell me! I'm sticking my neck out and it's going to hurt *you*, not me. Remember what I said about Sydney. She was in the same grave with Pat and Mary Anne, with the same cuts in the same manner. The pattern is the same."

"This again is what the police say. I won't be totally sure of that until we actually see any reports they have to prove this."

"OK, Tony," Goldman said, resignedly. "Whatever you say I go along with one hundred percent. If you're not telling the truth I'll be absolutely hurting you! Now, what do you want to say, finally, with respect to Patricia and Mary Anne?"

"Actually the same things I described previously."

"Why did Cory want to shoot them?"

"The only explanation I can come up with is that I owed Cory two hundred dollars for two ounces of hash. I told him I'd make it up to him in heroin, but things came to be and I considered that a mistake. I told Pat in his presence not to give him anything—this was while we were at the can. I said to her, 'Don't let anybody touch it until I get back.' The fact is I was going to give him just enough heroin to get high—I intended to give him the money I owed him after I sold some of the stuff. I didn't want to give him drugs; he was so screwed up to begin with."

"So why did he shoot Pat?" Goldman said. "Why didn't he shoot *you?*"

"He tried!" Costa said. "This is what really shook me up. He actually fired the gun at me."

"Was this before you cut up the body?"

"Yeah, it was way before. Pat was still on the ground. I didn't even know where Mary Anne was yet."

"Well, why didn't you leave him then?"

"I couldn't!" Costa said. "I freaked out. I don't know, it hit me like a ton of shit."

"After this you worked with him in the cutting up? A guy who was going to shoot you? Jesus! I should think you wouldn't have anything to do with him!"

"Well, see, I wasn't really stable. Coming upon this gore and blood and everything else, it was a pretty scary thing to me; I couldn't think straight. I just did whatever was brought out to me."

"So you're telling me nothing more today than what you've already told Zimmerman and Lester," Goldman said.

"There's nothing more I can say."

"That doesn't help me in the slightest. I've got nothing on Perry, I've got nothing on Monzon, and the police say Cory is absolutely innocent. The police say Cory wasn't even *there.*"

"That *can't* be so—"

"It *can* be so, because they're going to say so. Who's going to prove he was?"

"They must have found fingerprints on the car—"

"They did not!" Goldman said. "There are no fingerprints of him at all."

"They've got to have something!" Costa said. "They may say no, but that isn't so."

"There's no point in lying as far as Killen is concerned. If they can get another one it adds to their glory; they'd like to get another one if they could."

"I don't know what's going on," Costa said, "but there is definitely something wrong." He was hugging his sides, as if in pain, rocking back and forth in his chair. Goldman had never seen him so agitated, so close to losing control. "If we can't get these people to talk, there's nothing more I can do."

"Cory's going to say he wasn't even there, that he knows nothing about it," Goldman told him. "Your gun is the gun they've got. The fingerprints on the gun are *yours!* If Cory used the gun, why aren't Cory's fingerprints on the gun?"

"They just may be. See, I don't know."

"Tony, there are no fingerprints on that gun but yours."

419

"Well, I'm not sure about that," Costa snapped. His eyes darted about the small conference room as if seeking some means of escape. "I don't know what the hell is going on!"

"Well, I'm *telling* you, so you'll know!"

"And this is proof that you have? This is what they say?"

"This is what they *say,* Tony. *Proof?* No, sir! So, essentially, I haven't got any more than already exists in our previous records."

"That's about it," Costa said, "You guys wanted the truth and I told you the truth; and that's where it's at. I think I want to talk to Dr. Williams again and have him tell me a little bit more, to see what's happening."

"All right, Tony," Goldman said, without enthusiasm. "I'll have him talk to you again."

Goldman doubted whether a third interview would change Dr. Williams's opinion about Tony Costa. Acute and perceptive as his diagnosis might be, Williams's usefulness as an expert defense witness was limited. Williams had refused to confirm Goldman's theory that Costa had murdered the girls while intoxicated by drugs. Further, Williams could not, in good medical conscience, testify that Costa was psychotic—the magic word Goldman was seeking to support his defense of diminished responsibility. Williams's opinion that Costa was a psychopath fell short of meeting the legal requirements for an insanity plea.

Impatient with Costa's continued unwillingness to disclose the truth about the murders, Goldman grew furious when Costa told him that Herb Abrams had sought to interview Costa in jail and attempt to execute "an instrument of employment" as Costa's counsel. Further, Abrams had called *Life* magazine to demand that Vonnegut's article name him as co-counsel in the case. Goldman suggested that Abrams might be removed from the defense team when he called Williams to arrange for a third examination of Costa.

Williams suggested instead that "a fair and adequate" psychological examination of Costa would include "an electroencephalogram with sleep study, hyperventilation and strobe-light drive," since in his descriptions of certain behavior Costa had demonstrated some of the symptoms of temporal lobe epilepsy which should be considered as a possible diagnosis. Complete psychological testing was "essential" to an adequate psychiatric ex-

420

amination; Williams recommended a colleague at McClean Hospital. A thorough analysis and investigation of the drugs Costa had used around the time of the murders should be carried out, as well as a chromosome study made of Costa at Boston Children's Hospital.

Goldman was puzzled that Williams was so evasive with regard to his availability for a third examination of Tony Costa. Goldman found out why several days later when he received a letter from Williams which infuriated him:

> Let me reiterate that I think Mr. Abrams is essential to the case in terms of his special skills and experience, some of which I have shared with him. I work well with Mr. Abrams, he is close by and would provide excellent liaison with the case for me, and it was with this in mind that I entered the case. I do not feel I can be helpful to the defendant or to the court without Mr. Abrams' continued association with the case and would, therefore, terminate my services if he were not involved as one of the counsels for the defense.

Williams enclosed a bill for two psychiatric examinations of Tony Costa and consultations with Goldman, Cavanaugh and Avis Costa in the amount of $350.

Goldman sent a "forthright and explicit" letter to Herb Abrams. He told him that the fact that Dr. Williams did not care to continue his association with the defense unless Abrams remained on the case was, "to my way of thinking and within my experience, an attempt to dictate to me how Costa should be defended," Goldman said. "It leaves me with the impression that you played some part in Dr. Williams's ultimatum.

"Such bold behavior I have never, in my forty-four years as an attorney, experienced from an associate attorney whose services were to be used in the limited capacity of the required, if any, medical defense, and raises severe questions of judgment about your ability to associate with us in this matter," Goldman wrote. "I have discussed this with Tony, who now desires you to be removed from association in the defense." If Abrams would prepare a statement of the hours he had worked on the case, every effort would be made to reimburse him under the schedule of fees established by the Barnstable Bar Association, "when, as, and if money should become available." Goldman pointed out that payment of any fee could only come out of receipts from the sale of Costa's book rights. "And that possibility will not and cannot come to fruition until after Costa's trial.

"I regret it is your behavior and questionable judgment which requires me to take this action," Goldman concluded. He had tried to reach Abrams several times by telephone and was told that Abrams was talking long distance and would return the call.

Two weeks later Abrams turned up at a news conference to hand out biographies and photographs of himself and his new client, John Farrar, a scuba diver who had recovered the body of Mary Jo Kopechne from a submerged automobile. Farrar claimed an air pocket in the car's trunk could have provided sufficient oxygen to have kept the young woman alive for a time. Farrar was expected to testify at an inquest into the death called by District Attorney Edmund Dinis.

Struck by Costa's continued insistence that Cory Devereau had something to do with the murders, Goldman again approached George Killen. Despite a near-total belief in his client's guilt, Goldman wanted to determine exactly what Devereau's relationship had been with Costa at the time of the murders. That the polygraph test Devereau had successfully passed had shown some reaction to the name of Susan Perry seemed "significant," Goldman told Killen. Devereau had not been specifically questioned with regard to a visit to Susan Perry's grave. To encourage a second test on Devereau, Goldman had authorized Charles Zimmerman to cooperate with state police polygraphists by revealing where Costa's reactions on his polygrams appeared to indicate Devereau's possible involvement in the murders.

In his notes on Sydney Monzon, written at Goldman's request, Costa made a single and ominous admission: Sydney had participated in the robbery of Dr. Callis's office.

"She volunteered to provide transportation," Costa explained. "I repaid Sydney by granting her free use of the canister in the forest anytime she so desired."

Costa's statement regarding Susan Perry conceded what Goldman had suspected all along:

422

Susan and I never had any close relationship whatsoever, in public or elsewhere. She slept in the same bed as
I did and we *did* have sexual relations. I've had no other
relationship with Susan Perry . . .

16

"Tony," Goldman said when he met with Costa on August
25, "I was wondering what you're going to say when the district
attorney introduces the fact that the Perry girl lived at your
house; the fact that you were seen with Sydney Monzon and the
fact that you were seen with Walsh and the Wysocki girl, and you
had their automobile—I'm giving you an overall picture—and the
bill of sale with your signature on it . . . all these different matters. Have in mind that, in addition, they have your gun and a
knife your brother has identified as yours, and the fact that the
bodies were found in an area where you had a marijuana garden
and kept a store of drugs. They've got a direct tie-in of all these
things; they've made an overwhelming case. We haven't given up
hope of working on a tie-in with Devereau, or finding that first
fellow we chased and couldn't get—what's his name . . ."

"Chuck Hansen," Costa said.

"As things stand now, Tony, we can't put out a case that will
win," Goldman said. "Now, there are several approaches we have
in mind. We already have them over a barrel on a question of law.
For example, the grand jury indictment was obtained against you
absolutely on atmosphere and prejudicial publicity. The jurors did
not have a fair chance to consider the case; they just listened to
one police officer, Lieutenant Flynn. There was no testimony of
any kind on the autopsies, the medical examiner or the witnesses
that tied you into this thing. And based on that atmosphere—
which everybody recognizes—I've got a good fighting chance.

Second, Judge Beaudreau denied my motion for severance—that means we can't separate the crimes into different trials. Now, I ask you, what relationship is the alleged crime of the Perry girl got to do with the Wysocki girl, do you mind telling me that? There's *no* relationship! And I can show them that my motion for severance should not have been denied, so that I could trade.

"Now, in order not to gamble that deal, I've got to be able to prove your use of drugs during that period. If I could show *that* condition, I know I could get you out of first-degree murder. Then we take our appeal and I could make a trade. With the drug defense, even if a guilty finding is made, I've got enough exceptions to appeal the thing, to win new trials, and then make a deal to get you back out on the street—whether it's three years, four years or ten years. I know I can get you out. Do you follow me?"

"Yeah," Costa said.

"But if I do *nothing* in the defense angle to show that drugs controlled your motives, I'm left with a defense that takes you away from that position. I've got to be able to say: 'Now comes Antone Costa and he says *a* he is not guilty, and *b* if he *is* guilty of the crimes charged, he was in a condition under which he had no legal control or responsibility for what he did'—*that* should be the theme of my case, Tony. Give me a chance to keep you from being in jail for the rest of your life."

"Concerning that deal situation," Costa said. "How do you think that would come out?"

"Tony, it's the old story. When they haven't got an open-and-shut case, then I can trade. I say to the lawyer, 'Let's trade this off; instead of doing this, let's do that.' But if I put up *no* defense, you give me nothing to trade."

"What bothers me in a deal-type thing is there are four murders involved," Costa said.

"Tony, what we have is one murder case with four victims. They denied my severance. Do you understand what I mean? The legal point is: you cannot conscientiously and under the Constitution of the United States convict a man of one crime by introducing evidence of another crime. If you spit on the sidewalk two years ago, what has that got to do with spitting on the sidewalk today? They're two separate crimes. Now, they've ruled against us on severance and that was their big, big mistake in my judgment, just as it was a big mistake to send Lieutenant Flynn before the grand jury without a stenographer, to say anything he wanted to an inflamed group of people who'd heard the district attorney's stories. Think of it in those terms, Tony. Give a trading point. Don't tie my hands so I can't win this for you. Because I *must* win this for you.

"Now, tell me how I can do it any better, if you have any suggestions. There is plenty of evidence of drug use: the burglary of Dr. Callis's office, references in letters to your being stoned in your own words, and the observations of Avis, plus various people speaking of your conduct during that period to show that the guilty party was *drugs,* not Tony Costa. Do you follow me?"

"Yeah, I've contemplated this deal thing before," Costa said coolly. "The only thing that gets me uptight is the amount of time involved; because it's for four murders, right?"

"They're all being tried together, Tony. What difference does it make if I win three cases and they stick you on the fourth? Let me tell you what I did. I had a long talk with a fellow who idolizes you, who believes in you—Frank Bent, your uncle. He's a good, shrewd old fellow. He's been around for a great many years. He's seen things come and go. True, he's not a lawyer; he's not a psychologist, but he *is* a man of the world. He's certain you were under the influence of drugs; if you were not you would never have done any of these things at all. But right now the government's made a case against you of killing the girls to get an automobile away from them—a cold-blooded motive. Now I've got to meet that situation, Tony. I can't stand there and let them hit you in the jaw, hit the whole defense in the jaw and do nothing about it. I've got to be able to strike back, to set up a defense. Do you agree with me at all on this?"

"I agree with you . . . I want to say 'Go ahead,' but I'm afraid of what the judge will say."

"I don't *care* about the judge," Goldman said. "If I didn't have these legal obstacles it would be different. The papers are kicking the hell out of Dinis. He's in a bad way. *Newsweek* kicked his teeth in on the Ted Kennedy case. And they mentioned how he butchered the Costa case; it was the most devastating thing in the world. Think in those terms, if you would, Tony. You don't have to give me an answer today or tomorrow."

"How would this deal thing work? At the trial or afterwards?"

"I sure wouldn't make a deal *before,* " Goldman said. "I've got to see everything they've got. Maybe they can't prove the case at all. If they can't prove the case, then you're not guilty, period."

Costa unlocked his fingers, looked straight into Goldman's face and said evenly, "What have we got for a straight defense?"

Goldman was astonished. "Straight defense! You answer that yourself, Tony. You tell *me* what a straight defense is. Thus far, I've read every single one of your tapes, and all I'm faced with is a group of your statements which they will show are not the truth.

"You walked into the police station and voluntarily made statements that are admissible as evidence against you. Now, Goldman says they *can't* be admissible as evidence because you didn't know what you were doing when you went in there. You were under the influence of some type of speed, heroin or whatever; you were acting in a state of confusion. And everything you said is *not* admissible—to destroy all those statements you made which they say are lies. Do I make my point?"

"Yeah," Costa said. "What I was getting at was the fact that someone was trying to do me in and paying off money. And there would be a jury sitting there listening to this."

Goldman had been patient and forbearing throughout months of Costa's lies and evasions. Now he said, in a rare scolding voice, "You *always* jump the hurdle, Tony. And when I say always, I mean that you have been jumping the hurdle in the past in your explanations of these things."

Following his conference with Costa, Goldman reported to prison authorities that his client needed to see a doctor. Costa was pale, nervous, sleepless, unable to eat and had complained of gnawing pains under his breastbone and below his stomach. Costa had been bleeding into his intestine and was passing clots of blood. Goldman wanted to call in a doctor but was told that no examination could be carried out without consulting jail physician Dr. Cyril Rossten, who was treating Costa for gastritis.

"All they give me is Gelusil and Darvon; this is what I've been on now since I've been in here," Costa complained. "Darvon has aspirin in it, which is not good for an ulceric condition; aspirin only irritates the stomach and makes it worse. All I want is a doctor to check it out and make tests, not just theorize. I would like to go through a gastrointestinal thing, just to be sure. Because this guy in here doesn't do anything. No blood pressure test, nothing. He just talks to you and that's it. I've got horrible shortness of breath; and I've got pain. It seems like to be on this side of my left lung. The pain is agonizing. They just sit there and say 'If it gets any worse, let us know.' And it can't get any worse. It's at its peak," Costa said. "You've got to be dying in this place to get anything."

17

On August 27, the Boston *Record-American* published a story based on the release of statements Costa had made to police in which he had twice changed his story—statements Goldman had requested in his Discovery motions of July 9.

Goldman hit the ceiling when he read the headline:

SAY SUSPECT
IN TRURO GIRL
KILLINGS LIED

This was precisely the kind of pretrial publicity prejudicial to his client which had prompted Goldman's request to have the arguments of motions heard in chambers and the motions themselves impounded once they were ruled upon—an action Beaudreau had refused to take. Goldman promptly filed a motion to impound all pretrial Discovery pleadings.

"Notwithstanding the admonition of this court, there recently appeared a very serious and prejudicial statement to the effect that 'Costa lied' as a bold headline," Goldman said when he returned to Barnstable courthouse with a copy of the *Record-American* in his briefcase. By not impounding the motions, he said, the court would be allowing "a state of mass hysteria on the part of the public" to be further created against the defendant, and the climate of public prejudice growing out of "inflammatory publicity and prejudicial, extra-judicial accounts of the case would continue." Goldman was particularly concerned that there be no release of the autopsy reports—if he could ever get them himself.

Beaudreau made the newspaper Goldman had brought a part of the record during a lobby conference. "I am going to allow the impounding of these motions." Beaudreau was impounding any statements of the defendant now in court records, the bill of particulars and the autopsy and pathological report, as well as Goldman's request to inspect evidence gathered by the prosecution, the future publication of which was prohibited.

"I am still waiting for the autopsy reports," Goldman said.

"You haven't got those yet?" Beaudreau said. "What's taking so much time?"

"We contacted Dr. Katsas on many occasions and asked him for them and we haven't heard from him," Bernie Flynn said. He showed Goldman a copy of a letter the district attorney's office had written to Katsas.

"I think we ought to do something about that," Beaudreau said. "I might consider calling him."

"I wish you would," Flynn said. "Because we've tried and we haven't received any answer."

Beaudreau called Katsas from his chambers. Katsas promised the reports in a week. Beaudreau told Flynn, "You *cannot* issue or reveal the substance of these reports. I want to make that clear, because the impounding of the autopsy reports applies to the district attorney's office."

Costa, manacled to corrections officer Donald Parker, was brought to the courthouse, sitting impassively through the half-hour consultation in chambers. Dressed in a dark blue suit, white shirt and black tie, he chatted with Goldman and Cavanaugh before being led back up the hill by deputy master Irving Ellis. Costa appeared to be in good health, but Cavanaugh told reporters his client had been receiving treatment for a stomach ulcer and had lost weight.

Satisfied that some progress had been made in setting up the case, Goldman joined Charlie Zimmerman and Lester Allen a week later for another conference with Tony Costa.

"Tony, when did you first meet Dr. Callis?" Goldman said.

"I first went to him in 1965 with the intention of obtaining marriage counseling," Costa said.

428

"Am I correct in saying that's what started you on drugs?" Goldman said. "This is awfully important, Tony; because I've got something to lay this case on."

"This was the man who actually started me on drugs," Costa affirmed.

"How many times would say say you went to Dr. Callis from 1965 on?"

"Numerous occasions. I can't even keep count."

"See if you can refresh your memory between now and the next time one of us comes down. Try to tell us the number of times."

"I remember he let the bill run up to a hundred and forty dollars one time."

"Did he suggest that if there was any other person that you knew of who was having domestic troubles or other problems, he should come to his office?"

"Yeah, definitely."

"How many times do you think he suggested that?"

"Basically, I guess, every other time I went there. Like I took Joey Thomas and Chris Silva there. He was feeding them pills. And on one occasion Linda Monzon, who is Sydney's sister. She and David Salvador took an extreme amount of LSD and didn't know what to do about it. She was so out of her mind she couldn't understand anybody or anything. So I sent them to Dr. Callis to straighten her out; and he took care of her. Avis went to him on a couple of occasions. He gave her tranquilizers called Meprobamate. He more or less forced them into her hands."

"Don't say *forced*, Tony," Goldman said. "Because that's a conclusion, and it'll be objected to. He said she should have them; she wasn't particularly for pills, she said she didn't need them, but he said, 'As a doctor, take my advice, you should have them.' That's the point I'm trying to make."

Costa took the cue. "She said that she did not want pills under any circumstances. But he did say she needed them and gave her an envelope filled with Meprobamate. She came home and she took one—she discarded the rest. She called them 'shit pills.'

"Now, what was the date you took drugs out of his place?"

"That was in '68. April or May."

"The quantity of pills you took, was it a very little insignificant amount, or was it a very, very substantial amount?" Goldman said.

"It was a *tremendous* amount," Costa said.

"Would you estimate how many boxes of pills there were, quantity-wise?"

"There must have been at least ten thousand pills; these were strong pills, basically barbiturates. I walked out of there with many bottles. I mean there was a bag about three feet high filled chock to the top with stuff. Each bottle contained at least a thousand pills, and there would be at least, maybe forty bottles. Intermixed with those would be like bottles of five thousand."

"Did you get any morphine there?"

"Yeah, there was a good amount of morphine. There was four 20-cc vials of morphine. There was a little bit of Dilaudid, which is strong stuff. They give it to cancer patients for severe pain."

"When you got all the stuff out of there, did you put it in some container you had buried in Truro?"

"At that time it happened to be *four* containers about two feet high that I had," Costa said. "They were tank ammo cans."

"These pills you took, were they all in factory-packed containers?"

"Most of them were. The label on them said Rugy, the chemical company."

"Were there also packages that looked as if they had been unpacked and repackaged in any way, like paper-bag stuff?"

"There was a tremendous amount of stuff on the top shelf in little jars, regular mayonnaise jars or something, with powders in them."

"Any writing on them, any labels?"

"No, this is why I didn't touch them," Costa said.

"You only took the stuff you could identify at that time as drugs, or as pills of some type?"

"Yeah, cough syrup and stuff like that. Like he had little two-ounce jars of Robitussin-AC, which contains codeine."

"Tell me, very frankly and very honestly," Goldman said, "Do you think he's the one who started you on drugs?"

"Yeah," Costa said. "I mean, it's evident that he did."

"Well, it isn't *evident!*" Goldman snapped. "That again is a conclusion. Stop being an editorial writer and just give us the facts. You say he started you on this thing?"

430

Costa laughed, nervously, "Yeah, he did."

"Well, that's about all I want at this session," Goldman said. "I've covered what I came up here for today."

"Another thing about Callis," Costa went on. "He hired me to paint the trim and the gutters on his building. He had the paint in the garage and he left the door open. The entire garage was filled from wall to wall with boxes stacked about five feet high. There was samples that physicians get through the mail in the form of little jars and packets."

"Why do you use the word 'samples,'" Goldman said. "He wouldn't be getting samples in cartons, Tony."

"These were old cardboard boxes that he himself put there. All his samples and things were just thrown in. I rummaged through the boxes; and there was everything any drug user could want. Everything from strong narcotics . . ."

"Well, those weren't *samples,*" Goldman said. "You don't mean samples, you mean there was a stock of drugs there. The word is stock."

"What I'm getting at, is he deliberately left the garage door open—"

"You can't *say* that Tony!" Goldman said. "Did you take anything out of there?"

"Yeah, I did. I took Valium. There was some Nembutal and phenobarbital. I went through about three or four boxes; the ones that were easily accessible, right on top."

"Did you ever see Callis with a revolver in his pocket?" Goldman said.

"Yeah, he kept it strapped to his side all the time," Costa said. "He'd be sitting in a chair and on one occasion his coat flapped back and there was this big police revolver. I was nervous having the gun there."

"Tony, I'm going to leave you with a parting suggestion. Anything else you can tell us about Callis that we haven't already asked you, do so—but don't editorialize every answer. You're going to extend the trial by about two years by your telling why. Don't elaborate; just answer the questions either Mr. Zimmerman or Lester put to you without saying 'because'—it's one of your favorite words."

18

Zimmerman had little respect for Lester Allen's gifts as an interviewer after reviewing his tapes with Tony Costa. Costa had talked rings around Allen, easily getting him off the subject under discussion. Allen himself often changed subjects in mid-sentence and had difficulty keeping on the track of his own questions. Despite his boast to Costa— "Don't try to con me, because it's virtually impossible"—Costa had.

Zimmerman himself had left the six sessions he spent with Tony Costa exhausted. Costa, he could see, was a master of concealment. With the proficiency of a vaudeville juggler, Costa made a shambles of interrogation. He changed his story as casually as he changed his shirt, like as not to dismiss his previous lies "because I was uptight" or to protect a friend. Amoral, clever, manipulative, Costa had to be closely watched during questioning. At the least inattention, Zimmerman knew, Cost darted away from a subject he did not want to talk about with a dazzling display of obfuscation. Only when confronted by incontrovertible evidence discovered by investigators, and given no other choice, did he concede a fact having to do with his involvement in the murders. He was turning out to be the most cunning and slippery subject Zimmerman had ever examined. Costa was likely to begin a new interrogation session by asking, "What did I tell you the last time?"

Determined to wrest the truth from Costa, Zimmerman joined Lester Allen to question Costa again. "Tony, I'm not going to ask you any questions," Zimmerman said. "You can start where you did not tell the truth."

Costa insisted that Pat Walsh and Mary Anne Wysocki had returned to Mrs. Morton's rooming house around eleven o'clock on Sunday night. "The girls arrived first; then Cory came in. We had already been smoking pot by this time. And Cory had some hash. There wasn't much but enough to get us good and high. Then it was suggested we go for a ride and sort of cruise around town. I rolled another two sticks and we puffed some weed in the

432

car. I mentioned I had some stuff out at the hold. Cory was all up for going. He knew there was Dilaudid there, a little box of pills left over from the Wellfleet drugstore job—he wanted those. There was a round ball—maybe that big—of scag, heroin. This I was going to give Pat. I had promised this to Cory—he wasn't satisfied with the Dilaudid. I told Pat, 'Don't give him any of this stuff because it's yours.' And in running down to get his works, I don't know what happened at that point."

"There's no change with the exception of what you said the last time about Cory coming by and telling you he'd killed the girls?" Zimmerman said. "And the story about the heroin that was supposed to come in the girls had made a telephone call about. That's all out?"

"As far as the basic facts are concerned," Costa said smoothly. "You can forget the rest of that."

"Is there some compelling reason which either you don't re-call or you are reluctant to tell us why you were covering for Cory?" Lester Allen said. "*If* Cory played a part in all this?"

"I don't know," Costa said. "I guess I would cover for Cory the same way I would cover for anyone that I dug."

"You said prior to going to the woods with the girls you smoked some hash," Zimmerman said. "The question is, how much control did you have over your faculties. You say you can recall minute details of what happened. Obviously this is going counter to the defense your counsel is going to put out about drug use. The point I'm trying to get across is you've got to separate two things; your attorney has one set of facts for the defense, but the *true* facts don't have to be all to that defense. Defense is a matter of strategy but the facts themselves are a different kettle of fish."

"We're not going to come out and say I went riding out to the site with them, are we?" Costa said.

"Not if we can avoid it." Allen said. "But you're not giving us much chance to avoid it."

"What do you need to avoid it?"

"The *truth*, Tony!" Zimmerman said. "Then you can sit down with Mr. Goldman and say, 'This is what I want to do.' You cannot keep this information inside. Do you understand?"

"Yeah."

"Your attorney has to be in a position to prevent any damag-ing things from getting on the record. If he knows what happened,

433

he cannot inadvertently step on a hornet's nest by asking a question he never should have asked," Zimmerman said. "Tony, we go with the pitch. If you tell us you hit the ball to third base, we'll go dig in the third base area to find the ball. But we don't want to look at third base if the ball was hit to second base."

"I guess you guys are looking for legal things or something," Costa said.

"No, we are looking for *facts*," Zimmerman said. "Mr. Goldman will handle the legal elements very adequately. We have to know things that have an impact as far as Cory Devereau is concerned, if they put him on the stand, things he would know that could be damaging. The truth is not going to be exposed as far as *you're* concerned, unless you want it to be."

19

"The following represents a list of the drugs taken from Callis's office, their names and near-exact quantities." Costa wrote in a separate section of his exercise notebook:

Vials: Solutions, liquid:
(2) Nembutal (pentobarbital) sodium solution 30cc
(1) Seconal sodium solution 30cc
(2) Dextroamphetamine sulfate solution 30cc
(1) Amphetamine sulfate solution 30cc
(24) Scopolamine Hydrochloride solution 1cc ampules
(6) Syrettes Dihydromorphinone 1cc each (Dilaudid)

Bottles, plastic and glass
Nembutal–pentobarbital sodium
   1000 white tabs 100 mg
   1000 yellow capsules 100 mg
   1500 yellow/white capsules 50 mg

Amytal—amobarbital sodium blue caps 700
Librium—light green/white caps 1500 15 mg
" black/green 900 10 mg
Thorazine orange tabs 950 150 mg
Darvon gray/red 480 65 mg
Stelazine blue tabs 1000 5 mg
Butabarbital sodium blue tabs 500
Combid 3 bottles of 100 each 300 yellow/clear
Paragoric tabs (heart-shaped) 1000 w/opium
Digitalis grayish? 5000
Phenobarbital:
  1/4 grain 500 round tabs
  1/2 grain 1000 yellow round tabs
  1 grain 1000 round tabs

Rawolfia serpentina, red tabs 5000 plastic jar
Dextroamphetamine sulfate (Dexedrine)
  Brown/clear caps 15 mg each—1500
  with amobarbital, pink tabs—1900

Amphetamine sulfate (Benzedrine)
Canister of 5000, full strength   4100 left
  White with criss-cross on back

Dexamyl—green/clear   500
Valium—yellow tabs   500

Cough Syrup w/codeine
  Robitussin AC—16 4 oz.   24 1 oz.

Solacen—350 mg orange gelatin caps 400
Meprospan (Meprobamate) blue/clear caps 700

The following were in the form of sample cards and
containers.
Their quantities are as listed:
Eskatrol—orange/clear 300
Triavil—pink or blue 200
Tofranil—small, reddish 200
Deprol—(Meprobamate) big pinkish white tabs
36 sample bottles of 12 tabs each   432

Cavanaugh read the list with deep skepticism; it was a feat of memory he doubted Costa was capable of. Costa's encyclopedic knowledge of drugs through his study of the *Physician's Desk Reference,* his notoriously untrustworthy way with facts and his skill at fabricating elaborate lies all pointed to another fantasy dealing with his robbery of Callis's office.

Callis might not be the smartest doctor since the Mayo brothers, but Cavanaugh doubted he was the pill-pushing quack Costa was making him out to be now that Costa understood Goldman's strategy. Callis was a close personal friend of George Killen; Cavanaugh had too much respect for Killen as a judge of character to believe he would have a dope peddler for a friend.

Costa had steadily denied taking large quantities of drugs, until overwhelming proof from other sources so strongly contradicted him that Costa had been forced to concede the fact—particularly when it was suggested to him that it would be an advantage to his defense.

Cavanaugh admired the virtuosity of Goldman's plan for a drug defense, an adroit and skillful approach to a case difficult if not impossible to defend—the most difficult obstacle being Costa's stubborn refusal to allow the word "insanity" in his plea.

"Impairment" was the word that appealed to Costa's grandiose view of himself as an intellectual and rational person, and it avoided the stigma of an insanity plea. Cavanaugh was, however, dubious about Goldman's thesis of Callis as a villain who had trapped Tony Costa into a life of drug dependency. Tony Costa—drug pusher, thief, sexual psychopath and God only knows what else—was going to be represented in court as a gentle, hard worker, a faithful husband, devoted to his children and, in Cavanaugh's jaundiced view, "a man who was good to his mother, loved the American flag and Girl Scout cookies."

Costa's revelations to Charles Zimmerman had shaken whatever thoughts Cavanaugh had entertained of his client's innocence. Cavanaugh admitted that Tony Costa had fooled him completely at the beginning of the case, telling Goldman "I thought he was involved in some small-time dope deals with these girls; that's why he was lying. I never figured him as a killer."

Cavanaugh showed Costa a list of drugs that Dr. Callis had reported missing from his office to the Wellfleet police in contrast to the elaborate list Costa had written up.

"That's only about one-tenth of what I took," Costa said. "I

436

took enough stuff out of there to fill a laundry bag that stands about three feet high."

"Did Callis know you smoked pot?"

"He knew it because one time he told me they had marijuana capsules; he showed me a couple he had on hand. I did look for those marijuana things and I couldn't find them. There was nothing there; it was just a dull, dry place."

"What about the drugs you took from Murray's drugstore in Wellfleet?" Cavanaugh said.

Costa no longer denied the robbery. "There was only one container of speed, about twenty-five capsules of biphetamine sulfate; they were half-strength. That was the only speed that came out of the drugstore; the rest was all heavy morphine and Dilaudid. There was morphine with atropine, which is an intense speed; it's horrible! Most people don't like it, but Cory dug it because he got stoned and it kept him up at the same time."

Costa had sold a quantity of Dolophine to Ronnie Enos. "It's what hospitals use to take the place of heroin, it's not as addictive. You don't get a withdrawal thing from it. So Ronnie was happy with that. I gave it to him because it served two purposes: to get him high and to get him off other things."

"What were you using yourself at this time?" Cavanaugh said.

"I didn't do much of anything. I got into selling these drugs. I got into Nembutal and Tuinal, but mostly, I was just smoking pot and hash."

"What about the Dexedrine from Callis's office you gave Vinnie to sell for fifteen dollars a spoon?"

"Oh, I bought that from Larry Andresen," Costa said brightly. "He took some dextroamphetamine sulfate out of Adams Pharmacy. I bought a one-ounce jar from Larry for seventy dollars and sold it. There wasn't much speed from Callis's place. I remember saying that came from Callis; but that was only to protect Larry. Because Larry's a good friend of mine. And like Larry's uptight about my situation. He does want to help if he can. I wrote him a letter. I told him to tell you guys what he knows. To straighten this whole thing out."

20

On September 11, Costa gave a note to Lester Allen to be delivered to Maurice Goldman:

"The Sly Fly"

At this time, it seems evident to me that the DA might be in favor of a "constructive" approach due to his eminent failure in current events.

My idea is to attempt to persuade him to listen to reason. We could offer him a "package" deal. For example, I could or would cop out on a larceny charge, turn over the murderer to him plus the evidence we possess concerning the same, and ultimately offer my services to his office in cleaning up Cape Cod.

This would benefit him, his position, etc. and would appease his power-mad, glory-seeking desires.

Goldman was more interested in delaying the trial beyond November 3. The handicap of limited time to prepare the case was further aggravated, Goldman argued in court, "by continued publications of scurrilous and prejudicial accounts" of the crimes alleged in nationally circulated newspapers and magazines. Goldman cited the October issue of *Uncensored* magazine, whose cover advertised:

CAPE COD'S CANNIBAL MURDERS

Uncensored reported that Tony Costa "hung around with some of the pot-puffing LSD-gulping hippies who had established a more or less permanent base in Provincetown." Costa, the magazine said, had played the field after his divorce. "He was seen with a different girl almost every night. But, though he seldom slept alone, he formed no permanent attachments. Tony Costa was strictly a loner." *Uncensored* repeated Dinis's allegations that the murder victims had been dismembered "with surgical skill" and their sex organs cut out, indicting the murders had been sexually motivated. "Teeth marks on the torsos suggested the killer was a cannibal as well as a sex fiend. The breasts had been bitten and chewed as if part of the flesh had been consumed." *Uncensored* reported the reopening of police investigation into the death of Christine Gallant in New York; police were also checking reports that Costa had been in California. A young woman Costa knew had died "under mysterious circumstances" in San Francisco's Haight-Ashbury district.

The worst thing about it, Goldman knew, was that among the falsehoods was probably a great deal of truth.

Goldman also brought to the courthouse a copy of the New York Sunday *News* for August 31, containing a two-page story on Tony Costa, "The Murders in the Dunes."

George Killen had been appalled by the *News* story, counting more than forty errors of fact, including the time of arrival of Mary Anne Wysocki and Pat Walsh in Provincetown—"shortly before dark," when their car had stopped outside of 5 Standish Street "in the heart of the city," to be welcomed by a "motherly" Pat Morton. The *News* reported that Leonard Mattluck had walked the girls home from the Foc's'le on Friday night, where they had "read passages from an avant-garde book." The note Costa had written asking for a ride had been "slipped under their door." Carl Benson was represented to be "a Truro patrolman," who had picked up a teletype at the Truro police station on a missing Volkswagen. Costa was described as a "swarthy, black-haired young man sporting sideburns, a bushy mustache and black-rimmed granny glasses." A Burlington-to-Boston bus driver had reported Costa as a passenger to police. The *News* reported Susan Perry buried with Pat Walsh and Mary Anne Wysocki, while the body found on February 8 was that of "Cindy" Monzon.

The *News* had also taken liberties, Goldman charged, with the allegations and exhibits thus far disclosed by the district attorney, describing "a long-bladed razor-sharp machete" found at the grave sites which had apparently been used to carve up the corpses. Goldman said the story contributed "to the atmosphere of prejudgment, the effect of which denied Costa a fair and impartial trial, especially should the trial be heard in six weeks."

Dinis objected to any continuance; the prosecution was calling some sixty witnesses, many of them itinerant, scattered throughout the country. "We face a tremendous burden in any continuance because of our inability to hold them together."

Goldman pointed out that the mobility of Dinis's witnesses was reflected in the mobility of defense witnesses, too. He was also concerned about co-counsel Lawrence Shubow's inability to secure the services of competent psychiatrists. Shubow held conferences with three leading psychiatrists in the Greater Boston area; each had declined to participate despite their expressed interest in the case because of the early date set for the trial. They were, however, prepared to cooperate if more time were available.

Goldman kept up the pressure. "More specifically, I can't go to trial at this stage without having any autopsy report!"

"You haven't received it *yet?*" Beaudreau said, incredulous.

"I have not," Goldman said.

"We haven't received it, either," Dinis said.

"What happened to *that?*" Beaudreau said. "I called Dr. Katsas myself. He told me he would have it in a week."

"If there is a delay, it is not in our office," Dinis said.

"I am not holding you responsible for the autopsy delay," Beaudreau said to Dinis. "I understand all the other documents have been given to the defendant's counsel."

"They have been given to us, but I only have half an apple," Goldman said. "I haven't got what I mainly need. I can't do this piecemeal. This isn't one murder, this is *four* murders. They are all being tried together. I don't think my request for the period of extension is unreasonable because it will be within a nine- or ten-month period. The defendant isn't going anywhere."

Beaudreau took Goldman's request for continuance under advisement.

A week later, Goldman was back in the courtroom to complain, "Very plainly, Your Honor, I have not received the autopsy reports. I can't possibly go forward with this case until I get them."

Beaudreau was baffled. "I spoke to Dr. Katsas myself last Monday. He assured me that you would have them this week. It's not the commonwealth's fault; they would like to have them as much as you."

"I don't agree with the court," Goldman said. "It *is* the commonwealth's fault. There is a responsibility that I should be furnished with this information within a reasonable time. I have got to get somewhere in this case. I am not moving, because I am unable to move."

"I intervened personally in this; I talked to Dr. Katsas twice trying to get these autopsy reports," Beaudreau said. "I don't know why he is delinquent, but I will call him again on Monday and see if I can't get some action. You say you want to fix the date of trial from November third to sometime in March?"

"That's the very earliest I could possibly try it," Goldman said.

"Mr. Costa, have you consulted with your attorneys with respect to this continuance to March or April?" Beaudreau said.

"Yes, I have," Costa said.

"And you are in agreement that this should be?"

"Yes, I am."

"You understand you have the right to a trial in November, if it were not for this motion that you are making now to continue this matter?"

"Yes, I understand it completely."

"All right, I am going to continue this until April sixth."

"That's better," Goldman said.

"There was a motion for severance that I heard in July," Beaudreau said. "I might want to reconsider that. I'll want briefs filed by both parties by November third."

Goldman was very pleased with the session. Beaudreau had apparently talked with a justice of the Supreme Judicial Court who had warned him, "If you don't give severance and you make them try all the cases together, you are going to be overturned."

Goldman explained to Costa: "This business of filing briefs is just to save the judge's face. He'll grant the severance now."

Costa was taken to Barnstable County Hospital the next day and given an upper-GI series to determine whether or not he had an ulcer. "This wasn't a full test," Costa complained. "All they did was make X rays from the stomach up; they didn't check anything below. There was just me and another guy and it took fifteen minutes."

Costa was upset about the delivery of materials for which he intended to set himself up in a leathercraft business that he had received permission to conduct in his cell. "I'll have to turn in the tools at night when I get through working." Costa had received three packages from the Tandy Company and a bill for $105

441

which had been paid from funds provided by Maurice Goldman. "No tools arrived and I ordered them. I want to see the delivery slips to find out how many parcels were delivered. One of the guards told me there was four parcels out there; now today they bring in only three."

Costa was wringing his hands, pacing the conference room, alternately whining and angry. Cavanaugh had never seen him so agitated.

Charlie Zimmerman was uneasy when he met at state police headquarters in Boston on September 23 with George Killen and state police polygraphist John Cahalane to suggest that someone run a specific lie detector examination on Cory Devereau "with special emphasis on the death of Susan Perry."

Zimmerman, usually employed by either police or defense attorneys exclusively on cases, was bothered by the ethics of such a collaboration discreetly arranged by Maurice Goldman. Zimmerman had brought to the conference a transcript of Costa's statements regarding the killing of Susan Perry, alleged to have taken place at Devereau's house, and Costa's visit to her grave. Zimmerman was, however, at a loss to explain to Killen the role Devereau had played in the murders of Mary Anne Wysocki and Patricia Walsh. Costa had, once again, changed his story: After finding Mary Anne mortally wounded in some bushes, Costa had removed two empty shells from the gun and shot her. They had left the area in panic. Then, on Tuesday afternoon, the Gaspar brothers had taken Cory and Tony to Hatch Road. Costa noticed Pat's body had been disturbed—her jacket was missing. They had removed the girls' clothes for Cory to bury. Cory had cut Pat across the midsection; Costa had turned her body over and Cory cut the legs off and took "the top part" away. Cory had brought along doctor's instruments in a white pillowcase, Costa explained. "We used a very sharp, long chrome thing, with a blade that looked like a chisel almost. There were four other things that looked like scalpels, but they weren't. They were really long things. We put them back in the pillowcase after and brought them back to town with us. They were buried on the left side of Cory's house, between the hedges. We just tucked them under there." The instruments had been stolen from doctors' bags, Costa said. "One bag, I believe, came from Dr. Hiebert. I'm not positive which doctor the others came from. There were three bags I know he stole."

From George Killen, Zimmerman now learned the vital investigative facts about the murders and the condition of the bodies.

"It is believed, based on the blood found on the tree near the double graves, that a heavy branch was cut off, leaving a tree peg about eight to ten inches long, used to hang up the victims for purposes of cutting them up," Zimmerman reported to Goldman. To support his "peg theory," Killen pointed out Costa's known practice of tying up his ex-wife and having sex with her while she was suspended from a hook in their bedroom.

State police polygraphist John Cahalane had agreed to rerun tests on Cory Devereau after Zimmerman returned from Europe in two weeks to help frame test questions.

21

Maurice Goldman had still not received the autopsy reports when he appeared in court on September 26 to argue the defense's motion for severance.

"I can see where Walsh and Wysocki might be tried together, since they were the only two murders alleged to have been committed on the same date," Beaudreau said.

"There has been a series of events developing rather rapidly that suggests this motion should lie still with the eventual trial judge," Goldman said. If Beaudreau would reconsider and impose the original order to try the cases together or leave the matter to the trial judge to determine, Goldman would be content.

"I can't take the chance of this matter coming up before the trial judge and having somebody say, conceivably, 'We aren't ready for this one; we are ready for that one.' I am *definitely* going to make a decision on this." Beaudreau wanted to read briefs from both sides before he made up his mind.

To a defense motion for further psychiatric examination,

Beaudreau said, "I have allowed that motion with regard to Dr. Williams."

"My motion didn't limit itself to Dr. Williams," Goldman reminded him. "I merely represented that Dr. Williams was the one we had in mind. As a result of the dissociation on the part of Mr. Abrams, it seems that Dr. Williams apparently likes best to work with Mr. Abrams and not with Mr. Goldman."

Beaudreau smiled at Goldman's candor. "Do you have another psychiatrist in mind at this time?"

Goldman had in mind Dr. Jack Ewalt, former Massachusetts commissioner of mental health and presently the director of the Massachusetts Mental Health Center in Boston.

The following day Tony Costa was taken to the outpatient department of Cape Cod Hospital in Hyannis in severe pain. Costa had begun to feel the symptoms of "acute retention" two days earlier, reporting he was able to urinate only a "few drops," and complaining of nausea.

Urologist Dr. Austin O'Malley didn't think the pain was from kidney stones. Costa said, "He did quite a thorough examination. He couldn't find anything. It wasn't psychosomatic either. He thought it was that the muscle had relaxed from the tranquilizers I had been taking. And he took me right off the tranquilizers and gave me sulpha drugs, so there wouldn't be any infection." A catheterization had been performed. "It was really horrible," Costa said. "I was really sick."

Costa was feeling much better a week later, when Goldman and Lester Allen visited him.

Goldman had finally received the autopsy report on Susan Perry from George Killen.

Costa scanned the first page summary of the pathological findings, paled, and refused to read more:

1. Mutilation of the body into 8 distinct portions
2. Postmortem degeneration
3. Incised wounds of lower extremities and diaphragm
4. Pelvis evisceration with removal of internal genitalia
5. Amputation of the heart
6. Amputation of the breasts

"This is all going to sound pretty awful in court," Goldman said. "That is what we're concerned about."

"Right," Costa said.

"Such extensive dissection would have required a very sharp tool of some kind," Goldman said.

"The only tools I own are my carpentry tools," Costa said.

Costa wanted to talk to George Killen, telling Goldman: "I'd like to find out exactly where he stands, to see if he can do anything to help sway the cause. I feel we can get somewhere with Killen, because Killen seems very discriminate with his work. He can see what is right and what is wrong. Whereas I couldn't get through to Flynn. There's no doubt I'm involved in this thing, but we could present a thing to Killen where he could see that it wasn't only myself. If we have to come to the point of a psychological plea, I think that is where Killen could help."

Before Goldman and Allen left, Costa said, "Tell me something. How do you guys figure on getting me out of this? In five years or something?"

Killen sent Susan Perry's autopsy report and the "front sheet"— the summary of pathological findings—on Pat Walsh, Mary Anne Wysocki and Sydney Monzon to the New York state police who had asked for information regarding the murders of two teenage girls in Chili, New York. "We are particularly interested in the means employed in the homicides and whether any mutilation or removal of parts of the bodies took place," their request said.

Killen replied, "It is our belief that at least the Walsh and Wysocki girl were hung up to a tree feet first, before being cut up."

22

Goldman had secured Tony Costa's employment record from Starline Structures to compare with the narratives of his Labor Day weekend and his daybook journal entries. He found a tangle of contradictions and inconsistencies. For Goldman, however, the most serious time-gap occurred on Monday, September 9, 1968, the day Costa said he was arrested for nonsupport—and the time that Susan Perry disappeared.

"I am considerably upset about that date because the records show something to the contrary," Goldman said. "We find, Tony, that you were not committed here until September twenty-fourth. We have checked the docket at the court in Provincetown, the original papers and the admission records at this jail. We want you to reconsider your dates on that. We think you are slightly in error."

"Well, I can give you two sources: the newspapers, and the telegram I sent to Christine," Costa said.

"Let me tell you that you are wrong about the newspapers," Goldman said. "We checked and we find that the newspapers ran the story on September twenty-fifth."

"Get that telegram," Costa said irritably. "That telegram will straighten out a lot of things."

"It won't help me in the slightest," Goldman said. "Can I tell you why, Tony? It's no method of proof. You can't get past these records."

Costa leaped to his feet. White with fury he threw back his chair. "Well, they are *wrong,* then, man!" he said angrily. "I was delivered to this jail on September tenth! Jimmy Cook arrested me at ten-thirty in the morning of September ninth. Those dates I am *positive* on. I don't know how the hell they screwed these records up, but I knew they screwed them up!"

"Tony, follow me," Goldman said. "We saw the *original* papers; we didn't only take the docket."

"That needs checking," Costa said. "Somebody has been doing something."

"Tony, where do I do the checking now? They just made an out-and-out fool of me arguing that you were here on September tenth. I frame my whole case on the Perry girl around that date, all my pleadings. My whole date chart is useless! I can throw it into the wastebasket."

"Well, I don't know, Mr. Goldman. This has been the whole hang-up in this case. I tell you *exactly* what happened and Christ, there's always something to contradict it! I know it's hard for you guys to believe *anything* in this case."

"Tony, you know you haven't told us the truth," Goldman said.

"No, I didn't. Because it's not up to me to judge someone

446

else. I'm not going to play the part of God! They want to find out who killed the girls, it's up to them to investigate. But they have done nothing. This other guy, he's out there, running around—"

"Tony, you must admit you had some part in the cutting up."

"No, I didn't! I can't stand the sight of blood. I get sick. I had nothing to do with that! I said that because I was pressured into it by Mr. Zimmerman. When I'm pushed by anybody, I say the first thing that comes into my head, just to relieve myself, but now it's gotten out of hand. The fact is, there was a drug deal going on between me, Cory, the two girls and Danny. And the thing is, I didn't count on anybody getting killed. Yes, somebody did get killed in my presence! I was there! My part of the deal was getting rid of the car—I took that as my obligation. This was the extent of my goings-on in the case. I did my part and *he* did his part. And now I'm stuck with the rest of it. The only difference is that I'm in here and *he's* out there!"

"It's more than the only difference," Goldman said evenly. "It points to *you* too much. Your trouble is that you were on drugs; that is why you've got the dates confused."

"No, sir, that is *wrong*," Costa said, furious. "I was here September tenth! I was supposed to be in New York with Chrissie on the twelfth and I was here already two days. I stayed overnight in the Provincetown jail on September ninth."

"There is no record of you being in the Provincetown jail on September ninth!" Goldman said flatly.

"Then someone is doing a lot of caddiling with things out there," Costa said.

"Now, Tony, just hear me through, please. Give consideration to what I am saying. I believe that during those two weeks you were using LSD or speed extensively."

"Mr. Goldman, I was not using *anything!*" Costa shouted. "I was *here* September tenth! That is a fact. I know it, my mother knows it and Avis knows it."

"Avis doesn't know it," Goldman said. "Suppose Avis tells us that it was the twenty-fourth, what would you say?"

"Then I will say that *she* was on LSD, that's what I would say."

"Assuming that the date is not the date, then you have to tell me what you were doing in the way of drugs in that period," Goldman said.

"That is the date, Mr. Goldman. There is no doubt in my

mind!" Costa said. "I'm not going to cop out on drugs, because my mind isn't that bad."

"You lost two weeks there, Tony!" Goldman said.

"Mr. Goldman, I didn't *lose* anything! September tenth I was here!"

"There is no point in you and I fighting," Goldman said. "We have to meet the situation. We won't discuss it any further. All I can tell you is the records are against you. Just give it some thought now and we will pass it by for the moment. Now, did you have a chance to see the autopsy report on the Walsh girl?"

Costa was slumped in his chair. "No," he said, petulantly.

"I didn't think you did; it just came in," Goldman said, opening his briefcase. "Take a minute and read this report."

Costa was not interested. Pretending to read, his eyes scanned the margins, flipping over the pages before he contemptuously tossed the report on the table.

"Did you have sexual relations with her after you shot her?" Goldman asked.

"I didn't shoot her!"

"*Who* shot her?"

"Devereau shot her. And this is a fact which I intend to prove one way or the other."

"When did you cut up the body?" Goldman said.

"The whole thing happened on Sunday. I got a thing here . . . a report I did. It straightens this out, too. I have come around to what actually happened. And this is something else I think we should work on, too, to get myself out of this whole damn mess."

When Goldman left he took with him Costa's "definitive" version of the murders of Pat Walsh and Mary Anne Wysocki. "I have not diverted one degree, from the truth, no matter what you now think. I give you facts," Costa added in a note attached to his seven-page report of a night "of horror, confusion and panic, satiated by fear."

Goldman was disappointed to read a reiteration of the same story of the drug deal, the argument at the hold between Cory and Pat Walsh while Costa returned to the car to fetch Cory's works. Costa had not diverged much from his other version of how Cory had killed the girls except that the bodies had been put "to one side" before they had left the woods. The next day Cory reported he had returned to the area with Eddie Silva, dismembered and buried the girls. On Tuesday, Costa had gone to the woods with Cory to check the area, he explained. "Because I wanted to make sure everything was squared away and intact. We went to the graves and I felt like spongy soil, so I felt that was it."

23

"I didn't trust anybody, I checked every goddamned record and docket myself!" Goldman said to Costa when he returned to the Barnstable House of Correction two days later. "I also talked with Avis."

"I was so sure about that date," Costa said. "I was positive."

Docile and contrite, Costa seemed in an amenable mood for Goldman to test out the defense position he had formulated. "Tony, what we have to try to do is, if a man gets drunk and commits a crime, drunkenness is not an excuse, but it is a defense in mitigation of one's actions. It can result in a second-degree charge. With a second-degree you are able to defend yourself. We can get a sentence which can subsequently be reduced, paroled or pardoned. With a first-degree, you just won't have that situation. Now, if we could show the excessive use of LSD and whatever the hell else you used, I think we would have that mitigation. The point I'm getting at is, under the standards for knowing right from wrong—which is a question for a jury to decide—we have a problem to worry about medically and psychiatrically. If you committed these acts, all four of them—now, don't *jump* at me!" Goldman said when Costa gripped the arms of his chair and leaned forward. "And they were all committed by you under drugs, we are in the same position whether you tell me you had something to do with Pat and nothing to do with the Monzon girl or the Perry girl. It won't make a hell of a big difference. The outcome is the same if it's one or four or forty-four. Do you see what I'm driving at?"

"Yeah," Costa said.

"There is no way to relieve you of this if there is no drug situation involved," Goldman said. "If you were completely under the control and domination of drugs, it throws an entirely new phase into the case. It gives us a chance to work. Now, we spent three months in one direction, which was just a waste of time. Don't waste more time on our part, because it doesn't do you any good, Tony."

"Yeah, right."

"I don't care *what* you did, we are your *friends*, just the same. We are your *lawyers*. We are going to fight for you with the last drop of blood that is in us! In every way, shape or manner, we are going to make every move we know how. But we have got to get your full cooperation. Now, what can you tell me about Sydney Monzon? Did she ever go out with you to the woods where your canister was?"

"Yeah, she did. One time, right after the Callis thing, to pick up some stuff for Roland. She could go anytime she wanted to. That's all I had to do with Sydney."

"If you had anything to do with the Perry girl all you have to do is say so," Goldman said. "Now, with respect to September tenth, did you have sexual intercourse with Susan at your house in Dedham?"

"It would be long before that, way before Labor Day," Costa said. "The night before she left."

"Tony, do you suppose it's possible that you had something to do with all four murders and didn't even know you were doing it by reason of your being under the spell, or the influence of the combination of hash, pills, or from using speed, LSD or anything?"

"With Susan and Sydney I'd have to say no. Because I knew exactly where I was and what I was doing. There was no heavy drug use during Sydney's time. On the September thing, I was in Dedham at that time."

"The thing that bothers us, is the similarity of the dismemberment, the removal of the skin," Goldman said. "I haven't got the autopsy reports on the other two yet, but I'm told the patterns are all pretty much the same. Now, you had relations with Pat on Saturday night?"

"Yeah."

"How many times?"

"Once, as far as I can recall."

"Were you on drugs that night?"

"Just grass."

"Did you have anal intercourse with her?"

"Have *who?*"

"Anal intercourse."

"No, I didn't."

"How do you account for the sperm in her . . . fanny, as well as in her uterus?"

"That I can't account for," Costa said. "This is something new to me."

"Well, they found it in both portions of the body," Goldman said. "This is something we have to account for."

"Well, it has nothing to do with *me,* I can assure you of that," Costa said loftily.

"Was Patricia's head severed from her body?"

"I assume so. Like I said, I don't really know because I wasn't present. This is what I'm getting at—it is getting rather imperative to me anyway, that we do something on my counterpart."

Goldman was startled to hear Costa refer to his "counterpart." "Your *counterpart?*" Goldman said. "Who is that?"

"Mr. Devereau," Costa said. "This is what's getting me nervous. Because here we are going along a path where I am facing everything. The fact is, I don't know how much benefit it is going to be to me. The DA's office isn't doing anything. I think it's up to us."

"That isn't so at all, Tony!" Goldman said. "You can't say that they are not doing anything. Following up your original story involving Cory, they picked him up and gave him a lie detector test, and he came out of it with flying colors. Now, he is going back in again. The reason we want to hold him up again is I want to get all the autopsy reports first. Charlie Zimmerman is going to assist in preparing the interrogation, so we will make sure the right questions are asked. So you mustn't say they are not cooperating with us. They cooperated when I sold a bill of goods to let us do this trip to the Massachusetts Mental Health. No one else has ever done this before, no other murder case. They would have sent you to Bridgewater. That goddamned place! You take their report and they say that you should stand trial for first-degree murder; that you are a murderer—period. That is the substance of the Bridgewater report."

Costa was to be transported under guard to and from the center where he was to receive a complete psychiatric profile.

"There will be a whole troop of psychiatrists, some of them are graduate psychiatrists, some of them students," Goldman explained. "You are going to have a total take-out on your personality, on your physical well-being; they will do a complete series on you, so that when you get out of there we will know everything about your mental state. You are going to go starting next week," Goldman said. "And it is costing the state a fortune to do this; but we got away with it."

"Good for us!"

"Larry Shubow brought this off," Goldman said. "He is going to join us in the defense. He is the greatest lawyer sitting at the defense table with me. I got a hold of him because he is a lawyer, but also he is president of a chapter of Mental Health."

"I saw him the other day," Costa said. "He was the fellow with the gray hair."

"We'll have you going into Boston six or seven times," Goldman continued. "You are going to go under custody of a guard and come home here each night."

"If they ask me about the case, should I let them know anything?"

"Definitely," Goldman said. "Speak freely."

"That's good! I sort of am looking forward to it. I will discuss my drug problem openly. I have come to the point where I despise drugs, because of what they have done to me." Costa said. "I hope I don't have to urinate when I get up there."

"You hope *what?*"

"I hope that I don't have to urinate when I get up there. I urinate every twenty-five minutes to a half an hour now," Costa said. "The pain has subsided quite a bit; it's just the strain now, that's all."

Preparing to leave, Goldman said, "Now, Tony, you *did* some of the cutting up. You might just as well tell us."

"I can't really recall," Costa said blandly. "I mean, I am telling you what I remember to be true. Why I am stressing this is because you are going to do a cross-examination of this guy; and

452

he can't possibly say anything against me without incriminating himself."

"Tony, don't try to do the thinking. You tried to do the thinking before when you sent us into three months of wasting time. Let *us* do the thinking out. Under no circumstances are you going to get any cooperation from Cory. Cory is going to say that he knows absolutely nothing about it at all; that you went down there alone. I haven't got a man, for example, who can say he picked you and Cory up that night—"

"Did you guys investigate that truck thing?" Costa said. "There was a name and everything described on that truck."

"If you only *knew* what we went through on that truck thing!"

Goldman wanted Costa to concentrate again on the events that had occurred on Sunday night. Charlie Zimmerman had returned from Europe and had scheduled another test for Costa on Saturday, October 26.

Meanwhile, John Cahalane had run another polygraph on Cory Devereau.

Devereau was clear.

24

Charlie Zimmerman reviewed previous polygrams he had run on Tony Costa, listening to the tapes in the kitchen of the summer cottage he owned in Sandwich. Zimmerman realized he had reached his limit with Costa, having brought him from a position of no involvement in the murders at all to the edge of confession. Costa had admitted stabbing Mary Anne Wysocki— before he retracted his story—and being "responsible" for Christine Gallant's death.

Zimmerman could put no more pressure on Costa without

jeopardizing their whole relationship and risk having Costa renege on all his previous admissions. There was nothing to be gained by having Costa confess to him, then later repudiate his confession to Goldman by complaining that he had been "pressured," as he had done following the release of the autopsy reports. In Zimmerman's opinion, the case needed new blood.

"I said to myself, 'Charlie, you've had it,'" Zimmerman told Warren Holmes, a longtime friend and associate polygraphist. Zimmerman invited him to join in the October examination. A tall, handsome man, Holmes's "positive" approach to examinations was similar to Zimmerman's technique.

Holmes did a pretest interview. Costa was apathetic, disinterested in another test, when Zimmerman introduced Holmes to him in a vacant cell down the corridor from Costa's own. Zimmerman watched Costa's demeanor and attentiveness; when Holmes faltered in his questions, or Costa veered off the subject, Zimmerman took over.

Then Holmes ran a test.

Costa was still giving marked, multiple reactions and Zimmerman was discouraged during the session's break for lunch. Zimmerman had exhausted every technique in his considerable repertoire, feeling that Costa was very close to confessing, if only the right buttons could be pushed. He knew from experience that it was often a collateral issue, not the crime itself, which stood in the way of a subject's confession.

Zimmerman recalled only one occasion in his interrogations when Costa appeared to acknowledge his possible guilt. When Zimmerman had mentioned that if he *had* committed the murders, Costa would need medical help, Costa had leaped at the pretext to exclaim, "You're damn right I would!" Holmes wondered if they might not try the medical approach in view of Costa's forthcoming psychiatric examination. Goldman had so impressed Costa with Dr. Jack Ewalt's credentials and reputation that Costa regarded his approaching examination a signal honor. Stressing the medical elements and taking an objective, "scientific" approach might give Costa the pretext he needed to bring himself to confess. "Let's go after him," Holmes said.

Zimmerman thought the new approach might be better accomplished if Holmes led the questioning. Because Costa had already lied repeatedly to Zimmerman, he might find it easier to confess to a stranger.

Twenty minutes later, Holmes told Zimmerman, "I think he's ready."

Costa looked away when Zimmerman entered the cell.

Holmes said, formally, "Now, Tony, for the benefit of those interested in your case, and being the best defense in your behalf, I would like you, for the record, to disclose to us as fully and truthfully as you can, your involvement in this case."

"I will state exactly what I remember so that it will benefit the psychiatrist evaluating me, my psychological outlook, my psychological factors," Costa said, now parroting Holmes's voice and manner.

Costa paused. There was a slight grimace, as if to apologize in advance for some distasteful but necessary task which he was about to perform. "The fact is, I *do* remember committing these murders," Costa said quietly. "They were committed by me, for reasons I don't really know. There's a lot I don't really remember. I'd like to have someone study into it."

"What do you think now as you look back and try to understand yourself?" Holmes said. "What do you feel was the underlying cause?"

"I don't really know this either," Costa said earnestly. "There were drugs involved, I know this; but I don't think that's the total cause."

"You mean there's a psychological basis too complex for you to understand?" Holmes said.

"Right," Costa said. "Exactly."

"Do you recognize any force toward gratification of a sexual nature, Tony?" Zimmerman said gently.

"There could have been," Costa said meekly. "There was some drive there, an impulse."

"Did you ever feel that you were two people?" Holmes said. "That during the commission of these crimes you were actually watching someone else doing it?"

"Very much so," Costa said. "You realize that you are committing the crime, but it doesn't really seem as though it's you. It's another person; it's someone else."

"In looking back now, what can you tell us in reference to Susan Perry?" Zimmerman said. "What do you recall?"

"I can't really remember anything dramatic, other than the fact that she was gone and that she was buried. I know she was dismembered, but to what extent I don't remember."

"Was there any degree of sexual gratification involved in cutting up her body?"

"I don't think so," Costa said. "It just became something that had to be done."

"Was there a certain fascination about the dismembering the body, even though it may not have a sexual implication?" Holmes said. "Perhaps combined with a child's curiosity, like the dissection of an animal or a frog has a certain fascination? Not knowing the anatomy of a body, was there a certain curiosity as to what the different parts are, and that sort of thing?"

"Yes, I think this is true. As far as I can recall there was a certain fascination there," Costa said. "This is something I can't understand either. It was a little scary while it was happening."

"Do you recall any of the cutting up of Susan Perry?" Zimmerman said.

"No, I don't."

"Do you feel that because of the state of mind you were in at the time of the murders, you were not recording on your memory track precise details?" Holmes said. "So that now it's just a hazy, bizarre event which makes it difficult for you to recall?"

"I remember very little of what went on. I remember very little of the act. It's sort of like a dream, yet it really happened."

"Tony, if we talk about Pat and Mary Anne, you can recall more vividly, right?" Zimmerman said.

"Yes, very much so."

"What is your explanation as to why you can recall more here and less there? Is there fear involved?"

"I think there's an element of fear," Costa said. "I think there's an element of drug use. I think the LSD helped me to recall quite a bit because it's very vivid in its portrayal of anything."

"You mean it overactivates the senses so that everything seems to be dramatized in slow motion?" Holmes asked.

"Yes, everything is tremendously exaggerated to the point where a small piece of material that might feel smooth is suddenly rough and distorted. This is I think why I remember the Pat and Mary Anne incident in detail—*some* of the detail anyway. About three-quarters I remember and one-quarter I don't; that part is very vague."

"Does the effect of these drugs also heighten the mental response to the act of cutting up these bodies? The fascination of it?" Holmes said.

"Yes, it does. It's like—well, there's no comparison. You can't say it's like anything. It's something you just can't experience normally. With LSD, in looking at these things and going through this, it's like being in another world completely. You are not even in your own body, mind or anything."

"Do you find it difficult to reconcile the acts with your present mind, the mental state that you are in now?" Holmes said.

"There is no reconciliation for these crimes!" Costa said.

"Is there something you try to suppress from your mind because it's too painful to you?"

"Yes," Costa said.

"Is there disgust involved?" Zimmerman said.

"There's quite a bit of everything," Costa said. "There's disgust; there's hatred for the act itself; there's hatred for the use of drugs; there's fear. There's a little bit of everything; a lot of everything."

"Do you recall the difference in your activities pertaining to Mary Anne and to Pat as opposed to Susan Perry?" Zimmerman said. "How about Sydney Monzon?"

"With Sydney I can't remember anything. There's nothing I can remember, except being at the site of the grave."

"I want you to think about this very carefully," Holmes said. "Before you ever did this, did you ever have thoughts about killing? Did you have any fantasies about it? Any degree of fascination to see what it would be like to kill somebody?"

"Prior to this experience, no, I never had any," Costa said. "I've deplored any kind of hurt inflicted upon anyone."

"What do you think triggered this outburst of aggression toward these girls?"

"I actually believe that it was drugs in every sense of the word," Costa said.

"Your contacts with all these girls was when you were under the influence of drugs?" Zimmerman asked.

"Right," Costa said. "What kept our society together most of the time was drugs, the drug culture. *Everybody* used drugs! This is what we gathered for; to use drugs. Right up to that time I had an excellent supply; I was not lacking anything."

"How much of a feeling of guilt do you have, knowing you

457

killed these girls?" Holmes asked. "Can you remember any part of it?"

"A tremendous amount of it came back to me, that's why I stayed high most of the time; because it was tremendously hard to bear."

"Tony, when you speak of the horror of being there, what is projected in front of your mind? What do you see?" Zimmerman said. "When you are talking to us right now about these horrors, what is the outstanding thing you see in front of you?"

"What I see is the death, the shooting of these innocent girls; and then their dismembering."

"*You* pulled the trigger?" Zimmerman said.

"Right."

"What else? Is there noise?"

"No, it isn't that," Costa said. "It's the feeling that they were innocent young people; and for no reason whatsoever they were killed."

"In other words, you are finding it difficult to justify what you did?" Holmes said.

"There is *no* justification," Costa said fiercely.

"Tony what I mean is, do you *see* the dead person, or your activities?" Zimmerman said. "Do you see each of these people in front of you when you see that moment of horror?"

"I see the whole moment as it happened. I see the actual moment of causing death."

"Were there any actual screams with any of these girls? Was anything said?" Zimmerman said. "Was there anything outstanding that you recall? And I draw on my experience; because when there is a last call from somebody before they die, this is an extremely vivid experience. I have known in many cases that this was coming back and hounding a particular individual. What noises do you recall that are coming back continually?"

"I recall Mary Anne's gurgling sounds," Costa said. "That keeps coming back."

"Was that from being shot or from the knife?"

"That was from being shot," Costa said. "It was just a gurgling sound, a horrid sound."

"And that sound indicated to you death, or close to death?"

"Right," Costa said.

"Why did you shoot a gun when you heard that gurgling

458

sound?" Zimmerman asked. "Was there an area of fear, an area of force behind you? What was it?"

"My emotions were distorted, shattered," Costa said. "I think it was fear, and sympathy almost."

"Putting her out of her misery?" Holmes said.

"Yes," Costa said. "She took off about fifty, sixty feet up the road from the hold. She'd been shot; she was lying on the ground when I came to her and I just took the pistol. . . ."

"Did you cut up any of these girls while they were still alive?" Holmes prompted after a moment. He had decided to risk it.

"Pardon?"

"Did you cut up any of these girls, or dismember their bodies, while any of them were still alive?" Zimmerman put in.

"No."

"Why did you do it?" Holmes said.

"I don't know," Costa said softly. *"Why* didn't enter my mind. It just became something that had to be done."

"The cutting up was always a decision you made *after* the body was dead?" Zimmerman said.

"Yes."

"Now, Tony, are you sure that there was no sexual gratification at the moment of either killing or cutting up, to the point of ejaculation?" Zimmerman said.

"There was no sexual gratification whatsoever!" Costa said firmly.

"Did you masturbate at any of these sites?"

"No," Costa said. "There was nothing there. There was no sexual gratification whatsoever. The whole thing was so horrible, there *couldn't* be."

"Are you talking about it now?" Zimmerman asked, "or what your feelings were at the time?"

"No, at the time."

"It was also horrible then? The horror of the situation disgusted you as far as any sexual drive?"

"Right," Costa said. "I just became completely nil."

"Can you give us any explanation as to why sperm was found in Pat and Mary Anne?" Zimmerman said. "Is it possible you could have had sexual contacts with these girls and forgotten it? Is that within the realm of possibility, Tony?"

"I guess so," Costa said. "It's possible."

"Do you recall any such thing?"

"No, I don't recall anything whatsoever to do with anything like that."

"Why did you take part of Mary Anne and put her in the grave with the other girl?" Holmes said. "Do you feel that this was linking the crimes together?"

"I think, if anything, it would have just been for compactness."

"Less space available in one grave and more space available in the other?"

"Yes," Costa said.

"Did you ever go to these graves alone at other times?" Zimmerman said. "Before these bodies were found?"

"I went there on one occasion."

"To what grave?"

"To the Perry and Monzon ones."

"What did you do there?"

"I dug a little bit of the earth."

"For what reason?"

"To see if a body was really there," Costa said.

"You were trying to bring back the realization that you had actually committed these murders on a previous occasion?" Holmes said. "That it wasn't all just a nightmare?"

"Right," Costa said.

"Since we are making this tape for the purpose of allowing psychiatrists to analyze the situation, are there any other psychological aspects about these killings that you don't understand yourself?"

"I don't really understand any of it," Costa said. "Why it was done, what influence drugs had on me, or if they were only a part of the influence. I don't know exactly what was there. There's nothing else I can think of."

"After you committed your first murder why did you feel you had to do it again?" Holmes said. "What was there that prompted this type of behavior?"

"I don't know," Costa said.

"In reference to these girls, is there anything that you kept as a souvenir?" Zimmerman wanted to know. "Something to cherish because it was a part of them?"

Costa's eyes widened with horror. "No! I didn't want anything like that after I realized. I didn't want anything to bring them back at all!"

Holmes eased off. "As you look back on these acts and the realization that you are the person that did it, do you feel that you are mentally sick?"

"Oh, yes, I believe so," Costa said. "There's a problem there that has to be ironed out. There has got to be *something* there, otherwise the murders wouldn't have been committed. Somewhere there has to be something."

"Have you tried to analyze this yourself?" Holmes said.

"Yes, and I don't really come up with anything. It doesn't make sense. I can't find it at all," Costa said. "I don't know what it is."

Zimmerman ran a test. It was negative. Costa was still not telling the complete truth of what he knew about the murders. . . .

Goldman had observed that Costa's confession had made no mention of Cory Devereau.

Goldman saw no point in having Charlie Zimmerman run further polygraphs. Costa had gone as far as he was likely to go in his confession. Perhaps the memories of the murders were buried so deeply in his subconscious—whether committed by that side of his nature that was represented as Cory Devereau or the part that was the real Tony Costa—that they were beyond his powers to retrieve. Costa had not "beaten" the polygraph; rather, he had talked it to a stalemate. Goldman wondered if the real answer was not to be found between the lines of the disturbing poem Costa dashed off following his last session with Charlie Zimmerman:

You

(In memory of all
broken, desecrated men)

I

With love in my mind
peace in my heart
I welcomed you into my school
a school you blindly sought
to find, desperately, intensely
you asked me what I knew

I would teach you all I knew
The curriculum—love you said
life your goal. And me . . .
I was your teacher.

Through your eyes you saw nothing
Yet you sensed freedom
had approached you
you succumbed to its power
gracefully
allowed it to draw you closer
to its womb, magnetically
Then you envisioned me
"Come," I called, "I'll show you the way."
You came.
A child you thought. A baby
Freedom!
Independence. A mother, wife, lover.
A Free woman. And me . . .
I was your teacher.

With each new lesson
your plot unraveled
Soon my world would shrink
to black oblivion—lost!
You considered only you
You alone reigned supreme
casting knowledge aside
to grow damp and dusty
in the dungeons of your mind
The only book you had cherished
its pages blank,
now lies filled
cluttered with the decomposed
memories of your wickedness.
You have never read it
it speaks to you aloud
shouting the tales of all
those you have destroyed
And me . . .
I loved you.

I wait—listening to the echo
of your pain
haunting you as you stumble
through the stolid crypts . . .
crawling, searching for me
amidst the dung and stench
of dead men's bones
From the tombs of your mind
from the ebony past
I hear you scream,
"I will help you, you need it,
please allow me."
Yes—you are irony itself!
And me . . .
I lay silent.

Now you search the fortress
the citadel you once destroyed
but only the cobwebs remain
Even the spiders know you.
They hide, rushing from their webs,
to seek the secure dark crevasses
beneath the rubble you peruse
Yet, even some of them,
cannot escape your crushing foot
And me . . .
I lay broken

You stand in the vast expanse
of distance
stopping to look back
as a warrior queen
surveying the land she has left
charred, barren, conquered.
What you have destroyed
You can no longer repair
The grass will not grow
Flowers will not bloom
Amidst the garbage
The dead must die
Don't look back, travel on

You are a plague . . .
A dark, hideous plague
And me . . .
I taught you all I knew.

(by A. Costa)
Oct. 69

25

Before he was to examine Antone Costa, Dr. Jack Ewalt received a dossier of background material which included five of Costa's drawings in color and nine in charcoal. Costa had twice painted a picture in which a single, small figure was engulfed by his surroundings. Asked who the figure was, Costa had replied, "I think it's Tony."

Ewalt received a profile of the four murder victims, a taped interview of Avis during which she talked about her sex life, the autopsies of Susan Perry and Patricia Walsh and a short biography of Tony Costa along with—according to Goldman—"his somewhat involved recollections of what took place. In all his discussions of the murders," Goldman continued, "Costa has always given names to the mysterious 'other self' he claims to have been involved—Chuck Hansen, Danny O'Neil, Mark McClusky, Cory Devereau and sometimes just 'he,' or 'him.' In the interests of justice, there should be no limitations in your examination of Costa."

Accompanied by two corrections officers, Costa was taken to the Massachusetts Mental Health Center in the Roxbury section of Boston for the "diagnostic and evaluative study," by court order and at the request of his attorneys to determine his psychiatric, neurologic and psychological status.

Ewalt had agreed to examine Costa only if the sheriff's office took responsibility for his conduct and custody by bringing Costa to the center under guard and returning him to Barnstable at the end of a day's testing. The center, being open-doored, did not deal with patients who had committed capital offenses. At no time was Costa to be seen, except while in custody of the two officers who would also be present during all of Costa's tests. Admitted as a "day hospital guest," Costa was carried on the records as an out-patient.

Jack Ewalt was the architect of President Kennedy's program on mental health. He held the Bullard chair of psychiatry at Harvard, and was the former president of the American Psychiatric Association. He had resigned as Massachusetts Commissioner of Mental Health, fearing he was spending too much time in administration work. A slender man in his late fifties with a bony, aesthetic face, Ewalt presented an elegant, austere and chilly appearance that belied his great personal warmth. Originally from Texas, a slight drawl lingered in his measured speech. Held in enormous respect and admiration by colleagues and co-workers, Ewalt wore casually the honors bestowed upon his distinguished career. Ewalt himself conducted a first interview with Antone Costa in the presence of Dr. Steven Sharfstein, who would direct Costa's overall examination.

Despite his manacles, Costa greeted Ewalt and Sharfstein with a broad smile and a firm handshake. Sharfstein was impressed by the tall, broad-shouldered, handsome young man dressed in a blue turtleneck shirt and immaculate white denims, observing him to be "quite assertive, able to keep control of the situation, with excellent eye-to-eye contact and rapid, animated speech." Costa had little tolerance for silence. Sharfstein observed the well-developed, muscular body of a normal young person "in no acute distress," during Costa's physical examination. Costa complained of having suffered urinary retention and some "tenderness" over the abdominal area.

Costa was turned over to clinical psychology intern, Dr. Richard Bennett "to look for any psychotic processes." Over a period of four days, Bennett would administer the Minnesota Multi-Phasic Personality Inventory, a Wechsler IQ test, Rorschach, draw-a-picture, and a thematic apperception test (TAT), the same tests Costa had undergone at Bridgewater.

Costa appeared to Bennett to be "a thoughtful and quite controlled man who was obviously trying to win my friendship and sympathy. I often felt that he was speaking, not to me so much as to his jury. He used somewhat stilted speech which seemed to reflect his efforts at control. There were occasional indications, mainly in his posture, that the tests were putting a strain on him."

Costa was careful never to take the initiative or to participate spontaneously in the tests, being passively compliant to instructions. Bennett found Costa's TAT stories—a series of pictures from which Costa was asked to construct a story—particularly illuminating. Costa tended to give a great deal of unimportant detail, rather than a continuous, integrated narrative. Hostile or aggressive material was entirely absent from Costa's stories, even those matching pictures which most subjects who took the test saw as having aggressive content.

Bennett observed certain "childlike qualities" in Costa's stories, most of which took place in the span of a single day, all conflicts being resolved and the protagonist going home to enjoy hobbies and family life before "toddling off to bed."

"Another immature quality is his great interest in what people do in bed together and his inability to repress telling me about this," Bennett noted. Costa's stories seemed to be those of a child "who cannot resist the temptation of peeking into the grown-up world after the other children have gone to bed."

Many of Costa's stories suggested an ability to dissociate himself from his own behavior by assigning it to another time or state of consciousness, and his tendency to speak of himself in the third person. Costa told a story of a woman with a hangover who will have the courage to face her situation because the effect of the evening before "will do away with itself." Changes of state were also evident in Costa's use of such phrases as "has come out of his nap," instead of "woke up from his nap," and "changed themselves into," rather than "changed into" their winter underwear.

Costa's Rorschach ink-blot test demonstrated a preoccupation with eyes and faces, and showed much concern for the quality of their expressions, whether or not they were assuming an observing posture—such qualities usually assigned to the eyes. In fully half the blots, Costa described a face, always mentioning the eyes first. ("This face shows apathy because the eyes are blank";

"Looks hungry, because the eyes are sad.") Costa revealed that his own eyesight was "not as good as it used to be." Costa could recognize material that conveyed emotion, but was not spontaneously emotional himself.

"Whatever emotions he expressed were carefully controlled by intellectual processes, to give the outward appearance of emotional experiences," Bennett reported. "It remains questionable whether feeling experiences are available to him."

Costa demonstrated a high degree of skill at manipulating the impression others had of him, closely watching Bennett's reactions before committing himself to answers. Such a preoccupation with observing or being observed, and Costa's extremely guarded approach to new experience, and his need to structure, analyze and eliminate all unknown quantities of ambiguity, was part of a "paranoid style" Costa displayed throughout the tests, but was not seen by Bennett as "psychotically paranoid."

The most striking feature of the tests was the "almost complete denial of aggressive material," due to Costa's attempts to give "socially approved answers" with regard to self-control and moral values. Costa fervently denied any hostile impulses, expressing naive trust in others. Bennett reported, "He appears to have overplayed his hand in attempting to look passive and benign."

The overall test record did not indicate any psychotic condition of paranoia or other schizophrenia, or sufficient evidence to indicate "borderline" states. Bennett thought a diagnosis of "severe character disorder" was sustained.

Costa spoke freely at the ward meetings with dayroom nurses and staff and discussed those feelings of mutual fear being expressed by other patients toward him. Costa was very polite and spoke of getting help "to ascertain why the crimes occurred and to gain insight into my own motivations."

Costa also participated in two group therapy sessions. In the first, he tried talking to other patients about prison life and how much he missed his children. Costa spoke in a flat monotone with no change in inflection or rate of speech. Costa came to the second group session late, and asked what was going on. There was little response, much of the time remaining spent in silence.

Costa spent his free time playing cards and Ping-Pong, and expressed interest in going to the gym and using the swimming pool. The pleasant atmosphere of the center appeared to have a good effect. Costa told the officers with him that he felt "more like a patient than a prisoner."

On one of his drives back to Barnstable, Donald Parker observed Costa to be happier than he had seen him since his incarceration. Of his trip to Boston, Costa said, "It was one of the best days of my life."

During his consultation with Dr. Ewalt, Costa confessed he had found the responsibilities of marriage and fatherhood unbearable. From his review of the tape Avis Costa had made in connection with her married life, Ewalt deduced the marriage had been turbulent, marked with frequent separations and punctuated by "sexual irregularities." Costa had suffered problems with potency, going for long periods without intercourse. At other times he had contented himself by masturbating against his wife's back or thigh, after efforts to make her unconscious—"so he could do whatever he liked"—had failed because Avis became panic-stricken and refused. The marriage had grown increasingly tenuous as Costa became more and more involved with drugs.

The year prior to his arrest, Costa had been stoned most of the time and had difficulty remembering many details of the period. He had suffered a complete memory gap between September 10, when Susan Perry was murdered, through September 24, when he was jailed for nonsupport.

Costa had been deeply affected by the death of Christine Gallant who had committed suicide with the Nembutal pills Costa had given to her. He explained, "She knew my life had been threatened because of my knowledge of the first two murders that had already taken place."

Without drugs for the past eight months Costa pronounced himself "relaxed and relieved." Looking back, Costa referred to the drug scene as "the worst mistake in my life; it left me empty inside and was a waste of my life."

Ewalt found the tape Avis Costa had recorded with Lester Allen of questionable value in arriving at a diagnosis. "Because Mr. Allen, though well-intentioned, obviously asks many leading questions, all directed toward proving Mr. Costa mentally ill or sexually peculiar."

In the advance material sent to Ewalt, Goldman had pointed out that "in talking with Costa about girls, the distinction had to be made between those he has slept with and those he has engaged in sexual intercourse." Defense investigators had learned that Costa would sleep as closely as possible with women, expressing a desire for the warmth and closeness of a female body while he slept. Costa had denied any abnormality in the practice.

Costa was more subdued and "a bit depressed" during his second week of examination, Dr. Sharfstein observed. To begin, Costa saw Ewalt for an hour. Speaking freely, rapidly, Costa answered all questions unhesitatingly and rarely "blanked"; but was often vague and difficult to pin down. Costa struck Ewalt as often grandiose, seeing certain parallels in his life with the life of Christ, and calling the buildings he had helped construct on Cape Cod "monuments" that his children could be proud of.

Costa's interview with another psychiatrist, Dr. Richard Shader, did not lead to any major findings. Shader did not consider Costa overtly psychotic.

"What stands out is his severe psychopathy," Shader observed. "This is so severe that a diagnosis of 'borderline' would be appropriate as well. Shader suggested that Costa had "an over-idealized view of his father" since infancy. "Females, for instance his mother, had betrayed the father and him by remarrying and having another son. The episode with the girl from Somerville reinforces this fury and it is evident that, despite his protestations, Mr. Costa is a very angry man."

Costa's identification with the murder victims went into "a scheme of a sado-masochistic continuum," the murdering and cutting up of that part of himself that is "rotten" or "bad."

"It is unlikely that if he committed these murders he did so in a rational state of mind," Shader concluded. "Drugs—especially LSD—complicate matters, but a form of dissociative reaction is likely as well—that 'another' had actually done the killings."

Costa spent an hour discussing the murders with Sharfstein and Ewalt. Costa was tense, frequently blinked his eyes, and pushed his fingers through his hair, Ewalt observed. "His story gets a little confused as he attempts to rationalize why he was an accomplice, but not really involved. He then states he thinks he *was* involved to some degree, but can't remember. From that position, Costa went to a third level, explaining he was so 'out on drugs,' he didn't know what went on. He then contradicted this by recalling specifically leaving the scene with his alleged accomplice."

Costa described himself as "passive, tranquil and at peace now." He considered himself safe enough to go free, having himself and his impulses well organized and under control. "I believe I've learned my lesson, so that I would no longer get involved in drugs," Costa told Ewalt. "This, I believe, is what caused my problems in the first place."

Costa recalled a dream he had had the night before: "Everything is being flooded, the water is flowing in all around me and is washing everything away." Costa had awakened and been somewhat upset. "I ate a couple of cookies, then I went back to sleep; and the dream took up where it had left off."

Sharfstein observed water imagery in many of Costa's accounts: the death of his girlfriend in the bathtub in New York, the death of his father at sea, the term "gurgling" Costa used to describe one of the murder victims' last moments, the idea of death and purification associated with water.

Costa was friendly and cooperative during his final consultation with Ewalt, the opening subject of which dealt with the tape Avis had recorded about their married life. Costa had gotten the idea for suspending his wife by her heels from reading a book. "This was the time we got into this soul type thing, involving blood control and all this other trash which goes along with yoga," Costa explained. "It was more or less an agreement between Avis and I. She was uptight because she had never had an orgasm since we were married." Eventually Ewalt got Costa to admit to sexual relations with some of the murder victims while living, but Costa denied any "irregular sex practices" with them.

Ewalt found it difficult to determine whether Costa was lying or was actually describing periods of amnesia that he suffered while under the influence of drugs. Costa denied knowing any details of the murders, except in a "flashback" recollection of finding one of the girls lying on the ground covered with blood and making gurgling sounds. "The first time he told me he shot her, the second time he said he killed her with a knife. He maintained this was not done in anger, but to put her out of her misery," Ewalt noted. "It is difficult to fit the patient's blitheness in admitting this murder and stating he feels 'responsible' for the others, although he does not remember them, and his statement earlier that the evidence against him, as his attorney had told him, was all circumstantial and that he believes someone else is responsible.

When asked why he would admit to these things if he was not sure he had done them, he states that he feels that he must have."

Costa gave a long, rambling account of his fear of death. He claimed to remember seeing, when he was eight months old, his father in his coffin, and recalled other relatives who had died. . . .

Costa had more than thirty hours of observation by psychiatrists and social workers, and a complete physical, neurological and mental status examination including five psychological tests, blood chemistry, urinalysis, a Wassermann test and a chromosome smear. X rays had shown clear lungs, a normal heart and a skull with no abnormalities except the cranial bones were "rather large and heavy." His EEG was normal, as were all other laboratory studies. Ewalt had personally seen Costa on three separate occasions for one hour; his diagnosis was: "Borderline type schizophrenia":

> Such persons cope with their mental symptoms by over-activity and by a series of antisocial actions, often of a minor criminal type. Under great stress, the mental symptoms come to the fore. In this instance, while the patient was under drugs, aggressions and anger may have been uncontrolled, resulting in the death of the girls. What role deviant sexual tendencies played is unclear, although the mutilations of the bodies would suggest that this was an important factor.

> With regard to "technical, legal questions," Ewalt would have to say that Antone Costa knew the difference between right from wrong. When under the influence of drugs, and perhaps when in sexually stimulating situations, he may not have known right from wrong, but Ewalt had not been able to examine him when drugged.

> To a third, and more modern question sometimes propounded: Did this patient's mental condition contribute significantly to the commission of the crime? The answer is 'Yes.' The court might want to consider his commitment as a sexually dangerous person to that section of Bridgewater."

471

Goldman was delighted with Ewalt's report. Although Ewalt, like Williams, had stopped short of a definite diagnosis of insanity, he had left the door open sufficiently with regard to criminal responsibility for him to make a case. "Borderline" was vague enough to support Goldman's "impairment through use of drugs" defense—the backstop for an insanity plea. A witness with Ewalt's credentials would have considerable impact on a jury. Whether Tony Costa was Cory Devereau or anybody else didn't make any difference. For the purpose of the defense, "borderline" schizophrenia was as good a diagnosis as schizophrenia itself.

While Costa had objected vehemently to the mild diagnosis of "schizoid personality" following his examination at Bridgewater, he embraced Dr. Ewalt's report with pleasure, telling Goldman: "I find it extremely accurate and I agree with almost everything—that's basically the whole story right there. I'm not trying to boast or anything, but I have a tremendous understanding of everything. I know myself like a book. I could have written that report for them, if I wanted. The thing is, I can't tell anybody because I'm afraid of it. My ego interferes a lot. I can admit it to myself, but I don't like to. Because it destroys something else there."

26

Goldman was seeking to determine whether the murders had occurred in a territory of a national park. He had pictures of official "Area Closed" signs in the name of the U.S. Department of the Interior posted in areas contiguous to the grave sites to support his position that the murders had occurred within the boundaries of a national seashore park and were subject to federal jurisdiction.

However, George Killen put the issue to rest. Killen not only had a map from the national seashore park upon which he traced the area where the bodies had been found, but records showing the land in question belonged to the heirs of one Israel Lombard. While falling within the boundaries of the park, the area was private property.

Beaudreau held a hearing in the judge's lobby to hear Goldman's motion for a joint trial. Goldman had changed his mind on the basis of new evidence—primarily the autopsies, which revealed such a great similarity of execution in the dismemberment, method and place of burial that there was no hope of finding a jury that would not see the links among all the murders. At the time he had argued for severance he had not had the autopsy reports in his possession.

"It hardly seems possible to have any trial on one of these cases without some evidence properly related only to the other cases," Goldman said. "The district attorney, by his statements to the media pertaining to four bodies found on Cape Cod, forever denied Costa the opportunity to be tried on any one of the cases without at least some jury members remembering the other cases as well. The autopsy report in each case displays a complete similarity in the execution of the alleged murders, as well as the place of burial."

Beaudreau's examination of the autopsy reports did not, to him, warrant anything more than the possibility of a pattern. "As I interpret the law, a pattern is not a common design."

"Well, this is going to be another field day for newspaper exploitation," Goldman said angrily. "Every single juror will know something about *four* murders and they are only going to hear the evidence on *two*. I think it's very prejudicial to the defendant."

"It would be more prejudicial to go the other way," Beaudreau said. "That is why I am going to rule that the Wysocki and Walsh cases shall be tried on April 6—that includes the larceny of the motor vehicle in the Walsh case. There will be no further continuances."

Goldman had brought Ewalt's report to the hearing. "I will let a copy of this report be furnished to Lieutenant Killen."

Beaudreau read the report. He did not want it turned over to anyone until he had passed on a written statement signed by Costa that he wanted the report shown. "I am going to take action right now and see that it is impounded."

Furious that Beaudreau appeared to be impugning his integrity as a lawyer, Goldman was visibly shaking with rage when Beaudreau added, "I am now going to call Dr. Ewalt in the presence of the defendant and tell him the commonwealth has no right to ask for a copy of this report. Dr. Ewalt is the defendant's doctor and *not* the commonwealth's doctor."

"I want the record to show that I don't approve the calling of the doctor," Goldman said angrily. "You are now talking to a defense witness. I think Your Honor shouldn't do it."

Beaudreau called the Massachusetts Mental Health Center, telling Ewalt, "I want to make it clear that under no circumstances is a copy of this report to be given to anybody other than Mr. Goldman." Beaudreau said he was issuing a court order to that effect, but was not restricting the use of the report by the defense. "I do not mean you could not show it to another psychiatrist," Beaudreau said, "but no copy of the report will be given to anybody without the written order of the court."

"Oh, man, that was wild!" Costa told Cavanaugh after the session. "Goldie's all flipped out. I thought he was going to have a heart attack when the judge called Dr. Ewalt. He was *savage*. He sat there blowing his whole cool. It was the physical trauma he went through that got me upset."

"Don't worry about Mr. Goldman," Cavanaugh said. "He's a pretty good actor."

Beaudreau did not want Dr. Ewalt's psychiatric report made available to the prosecution, since it suggested that the court should review Costa's mental competence to stand trial. It was clear that Beaudreau wanted to preside over the trial. Cavanaugh told Costa that this was fine. "Beaudreau has made so many legal errors already that we *want* him sitting on the case." To Cavanaugh, Beaudreau seemed thoroughly confused; Cavanaugh explained that Beaudreau was limited to discussing law—not evidence. The mere discussion of evidence by a judge in a case was sometimes enough grounds to take it to a higher court.

"What boosted my hopes," Costa said, "was I got the impression that two of the charges might be dropped for lack of prosecution or something. I overheard a few little things Flynn was saying to Killen."

"What did you overhear?" Cavanaugh said.

"Flynn said something to Killen about dropping Perry for

lack of prosecution. He got uptight at what the judge said to one trial for Mary Anne and Pat because there were three bodies in the grave. And Killen said something like, 'That might be dropped, too.' "

Cavanaugh was interested in Killen's comment, "I don't think they've got much evidence in the Perry and Monzon cases. I think they're worried about proving those two. It's going to be very difficult to separate Mary Anne and Pat from Sydney, because she was in the same grave."

"This is what I was telling some of the guys," Costa said, excitedly. "Like I said, 'Man, how can they try Mary Anne and Pat without introducing some information about the other one?' "

"If they introduce any information about Sydney, it's a mistrial," Cavanaugh said.

"That's what I figured. Supposing while I'm being tried for these two murders, the papers come out and mention four bodies rather than two or something—that's grounds for a mistrial." Costa grinned. "Three of *them* and we're out on the street again."

Costa observed Christine Gallant's birthday on December 5 with a day of fasting and prayer. Otherwise he was busily engaged in his thriving leathercraft business, tools for which had finally arrived. Costa was working long hours in his cell to meet the demand for his belts, slippers and leather jewelry inscribed "A.C." A skilled craftsman, Costa's leatherwork was of such professional quality that deputy Donald Parker purchased a green belt with a border of delicate hand-tooled tracery to wear with his uniform pants. Displayed on the bars of Costa's cell along with other goods of his design was gun belt and holster, selling for twelve dollars . . .

On Sunday, December 21, Cecelia Bonaviri was Christmas shopping at King's department store in Hyannis. While admiring a pink angora cardigan, Mrs. Bonaviri collapsed from a massive cerebral hemorrhage. Rushed to Cape Cod Hospital emergency room by ambulance, she died two hours later.

Justin Cavanaugh was deputized to tell Tony Costa of his mother's death. Costa's eyes filled with tears, but he did not cry.

The sheriff's office received a tip the following morning from Cheney Marshall warning of an assassination attempt on Costa's life should he attend his mother's funeral.

Accompanied by sheriff's deputy Donald Parker and corrections officer Donald Grant, Costa was taken to Provincetown on December 24. He entered Nickerson's Funeral Home to pay his last respects before the sheriff's car joined a funeral cortege winding slowly through Provincetown's narrow streets to St. Peter the Apostle Roman Catholic Church for a 9 A.M. requiem mass.

The church's decor followed a motif of the sea, its stained-glass windows portraying fishermen tending their nets. The church's most striking feature, however, was one which had fascinated Antone Costa since he was a boy. On the undulating curves of the wall behind the altar, a mural had been painted depicting the turbulent, wind-tossed waves upon which a resplendently lighted and triumphant Jesus Christ walked, his feet lightly touching the surface of the water. In the dim light of flickering votive candles, the figure seemed to move across the front of the church. Costa kept his eyes on the mural during the funeral mass said by Father Leo Duarte, longtime pastor of the church who also presided over brief grave site rites in St. Peter's Cemetery, not far from the burial place of Susan Perry.

In a "new lots" section of the cemetery—barren, flat, close to the pavement of Winslow Street, the grave site was watched by a row of grim-faced Provincetown police. As Costa was led to the sheriff's car for his return to Barnstable, his shoulders sagged. Seated between two officers in the car he hunched forward. When he straightened tears were streaming from his eyes . . .

"Tony took it hard," Cavanaugh told Goldman afterward.

27

On January 15, Goldman received from Tony Costa a letter "just to let you know that all is well thus far":

I've been thinking about the case quite often recently. You have done an excellent job of crumbling the prosecution's case against us, it's really fantastic! I have great faith that you will succeed. If I were to plead gulty to larceny of the auto, what influence would it have in crushing the case further? . . .

Goldman was more concerned about the efforts the prosecution was mounting to undermine his defense, in the form of a motion for further psychiatric examination of Tony Costa. Held in the judge's lobby with Killen and Flynn present, arguments for the motion erupted almost at once in flashing tempers when Beaudreau "excused" Lester Allen from his chambers.

"I take exception!" Goldman said. "Lieutenant Killen represents the commonwealth. He has no greater right to be present than Lester Allen."

"That is true," Beaudreau said. "But I am going to excuse him."

"I don't think it's fair to have the commonwealth's investigators present here and not the defense's," Goldman said. "I just don't understand Your Honor's rationale."

Beaudreau had Allen escorted out anyway.

Armand Fernandes rose for the district attorney's office. Tony Costa had not been examined by the commonwealth for nearly a year, since the psychiatric evaluation at Bridgewater to judge his competency to stand trial, he said. "We know that the defendant was examined by his own psychiatrist. I suppose that counsel for the defense will say this case is going to be argued on its merits—a question of guilty or not guilty solely without medical testimony."

Goldman wanted more time to study the question. "If prosecution psychiatrists examine Tony, are any statements he makes admissible? Can he be asked any questions? Can his statements be used in his trial as an admission? There is a lot to consider here, Judge."

"I don't think under any circumstances could those statements be used in the trial," Beaudreau said.

"Then, I don't know what the purpose of the examination is," Goldman said.

"It may be that in the event that a . . . a specific defense is raised, Mr. Goldman, by your medical people . . . that the commonwealth's position could be in accordance with yours," Fernandes said—rather slyly avoiding the mention the word "insanity"—

"and save the commonwealth thirty thousand dollars or more for a trial."

Goldman was not amused. He stuck by his insistence on a week's time to study the motion, and added, "I would like to say for the record, I should have my right to consult with my investigator."

Beaudreau sighed. "Mr. Allen has no status, as far as I am concerned. The only reason I am having the lobby conference is to protect your client from newspaper publicity. I don't want any leaks to the press. I want reliable people whom I know; and I don't know Mr. Allen and I am not taking any chances." Beaudreau passed his glance to Tony Costa. "I am going to protect this gentleman as much as I can."

"Let *me* protect Mr. Costa," Goldman retorted, gathering his papers. "You just pass on the merits."

"We have reasons to believe that the defense may introduce evidence with regard to a medical examination as that relates to criminal responsibility," Fernandes said a week later in Beaudreau's chambers. Costa's examination at Bridgewater had dealt with his competence to stand trial. Fernandes wanted to revise the language of his motion to allow for an examination dealing with "diminished criminal responsibility."

Goldman said, "If the question arises concerning the defendant's mental capacity, it would serve no useful purpose. The crimes were committed more than a year ago. Moreover, I can't conceive how the defendant can answer anything other than courtesy questions. In no way can this court impose sanctions on Mr. Costa if he refuses to answer any questions. Certainly under Miranda, I am going to be present—or a member of our staff. We propose to advise the defendant that he refuse to answer any questions that he chooses on the grounds of the Fifth Amendment. That is my position."

"Well, I'm *opposed* to it," Beaudreau said.

"I can say for the record, under no circumstances is Mr. Costa going to plead guilty or not guilty by reason of insanity," Goldman said, putting it out on the table at last. "The defense is going to plead 'diminished capacity as a result of the use of drugs.' I repeat: there is no *need* to have this motion." Goldman cited Costa's examination at the Massachusetts Mental Health Center. "That examination was a full and thorough examination and involved some eight or nine days. In the expedition of justice, why don't I let the district attorney read the report," Goldman said. "Then we can have further conversation on this."

"I have no objection as long as I get Mr. Costa's written authorization, so there would not be any problems later on," Beaudreau said.

Costa gave his permission, but he was puzzled why Goldman would want the prosecution to have access to Ewalt's report. Privately, he told his lawyers, "There appears to me to be one or more extremely disastrous statements in it."

Goldman explained that he was looking for cooperation for a reduced plea to second-degree murder. He was using the report to convince the district attorney's office of the existence of mitigation.

Goldman did not have much hope that a deal could be made. Killen had been forbearing and cooperative in tracking down any "leads" the defense provided involving Cory Devereau, but Goldman had never been able to persuade Bernie Flynn to alter the course of his investigation. From his first interrogation, Flynn had set his sights on Tony Costa and never let up.

Goldman thought he had a chance to plea bargain, "because an intelligent person like Tony couldn't possibly kill the girls for a car, if he was sane." But his motion to suppress official statements about the case had so infuriated Dinis as to have closed off any chance of his cooperation.

Goldman handed over Ewalt's report to Armand Fernandes "with the understanding that none of the subject matters be introduced to trial for and in behalf of the government in accord with an agreement of February 7." Fernandes was also reading the transcript of the Quillen case Goldman had purchased from the court reporter for $324.45.

Goldman had received a letter from Costa with "instructions" for dealing with the district attorney:

> If I were to plead guilty to the larceny charge what effect would it have on the case such as:
> 1. Elimination of witnesses
> 2. Evidence in reference to murder charges
> 3. Etcetera
> I have also been wondering why I have not had the chance to become a state's witness in return for some-

form of amnesty. I have realized this in many other cases such as the Manson case, Robert Ranahan case, etc. It's a lot more secure than taking a chance of life or 20 years!

I feel that Lt. Killen, Sgt. Meads, etc. would help me since it would benefit them also. Justice is most important. I do not want to pay for a crime in which I am only a victim of circumstances, while the murderer roams free! . . .

Costa's mention of the Manson case disturbed Goldman. There were striking parallels in the cases: part of Manson's plan for the killings was to hang his victims from the ceiling beams in the living room and, according to one of the participants, to mutilate them. Manson and his disciples were a drug-besotted group involved in messianic delusions—too close to Costa for a jury aware of the sensational and recent California case not to recognize the similarity.

Costa also asked to discuss the contract he had signed with Goldman for dramatic and publication rights to his life story. "I would like this to be placed in my name. As you realize, my mind has returned to its proper functioning, so I can now decide more clearly concerning any royalties I may be entitled to."

Avis also was having second thoughts about the contract she had signed, telling Goldman she wanted it understood that 50 percent of the royalties she received was to go to her children in equal shares, the rest to be "retained and accounted for" to her. She would act as guardian of the children and their funds until they were twenty-one years of age and would "hold and disperse" all money for their benefit. "Please don't call me or have anyone (i.e., Lester Allen) visit me, unless it's absolutely necessary," Avis said. "It upsets me."

On March 9, Goldman received notice from the clerk of the Superior Court that "the Honorable G. Joseph Tauro, chief justice, has designated Mr. Justice Beaudreau to preside at the sitting of the court which is to begin at Greenfield on April 6, 1970."

28

After reading Ewalt's report, which Goldman had given to the prosecution, Armand Fernandes said, "The report doesn't tell me anything conclusively." Fernandes was not withdrawing his motion that Costa be examined again. "I don't want to get caught in the middle of the trial, where there is a specific defense raised and we are not able to meet it."

Beaudreau was inclined to grant Fernandes's motion. He had already made out an order for Costa to be committed to a state hospital to be examined by a qualified psychiatrist. Costa was ordered to cooperate fully, by answering each and every question put to him. Costa could have his own psychiatrist present, but not his attorney.

"Well, I would certainly quarrel with *this,*" Cavanaugh said after reading the order. "I don't think this court has any authority to order the defendant to cooperate fully with the examining psychiatrist or to answer his questions."

Beaudreau disagreed. Nothing coming out of the examination could be used by the district attorney for further investigation with respect to guilt, he said.

"It would only be available for our use in the event that the defendant raised the issue of criminal responsibility," Fernandes affirmed.

"Mr. Goldman's position was that if such a psychiatric examination was held, he would *definitely* be present to advise the defendant."

Beaudreau said, "I don't see how you can have a psychiatric examination with counsel interrupting to say, 'Don't answer this; don't answer that.' "

"Mr. Goldman also said that he could very well say to the defendant, 'Don't answer any questions at all,' " Cavanaugh told the judge. "So this examination would all be for naught."

"Well, he can do that if he wants to," Beaudreau said irritably. "I am not trying to control Mr. Goldman's defense."

"The second paragraph of your order indicates you *are* trying to control the defendant, in that he is to cooperate fully," Cavanaugh said. " 'Each and every question,' it says."

"Well, if his attorney tells him otherwise, that is the attorney's obligation, not mine," Beaudreau said, and he issued the order for an examination to take place within two weeks.

Furious when he learned of Beaudreau's order, Goldman promptly appealed to Justice R. Ammi Cutter of the Massachusetts Supreme Judicial Court, a maneuver which persuaded the prosecution to agree to a stipulation that Costa's lawyer could be present at the psychiatric examination. Goldman then turned his attention to a motion to revoke Beaudreau's order for a change of venue, since a survey Goldman had taken in both Franklin County in western Massachusetts and in Barnstable County showed that prejudicial pretrial publicity had been dissipated by time.

Beaudreau was displeased that Goldman had changed his mind on venue as he had on severance. Having made a shambles of Beaudreau's order for psychiatric examination by going over his head, Goldman was now asking him to revoke another decision.

The judge said he was reserving judgment on change of venue. As for a continuance, he thought April 22 would be acceptable but he was not sure.

Edith Thomas explained in a letter to Tony Costa the real reason why Maurice Goldman was seeking to return his case to Cape Cod. "Having been his personal secretary for a long time" she wrote, "I know his thinking."

I think he is concerned how a panel of Franklin County jurors would react, and that they might even wonder why a Provincetown murder trial was moved to be heard by small-town residents in western Massachusetts.

He was disturbed about the gruesome story appearing in the media, and he felt that what the jury will hear will not be pleasant, i.e. the autopsy reports. He rather thinks that people coming from a more cosmopolitan area now retired to the Cape, and Cape residents themselves, are now familiar with the drug situation. There have been all kinds of school programs, speeches being made and radio programs in and around Cape Cod dealing with the subject of drug intoxication. He believes that the Barnstable jurors would find it a little easier to be merciful toward the situation than the small town dwellers of Franklin County.

29

Dr. Frederick Whiskin of Plymouth came to the Barnstable House of Correction on March 25 to interview Antone Costa in the presence of Maurice Goldman and Lawrence Shubow.

Costa was getting a little shopworn from psychiatric examinations, having undergone examinations at Bridgewater, two interviews with Dr. Harold Williams and thirty hours of observation at the Massachusetts Mental Health Center. Nevertheless, he breezed rapidly through the two-hour interview with Whiskin with the aplomb of a professional.

"He showed no obvious physical defects or mannerisms, spoke fluently and well," Whiskin observed. "At times, he appeared tense, at others he was glib and relaxed. When he was tense, he scratched his hands or his arms."

Whiskin returned two weeks later for a second examination, conducted in the presence of Justin Cavanaugh and two stenographers from the district attorney's office.

"First I'd like to test your orientation," Whiskin said. "What day is it today?"

"Today is the twentieth—oh, no! the *thirteenth* day of April," Costa said.

"Do you know what a proverb is?"

"Yes, it usually is a saying similar to, 'Do unto others as you would have them do unto you.' "

"What does this proverb mean: 'People who live in glass houses should not throw stones.' "

483

"You should not criticize other people for what you yourself do."

"What is twelve times twelve?"

"One hundred and forty-four."

"One hundred minus seven?"

"Ninety-three."

"Would you keep going down subtracting seven from ninety-three."

"Eighty-six, seventy-nine, seventy-two, sixty-five, fifty-eight, fifty-one, forty-four, thirty-seven, thirty, twenty-three, fifteen, eight and one."

"What is seven into one hundred?"

"That should be fourteen and two left over."

"In view of your answer to the last question, what do you think of your answer to subtracting sevens from the one hundred series?"

"Sometimes I goof up on the first number," Costa said.

"What should your last number have been in the series?"

"Two," Costa said.

"As I talk to you today, do you feel you are a person that knows the difference between right and wrong?"

"Yes."

"How about during the period in question regarding the crimes that you are accused of?"

"I would have to give an honest answer to that of 'no,'" Costa said. "I didn't know where I was; I didn't know right from wrong. I was just looking to get high; just to satisfy my habit."

"Just to test your memory, what did you have for breakfast?"

"Pancakes and milk."

"I am going to give you a series of numbers to repeat after me: two, seven, five, four, eight, six.

"Two, seven, five, three, eight, six."

"Three, nine, one, two, one, five, seven," Whiskin said.

"Three, nine, one, five, one, two, seven."

"How are a chair and a table similar, and how are they different?"

"A chair and a table are both furniture," Costa said. "They are different in the manner of the making and are used for different purposes."

"If this morning you were able to rub a magic lantern and a

genie appeared and said make any three wishes, what would those three wishes be?"

"Freedom, peace in the world, conquering of disease," Costa said promptly.

"When you mention disease, what type of disease are you thinking of."

"All different kinds. Such as cancer and virus infections of any kind."

"Would you include mental disease?"

Yes, definitely. This country should take care of its people before it takes care of anything else. Instead, the United States throws thirteen billion dollars' worth of junk on the moon."

"What would you do if you had your freedom?"

"For me, my freedom means a beginning, like a rebirth, starting a new life. I'd go out and start my building business. Now that I know my mistakes, I know how to correct them."

"You have used the phrase 'a new birth.' Do you relate this to our discussion of reincarnation?"

"No, I relate it to the drug situation we talked about. I got into looking for some kind of representation of a father figure, someone that could help me decide some problem. It just wasn't there. This drug thing, I figure I sold my soul to the devil; it was like part of me dying."

"In one of the reports which has been made available to me, it states you have admitted to at least one of the crimes of which you are accused."

Cavanaugh broke in. "I advise you not to answer that question."

"Do you have any memory of the alleged incidents for which you are involved?" Whiskin said.

"I'm sorry, but I will have to advise you not to answer that question," Cavanaugh repeated.

"If you did know some act was wrong, do you feel your controls were impaired so that you would have done it anyway?"

"During this latter part of my drug period—the last few years, I had very little control of anything. I was like a vegetable. I don't think I could tell right from wrong, good from bad. All that mattered was getting high, nothing else."

"Is there any memory of the alleged night in which you were involved with the girls?"

"The only memory I have is at the rooming house," Costa

said. "You know, I have dreams that are clearer than anything I can recall about those girls. I couldn't recognize them now; I have no remembrance of them."

"How did your views of the world change after you were apprehended and couldn't get drugs any more?"

"After I was sent to Bridgewater State Hospital, I went through a few bad nights. I had some hallucinations and a lot of pain. I didn't see a doctor until I was there three or four days. The ceiling in my room was fifteen feet high; there was a mattress on the floor. A little mouse kept running in and out of the floor boards. At night I would put out crumbs for him from my supper. There was a window I would look out of and see the blue sky and say to myself 'What the hell are you doing in this room?' It seemed like a San Francisco crash pad; it was filthy and dirty. It was unreal! I thought I was just dreaming."

"How long do you think it was before you came back to reality?"

"It must have been at least June coming anywhere near reality, at least three months. I started realizing what I was being accused of, the seriousness of the situation."

"How did you feel then?"

"I became very nervous and edgy. There were many discrepancies in what I thought was real—like a lost weekend. For approximately four months I was trying to piece everything together . . ."

"Specific questions aimed at assessing Mr. Costa's intellectual functions revealed no abnormality," Whiskin reported. "Recent, remote and immediate memory was intact. Costa formed abstract concepts well; his mental calculations were well performed."

Whiskin was not able to assess Costa's state of mind at the time of the crimes, because of his reticence to discuss the subject and his attorney's advising him not to answer. Whiskin had, however, sufficient information to form an opinion regarding Costa's fundamental psychological makeup:

At the time of this examination he is not psychotic. His imaginativeness and idealism and value ideas for improving humanity are found in the schizoid person, but also in the immature individual who has not progressed much beyond adolescent ways of viewing the world. The

486

glibness and manipulativeness of which he is capable is more characteristic of the sociopathic personality.

Costa's history of abnormal sex relationships with his wife reported by Dr. Ewalt prompted Whiskin to entertain the possibility of a sexual perversion of some kind; but Whiskin found Ewalt's diagnosis of "borderline type schizophrenia" excessive. Costa was neither psychotic nor prepsychotic, although he showed some of the features of a "borderline," such as a certain "coolness," or lack of normal feelings.

Whiskin's diagnosis was, "Borderline personality disorder (nonpsychotic); sexual deviation (type undetermined) to be ruled out."

Charles Zimmerman had contacted Marshall Houts, a former FBI agent, attorney and writer. Goldman was hopeful that some arrangement could be made with Houts for the development of a book.

Goldman was not suggesting how the book should be written. Two publications had impressed him: *Trial* by William Harrington and *In Cold Blood* by Truman Capote.

Houts returned the material on Costa to Goldman with regrets. He didn't think he, or anyone else, could "clean up" Tony Costa sufficiently to make him a subject suitable for public consumption.

30

Beaudreau denied the defense's motion to return the trial of Tony Costa to Barnstable County, advising Goldman, "The trial is to begin in Greenfield as scheduled, April twenty-second."

Goldman promptly filed a petition to Massachusetts Supreme

Court Justice Jacob B. Spiegel to revoke Beaudreau's order for a change of venue. Spiegel ordered the Costa trial transferred back to Cape Cod.

Spiegel received a warm note of thanks from Tony Costa.

The revocation of the change of venue irritated George Killen, who had just completed elaborate arrangements for the accommodation and transportation of all prosecution witnesses to Greenfield.

Killen had recommended that state Trooper Edgar Thomas Gunnery receive a commendation "for several excellent pieces of police work" in connection with the Costa case. Gunnery, he wrote, had noticed a small piece of rope at the foot of a tree in a heavily wooded area with nothing around the ground to suggest it had been disturbed. Digging in the place, Gunnery had come upon the head and torso of Mary Anne Wysocki, which had led police to discover, some forty yards away, the second grave. Gunnery's persistence, after many unsuccessful searches, had then led to finding the murder weapon and "a human-blood-stained knife" buried some three hundred yards from where the bodies were found.

On May 4, Tom Gunnery was commended in special orders for "diligent effort and exemplary display of fortitude which reflect great credit on himself and the Massachusetts State Police." He was granted three extra days off with pay, to be taken at the convenience of his troop commander.

Bernie Flynn also won an official commendation. It hardly made much of a dent in the forty-one days of unpaid overtime he had put into investigating the Costa case.

On May 14, the United States Court of Appeals ruled in the John Von Utter, Jr., v. Donald P. Tullock case that an affidavit was insufficient for the issuance of a search warrant where there was no statement as to why a confidential informer's tip was believed to be trustworthy. "The decision whether or not to believe the informer is not for the police officer, but the magistrate who issues the warrant upon sufficient grounds for a finding of probable cause."

Goldman was too busy to give the ruling more attention than to share the irony with Cavanaugh that Tony Costa's singular act as a drug informer had been thrown out of court. Jay Von Utter was walking out of the Barnstable House of Correction a free man, a week before Antone Costa was to go on trial.

Lawrence Shubow was seeking additional psychiatric witnesses for the defense, explaining to Goldman that such witnesses need not examine Costa, but rather could be available to testify with regard to their expertise on the use and abuse of drugs. Shubow sent a copy of Dr. Ewalt's report to Dr. Jonathan O. Cole, superintendent of Boston State Hospital, with a list of drugs Costa had used.

Shubow told Ewalt that the defense was following essentially the suggestions implicit in his report. All possible data was to be shown to the jury to determine whether the offenses warranted a conviction of first-degree murder with or without clemency, second-degree murder with clemency, manslaughter, or a verdict of not guilty by reason of insanity.

"Our private belief," Shubow told Ewalt, "is that there is diminished responsibility by reason of drug addiction, superimposed upon underlying pathology short of conventional insanity." Shubow included in his letter to Ewalt the text of *Commonwealth v. McHoul*—"the most important recent decision showing the present philosophy regarding 'legal insanity' prevailing in the Massachusetts Supreme Judicial Court." The McHoul opinions would be key to the defense.

Tony Costa was also making preparations for his trial. Costa wanted to know, "Why is Goldman broadcasting that I have confessed to these crimes?" Costa was also complaining about "the distortion of the real story to Zimmerman and Holmes for purposes of my psychiatric examination."

For Goldman, Costa wrote a list of instructions he wanted followed during his trial:

The Defense

Police cannot place me at scene of crime, nor do they know location of scene of crime. Girls may have been dismembered in the forest but this does not indicate that the forest is the scene of the crime.

1. I was at laundromat the afternoon of January 25, 1969, with Peter. Witness available.

2. Wolf Fissler will testify that I was in Foc's'le Saturday night, January 25.

3. Mrs. Morton can testify that I was home in bed Saturday night, January 25. Also Sunday when she came in and I paid the rent.

4. Sunday morning I went to Joe Beaudry's to collect pay after calling him. He had already left so I returned to P'town via Paula Hoernig and friend. Then located Beaudry. Made arrangements to collect pay on Monday.

5. Met with Herbie, Judy, Patty and Timmy on Sunday afternoon.

According to the above, "when well presented in court," when could I have possibly committed the murders and buried girls also, plus destroying any of my own blood-stained clothing—as they certainly would be if I had dismembered anyone?

At least thirty (30) other persons had access to that can of drugs and the weapons. This *must* be brought out in court!

I will not allow any previous sexual activities testimony under any circumstances. Our private lives must remain private in court. These activities occurred seven years ago and have no relationship to the trial.

Devereau must be implicated and broken down on the stand with witnesses against him. Or I shall be forced to do so myself. We must place the blame in his hands and thereby influence the jury into possibly believing that I am a victim of circumstances.

Costa told Avis: "Many will be busted, one for murder; but they all had their chance. They should have kept their mouths shut. I predict some will run in fear, others will not testify, except to state they are incompetent by reason of drug use. But Cory Devereau will have no excuse if he shows his face. We are ready!"

PART FIVE

Tony

———

1

George Killen arrived early Monday morning to a still-deserted Barnstable courthouse. In his office, Killen rechecked eight Systematic brand storage boxes containing the forty-eight exhibits to be presented as evidence during the trial of Antone Costa. Killen had personally tagged the evidence, each piece identified in his precise and legible hand. Killen was joined by Tom Gunnery. As custodian of the boxes during the trial, it would be Gunnery's task to match up the exhibits with the testimony of witnesses so that the prosecution's presentation would proceed without delay.

Judge Robert Beaudreau pulled into a reserved parking space at the rear of the courthouse and went to his chambers. Beaudreau had previously inspected the courtroom with officers of the court; seated in the jury box. Beaudreau complained that, "The juror sitting in the end seat will have difficulty seeing the faces of the witnesses."

Beaudreau directed that the witness stand be moved, along with the tables and chairs that were to be used by the defense and prosecution. Beaudreau also gave instructions for the orderly management of the horde of spectators seeking to be accommodated in the 204-seat courtroom. A press headquarters in the courthouse basement was established for the more than one hundred reporters and photographers expected to cover the trial. No photographic equipment or "news apparatus" was to be allowed inside the courthouse. Only authorized persons would be permitted access to exhibits introduced during the trial as evidence. Witnesses could only be questioned by reporters outside the courthouse. The gallery behind the courtroom, where a straggle of

493

prospective jurors had commenced to gather, was roped off to prevent access to all but lawyers, witnesses and court officers.

Mobile television units were setting up in the parking lot when Antone Costa stepped from the sheriff's car that had brought him down the hill from Barnstable House of Correction.

Costa's appearance was drastically changed. Gone were his mustache and sideburns. His hair was neatly trimmed. He wore a navy blue mohair business suit, white shirt and maroon necktie, all borrowed from Maurice Goldman, who had told his wife to select something suitable from his own extensive wardrobe. Even fully let-out, Costa's trousers barely touched the tops of his new black oxfords.

Costa smiled for news and television cameramen, then strode briskly up the courthouse steps to be taken to a second-floor detention room by Deputy Sheriff Elwood Mills. A powerful man with massive shoulders, Mills was a full-blooded Wampanoag Indian whose high school athletic prowess had earned him the title "the Jim Thorpe of Cape Cod." Mills would stay close to Costa all during his trial.

The bell in the courthouse tower was tolling ten o'clock when Edmund Dinis arrived, now a celebrity as a result of his inquiry into the death of Mary Jo Kopechne. Dinis was accompanied by Armand Fernandes. Scholarly looking and self-effacing, Fernandes was regarded as the best lawyer on Dinis's staff and would present the prosecution's case.

Maurice Goldman wasted no time posing for photographers. Sweeping through a throng of reporters, he went immediately to the courtroom where ninety-eight prospective jurors were listening to Beaudreau deliver a preliminary talk on the importance of jury service. Sixteen jurors would be drawn to hear evidence in the Costa case to insure that, in the event of death or incapacity, twelve remained to deliberate, in order to avoid a mistrial. Jurors would be sequestered in a Hyannis motel for the duration of the trial.

Beaudreau introduced members of the prosecution and the defense, asking that any of the venire, or group of prospective jurors, with close associations to them so identify themselves. Introduced as a "defense investigator," Victor Wolfson was actually a novelist who had won an Emmy Award for writing the commentary for a documentary on Winston Churchill delivered by Richard Burton. Well-traveled and urbane, Wolfson was considering collaboration with Lester Allen on a book about the Costa case and would be seated at the defense table throughout the trial.

Beaudreau gradually excused forty-two of the prospective jurors for medical, job or family reasons, including real estate broker Antone Costa of East Falmouth—no relation—who had been called for jury duty. The courtroom was cleared of spectators; prospective jurors were called to be examined individually by Beaudreau, who asked if they had an "open mind" regarding the charges brought against Antone Costa, if they were conscious of any bias as a result of media accounts of the crimes, and if they would be willing to return a first-degree verdict that carried the death penalty or an innocent finding should the evidence warrant. After Beaudreau deemed a juror "indifferent," he or she was offered to Goldman and Dinis as candidates for the panel.

Goldman observed the prospective jurors with a practiced eye. Goldman facetiously told a colleague what kind of a jury he was looking for: "Six psychiatrists and six lawyers. They can't agree on anything." In fact Goldman was looking for a "regular" guy, "somebody who's been around and knows that smoking pot isn't the worst thing in the world." In particular, Goldman wanted to avoid "those guys that walk hand in hand with God." Nor was above-average intelligence necessarily a bar to jury service in Goldman's view; he quoted Mark Twain's famous admonition: "Let's knock him off the jury; he can read."

Goldman challenged all prospective jurors who were parents of daughters the age of Pat Walsh and Mary Anne Wysocki. Goldman sat in the jury box close to Tony Costa who was making notes on a copy of the venire list. Costa told Beaudreau, "I'm keeping track of the challenges myself." Asked why he consulted Costa before exercising every challenge, Goldman said, "Tony has the final say. After all, it's *his* life."

At the first session's close, six male jurors had been chosen, including Arthur Cahoon, a broad-shouldered foreman for Barnstable County's highway department. Cahoon admitted to Beaudreau: "I'm not for capital punishment."

Goldman was especially pleased to have Charles B. Horton, Jr. of Orleans on the jury. A pilot for Trans World Airlines, Horton said, "In all fairness, I question whether the death penalty serves as a deterrent."

2

Among the one hundred additional prospective jurors called to the courthouse on Tuesday morning was Mrs. Irene Mc-Coubrey. An attractive middle-aged blonde, she answered all questions without hesitation. Courtroom observers were surprised when Goldman found her acceptable; it had been assumed that Goldman wanted an all-male jury.

Goldman also accepted Mrs. Emma Sacht, wife of an officer at the Massachusetts Maritime Academy, and Mrs. Frances Leonardi, a retired schoolteacher. Mrs. Leonardi did not believe in the death penalty, but assured Beaudreau she could deliver a guilty verdict in the case. Her service on a sequestered jury would be a hardship on her seventy-two-year-old husband, she explained, "but he would want me to do my duty."

Jury selection was completed on Wednesday from an additional venire of eighty-four jurors. It was a well-dressed, sober, conscientious group of working people and housewives. Of the four women, two were retired schoolteachers. Retired machinist Russell A. Dodge was named foreman by Beaudreau. When the jury was sworn, Dinis explained that as their first task, they were to be taken on a "view" of areas in Provincetown and Truro.

A yellow school bus carried the sixteen jurors, counsel and eight court officers along the Mid-Cape Highway to the Wellfleet medical offices of Dr. Sidney Callis, from which Costa had stolen drugs.

"I want you to observe this garage, which is presently boarded up," Goldman said to the jury, "and the area of white paint on the trim of the building."

Costa was taken from the bus and transferred to the back seat of a sheriff's car. Entering Provincetown, the car was provided a bicycle escort by a long-haired youth who pedaled close enough to exchange pleasantries with Costa through the window. Parked on Standish Street across from Mrs. Morton's rooming house, Costa's presence quickly drew a crowd of young people who waved, held up their fingers in a V sign and called out, "Yea, Tony!"

Costa waved back and smiled. Deputy sheriffs had to chase away several young girls who pressed against the car's window for a closer look.

Dinis explained to the jurors gathered on Commercial Street, "Please observe this establishment, known as the Foc's'le."

Led by a deputy sheriff dressed in a traditional nineteenth-century frock coat with a double row of brass buttons and carrying a white staff of authority, the jurors walked in single file through the dingy premises, exchanging curious glances with the mostly long-haired and bearded patrons seated at rough benches and tables scarred with initials. The jukebox boomed, "We'll Sing in the Sunshine."

White paint was peeling from the shingles at 5 Standish Street when the jury was taken to a room Mrs. Morton had rented to Tony Costa.

Goldman said, "I particularly want to emphasize the toilet on the left, used by other residents of the house."

Mounting a steep stairway, each juror peering inside shabby room number 2 was told to note the half-closet door under a slanting dormer wall.

Dinis pointed out the corner of Conwell and Bradford streets, "where the girls were last seen alive."

The bus then traveled along scenic Route 6A to Beach Point and the location of the Royal Coachman motel. After passing Watt's garage, the bus drove to a staging area behind the old post office in Truro. Waiting there were five military jeeps, three blue park service trucks and a yellow van.

Judge Beaudreau stepped out of the bus to speak with military police and park rangers. "We have got to be particularly careful you do not talk to the jurors in any way. No small talk or anything, just driving."

The jurors were driven out of town from winding Depot Road to a turnoff at a sign that said: "Hatch Road—Dead End." To the left of a rotary was a space between over-reaching pine boughs, a barely perceptible one-track dirt road no larger than a path led into the woods. Tree branches scraped the sides of the vehicles as they bumped and jostled along the rutted roadbed into the stillness of the woods.

The convoy came to a stop at a clearing, three-quarters of a mile inside the forest. Handcuffed but smiling, Costa was helped from his jeep by a deputy sheriff. He listened attentively while

Dinis identified the clearing as "area one, parking space." Dinis also drew the jury's attention to a small hole by the side of the road where Mary Anne Wysocki's handbag had been buried and, a short distance away, the place where the gun and the knife had been hidden.

Led by a park ranger, the jurors walked in pairs down the rutted dirt road, the crunch of their footfalls on a carpet of pine needles the only sound in the forest. Little sunlight came through the newly leafed scrub oaks and clusters of high pine boughs. Unremarked upon was a hole on the roadbank were Susan Perry had been buried.

The jury was led to a narrow path through tangles of briars, chokeweed and eglantine to a small clearing.

"Mr. Foreman, and members of the jury, will you please observe the tree to my left together with the broken branches that protrude from the tree." Dinis said. "Please observe the depression behind this tree; it's simply a hole in the ground. This may be remembered as hole number one, in area nine."

Peering into the cavity as they filed past, the jurors saw that the grave was partially filled with leaves and sand.

Dinis led the way to another depression some thirty yards from hole number one. "This area where you are now standing is to be remembered as hole number two."

A space of uneven, weed-strewn ground was identified by Goldman. "This clearing in our immediate front is known as the defendant's so-called 'marijuana patch.' It will play a part in the case, in one manner or another."

Following a whispered conference with Goldman, Costa searched the woods for a place about one hundred feet from the graves, locating the two-foot hole behind a large tree where he had buried an ammunition canister.

"Mr. Foreman and members of the jury," Goldman announced. "Please observe this broken tree branch and the hole in this area, known as defendant's area A."

Returning to their vehicles, the jury was taken further along the dirt road into the woods. Dinis walked alongside the stopped caravan. "Ladies and gentlemen of the jury," he said, "there is no need for you to alight. This is a dead-end lane, fifty yards in length." Dinis pointed out a shady cul-de-sac strewn with leaves where papers belonging to Patricia Walsh had been recovered.

It was six o'clock when the jury returned to the staging area to wordlessly reboard the school bus.

Seated beside Goldman in the bus, Costa said, "That was very enjoyable."

In its coverage of the third day of the trial of Antone Costa, the Cape Cod *Standard-Times* published a profile of Justin Cavanaugh as a man "whose courtroom manner is anything but jolly." Like Maurice Goldman, Cavanaugh defended his clients "with an intensity that brooks no loopholes."

"I do my best to win for my client every time, that goes without saying," Cavanaugh told reporters. "What else is there?" He was proud to be a member of the team of lawyers defending Antone Costa. "Tony's a real charmer with the ladies. They just can't resist him."

3

Referring to "yesterday's nature walk," Beaudreau greeted the jury jovially at the start of the trial session on Thursday morning. "Had I known the trip would be as exciting as it was, I would have asked all of you if you had any Boy Scout or Girl Scout experience. I think that would have been an appropriate and qualifying question."

The packed courtroom grew quiet when Edmund Dinis stood at the prosecutor's table.

"The commonwealth says that Antone Costa, on or about the twenty-fifth day of January, 1969, did murder Patricia H. Walsh and Mary Anne Wysocki of Providence, Rhode Island, and, after murdering these girls, he stole the automobile owned by Patricia Walsh." Dinis spoke directly to the jurors, his rich baritone pouring out over them like warm honey. "The tragedy began when these two young women decided to take a weekend trip to Provincetown. They went to the rooming house we visited yesterday and were introduced to Antone Costa by Mrs. Morton, who will testify she saw a note on the closet door of the girls' room signed by Antone Costa to the effect, 'I would like a ride.' And he *did* go for a ride in Patricia Walsh's automobile; and that is the last evidence the commonwealth has that these girls were ever seen alive.

"The state pathologist examining the remains of these girls will show the defendant did murder these girls with deliberate, premeditated malice aforethought; and that he murdered them with extreme atrocity or cruelty," Dinis said. "The pathology will show these girls had been shot in the head by a revolver owned and possessed by Antone Costa that he had hidden in the woods of Truro. The pathology will reveal these girls were cut up in seven parts. Further, the pathological examination of parts of these butchered bodies showed that in the cavities of the vagina and rectum of these dead girls was found male sperm."

Maurice Goldman rested a benign and paternal glance on the jurors. In a voice as compelling as Dinis's, he said, "The defendant at this moment stands absolutely innocent. There is much that is going to be revealed in this case. We are going to offer evidence to prove, in substance, that the defendant was a victim of drug dependency; that at each and every stage of the proceedings he was under the domination, intoxication and use of mind-altering drugs; and what the effect of the use of those chemicals and drugs will do to a mind."

Following his opening, Goldman asked for a lobby conference. He had received a telephone call from his secretary, who had found an anonymous letter in the morning's mail.

"It is addressed to me saying, in effect, that Mrs. Irene McCoubrey—who is on the jury—is a personal friend of Mrs. Monzon, the mother of Sydney Monzon for whose murder Costa is presently under indictment. I am particularly disturbed because a portion of the alleged remains of the body of Sydney Monzon appeared in one of the graves exhibited in this case."

Judge Beaudreau had Mrs. McCoubrey brought to his chambers. With Goldman and Dinis present, he asked her, "Did you ever work with Mrs. Monzon at the A&P in Orleans?"

"Yes," Mrs. McCoubrey said. "In the summertime. I was on produce; she was on meat. I mean, it was like everybody else in the store, it wasn't social. There was no particular friendship."

"Do you know her daughter was allegedly murdered by the defendant, Costa?" Beaudreau asked.

"Yes."

"I didn't give you an opportunity to answer such a question because the Monzon case is not before us; I only asked you about Walsh and Wysocki, and you answered truthfully with regards to that," Beaudreau said to reassure the obviously nervous juror. "In view of the fact that you did know Mrs. Monzon, I am going to ask Mr. Goldman, would you feel better if this juror was excused?"

"I would, Your Honor," Goldman said. "I think this woman is a very honest woman, but I think, in the interest of the defendant, that she should be excused."

"We are going to excuse you," Beaudreau said. "You will be asked by the press why you were excused. I want to make it very clear you have the right to talk, if you want to; I can't restrict your freedom of expression. But I would caution you very strongly—don't say anything to anybody. They will press you for information; your telephone will be ringing and you will be asked questions."

"Will they *do* that?" Mrs. McCoubrey asked.

"You happen to be a very attractive woman," Goldman said. "You are in the papers already; you made the front page. You are the prettiest juror, so you photograph well."

"This is frightening!" Mrs. McCoubrey said. "I just got over being scared to death and relaxed, and now it's starting all over again—"

"There's nothing to be scared of," Beaudreau said. "There is bound to be some publicity. Again, I emphasize: say nothing—even to your family—until the case is over; then, you will have nothing to be disturbed about."

"I'm scared to death!" Mrs. McCoubrey said.

"You just smile pretty," Dinis said, "and you'll be all right."

"I have excused Mrs. Irene McCoubrey," Beaudreau announced in the courtroom. "You are not to be concerned, or draw any inference from that. One of the reasons why we have sixteen jurors impaneled is to take care of such matters as this."

Balding, stoop-shouldered and slender, Leonard Walsh took the witness stand as the prosecution's first witness. Armand Fernan-

501

des asked him, "When was the last time you saw your daughter, as best you remember?"

"It was Wednesday or Thursday, the twenty-second or twenty-third of January, 1969," Walsh said. "I cashed a check for her."

"Do you recall filing a missing person's report?"

"Yes, I do," Walsh said. "Coincident with filing the report, I called the Rehoboth barracks of the Massachusetts State Police. I asked them if they would try to determine for me whether or not my daughter had met with an accident on a Massachusetts highway and had been hospitalized, and for some reason or other, the family hadn't been notified. That was Monday morning, January twenty-seventh. Patricia should have been in school at that time."

"How did you find out that she was not in school?" Fernandes said.

"I received a telephone call from Mrs. Walsh who had been notified by Pat's principal that she hadn't shown up at school that morning."

Fernandes held up a framed studio portrait. "I show you this photograph; can you identify it?"

Walsh blinked his eyes behind black-rimmed glasses. "I sure can. That's my daughter."

"Mr. Walsh, did you know how your daughter planned on going to Provincetown?"

"She planned to drive her car."

Fernandes showed the witness a photograph of the light blue Volkswagen. Walsh touched the photograph glancingly, almost caressing it. He nodded his head.

"I am going to ask you to examine these items," Fernandes said. "Will you please tell the court and the jury what they are?"

"This blue booklet is a final-examination paper," Walsh said, his voice wavering. "And this is a term paper on psychological research methods. Both of them are in my daughter's handwriting."

Goldman had no questions.

Bernie Flynn watched Mrs. Catherine Walsh mount the witness stand. A heavy woman, wearing a brightly printed dress and a string of white beads, she carried a large handbag tucked under an ample arm. While she was being sworn in, her eyes, behind rimless glasses, fastened on Tony Costa seated in the first row of the spectator section. It was a look of fierce loathing and accusation.

"Are you the mother of Patricia Walsh?"

Mrs. Walsh shifted her weight on the stand. Her eyes never moved from Costa's face as she said in a strong voice, "I am."

Costa had answered her stare impassively, but he finally looked away.

Fernandes showed her a white turtleneck sweater. "Do you recognize it?"

"I recognize it as a sweater that Patricia came in to me with one day and said, 'Mommy, I'm getting like you. I got a bargain on this sweater; it's a Rosanna.' And I said, 'I think the sleeves might be a little short for you; you have long arms.' She tried it on, and it was all right . . ." Her voice trailed off.

Fernandes held up a handbag.

Mrs. Walsh took several deep breaths before she said, "It's a pocketbook that was made by a friend for her."

Fernandes unfolded a torn, wrinkled green smock whose delicate border of embroidery was streaked with dirt.

Mrs. Walsh stared at the garment for a long moment, her face frozen. "That is Patricia's; her long-sleeved overblouse."

Goldman had no questions.

Stepping off the witness stand, Mrs. Walsh opened the clasp of her handbag. Watching her go through the barrier to the courtroom's spectator section, Bernie Flynn grew apprehensive. Never taking her eyes from Tony Costa as she drew close to him, Mrs. Walsh removed her hand from the inside of the bag. Flynn tensed, half-expecting to see a gun. Mrs. Walsh brought a tissue to her lips. Walking down the center aisle of the courtroom, she joined her husband and two sons with whom she would sit throughout the trial.

Before giving testimony, Mrs. Walsh was sequestered in a conference room off the gallery with Sergeant James Sharkey of the state police bureau of photography and fingerprinting. Sharkey found her to be a "lovely person," later telling Flynn, "She couldn't justify what happened to her daughter in her own mind; she still couldn't accept it. She told me Patricia had been controlled, had been carefully supervised, had been brought up right."

Mrs. Walsh confided to Sharkey she had wanted to come to

the trial, "to hear from the witnesses themselves how it all happened."

The family of Mary Anne Wysocki was not represented at the trial of Antone Costa; her parents were reported to be seriously ill.

4

Barnstable County Treasurer Bruce Jerauld had issued $355 expenses for Russell Norton to travel from Boulder Creek, California, where he was now living, to Cape Cod.

Bearded and long-haired, Norton gave his occupation as "leathersmith," before telling Fernandes he had originally planned to accompany Pat Walsh and Mary Anne Wysocki to Provincetown for a weekend. "I couldn't leave on Friday, January twenty-fourth, and the girls went by themselves. We were to meet on Saturday afternoon. I was going to ride back to Providence with them on Sunday. I told them I would probably get to Provincetown somewhere around noon, and for them to be in the Foc's'le. I would meet them there."

"Did you see the girls when you arrived in Provincetown?" Fernandes said.

"No, I didn't."

"Did you make an effort to locate them?"

"Yes, I did . . ."

Mrs. Patricia Morton identified photographs of Patricia Walsh and Mary Anne Wysocki. "They came to the door of my office looking for a room on Friday, January twenty-fourth. I took them through the house first. I merely introduced them to Tony; I said he was present in that particular room and was one of our guests. They nodded faintly and we proceeded on our way and the girls registered. They decided they would stay two nights. I wrote out a receipt and that was that."

Fernandes held up a blue Pan Am flight bag.

"Mary Anne Wysocki had that in her hand when they registered," Mrs. Morton said. "Just their handbags and this little blue thing."

"Did you have occasion to see the girls after their registration on that day?" Fernandes said.

"Just before going to bed, I went upstairs in my bathrobe to check their room. I was afraid it would be cold because it was a bitter, bitter night; about five degrees. They were sitting up, fully dressed, on top of the bed with the spare blanket around each girl's shoulders. They were talking animatedly and seemed quite happy."

"Did you have occasion to go to their room at any other time?"

"Yes, on Saturday morning. I check all the rooms each day, the wastebaskets and general disorder. In the tongue and groove wood construction of the closet door was a note torn from a piece of brown paper bag. It was just stuck there carelessly with a pin, so I read it."

"What did the note say?"

"Something like, 'Could you possibly give me a ride to Truro early in the morning' or something. It was signed, 'Tony.'"

"On Sunday, January twenty-sixth, did you go to that room again?"

"Yes, I did."

"At that time what observations did you make?"

"Well, goodness, all their things were gone! The room was cleared out," Mrs. Morton said. "Then, I noticed the note tacked on the entrance door to the room. It was written on brown paper bag again, and it said, 'We are checking out. Thank you for your many kindnesses.' It was signed, 'Mary Anne and Pat.'"

"During this time had you occasion to see the defendant, Mr. Costa?"

"Yes, to collect the rent."

"Between January twenty-sixth through February first, did you have occasion to see Mr. Costa or go to his room?"

"Fleetingly, I think. I collected the rent again the following week. I noticed things were gradually being taken out of the room without any note saying, 'I'm leaving.'"

"Did you have occasion at a later date to go through Mr. Costa's room with anyone?"

"With three boys who came to my door on Saturday afternoon, February eighth," Mrs. Morton said. "One of them was young Turbidy, and they were looking for Pat Walsh and Mary Anne Wysocki. I took them up to the girls' room at their request. They looked at everything very carefully; they seemed to be searching for something. They turned the mattress over and lifted up the bed and opened the bureau drawers and looked in the closet—that sort of thing. Then we all went downstairs to the room that Antone Costa formerly had. Again, they searched and looked carefully. And they pounced on a hair dryer on the floor, and this turtleneck sweater that was resting on the lower shelf in his closet.

"Whose is *his* closet?"

"Antone Costa."

"Do you recognize Antone Costa in the courtroom?" Beaudreau said.

"Oh, yes!" Mrs. Morton said, and pointed. "I'm nearsighted, but I *do* see him."

"Was his appearance any different than it is now?"

"He looks fatter, and his hair is done differently; and he's dressed in business clothes."

In cross-examination, Goldman said, "Tony didn't dress as nice as he is dressed today?"

"He was always neatly dressed in mod clothes," Mrs. Morton said.

"What kind of clothes?"

"Mod. M-o-d, it's a modified hippie style," Mrs. Morton explained. "Hippies have styles. Some are all-out hippies and some are modified hippies; just sort of *dégagé* things—"

"I don't know what *dégagé* means," Goldman confessed.

"Casual clothes. Turtleneck sweaters, snug pants, and sort of boot things."

"*Tight* pants?" Goldman said.

"Well, no—not excessively."

There was nothing modified about Bob Turbidy's shoulder-length hair and full beard when he took the witness stand. Turbidy had operated the Leather Bench, a leathercraft shop in Provincetown during the summer of 1969.

Turbidy recognized Tony Costa from newspaper photographs. Costa returned Turbidy's curious stare, but Turbidy refused to play the game of chicken with him, looking away when Fernandes asked, "Did you know Pat Walsh?"

"We were sort of engaged, for about a year."

Fernandes held up a handbag. "Can you identify this?"

"That was Patricia Walsh's handbag."

"How do you know?"

"Because I made it for her."

"Did you have occasion to come to Provincetown on February eighth, 1969?"

"Yes, sir. Gerry Magnan and I went to the rooming house on Standish Street and we saw a hair dryer in a closet and a sweater I thought I recognized as Pat's. We called the Provincetown police, and they came to the house. We weren't satisfied, so we called the state police."

Fernandes held up a wrinkled, dirty army fatigue jacket. "Can you identify this?"

"It was my jacket; I wrote my name on the inside label," Turbidy said. "I gave it to Pat Walsh. She used to wear it."

Goldman had no questions.

Fernandes directed Gerry Magnan's attention to February 8, 1969. "Did you have occasion to come to Provincetown?"

"Yes, with Robert Turbidy and John McNally."

"For what purpose?"

"We had found out the name of the residence where Patricia Walsh and Mary Anne Wysocki had stayed. We went there to speak to the manager to see if we could find out anything."

"As a result of this conversation with Mrs. Morton, did you do anything?"

"We went to the room which had been occupied by a gentleman by the name of Costa," Magnan said coldly. "I saw a hair dryer on the floor in the closet. I had seen it before at Mary Anne Wysocki's house in Providence."

Magnan identified a round, mock-alligator hair dryer case and a Pan Am flight bag. "It's one exactly the same as Mary Anne owned and kept personal items in."

Fernandes held up several pieces of torn leather.

"That would be a pocketbook exactly like one Mary Anne carried," Magnan said.

Goldman had no questions.

Magnan was surprised his testimony had taken only ten minutes. "I expected a lot more questions about the rooming house evidence we found," he told Turbidy. "It was all very cut-and-dried; nobody had any feelings for what the girls might have meant to us." Magnan left the courthouse in disgust, convinced that Tony Costa was being "marketed" to get off.

Turbidy felt only sadness after his courtroom appearance. "It was obvious Costa was completely gone, mentally. I couldn't hold a grudge against him. Pat was not a vengeful person. She was an inspiration to me when she was alive, and she'll always be."

Neither Turbidy nor Magnan planned on attending the rest of the trial. The presence of the Walsh family in the courtroom had disturbed Turbidy. "They were like vultures, hovering over Costa, waiting for the kill," Turbidy told Magnan, as they left. "They were hoping he'd get the death penalty."

5

Fernandes guided Irene Hare through a recitation of the evening she and Brenda Dreyer had spent at the Foc's'le and the Pilgrim Club with Pat Walsh and Mary Anne Wysocki, then called James Zacharias to the stand.

Zacharias had worked with Tony Costa as a laborer, digging foundations for the Royal Coachman motel. He had been riding a motorcycle on Saturday morning, January 25, when Costa, a passenger in the front seat of a blue Volkswagen, had flagged him down.

"Did you have the occasion to note who was operating the car?" Fernandes said.

"It was a female," Zacharias said. "There was one more passenger in the backseat, but I don't know if it was a man or a woman."

"Did Tony get out of the car?"

"No."

"Which direction was the Volkswagen going?"

"It was going east," Zacharias said. "Towards Truro."

Carl Benson had come upon a blue Volkswagen, Rhode Island registration KV-978, in a clearing in the Truro woods about thirty feet off a dirt road when he was going down to get the Sunday papers the morning of February 2, 1969. After reporting his find to Chief Berrio of the Truro police, Benson had returned to the woods. "There was an object in the right-hand side of the windshield that wasn't there before," Benson said. "A piece of brown paper with some markings on it."

Benson had not read what the paper said.

William Watts, Sr., followed Benson to the stand. Costa had called Watts around the end of January 1969. "He wanted to know how much it would cost to paint a Volkswagen. I asked my brother; and he said about a hundred dollars, if it didn't have any dents. Tony said the car was in pretty good shape and he'd like to have it painted some exotic color. I told him it wouldn't cost no extra to have it painted any color he wanted. He said he'd stop by, but he never did."

Steve Grund took the stand wearing a brown leather jacket, striped bell-bottom trousers with a wide, big-buckled belt, and an orchid silk shirt. Grund's long hair was slicked back, held at the nape of his neck by two elastic bands. He glanced over at Tony Costa, sighed, and smiled nervously. Costa smiled back.

Grund had known Tony Costa since December, 1968. On the night of February 2, 1969, he had agreed to drive a Volkswagen to Boston. "I asked Tony as to where is the car," Grund said. "He said, 'It's in Truro.' We went out this road in back of the old post office that ends in a circle. We proceeded on foot into the woods, about a mile, and finally came to the car which was parked off the road.

"Tony said, 'I have keys,' and he patted his pants pocket or jacket, I can't remember exactly. We tried to find the gas cap so that we could put gas in. We took up the hood, and there was a bunch of stuff loaded in the car."

"Was there any further conversation about the car?" Fernandes said.

Grund paused, licking his lips. He was swaying slightly on the stand. "I was continuously asking Tony as to how he got the car, what he wanted to go to Boston for. And Tony said, 'I got to get my license back.' This was his main purpose in going to Boston. Then, I asked him, 'How did you get the car?' And he stated he got the car from these two girls that he knew. He said he had fronted the girls a pound of hashish they hadn't paid him for, plus he gave them a couple of hundred dollars."

"Could you explain, 'fronted'?"

"Fronted means to give something to someone so as they can sell it, and then reimburse you with the money that you are asking for the item . . ." Grund closed his eyes. His face was twisted and he had developed a noticeable nodding of his head from left to right.

Costa half stood up. Leaning over the railing, he whispered to Goldman, "Steve's freaking out. He's either on LSD, or coming down from speed; he's crashing."

Fernandes moved closer to his witness. "Now, there came a time when you arrived in Boston?"

"Tony gave me directions, and we got to 415 Beacon Street. We walked up three flights of stairs, to his brother's. We slept in an adjoining apartment. A few hours later, Tony came in to wake me up. He said, 'It's time to go to the airport.' I went back to Provincetown. Tony gave me fifteen dollars for the ticket."

"Did you have occasion to speak with Mr. Costa in Provincetown after that?" Fernandes said.

"Yes, it was during that week," Grund's voice was faint. Beads of perspiration had formed across his upper lip and forehead. "Tony was riding by Adams drugstore on a bicycle. He said he had to get out of town; the cops had been hassling him too much—" Grund's voice trailed off. His face was darkly flushed.

"Hassling?" Fernandes said.

"*Bothering* him!" Grund's knees buckled. He caught the witness stand's railing to steady himself. "Tony said . . . he just wanted . . . to get away . . . from everything . . ."

"Are you all right?" Fernandes said. "Do you want to take a rest?"

"I'd better," Grund whispered and staggered off the witness stand.

* * *

"What's the matter with him?" Dinis asked Killen in a conference room off the gallery.

"He's *on* something," Killen said.

"He's doing speed," Flynn told them. "He took it this morning to give himself courage to testify." Flynn sent Gunnery across the street to the Barnstable Apothecary for three dextroamphetamine tablets to get Grund through the rest of his testimony.

Grund stared hypnotically at the wall in the rear of the courtroom when he resumed testifying.

"Before we suspended, I believe you were relating a conversation you had with Mr. Costa in front of Adams drugstore in Provincetown," Fernandes said.

"Tony said he was going to split, because the cops were hassling him too much. Later on he asked me if I wanted to buy a gun."

"Was this the same day?"

"I believe so, yes," Grund said. "I asked him if it was the same gun he was going to sell to 'Weed'—that's Timmy Atkins. He said yes. I said, 'That gun is hot, I *know* it is. I don't want any part of it.'" Grund closed his eyes. Fernandes handed him a paper cup of water but Grund couldn't hold it in his shaking hand.

Fernandes turned the witness over to Goldman for cross-examination.

"Mr. Grund, I am not concerned with your use of drugs at all; I am concerned about the drugs that Tony used," Goldman said. "You are very friendly with Tony, aren't you?"

"Well, I know Tony," Grund said.

"You called him 'Sire'?"

"Yeah."

"What did that mean?"

"It's just a nickname."

Goldman showed Grund the letter he had written to Tony Costa at Bridgewater. "Did you write this yourself?"

"Yeah, I did."

"You have been called 'Speed,' is that right?"

"Yeah, it is."

Fernandes objected.

"That is excluded," Beaudreau said, and called a bench conference. "These witnesses are *not* to be put on trial. I'm going to exclude any reference to whether these witnesses use drugs."

511

"I'm only asking him what the meaning of 'speed' is," Goldman said innocently.

"That is what I want you to stay away from. You can lay your foundation for your medical here, but I am *not* going to allow you to ask these witnesses whether they are drug users . . ."

Goldman resumed: "Tony was pretty high on the way to Boston, wasn't he?"

"Well, as high as you can get off one joint," Grund said.

"Have you ever seen Tony high on drugs between the period of November 1968 and January 1969?"

"Yeah, I have."

"On how many occasions, would you say?"

"I couldn't tell you exactly how many, because it's been quite a while; maybe three, four, five times."

"It may be *twelve* times, too?" Goldman said.

"Correct, it may be."

"When Tony was high on drugs, how did he act?"

"He was always very easygoing, very congenial with everyone."

"Did Tony come to you sometime between November 1968 and January 1969 in some state or condition that led you to believe he was hung up on drugs?"

"Yeah, he did. He was nervous, distraught. He said he was getting really strung out on downs; that he had to get off them. He couldn't remember anymore, from day to day, or what day of the week or anything."

Goldman asked him, "What does 'strung out' mean?"

"Strung out is the excessive use of something, whatever it may be—drugs, coffee, cigarettes, whatever you want."

"Tony was pretty well gone on drugs, wasn't he?"

"Objection!" Fernandes said.

"I am going to allow that," Beaudreau said. To the witness, he added, "Finish your answer on 'strung out.' We want to know what that means in your language."

"It means, just . . . how do you explain something?" Grund said. "Just excessive use of anything, whereas you gradually lose your memory, or your ability to communicate well with people—"

Goldman pounced on the answer. "You lose your *memory*—"

512

Fernandes objected.

"Occasionally," Grund said.

"I will allow that," Beaudreau said. "Go ahead, Mr. Goldman."

"Strung out means *you lose your memory,*" Goldman said slowly for the jury. "What else does it mean, besides losing your memory?"

"Just the excessive use of drugs, in the general terminology with the so-called hippie sect."

"Thank you, Steve," Goldman said. "I have no further questions."

In Goldman's view, Grund's collapse on the witness stand had been an unexpected bonus for the defense. Despite Beaudreau's insistence that the witness not be questioned about his drug use, Grund had demonstrated it most convincingly to the jury. While the prosecution had sought through Grund to show Costa had been in full possession of his faculties the night he stole the Volkswagen, Grund's testimony had supported the defense's contention that Costa had acted while under the influence of drugs.

Mrs. Eva Atkins of 9 Alden Street, Provincetown, had tried unsuccessfully to have her son, Timmy ("Weed") excused from testifying at the trial of Antone Costa so that he could leave the area.

"He is being persecuted by the law in this town," Mrs. Atkins complained in a letter to the district attorney's office. "Neither I, his mother, nor he can stand it much longer; I would like to send him to my brother's in California." Mrs. Atkins pointed out that Provincetown police had kept Timmy under close surveillance, and had "harassed" the boy with constant interrogations. Atkins had been charged with "driving to endanger," only three days after his driver's license was reinstated . . .

From the witness stand, Atkins pointed to Tony Costa in the courtroom, then abruptly looked away.

Fernandes led him through the events of the night of February 2, 1969, then turned Atkins over the defense.

Goldman said, "We had a long talk about this case, didn't we, Timmy? And I asked you among other things, what drugs Tony was using. Do you remember that?"

"Geez, I can't remember," Atkins said. "Not offhand."

Goldman paused to appraise the sullen, unresponsive witness. "Why are you nicknamed 'Weed'?"

"I don't know. I just picked it up when I was in the sixth grade, that's all."

"How old were you when you were in the sixth grade?"

"I don't know, I can't remember," Atkins said. "I can't figure it out."

"Did you ever visit Tony at Standish Street?"

"Yeah."

"Were there any parties at Standish Street that you attended?"

"Just one."

"Can you give us the date?"

"I can't remember the date."

"Can you at least establish the *year?*"

"I guess it was in 1969. I can't remember what month."

"Was it around Christmastime? Would that help you?"

"No."

"All right, if you can't, you *can't!*" Goldman said, exasperated. "That was a *pot* party, wasn't it? You were all high, weren't you? Just say yes or no—"

"Objection!" Fernandes said.

"That is excluded," Beaudreau said. To the witness, Beaudreau said, "Was *Tony* there?"

"Yeah," Atkins said.

"You don't have a party without at least the *host* being there, Your Honor," Goldman said sharply. To the witness he said, "It was a pot party, wasn't it? By a pot party—we're not going to kid one another—they were all smoking marijuana, weren't they? Tony, in particular, was smoking pot that day?"

"Yeah."

"You know what the word 'stoned' means, don't you, Timmy?"

"Yeah, I guess so."

"Of *course,* you guess so," Goldman said, ironically. "Was Tony stoned that day?"

"Yeah, I guess so, I don't know. Geez, I can't remember back that far. Christ!"

"That ain't too far, Timmy. Come on, help us. Tell us what Tony's condition was that day."

"I can't remember if he was stoned or just—you know—a little bit high, or what."

"This was around Christmas wasn't it? Either the week before or the week after. Is that right, Timmy?"

"I guess so, I don't know. Geez, I can't remember!"

"Was there any hash used at the party at all by Tony?"

"Yeah, I think there was."

"Thank you, Timmy," Goldman said.

Atkins flinched when Fernandes got up from the prosecutor's table and approached the witness stand.

"What observations, if any, did you make of Tony Costa at this party?" Fernandes said.

"I don't know," Atkins said, frowning. "I don't understand what you mean by 'observations.'"

"You used the word 'stoned,' what observations did you make? What did you *see?*"

"I didn't really know if he was stoned or not."

"No further questions," Fernandes said . . .

Joining Steve Grund, Atkins made his way through a corridor to the little-used front door of the courthouse. Running down a steep hill, they vaulted a stone retaining wall. Press photographers who had waited outside the rear entrance raced around to the front of the somber, black granite courthouse in time to catch sight of flying coattails, as the two witnesses disappeared into a waiting car and drove off.

Tom Gunnery took the witness stand to tell of searching an area in the Truro woods where a Volkswagen had been reported abandoned. At the end of a dirt lane, Gunnery had found, among other papers, the cover of a Volkswagen owner's manual.

Fernandes held up the cover wrapped in cellophane. "Will you read what it says?"

"It says, 'Patricia H. Walsh, 241 California Avenue, Providence, Rhode Island,'" Gunnery read. "It has a ZIP code of 02405, and a key number."

Gunnery had also found a "Memory and Date Book," a Rhode Island Automobile Club membership card in the name of Patricia H. Walsh, a bill of sale from Kent County Motors of Warwick, Rhode Island, and Providence public school attendance record cards.

In cross-examination, Justin Cavanaugh asked Gunnery, "These items were not buried? They were all in plain sight?"

"That is correct."

"Did you or any of the enforcement officers find an ammunition can in and around the area you described?"

"The can was found by a Mr. Souza; I think he was just a citizen, not a police officer," Gunnery said. "I believe he turned it over to the Truro police."

"Did you have occasion to look inside the canister?"

"Yes, I did."

"What did you observe?"

"Nothing."

"Was the can submitted for chemical analysis?"

"No, it was not."

"When did you last see this can?"

"It was brought to the barracks at South Yarmouth by myself and Lieutenant Flynn. It was disposed of."

"When you say 'disposed of,'" Cavanaugh said, "what do you mean?"

"It was put out in the rubbish shed in the back of the bar-racks."

"Under whose orders?"

"Lieutenant Flynn's."

"Do you know whether or not there were any traces of drugs found in that canister?"

"I don't know," Gunnery said. "There was nothing in it."

John F. Walters of the FBI in Washington, D.C., had developed a latent print of a portion of a right thumb on the cover of the Volkswagen owner's manual.

"It is my opinion," Walters said on the witness stand, "that the latent print I developed was made by the same finger that made the right thumbprint appearing on the fingerprint card bearing the name Antone Charles Costa."

Francis "Cheney" Marshall had resigned from the Provincetown Police Department to take a position in the state attorney general's office, so James Meads was now acting chief of police of Provincetown. He had known Tony Costa for a year and a half, he testified. As a result of a telephone call from Bob Turbidy regarding two missing girls, he continued, Meads had checked with Mrs. Morton, then called Tony Costa's mother. Costa had called him at the Provincetown police station on Saturday, February 8, 1969. "Tony told me that if he heard anything concerning the girls' whereabouts, he would call me."

"Did you receive another call from him at a later time?" Fernandes said.

"Yes, I did," Meads said. "This was the following day, Sunday, February ninth. Tony said he would like to come to the police station. The words he used was, 'to straighten this matter out concerning the girls on my behalf.' He asked me if I could set up a meeting with Chief Marshall. I made arrangements for a meeting on Monday morning at the police station."

Justin Cavanaugh cross-examined. "Can you help us, Chief Meads, whether or not you know of any use of drugs by Tony Costa during the period that you have known him?"

Meads hesitated. In an affidavit that had accompanied his application for a search warrant in the Jay Von Utter case, Meads had characterized his confidential informant as "a known narcotics user." But on the stand he said, "I can honestly say I don't know of any drugs from my own personal knowledge."

"Then you can't help us?" Cavanaugh said.

Meads looked over at Tony Costa. "No, I'm sorry."

After Bernie Flynn finished testifying about three conflicting stories Tony Costa had given him in Provincetown on February 10, Justin Cavanaugh asked, "I understand you to say that Mr. Costa came to the Provincetown police station of his own volition the morning you had this discussion with him?"

"Yes, he did."

"After you talked with him for a time, you said, 'Clear your mind,' is that right?"

"No, I didn't."

"Didn't you tell the jury a few minutes ago that you said to Mr. Costa after he told you two conflicting stories, 'Clear your mind, and now tell me the truth?' Or words to that effect?"

"I told him that it was confusing. I said, 'Think it over.' I might have used the words, 'Clear your mind,' I'm not sure."

"Lieutenant Flynn, there has been some testimony that you gave orders to dispose of a canister about eighteen inches high and four inches square found in the woods. Is that the fact, Lieutenant?"

"That's the fact, yes."

"You don't know whether or not there was any evidence of drugs in that canister, do you?"

"I do not."

"You did not submit it for chemical analysis?"

"I wasn't investigating drugs," Flynn said. "I was investigating two missing girls. I wasn't interested in—"

"I didn't *ask* you that, did I?" Cavanaugh cut him off.

"No, I answered you." Flynn said.

"The canister was found in that district, wasn't it?"

"The can was handed to me by Chief Berrio. He told me he received it from some man. I looked in the can and there was nothing that connected with my investigation to any murders. I gave the can to Trooper Gunnery and told him to destroy it."

"Why was the can brought from the Truro police station to the Yarmouth barracks if it had no connection with this case?"

"We had no need for the can; it wouldn't help us in our investigation at all. And the can was subsequently destroyed."

"I assume you felt it might not help some eventual defendant who might be in court?" Cavanaugh said.

"I wasn't looking for *your* evidence at that time," Flynn said with a tense smile. "I was looking for two missing girls; and the persons that might have caused the disappearance."

"Then you want to leave it that you weren't looking for any evidence to help any defendant?"

Nettled by Cavanaugh's badgering, Flynn let his temper flare up. "No, I *don't* want to leave it that way!"

"Well, I have asked you a couple of times now why the can was sent from the Truro Police Department to the Yarmouth barracks," Cavanaugh said. "Why wasn't it destroyed at the police department in Truro, if it had no evidentiary value?"

"It was destroyed at the Yarmouth barracks. I *told* you that."

"Under *your* orders, and your orders alone?"

"I told Trooper Gunnery to get rid of the can because it had no evidentiary value to my investigation."

"That was *your* opinion?"

"Yes, that was *my* opinion."

"What other evidence found in that general area of Hatch Road was destroyed?"

"We found various items of clothing—a torn pair of man's pants, a carpenter's apron; we found a blanket, various papers. I picked up many things and just threw them to the ground after looking at them and believing they were of no value to my investigation. . . ."

Flynn recovered his composure under direct examination by Fernandes.

"With reference to your conversation with Mr. Costa on February tenth, what observations did you make of the defendant's physical or mental condition?"

"I observed him to be a very calm individual, unexcitable," Flynn said. "And I observed him to be intelligent."

"Did you have another conversation with Costa after that?"

"Yes, sir. On February twenty-fourth, at approximately six P.M. in my car, outside the Hyannis bus terminal. I said, 'Tony, at this time, the very least you are a suspect in is the larceny of that Volkswagen.' And I said, 'I don't want to be in Provincetown questioning people about you. I have other cases to work on.' I told him, 'Tony, if you hear from these girls, let me know immediately and I will get off this case; as soon as I hear they are alive.' At that point I told him we didn't have anything else to discuss and he left the car."

8

Francis Marshall, in his new position with the narcotics and drug abuse section of the state attorney general's office, was responsible for training all narcotics agents in Massachusetts. To assist him in the lectures he delivered throughout the state, he had obtained from Maurice Goldman abstracts from a case* in which the Massachusetts Supreme Judicial Court had ruled that the testimony of experts justified the conclusion that marijuana was "a mind-altering drug," the smoking of which could cause euphoria, hallucinations, mental confusion and acute panic. The court found smoking marijuana to be "a serious, chronic mental disorder," leading often to the use of more dangerous drugs and, when consumed by persons with personality disorders, could contribute to the onset of "psychotic breaks." Goldman had the case fully briefed for his defense of Antone Costa.

"On March second, I received a telephone call from Tony Costa's mother concerning a telegram sent to Mr. Costa at her house," Marshall said on the witness stand. "The defendant's mother brought the telegram to the station."

Goldman had no objection to Marshall reading aloud the telegram, signed by "Pat and Maryanne."

"Shortly after receiving this telegram, I received a collect call from the defendant, Costa," Marshall said. "He said he was calling from Boston. He asked if his mother had brought the telegram to me. I said, 'Yes, I have it right here,' and I read it back to him.

* *Commonwealth v. Leis*, 243 N.E. 2nd 898, decided January, 1969.

He said, 'I hope you're satisfied that these girls are all right.' I said, 'Will you go to New York and see if you can find these girls as prearranged?' And he said, 'Yes.' I said, 'If you do, call me back and let me know what happened.' And he said he would."

Western Union operator Margaret Procino testified that she had received a telegram from a coin box on March 2, 1969. The sender had given her a New York telephone number, 982-5763, where he could be reached. The unlisted number belonged to one Primitivo Africa, who followed Miss Procino onto the witness stand. The telephone number had been printed on a business card Africa had given Christine Gallant, a close friend of Tony Costa.

Lieutenant Richard Beaulieu of the Burlington, Vermont, police had received a stolen-vehicle complaint from George Killen regarding a 1968 blue Volkswagen, Rhode Island license KV-978.

"We checked the area specified by Lieutenant Killen, which was a Gulf service station," Beaulieu said. "The vehicle in question was parked in an area covered with snow and had no registration plates on it."

"Did you find registration plates at a later time?" Fernandes asked.

"Yes, sir. They were in the trunk of the car underneath a rubber mat."

Beaulieu had gone to a rooming house operated by Mrs. Stella Smith to examine a room rented to Antone Costa. In the room's wastebasket, Beaulieu had found the torn pieces of a bill of sale.

"Did you find anything else in Mr. Costa's room, Lieutenant, such as a book of any kind?" Goldman said in cross-examination.

"*I* didn't, sir, no," Beaulieu said. "Mrs. Smith, the landlady, did. It was a physician's reference book."

Goldman held up a red-bound, dictionary-size volume. "This is a 1968 *Physician's Desk Reference to Pharmaceutical Specialties and Biologicals,*" Goldman said. "Do you know whether this book contains information dealing with drugs and chemicals and their composite parts, such as amphetamines and all types of LSD? It deals with matters of cocaine, morphine, hashish and all the known soft and hard drugs, correct?"

"I don't think there is any reference there to hashish," Beaulieu said. "If there is, I haven't seen it."

Fernandes introduced into evidence a copy of *Hush Hush News* and an application to register a 1968 Volkswagen signed by Antone Costa. Then he announced, "To save time and the expense of bringing an FBI agent from Washington, the parties have agreed to the following stipulation: It was determined that the 'Anthony C. Costa' signature on the bill of sale was prepared by Antone Charles Costa and that the 'Patricia Walsh' signature on the bill of sale was not prepared by Patricia Walsh, nor was the writing on the torn Vermont papers, prepared by her."

"As long as it is further stipulated that the bill of sale was delivered to the police department at Provincetown by the defendant," Goldman added.

9

At the resumption of the trial, following a luncheon recess, a large map of the Truro woods attached to a portable display frame was wheeled up beside the witness stand.

Fernandes recalled Bernie Flynn.

"I direct your attention to March fourth, 1969," Fernandes said. "Did you have occasion to be in the woods in North Truro?"

"We had a small search party out on that particular day. While walking through this area here, I found a brown leather pocketbook, with a shoulder strap."

Fernandes held up the exhibit.

"That is the handbag I found in the woods," Flynn said.

"I direct your attention to the following day, March fifth," Fernandes said. "Were you again in the woods?"

"As a result of finding the pocketbook, we went to this area and searched a square mile," Flynn said, pointing on the map.

Fernandes emptied the contents of a green plastic bag on the prosecutor's table. "Will you identify the items that are there?"

"A piece of cotton, a small vial, bottle, piece of paper, another small bottle, bottle caps," Flynn said. "I was in the presence when Trooper Gunnery found this razor blade and small pieces of rope at the base of a tree. As a result of finding these items, we probed the area and started to dig beneath the surface. Trooper Gunnery was digging a hole when the dirt began to soften. He reached down into the hole, and as a result of what he felt there, we began to dig further."

The courtroom was absolutely silent. Costa sat listening attentively to Flynn, his eyes fixed on the map.

"Lieutenant Killen reached into the hole," Flynn continued. "And he came up with an arm, an arm protruded above the surface, the wrist and hand exposed. As a result of that, we started taking dirt out by hand. We dug down approximately twelve inches. I saw what appeared to be hair. I reached into the hole, and I pulled the hair. And, as I did so, it . . . removed itself from the scalp."

Flynn calmly held up a lock of brunette hair taken from hole number 1. "As a result of that, we dug further into the hole," he continued. "By that time it was approximately a foot and a half deep. I reached in and lifted up what appeared to be the head of a white female."

Mrs. Catherine Walsh turned ashen. Tears welled up in her eyes. Leonard Walsh put his arm around his wife's shoulders, drawing her close.

"Why don't we take a short recess at this time?" Beaudreau said.

Leonard Walsh led his wife to a water cooler in the corridor. Few others had left their seats during the recess. When she returned to the crowded courtroom, Mrs. Walsh was composed.

"Before continuing with your testimony, Lieutenant Flynn," Fernandes resumed, "would you identify these two photographs."

"Exhibit number seven is a photograph of Patricia Walsh which I obtained from her parents," Flynn said. "Exhibit eight is a photograph of Mary Anne Wysocki which I obtained from the parents of Mary Anne."

Fernandes passed the photographs to the jury.

"Prior to recess, you stated you had found what?" Fernandes said.

"I reached into the hole and I pulled out the severed head of a white female," Flynn said. "I held the head in my arms and I brushed the dirt, sand and gravel from the eyes. I brushed some sand and gravel off her face and opened her mouth and took the dirt and sand from the mouth. And as a result of doing that, I recognized the face as being that of Mary Anne Wysocki."

Fernandes showed Flynn a photograph from a group of five he held in his hand. "Is that a fair representation of what you saw after removing what you described as a head?"

"Yes, it is."

"What did you do next?"

"Along with Trooper Gunnery, we dug further into the hole to remove the portion of body that was exposed. By reaching our hands under the armpits, we pulled up the upper half of a female body, severed at the mid-abdomen. We placed that next to the head on top of a pile of sand."

Fernandes showed Flynn another photograph. "Is that a fair representation of what you saw at this time?"

"Yes, it is."

Fernandes brought a green plastic garbage bag to the witness stand. "Did you find anything else in hole number one?"

"At that time we pulled out a torn sleeve of a jersey, torn pieces of panty hose, this pair of shoes," Flynn said, holding up the exhibits. "This white plastic container, various pieces of cardboard which appeared to have contained pills, some small bottles, and a great number of bottle caps. And this piece of rope, approximately twenty or twenty-five feet in length."

"On that same day, did you have occasion to go to another area?" Fernandes said.

"Yes, I did. As we continued searching for items in hole number one, Park Ranger Kimple called to us. He pointed to an area in the ground approximately two hundred feet away." Flynn indicated on the map. "We began digging there. Down about two feet, I observed the flesh of a white female. We continued digging, and taking dirt out with our hands until exposed was the lower half of a white female, cut above the hips, the pelvis, buttocks and both legs. The legs were slashed down the side. I stepped into the hole and pulled out this portion of the body; I placed it on the ground above the hole. As we dug further down, I observed the

524

upper portion of a white female's body, including the head, chest and abdomen, and the arms and hands. I pulled this portion of the body out and placed it on the ground."

"I ask you to examine this photograph," Fernandes said. "Is that a fair representation of what you observed at that time?"

"Yes, it is."

"Was anything else found in hole number two?"

"Portions of body and clothing."

"What portions of body?"

"The pelvis of a white female, severed at the hip joints," Flynn said. "And also the left and right leg of a female."

Fernandes gave the photographs to Goldman.

Goldman had listened impassively to Flynn's devastating testimony, delivered in a tight-lipped monotone. Shuffling through the photographs, he was appalled that a depiction of such horrifying carnage was destined to go to the jury. There was nothing Goldman could do to prevent the photographs from being entered as evidence, since they were clearly admissible.

Goldman was not at first aware that Tony Costa had half risen from his place in the courtroom and was craning for a look at the photographs over Goldman's shoulder. Goldman shot him a sharp look of disapproval, then he called for a bench conference.

"As I understand it, these only concern Wysocki and Walsh, nobody else," Beaudreau said, looking at the photographs.

"That's right," Fernandes said.

"Who is *that*, allegedly?" Beaudreau asked, pointing to one of the prints.

"That's the top part of Walsh. And that's the bottom half of Walsh and Wysocki," Fernandes said. "Dr. Katsas will tie them in with the pieces."

Beaudreau addressed the jury. "The government is about to introduce a series of photographs. They are not introduced for any inflammatory or prejudicial effect on your senses; they are introduced merely to show the condition of the bodies found as Lieutenant Flynn has testified. You are asked to guard against any prejudicial effect that these photographs may have."

Goldman watched the first juror, Mrs. Emma Sacht, inspect the photographs, flinch, and quickly pass them along to Mrs. Frances Leonardi sitting next to her.

Fernandes resumed his examination. "Was anything else found in hole number two?"

525

"Just assorted clothing we took out of the grave."

Fernandes held up an off-white sweater darkly stained with dried blood. "Will you tell us whether or not you can identify this?"

"It's what I call a white cable-knit sweater which was taken from the hole." Flynn also identified a green army jacket, and a pair of torn dungarees. "We also took these pieces of boots from hole number two and also two bras, torn pieces of panty hose similar to that in hole number one and a left glove."

Fernandes entered into evidence the items Flynn had identified. "With one further stipulation," he told the court.

"Shall I make it?" Goldman spoke up.

"If you wish," Fernandes said.

"It is stipulated and agreed between the commonwealth and the defense," Goldman said, "that the boots contained in this exhibit are cut—not decomposed—by the use of some sharp instrument."

To Flynn, Goldman said in cross-examination, "The graves each contained some drug bottles, do you recall?"

"Objection!" Fernandes said.

"I will allow it—if the lieutenant can answer this question," Beaudreau said.

"They each contained bottles, yes," Flynn said.

"Do they resemble the style or type of bottle in which pills or drugs are contained?"

"Yes, they do."

"And there were plastic bottle caps?"

"Yes, sir."

"Did you notice that some of the bottle caps contained the name Wallace, W-a-l-l-a-c-e?"

"Yes, sir."

"And do you know that to be a pharmaceutical house?"

"No, I don't," Flynn said, but the point was made.

10

Fernandes recalled Tom Gunnery to the witness stand to testify to finding three expended .22 caliber short shells in hole number 1 on March 12.

"Did you return to the woods in Truro on March thirty-first?" Fernandes asked.

"Yes, I did," Gunnery said. "I resumed a search in area number three, near the parking space, right there." Gunnery pointed. "At the base of a pine tree, I uncovered the turf and I found a plastic bag. I observed in this plastic bag a .22 caliber revolver, make EIG, which had white grips on its handle." Gunnery had turned the weapon over to Lieutenant George Killen.

Sergeant Chester E. Hallice, Jr., of the Massachusetts State Police Ballistics Bureau had received the gun from George Killen. Taking the witness stand, Hallice said, "It is my opinion that the three .22 caliber discharged cartridge casings were fired from the submitted .22 caliber EIG revolver, serial number 549086."

After Lester Schrader, floor manager of the Bluefield Supply Company, identified the gun as one which had been sold to druggist John Taylor of Bluefield, West Virginia, Fernandes called to the witness stand, "Mr. Cory Devereau."

"I would like to sit down," Devereau said.

Shaggy-haired and bearded, Devereau passed his pale eyes to Tony Costa and nodded. Costa did not respond; he sat rigid with attention, staring intently at the witness.

"How old are you, Mr. Devereau?" Fernandes said.

"Eighteen."

"Are you acquainted with the defendant, Antone Costa?"

"Yes."

"How long have you known him?"

"I've known him for about two years."

"Have you any relatives that live in West Virginia?"

"I have a grandmother, Viola Taylor."

"Did you have occasion to visit your grandmother?" Fernandes said.

527

"I went down there in the spring of 1968, about the middle of April."

Fernandes showed him the gun. "Can you identify it?"

"That gun used to belong to my grandfather. I brought it back to Provincetown with me when I left," Devereau said. "It was in my possession until the end of June 1968, for about two months. Then I sold it."

"Did your grandmother know you took this gun from her house?"

"When I took it, she didn't know."

"Mr. Devereau, I believe you stated you sold the gun," Fernandes said. "To whom did you sell it?"

"Antone Costa."

There was a murmur in the courtroom.

"What were the circumstances concerning the negotiations of the sale of the gun?" Fernandes said. "Did you ask him if he wished to purchase it?"

Devereau hesitated. "I just want to make sure I remember this."

"All right, take your time." Fernandes wanted Devereau to get it right.

"I think Tony heard I had a gun. He asked me if I wanted to sell it—and I did, for twenty dollars."

"Thank you," Fernandes said. "You may inquire, Mr. Goldman."

Goldman approached the witness stand. Devereau was a poised and convincing witness; certainly not the drugged-out hippie Costa had painted him to be.

"Cory, you and Tony were close personal friends, weren't you?" Goldman said.

"I would say fairly close. We were good friends, yes."

"You socialized together? You went to his house, didn't you? And he went to your house, too?"

"Occasionally," Devereau said. "My father didn't like him. He didn't believe someone that old should be hanging around with me, because I was much younger than him. I was sixteen at the time, and my father didn't approve it."

"You didn't share your father's view, though?"

"No, I liked Tony."

"Did you ever go to Truro to visit his marijuana patch?"

"No."

528

"Did you ever go to Truro at all with Tony?"

"Yes, twice."

"And what did you go out there for?"

"Tony had a stash of pills in the woods," Devereau said.

"Where was the stash of pills located, to the best of your memory?"

"Behind a big, funny-looking tree," Devereau said. "There was some kind of a metallic container that was directly behind the trunk of the tree; it was round. We walked a while and we saw this big, funny-looking tree and he said, 'That's it.' And there was a hole there, covered with leaves."

"Can you tell us what was contained in the can, the type of drugs?"

"There was different kinds of amphetamines and barbiturates. Some of the barbiturates were Nembutal, Seconal, phenobarbital and sodium amytal. And some of the amphetamines were Dexedrine, methamphetamine . . . There was more, but I can't remember the names."

"Did you ever see Tony *use* drugs?"

"I saw Tony smoke marijuana, smoke hashish, use amphetamines and use barbiturates."

"How many times?"

"*Very* many."

"Did you ever see Tony stoned?"

"Yes."

"How many times did you see him stoned?"

"Too many to count. I would say, well over a hundred."

Goldman said, "I take it you were also with Tony when he was *not* using drugs. Tell us what Tony was like during those times he wasn't using drugs."

"He liked to sit down and talk, you know. People that are friends sit down and tell jokes between one another, talk about different things, girls, anything that comes to mind."

"How was he different with drugs than without?"

"He was still like a normal person. When Tony took barbiturates, sometimes he wouldn't talk to anybody. Sometimes, if he had a problem he would be depressed; he would sit down and just think. When he was on speed, he was more talkative about his beliefs; he would be overly happy, you know."

Goldman said, "In other words, there was never any change in his personality, whether he was using any 'acid' or not?"

529

"To my knowledge, Tony never used acid," Devereau said.

"When he used speed, was there any change in his personality?"

"The only thing I can think of is, he would talk more than usual."

"Other than that, there was no change?"

"In his personality, no. I don't think so. He was the same way when he was not on drugs."

"Was he ever violent when he was on any drug?"

"I have never seen Tony violent in my life," Devereau said emphatically.

"What kind of a person was Tony Costa?"

"I like him," Devereau said, earnestly. "I like Tony."

11

When his trial was recessed until Monday morning, Costa was escorted to the Barnstable House of Correction. A neatly typewritten three-page letter from Avis was waiting for him:

May 14, 1970

Dear Tony,

I've been wondering just exactly how I was going to tell you this and I can't come up with any good ideas, so the best thing is to tell it like it is. I am engaged. A few weeks ago I wrote you a letter about Peter (my old man) but I decided against mailing it, because I wanted to be sure about everything this time, before shooting off my mouth. I hesitate to tell you any of this for fear you will think I'm an asshole. NOTE: (Censor, please don't cut out the word asshole, any other word wouldn't have been descriptive enough. Thank you, Peace. A.L.C.)

But, Tony, you know me better than most people do, and therefore I think you know that any decisions I make concerning the future will be with much deliberation and with the kids best interest at heart. I, of course, am concerned for you, but they come first. You have planned your life, done your thing, and you will go on accordingly. They have a lifetime before them, and I want it to be normal and healthy. With a father and mother present. They feel that they are lucky 'cause they'll have two fathers. I think they're lucky in that respect, also. They'll have three times the love that any normal one-father-family kid would have.

Anyway, to go on. Peter is 27 years old and he knows what he's doing. I think you've probably met him before, but I don't think you'd remember. He's a friend of my family, oddly enough, and they are all very much in favor of the relationship. That, of course means a lot to me. Always did, and always will. He is a great person and I'm sure you'd really dig him. I wish you could meet him. In fact, I think one day I'll talk to Mr. Goldman and see if some Sunday, I can go to the jail with him and the kids and maybe they'll let Peter in, too. I would be much stronger with him there. He is working two jobs right now, and working really hard. I feel bad about it, but that's the way he is. He's a carpenter by day, and a fry cook by night. Soon he'll be cooking at the Inn full-time and will have a little more time off. That'll be a nice change.

After we're married, Peter wants to adopt the kids. I don't know how long it would be, but at least he's really serious about it. We've given it a lot of thought, too. It's not something we dreamed up overnight. Of course, first and foremost, I want to make sure that it is okay by you. I don't want to know right away. You can weigh all the possibilities in your mind. It'll give you something to think about other than this whole lousy trial.

Yesterday our son Peter asked if life was just one big dream. I think he wants to wake up. People keep asking who his father is. As for me, I am now under a doctor's care and am being kept mildly tranquil by way

531

of green and black librium. I will need a double dose on the days I may have to testify. I seriously don't think I am strong enough to handle it.

Well, I guess I've said everything I wanted to say. I hope I've brought you up, somewhat, and haven't put you through too many changes. It's all real. And I want you to know we're all happy about it. Peter, me and the kids. They absolutely love him. He is ultra-demonstrative when it comes to love and affection. He even lets my ugly dog slop all over him.

One favor to ask of you, please don't show this letter to anyone or repeat any of my marriage plans. I only wanted you to know. First, so that you can relax about the future of our kids. Also, if it gets around, it's going to fall into the wrong hands. I.E. YOUR FRIENDLY NEIGHBORHOOD NEWS MEDIA. That could get to be a hassle, and as a long range result, Peter could lose his job. Can you dig what I'm saying? So, the quieter it's kept, the better off we'll all be. If it gets out, I'll know it was the jail censor, as I don't think you want to make my life miserable. It's hard enough just being Avis Costa.

Well Tony, I want to wish you good luck and steady nerves in the weeks to come, and the same sentiments from Peter. Keep yourself together and I'll try to do the same. I'll be seeing you someday soon. If I don't expire in the meantime.

Much love,
Avis

Later, Lester Allen brought the letter to Goldman's office, explaining, "It knocked Tony on his fanny."

532

12

"I believe Your Honor directed counsel at the beginning of the proceedings to take whatever precautions they could to not be part of any news reporting that might be inflammatory, principally concerning the defendant," Edmund Dinis said at a lobby conference prior to the resumption of the trial on Monday morning. "This article that appeared in the *Standard-Times*—I don't think it's fair to be shooting at me at this particular time."

"I read it yesterday," Beaudreau said. "Fortunately, the jury is impaneled; they won't read it. Who is Charles Koehler?"

"He's a reporter around here," Goldman spoke up. "He asked me, 'When is the trial going to end,' and I said, 'I don't know.' He said, 'How about Mr. Dinis's case?' and I said, 'I don't think Mr. Dinis knows.' That is the only thing I said to him or any other reporter concerning the length of the trial."

Dinis was angered at the article's suggestion that he had botched the prosecution of the Chappaquiddick case involving Senator Ted Kennedy. Koehler's article had also represented Goldman as "feared, liked, hated and admired," his courtroom tactics described as "electric on occasion," and had reported, "Goldman takes payment 'in kind.' In his private life he operates a large summer camp in Brewster."

"I'm just as upset about the article as Mr. Dinis is," Goldman said. "I think it's a horrible thing that he implied I take it out in trade." Goldman was amused that Dinis would take umbrage at any publicity, since he had single-mindedly sought newspaper space in the Costa case. "Ed, you don't think that I had anything to do with that, do you, knowing me as you do?"

"I'm going to let this go by, Mr. Dinis," Beaudreau said. "I don't think he had anything to do with it. I certainly don't think he would want this in-trade business."

Goldman was not looking forward to the testimony he expected to hear from the next scheduled witness. Dr. George Katsas was being sworn in.

A graduate of the University of Athens, Greece, medical

school, presently associated with the Law-Medicine Institute of Boston University, Katsas was associate pathologist at Waltham Hospital. On March 6, 1969, Katsas had performed autopsies on two young women, identified by their dental charts as Patricia Walsh and Mary Anne Wysocki.

"The body of Patricia Walsh was cut in two pieces at about the midline of the abdomen, so that the upper part of the body contained the head, the chest, part of the abdomen, the hands and arms," Katsas said, in a lightly accented voice. "The body of Mary Anne Wysocki was cut into five pieces: the head and part of the neck; the chest; the pelvis, and two separated legs."

"With reference to the Walsh and Wysocki bodies, I ask you to examine these photographs," Fernandes said. "Are they a fair representation of what you observed?"

The photographs had been taken in Katsas's presence and under his direction. "Some of the pictures indicate the appearance of the bodies before I washed the sand and gravel off the skin," Katsas said.

Fernandes gave the photographs to Goldman.

"Please tell us what your examination revealed with reference to the victim Walsh," Fernandes said, returning to the witness.

"On the back of the neck was an entrance gunshot wound," Katsas said. "The skin was peeled off the chest in a fashion like a sweater, so that it was attached only about the shoulders. On the lower part of the body, predominantly, there were many slash wounds of the skin and deep tissues. Stab wounds were also present on the back of the chest. Most of the internal organs were present; the internal genital organs were unremarkable. I took smears from the rectum and the vagina of Patricia Walsh. When I examined this material under the microscope, I found sperm—spermatozoa—in both the rectum and the vagina."

Catherine Walsh bowed her head and stared at the floor. Costa was attending the testimony raptly, his hands resting in his lap. Goldman was studying a copy of the autopsy report at the defense table.

"Now, with reference to the other victim, Wysocki," Fernandes said. "Will you please give us what examination you performed?"

"The examination followed essentially the same pattern as the Walsh body: taking pictures, recording the findings, and examining the remains externally, then the internal organs," Katsas said. "Where the chest was separated from the pelvis, the skin was sharply cut. The pelvis was not separated through a relatively soft part; instead, the vertebrae itself was fractured. The bone of the spine was broken."

"You made the finding: 'This part of the body is covered with skin which is sharply cut along edges corresponding to the outline of panties.'" Fernandes said, glancing at his notes. "Is there any significance to the article of wearing apparel in that finding?"

"Merely for descriptive purposes," Katsas said. "The upper part of the cutting of the skin was about where the elastic waistband of a pair of panties would be, and the upper thighs was exactly where the legs of the panties would end."

"Somebody outlined the wounds to that portion of the female anatomy normally covered by panties?" Fernandes said.

"It looked that way."

"Can you tell us whether there is some sexual pathology indicated by that finding?"

"I have no opinion on that, sir," Katsas said.

"Now, continuing with your examination of Miss Wysocki . . ."

"At the back of the neck was an entrance gunshot wound," Katsas said. "Another entrance wound was present on the left side of the head, above the left ear. There was a bullet track which kept going through the skull, then to the brain. I found a bullet at the base of the skull on the right side. The lower extremities were completely cut off the body. The legs and the buttocks showed many stab wounds, which involved the skin and underlying muscles and soft tissues. Stab wounds were also present in the chest where the skin was again peeled off the underlying tissues and stuck on the body like a sweater. I obtained smears from the vaginal orifice and the rectum of Mary Anne Wysocki. Microscopically, I found sperm in both areas."

"From your examination, was there any evidence leading you to conclude there was a need for an abortion in either of the girls?"

"I found no evidence of pregnancy, and no injuries consistent with abortion," Katsas concluded.

Gray-haired, erect in bearing, Lawrence Shubow gave off an air of authority and confidence as he made his way to the witness stand to cross-examine Katsas. Goldman was counting on him to neutralize as much of Katsas's devastating testimony as he could.

Cavanaugh admired Shubow as "a fine, fine gentleman, and a brilliant lawyer—the best we could get." Shubow would conduct the "medical" aspects of the defense of Antone Costa.

"Is it fair to assume that the stab wounds on these bodies had been inflicted *after* death?" Shubow said.

"Yes, it is correct to assume this, with one exception," Katsas said. "Some of the stab wounds may have been inflicted while the person was still alive, but with low blood pressure. In other words, while dying."

"But you have no *evidence* that any such wounding was done during that period? The wounds are consistent with having been inflicted *after* death?"

"That is correct."

"The stab wounds were of a slash-type character and quite lengthy and numerous," Shubow said. "Would it be fair to characterize those wounds as exhibiting a great deal of uncontrolled aggression?"

"Frankly, I cannot answer that question," Katsas said. "It is a completely psychiatric question."

"I take it that the peeling of skin from the chest area of both these bodies with what you called a 'sweaterlike effect' was not connected with the dismemberment, but something in addition to it?"

"That was a separate process, yes."

"And is the peeling of the skin consistent with having been done *after* death?"

"Yes, sir, it is."

"That was a rather bizarre finding, was it not?"

"Yes, it was very bizarre; very unusual."

"In your examination of the sperm, which you found in two separate places, do you have any way of determining when that sperm found its way where you eventually located it?"

"No, sir, I have no way to know that."

"Your examination does not disclose whether the age of the sperm is the same as the time of death?"

"It is consistent with having been the same."

"From what you just said, can I draw the inference that the sperm was inserted into the body *after* death?" Shubow said.

"Yes, sir."

"As a forensic pathologist, have you ever run into the term 'necrophilia'?"

"Yes, sir, I have."

"What does the term necrophilia mean to you?"

"Necrophilia is a psychiatric term indicating the perversion of certain persons to have sexual attraction to dead bodies; 'necros' is the dead person."

"And your pathological findings are consistent with the conduct to be expected from a person with the psychiatric condition you have identified as 'necrophilia'?" Shubow said.

"If one assumes the sperm was inserted after death, one may be talking about a case of necrophilia, yes."

"Your findings *are* consistent with the sperm having been inserted after death?"

"They are consistent with having been inserted after death, *or* before death," Katsas said.

"I, of course, didn't ask you that, doctor," Shubow said pleasantly. "What I'm looking for is that your findings are consistent with the sperm having been inserted after death. Can you give me that?"

"Certainly."

"In connection with the approximately four thousand postmortems you have done, how many examples of necrophilia have you found?"

"There may be less than half a dozen cases in which sperm was present."

Fernandes took over questioning the witness. "With reference to the finding of sperm, it's as consistent with having occurred *prior* to death as with having occurred after death, is that right?"

"That is correct," Katsas said. "There is no way of determining that."

"You are not saying *this* is a case of necrophilia?"

"No, sir, I didn't say that."

Shubow resumed his cross-examination. "However, doctor, it *is* consistent with a case of necrophilia, is it not?"

"If there is sexual continuation after death, one may call it necrophilia. I'm not sure exactly what the psychiatrists would define as necrophilia."

"Can you think of any other term for it *but* necrophilia?"

"Just sexual intercourse with a body after death."

"Well, isn't that what necrophilia means?" Shubow said. "Sexual intercourse with a cadaver?"

"I'm not a psychiatrist," Katsas said. "Maybe I shouldn't answer."

"Will you agree it's a rare finding on postmortem examination?"

"Yes, sir. It is."

"I neglected to ask you in connection with the sperm finding whether the state of medical art has reached the point where sperm can be typed, as blood can be typed?" Shubow said.

"Yes, it can be typed, if it's fresh."

"Was it possible to type this particular sperm?"

"No," Katsas said. "As a matter of fact, I was surprised from the medical point of view that I did find the sperm, because of the estimated time of death. Usually, sperm decomposes as other parts of the body. It might have disappeared because of the time element between the death and the examination."

"Is it possible the sperm was not as old as the date of death?" Shubow said.

The courtroom was terribly quiet.

"No, sir. It is *not* possible."

"But if the sperm was deposited later than the time of death, wouldn't that be some explanation for its survival?"

"Of course, with several weeks having elapsed between the death and the examination, one or two days after death would not make much difference as far as the appearance of the sperm."

"What about a *week* after death?"

Katsas stared at Shubow curiously. "I don't know. No one knows."

"I really hoped you would be able to answer a question about whether these stab wounds required considerable amounts of force," Shubow said.

"Many of these wounds were deep," Katsas said. "One of the ribs was fractured beneath a wound; I would say this requires some effort. On the other hand, it depends on what kind of instrument one is using."

"And, I suppose, in part on the strength of the actor?"

"That is correct."

"In any case, the wounds showed considerable force?" Shubow persisted.

"To penetrate the skin, one does not need considerable force," Katsas said. "The wounds *were* deep enough," Katsas added, thoughtfully. Then: "I would agree with you that they would represent considerable force."

Shubow finally had the answer he wanted. "*Thank* you, doctor!"

Melvin Topjian testified that he had detected no barbiturates in the blood of Mary Anne Wysocki or Patricia Walsh. The length of rope taken from hole number 1 and placed into evidence by Bernie Flynn had disclosed varying shades of dark-brown human head hair consistent in length with female hair. The surface of the rope had indicated the presence of occult blood. "That is," Topjian explained, "blood not readily visible to the eye."

Topjian had also detected human blood on a snow brush found in the trunk of Pat Walsh's Volkswagen and the interior of the car itself, on a knife and knife case already in evidence and on the surface of a pair of work boots belonging to Tony Costa. A sample of earth taken from the graves was similar in character to the soil removed from the eyelets of the work boots.

Topjian had found residual amounts of long-acting and short-acting barbiturates in the rinsings of a white plastic bottle found in one of the graves.

"Did you also examine some little glass bottles and vials with rubber stoppers or metal vial seals?" Shubow said.

"Yes, I did."

"Can you characterize that type of bottle?"

"It would be a bottle that we use for injectable material, a pharmaceutical preparation intended for injection."

"By injection, you mean either under the skin or into the veins?"

"That's correct, sir."

"Did you examine those bottles for any traces of residual contents?"

"I found the *containers* for Triavil 2-10; I did not find the material itself."

"That is a psychoactive drug, is it not?" Shubow said. "It's dangerous when not administered by a physician?"

"It's a prescription product," Topjian said. "There are precautions that should be taken with the drug, yes."

When Topjian left the witness stand, Dinis said, "We would like to stipulate at this time that the chemist for the commonwealth examined the tree near hole 1. Where the branches were broken along the trunk some six or seven feet off the ground, he found evidence of human blood; and also on the trunk of the tree down toward the roots."

"And with that, Your Honor," Dinis said, "the commonwealth rests its case."

13

Goldman had listened with equanimity to the overwhelming circumstantial evidence brought against Antone Costa, admiring the skill and efficiency with which the prosecution's case had been presented by Armand Fernandes. Goldman had not challenged a single piece of evidence; nor had he lodged one exception to Beaudreau's rulings.

Throughout the testimony of prosecution witnesses, Goldman had received a steady stream of notes from Tony Costa, urging him to cross-examine. Costa was especially insistent that Goldman "break down" Bernie Flynn and Cory Devereau. Goldman had ignored such directives and, during a recess, had explained to Costa that there was no point in cross-examination if it did not benefit the case. The testimony Costa objected to was not only admissible, but virtually unassailable, Goldman told him. There was no legal advantage to be won by challenging it.

Convinced that Costa was guilty but sick, Goldman stood up at the defense table. He let the expectant quiet of the courtroom last a long moment before opening the defense's case.

"For over a week now, you have heard some very devastating and shocking evidence concerning the atrocities committed against two young ladies who were killed on a weekend visit to Provincetown," Goldman said. "A certain young man is charged with these atrocities. His name is Tony Costa. We propose to show that Mr. Costa has been fully made sick as a result of the use of

540

mind-altering drugs. We will show the impact of these mind-altering drugs. You are going to hear unfolded on the witness stand by lay people and by experts, what drugs will do. We want to show you that there was an underlying personality that, if left alone, wouldn't have created any problems. We are going to show you what happened to a personality such as this as the result of total, long-lasting drug dependence; what to a man who gets possessed of drugs. We are going to show you step by step how the use of drugs increased, increased, *increased,* until ultimately drugs will absolutely control you so you have no mental capacity to know what you are doing. You have no control over yourself.

"We propose to show that an unconscious force actually determined a man's deed; that he didn't possess the premeditation to commit a crime. He wasn't *capable* of committing a crime. He didn't know what he was doing, by virtue of being under the influence, domination and control of mind-altering drugs.

"Now, the government has set forth a very fine case. The police did a marvelous job; they should be complimented. But they fail to understand the consequences of one who is under the complete addiction, possession and control of drugs.

"Tony Costa is on trial today," Goldman said. "So are drugs."

Fernandes called for a bench conference.

"Your Honor, he used the defendant's capacity to know what he was doing," Fernandes said, turning to Goldman. "Are you maintaining this is an insanity defense?"

"You can figure it out," Goldman said. "It's a diminished mental capacity, under the McHoul case."

"If the issue is going to be a plea of insanity, then maybe we can shorten this trial tremendously," Fernandes said.

"You cannot plead not guilty to this charge by reason of insanity," Shubow said.

"I understand that," Fernandes said. "Mr. Goldman used the term 'diminished capacity'; that bothers me. Are you using this as a plea of insanity? Are you saying he couldn't form premeditation?"

"They are leaving the door open for, let's say, a legal gimmick, for want of better words," Beaudreau explained to Fernandes. "Or am I being too sloven in my talk when I say that?" he said, addressing the defense lawyers.

"We are introducing evidence of diminished capacity which is

541

relevant to the issue of clemency if the evidence warrants a conviction of first-degree murder, or to a conviction of second-degree if the jury decides this man does not have the requisite mental capacity for criminal responsibility," Shubow said. "We expect the court to propose instructions that one of the choices open to these jurors would be insanity."

"Then we have no problem," Beaudreau said.

"We are staying clearly within the mental capacity test under the McHoul case," Goldman said.

(A patient in a mental hospital, James N. McHoul, Jr., had been convicted and sentenced for assault with intent to commit rape. His appeal, heard by the Massachusetts Supreme Judicial Court, had provided the occasion for a restatement of the test for criminal responsibility, replacing the old M'Naghten rule which had held that to establish insanity, it had to be proved at the time of the commission of the crime that the defendant did not know right from wrong. In the McHoul case, the Supreme Court had adopted new wording for a dual test:

A person is not responsible for criminal conduct if at the time of such conduct as a result of mental disease or defect, he lacks substantial capacity either to appreciate the criminality [wrongfulness] of his conduct or to conform his conduct to the requirements of law.

Where the M'Naghten rule presumed every man to be sane until the contrary was proven, under McHoul the presumption of sanity disappeared from a case the moment evidence to the contrary was introduced. The opinion of experts on either side of the issue of insanity was not the conclusive factor; the decision of criminal responsibility was to be made by the jury.)

The defense called as its first witness Dr. Sidney Callis. To advance the defense's position that Tony Costa had been involuntarily addicted, it was Shubow's task in his examination to show that Callis was so inept a practitioner of the medical arts as to have hooked his own patient on prescriptive drugs.

Callis, a former resident in psychiatry at Bridgewater State Hospital, had graduated from Kansas City University of Physicians and Surgeons. He had been in the general practice of medicine in Massachusetts since 1942. "And I also practice psychosomatic medicine," he said.

"Would you explain briefly what 'psychosomatic medicine' is?" Shubow said.

"Psychosomatic medicine deals with the interaction between the mind and body, or emotional illness, treated by psychotherapy and medication."

"You do not profess to be a psychiatrist within the special meaning of that specialty, do you?" Shubow said pointedly.

"I do not confine my work to psychiatry," Callis said. "But I *do* practice psychosomatic medicine."

Shubow's questions led Callis to his first meeting with Antone Costa on December 8, 1965. "The patient complained of nervous tension, a gnawing pain over the stomach," Callis said. "He also complained of burning on voiding. He stated he had been treated by Dr. Daniel Hiebert for four years."

"And what findings did *you* make at that time?"

"After a careful examination and review of his history, I concluded that he was a strong, healthy fellow, and that there was some question of an emotional problem."

"Did you define this problem *medically* in any way?"

"I felt he was suffering from gastritis and that he was what I might call a psychoneurotic with anxiety," Callis said. "I prescribed Kolantyl, an antacid for his gastritis; and I dispensed thirty Solacen capsules, which is a mild tranquilizer."

"What was there about his physical condition that called for Solacen?" Shubow said.

"His physical condition was manifested by his nervousness," Callis said. "He stated he was having marital problems with his wife; that she was unhappy with him."

"Do you remember any discussions of a problem of sexual compatibility?"

"This was not mentioned by him, sir."

"Was there a time when you *changed* the medication for dealing with his psychoneurosis?" Shubow asked in a subtly disdainful voice.

"On July tenth, 1967, I placed the patient on Aventyl, which is an antidepressant. The patient was depressed; I felt, from his description of his problems at home, that he was in a mild depression, so I prescribed an antidepressant."

"What were you treating him for in 1967?"

"Gnawing pains in the stomach, nervous upset."

"And the treatment prescribed at that time?"

543

"Meprospan, four hundred milligrams, a mild tranquilizer similar to Solacen. He was given fourteen capsules and told to take one every twelve hours."

"Of course, the doctor never knows whether his patient takes medication as prescribed, does he?" Shubow said.

"No, sir."

Shubow paused to emphasize a question, crucial to the defense's position that Callis had prescribed drugs more potent than tranquilizers and had been responsible for Costa's involuntary addiction to barbiturates. "Did you ever prescribe Nembutal for Mr. Costa?"

"I have no recollection that I prescribed Nembutal at any time," Callis said flatly.

"At some time did Costa become an employee of yours?"

"In the spring of 1967 he was asked by me, and agreed, to help paint the outside trim on my office building. He was usually behind in his payments; he owed, as I recollect, about one hundred forty dollars. That was the reason for asking him to work off some of the bill."

"This bill he owed you was in part for the dispensing of medication?"

"That was included in his treatment, yes," Callis said. "And for the psychotherapy, counseling—face-to-face talking with the patient."

"What was the nature of the material he presented to you for counseling?"

"He complained of nervousness, tension, having marital problems. He was having fights with his wife. He didn't go into what the fights were about, *per se.* It was only in relation to arguing about their children."

"Was there a theft upon your premises some time in 1968?"

"Yes, there was."

"And was Costa at that time a suspect?"

"He was."

"And you so indicated to the police?"

"I reported it immediately to the Wellfleet police," Callis said. "I told them I felt he could be a suspect."

"You made a list of certain drugs having been stolen?"

"I did." Callis had brought the list with him to the witness stand.

"You reported stolen a thirty-cc. vial of amphetamine sulfate," Shubow said. "Are you familiar with the colloquial name for amphetamine sulfate?"

"It may also be called Benzedrine."

"Are there some people that call it 'speed'?"

"I think that's a fair statement."

"You also reported stolen, one thousand four hundred and eighty amphetamine sulfate, ten milligrams white tablets—that's one of the so-called amphetamines also known as speed?"

"That's right."

"Would you have had occasion during the course of your treatment of Mr. Costa to prescribe any amphetamines?"

"Never at any time," Callis said firmly.

"Why are you so *definite* that those were contraindicated?"

"They are not in the record," Callis said. "I do not recall ever having prescribed them, sir. I treated him with tranquilizers; amphetamine is the opposite."

"Was there something about this patient's makeup that led you to recognize that amphetamines were contraindicated?"

"The fact that I prescribed a tranquilizer, I think would speak for itself," Callis said. "If a tranquilizer were prescribed, then it should be evident even to a layman that a stimulant would not be prescribed."

"Did you have an inventory of all the prescription drugs on your premises at the time of the break-in, back in May, 1968?"

"Oh yes," Callis said. "I keep a day-to-day inventory of the drugs that are dispensed or prescribed."

"I am not talking about the ones dispensed or prescribed," Shubow said sharply. "Do you keep a record of the drugs on your premises *available* to be dispensed?"

"Yes, sir."

"In reporting the burglary to the police did you make an inventory of all the drugs on hand after the break, to compare with the inventory of drugs on hand before the break?"

"Yes, sir. That's how I derived what was stolen."

"Not having anticipated this next request, I take it you do not have the inventory of drugs on hand at the time of the break-in with you today."

"Not with me, no," Callis said. "Just what was stolen on May seventeenth, 1968."

"Are you willing to produce that inventory in court?" Shubow said.

If Callis realized that Shubow was setting him up, he gave no sign. "Yes, sir," he said agreeably.

"Will it be convenient for you to bring it here tomorrow morning at nine-thirty?"

"I'll check and see. It should be."

"Did you also have various sample cards of drugs distributed to physicians by pharmaceutical houses?"

"Oh, yes."

"Is your inventory going to include the samples on hand, too?"

"No, I don't keep a list of every sample I get."

"In making your report to the police didn't you include drug samples that were on the premises?"

"The Robitussin A-C, four one-ounce bottles were samples," Callis said. "They were included in the inventory because they contain a small amount of codeine."

"Do you know whether or not you had on hand on May eighteenth, 1968, two hundred sample cards of pink or blue Triavil tablets?"

"I would doubt that very much," Callis said. "I don't recall having that many sample Triavil."

"Doctor, you also reported stolen nine hundred capsules of Solacen. Would you tell us whether or not Solacen has a potential for becoming habit-forming?"

"I think *any* drug could be habit-forming," Callis said.

"I'm not asking you about *any* drug, doctor, I'm asking you about Solacen."

"Well, Solacen is a drug," Callis said evenly.

"Does *every* drug listed in the *Physician's Desk Reference* contain the statement: 'May be habit-forming'?"

"I don't know, sir."

Shubow opened the stolen reference book which had been entered into evidence and turned to the listing for Solacen. "Now, doctor, I'd like to read a sentence or two from this, 'Warnings: Simultaneous administration to psychotic patients of tybamate—' that's the generic name of Solacen, is it not?"

"Yes, it is."

" '—with phenothiazine and other central nervous system depressants has in a few instances been associated with the occurrence of grand mal and petit mal seizures.' Solacen would not be indicated in connection with the drug phenothiazine, would it?"

"I didn't prescribe phenothiazine," Callis said.

"I know you didn't *prescribe* phenothiazine, doctor," Shubow said. "Do you know whether Costa had it from another source?"

"I don't know anything about what he had," Callis said.

"I call your attention to the following words which I am reading from this exhibit: 'Like other psychotherapeutic agents, use with caution in addiction-prone individuals.' Do you agree that is sound advice with respect to the drug Solacen?"

"I do, and I *did,*" Callis said.

"The question is do you know whether *he* did?"

"I don't know what *he* did," Callis said. "I know what *I* did."

"Having in mind that Solacen is hazardous for addiction-prone individuals, did you make any judgment that Costa was an addiction-prone individual?"

"Not when I was treating him, he wasn't," Callis said.

"How did you *know* that?"

"From my observations and examinations of the patient. If he were addiction-prone, I wouldn't have been prescribing any drugs."

Shubow drew closer to the witness stand. "Did you know on or about May seventeenth, 1968, that Costa was using marijuana?"

"I don't know what Costa was using."

"Did you describe him at the time of your report to the Wellfleet police on or about May seventeenth, 1968, as a 'pothead'?"

"I have no recollection of that," Callis said.

"*Had* you described him as a 'pothead,' what would you have been meaning to convey by that term."

" 'Pothead' to me is one who smokes pot or marijuana," Callis said, "but I don't remember using that word."

"There is a record coming into this trial on the use of that word by *you,* sir, which will be offered tomorrow," Shubow said.

Callis looked genuinely puzzled.

"Now, Solacen and marijuana do not mix, do they? You wouldn't prescribe Solacen to a known 'pothead'?"

"I wouldn't prescribe Solacen for somebody who was using marijuana, no."

"Marijuana is a drug with dangerous potential for some people, is it not?"

"It's a moot question," Callis said. "It's been argued both ways."

"And you can have for us tomorrow the inventory of drugs on your premises as of May 1968?"

"I didn't know I would be asked about the inventory," Callis said, apologetically. "When I get through with office hours tonight, I will check my records. I should be able to bring the inventory here tomorrow morning."

14

Mark McCray wore a wrinkled double-breasted blazer to the witness stand. He had been brought to Barnstable courthouse manacled and under guard, a slender young man in his midtwenties, his weakly handsome face giving off a wounded air of defeat. McCray smiled wanly at Tony Costa when he mounted the witness stand. McCray was presently confined at the Bridgewater State Hospital addiction center. "I'm being rehabilitated, I suppose you would call it, for drug addiction," he said in answer to Goldman's question. "I've been there approximately three and a half months."

McCray had met Tony Costa in the spring of 1968. "I moved into the Crown and Anchor Inn around June seventh, for approximately two weeks. I was living in room 204 and Tony was living in room 200."

"Did you ever observe Tony's conduct while you were there with respect to drugs?" Goldman said.

"Yes, sir. I could always tell when he was speeding, or high on amphetamines. He was always, you know, moving around, doing something."

"Did he use any other drugs?"

"I have smoked marijuana and hashish with him," McCray said. "It was group gatherings with other people there."

"Did you ever go to a Bruce Collingwood's house?"

"Yes, sir."

"Did something happen there one night?"

McCray smiled faintly. "Something has happened there quite a few nights."

"Was it something with reference to a speed episode?"

"A friend of mine and I had been speeding one night and he got arrested the next morning," McCray said. "I went to Bruce Collingwood's house to hide from the police. I thought I had some speed with me, but I didn't. I tore his whole house apart, looking for speed."

"Did Tony tell you anything about his use of drugs with relation to a Dr. Callis?"

"He told me he was copping barbiturates from Dr. Callis."

"Did he tell you how he came to know Dr. Callis?"

"We had a conversation one day and he told me, you know, a story; but I can't remember how he said he came to know him."

"Did Tony ever appear violent to you?"

"No, sir. He was quiet, polite; just a nice, ordinary guy."

Fernandes took over. "You used the term 'copping' barbiturates from Dr. Callis," he said. "What do you mean by 'copping'?"

"Getting them from Dr. Callis."

"Was he *stealing* them?"

"He didn't define what he meant. He just said copping from him."

"Did he mention anything else he was taking from Dr. Callis? Did he mention Solacen?"

"No, sir."

Fernandes smiled. Then: "How was Tony when he was *not* on drugs?"

"I can't say I really ever saw him when he wasn't on drugs."

"How about high on marijuana?"

"You are more tranquil. You don't move around. You just feel like sitting there."

"You are telling us you never saw Tony when he was anything but high; yet, I think you said he was a calm, quiet, nice fellow."

"Sure."

"Even when he was on speed, he wasn't violent, was he?"

"No."

"A calm, quiet fellow?"

"More or less, yes," McCray said. "But he was active, you know."

"An *active,* calm, quiet, nice fellow, is that it?" Fernandes said.

"Yeah," McCray said.

15

At the resumption of the trial on Tuesday morning, May 19, Maurice Goldman called to the witness stand Benson R. Moore, chief of the Wellfleet police.

"Have you any records with you relating to Tony Costa?" Goldman said.

"Yes, I do."

"What does the record disclose with reference to Tony Costa on May eighteenth, 1968?"

"Do you want me to read this?" Moore said.

Fernandes objected. "I'd like to read it first. I don't know what he is going to read."

Beaudreau called a bench conference. "Is this going to connect up with Dr. Callis on the use of the word 'pothead'?"

"Yes, Your Honor," Goldman said.

"Dr. Callis was *your* witness," Fernandes said. "Are you trying to impeach your own witness's testimony?"

"I'm trying to *supplement* my testimony," Goldman said blandly.

"Dr. Callis certainly wasn't a witness that could be classified as a defendant's witness to the extent that he is here to testify only

550

for the defendant's benefit," Beaudreau said dryly. "He's what I would call an *impartial* witness."

Dinis asked Goldman, "Can you produce the man who made out the police report; the officer who had the conversation with Dr. Callis?"

Goldman could. He thanked Chief Moore and called Patrick Padden to the stand.

"Did you make out this report in your official duty as a Wellfleet police officer?" Goldman said.

"Yes, sir, I did."

"I am going to ask you to read this nice and loud so we all can hear it," Goldman said.

Padden cleared his throat. After reading out such preliminary data as the date and the complainant's name, Padden got to the information Goldman was most concerned with having revealed in the courtroom: " 'Callis stated he had been treating subject Costa for about three years, during which time he had prescribed the drug Solacen, issuing fifty capsules at a time and allowing two refills,' " Padden read. " 'Callis stated he was aware that Costa was a "pothead" and "pill user." However, stated Callis, he is a doctor and felt justified in treating the subject this way. Callis stated that Costa had painted his offices to pay some debts, therefore, Costa would have knowledge of the building's layout.' "

Fernandes moved in to diffuse the impact of Padden's statement. "When was this break-in?"

"May seventeenth, 1968," Padden said.

"When did you talk with the doctor?"

"On that date, at approximately ten-twenty A.M."

"With reference to the term 'pothead,' was that made as soon as you got there?" Fernandes asked.

"It was shortly after I arrived, yes."

"Is it safe to say that Dr. Callis was angry and upset?"

"Very much so, as I recall."

"Was there extensive damage done to his building?"

"To the interior of the building, yes, sir."

"And he wanted the person who was responsible for breaking and entering into his building and causing the damage and stealing his property to be apprehended?"

"That is correct."

"And he used some pretty strong language?"

"Yes, sir. I believe he did."

"Now, when he used the word 'pill user,' did that mean narcotics to you?"

"Yes."

"Is that what the *doctor* said?"

"No, sir. He referred to him as a 'pothead' and 'pill user.' "

"Could the pill he referred to have been Solacen?"

"Could very well have been."

"Or aspirin?"

"Yes, sir. It could have."

"The doctor did not say to you, 'He is on drugs'?"

"No, sir, he did not."

"Is it not a fact that the reason Dr. Callis suspected the defendant, Mr. Costa, was the amount of Solacen that was taken?"

"Yes, sir, that's correct."

"I object to that!" Goldman said. "That's a *conclusion!*"

"No further questions," Fernandes said.

Stephen Lipman approached the stand to examine Paula Hoernig. Lipman, a Boston University Law School graduate in 1966, was the youngest member of Tony Costa's defense team and was gaining experience in the conduct of capital cases.

Paula Hoernig said she had known Tony Costa to have used Nembutal. "And marijuana, hash and Solacen."

"Did you ever see Tony stoned?" Lipman said.

"Yes."

"What did he look like when he was stoned?"

"He seemed casual, normal."

"At some time Tony Costa drew something on the inside of a raincoat of yours, didn't he?"

"He made three drawings with a ballpoint pen. One was a picture of a pipe that was supposed to have hash in it. One was a picture of a face; it was sort of grotesque. It wasn't really made out to be a face. The features on it weren't—like—normal."

"What was the third drawing of?"

"A picture of a body with no arms."

"Was that a picture of a man or a woman?"

"Just a body."

16

After the drubbing he had taken on the stand the day before from Lawrence Shubow, Dr. Sidney Callis discussed his forthcoming testimony in advance with his good friend, George Killen. Killen revealed that Dr. Daniel Hiebert of Provincetown had treated Costa with Tuinal right up to the time of his arrest. "Then why don't they call Hiebert as a witness?" Callis said. "He was the guy who gave Costa barbiturates, not me."

Killen cautioned Callis about his court appearance. "You've got to be careful not to make Costa sound crazy. If he gets committed to Bridgewater, he could get out. We want to make sure this guy is put away forever."

When he returned to Barnstable courthouse, Callis was greeted warmly by Edmund Dinis, who told him, "You did a good job for us in your last testimony. This time, you take care of yourself."

Callis received permission from Beaudreau to have his wife present in the courtroom when he testified. He brought the inventory of drugs on hand in his office on May 17, 1968, to the witness stand.

"Is there any way you can tell us when that inventory was made?" Shubow said.

"This inventory was made last night," Callis said.

"Did you have a written inventory on May seventeenth, 1968?"

"I keep a list of drugs day-to-day," Callis said. "I was asked to bring a list of the inventory I had on May seventeenth and that is what I brought."

"Maybe I misunderstood you," Shubow said. "I thought you just said you prepared the list last night."

"From the list I had on May seventeenth, that's correct."

"Where is the list that existed back on May seventeenth?" Shubow said.

"I didn't bring that with me," Callis said. "I'm sorry, perhaps I misunderstood."

"The main point is the list that existed on May seventeenth is *not* in court this morning."

"It is not in court," Callis said, contritely. "This is the list."

"What you have is a *copy* you made last night of the list?"

"That is correct."

Shubow glared at the witness. "Is the list you left in your office physically more inconvenient to handle than the list you prepared last night?"

"Yes, it's a list of separate, individual papers giving the names of the drugs and the amounts. From that list, I compiled a list which I thought I was asked to bring this morning," Callis said politely. "I'm sorry if I haven't done what you asked."

"Well, assuming that this is an *accurate* copy of the list of drugs that were in your building on May seventeenth, 1968," Shubow said, "are there included on that list any amphetamines?"

"There were one thousand four hundred and eighty ten-milligram white tablets amphetamine, two thousand four hundred and sixty-four ten-milligram pink tablets amphetamine, and three hundred and thirty-three capsules of dextroamphetamine, fifteen milligrams. Those were the only amphetamines in my office."

"Does your inventory include a number of barbiturates?"

"Yes, sir."

"Nembutal?"

"Yes, sir?"

"Seconal?"

"No."

"Amytal?"

"No."

"Phenobarbital?"

"Yes, sir."

Having made a considerable issue over the inventory, Shubow proceeded to ignore it. "Yesterday, you told us you did not recall whether or not you had described Costa as a 'pothead' to Patrolman Padden," Shubow said. "Have you had a chance to think about that overnight?"

"At the time I testified yesterday, I did not recall having alluded to him as a 'pothead,' that's true."

"What about *today?*"

"Well, it's possible I could have called him that," Callis said, ruefully. "I might have called him some other things, too."

"You had pretty much decided who the culprit was?"

"Well, I had a suspicion, yes."

"Patrolman Padden was in court this morning speaking about his conversation with you back in May, 1968. I will tell you that the officer testified that you said 'pothead,' and 'pill user.' Did that express your resentment at things being stolen?"

"I don't recall that I called him a 'pothead' or 'pill user.' I might have," Callis said. "I was pretty angry to find my office broken into, after I had tried to help him."

"I will ask that that last remark go out, so that we don't go into collateral issues, namely 'After I had tried to help him,' " Shubow said icily.

"It should go out," Beaudreau said. "It has not been determined that Costa broke into his office. The only reason I would allow this testimony is to clear up this matter of 'pothead' and 'pill user' the doctor might have used."

"I hope you thought to bring your patient-treatment record with you this morning," Shubow said.

"Yes, I did."

"What are the total number of visits made by Costa?"

"I count thirty separate visits, from December eighth, 1965, to April nineteenth, 1968."

"Do you have a number of prescriptions that were written?"

"Eight prescriptions for Solacen, with refills."

"On other occasions when you prescribed drugs, they were dispensed from your premises?" Shubow said. "You gave the Solacen directly, rather than by prescription?"

"Yes, sir."

"Is it fair to say that on each of these visits medication was either dispensed or prescribed?"

"Not on each visit, no."

"On the overwhelming majority of visits?"

"Yes."

Shubow turned Callis over to Fernandes for cross-examination.

"Had you prescribed or dispensed to Mr. Costa amphetamines of any nature?" Fernandes said.

"No, sir, not at any time."

"A barbiturate of any nature?"

"No, sir."

"You certainly never prescribed marijuana?"

"No, sir," Callis said. "I don't have that in my office."

"LSD?"

"No, sir. I don't have that in my office."

"Morphine?"

"I have that in my office, but I never prescribed it."

"What was the medical diagnosis made by you that concluded that Solacen might be of service to Mr. Costa?" Fernandes said.

"The patient complained of nervous tension, gnawing pains over his stomach. I concluded from my examination that he needed a mild tranquilizer."

"What did he say to you, if anything, after taking this mild tranquilizer?"

"He said his nervousness was much improved."

"Did he ever complain to you about his use of Solacen?"

"No, he said that he would like to continue because it was helping him; he felt better with it."

"Was there ever any indication by your own observations or the defendant's statements which caused you to conclude that Solacen was having any kind of effect on him other than a therapeutic one which you desired?"

"No, sir."

"You have a special knowledge of Solacen?" Fernandes said.

"I was one of the original investigators on this drug for Wallace Pharmaceuticals in 1963," Callis said. "I wrote a paper, on a double-blind study of Solacen that appeared in the *International Journal of Neuropsychiatry.*"

"Is Solacen an addictive drug?"

"According to the 1970 edition of the *Physician's Desk Reference* I have with me, it is a *non*addictive drug."

Fernandes asked Callis to read from the Solacen listing in the directory: " 'There has been no evidence to date of the development of habituation or addiction.' "

"Did you give Costa Aventyl at one time?"

"Yes, sir."

"And Meprospan also?"

"Meprospan is also a Wallace product, a mild tranquilizer."

"Are these *addictive* drugs?"

"No, sir."

556

"Are they *barbiturates?*"

"No, sir."

"Are they *amphetamines?*"

"No, sir."

"I ask you to follow my finger," Shubow said, reading to Callis from the *Physician's Desk Reference:* " 'Solacen is prescribed or intended for persons with psychoneurotic disorders.' Right?"

"Yes, sir."

"In other words, Solacen is for treatment of somebody who has a *mental* problem?"

"Yes, sir."

"Is it fair to conclude that there are some circumstances in which the use of Solacen is hazardous, especially when used in connection with other medications or drugs?"

"Yes, sir."

"You assumed, in prescribing Solacen, that Tony Costa was not using anything else?"

"Yes, sir."

"Some of these other drugs identified here, particularly phenothiazine, monomine oxidase inhibitors are known—now, may I read: '. . . to potentiate the action of other drugs and may result in addictive actions—' "

"The word is *additive,* not addictive," Callis said.

Shubow hesitated, then frowned. "I'm sorry, you are correct. We will come to the other part of it—"

"I merely want to read what it says, I don't want to read what it doesn't say," Callis said, gathering courage. "I think the word additive is important."

"That makes perfect sense to me, Doctor," Shubow said. It had been a small, but critical, mistake, sufficient to throw Shubow momentarily off the track of his examination. He had lost mastery over the witness, having to concede to Callis an expertise that up to that moment his questions had sought to challenge.

Shubow tried to recoup, "I'm reading from the heading marked, 'Precautions': 'Solacen, like other psychotherapeutic agents, should be used with caution in addiction-prone individuals.' Correct?"

"That's what it says," Callis said.

"You obviously assumed that Costa was *not* an addiction-prone individual?"

"I did not feel he was when I was treating him."

557

"And if he *were,* you would never have given him Solacen, correct?"

"I wouldn't say that," Callis said. "Because Solacen is nonaddictive."

"We can agree that in the literature dispensed to the entire medical profession, Solacen is not recommended for addiction-prone individuals and has been known to produce confusion and panic reactions?"

"Yes, sir."

"Your suspicion of Costa as a suspect in the break-in of your office was based on the fact that he was on Solacen?" Shubow said. "Is it unfair to suggest that by 'on' Solacen you mean some form of attachment to the drug?"

Fernandes objected.

"No, he can handle that," Beaudreau said.

"He was *taking* Solacen," Callis answered. "That's what I mean."

"You said his dosage, if used normally, would have run out about the time of the break-in your office," Shubow said. "Do I understand you to say, therefore, he would have felt the need for some more, when his existing supply had been exhausted?"

"I don't know," Callis said. "Solacen is nonaddictive, but he might have felt he needed more, where it was helping him."

"Would you please explain why Solacen should be used guardedly with addiction-prone individuals, if you can?"

"Some drugs—and Solacen is one of them, according to the protocol—should not be used with certain other drugs because of synergistic or side effects. There are some drugs you just don't mix medically."

Fernandes took over the questioning for a moment. "During the approximately three years you treated the defendant Costa, did he ever suffer from any so-called side effects?"

"Never," Callis said.

"And none were observed by you, or told to you by this defendant?"

"Never, at any time. If there were side effects, you would notice them quickly."

Shubow came back to try to salvage what he could from the witness. "You never saw the defendant professionally after May sixteenth, 1968, did you?"

"I didn't see him professionally after April nineteenth, 1968," Callis corrected him.

"You don't know what effects he had from either Solacen or any other drugs after April nineteenth, 1968?"

"No."

"You don't know what side effects he may have had on those days he wasn't coming to your office, do you?"

"I only know what he exhibited when he was in my office, not when he wasn't there."

"And that led you, in your understandable anger, to characterize him as a 'pothead' and 'pill user'?"

"I have already testified to that," Callis said. "I don't remember saying it."

"You are not willing to deny you said that, are you?"

"I could have called him that; but I have no recollection of it. I may have called him those names you alluded to, and I may have called him other names at that time, too. I was angry."

"None of the other names presumably had any medical significance, did they?" Shubow said, as a parting shot.

"Objection, your honor," Fernandes said.

"We have no evidence of the other names," Beaudreau said, deadpan. "I think we can curtail this. You are excused."

"Thank you for your kindness," Callis said, and stepped off the witness stand.

Callis was pleased with his performance. He had at first been puzzled, then angry at the defense's attempts to impugn his integrity as a physician, but afterward he bore no animus toward Maurice Goldman, telling Killen: "I know it was nothing personal. Goldman's a damn good lawyer. He'd kick his grandmother in the butt to win a case."

17

Satisfied the defense had established Costa's longtime and chronic use of drugs, Goldman called Dr. Lawrence Barrows of Bridgewater State Hospital to the witness stand. Like Dr. Callis, Barrows could not properly be termed a defense witness. Shubow would undertake during his examination to dismantle the diagnosis of "schizoid personality" Barrows had made with regard to Tony Costa's competence to stand trial—no easy task, Shubow knew, when examining a psychiatrist and skilled interrogator.

Plump and balding, Barrows appeared at ease on the witness stand as he outlined the procedures and tests Antone Costa had undergone during thirty-five days of observation.

"And what diagnosis did you and your associates at Bridgewater make upon that basis?" Shubow said.

"We diagnosed him as having a schizoid personality."

"In reaching that diagnosis of schizoid personality, was there any information available to you as to the details of the commission of the crimes charged?"

"Not by the patient," Barrows said. "All we had were newspaper reports of that."

"Will you tell us whether or not you had available to you the pathologist's report, at any time?"

"No, I did not."

"Will you tell us what assumption you were operating on in reaching your diagnosis with reference to the use of drugs by the patient?"

"This patient denied the use of any drugs with the exception of taking marijuana for one year prior to his divorce," Barrows said.

"Would you describe for us the meaning of the word 'schizoid'?"

"This represents a patient whose personality makeup is such that he makes only a marginal adjustment to life in reality. Usually, these people have a spotty work record, maybe have problems relating to addiction, either to alcohol or drugs."

"Are you familiar with the diagnosis, 'borderline schizophrenic'?"

"Yes, I am."

"What is the relationship between a schizoid personality and a borderline schizophrenic?"

"A schizophrenic is in a psychotic state in which there is a loss of reality, a disturbance in the thought processes and judgment which makes decisions difficult."

"You have answered the question with respect to a schizophrenic, the question was *borderline* schizophrenic."

"This is someone who has made a satisfactory adjustment, either through intellectualization or other thought processes, so that the symptoms are not as florid as in a regular schizophrenic."

"Do you see any great inconsistency between your staff diagnosis of schizoid personality and what I will represent to you is the diagnosis of borderline schizophrenia?"

"I base my diagnosis on the observations made during the month I saw the patient. I don't know what other doctors may have diagnosed him as."

"Is the finding of schizoid personality inconsistent essentially from the finding of borderline schizophrenic?"

"Yes, there is an inconsistency. In a borderline schizophrenic there is some loss of reality, which is not present in a schizoid personality."

"Does 'borderline' mean the condition is not fixed and stable, but varies from one period to another?"

"It's not fully developed, is what it means."

"And on occasion the patient may go over whatever line is represented by the word 'borderline'?"

"Yes, and then become definite schizophrenic."

"I ask you to assume that this particular patient on January twenty-sixth shot and killed two young women and, after their death, had perverse sexual relations with each of them and, in addition, vigorously and forcefully slashed their buttocks and legs —all of this clearly *after* death. Would having that information have affected your diagnosis?"

"I think it probably would have," Barrows said.

"You did *not* have that information?"

"No, we didn't."

561

"I ask you assume, in addition, that there was a history of prolonged and chronic use of amphetamines, ingested both orally and intravenously; chronic use of marijuana, and its stronger form, hashish; chronic and excessive use of barbiturates and occasional use of LSD, to say nothing of other pharmaceutical properties, including Solacen and various other medications. With those facts in your history would your diagnosis have been the same?"

"Knowing those facts, my diagnosis of schizoid personality would have changed, probably to a sociopathic personality with drug addiction. The two are very closely allied; it's just a shade of gray, really."

"Is it fair generalization that among those predisposed to drug addiction are people with the diagnosis of schizoid personality?"

"Yes."

"And also with the diagnosis of borderline schizophrenic?"

"I refuse to answer that," Barrows said. "I don't use the word 'borderline' in my diagnostic workups."

"There is no question that some competent, qualified people *do* use that term?" Shubow said.

"Yes."

"You weren't studying Costa from the point of view of the impact of drugs upon his underlying makeup, because you had no significant history of drugs?" Shubow said.

"He denied all drugs, except for what I have stated."

"You and your associates accepted that denial?"

"We had no other information available."

"There was no discussion of his conduct at the time of these alleged offenses?"

"I think on the advice of his lawyer, he declined to discuss the alleged offenses."

"Does a schizoid personality suffer from any impairment of mental function?" Shubow said.

"No, I wouldn't say he suffers from impairment of mental capacity."

"It *is* a mental disorder, is it not?"

"Yes, it is."

"And, therefore, affects the mental processes by reason of the illness, does it not?"

"Yes, it does."

562

"And when it exists in association with harmful drugs, may it become intensified?"

"It may become exacerbated, yes."

"And have effects upon behavior?"

"Well, *all* drugs have effects on behavior," Barrows said.

"I have asked you to assume there are facts here about multiple slashings of deceased young women; does that sound like psychotic behavior?" Shubow asked.

"Ordinarily anyone who does such a thing would be mentally disturbed. I don't know whether or not they would be psychotic."

"That mental disturbance would play some part in the conduct?"

"It may not account for all the conduct, but it accounts for some of it, yes."

"I ask you to superimpose on that mental disturbance chronic abuse of marijuana, chronic abuse of amphetamines, chronic abuse of barbiturates—all in combination."

"I doubt if such an act could occur if they were used in combination, because they counteract one another. Anyone taking excessive doses of amphetamines, coupled with excessive doses of barbiturates is going to have periods of 'ups' and 'downs,' but it's not necessarily psychotic."

"But psychotic episodes *are* a known hazard of this kind of conduct?"

"Yes, in some patients."

Barrows looked relieved when Beaudreau called a recess.

"Dr. Barrows, did you elicit some history during your examination of the defendant, Antone Costa?" Fernandes said when the session resumed.

"He gave a history of his education, the fact that he had been on marijuana for a year before his divorce, his relationship with his wife, the fact that he had deliberately impregnated her at fourteen so they could marry, because she was underage. Things of that sort were all brought out in the history."

"In addition to the history, was a physical examination given?"

"Yes. It was a general physical examination," Barrows said. "And in all, he was normal."

"There was nothing in the physical examination which led

you to conclude that he was addicted to anything?" Fernandes said.

"There was no possible way of determining that from our examination at that time," Barrows said. "When I first examined him I felt there was no major psychiatric disease. He was very well composed, oriented, clear of memory, understanding, everything. Of course, we changed our diagnosis from no major psychiatric disease to a schizoid personality as a result of our testing and other information available to us."

"What behavior did the defendant exhibit while he was at Bridgewater those thirty-five days?"

"I was impressed with the candor and coolness that he had, considering the gravity of the charges," Barrows said. "He did not appear to be concerned at all about the testing or anything. This was unusual in my experience. Anyone charged with such a serious crime is usually somewhat upset or apprehensive for a short period of time."

"Your first diagnosis was a schizoid personality," Fernandes said. "That does not represent psychotic behavior, does it?"

"No, it's not a psychotic behavior problem."

"Will you describe for the court and the jury what *is* psychotic behavior?"

"Psychotic behavior is the loss of sense of reality. There is gross misinterpretation of incoming thoughts and senses, such as sight, hearing. People who are psychotic frequently have auditory or visual hallucinations. They may see snakes, or pink elephants; they may see pictures of the Blessed Virgin, things of that sort. This is not found in the schizoid personality."

"Did you at any time find the patient was suffering from a psychosis of any kind?"

"No, he was not psychotic."

"Sometime after the diagnosis of schizoid personality you met with me and other members of our staff and at that time the nature of the crime and the charges against the defendant were fully explained to you, and the evidence the commonwealth had," Fernandes said. "Now, based on that information which essentially was given to you earlier in Mr. Shubow's hypothetical, I believe you said you formed an opinion that he was a 'sociopathic personality with drug addiction.' Would you explain exactly what that is, in lay terms?"

"This is a person who, very much like a schizoid personality, makes only a marginal adjustment to life's stresses and strains. The chief difference is that the sociopathic personality is inclined to get into more conflicts with the law, to make poor marital adjustments and frequently has a criminal record as well as addiction to either alcohol or barbiturates."

"Is that a diagnosis of a psychotic?" Fernandes wanted this repeated for the jury.

"It is not a psychotic person," Barrows said.

"Based on these factors which Mr. Shubow gave you, and the history you elicited from the defendant, do you have an opinion whether Tony Costa had sufficient mental capacity to appreciate the wrongfulness of his conduct on or about January twenty-fifth, 1969?"

"In my opinion, this man had substantial capacity to appreciate the criminality of his acts, and to conform his conduct to the requirements of the law."

"What is an 'amphetamine psychosis'?" Fernandes said.

"That is a highly toxic dose of either Benzedrine, Dexedrine or biphetamine, in which there is an exaggeration of one's innate abilities to perform life's functions. For example, if he were in a barroom and someone threatened him, he would probably say he could knock the man over without any difficulty—it's an exaggeration of one's normal pattern of living."

"Now, Doctor," Fernandes said, "I would ask you to assume these facts: assume that a person leaves a note on a door requesting a ride to a specific location. Assume further, that he procures this ride, and it takes him into a specific wooded area. Assume that while there he shoots two people. Assume that these two women are assaulted sexually in both orifices, vagina and rectum. Assume further that either before or after the assault, they were mutilated and cut up—one into two pieces and the other into five pieces. Assume that these pieces are buried in two graves. Assume that the weapons used are buried in a specific location. Assume that the vehicle owned by one of the victims is taken from the area to another location. Assume further that this person, when confronted by the police, relates contradictory stories as to the whereabouts of these girls. I ask you, doctor, assuming all these facts, and the further fact that this person was on drugs, have you an opinion as to whether or not the person who did this was suffering from an amphetamine psychosis at that time?"

"In my opinion, he was *not* suffering from an amphetamine psychosis," Barrows said.

"Why not?"

"Because a person suffering from a psychosis could not perform such organized activity such as you outlined in your rather lengthy hypothetical question."

"Would a person exhibit that kind of conduct if he were under a substantial dosage of barbiturates?"

"No, he would not," Barrows said. "He would be asleep."

"Are you saying he could *not* engage in the sexual conduct described in the hypothetical?"

"No, he couldn't."

"Would he have the strength to slash and mutilate the bodies?"

"If he were on an overdose of barbiturates, he would be sleeping. He would probably sleep twenty-four to thirty-six hours."

Shubow said, "As I understand your description of amphetamine psychosis, there is an exaggeration of the normal pattern of living. Is that the principal way of characterizing that?"

"I would say so. At least, that's my interpretation of it."

"Am I being unfair in characterizing the conduct as described both by the prosecution and myself as deserving of the label, 'an exaggeration of the normal pattern of living'?"

"Well, certainly it was abnormal."

"Just so that we will be clear about this, regardless of the particular label you put on this conduct, it *is* an expression of some disorder of the mental processes?"

"I would say so, yes."

"The borderline between nonpsychotic and psychotic conduct is not very precise in the science of psychiatry, is it?"

"No, it is not."

"And honest experts can disagree about whether the borderline has been crossed or not?"

"They frequently do."

"You cannot measure this like you can measure a patient's temperature with a thermometer?"

"No."

"If I understood you correctly, the main reason for your saying that Costa could not have been under the influence of any

566

amphetamine psychosis was that he showed no signs of it when you saw him six weeks later?"

"Yes."

"And you didn't think the organization of his activities was possible?"

"I didn't think that was psychotic activity."

"Are you saying that *any* conduct that was well organized, in the sense that an actor pursues a certain object, is never psychotic? Like aiming a pistol, that can never be a psychotic act because it is organized?"

"Oh, it *could* be—"

"Then, the organization isn't what makes the psychotic state; it is the patient's state of mind that determines whether it is psychotic or not, isn't that so?"

"Yes."

"And we get some clue as to the state of mind by the conduct itself, is that a fair statement?" Shubow said. "One of the bits of evidence you use to determine a person's state of mind is how they behave?"

"Yes."

"Will you agree that necrophilia is abnormal behavior?"

"Yes, it is."

"Would I be unfair in saying it *always* is an example of a pathological state of mind?"

"Yes, it is."

"And if this defendant committed acts of necrophilia he was, to some degree, mentally ill?"

"I had no knowledge of that," Barrows said.

"I'm asking you now to *assume* it," Shubow said.

"If this were substantiated—that it was a case of necrophilia —he was mentally ill."

"You agree that if there *was* sexual intercourse with deceased bodies, that is pathological?"

"Yes."

"The diagnosis reached at the hospital obviously didn't include this data, because you didn't have it?"

"No, I didn't know about it."

"And the very least that can be said, it raises some serious questions about what is the correct diagnosis?"

"Possibly," Barrows said.

"Well, if there is conduct that is *always* evidence of mental sickness that you weren't aware of, that item of the history inevitably undermines the diagnosis reached at the hospital, doesn't it?"

"There are persons with mental illness who can commit crimes and still know what they are doing," Barrows said.

"The underlying illness is, in your opinion, that of a schizoid personality?"

"Yes."

"This schizoid personality whom you saw in Bridgewater State Hospital was under control?"

"Markedly so."

"And *cool?*"

"Yes."

"Would you agree that the slashing of dead bodies is not an example of *cool* behavior?"

"No, I would agree that is abnormal behavior."

"And that necrophilia is inconsistent with *cool* behavior?"

"Of course."

"Did the underlying illness which you diagnosed play a part in that conduct?"

"Yes, I imagine it did."

"Well, it's more than imagination, I hope, doctor," Shubow said. "That is your *conclusion,* is it not?"

"I would conclude that the underlying diagnosis played a part in the events which you hypothetically put to me, yes."

"And the underlying diagnosis is a condition of the *mind,* not of the body?"

"Yes."

"And a person with that mental condition is predisposed to suffer from the dangerous consequences of the drugs I have enumerated, namely LSD, marijuana, amphetamines and barbiturates, and the synergistic effects of their use in combination?"

Barrows sighed. "Yes!" he said.

"Thank you, sir!" Shubow said.

Fernandes hastened to repair the damage of Barrow's admission. It was the second time he had had to rescue a defense witness from the assault of Shubow's examination. "Doctor, would you agree that marijuana causes alterations in sensory perception, psychomotor discoordination and an inability to concentrate?"

"It does all three."

"Relating to the conduct which I described to you in my

568

hypothetical earlier and in Mr. Shubow's statements about the facts surrounding the killings in the case, would it be your opinion that a person who performed this action was under the effects of marijuana?"

"I don't see how any of the drugs that we have discussed—if taken in sufficient quantity—could have permitted him to have performed those acts," Barrows said.

"Would you say that someone who suffers from the mental illness described to you by Mr. Shubow would have sufficient mental capacity to appreciate the wrongfulness or criminality of his conduct and to conform that conduct to the requirements of law?"

"Someone with a mental illness could perform these disorders and still be able to have substantial capacity to appreciate the criminality of the acts and to conform his conduct to the requirements of the law."

Fernandes sat down.

Shubow stood at the defense table to deliver the coup de grace. "A person suffering from a mental illness, who is not psychotic, may well suffer psychotic *episodes,* may he not?"

Barrows hesitated before he answered, "Oh . . . yes."

"And then return to his preexisting nonpsychotic state?"

"That's true," Barrows said.

Despite his stubborn effort not to be, Barrows had ended up a witness for the defense after all.

The first medical witness who was unquestionably a defendant's witness appeared on the eleventh day of the trial of Tony Costa.

Dr. Jack Ewalt took the witness stand to give an offhand and modestly brief summary of his distinguished career as former Massachusetts Commissioner of Mental Health and, since 1959, the superintendent of the Massachusetts Health Center. "I'm also the Bullard professor of psychiatry at Harvard," he added. "That's a kind of an honorary thing. It means somebody named Bullard left money to Harvard with which they pay part of my salary."

"Have you ever seen the defendant, Antone Costa, who is sitting over there on my right?" Shubow said.

Ewalt looked at Costa and winked. Costa smiled back. "Yes, at the Massachusetts Mental Health Center. He came there on eight different occasions. He had more than thirty hours of observation by skilled psychiatric nurses, physicians on the staff, social workers and so forth. He had the usual physical and neurological examination, X rays, blood and urine tests and whatnot," Ewalt said. "This patient had five different types of psychological tests, so-called mental measurements for different capacities, and an electroencephalogram. This is like an electrocardiogram, except it works on the brain. You can measure brain functions in some categories by picking up these little electrical currents—to rule out things like epilepsy, brain tumor, damage to the brain of that sort. And we had chromosome smears made by one of the research people in my Harvard department."

"And, in addition, did you obtain some history from the patient himself?" Shubow said.

"Yes, and we had the benefit of materials that were produced from the defense, some tape recordings."

"Having in mind these various tests, what findings did you make based upon the studies that were done at the hospital?"

"Well, in the first place," Ewalt said, "none of these tests revealed any organic pathology of the brain, such as tumor, epilepsy, anything like this. The tests did reveal that he had a superior intelligence. He was described in some parts of the record as 'cool.' When he was observed in a free situation, that is, mingling with other patients, he conducted himself very well. I think the patients were rather apprehensive about having this individual in the group because of the publicity that accompanied his coming there; but I think after a while, they found him a very likable person.

"However, when we gave him what we term an 'open-ended' question, he would talk on quite rationally and reasonably for a while, then he would begin to sort of spew off into not-such-sensible directions. When we put him under stress by discussing some of the things he was accused of, he would begin to blink his eyes very rapidly, get quite restless and become evasive; and his speech was much less well organized.

"These findings all combined to make a diagnosis of so-called 'borderline state,' or 'borderline schizophrenia' which is a sub-category of a very common, very serious form of mental illness. These people are called borderline because under ordinary circumstances they are quite normal in their conduct, and in their ability to manage things. When placed under any undue stress of a major sort, they do what we call 'regress'; they begin to show psychotic symptoms. These people actually become mentally ill— or "crazy" if you like, only when they are under stress. It can be a head injury, some great emotional trauma, or it can be drugs. And then, they tend to recover. . . ."

"Doctor, I am going to ask you to assume certain facts which I know are not in your record," Shubow said. "I am going to ask you to assume that this patient on or about January twenty-sixth, 1969, killed by gunfire two young women, and after their death— and I emphasize *after* their death—he peeled off the skin of each of these young women in what has been described as creating a sweaterlike effect and, in addition, made multiple slashing, forceful stab wounds of the lower extremities, buttocks and other portions of the anatomy. I am going to ask you to assume that there is evidence consistent with sexual contact with the bodies after death. Is that conduct as represented by those facts consistent with your diagnosis of schizophrenic reaction?"

"Well, it's not a common finding in borderline states, but it's not inconsistent with it," Ewalt said. "If I may explain that a bit; it sounds a little screwy. Schizophrenia in any of its forms is a disease or pathological condition that I might get, or any of you might get. We have priests, nuns, businessmen, stupid people, smart people, all kinds of people with this kind of a disease. Some of these people are very aggressive and hostile sadistic types. One of those persons getting schizophrenia, if his behavior gets out of control, might do very aggressive, sadistic and hostile acts. Others who are more the pious, quiet types, go around espousing themselves as saviors of the world, and this kind of thing. So different people have different kinds of symptoms. But they have a consistent pattern of disturbance in emotional control with other people, and the way they put their language together."

"Would this underlying disease reduce the capacity of a person to appreciate the wrongfulness of his conduct?" Shubow said.

"Yes."

"Based upon what you know of this patient—namely, Antone Costa—at the time you saw him, and what you know of the disease borderline schizophrenia, does that disease reduce his capacity to conform his conduct to the requirements of our legal system?"

"It *would* reduce his capacity," Ewalt said. "The amount it would reduce it would depend on the severity of the symptoms at a particular time—"

"I move that be stricken, your honor," Fernandes said.

"No," Beaudreau said, "I'm going to allow that to stand." Beaudreau addressed the witness, "Excuse me, Doctor. When you say 'at a particular time,' does that mean January twenty-sixth, 1969?"

"Well, one can refer to that only by inference," Ewalt said. "This illness is not something that comes and goes like a cold or the measles. If he had it when I saw him last November, I am assuming he probably had it before. I did not examine him in January 1969; I saw him ten months later."

"Can you draw that inference back to January twenty-sixth, 1969, with reasonable psychiatric certainty?" Beaudreau said.

Shubow asked for a bench conference.

"Under the conditions laid down by the McHoul case, the defendant is entitled to offer any evidence of his mental capacity, whether or not it amounts to legal insanity, as relevant to the issue of clemency and premeditation," Shubow said. "We are not going to take an advocacy position on insanity versus second-degree murder. The present law is clear on this point. Give the jury everything you psychiatrically can, and let the jury decide."

"Are we shooting for a defense of not guilty by reason of insanity?" Beaudreau said. "Or are we just trying to reduce this from premeditation to second-degree?"

"Our position is that the evidence will permit the jury to make one of four or five findings," Shubow said. "We don't want to elect on them."

"Let's have an understanding on ground rules," Beaudreau said. "If you are going into this question of borderline schizophrenia, you have got to establish we are talking about this period around January twenty-sixth, 1969."

"That is the *only* question," Fernandes said.

"You made a diagnosis of borderline schizophrenic at the time you saw this man," Shubow resumed. "Can we infer that the man had the condition of borderline schizophrenia back in January 1969?"

"I think so, yes," Ewalt said.

"And that condition would reduce his capacity to appreciate what he was doing?"

"*Reduce,* yes," Ewalt said.

"And also reduce his capacity to conform his conduct to the requirements of law?"

"Yes."

Fernandes rose from the prosecutor's table to cross-examine. "Dr. Ewalt, I am going to ask you for some help occasionally because I'm certainly not a psychiatrist. I have trouble being a lawyer."

"Not very much," Goldman called out.

"What is your connection with this case?" Fernandes said.

"We were asked to examine this man. We usually don't take cases where there has been a capital offense because our hospital is open-doored," Ewalt said. "I agreed to take him if the sheriff's office would be responsible for his conduct. So he was brought each day with two officers, and then he was taken back somewhere at night."

"You are not testifying on behalf of the commonwealth?" Fernandes said. "You are here at the request of the defendant?"

"Yes, that's correct."

"You also said that as part of the procedure by which you formed an opinion in this case, you elicited a history from the defendant. Could you tell us what was in this history that you remember? You may allude to your notes."

Beaudreau called another bench conference. "I think we have got to get the doctor over here to make sure he doesn't overstep under any circumstances. By statute, the defendant can object to any incriminating statements he might have made in the history. It can be waived if the defendant wants to, but otherwise, incriminating statements made during the course of a psychiatric examination are not admissible in court."

"We are waiving that," Goldman said, "as to the offenses under trial in this case."

Beaudreau asked Ewalt to join the conference. "Doctor, we have a problem here. The only two murder cases involved here are Walsh and Wysocki. We want to be careful not to inject inadvertently the names of Monzon and Perry in this case when we go over this history."

Ewalt suggested he be asked what in Costa's history made him come to his diagnosis.

Fernandes said, resuming his cross-examination, "What in the history of this defendant prior to January 1969, did you consider in evaluating his condition and forming your opinion?"

"Well," replied Ewalt, "he mentioned he had been on drugs for a long time; that he had been part of what the kids call 'the drug scene.' He mentioned some difficulties in his marriage, and the manifestation at times of generally unstable or aggressive kinds of conduct—so much so that I think one could make some case for this being a so-called psychopath, or character disorder, if it hadn't been for these other findings that we had."

"What are 'these other findings'?" Fernandes said.

"The fact that he doesn't put his language together well under stress; his conversation gets a little fragmented; the evidence of abnormal acts of one sort or another with his wife, these kinds of things."

"Did part of this history relate to the crime for which he is now put on trial?"

"I didn't go into that very much; that is not relevant to making a diagnosis. We are not interested," Ewalt said.

"Are you telling this court and jury you would form the same opinion irrespective of the conduct that was exhibited by him, as described to you in Mr. Shubow's hypothetical, which related to the crime?" Fernandes said.

"Making this diagnosis was a medical operation. Whether, in fact, this man has committed a crime doesn't have anything to do with this diagnosis. 'Borderline state' is a very common kind of illness. The vast majority have not committed any crime other than assault and battery or drunk-and-disturb, minor sorts of things. A major crime is a possibility in these people because at times they're aggressive and act up; but it's not a necessary part. The fact that he is accused of murder has nothing to do with our medical diagnosis."

"What did the defendant tell you about the crime?" Fernandes asked.

"Frankly, I did not encourage him to tell me," Ewalt said. "He denied any knowledge of having done any of them. In effect he said he was 'out' on drugs; that he thinks he was involved to some degree but can't remember. He does recall in a flashback, finding a girl lying on the ground making gurgling sounds in her throat. It was too late to get her help because they were so far from civilization so he sort of killed her to put her out of her misery; but it wasn't done in anger. This is all he told me about the girls."

"What about sex with these victims, Doctor?" Fernandes said. "Did he admit to any?"

"He admitted having sexual relations with one of them; but I'm not sure which one. He denied any irregular sexual practices with those victims."

"What is necrophilia?" Fernandes said.

"That is supposed to be sexual relations with dead bodies."

"Would you consider that to be an 'irregular sexual practice,' if it occurred?"

"Yes."

"So there will be no question, Doctor, is it your opinion that the defendant, Antone Costa, was legally *insane* at the time of the commission of these offenses—"

"I pray Your Honor's judgment!" Shubow called out.

Beaudreau called Shubow, Goldman and Fernandes to the bench. "This question is admissible," the judge said, "but I think before we get to this conclusion we have got to ask the question along the lines of the McHoul test; then, if you want to end up with the question, 'was he insane,' all right. I don't think Mr. Shubow elicited the McHoul test correctly. He left out the word 'substantial.' "

"I think it was deliberate," Fernandes said.

"I don't know if it was deliberate or not," Beaudreau said. "He's pretty adept."

"You'd better *believe* it," Fernandes said.

"I know what the doctor's answer would be," Shubow said. "At the time he saw Costa at the hospital he was not legally insane. As far as January goes, he doesn't know."

"I've got to clear that up," Fernandes said. "The jury has

been left with an impression of reduced responsibility. Are you saying drugs is a complete defense?"

"A drug-induced psychosis is insanity," Shubow said. "I don't care what caused it: his mother, his father or drugs. Some of the doctors take the position that this guy had a psychotic breakdown at the time of the killings, caused by the complication of his underlying mental condition by drugs—what we are trying to sell is a temporary psychotic episode."

"I am going to give Mr. Shubow the opportunity to rephrase those questions and use the word 'substantial,' " Beaudreau said. "I don't think you can leave out that word and then say we got an opinion from the doctor stating he was insane; I think you've got to use that phraseology. And I want to give Mr. Shubow that opportunity, because I don't know if it was deliberate."

"It was *very* deliberate," Shubow admitted without apology.

"It certainly *wasn't,*" Goldman said hastily. "I don't think it was deliberate at all!"

"I am going to exclude this question at this time to give you an opportunity to rephrase your preliminary questions along the McHoul case," Beaudreau said. "Then you can put in your final question, 'Was he legally insane.' I don't want to skip the McHoul test."

"If I rephrase the question in terms of 'substantial capacity' of the McHoul test, you have no objection to me asking the question now?" Fernandes said. "You don't want me to wait until Mr. Shubow finishes?"

"That's right," Beaudreau said. "Just as the McHoul test."

Fernandes said to Ewalt, "Is it your opinion, Doctor, that the defendant, Antone Costa, is not responsible for his criminal conduct as a result of a mental disease he had on or about January twenty-sixth, 1969? And that as a result of such disease, he lacks substantial capacity either to appreciate the wrongfulness or criminality of his acts, or to conform his conduct to the requirements of law?"

"It has to be by inference, because I obviously didn't see him on January twenty-sixth, 1969," Ewalt said. "I think he certainly was not responsible for things he did then."

"In that form that I gave you?"

"Yes," Ewalt said, firmly.

Fernandes looked surprised. He was angry as hell. Shubow had unequivocally stated during the bench conference that Ewalt

576

had no opinion as to Costa's sanity under the McHoul test. Fernandes had, inadvertently, scored a major point for the defense.

"Is it therefore your opinion that the defendant, Antone Costa, on January twenty-sixth, 1969 was legally insane?"

"How are you defining that term?" Ewalt said. "That's not a medical term."

"I'm defining it in terms of the 'substantial capacity' test I just gave you."

"His capacity to know what he was doing and control his behavior *was* substantially impaired, in my opinion," Ewalt said.

"To the point that he lacks substantial capacity to appreciate the wrongfulness of his acts and to conform his conduct to the requirements of law?"

"That's right."

"And if that's what I mean by 'legal insanity,' are you saying that the defendant, Antone Costa, was legally insane as of that day?"

"Yes," Ewalt said.

"I object to the question, Your Honor, on the grounds that it calls for a legal conclusion!" Shubow said. "That is the job of the court."

"And the *jury,*" Goldman added.

"Well, the doctor said that he differentiated between legal and medical terms of insanity." Beaudreau said. "We appreciate that 'sanity' and 'insanity' are legal terms, not medical terms with regards to this test that is being put here."

"Are you saying that this defendant is suffering from a psychosis brought on by drugs?" Fernandes said.

"No," Ewalt said.

"You did refer to the use of drugs producing certain psychotic episodes, did you not?"

"Drugs is one of the things that can produce them, yes."

"Let's talk about amphetamine psychosis," Fernandes said. "What would the psychotic event be?"

"One of the common forms is that they look like they have a paranoid schizophrenia. Another form is they get very aggressive, hostile, almost like an epileptic in a furor state. You have probably seen older people get into senile tantrums; they sometimes look like that. If he was on amphetamines and there were other people around him and they say he was calm, cool and relaxed, he might be."

577

"And yet he might be psychotic?"

"Yes, of course."

"If a person meets two people he does not know and leaves a note on the door asking for a ride to a specific location, and is seen by others wherein they have a discussion concerning a payroll check, and then secures the ride to the woods, does that depict someone undergoing a psychotic episode caused by amphetamines?"

"I don't think you could answer that 'yes' or 'no,'" Ewalt said. "It could happen, and—"

Fernandes cut him off. "What you are saying is, you don't know!"

"That's right."

"Now, we are in the wooded area. A gun conveniently happens to be nearby. Three shots, one into one victim, two into the other victim; then there is the mutilation, the sex described by Mr. Shubow. Then there is burial of the victims, and of the weapons. Is that conduct equivalent to a psychotic episode?"

"Psychotic patients *could* do that, yes."

"May one who is *not* psychotic do it?"

"Of course."

"You don't know whether Mr. Costa was psychotic at this time, do you?"

"Not for sure."

"Your answer would be, 'I don't know if Mr. Costa was psychotic at this time.' Is that a fair statement?"

"That would be fair," Ewalt said. "You can only infer. It's an educated guess."

"Doctor, we are not interested in guesswork in this case!" Fernandes said.

"An educated guess is different," Ewalt said.

"What do you mean by 'an educated guess'?"

"Well, we have evidence that this man had this disorder. We have evidence that he was on drugs. So, one could assume with fair safety that he was under a drug affection and probably psychotic."

"That's a big assumption," Fernandes said. "He may *not* have been?"

"He might not be," Ewalt said. "There are many people in this courtroom. I can't sit here, being somewhat of an expert, and tell you whether any of them are psychotic or not."

578

"Except *me?*" Fernandes said, smiling.

"I can't even tell on *you,* sir," Ewalt said.

"Was there anything you could *see* in the tests you gave him which would conclude that defendant, Antone Costa, was suffering from an organic psychiatric malfunction?"

"I didn't testify he had an organic malfunction. I said he had borderline schizophrenia."

"Was there a mental disease that you could see from those tests?"

"See?" Ewalt said. "It was a *diagnosis!* You can't see pneumonia, either."

"All right, *prove?*"

"Yes," Ewalt said. "That is what I testified to."

"The basis of your opinion, then, is on what?"

"Mostly on the mental examination."

"Which consists of what?"

"Questions, answers, observations, the way they put their language together; the way they handle their context."

"Is it not fair to say that the basis of your opinion depends, to a great extent, on what the defendant told you?"

"No."

"Even though it is done with a question and answer, as you described?"

"No, it's how he says it, which is not possible for an uninformed person to fake; or even me."

"But the source of the information comes from the defendant? That can be answered 'yes' fairly, can't it?" Fernandes asked.

"That is true of any illness," Ewalt said. "The evidence of a broken leg comes from the victim, too."

"How long would a psychotic episode last?"

"There are many kinds of psychoses. Borderline schizophrenia tends to be a long-term kind of illness, interspersed with shorter episodes which are much worse. An analogy would be epilepsy. A person is always an epileptic, but he may only have seizures periodically."

"If a person took a substantial amount of barbiturates, what would be his physical behavior?"

"He might go to sleep. He might be walking around, and not be particularly unusual in appearance or behavior."

"Is it likely for him to have sex?"

"He might, particularly if he was young. Barbiturates do not greatly impair the sexual function, although they do a little."

"They *depress* you as a rule?"

"No, some people get fairly high on them," Ewalt said. "They're very much like alcohol that way. Some people get depressed, some people get high."

"Do you lose control a little bit?" Fernandes asked.

"A little bit."

"And it reduces the desire for sex occasionally, is that it?"

"It might," Ewalt said. "It might *stimulate* it. It depends on the individual."

"Is it likely to produce a situation where intercourse may have been had *four* times?"

"Well, that would depend on whom you started with," Ewalt said. "I don't think a person who is a one-time performer would become a four-time performer on barbiturates, no."

"You don't know what the defendant's response was?"

"No, I have never seen him on drugs."

"Did Antone Costa say to you, 'On January twenty-sixth I was under the influence of drugs'?"

"We didn't discuss January twenty-sixth as a specific day. I was trying to make a *medical* diagnosis. Pinning him down as to whether he did or didn't do this is not my affair. I was supposed to find out this man's mental condition. What one day was as opposed to another is none of my concern."

"Therefore, you don't know *what* he was on January twenty-sixth?"

"No, except I know what he is now," Ewalt said. "And I can be pretty sure what he was like on that day."

"You are saying if he is borderline schizophrenic now, he probably was on January twenty-sixth?"

"That's right."

"But you can't tell me what kind of conduct he displayed on that day, because you don't know."

"I don't know, that's right."

"You don't know whether or not he had the mental capacity to conform his conduct to the requirements of law, or appreciate the wrongfulness of his conduct?"

"I think you *do*."

"How do you *know?*"

"He could have done this crime on many days, and the answer would be the same," Ewalt said. "I don't even know if January twenty-sixth is the right day."

"There is no evidence as to the right day," Goldman interjected.

"Now, doctor, I am going to make reference to your report. 'While the patient was under drugs, aggressions and anger may have been uncontrolled.'" Fernandes said. "They may *not* have been?"

"That's true, absolutely."

"You are not saying that Antone Costa's taking of drugs resulted in the death of these girls?" Fernandes asked, attacking one wing of Goldman's defense.

"I didn't say that."

"Does the mutilation of the bodies in this case necessarily suggest psychotic behavior?"

"I would think so."

"You are saying that persons who mutilate bodies are psychotic?" Fernandes said.

"In my opinion, they probably are; I haven't seen all of them," Ewalt said. "If anybody in this audience—including me—kills somebody, we might be angry; but if we then mutilate the body, we must be nuts."

"How about burying the bodies, hiding the gun, getting the girls to the scene, is that 'nutty' behavior?" Fernandes managed to make Ewalt's folksiness a moment before now sound distinctly unprofessional.

"Not necessarily. It may be."

"And might mutilation of the bodies *not* be psychotic behavior?"

"It would be hard for me to say that it's not," Ewalt said. "I think anybody who mutilates a body, alive or dead, in this type of manner that is alleged is psychotic. Yes, I do."

"You don't know what Antone Costa's actions were, or his responsibility for them was on January twenty-sixth, is that right?"

"I don't know about January twenty-sixth, but by inference, if he committed these crimes, that certainly was not the act of a normal person. I don't know that he committed the crimes."

"In your opinion, anytime anyone kills anyone, it is *not* normal?"

581

"No, I didn't say that at all," Ewalt said. "But anytime anybody kills somebody and cuts them up, *that* is not normal."

"Is it a sign of a mental illness?"

"That's right."

"A mental illness which will *always* render one not responsible?"

"I would think so."

"You have never heard of sadistic crimes?"

"Sadists that kill are mentally ill," Ewalt said. "They really are, sir."

"We are concerned with whether or not as a result of that mental illness the person has substantial capacity to conform his conduct to the requirements of law, or to appreciate what he is doing is wrong."

"I don't think they have."

"In this case, when a person buries the bodies, having first put the note on the door to get these people to the scene of the crime, buries the weapons, and does everything which one might say is flight, avoidance of guilt—*that* is not knowledge of right and wrong?"

"The right and wrong test is a very difficult one—"

"*That* is not what I asked you," Fernandes said. "I asked you if it was not evidence that the person knew what he was doing was wrong?"

"It could or it could not be. That is not a medical question. That is what these people have got to decide," Ewalt said, nodding toward the jury. Ewalt expected a rebuke from Fernandes, or from the judge, but none came.

"Continuing with your report, doctor, did you not say that at the time you examined this defendant, *he knew right from wrong?*"

"That's right," Ewalt said. "But in our opinion, during the time of this alleged crime, this individual was having one of those attacks or episodes precipitated by drugs which rendered him mentally ill."

"That is an *assumption!*" Fernandes said.

"It's a pretty good one," Ewalt said, and smiled.

"Did the defendant tell you that he was under a specific drug at a specific time, and that it had a specific effect?"

"No, of course not—"

"What he told you was, 'I have a loss of memory.' "

"No, he told us that he had been on drugs for a long time,

582

and that he had gaps in his memory. I also point out that the description of the condition of these bodies would suggest that whoever did this was mentally ill at the time—"

"You never answered the question of burying the bodies," Beaudreau said. "Is that also related to the mutilation?"

"I don't know as much about the burying," Ewalt said. "From the information we produced, they were rather crudely buried and not very carefully concealed. It would seem anybody could do a better job than that in trying to conceal something."

"If I represent to you that for one solid month police were in the woods in search of those burial holes and they were not found, would you say that was a pretty good job of concealing?" Fernandes said.

"No, I wouldn't," Ewalt said. "I have seen people look for months for a downed airplane in the woods and not find it."

"How about the burial of the gun?"

"I don't know anything about the burial of the gun."

"Did they tell you it was buried a good distance away from the graves?"

"It would suggest he thought he might want it again, but that is pure speculation on my part," Ewalt said. "That is why *I* would bury it away—if I was going to do it."

"Where you could get at it again when you had your next psychotic episode?" Fernandes said bitingly.

"Maybe," Ewalt replied evenly. "But that would not be evidence for or against the man being mentally ill. Mentally ill people behave very rationally in some behaviors. They go to church, conduct businesses."

"Can we say with all fairness that the defendant, Antone Costa, is a very intelligent young man?"

"That's right."

"Would you say that the outcome of this case is very important to him?"

"I would think so."

"And is it your opinion that he might tend to exaggerate because of the importance of this case?"

"I think that is true, yes."

Shubow countered, "In addition to being a very intelligent young man, is it your sober medical judgment, based on everything you know, that he was also a very *sick* young man, mentally speaking?"

"He was and *is*," Ewalt said.

Ewalt left the stand. Fernandes had matched Shubow with a penetrating and brilliant cross-examination, but Ewalt had stuck by his conviction that Tony Costa had been psychotic at the time of the murders of Patricia Walsh and Mary Anne Wysocki. His testimony had been a triumph for the defense.

19

Dr. Jonathan Cole was a pleasant, balding man in his early forties. Superintendent of Boston State Mental Hospital in Mattapan and professor of psychiatry at Tufts University Medical School, Cole had been chief of the psychopharmacology research branch of the National Institute of Mental Health studying drugs that affect behavior.

"Doctor, you have been asked to testify in this case at the request of the defendant's lawyers," Shubow said. "But you have never seen the defendant, Antone Costa, or treated him?"

"That's true," Cole said.

"Doctor, I am going to ask you a very long question," Shubow said. "I am going to ask you to assume one Antone Costa, who has been diagnosed as a drug-dependent person, married a fourteen-year-old woman whom he had impregnated; that he engaged in the practice of suspending her by the feet from the ceiling and then performing various perverse practices; that in 1965, having difficulties in his marriage, he went to a physician who put him on a regular therapy basis with a product known as Solacen, and he says thereafter on barbiturates—but the doctor says there were no barbiturates prescribed; that in May of 1968 he made a theft from this doctor's office of a barracks-bagful of drugs—the doctor says it was a much smaller quantity of drugs; and that he is implicated in another drug theft in July 1968. He was described by friends and companions as stoned over one hundred times and to be a very frequent user of amphetamines and, in addition, is known as a regular smoker of marijuana and hashish. And there is evidence of occasional use of LSD.

"I ask you to assume that toward the end of January 1969, while living in a rooming house in Provincetown, he met for the first time two young women and that sometime on or after January twenty-sixth, the evidence indicates that in the woods in Truro where he had secreted a container of drugs, he shot and killed each of these women; that after he killed them, based on the evidence given us by a pathologist, the chest was sliced vertically and the skin peeled open to create a sweaterlike effect; and in addition, there were multiple slash wounds of other portions of the anatomy. Each of the bodies of these young women was cut up and buried in that wooded locale, and there was found in one of the graves a plastic bottle with residuals of barbiturates and a sample card for the drug Triavil. There is further evidence that following these acts, the defendant, having taken a Volkswagen belonging to one of these girls, called a local garageman and said, 'How much does it cost to paint a Volkswagen an exotic color?' There is evidence he went to Vermont and among the possessions he took with him was a copy of the *Physicians' Desk Reference* for the year 1968. There is evidence he went to the police while under no legal compulsion to do so and gave three inconsistent and mutually contradictory explanations of his knowledge of the whereabouts of these two victims. There is evidence also that warrants us to assume he sent a telegram from New York trying to indicate the girls were still alive. Now, having made all those assumptions, do you have an opinion as to whether the behavior I have described to you, based upon your expertise as a psychiatrist, was psychotic or not?"

"Yes, I think I would judge that as psychotic behavior," Cole said.

"Would a drug-dependent person as I have described to you have his mental processes affected by his drug dependency?"

"Yes, he can."

"What about the capacity of such a person to control his behavior in the way the law requires?"

"I think it might well be impaired," Cole said. "I would include whatever drug effect was present during the crime as part of the mental disease."

Fernandes said, in cross-examination, "Doctor, there are diagnoses known as 'personality disorders.' Are these psychotic?"

"They are generally not considered to be psychotic."

"Is there a personality diagnosis, 'with sexual deviation'?"

"Certainly."

"On the hypothetical given to you by Mr. Shubow, a proper diagnosis might have been 'personality disorder, sexual deviation, *nonpsychotic?*" Fernandes said.

"These would all be diagnoses which a psychiatrist could make in clear conscience," Cole said. "My personal clinical judgment is that where the behavior is somewhat understandable—the soldier who goes AWOL a lot to get out of duty, or is always in trouble because he is goldbricking—I would call it a personality disorder. Somebody who is very bizarre, I would feel is clearly a borderline psychotic. Other people would disagree with me, but I would stick to my guns on my diagnosis."

"What is the effect on sexual behavior of being high on barbiturates?"

"Barbiturates do not generally enhance sexual behavior, even as alcohol tends sometimes to interfere with performance," Cole said. "A low dose might enable someone whose sexual behavior was inhibited by anxiety to perform more effectively."

"What about sexual relations *four* time?" Fernandes said.

"It seems to me unlikely," Cole said, dryly.

"Is it your opinion that the mutilation and sexual conduct that occurred either before or after death is clearly and positively *only* psychotic behavior?" Fernandes said.

"Yes, I would say that was psychotic behavior."

"Sexual deviation of that character does not, and can never be, nonpsychotic?"

"Yes, that's what I am saying."

"Why?"

"Because that is what I believe," Cole said. "It's an emotional belief as much as an intellectual belief."

"I am not interested in your *emotions,* Doctor," Fernandes said. "I am interested in your intellectual beliefs. And I am sure you have a lot of intellect. Would you try to give us some?"

"I think certain kinds of behavior are understandable as aberrations of personality," Cole said quietly. "Certain kinds of drug behavior go so far beyond what is understandable in terms of motivations of ordinary people that I have great difficulty in calling it anything but psychotic."

Before Costa was returned to the Barnstable House of Correction, he met with Goldman and Cavanaugh in a conference room off the courtroom's gallery. He wanted to go on the witness stand. "I can do it, Mr. Goldman. I *know* I can do it!"

"Tony, there's no way you can take the stand," Goldman said. "No way at all you can take a cross-examination."

"Don't say that," Costa said, angrily. "Don't say I can't."

"Well, you can't, Tony," Goldman said. "What are you going to say when they start asking you about going to the woods with the girls? What about the history you gave Dr. Ewalt, about stabbing Mary Anne. That's an admission that's in the record!"

"It's just a circumstantial case," Costa said. "All they've got is circumstantial evidence."

"Tony, listen to me. There's nothing wrong with circumstantial evidence. Circumstantial evidence is damn good evidence. For example, you say you saw me put your wallet in my pocket. That's eyewitness evidence, right? But you could be *wrong*. The light might be bad, or you had a couple of drinks, and you don't know *what* you saw. I could have put something else in my pocket, a prayer book, a memo pad, any damn thing. Or you might not like me, might want to get me in trouble because I was fooling around with your wife. Eyewitness testimony, Tony, you can break down. If you only knew how many eyewitnesses get things wrong. But, if you *find* your wallet in my pocket, that's circumstantial evidence, but it's damn good evidence I took your wallet."

Goldman suggested another way for Costa to be heard in the courtroom. In capital cases, a defendant was permitted to make a statement to the jury in his own defense. The statement was not evidence, because it was not made under oath or subject to cross-examination. He wanted Costa to consider it. "There's time yet to let me know. Tomorrow or the next day."

"Mr. Goldman, I want to take the stand," Costa insisted.

"Tony, if you take the stand," Goldman said, "the jury will be out just long enough to take a piss."

20

Avis Costa arrived at Barnstable courthouse at 9:30 A.M. on Thursday, May 21. She wore a crocheted magenta wool vest over a brown, long-sleeved cotton turtleneck and a plaid miniskirt. Giddy with nerves, she greeted waiting photographers with an open-armed gesture of mock fanfare, grinning and posturing for the cameras. Goldman stood beside her, stony with disapproval.

Avis Costa brought to the witness stand a small bouquet of white lilacs she had picked from the courthouse grounds.

"What are those flowers for?" Goldman said.

"Security," Avis said, giggling.

Sitting in the witness chair, she swept her long hair from her eyes, grinned broadly and waved at Tony Costa. Costa smiled back and nodded.

"Now, don't you be nervous, Avis," Goldman said. "How old are you now?"

"Twenty-one."

"How old were you when you married Tony?"

"Fourteen," Avis said. She giggled again, bringing a hand to her mouth.

"You had known him how long?"

"I had known him when I was about five. Then, I didn't see him for a while. I had known him well for over a year before we got married."

"Sweethearts, then?" Goldman said.

"Yeah."

"And out of this marriage did you have any children?"

"Three."

"And what are their names?"

"Peter, Michael and Nico."

"How old are they?"

"Peter is six; Michael is five and Nico is three."

"Where did you live when you first got married?"

"In North Truro for, I think, probably two years. I don't remember."

"And were you happy during those first two years?"

"Yeah."

"I see you looking over; you still like Tony?" Goldman said.

Avis grinned and swept her hair back. "Sure!" She giggled and brought the hand over her mouth.

Costa bowed his head. He removed his glasses, rubbed his eyes. Tears glistened on his cheeks.

"I think you ought to talk a little bit louder," Goldman said. "If you would put your hand down . . ."

"OK," Avis said.

"Did some family disagreements take place in your household between you and Tony?" Goldman said.

"Yeah."

"When did that start?"

"I'd say in 1965."

"Up until 1965 did Tony use drugs in any way, form, shape or style?"

"Not that I know of, no."

"When did he first commence to use drugs, so far as you know?"

"When he first visited Dr. Callis in Wellfleet."

"Avis—again—when you put your hand up, we just can't hear you," Goldman said. "Try to keep your hand down, would you?"

"Hold the flowers in both hands," Beaudreau suggested.

"Is that an *order?*" Avis looked up to the bench and grinned. "OK."

"Now, was there trouble in the family?" Goldman said.

"Yeah," Avis said. "Mostly because I'm a very lazy housewife." Avis giggled, her hand at her mouth.

"Was that what Tony said?"

"Yeah."

"Why did he call you a lazy housewife?"

"Because his mother was a very fastidious person, and I'm not."

"Do you know whether Tony went to see some doctor as the result of some problem?"

"He was having trouble with his stomach because of his

589

nerves, because of all the arguing we were doing. We were hassling each other all the time."

"This was following—" Goldman discovered Avis furtively waving to her ex-husband. "I think you should pay attention to us here!" Goldman said sharply. "It's not fair!"

"OK!" Avis said.

"Now, what happened after Tony started going to see Dr. Callis?"

"Dr. Callis prescribed tranquilizers for him. When Tony was taking tranquilizers, he was very calm and collected, I believe, and really pleasant, you know. Just a passive, nice person."

"Did he like the children?"

"Yeah, I think so."

"And was he attentive to the children?"

"Not all the time, but yeah, I'd say he was."

"Now, what happened following Tony's various visits with Dr. Callis?" Goldman said.

"The more Tony saw him, the more he took the tranquilizers. The more tranquilizers Tony was taking the more uptight he got when he wasn't taking them. He was very hard to live with."

"By 'uptight' you mean what?"

"Argumentative, nervous," Avis said. "You know, anxieties."

"Did he use any other type of drugs from that period on?"

"Amphetamines—that's speed. All sorts of barbiturates, LSD, marijuana. Everything."

"Following your divorce, did he come to your house to see the children?"

"Yeah."

"How often would he come?"

"Gee, I don't know. He was living in Boston for part of that time, so maybe I'd see him once or twice a week."

"Would he come regularly once or twice a week?"

"No, he wasn't regular about too much."

"On those occasions when he came to visit the children, would he ever be under the influence of any drug, if you so observed?"

"Most of the time that I saw him he was stoned," Avis said. "He was dealing hash at that time; and he was smoking hash. Every time I saw him he was stoned."

"*Every* time?"

"I've never seen him not stoned," Avis said. "I mean, you know, there weren't very many times he wasn't stoned."

"You're *sure* about that?" Goldman said.

"I'm *positive!*"

"Did you observe his condition in the latter part of 1968?"

"I saw him a few times around the last of January, off and on until he was arrested."

"Did you ever see Tony in December or January take any amphetamines or barbiturates in your presence?"

"Yeah."

"How many times?"

"I can't tell you how many times, but a lot. You know . . . maybe . . . almost every day. He could take handfuls of them. He'd try to give them to everybody, you know." Avis grinned. "He was playing Santa Claus."

Goldman turned the witness over to Edmund Dinis.

"Mrs. Costa, did you live on Hughes Road in Truro when you first married?"

"Yeah."

"Do you recall an incident where Dr. Hiebert was either called or you were taken to him?"

Avis's grin froze. "Yeah," she said, uncertainly.

"Would you tell us about that?"

"I really would rather not," Avis said.

"Did it involve a situation where you needed medical attention as a result of something you ingested?" Dinis said.

Avis looked down at the lilacs in her hand. "Uh-huh."

"Did you take a chemical of some kind?"

"Chloral hydrate."

"Is that a drug?"

"Yeah, I guess it is. I don't know."

"Who gave you that drug?"

"Nobody *gave* it to me," Avis said.

"You took it of your own volition?"

"Yeah."

"You got it from Tony Costa, didn't you?" Dinis said.

"I got it in my house. I didn't get it from him."

"Who brought it into the house?"

"I imagine Tony did."

"What prompted you to take this drug?"

591

"That's really *personal*," Avis said, indignantly. "I really would not like to go into that."

"Isn't it a fact that your husband gave you that drug so that you could take it at that time?"

"He did *not* give me that drug, no."

"Did you become unconscious?"

"Yeah, I did."

"Wasn't it the practice of your husband, at that time Tony Costa, to give you that drug to make you unconscious?" Dinis said.

"That's *not* true!" Avis said. "You have your story a little mixed up."

"You were interrogated after Tony was arrested, were you not? Lieutenant Flynn of the state police?"

"I was interrogated quite a few times," Avis said with annoyance.

"Do you remember saying that early in your marriage, your husband, Tony Costa, liked to put a plastic bag over your head?"

"That's not the way I put it, no!"

"Can you tell us *how* you put it?"

"Look, I really would not like to talk about this in front of all these people. I'm sorry, but that's just the way it is."

"You told us, did you not, that you were happy in your early years of marriage?" Dinis said.

"Yeah, I was."

"Is it true or not that Tony Costa would put a plastic bag over your head, endeavoring to knock you out, before he had sexual relations with you?"

"I am not going to agree to that! You have that *completely* wrong. I am not going to say, 'yes' to that, because it's *not* true."

"As a result of using the plastic bag, were you not afraid of Tony Costa at that time?"

"No, I was not afraid of him," Avis said. "I was never forced into anything."

"Did you tell investigators that Tony Costa would try to smother you with pillows?"

"I don't remember saying it in those words, no."

"Can you tell us what words you *did* use?" Dinis said.

"I don't want to *talk* about that," Avis said. "I'm telling you, you are *wrong*. You're trying to make it sound like these were acts of violence that he insisted upon, or forced onto me; and that's not the way it was."

"There *was* the use of pillows in order to cut short your breath, was there not?"

"Maybe *once*, yes . . ."

"And the same thing with the plastic bag? Your cooperation was required with the plastic bag?"

"At one time, yes."

"Did that knock you out?"

"No!"

"At one time did your husband ask you to hang by your heels?"

Avis glared at Dinis. "Yeah."

"Was that involving a sexual experience?"

"Do I have to talk about this, *really?*" Avis appealed to Goldman at the defense table. "This period of things you are talking about lasted a week. It was an experiment that I wouldn't have anything to do with. After that was established, we got along fine."

"Did you tell investigators that this happened six or seven times?"

"I *never* said six or seven times!"

"These incidents that I just asked you about occurred prior to 1965, didn't they?" Dinis said.

"I don't know; I can't remember the date. If you want the date, get it from someone else."

"This was before Tony went to see Dr. Callis? The plastic bag, the pillows, the hanging upside down on the hook, the fact that you had to call a doctor?"

"I guess so, I don't know."

"Was it these conditions that prompted him to seek out a doctor?"

"No, it wasn't!" Avis said. "I just got through explaining to you that these 'conditions' as you put it, was a period of experimentation. It was never anything inflicted on me. It was never a horror scene. It lasted a week; and then it was complete. That's all there was to it."

"Did you tell investigators you would turn the clock back in order to avoid . . . ?"

"One day I did that to make the time look later because I didn't want to go through . . . the hassle that we just got through talking about," Avis said. "I *don't* want to talk about it—"

"The plastic bag and the pillows—"

"You keep talking about them like the same thing, and it was separate incidents, maybe once or twice, three times at the most during the week; and then that was over!"

"Was there an incident involving a belt?" Dinis said. "Somebody, either you or Tony, beating each other with belts?"

"No!"

"You never told the investigators that?"

"Not that I remember, no."

"Did Tony ever burn you with cigarettes?"

"That is absolutely *absurd.*"

"How was he with the children?"

"I don't know. They were his kids."

"Did he beat them once in a while?"

"Not beat them, no."

"Did you tell investigators that he beat their heads against the crib when he was angry?"

"I *never* said that!" Avis shrieked.

"Did you say earlier that when Tony is on drugs, he appears to be normal?"

"He appears very calm, yes."

"And when he is off drugs he is uptight, he gets irritable?"

"Yeah, somewhat. He just gets nervous."

Dinis returned to the prosecutor's table, wheeled about and said, "Mrs. Costa, are you writing a *book* about this case?"

"No!" Avis said.

Leaving the witness stand, Avis blew a kiss to Costa, transformed in midgesture into a peace sign. She gave the lilacs to a deputy sheriff to be delivered to her ex-husband. The lilac stems had been wrapped in paper which contained "objects" belonging to her three children and a friend. She explained, "It represents life."

Avis stationed herself at the rear entrance of the courthouse to await Costa's appearance at the lunch recess. When he emerged, she reached out to touch him. Deputy sheriff Elwood Mills knocked her hand away. Avis flashed a crooked grin for photographers who had observed the scene, holding up both hands in a double peace sign.

Maurice Goldman followed Costa up the hill to the Barnstable House of Correction. Costa had changed his mind about taking the witness stand to testify in his own behalf. He would, instead, make a statement.

"Tony will be heard," Goldman promised reporters when he returned to the courthouse for the afternoon session of the trial.

"I'd like to read the following into the record," Goldman told Beaudreau during a bench conference. Goldman consulted a single memo page upon which Tony Costa had written:

It is my considered opinion after much deliberation that I do not prefer to take the stand.

"It's dated today," Goldman said. "I want that made a part of the record."

"With that, are you going to rest?" Beaudreau said.

"I am going to rest," Goldman said.

Fernandes called Dr. Frederick Whiskin to the stand as a psychiatric rebuttal witness. Whiskin had changed his earlier diagnosis of "borderline personality, sexual deviation, type undetermined."

"My diagnostic impression has changed since that time to 'antisocial personality, severe, manifested by deviant sexual behavior of a sadistic nature, stealing, lying and illegal use of drugs.' "

"Is that a psychotic diagnosis?"

"No, it's a personality disorder."

Shubow swiftly demolished the witness. "Was there some *dissatisfaction* with your original diagnosis which caused you to reconsider it?"

"Since I made the original diagnosis, I had access to Dr. Ewalt's report. When I examined Mr. Costa I could not make the assumption that he had, in fact, committed the crimes."

"Do you agree that a person in a borderline state may erupt into psychotic episodes?"

"I can agree with that."

"Leaving all labels aside, what we are really discussing is conduct, are we not?" Shubow said. "And the mental condition underlying that conduct?"

"We could talk about that, yes."

"This crime has been described by a pathologist as 'the most bizarre he's seen in his practice.' Would you consider this conduct that has been described to you bizarre?"

"Yes."

"Well, you agree that persons with personality disorders can engage in psychotic conduct."

"The behavior may be psychotic, bizarre and so forth, but the person exhibiting this bizarre behavior need not be psychotic at the time of his commiting the act."

"But *may* be?"

"Yes."

"Are you willing to concede that even though his underlying condition was nonpsychotic, his behavior was psychotic?"

"I find it difficult to label behavior psychotic," Whiskin said. "Psychosis involves the total personality."

"I thought I was quoting you when you said sometimes nonpsychotic persons can engage in psychotic behavior."

Whiskin smiled uncomfortably. "I think I did."

"If nonpsychotic persons can engage in psychotic behavior, would you not then concede the behavior in this case was a good example of psychotic behavior?"

Whiskin paused, realizing too late the trap Shubow's questions had led him into. "It would serve the purpose, yes."

"Would you agree that necrophilia is almost always a manifestation of a very severely ill mental state?"

"I would agree as long as you are not indicating that it always means psychosis."

"You do *not* agree that acts of necrophilia are always pathological?" Shubow said, incredulously.

"I do not agree that acts of necrophilia always mean psychosis!"

"Would you consider necrophilia an example of psychotic behavior, regardless of the underlying state of mind?"

Whiskin couldn't dodge the question any more. "Yes," he said quietly.

"Your answer is *yes!*" Shubow repeated in triumph. "Thank you, I have no further questions."

21

For his statement to the jury, Antone Costa wrote out a list of instructions for Goldman to follow:

1. The prosecution has failed to place me at the scene of the crime—wherever that is!
2. Bullet heads which match those found in the girls' bodies are not lodged in the walls of my room, but I can tell you whose room they may be found in!
3. The gun that killed the girls was not stolen by me from West Virginia.
4. The gun used to kill the girls was not used by me but I can tell you who used it to kill them.
5. My room was not redecorated many months ago to conceal and cover up the bullet holes in the walls and the bloodstains.
6. I did not steal any doctors' bags containing surgical instruments.
7. I can also tell you that these girls met this same person by prearrangement at his mother's cosmetic shop after purchasing certain items. It is also remarkable that these girls, strangers in town, should know where to find this shop or should go there at all for two reasons:

   a. The shop had just opened for its first day of business on January 25, 1969. No one else in town seemed to know that this shop had opened for business. Yet, the girls knew, somehow.

   b. The local pharmacy, just two short blocks from where the girls were staying, could supply them with any cosmetics necessary and at a lower cost.

   After their subsequent meeting at the area di-

rectly surrounding this shop, the girls were never
seen alive again! . . .

I did not kill the girls but I have told you who did!

Goldman hastily called a conference that evening, during which
he, Cavanaugh, Lester Allen and Victor Wolfson took turns re-
writing drafts of a statement Costa would deliver the next morning.

Costa had a cleanly typed manuscript with him when he entered the courtroom on Friday morning, May 22.

Beaudreau had prepared a "box-score" sheet with various
verdicts to be checked by the jury, and Shubow complained about
it. "There's no box here for 'Not guilty, period,'" Shubow said.
"The jury might disbelieve everything they heard and say that a
circumstantial case was not proved beyond a reasonable doubt."

"I think, for the record, it should go in," Goldman said.

"Can we write 'not guilty' in pen?" Fernandes said.

"I will do that before I charge the jury," Beaudreau said,
then settled into his chair and looked out over the courtroom.
"All right, Mr. Goldman."

Goldman walked slowly to the jury box.

"Might I start my summation by saying that I would be
lacking in common courtesy and ordinary manners if I didn't say
thank you very much for your patience in these days that have
preceded us during this trial," Goldman said. "I want to take this
opportunity also to thank the police, the district attorney, and the
sheriff's office who have fully cooperated with us in an endeavor to
get at the truth in the Costa case.

"There is a serious problem in the search for truth in this
case," Goldman continued. "I think in every courtroom there
should be the statement: 'In God We Trust,' because today, in a
real sense, you are sitting in judgment of your fellow man; you are
performing a godlike function.

"If you recall in my opening, I told you the defense was going
to prove that drugs, and drug abuse—and it is horrible—are on
trial before this court *with* Tony Costa," Goldman said. "Now,
what did you hear for some eleven days? First, you heard a little
bit about Tony Costa's background. You heard he graduated from
Provincetown High School, and while there he met and married a
young girl, he himself at a young age. There is no evidence of any

kind introduced at this trial to indicate that Tony was anything other than a good boy. As I recall the testimony, he had a reasonably happy marriage at the start. Two children were born, and a third followed their domestic difficulties. Sometime in 1965, his marriage was falling apart at the seams. There was tension and a lot of friction in the household. Tony Costa was sick; he had some stomach disorder and he was nervous. He needed some medical help and attention, so he went to see a doctor. He went to what was purported to be a medical center in Wellfleet, and there he found one doctor; and I think his name was Dr. Callis. He went there seeking *help*. What did he get? Pills. Pills. Pills!

"Up until that time Tony Costa never took a single pill, even so much as an aspirin," Goldman continued. "When he went to that doctor, the doctor started him on pills. I am not passing upon Dr. Callis; he is not on trial here today. But I want you to consider how Tony got started on his downfall in life. Drugs took possession of a sick man; and we know now what happened. We watched the gradual deterioration of Tony through all those witnesses you will recall, the little girls of all ages and sizes. And Tony started on the drug path. One drug led to another: Solacen, barbiturates, marijuana, hash—followed step by step. We watched Tony's physical and mental condition, triggered by the use of drugs, deteriorate and fall apart. And then, finally, the crime.

"The crime was described best by Dr. Katsas, the pathologist. He said it was the most bizarre killing he had ever seen. Let's see what that amounts to: Mary Anne Wysocki, mutilation of the body in five distinct portions, gunshot wounds, stab wounds of the chest, abdomen and legs, with peeling off of the skin. And present, as you recall, spermatozoa in the vagina and the rectum."

Goldman glared at the jury. "Is that a *sane* man? Do I have to tell a Barnstable County jury that any man that does that can possibly be sane?

"We find the same mutilation of the body into two distinct portions of Patricia Walsh, the gunshot wound, the stab wounds of the chest, abdomen, legs; and, again a peeling of skin, and the presence of spermatozoa in the vagina and the rectum! Is that the action of a mentally well-balanced person? Or is that the action of a truly sick person?

"We don't need expert witnesses because it doesn't make any difference what I say or what the witnesses say so far as the mental capacity of Tony is concerned. It's what *you* say. You alone are the judges of that. You heard the leading psychiatrists in America on the stand say Tony is nuts, Tony is crazy. There's no question about that in *my* mind. And I trust there is no question about that in your mind.

"No, Mr. Foreman, and ladies and gentleman of this jury, the defense in this case does not and will not ask you to set Tony Costa free," Goldman said. "But I want you to consider that you are dealing with a mentally sick person—and all triggered by the use of drugs. His mind was completely gone at the time of the killing of those girls—that terrible tragedy in January of 1969.

"You are going to be told by the able district attorney that Tony Costa is a killer; that it's true that Tony Costa used drugs, but that every drug user is not a killer. That's only partly true. Every other drug person is not mentally sick. They don't possess a psychosis. But a mentally sick person will kill through the use of drugs.

"You are going to be told by the district attorney that Tony is a schemer, a conniver; he's going to refer to Tony doing everything possible to conceal his crime." Goldman said. "Tony is a mentally sick person. Now, what does he do? Let's see the inconsistencies of a mentally sick person. He takes an automobile. He doesn't drive it from Cape Cod, he gets someone else to drive it to Boston. It's left in the middle of the street, not hidden around the corner. He drives the car up to Vermont; he leaves it in an open-air parking space. When he is asked in whose name, he says, 'Tony Costa.' He checks into a rooming house and registers under the name, 'Tony Costa.' He writes out a bill of sale, and to make sure you know it was written by him, *he puts his name on it:* 'Tony Costa.' Is that the normal action of a man who is concealing, or is that the action of a man in a mental state of confusion, a man who is sick?

"What else does he do?" Goldman turned to face the prosecution's table. "He walks into the police station and he gives the bill of sale to the police! He says, 'You're looking for somebody; I didn't do the crime,' and he tells a series of lies.

"Dr. Ewalt says a person acting in that fashion is consistent with a man suffering drug dependency in the mental state of psychosis. Tony Costa was so sick he didn't know what he was doing from minute to minute. His lies are a truth to him; and the truth to him are lies.

"In this case, Tony Costa couldn't plan these murders rationally; he was so seriously ill at the time of these crimes that he hadn't the slightest idea what he was doing out at Truro on the day in January when these girls were killed. The evidence clearly shows that Tony Costa was incapable of any premeditation, because his mind was so diseased and sick.

"I think there is time for me to talk about one of the possibilities here in the case you might consider. I think you are satisfied that Tony is sick. Incarceration is the place for a sick person. The way the law handles that situation is that your verdict of not guilty by reason of insanity puts Tony away for life. His Honor will instruct you more fully on the subject, but that is the position the defense takes in this case. Tony is a sick man, a drug-addicted man. I think in this temple of justice, you folks as jurymen with good common sense know that a sick person must be treated. And everybody must know that drug dependency is a curse in America.

"Drugs are now on trial in the Costa case," Goldman concluded. "May God bless you in your verdict, in the consideration of a mentally sick and drug-dependent defendant."

22

Edmund Dinis rose from the prosecutor's table.

"The defendant stands before you today charged with the double slaying of Mary Anne Wysocki and Patricia Walsh," Dinis said. "I submit to you that the defense has endeavored to introduce into this trial the complication in our society involving the use and abuse of drugs. They say, in defense of these murders, that drug abuse bringing mental illness interferes with deliberation, premeditation or malice aforethought, which is the requirement for a conviction of murder in the first degree.

"I think we should examine the testimony of the psychiatrists

601

in this case. Although a needed profession that is making a contribution to curing the ills of mankind, psychiatry is not an exact science. You can draw, from your own observations of your fellow man, the conclusion that we never know what's in the mind of the other fellow, and that includes psychiatrists. You cannot accept the opinion of a psychiatrist over your own judgment.

"Some of the doctors said they felt the defendant suffered nothing more than a personality disorder," Dinis continued. "I would interpret that to be that he is a vicious person; that his appetite cannot be satisfied as a normal person. That is not insanity under our law or under the opinions given to you by the psychiatrists. In other instances, the psychiatrists said they didn't know what happened at that particular time of the butchering of these girls in the Truro woods. Other opinions were that anyone who did this had to be mentally ill and, further, psychotic.

"There is a tremendous challenge among the psychiatric profession as to the definition of terms. They themselves do not agree on terminology. There is a disagreement as to what different terms may mean, whether a person is psychotic, schizophrenic, borderline schizophrenic, personality disordered, and the like. But I submit that even though he has a mental illness, the defendant was never deprived of a substantial capacity to understand the wrong that he was doing when he did it. He *knew* what he had in mind when he asked those girls for a ride to Truro that morning, when he rode out of Provincetown with these girls to their unfortunate and most tragic death in the woods.

"There is no evidence that Costa was under drugs in that rooming house. Did you feel for a single moment that these two girls, one a schoolteacher, one a junior in college, would drive off with a man they did not know if he was under the spell of drugs— or so changed in personality by drugs? I submit to you that he was his charming self; that when these girls walked into that rooming house and were introduced to him by the landlady that he began making plans for them; and he subsequently lured them to their deaths.

"You examined the woods of Truro with me," Dinis said. "You saw that the area in which this tragedy occurred involved distances of almost a mile from one area to another. The place where he took the girls to be slain was deep in the woods; yet the area where he kept the gun and other items he was hiding wasn't so far off the road. Does this indicate that this man didn't know

602

what he was doing, or was not able to appreciate the wrongfulness of his act? Or was this a plan that he had to satisfy his sexual appetite, to satisfy his lust, his need to kill? Why did he divide this area and spread it out through those woods? Because he wanted to engage in his evil acts without being detected! Was he aware of right and wrong? He *was*. He plants a note on the door of the room belonging to these girls saying, 'We're leaving. Thank you very much for your kindness,' signed, 'Patricia Walsh and Mary Anne Wysocki,' because he wants to satisfy the landlady's curiosity; and he removes items of clothing and personal belongings to his own room. He calls a garage and asks the owner, 'How much to paint a Volkswagen?' He knew at that time that his conduct wasn't conforming to the law. He wants the car painted so that nobody will be on the lookout for a blue Volkswagen. In addition to his evil gratification, he wants to keep the automobile, because he can use it. He *knew* at that time that his conduct wasn't conforming to the law! Shortly thereafter the car is spotted in the Truro woods by Mr. Benson. When he went to the police station there was nothing on the windshield; when he came back there was a note on the windshield. Why are these notes left? They are left to appease curiosity and not to arouse suspicion; because there is *wrong* involved. And the defendant *knew* it.

"When he moved the automobile from the Truro woods, who drove the car? Not Tony Costa! Why not? Because he had lost his license. He didn't want to get involved with the police at this time; he knew right from wrong. So he let friends drive the automobile to Boston, and when he got to Boston he asked how to make out a bill of sale so that he could justify registering this automobile in some locality.

"Why did he go to Burlington, Vermont?" Dinis said. "Sure, he left the car in an open parking lot, but the number plates had been removed. For what reason? Because he suspected that the registration would be broadcast to police and they would be looking for a Rhode Island registration with that number.

"Now, when the items that were found in the rooming house caused the police to talk to Antone Costa, he gave them different stories about the girls going to Canada; about the fact that abortion may have been the situation; about the involvement of marijuana. He is telling stories, hoping he can outwit the police, hoping he can defeat them in their search, so that he will not be associated with the atrocity that he has committed. He *never* had a loss of memory while he was involved in these macabre operations, during all these bizarre actions and murder. He knew *exactly* where to go and what he wanted to do. And I submit to you that after shooting these girls, he carried out whatever satisfaction he wanted from them; that he cut them up on that tree by one of the grave sites; and he buried them, not in one grave, but in *two* graves, and covered those graves with leaves deep in the Truro woods so that he would not be detected. Because while he was carrying out this grotesque, this inhuman, unbelievable butchery, he was mindful that what he was doing was wrong! He was mindful that he could be detected; that he was violating the law, and the law would require punishment for these deeds," Dinis said forcefully. "Mentally ill? Yes. But not substantially ill as not to know the consequences of his doings, and the consequences of the law. He was mindful of that all the time.

"The use of drugs is an endeavor to bring a smoke screen before you, because this is a national problem. Tony Costa was never hooked! He's been sitting in jail for thirteen months and we haven't had a single bit of evidence that this man ever had any problems. We had a doctor testify that he saw nothing of the application of needles or other complications involving drugs the day after the defendant was arrested," Dinis said. "Tony Costa wasn't addicted. He was on kicks, self-gratification, playing with himself. He was always conscious of what he was doing. In every phase of this man's life he was trying to manipulate people for his own gratification, to the extent that he would lure them into the woods and butcher them. He has a 'problem' because he has been detected, apprehended and tried.

"The final adjudication of this matter lies with you," Dinis said. "It is your duty to impose a finding as to guilty or not guilty under our system of law. And I submit to you that Antone Charles Costa should be found guilty of murder in the first degree; that he is guilty of murder with premeditation, with malice aforethought.

"Although I ask you to find him guilty of murder in the first degree in both of these butcherings of Mary Anne Wysocki and Patricia Walsh, I ask you to temper that finding with clemency," Dinis said, concluding with his most important piece of strategy to make it easy for the jurors to convict. "Let Costa live, so that he can think and meditate, because he is a man of high intelligence. Let him think about the unwarranted butchering of these

604

two helpless souls on that day in January in the woods of North Truro. Let him *live* with it, because that is what he deserves, to live with that. But he deserves no other consideration."

23

"Mr. Costa, at this time you are privileged by the law of this commonwealth to address the jury," Judge Beaudreau said. "This is a matter left solely to your choice."

Costa stood up. His face showed extreme tension.

"If the court please," Costa said. "I would like to address the jury."

"You have that privilege," Beaudreau said, as interested as anyone in his courtroom at what the defendant would say.

Costa gripped the railing that separated the spectator side of the courtroom. "At this time, Your Honor, I would like to thank you for your kindness and consideration in this matter. I have always had a high respect for the legal system of this country and your considerations have reinforced that one-hundred fold. I would also like to thank my chief counsel. Mr. Goldman and his assistant, Mr. Cavanaugh, who I consider dedicated pursuers of justice, along with Larry Shubow and Stephen Lipman. And I want to apologize to the jury for any inconvenience in having you sequestered, and keeping you from your loved ones.

"I now realize that I was involved in some nightmarish events, and I can't explain how or why. I do know that it is one heck of a thing to have to live with . . . and to realize at this point," Costa said in a quavering voice. "Before this event took place, my wife and I led a very good, very decent life. And marital problems developed; and I realized I needed help. At that time I sought that help. I did not receive help; I received drugs instead. And in receiving these drugs, I became dependent on them. I could no longer carry on as I had in the past; I was no longer the person I used to be. It became a constant downhill fall. I lost everything that I had worked for. I had a business, I had a good life, I had a home and I had children. And in using these chemicals, I lost all this. And I started to lose contact with reality.

"And I held great contempt for myself for getting involved in this situation; but at this point there was nothing I could do. My mind was shackled by chemicals."

Gaining authority and confidence, Costa went on. "I tried to decrease my capacity and tolerance for drugs. In these attempts I got into what I believed to be much milder drugs. And this only led to a complete state of further confusion. And I met a girl who I was very much in love with; and I made the determination to stop using drugs at that time. Then, one unfortunate evening when I was in Provincetown, I received word that she had taken an overdose of drugs and had passed away. And with this knowledge I just fell to pieces; I went right back to drugs. I felt that everything had collapsed around me; I felt I had nothing anymore.

"In February I had access to great quantities of LSD," Costa went on. "I had heard that it was an enlightening drug, that it could possibly open one's mind and help one's self. And in taking LSD, I simply found that it did nothing but cause nightmarish hallucinations. It caused me to become so far from reality that I couldn't exist as a man any more. All I wanted to do was just go somewhere and die. I had flashbacks, or bad trips from LSD, without even using any drugs. And it was at this time that I decided to stop taking drugs. And I realized that I was mentally ill. I was attempting to seek help; I was deciding where I should seek that help, because I had been disillusioned in attempting to seek help in 1965. I felt that a great part of my problem was that in seeking this help I didn't get the help I wanted. I felt I had to make a very harsh decision on which doctors I could trust for this help, where I could go. And in my state of confusion at that time, it was one heck of a decision to make.

"And I gradually diminished my capacity for drugs," Costa said, unconsciously paraphrasing the McHoul test on which his defense was based. "I was not using any drugs, but I still had a loss of contact with reality. I realized that I was on my way to rehabilitation, but there was a long way to go; one heck of a long way to go. And then I came to the final decision in March that I

606

was going to return to society and be the man I once was; to be the man that people had loved and had faith in. I got a haircut; I cleaned myself up and I went out and got a job. I was to start work the next day, but, unfortunately, I was arrested. And that is about where I had stopped along the line of rehabilitation. I was not allowed to go any further; because I have been confined since that time.

"I am hoping now that I can seek the help that I desperately sought then. I am hoping that you will give me this chance to accomplish my achievement in life, with the help that I need. All that I can ask of you is that you grant me the chance of getting the help that I desperately need so that some day, perhaps in the far-off, foreseeable future, I may be able to return to society as the man that I once was.

"And I have a message at this time that I would like to give to young people," Costa said. "I want these people to know from what I have experienced that drugs are destruction. You cannot find happiness in a capsule; you cannot find happiness by shooting it into your veins. You can only destroy yourself. And I hope these young Americans realize the power and the potency of destructive drugs, and exactly what they can do to a mind. At our birth we are given the most precious, God-given gift that we could have, and that is our brain. And I pray that these young Americans will start using their brain and stop using drugs.

"I now realize that I must suffer the consequences of my drug domination. And I leave my fate in your hands."

Beaudreau took a short recess.

Goldman spoke briefly with Costa in the courtroom, congratulating him on his performance. Costa was high after his speech, thrilled with himself. "I think I did it!" he told Goldman. "Christ, I think I just won the case!"

George Killen sat back in his seat, stunned by his realization that Costa had, in winning his righteous personal crusade to be heard, all but demolished his lawyers' portrait of him as a psychotic.

24

Three of the fifteen jurors, drawn by lot, were dismissed before the jury entered the deliberation room at 12:30 P.M. to determine the fate of Antone Costa.

Costa was optimistic when he returned to the Barnstable House of Correction, telling Donald Parker, "I don't think the prosecution proved their case against me; it was all circumstantial evidence."

Costa washed his face, combed his hair and stretched out on the bunk of his cell to listen to a portable radio predict temperatures in the eighties for the start of the Memorial Day weekend which traditionally marked the start of Cape Cod's tourist season.

Costa was brought back to the courthouse at two-thirty that afternoon and held in a detention room.

At six-thirty the jury returned to the courtroom with a query.

"One of the jurors," Beaudreau announced from the bench, "would like to be assured that Mr. Goldman in his final argument remarked that he did not want the defendant loose on the streets."

Beaudreau read from the stenographer's transcript of Goldman's summation: "The defense in this case does not and will not ask you to set Tony Costa free. But I want you to consider you are dealing with a mentally sick person—and all triggered by the use of drugs . . ."

As the jury was led back to the jury room, Goldman was encouraged to hope that the question meant that they were deliberating a verdict of not guilty by reason of insanity.

The jury returned to a packed courtroom at 7:05 P.M., and this time Costa was brought in.

From a desk forward and below the judge's dais, the clerk of the superior court, Barbara Holmes Neil, addressed the jury: "Mr. Foreman, have you agreed upon your verdicts?"

"We have," foreman Russell Dodge said.

"In case number 27664, Commonwealth versus Antone

Charles Costa, what do you say, Mr. Foreman: is the defendant guilty or not guilty of any offense charged in this indictment?"

"We find the defendant guilty of murder in the first degree," Dodge said. "but we recommend that the sentence of death be not imposed."

Costa did not react. He sat unmoved, staring at the jury.

"In case number 27666, Commonwealth versus Antone Charles Costa," Mrs. Neil said, "what do you say, Mr. Foreman, is the defendant guilty or not guilty of any offense charged in this indictment?"

"We find the defendant guilty of murder in the first degree. The jury recommends that the sentence of death not be imposed."

Dinis stood at the prosecutor's table in a sudden flush of victory. "The commonwealth moves for sentencing at this time."

Beaudreau called a bench conference. "We have two murders here. It's a question of concurrent or 'from and after.' "

"We move 'from and after,' " Dinis said, out for blood and wanting the sentences to run one after the other.

"I don't know if you can or not," Beaudreau said. "My memory is you cannot; it has got to be concurrent sentences."

"This is murder one; there's no parole anyway," Cavanaugh said dispiritedly. "What difference does it make?"

"Antone Charles Costa, please rise," Mrs. Neil said. "Under indictment number 27664 the court, having considered the offense whereof you stand convicted, orders that you be punished by imprisonment in the Massachusetts Correctional Institution at Walpole for and during the term of your natural life; and that you be remanded to the jail in Barnstable until you are removed in execution of this sentence."

After repeating the identical formula for the second indictment, Mrs. Neil added, "You have the right, within ten days, to appeal to the Appellate Division for review of your sentence."

Costa blinked, nodded, then mouthed the words "Thank you" before he was taken from the courtroom.

Beaudreau thanked the jury before dismissing them and adjourning the trial. Several jurors stopped at the prosecutor's table to shake hands with Fernandes and Dinis.

"I feel the weight of the evidence warranted the findings of guilty on both charges," Dinis assured them. "This is a most terrible tragedy and a most unfortunate incident in the lives of all concerned."

One juror made his way to the defense table to explain, "It was a really difficult decision." Two jurors had voted not guilty by reason of insanity, but had been won over for conviction.

Shubow was talking to reporters milling around the defense table. "I believe the law should be changed to offer a finding of guilty, but insane, instead of not guilty by virtue of insanity. Everyone knows Costa is mentally sick; but it is an insuperable task to get a jury to convert that finding into saying 'not guilty,' even though the insanity clause is added."

Goldman told them, "The verdict upset Tony; but his spirits are still very high."

That night, from his cell at Barnstable House of Correction, Costa wrote to Barbara Holmes Neil.

> Dear Miss Neil,
> This is to inform the Barnstable Superior Court that I desire to have my case appealed, concerning the first-degree murder indictments of which there was a guilty finding in the first degree.
> At this point I am not certain but a change in counsel may be imminent and necessary. Anyway, the request for appeal is hereby entered by myself, regardless of the desires of my present counsel. Please acknowledge my request as soon as possible and advise me of any other information or proceedings necessary.
> Your consideration in this matter is appreciated.
> > Respectfully,
> > Antone Charles Costa

Costa also wrote to Maurice Goldman.

> This is to inform you that I have entered a request for appeal of my case to the court, this day. I realize that you may not agree with my decision but I cannot disperse it from my mind, and will not. If you will contact me I shall explain my reasons. I remain adamant on my request for appeal.
> The evidence in this case was circumstantial, as you know—no fingerprints, destruction of evidence by Lieu-

tenant Flynn, etc. We could have used all of this to our advantage.

I now believe that if I had taken the stand, we definitely would have refuted and thrown out much of their case. I feel that you did an excellent job in handling the case as a drug issue, but it also cast no doubt in the jury's mind but that I was guilty, as I see it now.

Please contact me as soon as possible so that we may come to an agreement one way or another. I would rather be free than a martyr.

Respectfully,
Tony Costa

Costa was taken the following morning to Walpole, where he again wrote to Goldman.

Dear Mr. Goldman:

It is my desire and wish that we appeal for a retrial. I now realize what a fool I was to allow myself to be persuaded and coaxed into such a pathetically insane defense. You never once indicated, or even insinuated that I was innocent! I believe I foresaw a "conflict of interest" on your part and many friends warned me of same. But I trusted in you. They were right, though; if I were acquitted your book is worthless!

I am sorry that I allowed you to coax me into making false statements on tape for Dr. Ewalt, etc. But now I want to be tried on the *facts* as I know them. And this time I *will* take the stand, instead of reading a statement! This appeal for a new trial is most important to me, so I suggest that you or Mr. Cavanaugh contact me before this week is over.

I shall not spend my life in prison for a crime I could not have committed. This time around I shall be the captain of my ship. I only regret now that I didn't take everyone's advice and get myself "a fighting man." This case is totally circumstantial. I should be free now if you had acted as I wanted you to. I realize Dinis is a comrade of yours but I also discovered this too late. I won't make the same mistake twice.

Please advise me of your feelings in this matter so that I may make arrangements for future plans. I also want to discuss "the book," finances, etc.

I will anxiously await to hear from you, *very* soon.

Sincerely,

Antone Charles Costa

Goldman was more distressed than angered by Costa's two letters. "I am more or less shocked," he told his client. Goldman had already filed a motion for a new trial. "The motion will no doubt be denied, but it must be filed so all your rights are protected," he explained. "Don't be disturbed; everything in our power will be done for you."

Costa said nothing about the letter he had written to Barbara Neil.

25

Costa's appearance was changed when he returned to Beaudreau's courtroom at Barnstable superior court on Friday, May 29, for a hearing on a motion for a new trial. Thin and pallid, he wore a suit of baggy, unpressed prison clothes instead of the business suits he had borrowed during his trial. George Killen and Bernie Flynn attended the motion, sitting with Fernandes at the prosecutor's table.

"The commonwealth never proved Costa's sanity beyond a reasonable doubt," Goldman said, arguing the motion. "I think the evidence in this case clearly shows that Mr. Costa was seriously disordered at the time of the crimes and was incapable, by reason of a diminished mental status, of deliberately premeditating his deeds or weighing their consequences.

"I think further, that Mr. Costa was first induced to use drugs involuntarily by his visits to the office of Dr. Callis at the Wellfleet Medical Center," Goldman went on. "It is clearly uncontradicted that Costa never once used drugs of any kind, name or nature prior to his entering the office of Dr. Callis.

"The finding of murder in the first degree was not warranted by the weight of the evidence," Goldman said. "First-degree murder? No, it is wrong. It is an injustice. It is unfair. It is unconscionable! Because it wasn't a voluntary act on his part. And I ask your honor to give consideration to the reduction to second-degree murder, and a new trial on that basis."

"Mr. Costa, do you want to say anything with regard to the motion for a new trial?" Beaudreau said.

"No, I don't, Your Honor," Costa said. "My counsel has covered it quite clearly, I believe. I have, you know, full respect and faith in him."

"I note for the record," Armand Fernandes broke in, "a letter from Mr. Costa addressed to Mrs. Neil. Part of this letter states: 'At this point I am not certain but a change in counsel may be imminent and necessary.' Is it safe to say that Mr. Costa is satisfied with Mr. Goldman's representation at this time?"

Goldman turned around to stare at Costa in astonishment.

"I'm quite satisfied with Mr. Goldman and Mr. Cavanaugh," Costa said.

"As I recall the testimony," Fernandes said, "Dr. Barrows said that in his opinion the defendant, Mr. Costa, had substantial capacity to appreciate the wrongfulness of his conduct and to conform his conduct to the requirements of law. Dr. Ewalt said that in his opinion, Mr. Costa lacked that capacity; and Dr. Whiskin said Mr. Costa was mentally ill, but had a nonpsychotic personality disorder. The jury had the opportunity of observing Mr. Costa and to listen to the evidence as to his behavior. Taken as a whole, the jury certainly was warranted if it believed Dr. Barrows; if it believed those witnesses who testified Mr. Costa deliberately put the note on the door; that he buried the gun; that he didn't have a loss of memory; that he knew what he was doing; that he, in fact, *did* have substantial capacity to appreciate the wrongfulness of his conduct and conform it to the requirements of law.

"With reference to Dr. Callis," Fernandes continued, "nowhere did I hear any evidence that he prescribed marijuana, LSD, or even barbiturates. By innuendo, Mr. Shubow sought to draw out that Dr. Callis had prescribed Nembutal; Dr. Callis said he never did. He only prescribed Solacen, then subsequently, two other drugs, neither of which were addictive. There was no evidence that the defendant was under the influence of drugs on or about January twenty-sixth, 1969; the evidence, again, was to the contrary. The jury could have found that when Mr. Zacharias observed the defendant at the intersection of Bradford and Conwell and gave him his check that an inference could be drawn that Costa was behaving normally; that he suffered no irresistible impulse or lack of control. The jury was certainly warranted in finding as they did, based on the evidence introduced at the trial."

In rebuttal, Goldman said, "With reference to Dr. Barrows's testimony that my learned brother made mention of, he forgot to add that if Dr. Barrows had known all the facts concerning the drugs, he would have had an entirely different opinion. You will find that on the record. That Tony was on drugs in January 1969, was told by the witnesses that spoke of the period. We had four of them testify to the use of LSD in the month of January, a period following the use of amphetamines. One witness described it as 'handfuls.' So, in each of these cases, I must remind the court that the facts are slightly to the contrary on that."

"Mr. Costa," Beaudreau said, producing yet a third letter, "you wrote me on May twenty-fourth, 1970. The letter reads:

Dear Judge Beaudreau,
I want to thank you for your much appreciated efforts made both prior to and during my trial. I realize you did much more than you had to on many occasions. For that, I am grateful.
I wish to appeal my case, as you probably know already, due to the fact that I have written to Mrs. Neil yesterday, informing her of the same. My reasons are many: my defense counsel has failed to defend me according to a prior agreement assented to, due to a conflict of interest concerning a book being written (which I was informed is almost now complete) about this case. If I were to be acquitted, the book would be worthless.
I possess many facts of evidence concerning my innocence. I believed these facts would be presented; yet, they were not. Only drugs were discussed to spice up the book.
I pray that Your Honor will hear me on this matter of appeal in the interest of true justice. Since I lack knowledge of legal proceedings, I trusted fully in my counsel. I —

have been through a nightmare of events concerning this case, but I am a much wiser man for it.

I am almost certain that a change of counsel is imminent and necessary to vindicate myself. I wish to be retried on the facts in rebuttal of evidence—not on drugs, and a story I was told to give to Dr. Ewalt . . .

These are but a few of my reasons that I pray your honor will hear me. Your consideration is most gratefully appreciated in this matter of prime importance to the ideals of justice in our nation.

> Most respectfully yours,
> Antone Charles Costa.

Goldman had been through enough of this to remain impassive, but Cavanaugh's face was flushed with anger.

"You *did* write that letter to me?" Beaudreau asked Costa.

"Yes, I did, Your Honor."

"Since this letter was addressed to me, personally, I feel I cannot pass it over," Beaudreau said. "I am giving you an opportunity now to take your position on it."

"My position, Your Honor, is that at the time of writing that letter I was, you can say, in a state of shock due to the first-degree verdicts brought against me," Costa said. "I couldn't comprehend quite what had happened. I didn't understand legal proceedings; I didn't know exactly what effect any other evidence that, you know, we possessed, would have. I do possess a very deep hatred for drugs," Costa continued, pleased to at last be given his chance to answer some questions in a courtroom. "And just the thought of having a defense on drugs, it sort of binds me up psychologically. When drugs are just constantly reiterated, it presents like a nightmare in front of me. I don't like to see it; it makes me nervous. And I am just, you could say, mentally unstable in discussing drugs or hearing anything discussed about my use. It was drugs that got me into this mess, and when I hear people presenting evidence against me in this fashion, it brings back a lot of bad memories. I just don't like to discuss them at all. And when I got up to Walpole I was put in a little cell there, I just more or less fell to pieces."

"Do I understand that you wish to retract these remarks you made—that your defense counsel has failed to defend you according to a prior agreement, due to a conflict of interest concerning a book being written?" Beaudreau said.

"Yes, Your Honor, I would like to retract the entire letter."

"Do I also understand you are going to be represented on your appeal by Mr. Goldman?"

"Yes, sir."

"I do not want to receive any further letters from you with respect to appeals or any other matters," Beaudreau said. "You can refer them to your lawyer, and he will take them up with me in accordance with the procedure that's set up. I want to make it clear, you have every right to appeal, and I hope you do. But I think it should be done through proper channels. So, with that, I am constrained on the evidence that I heard in this case and the arguments made here today, to deny the motion for a new trial."

George Killen and Bernie Flynn got up wearily from the prosecutor's table and watched Tony Costa being escorted out of the courtroom to be returned to Walpole to being serving two concurrent life sentences for murder—one for each side of his personality, someone had observed.

"He won't last very long up there," Flynn predicted.

EPILOGUE

Walpole

1

The Massachusetts Correctional Institution at Walpole stood like a medieval fortress behind huge gray walls.

Antone Costa was passed through an electrically controlled, robin's-egg blue, two-inch-thick steel door, then through three grilled barriers to a vacant concrete plaza. Yellow lines painted on the pavement created a pathway to a barbed-wire gate in the prison's inner wall; the lines traced the perimeter of the exercise yards, supervised from armed turrets. Of an inmate population of more than six hundred, none stepped over yellow lines.

Costa removed his clothes for a "strip shake" in a small, windowless room outside the cellblocks. Corrections officers examined his mouth, ears, hair, armpits, rectum and testicles for contraband. He was taken to Block-8, forty-five cells in two tiers and ground-level "flats" reserved for the orientation of new inmates. Costa was locked into cell 29, a narrow cubicle furnished with a toilet, cold-water sink, bunk bed and a fluorescent light.

A letter from Maurice Goldman awaited Costa. "Be as calm as possible, knowing that every avenue will be pursued," it said. "Don't get discouraged and don't get 'jail jitters.' We are with you one hundred percent."

Costa realized the process of his appeal could take up to a year or more. "But I have the patience to wait," he replied. "I hope a new trial is granted. I firmly feel that you could make a shambles of the prosecution's case with a strong rebuttal of evidence and cross-examination of witnesses."

He had considerable time to think over all aspects of his case while at Walpole. Costa wrote Goldman in July:

619

I hope you understand thoroughly that I do *not* give consent to publish any book before my appeal is decided. I feel that the book would prejudice a new trial severely. I have never seen or read any contract concerning the book. Since I was in a state of confusion and despondency at Bridgewater, I am not sure what I signed. I would, therefore, respectfully request that you produce such papers so that I may read and understand same for clarification purposes.

Costa also wanted to examine the writs of errors, exceptions, and petitions Goldman intended submitting to the Supreme Judicial Court of Massachusetts as a basis for his appeal.

This time *I* must know and understand thoroughly any procedures carried out. I must be informed concerning strategy, tactics and the total defense. I will accept your counsel, but the final verdict will be mine.

Costa nevertheless sent greetings to Justin Cavanaugh and Goldman's staff. "I sure wish I could be with you! Maybe, someday soon. I pray the future will be brighter and hold promise for all of us."

A week before he celebrated this twenty-sixth birthday, Costa wrote Goldman, "I am in need of financial assistance. Can you help? I honestly don't like asking you since you have spent so much already." Costa planned to be working in leathercraft as soon as prison authorities gave him permission. "Then I should be fairly self-sufficient."

Costa had joined the Special Narcotics Addiction Program (SNAP) made up of former drug addicts and was helping in a "poster campaign" against drugs. He was also engaged in writing a novel "concerning this horrible situation I have been convicted of."

Goldman made no mention of Costa's book when he sent him a check for fifty dollars with his best wishes. Goldman had given his blessing to Victor Wolfson, who was writing a screen treatment and rewrite of *A Shuddering of Girls,* the 277-page "raw narrative" assembled by Lester Allen from defense tapes and investigation reports. "Wish me luck," Wolfson wrote Goldman from his place, Amity Farm, in Wellfleet. "Wish us *both* luck."

In October, Costa spoke with administrative personnel at Walpole with regard to petitioning the governor for a commutation of his sentence to a state hospital.

2

"I'm holding a steady keel, but depression is profound and common," Costa wrote Goldman in November. "Reflections on the past cause the greatest anxiety. I can't understand how I allowed myself to become a slave to drug abuse, or to the life I led. It's not the real *me* at all! We can't retrace the past and mend the errors, I only wish I could. There is so much I would like to do over, the *right* way this time!"

Costa had acquired an "avocational bench" at Walpole from which to carry on a jewelry business. "I wish to order supplies to begin work but I have no money to do so," Costa continued in his letter. "I've attempted to borrow money from some of the guys here, but they want twice the amount returned as interest on the loan, so that's out of the question. Can you spare a few more dollars for my business venture? Once I get started in business my finances will remain stable. I realize you sent me $50 not long ago, but I paid bills with that and bought underwear, soap, and postage stamps. Now I'm broke again."

Goldman sent a second check for $50 along with "kindest regards from all of us, and good luck with your new venture."

Costa was transferred to A-Block, a minimum security section. On December 28, he thanked Goldman for a package of Christmas gifts he had received "and your past kindnesses."

> Due to my mom's death last year, three days before Christmas, the holidays can only be depressing for me.

The past is profoundly regrettable; but there is no way I can correct the harm that has occurred. I can only look toward the future, if there is one for me, and hope to be free again some day. I can now trust myself.

I am *not* a murderer! I am a victim of a drug-pushing doctor and ultimately of drugs. If my conviction is over-turned, I would like to take the stand and tell people what the past was like. I'd like them to know it wasn't all peaches and cream.

Prominent among the Christmas cards Costa displayed on the wall of his cell was one upon which George Killen had written "Best regards Tony—I will stop in to see you next time I am in the area if you want."

Killen's card showed a painting of children skating on a frozen pond. "When you see Lieutenant Killen again, please thank him," Costa said. "I hope he will be as understanding if we do get back in court."

"The thought of being here with no hope of parole or otherwise at times gets to me," Costa confessed to Goldman in January of 1971, "but I cling to the hope that my appeal will restore justice."

I look back on my life with profound regret. The horror of the past is an overwhelming load for my mind to bear. I can see it all now; my greatest regret is that I could not see it before it happened. But, God willing, given an-other chance, it won't happen again. *That* I can guaran-tee!

Costa was ebullient and in good spirits when Stephen Lipman visited him at Walpole in February. "Lipman did not seem too overly optimistic concerning the outcome of the appeal," Costa reported to Goldman. "I'm hoping you are more enthusiastic about it."

I'm most interested in what grounds you intend to argue the appeal on. There are many factors which were lack-ing at the trial that concern me greatly: bloodstains were grouped, but no further typing was done. No sperm prints were taken. There were no witnesses against me, only inferences by the district attorney. Lt. Flynn gave conflicting testimony as well as destroyed evidence. That's the way I see it.

Costa had been working steadily on his novel. "It's an epitaph to drug abuse, and the hope for a drug-free future for the youth of the world. If nothing else, it will provide me with some money so that I don't have to keep scrounging around or begging a few dollars in order to sustain myself here."

My jewelry business flopped out on me. I've gone bankrupt. A friend is trying to get me started in the leather business, but it's difficult to squeeze into the so-called "union." It's the usual clique and they're uptight about letting newcomers in. If you have any spending change available, would you send it along to hold me over until I can regain my financial status again? I dislike asking you, but I don't know who else I can ask.

Goldman was sorry to learn Costa's jewelry business had failed. "I will try to help you again if you get permission to go into the leather business." He sent a third check, for twenty-five dollars this time, to help with Costa's "immediate needs."

Costa wasted no time in picking up on Goldman's offer. A leather business was available at Walpole:

The guy is receiving a parole and is selling his business complete with tools, leather and some already fashioned items. He wants $300 for everything. *If* you can help, I will need a loan of $275 at your earliest convenience. My first endeavor will be to pay you back. I feel like a leech asking you for money; it really bothers me! I've always been so independent, but but now I must rely on others. I hope someday to return the favors. And I *will!*

When two weeks passed with no reply from Goldman, Costa sought the aid of the prison's chaplain, John J. Foley. Failing to reach Goldman at his office by phone, Foley sent a note "regarding the $275 loan you were agreeable to make to Tony Costa. He must have your support within the next week to complete the transfer of the business."

Two days later Goldman received a telegram:

I WILL NEED BUSINESS MONEY BY WEDNES-
DAY IF YOU CAN HELP PLEASE REPLY
THANKS

                                    TONY COSTA

Goldman regretted he could not make the loan.

I have previously financed you in the leather goods and
jewelry business and from neither of these ventures did
you return the capital I invested. So far, I have not received any money from any source in connection with
your case and just don't feel I can add this additional
expenditure.

Costa made no mention of his aborted business plans when
he wrote Goldman in April. He was typing the "finished manuscript" of his novel and was "in dire need" of a typewriter. He was
currently borrowing machines from other inmates, "which can be
a very precarious situation in prison."

If you can afford it, I would like a loan or an advance of
$90 or $100 so that I may purchase wholesale a typewriter and have $20 left to spend this summer. I would
appreciate it greatly and may even dedicate one of my
books to you. (chuckle)
If you send me the money I'll put it to excellent use.
And thanks again. You're like a father to me, and that's
something I've never had, unfortunately. Perhaps if I
had some paternal guidance I'd have been a better person. But God didn't see it that way for me. Mom did her
best under the circumstances, until I sent her to her
grave. It took a lot of tragedy and hurt to get me to grow
up and mature into a man. Now I wonder if it was all
necessary.

In a postscript, Costa added, "Someday I'll write you a letter
that won't be a request for anything. I hope that day comes soon."

624

3

Costa said he was "devoting myself and my talents" to anti-drug efforts at Walpole. Major changes were taking place in the rehabilitation of young drug offenders in Massachusetts. "I'm hoping I can become part of that program in the future," Costa wrote Goldman. "Since I've been through it all and have learned my lesson the hard way, I figure I have a lot to offer."

Soon, however, Costa no longer attended many SNAP meetings. He explained: "I strongly disagree with the asinine, ridiculous proposals they expound. Most of them were junkies when they entered this institution, and they will still be junkies when they leave. They haven't learned a thing!"

Hardened, street-wise, many of them former "high junkies" hooked on heroin, SNAP members refused to take Costa's pretensions of intellectual superiority seriously, rejecting his high-flown talk and fancy accent with hoots of derision. The inmate grapevine classified him as a "wimp." Costa flinched when he was addressed by the nickname he had acquired at Walpole: "Choice Cuts."

In a letter to Goldman, Costa cited his activism in drug-related programs as "evidence of my dedication to help young people avoid the pitfalls of drug abuse I fell into and my sincere desire to straighten out my own life. Hopefully, if I am granted a new trial, my self-help efforts will be considered. Perhaps what I have accomplished this year may influence the case in showing I have assumed some responsibility and have not wasted my time."

Costa had received permission from prison authorities to establish an "experimental dramatic theater" at Walpole. As executive chairman, he was seeking "only members of the highest quality character and dedication, possessing above-normal intellectual values." He wrote to Goldman:

> I am now in the process of recruiting fellow actors for the project. We will eventually stage major theatrical productions in the auditorium here for the benefit of the

inmates and personnel. Perhaps in the autumn I will be able to obtain permission from the super to allow you and Mrs. Goldman to come up and "dig" the theater. If a man puts his mind to it, he can accomplish wonders.

Costa had been in contact with a publisher who was interested in his novel, "But no agreement has been entered into because I want to peruse the contract you possess."

Whatever happened to Lester's book? I heard it was a flop, is that true? Don't worry about it, because we've got a best-seller anyway, written by the defendant himself. I'm telling it like it is, as only *I* can since I experienced the whole thing.

"As you recall," Goldman reminded Costa, "you gave me an assignment of all rights, title and interest in the subject matter of the book. Until I know exactly what you are doing, I cannot consent to any other arrangement, the same already having been assigned to me by prior agreement. I have expended thousands of dollars on your behalf and to the present writing have not received a single penny." Goldman was finishing the brief on Costa's appeal to be filed in July. "Shortly thereafter I am planning to come and have a long talk with you."

Goldman did not elaborate on "Lester's book." Unable to sell chapters of his work during several trips to New York, Lester Allen had proved to be a difficult collaborator. Victor Wolfson had bowed out of the project following a disagreement with Allen over the division of anticipated royalties.

Goldman was furious, complaining to Cavanaugh, "Allen's no writer! He's never sold a story in his life." Fed up with the entire enterprise, Goldman had virtually given up hope of placing book or film rights and was considering filing a motion for fees due him as court-appointed attorney.

Evelyn Lawson had fared no better with her book on the Costa case. Having struggled for more than a year over a first draft, she had thrown her hands up discouragement and turned her attention to *Murder, Now Playing*, a mystery novel with a summer-theater setting.

* * *

"I think you misunderstood my last letter," Costa wrote Goldman in July. "Part of the reason I wrote the book was to have something to offer you for all the time, money and exhaustion you have put into the case, and are *still* putting into it."

> In the beginning, I was uptight because I feared you would cop out on me in favor of Lester's book. Now, I feel much more secure in understanding your trial strategy and in knowing you didn't cop out on me. I have been corresponding with Houghton-Mifflin publishers, but I informed them I can do nothing without your approval. So don't worry about my doing anything to endanger the appeal. I've grown up a lot in the past year. I stop and think now before I do anything.

It was not necessary after all for Goldman to send him the contract he had signed at Bridgewater, Costa explained. "If you will only revise it so that I myself receive any income at the percentage you allotted in trust. As such it should provide me enough money to supply my basic needs, should I have to remain here too much longer."

> I prefer assuming the responsibility of doling out any cash to my children as I see fit, then I will be certain they are properly receiving it and certain members of my family will not squander any money foolishly. Don't misunderstand. The rest of the royalties are *yours*. Let me know if you would like to have a copy of the book when you come up. I am looking forward to seeing you again. It's been a long time.

Costa did not mention Avis. Since her remarriage and his refusal to give his permission for his children to be adopted, Costa had cut off all communication with his ex-wife.

Costa also wrote Barbara Holmes Neil, clerk of the superior court. "I have contacted my attorney within the past year on numerous occasions in an attempt to obtain the trial transcript, but have received no reply from him."

In another letter to Goldman, Costa explained: "Please don't think I wanted the transcript for any other purpose than to write

627

another book from it, using the contents as my base outline. I will in no way interfere with your planned legal maneuvers." He continued:

I cannot, in any manner, condone my actions. It is truly unbelievable what drugs can do to a human mind. I only wish people knew how many tears I've cried because of what I've experienced and realized. I'm not too proud to admit that I cry, that I feel, and that I'm sorry. I realize that I have been partially the victim of circumstances, but I also embrace the power and willingness to forgive. In essence, that's all I'm asking these whom I've hurt, that they find in their hearts the power and willingness to forgive and give me the chance to prove myself worthy of their sentiment. I pray every night that God stands by us and will grant you success in your attempts to seek justice. I am hoping you gain a complete reversal.

In September, Costa sent Goldman the benefit of some legal research he had accomplished at Walpole. He had followed the case of seventeen-year-old Debra Puopolo of South Boston who had stabbed her boyfriend to death after taking LSD at a party.

She was tried by the judge only and sentenced to five years! I realize the implications of her being a minor where the law is concerned, but I want to stress the short sentence she received after being charged with first-degree murder! I certainly hope the court sees fit to consider *my* state of mind to such a degree as they did hers.

Costa's novel was finished. "It will be ready for submission following a decision on the appeal or whenever you give me the 'go ahead.' "

I've already started a second book concerning a majority of the answers to the drug problem as I see it. That shall occupy a large portion of my restless time here. The closer we come to the appeal, the more anxiety-filled are my days. But now, thank God, I am able to employ my anxieties and ambitions constructively. Writing is one of my outlets.

In a postscript, Costa added, "If you see Lieutenant Killen, tell him I asked for him and said, 'Hello.' "

4

On September 21, 1971, Goldman went before the Massachusetts Supreme Judicial Court.

"There is not, in this case, a scintilla of evidence as to whether there ever was a conscious intent to kill; or if there was, whether it arose suddenly, stimulated either by sexual drives of a pathological type within the defendant, or by other external circumstances arising suddenly," Goldman argued.

Antone Costa's sanity was the central issue in the case. Doctors Ewalt and Cole had agreed that the tests for irresponsibility laid down by the McHoul case were satisfied by the defendant's mental state. Other doctors testified that while basically responsible, Costa may well have, on drugs, crossed over the borderline between sane and insane conduct.

The crimes had involved necrophilia, Goldman said, a pathological manifestation all four psychiatrists agreed was psychotic, tending to contradict the presence of the rationality necessary to form a premeditated and deliberate design to kill. Under Massachusetts law, the verdict in the Costa trial—guilty of murder in the first degree with a recommendation that the sentence of death be not imposed—was not lawful where the murder was alleged to have been committed in connection with rape. "By itself asking the jury for clemency, the government conceded that the sexual congress was *post mortem,*" Goldman said.

Both motive and a specific intent to kill were necessary elements of the crime of murder; when either element was missing, the defendant could not be found guilty of murder. The bizarre character of the acts themselves made a finding of premeditation insupportable, Goldman argued. "The savagery and brutality of the attack upon the girls suggests either insanity or such great provocation to give rise to the so-called 'sudden heat of passion,' which would entitle the jury to consider the possibility of finding the defendant guilty of manslaughter."

Based on the absence of sufficient evidence to warrant a finding of premeditation, the charge of first-degree murder should have been withdrawn from the jury. Goldman asked that a new trial be ordered because of Judge Beaudreau's failure to instruct the jury that manslaughter was one of the possible verdicts. "This court," Goldman said, "under its broad powers of review, should either direct the entry of a verdict of guilt to a lesser degree of homicide, or order a new trial on the issue of the defendant's mental responsibility."

After his appearance before the Supreme Judicial Court, Goldman paid his first visit to Walpole, meeting with Costa in a small room near a cluster of program services offices outside the main cellblocks.

Costa was pleased with the appeal brief. "I think it's an excellent argument and is visible proof of the immense amount of work that went into it," he told Goldman. "I'm certain your efforts will culminate successfully. I'm praying real hard they come back with a manslaughter verdict or a new trial, but I suppose we'll have to wait and see what the future holds."

When Goldman left Walpole, he took with him a manuscript:

Resurrection
A Factual Novel
by
A. Charles Costa

"The writing of this novel involved raw courage, but Truth always demands courage!" Costa announced in a preface. "The pages of this account contain pure, unexaggerated, brutal fact, exactly as it happened, all of it true to the last detail . . ."

> Herein the reader will discover an autobiographical epoch; a tragedy. As each episode develops, I fathom the psychological trauma, torment and disillusionment I suffer as I plunge profoundly deeper into the black vortex of drug abuse. As the grievous culmination of my involvement with drugs, I am arrested and charged with a most deplorable crime—a crime I could not have committed!

Costa opened his "novel" with a reflection on his "calamitous marriage," the first few years of which had been "simple but beautiful." . . .

> Avis cooked food exactly the way I liked it. The house was kept clean and tidy. As a mother she was perfect.

Returning home unexpectedly early one afternoon, Costa had encountered "a very pungent aroma similar to burning rags," surprising Avis in the act of smoking marijuana. . . .

> For many weeks I had noticed Avis's personality had undergone minute but recognizable changes. Now, I understood why. My wife had turned into a dope fiend!

Costa had sought help from Dr. Hiebert who suggested he consult a psychiatrist or marriage counselor. Costa went to the office of a "Dr. Calder" in Wellfleet, where Dr. Calder, after disappearing into an adjacent hallway, had returned with two envelopes filled with "extremely large and ominous-looking" yellow cap-

631

sules. Costa observed, "They looked like tiny yellow submarines without periscopes, an entire fleet of them. A mild shudder rolled through me."

When he returned to the apartment on Hughes Road, Costa had attempted to embrace Avis affectionately, "As usual, she shrugged disdainfully—one of her 'Delilah' games, quite common among women seeking to test their alluring capabilities."

Avis was furious to learn Costa had been to "Dr. Calder" and given tranquilizers. All the same, he had taken his first Solacen capsule fifteen minutes before dinner. . . .

I felt as though someone had dumped a bucket of warm, liquid placidity over me. I loved the effect of the pill! It was like the aftermath of an unholy orgasm. A beautiful experience. I thoroughly enjoyed every moment of it.

He had been unable to lift the spoon from the table to eat the "Whip 'n' Chill" Avis had made for dessert. "The spoon felt as though it weighed fifty pounds!"

After several months of treatment, Costa told "Dr. Calder" he was becoming addicted to Solacen and had been given new medication Costa had learned later was 100-milligram Nembutal capsules. "The Nembutal eased the tension of withdrawal from Solacen dependency while creating one of its own," Costa wrote. "I had inadvertently become a drug addict!"

Because of the medication, Costa had lost all ambition to work and accept responsibility. . . .

I had blown my construction business. I had been treated by a quack who had gotten me strung out on dope and tried to run away from it all by going to Haight-Ashbury.

Costa's only reference to Barbara Spaulding dealt with the occasion when he had been hospitalized for an overdose before returning to Provincetown. . . .

Employed at the Crown and Anchor Inn, Costa had been too stoned on Nembutal and hashish to accomplish anything but menial tasks.

Costa had managed to conceal his barbiturate addiction. "Many of my loved ones never really knew I had a habit, although

632

they thought it unusual I should be visiting the doctor so often. In my condition I could not afford to get busted. Getting busted would only bring shame and disgrace upon the people I loved." Afraid of keeping drugs in his room, Costa had buried a cache of acid and speed in a glass jar on the beach behind the inn. . . .

After burying the dope I returned to my room. I prepared a good heavy hit of Meth and LSD in the Bayer aspirin bottle-cap cooker. I crushed up the acid tabs and dropped them into the cold water solution. I grabbed my guitar strap, tied off my arm and mainlined the brew. An instant rush of blazing color and sound overpowered my mind seconds after I released the tie. I ran through the corridors and made my way to the beach and walked the stretches of shoreline. Everything was so fabulously exquisite, the LSD serving only to heighten my perception of things around me—a brilliant cinerama of God and nature!

I perched myself atop a huge boulder in the middle of a sandbar. I pondered the problem of securing enough pills so that I could gradually reduce my intake to the point where I would no longer need any more of the doctor's abhorrent drugs. They had destroyed enough of my life already! I also wanted to retaliate against the doctor for what he had done to me. The answer seemed suddenly apparent. All I had to do was to rob his office! Then I'd have as much dope as I needed to accomplish withdrawal without any hang-ups.

Costa had conspired "with a friend and lover" for a ride to Dr. Calder's office in Wellfleet. "I mentioned the fact that we might get busted, but this revelation did not sway her in the least. She was a spunky little creature. . . ."

She was to pick me up at the inn at eight o'clock that night. I lay on my bed, relaxing when someone rapped on the door. I opened it and greeted Syd. She was outfitted in skin-tight Levi's cut off above the knees. A sleeveless orange blouse revealed her petite, voluptuous body. Her long, silky brown hair cascaded down her back and shoulders. An aura of innocence and exotic feminine

633

beauty surrounded her. She embraced my head gently and kissed me sensously, strongly. "I don't have the car yet," she said. "I've got to pick it up later."

"Would you like to smoke some hash now?" I said. "We've got a few hours to burn before we move out. Shall I get the pipe?"

"Sure," she replied. "I'm up for anything."

When the miniature pipe was filled she lifted it to my mouth and lit a match for me. We passed the pipe mutually between us and soon we were both quite high. I fell back on the bed and Syd joined me. She draped herself over me, running her hand over my chest and stomach. Her knee gently massaged my swelling manhood. For the moment no one else existed, just the two of us. . . . She kissed my ear ever-so-gently. "Other guys turn me off; they really sicken me. You're different," she sighed. "Tony, I think I love you."

After making love, Costa asked Syd, "What kind of dope do you want to do before we set out on our excursion? I could dig a hit of Meth to give me some energy. How about you?"

Costa had found it easier to contemplate the robbery with Methedrine and the remnants of a hash high peaking through his brain. "Speed created a certain synthetic courage, assuring me I could handle the situation." When Syd left to fetch the car, Costa had gathered up the implements necessary to accomplish the robbery: a pair of gloves, a green nylon laundry bag and a screwdriver. He had waited only a few moments in the inn's parking lot before Syd drove up. Costa instructed her to drive by "Dr. Calder's" office, so he could inspect the building before being dropped off at a telephone booth near a hamburger stand. . . .

"When I'm through pillaging his office I'll wait for you in the phone booth," I told her, gasping nervously for breath. I grabbed my equipment and leaped out of the car.

"Good luck," Syd offered.

She drove away. I watched the taillights grow smaller and vanish in the night. I hopped over the guardrail and slid involuntarily down the embankment. I crouched down amongst the bushes, panic-stricken, clutching my laundry bag so tightly my hand grew numb. Without pausing to catch my breath I darted up the embankment and scurried across the highway to the doctor's office. I hid in a small grove of pines waiting anxiously for about half an hour until I saw the local police cruiser pass by on its regular patrol. Then I scampered to the rear of the building and tested a window to see if it might be unlocked. I wedged the screwdriver between the muntins and tripped the lock. I slid the window open and literally jumped through it after peeking in to make sure nothing was in the way.

The pill closet was located in front of the building. To get there I had to remove numerous doors by pulling out their hinges . . .

At this time I had used a penlight, but the battery was weak; it barely shone at all. I had filled my pockets with at least twenty books of matches, and a small glass vial of denatured alcohol. I used a piece of clothesline for a wick. It was a compact kit I had used often on the road to cook up dope. Now it was handy as a lighting device.

I burned up a few books of matches while assembling the alcohol lamp. I was so nervous and uncoordinated that I could not put the lamp together. My whole body trembled in excitation and apprehension. With the lamp assembled I scrutinized the shelves of pills. I had never seen such an abundant supply! Every shelf had been stacked to capacity with jars and boxes of pills and powders. I noticed many jars of barbiturates, and an equal amount of amphetamines. A gold mine! I began dumping boxes and bottles into the laundry bag to the brim.

I dragged the laundry bag out of the closet and headed for the window in the rear of the building. I thrashed open the window, picked up the heavy bag of dope and shoved it through the opening and dashed down the highway to the telephone booth to wait for Syd.

Only two cars passed by. The third car was Syd's. She pulled up to the booth. I ran around the front of the car and got in.

"What happened?" she asked. "Did you get anything?"

"That guy had more dope in there than a pharmaceutical warehouse. There's enough stuff to last an army of junkies a year!" I said. "The bag's in the pine grove. Let's get it and get out of here."

"Do you want to go out to the stash in the woods and sort the stuff, then put it in the ammo cans?" Syd asked.

Syd knew the way well. She had been there many times before to get hash or grass for us.

We approached the parking space near the ammo-can stash. Nature had created a clearing into which one car could fit perfectly. Syd turned off the ignition. She squirmed out from behind the steering wheel and threw her arms around me. I ran my hands sensuously over her voluptuous figure. . . .

In the pouring rain we carried the drugs in the darkness to the cans that lay buried in the forest. The cans were filled to capacity. Before leaving, we swallowed a few "black beauties" to celebrate the successful accomplishment of our marvelous feat. When we arrived in Provincetown, I got out at the inn and Syd returned the car to its owner. She rejoined me later in my room. We spent the next three days and nights together. High!

Of Christine Gallant, Costa wrote: "Her personality was that of a child of God, an innocent young creature who, like me, lived strictly by the word of the New Testament, the word of Christ!"

Jailed for nonsupport, Costa had suffered from a lack of drugs his first days at the Barnstable House of Correction, but had not experienced severe withdrawal. Released on parole, Costa went to New York. "With my addiction left almost in the past, I resolved to go straight, marry Chrissie and live a decent life." . . .

After he returned to Provincetown, Costa had learned of Christine's suicide and observed at her funeral, "Drugs had taken from me everything I loved."

Apathetically going through his mail several days later, Costa discovered a note written on scented green paper:

Dearest Tony:

I realize your sentiment toward Avis. As you have said many times, she is the mother of your children. I don't think you could ever love me as much. I love you, Tony. I'm sorry.

> Love,
> Chrissie

The note was dated the day she died! I began screaming and pulling at my hair in a state of explosive frenzy. "Why did this have to happen?" I shouted, gnashing my teeth insanely. I couldn't handle it. I needed a way out, a cop-out on life! . . .

I made my way to the hallway and grabbed my set of works from under the staircase molding and staggered back inside. I poured the powder from six 100-milligram Nembutal capsules out into my bottle-cap cooker, added a little cold water and stirred the solution with a bobby pin.

I tied off my arm with a guitar strap, painfully forced the huge spike into my arm and shot the dope into my vein.

I swallowed the remaining thirty Nembutal capsules with a glass of water. I reckoned death would come easily. Soon I would join my love, wherever she was. . . .

Costa had awakened two days later with a midafternoon sun at the window of his bedroom. His vision was blurred; he felt a sharp pain in his stomach, and a thundering headache. He tried getting out of bed but couldn't coordinate his movements. He remained in bed until nightfall when someone knocked at his door, opened it and poked her head inside. Costa couldn't remember who it was.

Goldman had to read nearly a hundred pages before he
reached that portion of the novel dealing with the events which
had occurred on January 24, 1969—a day Costa described as
"cold and dismal."

Costa had awakened "with an overwhelming sick feeling,
cold chills and a general increasing sense of irritability." He put
"Dylan's Greatest Hits" and "Saturday's Children" by the Rolling Stones on his stereo. "My body cried out for dope. The only
way I could quash the gnawing, unbearable, excruciating pain was
to surrender to my physical and psychological need for dope. I felt
as though I were being forced to feed some evil creature that had
taken possession of me without my being aware." Costa had shot
up seven Nembutals and smoked some "black gundji," a pure
form of hashish laced with opium. That afternoon, Costa had
picked up a paperback copy of *Demian* by Hermann Hesse. . . .

Suddenly the landlady appeared in the passageway. "Hi,
Antone," she said. "I want to introduce you to two new
guests. They've just arrived."

I arose and began walking toward them. I experienced a ferocious dizzy spell, a sort of rush from the
combination of hash and standing up took quickly.

"This is Patricia and this is Mary Anne," the landlady said. "I've given the girls the small room at the
head of the stairs. All those hippies up there are using
the combination kitchen and bath so I was wondering if
you would mind if they used this bathroom."

"It's no hassle at all," I said. "Make yourselves at
home, girls. You'll get used to all the hang-ups this place
has after a while. Feel free to do your thing."

Both girls seemed understandably shy on first meeting. Yet, Patricia came through with a vibrant personality. Mary Anne appeared a bit withdrawn, but very
pleasant.

The landlady returned to her basement apartment. I invited the girls into the room to sit on the bed and be comfortable.

"You've got a nice name," Pat said. "It sounds sophisticated, and intellectual. You speak well, also. I notice you've been reading Hesse. Do you do much contemporary reading?"

"I'm not partial to any particular type of literature." I paused momentarily, contemplating my next question. "Do you smoke?"

Pat produced a pack of Pall Malls from her purse and offered me one.

"I didn't mean that kind of smoke. I mean grass or hash. I have some excellent hash and will gladly share it with you. It's a drag turning on alone."

"Your offer sort of caught me off guard," Pat said. She reached into her purse, hauling out a plastic Baggie. "I do smoke grass. *See?*" She held up the Baggie.

"I've only smoked pot once or twice," Mary Anne said. "You two go ahead and enjoy yourselves, I might try some later. Right now I want to take a shower." She grabbed a towel and some underwear and trotted off to the bathroom, closing the door behind her.

Pat placed some records on my stereo as I filled the hash pipe.

I gave the pipe to Pat, offering her the pleasure of the first toke, usually the sweetest and strongest. She held it to her lips while I held a match to the bowl. She drew in a deep breath of aromatic smoke. I took the pipe from her and took a super-toke from it. The hash tasted like ambrosia. We continued smoking until the shavings in the bowl were dust. At least ten minutes passed without either of us uttering a word.

"This is good stuff, Antone, I feel high already," Pat said.

I began shaving more slivers of hash from the chunk. "We'll use these to turn on with Mary Anne when she comes out."

While we waited, Pat and I lay back on the bed. I held her to me, kissed her soft, damp lips and ran my hands over the contours of her body. I slipped my hand under her blouse and lifted her bra up over her breast to feel the warm, firm mound. We spent the next few minutes lost in love.

"Are you happy?" I asked.

"Yes, very. And you?" Pat said tenderly. She rolled her hand over my manhood, squeezed gently, then lay flat on her back staring up at the ceiling.

Pat bore a remarkable resemblance to Avis, the long dark hair, high cheekbones and other facial features, expressions and mannerisms. Pat was fifteen pounds heavier and more full-bodied, but she could almost have been Avis . . .

Mary Anne opened the bathroom door and came walking out wearing only her bra and panties. She went over to the bed, dropped her wet towel to the floor and grabbed a dry one to wipe her hair with. I took in the full beauty of her body. She was a solid chick with long slender legs, well-shaped hips and gorgeous breasts, full and firm and creamy white. A perfect woman! She quickly jumped into her slacks and sweater and put on a pair of heavy wool socks. "Now I'm ready to try some hash if you want to," she informed us. "Is it all right if I dry my hair while I smoke?"

"She's only turned on to grass a few times," Pat informed me as she ran her hand over my manhood and along my thigh. "It's done the same way as grass, Mary Anne. Just hold it in as long as you can."

We passed the pipe around and continued turning on. I held the pipe for Pat when her turn came so she wouldn't have to change position. She was comfortable and I enjoyed her hands running over me. When the pipe was empty we watched Mary Anne come out of her fixation, place the dryer bonnet on her head and push a button. The hair dryer produced a low, mesmerizing tone. I nodded out for ten or fifteen minutes, comforted by Pat's presence.

Costa left the rooming house to keep an appointment. "I wrenched Baby Blue, my English racer from its icebound ties on the side porch and tested the hand brakes to determine whether they might be frozen. Baby Blue proved to be a trustworthy companion. She was like a woman," Costa observed. "She necessitated pampering to perform well." Costa went to see Cory Devereau, thinly disguised as "Carl" in his story. . . .

In numerous facets of our character and personality, Carl and I were alike. We were both searching for something vague yet profound which we suspect we had lost as children. Carl had not known the love of a real father either.

Carl had received a shipment of drugs, telling Costa: "It's groovy head acid, the best I've ever had, but it fucks your head around, funny-like." Scattered around Carl's bedroom were thousands of orange tablets and several large chunks of hashish wrapped in polyethylene. Intending to sell the acid and hash, Costa and Carl had discussed ways of getting the dope to the canisters in Truro. "I've been thinking about asking the two chicks I just met at the rooming house for a ride to the motel to pick up my paycheck in the morning. I suppose I could ask them to give us a ride out to the stash area also."

Costa had spent the evening at the Foc'sl'e "lost in drink, conversation and other trivial matters." Costa returned to Mrs. Morton's around midnight and wrote a note requesting a ride, pinning it to the door of the girls' room. He had been awakened the next morning with Pat Walsh playfully tugging at his blankets. Pat had agreed to drive him to Truro. That afternoon, Carl had arrived at Costa's room, high on scag. Everyone had dropped acid before leaving in the car for Truro.

In a chapter he entitled "The Apocalypse," Costa described smoking hashish in the car and stopping at Dutra's general store in Truro "before I got too high to act normal in front of straight people." Purchasing four pints of Wild Irish Rose wine and a bottle of Chianti, Costa had returned to the car to share the bursts of uncontrollable laughter accompanying an "acid laugh jag," when the LSD began taking effect. Then Pat Walsh drove the four of them to Hatch Road. . . .

It was only a matter of minutes before we arrived at the dirt road which would lead us to the cache. I directed Pat to turn off the paved surface and follow the wagon-rutted road. When we were about half a mile down the road, I heard someone say: "Oh, look, there's an old cemetery way out here in the middle of the forest."

"Yeah," I said. "In the middle of nowhere." That's exactly how I felt at that moment, "nowhere." For the past few minutes I had been silently meditating, looking inward. I felt depressed and forsaken. Although I was in the company of much-loved friends, there seemed to be something lacking. The friend I truly desired was no longer mine; I saw her no longer . . .

I opened the car door and ambled over to the nearest tree. With LSD and the combination of other drugs in me, the tree became a hugh spectral silhouette. The trunk bore the image of a gigantic wrist protruding from the ground. The top of the tree, completely divested of foliage, appeared to be the hand and fingers of a colossal and fearfully gruesome skeleton. I felt as though it were trying to grasp me in its cold, deathlike grips as I trod the unearthly cemetery.

I was completely surrounded by gravestones, most of them so ancient they no longer stood erect but leaned toward the ground seeking their namesakes deep within the bowels of the earth. Some slabs had long ago toppled to the ground. An ugly, horrible greenish-yellow moss covered many of the stones. If I stared long enough, the moss began oozing its way over the gravestones like honey flowing from its container.

I looked into the sky and settled my gaze on the horizon. The sun had faded, leaving gray, steel-wool clouds. The wind blew harshly, caressing my face like the gelid hands of some incipient phantom seeking to infect his unwary victim with terror. The icy breeze carried the stench of death while sea gulls and crows—the carrion birds—drifted high in the somber-colored sky.

Ever since I was a child I've despised and feared cemeteries, but never knew why. I always avoided walking near them, especially at night! Now I found myself unexpectedly in the center of this small but eerie depository of death. I turned away from the tree after urinating, picked up the paper bag with the empty wine bottles and tossed it over the pipe railing encompassing the perimeter of the cemetery. My ears registered the sound of the bottles breaking when the bag hit the ground.

I intended returning to the car, but as I focused, I viewed my three friends approaching me.

"What are you guys doing out here?" I questioned. "It's cold out."

"We'd like to read the inscriptions on the gravestones," Mary Anne replied.

I began to shiver. The cold had penetrated through my body. We walked over to a large slab of stone under the spectral tree. I didn't much care for the idea of sitting there in the chilly atmosphere, but Pat was passionately catering to my needs as a man, thus drawing my full attention toward her. Though we had met only a short while back, our relationship was definitely becoming a beautiful love story. Because I had lost Chrissie only two months prior, I found it terribly difficult to crack the tragic shell that encased me; but Pat helped fabulously. I wanted so desperately to respond to love's touch unrestrictedly, but painful memories of a once-shattered love glared at me from every crevice of my mind. Often, when in bed with a chick, I'd unconsciously whisper either Avis or Chrissie's name, which on numerous occasions became quite embarrassing. A few times at breakfast the next morning, my woman for the night would ask: "Who's Avis?" or "Who's Chrissie?" . . .

I helped Pat to her feet. As we started for the car I chanced to look upward. Suddenly a pocket opened in the sky exposing what I thought to be some sort of astral plane. It first appeared as a brilliantly burning light, as though the entire earth no longer existed. I could not see or hear my friends or the ground beneath my feet.

I peered deeper into the heavenly fissure, while my body seemed to be melting into the light. I was being sucked up into the crevice. I wanted to go! Never have I witnessed anything so profoundly exquisite or fantastically peaceful! It was as though the Holy Master had opened heaven's gate to me! Magnificient hues of red, purple and yellow pulsated from within the fissure while streaks of other colors bolted out at me like sparks scratched on a flintstone. Ten thousand angelic voices, the Holy Cherubim, sublimely chanted in resplendent harmony while a tranquil essence echoed within the void surrounding me.

For what seemed an eon my inner being traversed the planes of infinity! It was so strangely marvelous, beauteous and placating! Then, as quickly as it occurred, it vanished. My mind returned to earth and my friends, with a much better understanding of the universe and man's insignificance in it. I compared my mystical experience with those of the prophets as set forth in the Bible. For me, it was a true spiritual awakening, an experience I shall never forget and one that I needed badly in order to understand myself and my fellow man better— the most powerful and enlightening experience that LSD had ever provided.

Goldman was astonished by what he had just read. Costa had described the precise moment that his personality had undergone the monstrous transformation into "Cory," still disguised sometimes as "Carl." It was typical of Costa to transform a psychotic episode into a moment of transcendental revelation. Goldman knew what to expect when he picked up the narrative again: from now on, Costa's novel would alternate between two narrators; "Cory" would be telling part of the story.

We arrived at the Volkswagen and crawled inside, chattering incessantly while the engine poured out hot air. It had been late afternoon when we reached the cemetery area. Now, darkness began to settle around us. The night crept in, catching us off guard. We had rapped so long while warming ourselves we failed to witness the sunset. Acid had messed with our heads.

Pat inserted the key in the ignition and the car bounced along the rutted trails. Within minutes we came to the customary parking space, a niche off the rutted road.

"We have to decide who's going out into the cold to stash the dope," I said. "We can't all go!"

"Why not?" Pat questioned. "I'd rather not stay here in the dark alone while you guys are out there somewhere. I'm tripping and these trees look so freaky. I'd be scared to death to stay here with just Mary Anne."

We pulled up our zippers, buttoned our coats and

prepared to enter the gelid darkness. "Do you still have those Dilaudid out here, Sire?" Carl asked. "I'd like to do some."

"Do you really intend to do Dilaudid on top of all the other dope you've got in you?" I said. "Why not?" Carl retorted. "I'm going to drop some more of these acid tabs, too. Do you people want any more before we stash them?"

Carl received a unanimous, "No, thanks!" The rest of us had had enough dope for one night.

Carl popped a few more tabs into his mouth. "I've got my set of works here," he said. "What do you want to do with them?"

"Give them to me, Carl. I'll stash them outside the car just in case any nosy park rangers decide to search the car while we're gone. It doesn't happen often, but it would be foolhardy to push our luck."

I got out of the car and hid Carl's works under some pine needles. Through the treetops the wind shrieked and howled, penetrating the entire forest. LSD greatly exaggerated the wind's shrill screech beyond any realm of reality as the four of us tramped through the woods in the darkness. I locked my arms around Pat's shoulders. She had intertwined her arms around my waist. Her head rested against my chest as we walked along, secure in each other's tender affection.

Ten minutes later we were standing atop the moss and pine needles covering two ammo cans, side-by-side. I uncovered one, reached in and hauled out the dope it contained. Carl took the flashlight from Pat and joined me in placing the blue bag of acid and hash in the can. We then perused the pile of dope on the ground we had removed from the canister. Polyethylene Baggies, glass and plastic bottles and small cardboard boxes formed a pile upon the earth. Carl pointed excitedly to a small plastic vial. "There's the Dilaudid!" he said. He slammed into me so that I almost fell over, unaware that he had shoved me out of the way. "There must be at least two dozen of them in there!" Carl grinned insanely, ogling the pills.

"That's the last of the Dilaudid, Carl. We'll have to

cop some more," I said. "You can do whatever you want with them when we get back in town."

"Where's the water thermos?" Carl said frantically. "It's here somewhere." He began searching for the insulated water container in the pile of dope until he located the thermos we usually kept in the can. "I only need a little bit of water to shoot some Dilaudid with. This acid is doing strange things to my head, I want to come down. Where is my set of works?"

"I've hidden it near the car, Carl, remember?" I said.

"Who gave you the right to hide my works? That's not a very funny joke!" Carl said, his mind evidently in a frenzy. "I want to do up some stuff now. Would you go get my works for me, Sire? I'd go and get them myself but I don't know where they are."

"What do we do, people?" I asked Pat and Mary Anne. "He can be a real bring-down at times, and unfortunately, this is one of those times."

My prime idea was to escort the girls back to the car and return alone with Carl's works, but the girls didn't wish to remain alone in the car while I journeyed back to the stash. Instead, they chose to remain with Carl. Informing them that I'd return within ten minutes, I disappeared into the darkness.

I ran most of the way, acid flashes and all.

Costa arrived at the Volkswagen out of breath. "I scrambled through the bushes and came out with Carl's works. I tried to get into the car for a cigarette but it was locked. Although Pat had given me the spare key she kept secreted in the engine compartment, I decided to head back through the forest. I began running slowly up the trail toward Carl and the girls. . . ."

The tree tops loomed over the road, forming a tunnellike effect. Brambles and briar patches reached out into the pathway, grabbing at my ankles. I detested those thorny vines! It was always a royal hassle attempting to extricate myself from those horrible Satanic creations. Otherwise, it remained a beautiful stroll through the tunneled forest; a bit cold, but nice. Acid played with my mind as I sauntered leisurely along the path. I focused on the stars and watched the tiny pinholes of light swirl vibrantly through the blackness.

Suddenly, a thunderous explosion shattered the air around me! At first I didn't recognize the sound, but it penetrated the forest a second, then three times consecutively. My mood changed from carefree spirit to concern and fear when I realized what those frightening sounds were: five gunshots in the night!

Carl must have opened the other ammo can in which the clique stored their weapons, loaded one of the pistols and began firing foolishly at some imaginary target. I became furious to think that Carl would have performed such a stupid stunt. His actions could bring the forest rangers down on us, thinking we were poachers, and we'd end up getting busted.

After the barrage, a mystifying silence ensued. When I reached the summit of the road I turned onto the vine-entangled path that led directly to the ammo-can stash. I noticed the illumined flashlight dropped on the ground. Its beam aimed at my eyes, temporarily blinded me.

My three friends were nowhere in sight. I stooped to pick up the flashlight and projected its beam in a circular pattern encompassing the general area. The weapons container had been opened, its cover askew on the ground. Fear held me tighter in its grip. I thought perhaps the rangers had chanced to sneak up on my friends and had busted them. That could also explain the shots—perhaps a warning fired by the rangers as my friends tried to escape capture. I listened intently and uneasily to the blackness of night. Nothing was to be heard so I decided to check out the ammo can to ascertain whether or not the drugs were still there. They were.

I beamed the flashlight at the ground level, stopping at an unnatural clump on the ground that appeared to be a body. I gasped fearfully, swallowing my fright. Dizziness and nausea prevailed, momentarily overwhelming me. I crawled over to the clump, hoping that I was hallucinating. It was Pat's body! Barely conscious, she lay on her side, her right arm extended above her head.

I prodded her shoulder gently. "Pat?" I called, fearfully. She tried to move. "Tony . . . please hold me," came her soft, deathlike whisper. "I'm so cold . . . I love you."

"Pat," I mumbled, "what's wrong?" I was so powerfully dominated by fear that the words hardly scrambled from my lips.

There was no answer! I listened to see if she was breathing, lightly resting my hand on her chest, hoping to sense the expansion that carried with it the breath of life. I lowered my head into a position a few inches from her face. I heard and felt nothing significant of life in her!

On the brink of insane panic, I forced myself to banish the thought of death from my mind. I kneeled beside her and placed my right hand under her neck, gripped her shoulder and lifted her to a sitting position. Her head bobbed forward as I lifted her limp body. She felt as though she were composed of rubber. I shook her mildly and called to her again. No response.

I was suddenly startled by a simultaneous hot-cold reaction flowing over the hand that caressed her neck. *Acid games, or reality?* I gently lowered her body and tensely withdrew my hand. It was covered with fresh, warm, dripping blood! I now saw the blood on the back of her jacket collar. Blood oozed its way through her soft hair. The terrible horror of reality covered my hand. I panicked! In a nauseous frenzy I leaped back from her body and rubbed my hand furiously in the dirt and pine needles. I felt sick, like barfing! My head was about to explode. This was *real*, not acid! For undetermined minutes I stood there, totally shocked, stunned. I thought perhaps someone had learned we were to hide the dope on this particular evening and had been lurking in the shrubbery planning to kill us all and take our dope. We had a great deal of hash and thirty thousand tabs of acid. Worse crimes have been committed for much less!

I was plagued by the thought that Mary Anne and Carl were nowhere in sight. Could they have been killed, too? I feared for my own life! I sensed that someone would ultimately return to the ammo cans. Then perhaps, it would be my turn to die. Yet I couldn't move, although I wanted to, desperately! My mind was a vacuous chamber impregnated with fear. I was incapable of rational thought or action. I attributed such a reaction to LSD, but I believe it would have been the same without acid. I had encountered a real-life, horror-filled nightmare! With or without acid it would have been a super-bummer!

Behind me, I heard someone furiously thrashing through the bushes, heading my way. Fear and confusion overwhelmed me to such an extent I was powerless to move. I waited and listened through agonizing seconds while the sound grew louder and nearer. Suddenly, with one huge collision, whoever it was raging through the bushes smashed into me, knocking us both to the ground.

I screamed insanely as we scuffled and finally realized it was Carl I was rolling around with on the moss-covered earth. I attempted to let him know it was me he was attacking. I called him by name and tried to calm him down so he'd curtail his assault. Carl had wrapped his hands around my throat while he kneeled on my chest. He loosened his grip. With one hand he quickly produced a .22 caliber revolver. I stared directly into its barrel.

"Carl!" I screamed, "It's me. Be cool! What's wrong with you? You're acting insanely. Get yourself together, man!" His distorted facial movements expressed anger, fear and pure insanity. I'd never witnessed Carl in such a berserk state. I dared not flinch a muscle. He had the gun pointed at my head. He began mumbling, "You'll die too, motherfucker, just like the rest of them!" He cocked the hammer back; it clicked into place. His hand began shaking vehemently as he continued his insane utterances. "You're the cause of all this, you bastard! You brought me out here. You tried to take my dope! You gave it to that douchebag! *My* dope! What belongs to me is *mine!* You shouldn't have offered those Dilaudid to that crazy chick, Pat. I knew you two were trying to steal my dope. Now, you'll die for it, like the rest of them!" Carl muttered through gritted teeth.

His grip tightened around my throat. He butted the gun muzzle to my temple and squeezed the trigger. *Click.* Nothing happened!

My mind snapped. I became enraged, empowered with strength. My arm sliced the air, violently knocking the gun from his hand and simultaneously throwing Carl off-balance. I sprang to my feet and kicked him viciously in his left side. He groaned in pain and writhed on the ground, mewling helplessly.

I came to my senses and decided to help him to his feet. I leaned over to assist him, extending my hand. He reached into his jacket lining and withdrew a huge, scary-looking bowie knife. The brilliant glint of shining steel flashed in the moonlight. He swung at me with the knife again and again, wielding it wildly, insanely. I could hear it cut furiously through the air. I jumped back, but not quick enough! The knife ripped into my sleeve, slashing it wide open lengthwise. I freaked!

Focusing my total attention on the knife, I kicked fiercely and the weapon leaped from Carl's hand and soared through the dense night air. I pounced on Carl savagely, thrusting him to the ground, and pinned him securely.

"Listen, you little son of a bitch!" I commanded, seething with rage. "You better get yourself together or I'll pound the hell out of you! Do you understand that?"

I stood back, allowing plenty of distance between us. Carl maneuvered himself into a sitting position on the ground, facing me. He began sobbing. "You've got to help me, Sire," he wailed. "I didn't mean to do it. It was all a horrible mistake."

"Carl, Pat's dead, I think," I said soberly, on the verge of tears myself. But I had to maintain my composure. Should I surrender now I would definitely relinquish any tangible scrap of reason I still clung to. My strength began seeping out of me like water through cloth. Acid permeated the entire caper with an absurd essence of non-realism. It became virtually impossible to decide what to do next. I was incapable of determining my motivations or actions. To decide whether something was right or wrong seemed of no importance. Like a circuit breaker, my rational mind had kicked out.

Carl muttered, "What are we going to do?"

"I don't know where you get this 'we' stuff," I said, "but I'm getting the hell out of here. And quick!" I began walking away.

"Wait!" Carl shouted. "Please, wait!"

"I don't know what happened out here, but I don't want any part of it!" I spouted off angrily. "My God, man, what's wrong with you, anyway! You're sick! There's an innocent dead girl lying over there, Carl and *you* killed her! Where's the other chick, Mary Anne?"

"She's in the bushes," Carl said, pointing to a clump of foliage in the darkness. I grabbed Carl by the shoulders. "Get off your lousy ass and take me to her!"

"For what, Tony? She's dead, don't you understand?"

"Get moving, bastard!" I shoved him in the direction he had pointed to. "Lead me to her. Fast!"

After searching the area a while we came upon Mary Anne's body lying face down in the shrubbery. Clotted blood saturated her blonde, curly hair. She appeared not to be breathing, but as I rolled her onto her back a strange gurgling sound emanated from deep within her throat. For a brief moment I hoped she was alive and able to be helped—but lack of breathing, pulse and no retinal response to the flashlight ruled against it.

"Wait here, Carl," I ordered. I handed him the flashlight. "Hold onto this."

"Where are you going?" he asked.

"I'll be back in a minute. Just hold steady."

I returned to the area where Carl and I had scuffled, located the knife and walked back to Mary Anne.

Carl eyed me fearfully as I approached. Pointing to the knife he asked, "What are you going to do with that?"

"It's obvious there is nothing we can do to help her back to life," I said. "From the gurgling sound she made, she may be suffering. I will try to make it easier for her. It's what I would want done to me if I were in her shape. I hope I'm doing the right thing. I wish I could think straight, damn it!"

"Do you have the courage to do it?" Carl asked contemptuously. "I don't think you can." He grinned. "She'll die anyway. I made sure of that, so what's the sense to it?"

"She may be in *pain,* you bastard!" I shouted, gnashing my teeth. "This is all your asinine doings! And to think that I loved you like my own son! What a fool I was!" Tears welled up in my eyes. Never before had I been so torn between love and hate.

I brushed Mary Anne's jacket flaps open. I rested the knife point against her sweater just beneath her breastbone and aimed it inward toward her heart. I held it there for what seemed a millenium while I tried to build up courage. It was the most difficult thing I've ever had to do. I stiffened my arm and allowed my full body weight to pressure the knife. It sunk into her chest, deeply. I pulled the knife out, flung it disdainfully to the ground and fell limp upon Mary Anne, weeping uncontrollably, stunned by the deed I had done.

"See?" Carl said. "She didn't even move. I told you she was dead!"

Carl's words shocked and infuriated me. How could he be so insensitive? I clenched my fist and swung with all my strength, walloping him on his shoulder with a solid backhand. He fell to the ground, moaning. "What the hell did you do *that* for?"

"Come on!" I commanded. "Let's get the hell out of here!"

"Wait!" Carl said. "We've got to bury the bodies.

652

We can't leave them here like this! Either you help me bury these chicks or we'll both end up behind bars. We're both in this up to our necks. If I get caught I'll say you were here when I killed them, then what will you do? So are you going to help me or not?"

"How the hell are we going to bury anybody when the ground is frozen solid?" I said.

"At least help me carry Mary Anne back to the other body," Carl pleaded. "Then we'll cover them and split."

I shivered, not certain whether the ten-degree temperature caused it or the shock of what had happened. My only desire was to leave the area quickly.

I walked over to Mary Anne's body and slid my arms under her knee joints, gripping her legs firmly. Carl sat her up and grabbed her from behind around the chest and slid his arms under her armpits. We carried Mary Anne's lead-heavy body back to the ammo cans beside Pat.

Carl gathered up the gun and the knife and placed them in his pocket. After dumping in the drugs, I replaced the top of the ammo cans and spread a light covering of leaves. Together, Carl and I scraped up a pile of leaves and pine needles to sprinkle over the bodies of my senselessly murdered friends. . . .

"When you come up to visit me," Costa wrote Goldman in October, "please don't forget to bring the book manuscript with you. I am attempting to write a screenplay from the novel so if you cannot visit within a week, please send the manuscript first-class mail, with your comments, if you desire. When the time comes to publish it, I shall contact you for advice."

When he returned to the novel, Goldman was curious to read how Costa had resolved his dilemma. Following a long walk on the beach the morning after the murders, Costa had returned to his room at Mrs. Morton's. Carl had paid him a visit that afternoon to turn him onto some good grass. . . .

"I don't want any! I snapped. "All I want is some answers from you as to why you killed those chicks!"

"It all began as a joke when you went to get my

653

works," Carl said. "You had given the Dilaudid to that chick Pat. She wouldn't give me any until you came back. She got real bitchy and talked to me like I was just a kid. I figured I could scare her if I got the gun out of the other can." I told Pat more than once to give me the dope but she wouldn't, so I pulled the trigger. I was only fooling around, Sire."

"I still don't understand why you shot Mary Anne also," I said. "It all seems so senseless."

"My head got freaky," Carl said. "I don't know what happened. I sort of went mad, like before."

" 'Like before'?" I asked. "What do you mean by that?"

"Nothing that should interest you!" Carl retorted. "What I need is help. I was counting on you. I don't know what to do!" Carl began weeping intensely. Lollipop tears dropped from his eyes and rolled over his cheeks. "Please don't desert me, Sire. I need a friend so bad."

I handed Carl my handkerchief so he could dry his face. Seeing his tears and feeling as I did from lack of sleep and constant mental turmoil, I felt like weeping myself.

"I have sort of a mutual friend," Carl said. "He's offered to help me bury the bodies tomorrow if I give him all the dope we stashed."

"How many other people know about this, Carl? I think you're trusting too many people. Who is this friend?"

"It's Eddie Gold."

"Oh, man! Are you serious?" I exclaimed in disbelief. "He's had a personal vendetta against me for quite a while now and it's growing stronger day-by-day. I despise him almost as much as he hates me. He can't be trusted!"

"I didn't ask him to help *us,* I asked him to help *me,*" Carl said. "I didn't mention you at all. I know you two don't dig each other. Eddie got super-hot and bothered sex-wise and more than ready and willing when told him he would be helping me bury two chicks," Carl sneered. "You know what a pervert he is. Just mention chicks and he froths at the mouth. Mention *dead* chicks and he practically has an orgasm. You should have seen how excited he got. He couldn't keep his dork in his pants; he kept touching it while I explained things to him. Really weird! But he'll help. Because I've put you through enough already, all you have to do is get rid of the car, I'll worry about the rest."

Because of Carl's state of mind and because I loved him as I would my own son, I agreed to help, but I attached a stipulation. "You've got to tell me what you meant by 'you went mad like before.'"

Carl took the hash pipe out of his pocket. "Do you want to smoke some hash with me? I'll explain things while we're turning on, OK?"

I lit the pipe and propped the bed pillows against the wall and prepared to relax. My lungs were filled to capacity with the sweet oriental smoke.

"All right, Carl," I said. "Start rapping."

"All I can say is this all happened to me before." Carl stared discontentedly at the ceiling. "There were two other girls I killed once. That's why Eddie has volunteered to help. He was at my house when one of them died. Bad scag, you know. There was nothing left to do but get rid of her."

"You're telling me you were actually involved in killing two other girls? I can't believe that!"

"I'm not telling you I killed them, Sire. They died on their own," Carl said. "They were nice kids, but they got hung up on dope and trusted too many people. Now you know why I do so much dope. I can't live with knowing what I know. Especially with what Eddie did to them poor chicks after they died I'll never forget that! He made me help him, too!"

"What are you talking about?" I said. "If my assumptions about Eddie are correct he most likely had sexual relations with them. Necrophilia! That's ugly!"

Carl squirmed nervously in his chair. "Well, yeah, he did fuck them, but he did a lot worse than that. With Sydney he did it to her in the woods, but with Susan, he did it in my house. In the bathroom."

"What's worse than sexually abusing a girl's body after she's dead?" I asked.

"Cutting them up into pieces, that's what's worse!" Carl said. "I didn't see him cut up Sydney, but I saw the pieces of her body he put in the grave I dug. It was horrible!"

Tears welled up in his eyes as he spoke. He was going through so many changes I felt sorry for him. Now I understood why Carl had plunged headlong into the drug escape. Why he preferred to drown his life in drugs.

"You say you saw Eddie cut up Susan in your house?" I said. "God, that's ghastly! Where was your mother and stepdad?"

"You haven't heard anything yet! You'd better brace yourself," Carl said. "My mom and old man were working. Susan died in my room and Eddie and I carried her downstairs to the bathroom and put her on the floor. Eddie went out for a while to borrow a car; then he came back. I was in the bathroom shooting some speed. Eddie came in and shot some, too. We were trying to decide how to get Susan's body out of the house when he came up with the idea of cutting her up into chunks. When he came in he brought a duffel bag he got in the army. I guess he expected her to fit into the bag but she was too big. I tried to tell him we could just wrap her in a blanket and take her out to the car but he wouldn't listen. There was an insane look in his eyes. Susan's body was still on the floor and Eddie leaned over and was ripping her clothes off.

Carl paused to relight the pipe. He passed it to me again. A grim expression veiled his face.

"She still had her bra and panties on, but Eddie ripped those off, too, and ran his hands all over her naked body. He even leaned down and started sucking on her boobs. I just stood there watching him. I didn't know what to say. He asked me what time my folks would be home and I told him we had about three hours yet. I didn't think they'd be home before that. He kept running his hands all over her and grabbed her other tit and kept squeezing real hard. He stuck his finger in her and said some stupid thing about Susan having a nice body! I didn't say anything to that. I could see it was nice; but she was dead and I was scared. I told Eddie to hurry up and get it over with so that we could get her out of the house. He said she was still warm and he wanted to fuck her. He told me to leave for a few minutes and closed the door. I really didn't want to but I did as he told me. It seemed like hours before Eddie opened the bathroom door. His face was all red and he breathed hard. Susan's body was in the middle of the floor with her legs spread wide open. I could look right into her snatch. She really didn't look too dead. She looked like she was sleeping. That's when I noticed how nice her body was. She had real nice legs and groovy breasts. It's too bad. I wish it hadn't happened."

Somber silence prevailed momentarily as we both gathered our thoughts.

"When I went back in the bathroom," Carl went on, "Eddie grabbed Susan by the legs and told me to grab her arms so we could sit her up against the outside of the tub. Then he ran some cold water in the tub, just a few inches. We picked her body up and put it in a kneeling position facing the inside of the tub, like this." Carl slid out of the chair and positioned himself on the floor, evidently as Susan had been propped against the tub. He then returned to the chair, sinking heavily into it and resumed his tale.

"Her head dangled down floppily into the tub and almost went in the water. We lifted her up so her breasts just made it over the inside railing of the tub. Eddie told me to hold her in that position and to keep her hands and arms outside the tub. I wrapped my arms around her from behind and held her body there. She felt real nice. Eddie came over to the tub with a huge hunting knife. He gripped her by the hair and tilted her head straight back. He told me to hold her steady. Then he reached over the tub and stuck the knife straight in her throat saying, 'We'll fix this bitch!' He just kept sticking the knife in her throat and hacked away while holding her by the hair. Finally, he stood there grinning, holding her head up in the air! He got it near me when he put it

657

in the tub, and I freaked and let go of her body. Blood dribbled out through her neck. She began to slump toward the floor when I let go. Eddie got super pissed-off and grabbed her real quick! He picked her up and slid her into the tub with her legs hanging over it. I couldn't take it! I leaned over the tub and barfed my guts out. The smell of blood in the water made me even sicker! I thought I was going to die. I couldn't hardly breathe. I was crying, too. And that pissed off Eddie all the worse. He got more uptight and started hollering. He grabbed me by the collar and shook me. He said to either help him or get out of the way!"

Carl paused and gazed blankly at the floor then turned and stared at me. Gumball tears trickled over his cheeks forming heavy droplets on his chin. "I did help him," Carl continued apathetically, "but something happened to my mind. It went blank or something. I didn't look when he cut into Susan because I felt really sick. I just held parts of her body and put them in the duffel bag.

"We were almost finished when my mom came home. Christ! I didn't know what to do! You should have seen Eddie's face! He panicked when he heard her come in and ran out through one of the windows."

"Did she see him?"

"No, she didn't. I was so uptight I couldn't move. What a hassle she gave me!" Carl emphasized his statement with distorted facial expressions. "Man, she flipped right out when she saw the blood and Susan's ass and some of her guts in the tub! She told me to clean up the mess *fast* and hope for the best. She leaned over the toilet and started barfing. Then she took some of those stupid tranquilizers out of the medicine chest and began hollering at me saying that dope had caused all this trouble, and she swallowed a bunch of pills!"

"What happened to Eddie?" I asked. "Did he ever come back?"

"Yeah, he sure did," Carl replied. "He was waiting for me in the car. He'd been hiding there. My mother had gone out somewhere, but I told Eddie what she said. He just laughed it off like it was a joke or something. I was scared shitless! If she ever got drunk or started blabbing about what she saw, it would be the end! So, Eddie and I ran into the house again and put the ass and the guts in the bag and washed up the bathroom real good. Both of us carried the bag out to the station wagon. I got a shovel that was leaning up against the house and stuck it in the car."

Never had I heard such a strange, grissly tale. A horror story! I sat entranced, experiencing odd, vicarious sensations as Carl's tale unfolded. "Where did you bury her?" I asked.

"Out near the dope stash," Carl replied.

My head swirled dizzingly. "So Susan has been buried out there all this time and only you and Eddie knew about it?"

"Yep, and Sydney, too," Carl said. "Eddie says we can put Pat and the other chick in the graves with Susan and Sydney. It'll save time digging."

The shock of learning of Susan's and Sydney's deaths, added to the murders of Pat and Mary Anne, had caused Costa such mental turmoil that he hardly left his room, the novel said. He waited a week before moving the car from the woods, parking it behind his brother's apartment house in Boston.

I still had not decided what to do with the car. My conscience and moral ethics stressed the importance of holding on to it. The more I thought about what happened to the girls, and what I should do about it, the more confused I became.

Then Costa had packed a laundry bag full of clothes and gone to Burlington, Vermont.

I just got on a bus and went wherever it was going. After two sleepless days and nights, I could no longer bear the pain, I decided to go back to Provincetown and discuss the matter with police so they could either impound the automobile or return it to Rhode Island. When I entered the police station I intended to relate exactly what I knew concerning the crime, but under no circumstances would I involve Carl. My reason being that I am subject to a higher law than that of man. God's Law commands me not to speak against my brothers! I told the police nothing but a conglomeration of misinformation concerning myself only—each story related while on LSD and other drugs. A super-trip!

"I'll go to New York for a while," Carl had said. "I'll send a telegram to your place and sign it with the girls' names. That should help clear you, don't you think?"

Costa disposed of his trial in a three-page "Epilogue".

Selecting a jury became an impossible task due to each member admitting that he or she believed me to be guilty based on what they'd read or heard from the news media. Because of the few negligible facts the district attorney possessed, he had no alternative but to convict me before I came to trial, otherwise he had no case against me—an indication of the power of the press in America to interfere with justice solely for the purpose of selling a ten-cent newspaper! To the press, justice and a man's life are not worth a dime!

My chief counsel, attorney Maurice Goldman, did a marvelous job at the trial in pointing out the inherent dangers of drug abuse and that I had been victimized by a "quack" posing as a qualified physician. After an eleven-day trial, the jury deliberated for approximately six-and-a-half hours, returning a verdict of guilty of first-degree murder!

On May 23, 1970, I was escorted to Walpole State Prison. The heavy steel doors clanged shut behind me, sealing me in a concrete grave.

Goldman was appalled, in spite of everything he had been through in the case. Costa had taken information gathered from defense investigators to elaborate a portrait of himself as the put-upon hero of his "novel." More incredible still was the remorseless rationalization of his crimes. Despite an often-reiterated hatred for drugs, Costa's lovingly-recalled accounts of his former addiction—particularly the lip-smacking details of shooting up—

660

made it clear that he was far from recovered from his psychological drug dependency.

Goldman was particularly upset that Costa should have his victims declare their love for him before he killed them: Sydney Monzon in a car en route to Wellfleet; Christine Gallant in a "suicide note" Costa had never mentioned before, and Pat Walsh's last words as she lay dying in the Truro woods. Goldman had never given credence to the story Costa had told about having his sexual relations with Pat Walsh at Mrs. Morton's—his attempt to explain the presence of sperm mentioned in the autopsy report.

The monstrous duality of Costa's personality was never more transparent than in his horrifying account of necrophilic sex play and Susan Perry's dismemberment. To Goldman, such graphic, closely-observed details were redolent of eyewitness testimony rather than the repetition of information given by another. It was more likely that Costa had overdosed Susan Perry at his mother's apartment *and been caught by her in the process of disposing of the body.*

Putting the manuscript aside, Goldman was reminded of a portion of his own summation at Costa's trial: "His lies are a truth to him; and the truth to him are lies."

Costa had dedicated his novel,

> "For Peter, Michael and Nico
> I pray they will understand."

On November 1, 1971, Goldman's office received word that the Massachusetts Supreme Judicial Court had affirmed the judgments in *Commonwealth v. Antone Costa*. The opinion was unequivocal with regard to Costa's mental status not warranting a finding of deliberate premeditation. There was much circumstantial evidence from which the jury could properly infer that Costa was sane: he had left a note on the door of the girls' room and maneuvered them to an isolated wooded area for the purpose of killing them. He had carried a pistol or had it hidden at the scene in advance; he had a knife and other cutting instruments available. Costa had concealed Pat Walsh's car "in remote cities" and had inquired about having the vehicle painted and registered.

Considering all the "substantial and weighty evidence," together with "permissible inferences," it was the opinion of the justices that no finding for manslaughter was warranted, particularly in view of the fact that Costa had accomplished two successive killings by gunshots. The court declined to award a new trial or direct a verdict of a lesser degree than homicide.

Cavanaugh was not surprised the court had turned down the appeal. "We didn't have much," he told Goldman. "Beaudreau didn't make a reversible error during the trial. He made all his mistakes during the pretrial motions."

"I'm disappointed in the supreme court (not in *you*)," Costa wrote Goldman. "I don't know what went through their heads, but I can understand their political position just before the elections. This is certainly not *your* fault! I reckon we'll just have to try again."

Costa was concerned for the return of the manuscript of his novel:

> I can assure you I will not release it to anyone before you feel the time is ready. What I plan is the sale and publication of another book entitled, "Polyethylene People of the Plastic Society." It is *not* related to the case whatsoever, but is simply a commentary on society. Houghton-Mifflin just rejected it saying it was beautifully written, extremely articulate, but too overwhelmingly angry for their taste. If you can afford it, could you please send me fifty or sixty dollars so I may send this manuscript to one of the literary agencies? . . .

Goldman promised to return "a copy" of the novel either in person or by mail, cautioning Costa:

A reading of the book suggests that you do *not* allow it
to get outside of your hands until such time as we talk
about it. I can't urge you too strongly to be mindful of
the folly of your doings should your book fall in anyone's hands other than your own.

On further consideration, Goldman decided that the greater
folly would be to let Costa get his hands on the novel again.

Increasingly unhappy about the failure of his appeal and disappointed over Goldman's reaction to his novel, Costa's frustration reached a bursting point; on November 16, he exploded, demanding the immediate return "of the perfectly typed original. I
also wish to see you as soon as possible to discuss certain matters,
particularly my future! Since legally, nothing has been done to aid
my cause and absolutely no headway made, I must now think very
seriously about any further action pending."

The lack of evidence in this case is secondary only to the
lack of objections raised during the course of the trial!
The majority of the police evidence presented should
have been objected to and fought rigorously.

You know as well as I do that my so-called "friend"
led Lt. Flynn to the area and provided him with all the
evidence he needed, then granted him amnesty, wiped
out his criminal record and set him free (to murder
again). Only *he* could have shown the police the evidence they needed because only *he* knew where the
graves were. *He* buried them!

I am *not* a murderer! And I intend to prove that if I
have to go to hell and back! . . .

This case can now provide any attorney with the
power, glory and prestige he desires. All he has to do is
provide a little action in court! In the beginning you
promised me roses and lollipops. "Five years," you said.
That's all I'd get, because everything was circumstantial!
Whatever happened to that five years? It was not the
circumstantial evidence that copped out on me!

Because my life depends on it, I am presently in the
process of seriously contemplating my future and what
to do with it. I can remain here and rot! Or I can take

action and walk out the door! Two and a half years with no progress is too long to consider reasonable.

Astonished by Costa's accusations, Goldman had Gerald Garnick, an associate in his law office, sign the letter he dictated in reply:

Because of the intemperate nature of your letter, Mr. Goldman suggested he would write you at some future date when he feels you have cooled down.

Mr. Goldman points out that any rights in the book were your payment for services, and hence you have no rights in the book. I might call you attention to the fact that Lester Allen's book has been rejected by publishers as not having any significant value.

I would also remind you that, under provisions of the law, the supreme court reviewed the entire record of your case and came to the conclusion that there was substantial and weighty evidence to support all the findings implied in the jury's verdict.

Garnick's letter only added fuel to the fire of Costa's fury. "Although I don't know who the hell you are, nor do I care," Costa answered, "I must say that I expected such asinine gibberish from you!"

If, as you say, any rights in the book were payment for services, then please have the kindness to inform Mr. Goldman that I request a bona fide copy of the contract signing such over to him, if such a contract *does,* in fact, exist. I am also interested to know just when these so-called "services" are to begin! I should have been tried on the *facts* of the case, not on the basis of a book, or movie rights or any other rights!

You state in your letter there was substantial and weighty evidence to support the jury's findings. That may be true *only* because Mr. Goldman conceded to the prosecution as well as to his own ulterior motives, hence he caused the jury to believe I *was* guilty! They could not have reached a guilty verdict if Mr. Goldman had fought the case, which any competent attorney could

664

have won. But you are the kind of nincompoop that is not interested in justice. Your wallet is your justice!

I wish to inform you also that I have been granted an interview in *two* national magazines. Although the truth was suppressed during the trial, I will no longer suppress it! The payment contract and publication release papers for the interviews are presently in my possession. I can assure you that I shall no longer remain silent while you and Mr. Goldman reap the profits of my time and freedom! You have all *used* me to build yourselves up. Your letter, as well as Mr. Goldman's lack of responsibility in returning my original manuscript may be of prime interest to the news media. I will wait one week, until December 7. If I have not received the book manuscript by that time, I shall send off the contracts for the interviews. I can assure you that the answers I will provide the media will not be to your liking.

Since I believe Mr. Goldman to be my attorney, not you, let him speak for himself! I'll be waiting. Seven days . . .

Three weeks after his ultimatum, Costa thanked Goldman for a Christmas package of gifts he received:

Please tell me what's next on the legal agenda. If you have a course of action planned, please outline it briefly for me.

Costa also received a copy of the book contract he had signed at Bridgewater, along with a letter from Garnick, "I showed your distemperate letter to Mr. Goldman, who is somewhat disturbed by same." Since it was necessary for him to carry on some of the correspondence in Costa's case, Garnick explained, "I do not think you should be so abusive to me when I am simply carrying out Mr. Goldman's suggestion in writing to you."

9

March 13, 1972

Gentlemen:

I hope you do not think it terribly rude or arrogant of me but I have a request of you, or rather, two requests. First, would you please inform me as to what is the next step legally concerning my appeals? A brief outline will be sufficient and will alleviate some of my anxiety.

Second: I have acquired permission from the administration to start a business here in prison. The business involves the making of "rubber stamps" and will be quite a successful endeavor. It will also offer me a chance to express my artistic talents in a beneficial manner, as well as to profit financially from my efforts. To begin the business I will need $250. . . .

"Please have the courtesy to reply to my letters," Costa wrote Goldman a month later. "I realize you are very busy but a short note from the secretary will suffice. What is the next step in my appeal? Will you supply me with a copy of my trial transcript?"

On April 28, Costa's aunt, Lucy Medeiros (sister of Costa's uncle, Frank Bent) left a message "from Tony" at Goldman's office:

What are you going to do about sending Tony's manuscript? Are you still handling his case? He must hear from you by Wednesday or he will dismiss you.

"I wish I could send you some money, but it seems all your letters ever do is request money," Goldman finally wrote Costa on May 1:

I have laid out thousands of dollars for you, and thus far have not received a penny from any source. I have set

666

you up in two businesses and did not get any return on
my investment. I at least expected to get my initial investment back. You ate up the profits (if any), and also
ate up my investment. Obviously, I am not in a position
to finance you again.

Goldman hoped to get in touch with Costa again "very
shortly."

On the same day, Costa wrote to Chief Justice Walter Mc-
Laughlin of the Massachusetts Supreme Judicial Court:

I realize you are quite a busy man with a burdensome
schedule, but I feel I must seek your assistance. On numerous occasions since my first-degree murder conviction in May, 1970, I have written both the Barnstable
superior court and to my attorneys in an effort to obtain
a copy of my trial transcript, but to no avail.
During and shortly after trial proceedings began, I discovered that a severe conflict of interest concerning a
novel based upon the case was a major factor in any
decision my attorney made. Unfortunately it was too
late for me to stop the trial and seek new counsel. I am
now requesting that my attorneys, Maurice Goldman
and staff, make a disappearance from any further legal
proceedings in my case and I pray the court will appoint
another attorney to handle my appeals hereafter.

Costa enclosed a copy of his letter to Justice McLaughlin
when he wrote to Goldman at the same time:

As you can see I have made the final decision necessary
to secure assistance with my further appeals. As I've
told you before, there are numerous lawyers, media and
individuals interested in the case. They are all seeking
answers. Why did the police destroy evidence found in
the graves with the bodies? Why did Grund collapse on
the stand? Who was I covering for? I am now prepared
to answer these questions for the people,
And so I must ask you for your withdrawal from the
case, since I can no longer prejudice my appeals. I regret

667

any pain this letter might bring you, but a man can dig a hole only so deep, then he buries himself!

Perhaps the next time we meet, I'll be free. That's my goal.

Justin Cavanaugh was astonished when Gerald Garnick showed him Costa's letter. He knew that Goldman had provided far beyond anything a client could reasonably expect by way of legal services. "He never pressed Tony's family for money. He provided for private investigators and hired his own experts, like Charlie Zimmerman. He even saw to Tony's personal needs while he was at Barnstable. Goldman went in the hole for something like six thousand bucks on the case." Cavanaugh himself had written off out-of-pocket expenses of nearly two thousand dollars.

According to law, Goldman was permitted to charge up to ten dollars per hour for work performed outside of court, and fifteen dollars per hour for time in court. Over the three years of his representation of Tony Costa, Goldman logged more than sixteen hundred miles of automobile travel, over one hundred telephone calls, three hundred hours for "clerical services," and more than one hundred fifty hours in trial preparation, research and conferences with police, polygraph and psychiatric experts and approximately fifty witnesses. Goldman had argued seventy pretrial motions, an eleven-day trial, and Costa's appeal before the Massachusetts Supreme Judicial Court. Goldman estimated disbursements of $5,829 "for certain items of expenses incurred" for a draft motion for the payment of attorney fees submitted to the Barnstable superior court. Goldman certified that he had received no compensation for professional services as counsel for Antone Charles Costa, "and does not expect to receive any such compensation and if offered he would refuse same."

On May 11, 1972, Goldman was advised that Arthur D. Serota of Springfield, Massachusetts, had been retained as counsel by Antone Costa "in furtherance of his appeal from a first-degree murder conviction at Barnstable Superior Court."

In advising me that he has requested your withdrawal from the case, Mr. Costa tells me that you have not made the trial transcript available to him. Since further appellate process will be initiated forthwith, it is imperative that you forward the transcript, together with all papers and information in your file which will be beneficial to the appeal, to my office by registered mail immediately.

May I further advise that since a motion for a new trial remains a possible future remedial measure, that any efforts in which you are presently engaged to seek publication of this entire matter be halted.

10

By his own description, Arthur Serota had been a follower while attending the University of Maine. A "loyal American" who supported the war in Vietnam, he had joined the ROTC and endured boot camp at Fort Devens. In his senior year, Serota had been moved by the squalid living conditions of the Penobscot Indians living four miles from the campus. When he volunteered to act as "correspondent" to area newspapers to publicize conditions on Indian Island, Serota had encountered indifference, racial slurs and local prejudice.

After graduating in 1966, Serota arrived in Boston in September with one hundred dollars in his pocket, and a job with the Beneficial Finance Company. He had driven a cab at night to put himself through Suffolk Law School. The ferment of student activism in Boston and the death in Vietnam of his best friend's brother had combined to persuade Serota to take part in demonstrations against the Vietnam War. His military service at an army medical field services school at Fort Sam Houston in Texas had hardened his resistance to the war. Serota used a history of childhood asthma to secure an honorable medical discharge in June 1970, moving to Springfield, Massachusetts, where a friend from law school had set up practice. Proximity to Westover Air Force Base had allowed him to continue his antimilitary legal work as well as join a "penal task force" of the Springfield Council of Churches to protest the abuse of prisoners at the Hampden County Jail. Serota's interest in prison reform had led him to Walpole where several of his clients, mostly poor blacks and Hispanics who made up the largest share of his law practice, were imprisoned.

Introduced to Antone Costa by a client-inmate, Serota found him to be a terribly earnest young man, deeply concerned that young people not follow his own pathway to drugs.

Serota knew nothing of the murders Costa denied having committed, insisting he had been a victim of circumstances. Serota agreed to act as counsel for Costa's further appeals only if private investigators reexamined the case. Unlike Maurice Goldman, Serota could not provide such services for him; nor would he be able to consult with his client very often. Walpole was more than one hundred miles from Springfield.

Serota was not "comfortable" with the contract for book and film rights Costa claimed had been the source of a "conflict of interest" which had motivated defense tactics. Most of Serota's practice was devoted to "representing indigent people at indigent prices," in keeping with his conviction that "Anybody lucky enough to be a lawyer shouldn't be making money at it."

Costa could not complain that a generation gap prevented him from communicating with his attorney. At twenty-seven, Arthur Serota was six months younger than his new client.

Serota was ready "to start on a new case" for Antone Costa in August, when he again requested the trial transcript from Goldman. Growing impatient with Goldman's "unfulfilled promises," he wrote in February: "If the transcripts are not received in my office by next week, I shall feel warranted in taking further action."

Goldman had loaned the transcript to Stephen Yeager, a sometime journalist and aspiring filmmaker who summered in Provincetown. Yeager had disappeared without a trace. Serota learned from the Hagopian Court Reporting Service that a copy of the eleven-volume, 1,553-page transcript would cost $2,150.

11

Costa greeted George Killen with a broad smile when the
policeman visited Walpole. Killen had been puzzled at first to
receive friendly notes from Tony Costa. Costa had confided to
him: "I doubt whether my life will be 'normal' again," and had
asked him to return two diplomas contained in the Pan Am flight
bag which the police had confiscated on the day of his arrest.

Killen was curious to see if he could find out if Costa had
buried other victims in the vicinity of his former marijuana garden
in Truro.

Costa was in no mood to confess to any crimes. He assured
Killen instead that an independent investigation undertaken by
his new counsel would bring about a new trial. He had "important
information" about his case, but "could not disclose it at this
time." He had "rehabilitated" himself during his two years at
Walpole, telling Killen: "I think I'm a fit subject to be released,
and be of some benefit to society."

"I saw your friend Costa yesterday," Killen said to Bernie
Flynn in his office the next morning. "It hasn't hit Tony yet that
he's never going to get out of Walpole."

In January 1973, Costa petitioned prison officials to be transferred to the treatment center at Bridgewater State Hospital. Dr.
Daniel Weiss of the State Division of Legal Medicine, making the
required visit, found Costa's cell in immaculate order, furnished
with his own television set, radio, typewriter and drawing board.
Costa's private library included copies of *The Satanic Bible, A
Treasury of Witchcraft, Ceremonial Magic,* and *Zen Buddhism.*

Costa had fired his attorney and was "employing certain legal
maneuvers to get himself out of this," Weiss said in his examination report to superintendent Raymond Porelle. "He claims he did
not kill anybody; that his attorney was writing a book about the
murders and in that book the outcome was that the murderer was
found guilty. Therefore, he says, his attorney arranged things so
that he would be found guilty."

Weiss recommended Costa be transferred to Bridgewater for

671

a period of observation not to exceed sixty days. "This man has a very great deal of time left to serve, unless some gross change is made in his disposition," Weiss pointed out. "More important, however, than the length of time involved is the question of whether or not he is a sexually dangerous person."

Committed to Bridgewater in June, Costa denied the perverse sexual practices reported by his ex-wife but now admitted to two brief homosexual encounters. He was observed to be "an oriented, alert, intellectualizing individual who under stress-type interviews becomes restless and tangential," during seven examinations by consulting psychiatrists Leonard Friedman and Newman Cohen. He appeared, on testing, to be "an inadequate male with some sexual confusion who needs to manipulate people, especially women."

"He *is* a sexually dangerous person," Friedman and Cohen reported. "We recommend his *return* to the Massachusetts Correctional Institution, Walpole."

> It is probable that commitment to the Treatment Center at this time would guarantee failure of rehabilitation as it would add to his sense of hopelessness in superimposing a commitment for life on top of two concurrent life sentences. Nor would he be at all treatable in view of his preoccupation with legal efforts to gain a new trial. It is doubtful that any treatment presently available in medicine could offer the slightest hope of an early dissipation of his dangerous potential."

Dr. Harry Kozol, director of the treatment center, concurred with the diagnosis in a report to the Barnstable Superior Court. The report suggested that Tony Costa be reexamined "after a substantial period of imprisonment."

His diagnosis as "a sexually dangerous person" had been predicated on the assumption of his guilt in the murders on the part of examining psychiatrists, Costa explained to Serota.

"My tests were conducted under an atmosphere of extreme tension and anxiety. Neither my rehabilitation, or imprisonment for three years under the abnormally violent environment at Walpole, was taken into account."

Costa's half brother Vincent visited Bridgewater and had brought "good news." Costa's family had promised to raise the money to hire investigators by the end of July.

Serota had been in contact with a branch of Costa's family living in Swansea, Massachusetts. Costa's cousin, Maureen Gaspar, in particular had indicated her willingness to raise funds for a new appeal.

Costa was returned to Walpole in August, despite an eruption of inmate violence there. Worried, he asked Serota whether his family had provided money for investigators "as promised."

"If they don't provide the money, I'll try something else," Costa told Serota in November, suggesting he could sell his artwork to greeting card companies. Costa had duplicated from memory an approximate version of his novel—retitled *Trip! Stumble! Fall!*—but had given up trying to find a publisher.

"I still have hope for the future, but my anxiety sometimes gets the best of me," Costa confessed. "I'm finding it harder to do time with every day that passes. All I want is a second chance to live a decent life."

Costa was enrolled in electronics technology classes at Walpole. "Should I be released from prison, I'd like to specialize in marine electronics." He also planned on taking a correspondence course in accounting, Costa said. "Studying is my only solace."

Serota had tracked down Steve Yeager and the missing transcript—in Baltimore. Yeager was organizing an independent production company to film his screenplay of the case. When he asked to read Costa's novel, Serota turned him down.

Serota's reading of the transcript did not persuade him that Maurice Goldman had misrepresented Costa's defense. There remained the question of whether police had covered up or fabricated evidence to "slant" the case against him, as Costa charged. Serota insisted that a prerequisite for further appeals was a professional reinvestigation of the case—i.e., money was needed. After eighteen months as Costa's counsel, Serota had yet to file a single motion on his behalf.

"How's everything going?" Costa asked Serota in January, 1974, promising to redouble his efforts to secure his family's financial backing. "Please let me know what to expect . . ."

In April, Costa wanted to know if he could be remanded to the Barnstable House of Correction to await a hearing on his appeal, once a motion for his new trial was filed. Barnstable corrections officers had indicated their willingness to assist him in any way, Costa explained. "When they were driving me back and forth to Boston, I could have easily escaped, but I didn't even try. And they respected me for that."

Costa had reestablished his jewelry business at Walpole.

"I'm still praying for my future," he said. "But it's been so depressing . . ."

13

On Sunday, May 12, 1974, a Walpole corrections officer making a routine tier check at 8:10 P.M. discovered Antone Costa hanging by the neck from a woven leather belt knotted around the upper bars of his cell.

Costa's eyes bulged open; his darkly mottled face was frozen into a grotesque mask. Blood foamed against his gaping lips from his having bitten his tongue nearly in half. One unlaced sneaker had been kicked off during his death struggles, revealing a mended white sock. Costa had urinated down the front of his unpressed prison trousers.

Medical examiner Harold L. Shenker certified that Antone Charles Costa had died "of asphyxiation by hanging—suicide."

Costa was twenty-nine years old.

Arthur Serota heard of Antone Costa's death on his car radio. During the period of Costa's confinement at Walpole, eleven inmates had been murdered. Serota did not believe that Costa had died by his own hand.

George Killen also heard about Costa's suicide over a car radio, while visiting Martha's Vineyard with Assistant District Attorney Jimmy O'Neil.

"George turned *white*," O'Neil reported to associates back in his office. "He was really upset about it."

Killen was convinced Costa had hanged himself.

Justin Cavanaugh also questioned whether Tony Costa's death was self-inflicted, to the extent that he inquired of state police in Boston about any investigation undertaken at Walpole. He reported to Goldman that police were "satisfied" Costa had killed himself.

Goldman was anything but satisfied, telling Cavanaugh: "Tony was a good-looking young man. He'd been under considerable sexual harassment from the other inmates ever since he went up to Walpole." Goldman thought Costa had been murdered.

Maurice Goldman had never gotten around to filing his motion for expenses in the Costa case. Now, shaken by the abrupt news of Costa's death, he was reminded of the epitaph Costa had written for himself in his novel:

I hope that when I die, that I will be remembered for the benevolence I have displayed during my life. It is true I have committed many mistakes, that is a human characteristic, but I have never intentionally hurt anyone in my life. For me to needlessly injure someone would be to inflict pain upon myself.

Neither Goldman, Cavanaugh nor Serota was asked to attend Tony Costa's funeral in Provincetown. There were no "calling hours" given for the Carlton-Roth Funeral Home on Shank Painter Road. In the cryptic funeral notice that appeared in the

Cape Cod *Standard-Times,* it was announced only that a requiem mass would be celebrated "at the convenience of the family." . . .

A small cluster of mourners was gathered on either side of the plain oak coffin wheeled up near the altar of St. Peter the Apostle Church where Tony Costa had said he often sought "to be at peace with myself." Father Leo Duarte had given permission for Costa to be buried in consecrated ground, a privilege usually denied Catholic suicides.

The misting morning rain turned into a steady downpour by the time the cortege found its way to St. Peter's Cemetery to the canopy flapping under an assault of wind gusts. Following a brief ceremony, grounds keepers lowered the coffin and filled in the grave, leveled the sandy earth and replaced squares of damp sod over Tony Costa's final resting place—next to his mother.

It was, according to Dr. Harold Williams, exactly where Costa wanted to be—the consummation of the state of grace in death which he had enacted in terrible rituals at a clearing in the woods of Truro.

Yet, except for the fading edges of disturbed greensward, no marker acknowledged Costa's presence. He was, in death, deprived of that recognition of his identity that had, during his life, driven him over the edge of madness. . . .

By Memorial Day, 1980, a visitor bending to read the inscription on Cecelia Bonaviri's modest headstone would not suspect from the undisturbed ground that her son lay beside her. It was necessary to seek out the cemetery's grounds keeper to inquire where Tony Costa was buried.

The grounds keeper, an earnest man in his middle thirties, pointed and said, "Right there, next to his mother." Then, he added, "You know, I went to school with Tony. He was a nice boy; a quiet boy. He never got into any trouble."

His eyes passed once more to the place where the short and terrible life of Antone Charles Costa had been consigned to the anonymity of an unmarked grave. "But you never know which way a life is going to turn."

SPECIAL ACKNOWLEDGMENTS

Most of the people who appear in this book provided me with the benefit of their cooperation, which I gratefully acknowledge here.

However, I do wish to thank those whose specific contributions were invaluable: District Attorney Philip Rollins and his assistant, the late David Riley, for unrestricted access to official records; State Police Detective Lieutenants George Killen and Bernie Flynn for their unstinting assistance during my researches; and Maurice Goldman, without whose generosity this book could not have been written.

L.D.

ABOUT THE AUTHOR

LEO DAMORE was columnist on the Cape Cod *News,* cited for "outstanding feature writer," when the events of *In His Garden* took place. He received an award from the New England Press Association in 1975 for "the best editorial of the year." He gathered the details of the Costa case for over six years, conducting more than 240 interviews, examining tens of thousands of pages of official and private documents, and traveling extensively throughout the eastern United States and Canada to virtually every location visited by Antone Costa. Leo Damore's other books include the trial documentary *The "Crime" of Dorothy Sheridan,* the novel *Cache, The Cape Cod Years of John Fitzgerald Kennedy,* and *Senatorial Privilege: The Chappaquiddick Cover-up.* A graduate of Kent State University, Mr. Damore lived on Cape Cod for eighteen years, several of them in Provincetown. He makes his home in Connecticut.